The Duck Hunter's Book

The Duck Hunter's Book
Classic
Waterfowl Stories

Drawings by Tom Hennessey

THE LYONS PRESS
Guilford, Connecticut
An imprint of The Globe Pequot Press

Copyright © 2004 The Amwell Press

First Lyons Press edition, 2004

The Lyons Press is an imprint of The Globe Pequot Press.

10 9 8 7 6 5 4

Printed in the United States of America

ISBN 978-1-59228-422-1

Library of Congress Cataloging-in-Publication Data

The duck hunter's book : classic waterfowl stories / edited by Lamar
Underwood. – 1st Lyons Press ed.
     p. cm.
   Originally published: Clinton, N.J. : Amwell Press, 1982.
   ISBN 978-1-59228-422-1 (tradepaper)
   1. Duck shooting. I. Underwood, Lamar.

SK333.D6D83 2004
799.2'44—dc22

2004048978

DEDICATED TO
GENE HILL

No matter whether the skies over the marsh were empty or filled with wings, I've never shared a duck blind with a better man.

CONTENTS

INTRODUCTION

Lamar Underwood

THE SMOOTH, rhythmic dip of the paddles suddenly went quiet, and the nose of the duck boat plunged into the dark wall of marsh grass and stopped abruptly. Ted DeCharme clambered over the side, grabbed the bow, and muscled the craft deeper into the rustling, frosty reeds, his boots making sloshing and sucking noises in the water and mud. Jimmy Robinson braced a hand on my shoulder and stood up, looking around and stretching. "This is the place," he exclaimed. "This is a heck of a place!"

The qualities that made this particular marshy point better than scores of others that had loomed in the pre-dawn blackness were lost on me. Ever since Ted had begun rowing us through the inky darkness an hour before, three sounds had been continuous: One was Jimmy's constant chatter of places and adventures and people remembered. The others were the splashes and alarm calls of countless ducks and geese being spooked into flight. "They'll come back," Jimmy kept saying. "We could set up anywhere along here and get shooting." But every time DeCharme shipped his oars and reached for the sacks of decoys, Jimmy had barked, "No! No! Not here, Ted!" and so we beat on.

Now the decoys were blobs of shadows that seemed frozen to the smooth, star-lit expanse of water out front. "Could use some wind," Jimmy said, picking up an oar and beating on the perimeter of marsh grass to reduce its height. "It'll come with the daylight, more'n likely." When he had finished manicuring our hideout, he sat down on an old wooden shell box at the right end of the boat, while I took the left. Ted sat in the middle with Buck, his Yellow Lab, trembling between his legs.

Overhead the black vault of the sky was dominated by the constellation Orion, The Hunter, which would rule the night skies of winter until March. On the horizon, the misty-green glow of the Northern Lights showed in a wavering, teasing dance. "We're awfully early, Jimmy," I said as I dug into my shell kit for a Thermos of coffee.

"What? Why, where else would you rather be than the marsh?"

That year Jimmy was experiencing his fiftieth uninterrupted opening day on Manitoba's Delta Marsh. I knew I was doubly blessed, both with his company and the kind of pre-dawn splendor most duck hunters miss, either because they linger abed too long or have it smudged out by dull weather. What I didn't know was that I was about to experience some lessons in shooting that would bring about a self-examination of all my hunting abilities.

As the darkness melted, we saw that so many ducks were trading back and to in the vicinity of our point that a terrific shoot seemed likely. As the sun neared the horizon, guns began to thud in the distance. Ted looked at his watch for the hundredth time. "We're legal," he said. "Load 'em up."

Jimmy was right in the middle of his story of the time Clark Gable came to gun with him on the Delta Marsh, and he went right on talking as he loaded three shells into his veteran Remington 870 pump gun and worked the action. I looked down the tubes of my Winchester 21, dropped in a pair of magnum fours, and enjoyed the tight *snick* as the action closed, signaling the start of a new gunning season.

"Mallards, 'way out front," Ted whispered, hunkering down and putting his duck call to his lips. As Jimmy and I crouched lower, we tried to peer past the wall of marsh grass to see the distant flock Ted was hailing with the long, clarion notes of a greeting call. His head turned constantly, his eyes searching the nearer skies, as the pleading quack, q-u-a-c-k, q—u—a—c—k notes rang out. Suddenly, he dropped the call and whispered, hoarsely, "Mark left! Bills! Take 'em!"

I came up quickly, and there they were, by God, right there—a score or more bluebills had already crossed the outer fringe of the decoys, the leaders with wheels and flaps down settling toward the open water of our fishhook spread, the trailers boring low and hard to catch up. As I finally got my gun to my shoulder, I felt a disturbing awareness that everything was happening too fast. I heard Jimmy shout, and one of the front birds crumpled from the pattern, then I was searching down the broad plane of the double for an incomer— and there weren't any! White breasts and dark heads flashing in the sun, the entire flock was whipping across the decoys with sickening speed. I saw a bird cartwheel from the lower edge of the bunch than I finally got my trigger pulled as the nose of the 21 wavered in the vague direction of a tail-ender. The shot pattern raked a swath across the water ten feet behind the hurtling form, and they were gone. Blast and damn!

"Too slow!" Jimmy barked at me. "You're 'way too slow."

Ted restrained Buck from doing his thing and told us to get down. Retrieving chores would have to wait while other customers were in the area.

This time a flock of mallards decided to investigate Ted's invitation. The dozen or so birds circled warily as Ted changed the tempo of his calls to the quicker greeting notes. "Don't look up," he admonished. "They'll come around." I heard the whisper of wings in the frosty air as the birds passed behind us. Head down, body stiffened, I cut a glance at Ted's face. He was calling in the low, guttural feeding chuckle, his eyes narrowed expectantly toward a left-hand quadrant of sky. Suddenly, he dropped the call and barked the magic words, "Take 'em!"

Don't mess this up, I told myself, with visions of a double on hefty greenheads dancing in my mind as I came up quickly, ready to start blazing toward the low angle of water and sky that had brought the bluebills. But no—they weren't there! They were high, high, dropping straight down, their wings braking to check their descent, their legs outstretched. Before I could get the barrel of the double pointed skyward from the horizontal plane where I had expected to fire, Jimmy's pump spoke, dumping one of the leaders, and once again I was far behind the flow of the action. By the time I was looking down the tubes, the flock had exploded into confusing, individual forms, all hurtling toward the heavens as though they had bounced from some unseen trampoline. Jimmy's next shot mauled a vaulting greenhead as I picked up a bird over the ivory sight, then whipped the tubes past. *Wham*! Nothing! The lead is up, my mind screamed, not to the side! But my target was really getting high now, and far out over the decoy perimeter, and the second shot I poked his way was an ineffectual salute.

You would have thought I had never been in a duck blind in my life, the way I shot during the early part of that morning. And I had, in fact, been away from the sport for five years due to various circumstances. But still, I should have fared better. Birds came and went. Jimmy filled out and waited patiently while I hacked my way toward the bottom of a second box of shells. He had no desire to leave the marsh and was, in fact, rather bemused by my agony.

That marsh is particularly interesting in that both divers and puddlers share the same water. I had all kinds of angles and chances, but for hours my gun-handling seemed to be totally out of synch with the action.

Then, magically, the demons seemed to release their grip, and I started to score consistently. *Wham*, splash! *Wham*, splash! The skies continued their bountious yield, and in no time I had my limit.

We were about to pick up when suddenly Ted barked, "Listen!" From the horizon came a distant but unmistakable chorus, not unlike a hundred yaps and barks all going at once. Canadas! Ted opened up with his call as Jimmy and I dug in our pockets for two's. The flock appeared across the marsh, a long wavering line headed in our direction. "Take 'em if they cross," Ted whispered. "They'll never decoy."

Ted was right. The flock did not decoy but did respond to his insistent calling by passing directly over our blind. They were well within range. An easy double, I thought, confident of my newly discovered smoothbore ability.

The easy double came, all right, for Jimmy! I fanned with both barrels. Go back to Go. Do not collect two geese.

"To hit is history; to miss is mystery," once spoke the father of modern shotgunning, Fred Kimball, the man who invented choke boring. I kept thinking of that quote all that day while doing some mental gymnastics with the possible reasons for my erratic comedy of shooting errors. At one point I stood in Jimmy's duck camp living room making imaginary swings with my 21 on speeding birds, checking my head position, arm extension, grip and trigger pull. Flinching, maybe? No that wasn't it, either.

Finally, I came around to some conclusions that many might share: My poor shooting had nothing to do with basic gun-handling ability. The name of the game is the game itself: Knowing your quarry so well that its movements and appearances are as grooved into your expectations as the flight path of a skeet target. Never mind that fowl and game sometimes do unexpected things. I'll accept the misses that occur on uncharacteristic chances and still end up with more birds in my coat or game in my freezer than the gunner who can shoot circles around me but doesn't understand the habits of the quarry.

When the bluebills had whipped across the decoys that morning, I had been unprepared for the spectacle that greeted my eyes when I stood up to shoot: First, the rocking, wing-cupped forms low to the water in a long smooth glide over the decoys; then boring straight across the blocks as the shooting started. Then when the mallards dropped in, the target was totally different, dropping straight down toward the decoys, then scattering up and out. All morning I was behind the action because I looked too long to see what the birds were doing, instead of anticipating like Jimmy: As he stood, his gun was coming to his shoulder in one fluid motion; instantly he was looking for one of the lead birds in the landing pattern, firing quickly before the target turned on its afterburner and started to get the heck out of there, then swinging on the path he knew the survivors would take.

Then after I had started getting enough hits to limit out, I had reverted to form on the geese for exactly the same reason. Fooled by their enormous size, I did not anticipate that they were, in fact, flying as fast as the ducks had been! They have to be led—and led plenty—with a long fast swing. Ray Holland once reported seeing a Canada goose flying with a flock of teal. The honker was having no trouble keeping up with those speedsters.

It has always seemed to me that duck hunting's great appeal stems from the variety of episodes that can occur on a good marsh or bay on any given day, with plenty of birds flying and opportunities for action outnumbering the sandwiches eaten or cups of coffee downed. In fact, I shall be so bold as to say that no shotgunning sport presents the variety of shot angles and distances that occur in duck hunting. But the charm of the sport does not end there; What makes duck hunting the sport of dreams, tales, paintings—what sustains the duck hunter's efforts to cope with the sport's considerable logistics of guns, gear, boats, and dogs—is the fact that the duck hunter is part of a magnificent tapestry of land, water, and skies alive with the stirrings of elemental nature.

Ducks are a kind of magic, they come to us from the secret far-away places of their summers, riding the winds of seasonal renewal, stirring and rekindling the fires in our hunters' hearts. In late summer we pour eagerly over scouting reports, seeking some clues of the numbers to come. Will this be the year of the many, or the few? In early season we enjoy local birds as much as possible, still waiting for the curtain to go up on The Big Show. Then, somewhere to the north, the mercury is plunging, winds are stirring through the marsh grasses, and the flight is on.

This is a book about that tapestry. I hope you will find it to be as warm and friendly as a fireside drink with your best hunting buddy. If you want it to, the book can probably improve your duck-hunting skills. That will be a bonus as far as I'm concerned, because these selections have been chosen not to make you better, but to make you richer. For in the pages ahead, you will be sharing the accounts and observations of a number of rare men (many of whom have taken in the decoys for the last time) who write about ducks and duck hunting in prose that is engaging and illuminating.

My personal duck hunting odyssey has been a rich and varied one that has taken me from ambushing wood ducks beside a Georgia pond, to pass shooting red-legged mallards under the Wrangell Mountains in Alaska. I have truly been blessed with the fortune of having numerous days afield, some empty of action, some outstanding. Even though I'm only now in my mid-forties (is the flask half empty, or half full?) as I write this, if I were to be deprived of ever hunting ducks in the future, I could only look at our Creator and say, tearfully perhaps, "Thank you!"

A duck hunter can be alone, but never lonely. The marsh is never empty. Sometimes, it's just that the ducks are flying someplace else —someplace perhaps where there's a Gene Hill or Nash Buckingham or Charlie Waterman waiting. Let's go hear what they have to say.

Lamar Underwood
Hopewell, New Jersey

ACKNOWLEDGMENTS

FOR ARRANGEMENTS made with various authors, their representatives and publishers, where copyrighted material was permitted to be reprinted, and for the courtesy extended by them, the following acknowledgments are gratefully made:

"Wings and Water, Guns and Dogs," by Ed Zern, originally appeared in *The American Sportsman*, Volume 1, Number 1, Winter 1968, published by The Ridge Press, Inc., New York, and is reprinted by permission of the author.

"This Mania Called Duck Hunting," by Ted Trueblood, is from his book, *The Ted Trueblood Hunting Treasury*, David MacKay Company, Inc., New York, copyright 1978, by Ted Trueblood.

"Portrait of a Sweet-Water Marsh," by Robert Elman, is from his book, *The Atlantic Flyway*, published by Winchester Press, New York, in 1972, and is reprinted by permission of the author.

"Duck Blinds," by Charles F. Waterman is from his book, *The Part I Remember*, published by Winchester Press, New York, in 1974, and is reprinted by permission of the author.

"What Is a Duck Hunter?" By Charley Dickey, originally appeared in *Field & Stream* and is reprinted by permission of the author.

"North Again," by John Madson, originally appeared in *Audubon* magazine, and was later included in the Madson book, *Out Home*, published by Winchester Press, New York, 1979. It is reprinted by permission of the author.

"Have Ducks the Power of Scent?" by Ray P. Holland, is from his book, *Scattergunning*, published by Alfred A. Knopf, Inc., New York, in 1951.

"Waterfowl Speeds," by Ray P. Holland, is from his book, *Scattergunning*, published by Alfred A. Knopf, Inc., New York, in 1951.

"Mysteries of Migration," by Robert Elman, is from his book, *The Atlantic Flyway*, published by Winchester Press, New York, in 1972, and is reprinted by permission of the author.

"Secret Life of the Salt Marsh Barrens," by Robert Elman, is from his book, *The Atlantic Flyway*, published by Winchester Press, New York, in 1972, and is reprinted by permission of the author.

"Canada and the Provinces," by Raymond R. Camp, is from his book, *Duck Boats: Blinds: Decoys and Eastern Seaboard Wildfowling*, published by Alfred A. Knopf, Inc., New York, in 1952.

"Big Sky," by Charles F. Waterman, was originally published in *Gray's Sporting Journal*, Fall, 1973, and is reprinted by permission of the author.

"Ice, Ducks, and Good Strong Rye," by Martin Bovey, was originally published in his book, *Whistling Wings*, published by Doubleday & Company, Inc., Garden City, New York, in 1947.

"The Susquehanna Flats," by Norris E. Pratt, was originally published in the book, *Chesapeake Bay Decoys: The Men Who Made and Used Them*, edited by R.H. Richardson, and published by Crow Haven Publishers, Cambridge, Maryland.

"And Keep Your Powder Dry," by Colin Willcock, is from his book, *Landscape with Solitary Figure*, published by Longmans Green and Co. Ltd., London, in 1966.

"Maine and New England," by Raymond R. Camp, is from his book, *Duck Boats: Blinds: Decoys and Eastern Seaboard Wildfowling*, published by Alfred A. Knopf, Inc., New York, in 1952.

"Skyful of Bright Wings," by Russell Annabel, is from his book, *Hunting and Fishing in Alaska*, published by Alfred A. Knopf, Inc., New York, in 1948.

"Bait: The Use of Corn," by Harry M. Walsh, is from his book, *The Outlaw Gunner*, published by Tidewater Publishers, Cambridge, Maryland, in 1971, and is reprinted by permission of the author.

"Duck Talk," by Jim Rikhoff, originally appeared in *The American Rifleman* and later in Rikhoff's anthology, *Mixed Bag*, published by The Amwell Press and the National Sporting Fraternity Ltd., in 1979, and is reprinted by permission of the author.

"A Christmas Present to Myself," by Robert C. Ruark, originally appeared in the December, 1952, issue of *Field & Stream*. Reprinted by permission of Harold Matson Company, Inc.

"Are We Shooting 8-Gauge Guns?" by Nash Buckingham, originally appeared in *Gun Digest*, 1960, and in the Buckingham book, *De*

Shootinest Gent'man and Other Hunting Tales, published by Thomas Nelson & Sons, New York, in 1961.

"Calling Ducks," by Gene Hill, originally appeared in *Sports Afield* and later in the Hill anthology, *Mostly Tailfeathers*, published by Winchester Press, New York, in 1975. It is reprinted by permission of the author.

"Painting Decoys," by Eugene V. Connett, III, is from his book, *Duck Decoys*, published by William Morrow & Company, New York, in 1953.

"The Craft of the Blind," by Raymond R. Camp, is from his book, *Duck Boats: Blinds: Decoys and Eastern Seaboard Wildfowling*, published by Alfred A. Knopf, Inc., New York, in 1952.

"Setting Decoys," by Norman Strung, is from his book, *Misty Mornings and Moonless Nights*, published by Macmillan Publishing Co., Inc., New York, in 1974, and is reprinted by permission of the author.

"Make the Ducks Come to You," by Ted Trueblood, is from his book, *The Ted Trueblood Hunting Treasury*, published by David MacKay Company, Inc., New York, in 1978.

"Dusky Ducks in the Wilderness," by Bert Claflin, is from his book, *American Waterfowl*, published by Alfred A. Knopf, Inc., New York, in 1952.

"Hunting the Pothole Ducks," by Hart Stillwell, is from his book, *Hunting and Fishing in Texas*, published by Alfred A. Knopf, Inc., New York, in 1946.

"Black Ducks Here and There," by Van Campen Heilner, was originally published in his book, *A Book on Duck Shooting*, published by the Penn Publishing Company, Philadelphia, in 1939, and later republished by Alfred A. Knopf, Inc., New York.

"Bayman's Solstice," by Norman Strung, was originally published in *Gray's Sporting Journal*, Fall, 1980, and is reprinted by permission of the author.

"Beyond the Limit," by Nelson Bryant, was originally published in *Gray's Sporting Journal*, Fall, 1976, is and is reprinted by permission of the author.

"Canvasbacks From North to South," by Van Campen Heilner, was originally published in his book, *A Book on Duck Shooting*, published by the Penn Publishing Company, Philadephia, in 1939, and later republished by Alfred A. Knopf, Inc., New York.

"Redhead Ridge," by Hart Stillwell, is from his book, *Hunting and Fishing in Texas*, published by Alfred A. Knopf, Inc., New York, in 1946.

"The Meaning of Canvasback," by Gene Hill, was originally published in *The Complete Hunter's Catalog*, edited by Norman Strung and published by J.B. Lippincott Company, New York, in 1977. It is reprinted by permission of the author.

"To Ride the Wind," by H. Albert Hochbaum, is from his book, *To Ride the Wind*, a Richard Bonnycastle Book, published and copyrighted by Harlequin Enterprises Limited in Toronto, Canada, and London, England, in 1973.

"A Shift in the Wind," by Sigurd F. Olson, is from the book, *Outdoors Unlimited*, edited by J. Hammond Brown, sponsored by the Outdoor Writers' Association of America, and published by A.S. Barnes and Company, New York, in 1947.

"A Duck Looks Different to Another Duck," by Robert C. Ruark, originally appeared in *Field & Stream*, and later in the book, *The Old Man and the Boy*, published by Henry Holt and Company, New York, in 1953. Reprinted by permission of Harold Matson Company, Inc.

"Times Past on the Eastern Shore," by Gene Hill, originally appeared in *Sports Afield*, and later in Hill's anthology, *Mostly Tailfeathers*, published by Winchester Press, New York, in 1975. It is reprinted by permission of the author.

"Pintail Point," by Kendrick Kimball, originally appeared in *Field & Stream* and in the anthology, *The Field and Stream Reader*, Published by Doubleday & Company, Inc., Garden City, New York in 1946.

"Great Day in the Morning," by Nash Buckingham, originally appeared in *Field & Stream* in 1941, and was included in Buckingham's *Tattered Coat,* published by G.P. Putnam's Sons, New York, in 1944.

"Pothole Guys, Friz Out," by Gordon MacQuarrie, originally appeared in *Outdoorsman* magazine and was included in the anthology, *Outdoors Unlimited*, edited by J. Hammond Brown, sponsored by the Outdoor Writers' Association of America, and published by A.S. Barnes and Company, New York, in 1947.

"Moss, Mallards and Mules," by Bob Brister, is from his book, *Moss, Mallards and Mules*, published by Winchester Press, New York, in 1973. It is reprinted by permission of the author.

"Pot Luck," by Roland Clark, is from his book, *Pot Luck*, published by A.S. Barnes, New York, in 1945.

"One to Get Ready"—"And Two to Go," by Colonel Harold P. Sheldon, are from his book, *Tranquillity Regained*, originally published by Derrydale in 1936, and reprinted by Countryman Press in 1945.

"What Rarer Day?" by Nash Buckingham, is from *De Shootinest Gent'man*, published by The Derrydale Press in 1934 and G.P. Putnam's Sons, New York, in 1943.

"Trash Ducks," by Harold P. Sheldon, was originally published in *Field & Stream* and was included in the anthology, *The Field and Stream Reader*, published by Doubleday & Company, Inc., Garden City, New York, in 1946.

"Meditations in a Duck Blind, " by A. Starker Leopold, originally appeared in *Gray's Sporting Journal*, Volume Two, Issue Six.

"The Ducks of Tranquillity," by Archibald Rutledge, is from his anthology, *An American Hunter*, published by J.B. Lippincott Company, New York, in 1937.

"Danky Knows His Ducks," by Archibald Rutledge, is from his anthology, *An American Hunter*, published by J.B. Lippincott Company, New York, in 1937.

"Nothing to Do for Three Weeks," by Gordon MacQuarrie, was originally published in *Field & Stream* and later included in the anthology, *The Stories of the Old Duck Hunters & Other Drivel*, edited by Zack Taylor and published by Stackpole.

"Hail and Farewell," by Nash Buckingham is from his book, *Mark Right!*, published by G.P. Putnam's Sons, New York, in 1944.

ONE

A Celebration

WINGS AND WATER, GUNS AND DOGS

Ed Zern

He is the ultimate court jester. He is a Mark Twain, a Ring Lardner, an Irwin S. Cobb—all rolled into one incredible character who has looked into every corner of outdoor sport and found mirth in it all. There is something of a mischievous little boy in him—and at the same time the wisdom of one who has seen and knows much. He is the all-time ego-deflater, the champion of reminding the world not to be serious about unserious things. He has virtually single-handedly put humor into the important outdoor literature of this century. He puts serious would-be achievers of field-sport feats before a firing squad of barbs. He puts fun back into things that are always supposed to be that way but get mixed up when people lose their perspective sometimes. We are all human, he says, and we are all potential victims who need more luck than we think we do. Ed Zern has done all these things in his magazine articles and columns, his books, and his masterful speaking appearances. The humorous side of Ed Zern sometimes obscures the fact that he really is an accomplished out-doorsman with experience and expertise in most areas of sport. There are some chuckles in the piece ahead, but basically the piece is a celebration of waterfowling by a man who holds the sport very dear to his heart. It appeared in Volume One, Number One of The American Sportsman, *the hard-cover magazine-format book published by Ridge Press and ABC in 1967, in conjunction with the television series. The TV show is still on as this is written (although hunting has virtually been dropped due to pressures on the gutless wonders who run the network), but alas the book project did not work out and was abandoned after several were published. If you met Zern in person you would be amazed at how like his words he is in the flesh. He is a gracious man with a twinkle in his eyes and softness to his voice that can sting the mighty.*

AT THE BAR in the Shannon Airport the bartender sees the gun cases with the luggage and says, "Snipe?" "Yes," I say, "and ducks." "Ah, that's my sport," he says. "Tell me about wildfowlin' in America, now. What's it like?" I try to tell him, but . . .

In the half-light of a December dawn, a man stands on an abandoned railroad causeway, slapping at mosquitoes with his left hand; the right clutches a beat-up pump gun. One pocket of a frayed canvas vest bulges with cartridges. Around him stretch the Florida Everglades, here thick with moss-hung scrub trees. He has walked four miles down the causeway to be here at sunup, now he waits. . . .

The dusty station wagon comes up over the rise of the dirt road and stops. Both men in the front seat raise binoculars and scan the rush-rimmed two-acre pond half a mile across the Montana Valley. The man in the back seat shivers, partly from cold and partly from excitement. "Greenheads at the south end," the driver says, "and looks like sprig on the far side. Charley, I'll drop you at the foot of the hill, so's you can sneak along that cut-bank. Ollie, you and me'll drive around and leave the car beside the culvert; then we can spread out and cover that end. We'll bushwhack 'em good . . ."

The bare, cold rock juts out into Long Island Sound, and with the early-morning mist you hardly notice the rowboat pulled halfway up on the ledge. Then, because the boat couldn't have got there by itself, you look harder and see the man squatting in the angle of rock, the three-shot automatic in his lap and his eyes searching the mist. . . .

The smooth-faced, heavy-set man leans back in the blind, turns up the collar of his custom-made shooting jacket and says, "Gus, California weather or no California weather, it's going to feel good to get back to the clubhouse and a large hooker of bourbon." Gus, whose face is no stranger to sleet and wind, whose set isn't heavy, and whose shooting jacket isn't custom-made, keeps peering between the bundles of tules in front of them. "It'd feel even better, Mr. B., if them so-and-sos would start flying," he says, taking a wooden cylinder from his pocket. "I'm gonna give 'em another toot on the tooter . . ."

A lot of people (including me) have wondered why duck hunters (including me) are willing to endure the discomfort and misery that usually afflict the wildfowler, especially in the northern states. I don't know the answer, but I shared a Long Island blind one bitter-cold December day with a fairly distinguished psychoanalyst who felt the answer was simple. As we huddled, with sleet blasting the skin off our faces and our feet too numb for feeling, he explained to me, through frost-chapped lips, that this nation was nurtured in the Puritan ethic, one tenet of which holds that anything pleasant or enjoyable must, per se, be wicked or sinful, and that wickedness must sooner or later be explained in pain and suffering. Duck-hunting, he declared, provides expiation, with the degree of suffering in direct relation to the quality of the sport—since ducks fly best when the weather's worst. I'm not enough of a psychologist to know how valid the doctor's theory is, but I recall that, as I sat there in the blind with my teeth chattering and my hands so chilled I could barely hold a gun, it made a lot of sense.

Although someone defined duck-hunting as the most fun you can have while in agony, the fact is that not all of us are enthusiastic about suffering for our sport. A friend of mine once said that in his opinion the only indisputably great Americans were George Washington, Abraham Lincoln, and the man who invented thermal underwear; personally I would have included the inventor of the insulated boot-foot wader and possibly Thomas Jefferson.

About ten years ago I had to have an operation during the first week in November. I was up and around before the duck season ended, but was told by my doctor that I must shun all exercise, however mild, for at least six months. I explained that except for lifting a seven-pound gun occasionally, there wasn't any real exercise involved in shooting ducks over decoys, but he was adamant.

The day before the season ended, my friends Pete and Mac telephoned, inviting me to shoot from Pete's blind on an island in Barnegat Bay. I told them what the doctor had said, but they insisted I wouldn't have to lift a finger. If necessary, they said, they would hold the gun and I could simply pull the trigger. Since I felt fine, and since Pete is a rugged two-hundred pounder in prime physical condition, I agreed to meet them at the Tom's River diner at four the next morning, and did.

Or rather, I met Mac, who explained that Pete had been called to an emergency conference, but that he, Mac, would do all the necessary physical chores. I listened with some misgivings, since

Mac weighs about a hundred and eighteen pounds with a box of high-brass 6's in each pocket, but having driven a hundred and fifty miles through a snowstorm I said okay, and we loaded gear, guns, deeks, and dogs into Pete's 16-foot Garvey, and off we went across the bay.

On the way, we noticed that the temperature was dropping fast, and by the time we had the decoys out it was several degrees below zero. We had pretty good shooting for about fifteen minutes, and then Mac pointed out that the bay was beginning to freeze up, and that some of the decoys were already frozen in solid. We had visions of being ice-locked on that island, two miles from the nearest land, with no provisions except a fifth of whiskey and some dog biscuits, and so began chopping the decoys out of the ice and stowing our stuff back to the boat. Then, from ten o'clock in the morning until four that afternoon, with only occasional two-minute whiskey-breaks, we chopped, smashed, and slogged our way through and over two miles of ice and slush-ice, and eventually got back to the landing after I had committed more strenuous physical exercise in a day than I usually do in an entire duck season. I sat around the rest of that winter waiting for adhesions to set in or for something to pop. but nothing ever did, and I guess after ten years nothing will.

 DECOYS

A subject that divides duck hunters is how decoys should look. There are a number of schools, ranging from purely impressionistic to exact imitation, somewhat like the several schools of trout flies, and each has its impassioned adherents.

The most beautifully realistic wildfowl decoys I ever saw were a set of a dozen black ducks—six hens and six drakes—made by having a taxidermist mount the actual skins of shot birds on carved cedar bodies in various natural positions. When they floated on a pond, you could watch them from ten feet and feel sure they were alive, until absence of movement betrayed their fraudulence. The most interesting aspect of their realism and beauty was that on several occasions when the owner had rigged them in front of his St. Lawrence River blind—a proven hotspot for black ducks—not a single duck of any species had come into the rig.

On the other hand, I once shot ducks in Yucatan over decoys made by hastily blackening coconut husks with a blowtorch and tossing them into the lagoon in front of the crude brush-blind. Ducks came barreling in so fast that I restricted my shooting to drake pintails quartering in from left to right, an angle at which I've always been especially lousy, and had my limit of twenty-five in less than two hours. Since these were the same pintails that had come down the Mississippi and Pacific flyways a few days or weeks before and had no doubt spurned a lot of high-priced, hand-carved decoys along the way, there is probably a moral here somewhere; or it may have been the aroma of roasted coconut that brought them in. My friend Tap Tapply, in Massachusetts, has killed black ducks over decoys made by filling canvas bags with chunks of cork and spray-painting them black. The nice thing about this argument, of course, is that nobody can win it, because it can't be proved that someone might have killed more blacks if his decoys had been more realistic.

There's also the controversy about normalsize versus oversize blocks, and some of the old-timers along the Atlantic coast still prefer an undersize decoy, pointing out that they can pack more of them along the rails of a sneak-box when going into the marshes, and that the ducks don't seem to mind. Personally, I belong to the oversize school on the likelihood that a bigger object is visible at a greater distance and may also look better-fed and therefore more persuasive to a hungry duck.

A few years ago I persuaded one of the remaining old-time New Jersey decoy whittlers to make me a dozen hollow-cedar black-duck decoys for shooting. I put them in the station wagon with a six-months-old Labrador Retriever puppy, and while I was paying my bill chatting with the old man the puppy chewed the heads off all but two of the decoys. I patched the tooth-holes in the two survivors, and recently sold the pair of them to a collector for more than I had paid for the dozen.

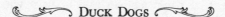 DUCK DOGS

One of the fringe pleasures of duck-shooting is owning dogs, training them, reciprocating their affection, and watching them work—

and of course knowing that, thanks to the dog, you're putting cripples into the bag which would otherwise die lingering deaths from infection, or be eaten alive by gulls. One of the most effective steps that might be taken to conserve wildfowl would be a Federal rule requiring every duck hunter to have a bona fide retriever with him while shooting, unless accompanied by a guide whose duties would include retrieving.

My own preference in duck dogs is the Labrador Retriever, partly because it's the breed I know best and partly because they're usually easier to train and better dispositioned than the Chesapeake Bay Retriever. The Golden Retriever is a beautiful and useful breed but with all the obvious disadvantages of a long-haired dog and without the Lab's or Chessie's indifference to icy waters and subzero temperatures. The Chesapeake is a marvelous breed for hard, cold-weather work, but some strains are inclined to be surly and bad-tempered, quick to snarl at strange men or dogs, poking around their boats, perhaps checking for out-of-season or undersize fish and game or illegal gear, and wanted a one-man dog that would just as soon bite a chunk out of a stranger as look at him. (One time, a week after a duck-hunting threesome of which I'd been part had admired and petted a ten-month-old Chesapeake on a Maryland Eastern Shore wharf, I heard that the owner, an oysterman and clammer, had shot it and kicked it off the dock on the outgoing tide, because he considered it too chummy with strangers.)

I use my Labs for upland shooting as well as wildfowling, as do a lot of gunners who can't afford to maintain a kennel of pointing, flushing, and retrieving dogs, but it's on water that the Labrador shines, and there are moments that repay many times over the work and expense of having several large, hungry, and opinionated dogs around the house.

I sat one morning in a sunken blind in the Tuckerton marshes of New Jersey, where a few months earlier I had walked up a limit of clapper rails. I was with my friend Hugh and my three Labs, and the fog was so thick that we could barely see the nearest decoys in front of us. We could hear the whistling of wings as ducks flew past, but we couldn't see them until suddenly three blacks came over us low from behind. Hugh fired twice, I fired once, and we heard the splash of ducks tumbling into the water. I sent all three dogs off into the fog, wondering if they'd get lost in it and I'd have to whistle them back. A few minutes later we saw the three of them materialize out of the mist, swimming abreast like a team of canine aquacaders, each with a dead black duck in its mouth. It was good man-work and good dog-work, and a moment that Hugh and I (and perhaps the dogs) have run off on our minds' instant-replay screen a thousand times since then.

Another day I was shooting alone over a small marsh pond near Watchapreague on the eastern shore of Virginia, with a Lab sitting on either side of me on the bench of the two-man brush blind. One of the Labs was Rocky, an erstwhile top performer in field trials but never an enthusiastic field worker. The other was Wullie, who hated field trials as much as he loved hunting and who scanned the skies for ducks with such eagerness that he trembled. Then a flock of fifty or sixty marsh sparrows settled on the blind, paying no attention to me or the dogs and hopping from twig to twig. Rocky had dozed off, but Wullie kept looking for ducks on the horizon, and each time a sparrow would settle on a branch in front of him, obscuring his vision, he would reach up gently with one paw and brush it aside, like a man brushing gnats while he's watching a trout pool for rises.

Wullie's now twelve and aging with grace and dignity, but in his prime he knew—as a few duck dogs do—when a duck had been hit, even when the gunner thought he had missed cleanly; a score of times he has insisted on taking off after a bird I was sure had been unscathed, and in every case but one he came back with a duck. One time I shot at a teal and Wullie came back with a crippled widgeon. But almost every time, I'm sure, he retrieved the right bird.

 GUNS

The subject of duck guns is capably covered elsewhere, but for the record my own preference is a 12-gauge over-and-under with 28-inch barrels bored modified and full choke. For shooting over decoys I want 7½ shot or even 8, since the denser pattern is more likely to break wingbones and get the bird down on the water where the dogs can retrieve it, and because I hate to see a duck that has been hit with 4's or 5's fly half a mile out into the bay before collapsing. By the time the dogs can get to him he may have drifted half a mile farther out. Only once have I had to retrieve a retriever being swept out the inlet on a strong outgoing tide, but that was enough. On the other hand I once found myself in a pothole blind in northern Montana with nothing but a box of 2's, and killed every duck I shot at stone dead. Perhaps the important thing is getting the duck centered in the pattern no matter what size the pellets.

I'm unable to see any sporting virtue in a gauge smaller than 12, since the size of pattern is almost identical in 20, 16, and 12 gauge (or even .410). The only difference is density of shot, and although I don't mind missing a duck, when I do hit it I want to kill it.

Years ago I spent a week shooting in Currituck Sound with an elderly North Carolinian farmer whose only gun was an ancient three-shot automatic, held together with friction tape and wire. Every time he pulled the trigger all three shots went off—blam-blam-blam! As a result he wouldn't shoot unless there was a fair-sized flock of birds within range, and each barrage he laid down would kick him halfway out of the blind, without doing the ducks any appreciable damage, as he flinched too much to be accurate. I asked him one time why he didn't put just one shell in the gun, or two at most, and his jaw dropped in astonishment. "God-dammit, bub, it's a three-shot gun!" he said, and I bowed to the compelling force of his logic.

And my friend Pete McLain, a wildlife biologist with the New Jersey Conservation Department and one of the best black-duck hunters in that state, shoots a three-shot automatic that he paints dead-grass green from muzzle to butt-plate and even inside most of the receiver, so it won't flash in the sun to spook wary ducks and won't rust even after lying in the bottom of a leaky sneak-box. I watched a gun-loving friend of mine turn pale one time when he saw Pete slosh duck-boat paint on a brand-new automatic, and it took three slugs of applejack to restore his pulse.

BLACK DUCKS

Throughout the northeastern United States the duck valued most highly by most gunners is the black. Not only is it a fine table duck, but it is also an extremely wary bird; the duck hunter who consistently scores on this species is a real expert. Even with a strong wind blowing, a black duck will usually circle the decoys once or twice, looking into the blind over the gunner's shoulder, before coming into the rig. If he sees the slightest movement or spots anything unnatural—the flash of light on metal, the glint of shooting glasses, a white handkerchief, or whatever—he'll go look for a more congenial landing strip. I know two black-duck hunters who recently traded in their spectacles for contact lenses, at considerable cost and bother, because they suspected that light bouncing off their glasses sometimes spooked black ducks coming into their decoys.

Actually, the black is a close cousin to the mallard, the most popular duck in the Midwest, and there are gunners along the Atlantic seaboard who speak of the black as "black mallard." But I've found the black a lot warier than his green-headed cousin, perhaps because he's been subjected to heavier shooting pressure for a longer period of time and only those of his tribe with suspicious natures survived to transmit their caution.

BUSHWHACKING

One of the most exciting ways of shooting ducks in some of the western states is bushwhacking them in small ponds and large potholes. I've enjoyed great sport, if not many ducks in the bag, while cruising along dirt roads with one, or preferably two, companions, looking for ducks on water. When we'd spot a pair, or a small flock, on a reed-rimmed pot-hole, we'd park the car and stalk them from two or three sides, in hope that at least one of us would get some shooting when the ducks flushed. Sometimes we did, and sometimes we even got a duck or two.

One time, just across the Canadian border in the Milk River Valley of Alberta, I stood in a field with no blind or cover, along what was obviously a tradeway between a feeding area and the reservoir a hundred feet behind me, and lowered a limit of fat drake mallards in broad daylight. One of them set his wings and planed clear to the reservoir. I walked half a mile to a farmhouse, borrowed a bait-casting rod and bass plug, and was finally able to hook the duck and reel it in. When I took the gear back to the farmhouse and offered the farmer's wife a brace of plump grain-fed mallards she laughed and said, "No thanks! We lived on them critters for ten years when things was tough, and we don't want to taste a duck or goose ever again!" I could see the scrawny cold-storage chicken thawing on the kitchen sink, and wondered about market research.

LIMITS

A lot of gunners today are troubled by what seems to be a growing disregard for game laws, and some feel that the setting of two-, three-, and four-bird limits is bound to make scofflaws of normally law-abiding citizens. The problem is that a man may start out at midnight to drive two hundred miles to his favorite shooting spot, arrive at four A.M., spend the better part of two hours rigging decoys, grassing and pumping out the blind, and setting up housekeeping. Half an hour before sunrise he settles himself and his dog in the blind, when suddenly in come the ducks. Five minutes later (as sometimes happens) he has his limit. I don't know what you, the reader, would do in this situation, but most of the duck hunters I know, whether bankers, bishops, or burglars, do not immediately jump out of the blind, gather up their rig of decoys, change their clothes, and drive two hundred miles home. Generally, they keep on shooting, reminding themselves that after all they get out only two or three times, unlike some of their friends who are able to shoot every legal day of the season. This line of reasoning doesn't do them much good if they're checked by a warden, but it does assuage the pangs of conscience.

One way to solve the problem might be a *season* limit of ten or twenty or a hundred ducks, with the license holder having the option of killing all of them in one day or spreading them out over a season. In either case, when he had shot his limit he would be through for that season. This is the same system that the state of Washington uses for steelhead trout, and although some people say it wouldn't be enforceable, the fact is that with the pitifully small number of wardens in the field and the vast army of hunters, no game or fish laws today are "enforceable" except in token fashion. Personally I'd prefer a season limit, with the feeling that if I wanted to use up all my tags or stamps or card-punches in one shoot-the-works spree I could do so, and then shoot skeet or trap or hang around poolrooms until the next season.

DOG TRAINING

One advantage of owning a well-trained dog is that during the off-season you can have a lot of enjoyment, and incidentally help keep the dog in condition, by running it in retriever field trials.

Generally, a dog trained for field work doesn't do as well as those trained primarily for trials, but you can have fun and pick up useful pointers on training and handling by attending local trials. Field-trial dogs get marked down for dropping the retrieved bird to shake the water from their coats before delivering it to the handler, whereas most of us who shoot would rather have the dog shake himself outside the blind than inside. By the same token, we want our dogs to take a land route to a fallen bird when it's faster than swimming across a pond, while the field-trial dog is expected to take a straight line across the water even if it takes him several minutes longer to retrieve the bird. But basically the field trial duplicates field conditions, and the top field-trial dog is usually a top performer under actual shooting conditions.)

The ideal duck dog is not only completely steady under all field situations but will respond to whistles and hand signals when he is after a bird that you saw fall and he didn't. The problem is to get a fully disciplined dog that still retains his drive and enthusiasm for field work. Unless you're able to spend a lot of time with a puppy, and are blessed with great patience, it might be best to have the dog trained professionally after you've taught it the basic disciplines of sitting, staying, walking at heel, and coming instantly on command. If you're going to train a puppy yourself, there are a number of good books on retriever training; read at least three of them, and compare viewpoints, before you accept any one of them as your bible.

WALKING THEM UP

One of the most sporting and challenging ways to shoot ducks is by walking them up, or jumping them, in marshes—preferably on a windy day in areas with fairly high grass. By walking upwind you can frequently flush blacks, mallards, and other puddle-ducks out of pot-holes and tidal creeks where they've taken shelter from the wind, although unless you keep low and there's enough wind to damp the sound of your movement through the marsh, most of them will get up well out of gunshot.

This is always tricky shooting, and you have to remind yourself that even though the duck doesn't seem to be going fast his airspeed is the same as it would be on a still day, and you must lead him just as far. Incidentally, there's a temptation to try your second barrel when you miss with the first (or your second shot, if you're using a pump or three-shot auto). Usually the duck has got up near the outside range of your gun and is out of gunshot by the time you get off a second round. Also it's virtually certain that if you fire that second barrel two things will happen: 1) the duck will fly on, unpunctured, 2) a second duck will get up well within range, and be out of it by the time you reload.

Duck-Boats

Basically, most duck-boats are the same. It's the local variations that make them interesting. The one I know best is the Barnegat sneak-box, which, like most successful duck-boats, was perfected by market hunters and adapted to sporting use when these shoot-to-sell experts turned to guide work after being legislated out of business. I once had one of the old New Jersey craftsmen make me an eleven-footer, with the traditional white-cedar construction, balanced to take a three-horsepower outboard motor, and for several seasons used it as a sort of mobile blind. I had leased a few acres of marshland between two good-sized clubs in Barnegat Bay, and instead of constructing a permanent blind I simply dug the sneak-box into the edge of the marsh, grassed it with reeds and a piece of tank-camouflage netting, put out half a dozen black-duck decoys and was in business. Stretched out in the box with the dogs beside me I was warm and comfortable; frequently, when things were slow, I dozed off. Usually the dogs' excitement was enough to awaken me if ducks stooled into the rig.

Going out to my leasehold at four one December morning, in total darkness, I was overtaken by a commercial trawler in the narrow main channel and swamped, fortunately in just three feet of water. Standing in the icy water, grabbing at floating decoys, shell boxes, netting, my hat, and sundry paraphernalia while two Labrador Retrievers paddled around helpfully, I thought of the millions of people sleeping soundly in warm beds and hoped nobody would come by and subject me to a sanity test. Nobody did. I went on out to the marsh, dried out reasonably well, and had a fair day's shooting for myself.

JUMP-SHOOTING

Another kind of jump-shooting is done from a canoe of skiff on rivers or creeks, either drifting with the current or paddling until a duck gets up. This is sporty shooting, since the ducks usually jump on the outer edge of the gun's range, and by the time you've dropped a paddle and grabbed a gun it's likely to be a barrel-stretching shot from a very unstable position.

One of the most enjoyable days of duck-shooting I ever had was on a creek in central Arkansas, with a guide poling a john-boat down the muddy, slow-moving waterway. There were cottonwoods and willows on both sides of the creek and generally a duck, or two around each bend. Frequently they'd jump and climb almost straight up to clear the trees, and when I fired at one almost directly overhead and then swung on another, the first duck fell directly onto my head and, as the guide observed, like to damn near broken my neckbone. Altogether I've been hit five times by falling ducks —and when four pounds of duck drops onto a man from a hundred feet up, it can jar him considerably. My friend Gene Hill was walking a Delaware marsh one time and shot an overhead Canada goose, then swung to shoot its partner; when the goose fell on him, Gene told me, it drove him ankle-deep into the muddy marsh bottom.

HARD RETRIEVES

Sometimes, of course, a duck simply isn't retrievable. I was shooting one cold November day in a cornfield in Lancaster County,

Pennsylvania, with a blacktop road running along one edge of it and local ducks, mostly mallards, trading back and forth from the field to the lake a mile away. Some over-hanging tree limbs at one end of the field served as sort of a stand-up blind, and when ducks would come over the trees I'd step out and shoot. I had promised the farmer who owned the field a brace of ducks, since it had looked like easy shooting, but it took me four missed ducks to realize they were flying into a stiff breeze and their airspeed was twice what it seemed. I doubled my lead and lowered one fat hen, but after that they stopped coming in.

Finally, after an hour's wait, a single greenhead came over and I stepped out, gave it a big lead and saw it fold its wings and start to tumble. Unfortunately it tumbled into the open back platform of a passing Ford pick-up truck, and since it would have taken me five minutes to get to my car and start chasing it, I called a baffled Labrador Retriever back, took the one duck, and walked down the road to the farmhouse. When I told the farmer about the truck-duck caper he asked which way the Ford had been headed, said "H-m-m!" and went into the house. In a minute he came out, said he'd telephoned his next-farm neighbor, asked him to look in the back of his truck, and had been told the duck was there. I drove down the road a mile and picked it up, to complete the promised pair.

THE ROLE OF PREDATOR

I've spent considerable time sitting in duck blinds in various parts of the country, and only a tiny fraction of that time—probably less than one percent—was spent in actual shooting. Sometimes it was a bluebird day and I didn't fire a shot. And since I always have binoculars with me, I've spent much of that time observing the gulls, herons, wading birds, songbirds, marsh hawks, sparrow hawks, ospreys, marsh rabbits, marsh rats, raccoons, crabs from fiddlers to horseshoes, fish singly and in schools, dragonflies, spiders—all the myraid, complex life that goes on in a coastal marsh. If the bluebird days don't provide shooting, at least they provide a free show, for those who care to watch it.

I told a nice old lady about this one time and she said, "Why don't you leave that nasty gun behind and just take the binoculars?" I tried to explain to her that even though I often didn't fire a shot for hours on end, it was important that I be *prepared* to shoot, that only when I was there in the role of a predator could I be a part of the whole ecological community of the marsh. Everything in that community, including me, had been preying on some lower, or at least smaller, form of life, and I had been there prepared to prey on ducks, brant, and geese. Without the gun, I tried to explain, I'd have been there merely as a spectator, with no more relationship to the life of the marsh than I have to the Green Bay Packers or the trained seals on a TV show.

I believe it's this establishment of a basic kinship to the whole of nature and to the fundamental patterns of natural life that makes the duck hunter hunt ducks. He may not be aware of it, and certainly isn't articulate about it, but I've known and talked to and drunk with enough duck shooters to be convinced that this is the root of their deep feeling about their sport—and, perhaps, the root of all modern man's urge to hunt and fish.

First Duck

I shot my first duck only twenty-six years ago, which qualifies me as a promising novice in a sport that takes a lifetime of learning. I remember the occasion as clearly as this morning's ham and eggs. I had been lying flat on my back for twenty minutes, on the bottom of a flat-floored skiff anchored in Shinnecock Bay on the ocean side of Long Island. The temperature was a few degrees above zero, and a northerly breeze whipped the bay into a chop that rocked the skiff jerkily. Each jerk sent two inches of slush and seawater sloshing across the floorboards, with each slosh sluicing ice water into the gap between my parka and my pants. I was soaked and starting to get seasick. I had been warned not to raise my head lest it spook incoming ducks, but sometimes when the skiff pitched I could see part of the rig around me—nearly two hundred block-decoys strewn cunningly over half an acre of bay.

The skiff was a special Long Island variety called a scooter, designed to lie as low in the water as the old, now-illegal sink-box and presumably resemble a floating cake of ice—an illusion enhanced by the white tarp that covered all of me but my face. The quarry was "coot," a New England misnomer for that coal-black, hump-beaked, fish-flavored, incredibly ugly duck, the sea-scoter, a species then so abundant that the limit was twenty-five a day. (It's still abundant, comparatively, with a daily limit of eight last year.)

Half a mile downwind, my guide waited in a beat-up cabin cruiser and kept himself warm by tonging quahogs from the bay bottom; eventually, when he reckoned I had reached the outer limits of human endurance, he would up anchor and come by to pick me up and deposit my partner in my place.

Then, from the corner of one eye, I saw a flock of white-winged scoters come barreling downwind across the spread of decoys—perhaps twenty birds bunched tight, with one lone straggler twenty feet behind. Grabbing for the double-barreled 12-gauge on the gunwhale rack, I thought, *One shot into the middle of that flock and I'll have half my limit with one shell. Bam!*

When the tight-bunched flock continued on its way unscathed, I was so astonished that I failed to fire the second barrel, and was only slightly less surprised when the straggler folded his wings and tumbled into the bay, stone dead. When the boat came down to pick up the coot and me, my companion said, "Chum, that was a classy shot. And I'm happy to see you're a sportsman, not one of these pot-hunting flock-shooters."

THIS MANIA CALLED DUCK HUNTING

Ted Trueblood

Despite my good fortune of having been able to edit Sports Afield *and* Outdoor Life, *one regret about the period that I'm stuck with is that I never had the chance to go hunting or fishing with Ted Trueblood. Friends like Ed Zern and Pete Barrett, regular True-blood companions, regaled me with accounts of their outings with Ted, but the opportunity to get into the field with him never came my way. If it ever does, it will be most welcome, for I have ad-mired him literally since boyhood. As a teenager, at one point I even began clipping Trueblood pieces to save in a loose-leaf binder, wanting to keep them to reread whenever the mood struck me. Today, I am no less a fan of Trueblood's clean, engaging prose. I find it illuminating and warm with feeling. Every month I look for-ward to his column in* Field & Stream, *and when the* Ted True-blood Hunting Treasury *was published by David MacKay Com-pany, Inc., New York, in 1978, I got one of the first copies. This is the first of two Trueblood's from his book we are happy to in-clude in our waterfowl book. Among other things, Trueblood knows ducks and duck hunters. He has been there, my friend, and will never need the power of invention when he talks about what he saw and felt.*

LAWS OF DUCK HUNTING

AFTER HUNTING ducks with varying success but with unflagging en-thusiasm for more than thirty years, I have finally come to the con-clusion that certain inflexible laws govern the sport of wildfowling. They are not man-made laws. They have nothing to do with the num-ber of times your gun will shoot without reloading, whether you can have a motor on your skiff, or the kind of decoys you must use.

In fact, the laws to which I refer are much more rigid than these. A man-made law can be broken. Doing so might not be a good idea, but it is possible. It is not possible to violate the laws to which I refer. They are laws of nature, as inexorable as the law of gravity. Every old hunter will recognize them. Let the newcomer read and beware.

There is a law to fit each situation, and each situation has its law. For example: You have been sitting in the blind for hours and not a duck has come near. The only thing to fly across the area of sky that you can watch has been an occasional dickeybird. You are cramped and stiff, and you decide to walk around (or take the skiff) and see if you can jump a few ducks.

The law: As soon as you are too far away to get back in time, they will start pouring in like bees to honey.

Young hunter, do you doubt this law? Let me tell you. One New Year's Day, Clare Conley and I went duck hunting. We made our setup before daylight on a bar in the Snake River. When the water is low, the gravel is exposed in a narrow strip about 50 yards long, and it is a great spot for mallards to loaf and rest. Right in the middle of the bar is a tiny, brushy island, just big enough to conceal a couple of hunters.

For some reason, however, the ducks didn't like our bar that day. We got four or five right after shooting time and then for the next three hours we might as well have been in the middle of a desert. What few ducks were flying knew exactly where they were going—and it wasn't to our bar, either. Our decoys, on the bar and in the water, looked good to us, but they obviously didn't look good to the ducks.

Conley, at that time, was fairly new to duck hunting. About 10 o'clock, he said, "Nuts! I've had enough of this. I'm going down the river and try to jump-shoot a few."

Although I did advise him not to leave the blind, I was wicked enough to be secretly glad that he was going. I knew what would happen.

Sure enough, he had been gone scarcely ten minutes when a little wad of mallards saw the decoys and came in like long-lost friends. I managed to drop a couple on the bar. A flock of bluebills whisked over almost low enough to knock my cap off, but I didn't see them in time to shoot. One greenwing teal lit among the decoys. I didn't disturb him.

When Conley had been gone thirty minutes, I saw a flock of Canada geese flying up the middle of the river. They were low and apparently looking for a place to sit down. I waited until they were opposite the blind, then gave them just a little soft, confidential mallard talk on the call. They turned, set their wings, and came straight in, and I killed two.

Conley had seen the geese, and he came back upstream in time to pick mine up. He was disgusted. He tied the boat under the overhanging brush that concealed it and got into the blind without a word. Then we sat until 1 P.M. without breaking another cap and finally went home.

There are laws that govern various other aspects of the sport of duck hunting, too. Take the matter of weather. Everybody knows that good shooting depends on the weather. I never miss a forecast during the duck season, but the problem is more involved than that. If I plan a trip far in advance I am certain to draw a bluebird day; if I wait until the last minute, the boss piles on more work or relatives come to visit and I can't go at all. In the spring when I am trying to fish the wind blows all the time; in the fall when I need it to make the ducks fly, it never blows at all. Therefore, I have arrived at this law: No matter what you do, the weather will be wrong 95 percent of the time.

Once I had discovered the law of weather, the solution was fairly simple. I just went duck hunting as often as I could, and approximately one day out of twenty was perfect. Knowing this, I was spared a great deal of fretting.

Then there is the law of arrival. It is so simple that it requires no explanation. It states: If you arrive at the chosen spot early and get your decoys out well in advance of shooting time, the flight will be late. If, however, you arrive a little late and are still putting out decoys when shooting time comes, the flight will be early.

There are two minor laws that might well be grouped together, though in the aggregate they save a great many ducks. The first is the law of smoking: If after a long dry period, you set down your gun to light a smoke, a flock of ducks will immediately whip over the blind and be out of range before you can recover. The second is the law of coffee: If, likewise after a long dry spell, you decide to have a cup of coffee, a flock will swing over while you have vacuum bottle in one hand and a half-filled cup in the other.

Normally during the duck season, I carry lunch, coffee bottle, dry gloves, camera, shells, and various useful odds and ends in a waterproof box. I take it home each evening to be restocked and return it to the boat next morning. One bleak day several years ago, my wife and I set out our decoys in a likely spot, and since we both had quite a few shells left in our coat pockets from the last hunt, we didn't attempt to get more out of the box at first.

The flight was slow, but we eventually began to run low on ammunition. A few snowflakes began to curl down about this time and, judging from past experience, I decided that I'd better get more shells. I walked along the shore to the boat, which was hidden 50 yards away, and opened the box. There was not one shell in it! I had forgotten to put more in the night before.

When I returned to the blind with the bad news, we counted up and discovered that we had just six shells between us—and we still had six ducks to go. Judging from the way we had been shooting so far, this was definitely too many ducks to go. Sure enough. We did the best we could, but we ran out of shells when we were still short of our limit by three birds.

Meanwhile, the snow fell harder and harder. When it snows, mallards feed in the fields all day, but every time they get a neckful of corn or wheat they have to make a trip for water. They also need gravel, and if you are in a convenient spot that offers both you will see shooting out of this world. We were in such a spot, and an hour after the first snowflakes fell the ducks came.

We could no longer shoot, of course, but we could look. The air soon was full of ducks as far as we could see. The water was black with them. Mostly, they were mallards, a few pintails and green-wing teal and some baldpates.

They plummeted down so close that we could have hit them with a stick. They splashed and gabbled among our decoys with no concern whatever and walked out on the bar, almost at our feet.

For two solid hours they came and went in a steady procession. Very likely they continued all day. It was something I'll never forget, but two hours of it with empty guns was all we could endure.

This experience, coupled with similar ones in the days when limits were bigger and running out of shells not so unusual, led to my discovery of the law of ammunition: The one sure way to bring on a spectacular duck flight is to run out of shells.

No doubt all duck hunters are familiar with the law of lunch—the quickest way to bring a flurry of activity on a dull day is to start eating your lunch—but I question whether most duck hunters know about the equally infallible law of decoy moving. It was one of the most difficult to discover, but after getting the hang of it I have profited many times.

It works best on a dull day—a time when only a few ducks are flying and all of them are going somewhere else. About the middle of the morning, you decide your decoys aren't placed right. You will move some of them. As soon as you are up to your boot tops in the water with a bundle of blocks in each arm, you hear a cautious "Psst" from your partner, who is still in the blind. You look up, and there is a big flock coming straight at you, wings cupped for a landing. Of course, it too late then and the first willing ducks in two hours flare off out of range.

This happened to me so often that I finally began to get wise. I kept an eye cocked skyward at all times. Sometimes I saw the approaching birds in time to rush back into the blind. Once I flopped face down on a gravel bar and my partner dropped mallards on both sides of me. I felt quite clever about this maneuver until I discovered that I had somehow broken my pipe in the process.

At any rate, the law is this: When things are desperate, go out to move your decoys. It will bring ducks nine times out of ten.

I shouldn't have to mention the law of sleep. Every old-time member of the clan has discovered it to his mortification. But for the benefit of the younger generation, this is how it works. The situation calls for a flat-calm, sunny, warm, bluebird day. No ducks are stirring. You are sleepy because you were up late getting ready and up early getting where you are now, and you finally give in to Morpheus. The law: As soon as you are sound asleep, a big flock of ducks will light among the decoys. They will remain until you wake up. Then they will fly safely away before you are able to collect your senses, pick up your gun, and get ready to shoot.

There are two laws concerning friends. The first is the law of special friends: If you have a special friend that you are particularly anxious to show good shooting, and you take him to the best spot you know during the best part of the season in the best kind of weather, the shooting will be miserable.

I took a special friend duck hunting twice one year. One day we got one duck and the other day we didn't get any. I am sure he is now convinced that I never do kill one and that all my duck killing is purely imaginary.

The other friend law concerns conversational friends. If—as all duck hunters are forever hoping to do—you discover a new and wonderful place to shoot and make the mistake of telling a talking-to (as distinguished from a hunting-with) friend, there will be a hunter behind every reed when you go back. Futhermore, each hunter will have a nervous dog, a loud call, and an inexhaustible supply of ammunition.

Although I consider it inexcusable, people do have parties during the hunting season. This led to my discovery of the law of society, which follows: If you offend your friends by not attending their party so that you can go duck hunting early the next morning, the shooting will be terrible; if, however, you do go and give up hunting you will learn later that you missed the best day of the year.

Consider, too, the law of the upwind ducks. The situation is this: You are pass-shooting at ducks that are beating their way into the wind. It is a hard wind. Some of them seem to be hanging almost still in it as they slowly approach and others are drifting back and forth. You burn up a scandalous amount of ammunition. Finally, after leading them farther and farther out of sheer desperation, you connect twice in a row. You have it made! Law: The flight will stop immediately.

My last law is one that no experienced duck hunter will challenge. It had been a miserable day. Only a handful of ducks flew early and still fewer later on. Those that did pass by were both high and far, and if they saw your decoys they failed to give them a second look. After hours of waiting, during which your feeling of hopelessness steadily increased, you decided to pick up and go. Law: As soon as the last decoy is in the bag a great flight will commence.

Thus we see that the lot of the duck hunter is not a happy one. He is the child of frustration, the collector of mishap, the victim of misfortume. He suffers from cold and wet and lack of sleep. He is punished more often than he is rewarded. Yet he continues. Why? Because one great day—and great days do come, days when the ducks are willing and the sun swings true—repays him manyfold for all the others.

That is why there are so many of us. We are all waiting for the next great day—whenever that may be.

PORTRAIT OF A
SWEET-WATER MARSH

Robert Elman

As this is written, Bob Elman's chores as Editor-in-Chief of Winchester Press have thrown a half-hitch on his typewriter. Until taking the Winchester reins, he was one of the most prolific and sought-after professionals in the outdoor field. Of his many books and hundreds of magazine articles, my personal favorite is the magnificent The Atlantic Flyway, *published by Winchester Press. In the book, Bob's lively yet precise prose deals with masses of information and background on waterfowling's present and past. The book, a must for the serious collector, is enriched by the superb photography of Walter Osborne, who passed away just after completing the work. The true and mature duck hunter knows that the marsh is the place to be, whether the ducks are flying or not. The marsh is alive with eternal rhythms that will make you grateful to be a part of them. Once you know what to look for, the feeling of enjoying the marsh world in total will never leave you.*

WITH THE moon beyond the last quarter and the sun not yet up, a grove of scrub pines is barely discernible above the marsh. A gunner trudges along gingerly, intent on getting his decoys set out before the legal shooting hour. He hears only the crunch of sand underfoot as he passes among the pines, then the gurgling of running water and the suck of ankle-deep mud in a narrow cedar swamp. He is mildly startled by the rustle of cordgrass whipping against his waders as he descends a meadow. Thinking about the morning to come, remembering other mornings, he is hardly aware of the sound his dog makes, padding, panting, splashing through each puddle. Several meadowlarks dart chest-high across the gunner's path, close enough to have touched but visible for only an instant as a black-on-black flickering. He smiles, reminded of the hidden life surrounding him.

This, in part, is why he has come here. This, and the difficult beauty of patience in a cold wind, of enticing ducks and geese that have seen decoys before and survived other calls; this, and the smooth gun swing, the report, the plummeting bird, the eagerness of the big black Labrador Retriever. It is atavism, no doubt, but also the craftsman's pride and the naturalist's curiosity.

The gunner pauses at the shoreline of the slough, listening to the rhythmic lap of water and the whisper of feather grass, and another whisper contending with the breeze. He has heard no wild-fowl cry, but he recognizes the sibilant throb of wings. Then he hears the voice of a flight, a reedy stutter of quacks followed by a staccato rattling. Black ducks, he guesses. It sounds like their feeding call, yet the tone seems both urgent and plaintive. The weather has been cold to the north. Perhaps, despite the waning moon, the flock is setting down after a long migratory flight. Ducks and geese often travel far at night.

Before the morning is over, the gunner hopes to see mallards, pintails, and Canada geese as well. Literally dozens of waterfowl species rest and feed at this marsh on the Atlantic Flyway. Many can be legally hunted, though the regulations and bag limits often vary from fall to fall, based on hunting pressure and a careful watch of the northern breeding grounds. Game biologists have studied water and food levels through the spring and summer, checked hatching and fledging success, taken a census of the anatidine population, closely observed the fits and starts of onsetting migration. The gunner carries a copy of his state's regulations—which, of course, conform to applicable federal regulations—but he will probably have no need to consult it. He knows this year's bag limits, and he can recognize the species along his flyway.

In the pale glow that has now inched upward from the horizon he sees a wavering line of dots curve across the sky toward him. A few of the dots pass the others and a few slip back, forming a wide bow that quickly stretches and sharpens to become a massive chevron. The black silhouettes are Canadas. Now he can hear the resonant calls of the wild geese, bugling cries above the dim, echolike chorus of distant stragglers.

Clambering down the bank to where his boat is tied, he throws back the protective tarp, carefully props his long 12-gauge double against the stern seat, sets his shell box next to it, and stiffly climbs in. His side-by-side is prized for its efficiency as well as its traditional beauty of contour. Only in recent years have such fowling pieces been over-shadowed by over/unders and repeaters—the latter equipped with magazine plugs limiting their capacity to three shells in compliance with a sensible federal law. But since few men are quick enough to get off three effective shots before a flight is gone, the choice of gun is hardly more than a matter of personal preference.

The gunner on this marsh has used the same double for years, and he lays it in the boat with a tenderness not usually displayed in handling mechanical contrivances. His big Lab has jumped aboard and clambers among the decoys, whining impatiently.

Keeping near the shoreline, the gunner poles quickly to his blind and then works quickly but methodically to set out his decoys. He starts with several strings of two or three blocks each, lined together and anchored so that they will bob on the current with a lifelike movement. He scatters other blocks about in what appears to be a random positioning. His father, an old Eastern Shoreman, would have set them in a careful "fish hook" pattern, but the value of those traditional arrangements was never more than myth. The gunner follows simpler rules, separating each decoy by several feet from all the others to ensure that all can be seen readily and recognized from the air. In the midst of the spread is a vacant area—landing space. The innermost decoys are a bit over twenty yards downwind from his blind, so that the birds will pass before him as they set down into the wind.

The blind is built on the lee side of a great curving spit, overgrown with tall grasses. On the far side of the spit is a river, a second shoreline, and a sprawling farm. Reeds and sedges line the shores, with meadow foxtail growing beyond. Farther off, on the farm, are potholes adorned with sago and rimmed with Japanese millet. Best of all, there are the fields of corn that have drawn gigantic concentrations of waterfowl to the middle portion of the flyway in recent years.

As the gunner places his decoys, he reflects on two recent days of rather mediocre shooting. The birds had been foraging nocturnally under a full, bright moon, and there was little movement after sun-up. Then, too, there had been calm, bright high-flying weather on the first day, and on the second a variable breeze that frequently brought ducks over with the wind at their tails. But today, he notes, the wind will be at his back, and a heavy overcast will keep both ducks and geese flying low, watching for landmarks and staying under a layer of turbulent weather. Different conditions may be advantageous in some spots, depending on local terrain and type of habitat, but this is the kind of day when many blinds are occupied on the marshes of the Altantic Flyway.

The gunner is using two dozen mallard blocks and a pair of Canada goose decoys. If he had a partner with him, he would prob-ably set out more, but even a dozen mallards will usually entice the puddlers. On one of the big coastal salt marshes, or a bay, or on good deep wild-celery water, he would substitute several dozen scaup or canvasback decoys, for these will lure the diver species of the flyway. It takes a big raft of decoys to interest the flights of divers on the open waters of the coast.

A wildfowler of long experience, he sets out a pair of "confidence" decoys—oversized Canada goose blocks representing two old tradi-tions of the Atlantic Flyway. Decoys carved in feeding or preening position, or with their heads turned back upon their bodies in an attitude of sleep are sometimes called confidence decoys, the theory being that their serenity proclaims all is well. But a true confidence decoy imitates a species not being hunted, particularly a bird known for wariness and intelligence, and therefore calculated to impart a sense of security to any wildfowl flying over to inspect the rig. Con-fidence decoys have been in use along the flyway since the mid-nineteenth century, and their use has spread westward. They have included geese, shorebirds, gulls, herons, terns, and even loon in upper New England. Occasionally one still sees a gull—the creation of a wood sculptor or a taxidermist—perched upon the camouflaged bow of a sneakboat.

The other tradition, that of mammoth decoys, is thought to have originated with the market shooters and guides at the famous "shoot-ing stands" erected at Cape Cod during the nineteenth century. These men used live decoys near the blinds, and farther out they floated huge, barrel-bodied "slat" decoys to attract flights from great distances. The idea soon spread southward and appeared in the form of solid blocks as well as slat decoys. A number of them can be seen at the Shelburne Museum in Shelburne, Vermont, where the collections include that of the late Joel D. Barber whose 1932 book, *Wild Fowl Decoys*, was the first treatise on the history and use of American decoys.

The oversized Shelburne decoys include a primitive solid wood black duck made by Wilbur Corwin at Bellport, Long Island, in about 1850; a solid canvasback made by Wilton Walker of Tulls Creek, North Carolina, in about 1900 and used at Knotts Island, on Currituck Sound; another oversized can, of unknown date, by the renowned Shang Wheeler; and a massive slat goose by the great Cape Cod maker Joseph C. Lincoln. Probably built at about the turn of the century, the Lincoln decoy is over five feet long and bears a passing resemblance to an upturned boat. The use of mammoths spread to other flyways, and such well-known commercial manufacturers as Mason's Decoy Factory of Detroit produced them in the late nineteenth and early twentieth centuries.

Oversized canvasbacks and redheads were popular among market gunners from Back Bay, Virginia, down through Currituck Sound in North Carolina. Even more imposing than the ducks or the giant Canada blocks were the swan decoys used from Currituck north into Chesapeake Bay until swan shooting was prohibited in 1913. Professional gunners sometimes included a few swans in their rigs, and when that law was passed, Joel Barber recalled, many men knocked the long necks and heads off the blocks and converted the decoys into geese. Some of those swans were truly works of art. A specimen from the Barber-Shelburne collection, made in about 1890 by Samuel T. Barnes of Havre de Grace, Maryland, is among the finest examples of tidewater sculpture.

Fifteen-pound wooden swans are no longer encountered on the coastal marshes, but somewhat oversized Canadas are still occasionally seen. Bobbing ponderously on the waters of today's Atlantic Flyway are plastic mallards and even blacks over two feet long and nearly a foot wide, about a third larger than the more common standard decoys. The manufacturers sometimes advertise these looming figurines as "Magnums," a term as apropos of decoys as of shotgun shells or champagne bottles.

If the gunner were out primarily for Canadas, he would use as many goose decoys as possible, whether on water or at a feeding field. It is the nature of these birds to be skeptical, and reassurance is most effective in the form of large numbers of their own kind. Just a pair of them, used as confidence decoys, may or may not draw any Canadas within range. Possibly they will attract a few stray singles or pairs. And they will reassure some of the less wary ducks such as mallards. One of them is a floating block, and the gunner places it at a dignified distance from his duck decoys and very close to shore. The second is a "stick-up," with a pointed stake protruding from its base. He drives this into the mud, standing the decoy on shore near its mate.

It is almost sunup when the last decoy is set. The legal shooting hour has arrived. The sound of chuckling, gabbling calls has become closer and more frequent. The gunner poles his boat over to the blind, an elevated affair constructed on stilts a little out from shore. He had originally planned to build his blind on the bank, where tall grasses would add to its camouflage, but he had found no way to conceal his boat. With the blind on the water, he can slide the craft beneath the elevated floor. The dog jumps out and sits in a corner of the blind, trembling slightly. The gunner opens his shell box, loads up, and settles himself comfortably on the battered piano stool. He thinks about shifting a couple of the nearest decoys. There is no need for the boat since he is wearing his waders.

As he is about to stand, he hears a sudden loud chorus of quacking. A score of mallards rises out of the tall grass sixty yards behind the blind and wheels away. He grins, realizing that the ducks have been quietly resting or feeding there since before his arrival. His activity has finally alarmed them, but he has not actually flushed them and he has not fired a shot. They will probably return later, a few at a time. They will circle his rig, and he will be ready.

A small bunch of sprig passes, fast and too high, their wings flailing so rapidly as to appear blurred. He hopes there will be more pintails—more and closer. A trio of tiny greenwings darts by, dipping and turning erratically. The teal season has already closed for the year and he does not raise his gun.

Beginning to feel chilled and dejected, knowing that the best period for shooting is passed too quietly, he sips hot coffee and remembers other mornings. For a moment he thinks the call of a single wild goose is part of his reverie, but then he sees the big, lone Canada, wings thrusting deeply, neck curved slightly downward, flying low, searching. The bird has seen his confidence decoys and will pass just close enough. The gunner is on his feet, swinging the muzzle past the great gray body before a blast from the right barrel reverberates over the water.

In a few moments the dog is back in the blind, dripping, tail thumping. The goose lies in an opposite corner of the blind.

At mid-morning, the gunner stands and stretches. The goose is flanked by two pintails now, both drakes, one with its iridescent brown head and slender white neck draped across the brownish-gray wing of the Canada. The long tail feathers of the second sprig are cocked upward from the floor of the blind, peculiarly jaunty even when lifeless.

The gunner has not filled his limit, but with the day growing warm and still, he has half decided to quit when he hears the low, chattering feeding call of mallards. He crouches, gun ready, and answers their call with his—tolling them in, not overdoing it, coaxing. Five birds come over, setting their wings to pitch in among the decoys. A hen plummets into the water directly in front of the blind. A large drake arcs downward and crashes on shore with a thudding sound. A double. He is still one bird short of this year's daily bag limit in his state, but he does not care.

As his Lab fetches the drake—the farthest bird first—he is already putting his gear back into the boat. The sky is still overcast and gusts are again rippling the water. For a wildfowler on the Atlantic Flyway, it has been a beautiful day.

DUCK BLINDS

Charles F. Waterman

Since its founding in 1969, Winchester Press has made some solid contributions to outdoor literature. Among these, one nearest to my own heart was the publication of Charlie Waterman's The Part I Remember *in 1974. The book's appearance was a clear acknowledgment of the outstanding writing Charlie had been doing in his numerous magazine pieces. This piece from the book shows the Waterman talent at its typical best. Charlie divides his time between Florida in the winter and Montana in the summer and autumn. Nice work if you can get it, and I guess you can if you can write like Charlie. Me? . . . I live in New Jersey, all year!*

LONG BEFORE dawn the traffic lights blinked for us alone in our small town. Our tires crunched against dry snow on the pavement and a single mongrel dog trotted under a street light, pursuing his route at a slight angle. Our windshield wipers grated against some icy streaks not yet thawed by the heater. We drove slowly on the highway, slippery in spots.

The hot coffee still seemed warm against my ribs and I squirmed cozily in my layers of wool and down. The blind would be cold and dawn would come slowly.

We turned into the rough side road. I was careful not to miss the lane toward the river, its two tracks white with fresh snow. When we had stopped by the creek we stood silent outside the little truck for a moment, listening to the mutter of running water and hoping to hear ducks or geese, but we caught only the barking of a farm dog somewhere. That reminded Jack of something.

"We should have a retriever," he said. "You don't go after downed birds as fast as you used to."

I thought of the time I'd peeled to my underwear, walked through a little snow and swam after a pair of fat mallards lodged with their orange feet up against a clump of grass. It had been years ago and I had no intention of repeating that performance.

You'd be better off if you'd think more about Labs and less about pointing dogs," Jack accused. "There are lots of shots we pass up because we don't have a Lab. I'm gonna get me a Lab or a Chessie, or maybe one of those water spaniels."

He had been announcing that for years so I didn't take it too seriously. Jack's wife, Norma, had put her foot down. Two dogs were enough and if Jack wanted a Lab he'd have to give up one of his pointers.

"If he'd just treat them like members of the family, I wouldn't care," Norma had said. "But he treats them better than people. When the kids were home their milk came right after the dog food."

We got into our waders with grunts and puffing because our extra clothing made it difficult to stoop. We gathered up the ammunition, more than we could possibly use, the bags of decoys and the duck guns.

"That damned fence," Jack grumbled, his little flashlight playing along four tight strands of barbed wire.

We tossed the decoys over the fence, pushed the guns through, and crawled under like overweight bears, trying to keep the barbs out of our chest waders.

Next was the creek, friendly and shallow in daylight but dark, mysterious and ominous at night. From midstream, we heard the startled quacks and slapping wings of a little bunch of mallards that went almost straight up to clear the cottonwoods. For an instant we made out dark blobs above us.

We waded with our eyes on the white opposite bank, feeling the bottom stones with our feet; after that we came to the slough with more ducks and then to where the creek slowed and broadened toward the river. The blind was only a dark clump roofed with snow, much like the bushes along the backwater's shore, and we hurried a little with the decoys, trying to keep our hands dry as we placed the blocks in a foot of water, and sloshed back to the willow blind and its improvised seats.

Once there was a hissing rush when birds set their wings over the decoys and then hurried on to fade from hearing. We heard Canada geese going high and following the river, their honks and softer gabbling sparse and unhurried.

Dawn was gradual but there was a point when we knew shoot time had arrived although we checked our watches to be sure. The decoys showed plainly out there, bobbing a little in a chill breeze and collecting a few small flakes of snow. We never saw the two green-winged teal until they plummeted from nowhere and struck the water with loud plops to sit with stretched necks and eye the decoys with suspicious disapproval.

"Let's let them go," Jack said, and a few moments later they left almost as suddenly as they had arrived. We swung our guns at them.

"They look easy when you aren't going to shoot," Jack said.

A flock of mallards went over high, too many birds to be interested in our little slough and dozen decoys, but I quacked hopefully on the call.

"You sound better," said Jack, who has been critical of my duck calling for twenty years, "but if any look as if they might try to come in you leave that damned thing alone. It's hard enough to get birds into this puddle without you squawking at them."

Jack is getting older and I am very tolerant of him.

There was a speck low against the gray sky, coming fast, and it became a duck, then a big duck, then a mallard, then a drake, and he set his wings briefly as if about to come in but changed his mind and headed on. Jack has missed a lot of ducks but he didn't miss that one. He stood up with his old Model 12 pumpgun with the solid rib and the shiny receiver where the blueing is worn off, and he caught the drake in a smooth swing with an ounce and a half of fives. The duck splashed and then bobbed with its feet up.

"I wish I could do that every time," he said.

Other mallards went over high, the storm pushing them from frozen potholes to the north, but they gave no sign they had seen our decoys. There were some goldeneyes that whistled past behind the blind, and we saw a young whitetail buck on down the shore fidgeting about something, perhaps a thread of our scent he couldn't quite catalog. A cock pheasant crackled over near the main river near the thick brush, and a mink prospected the far side of our backwater, appearing and disappearing in shoreline growth.

They say that great industries have had their beginnings in

duck binds and that national policy has been influenced there, but Jack and I have never talked about such things as far as I can remember. We once decided that number five shot is a pretty good compromise between sixes and fours and we concluded that manufacturers should test their new waders better, but I don't know who Jack voted for in any presidential election.

"There are no bad days in a duck blind," Jack said. "Everybody likes pretty weather but ducks generally fly better when it's stormy. When I was younger I used to think I could hunt ducks every day forever but now that I don't work any more there's one thing missing —a day like this would be more fun if you could take it off from something. When I don't work I don't appreciate leisure, I guess.

"And now that I'm past seventy," Jack said, rubbing a speck of mud from his gunstock, "I find there's a new problem in growing older. When I was forty I couldn't do the things I did when I was twenty but I didn't care because I didn't want to do the things I did when I was twenty. But now that I'm seventy I wish I could still do the things I did when I was forty or fifty."

Jack doesn't go sheep hunting any more and he doesn't wade the deeper, faster trout and steelhead rivers.

At around noon we stood up and got the kinks out of our muscles and then we waded out after the decoys. As they always do in the sporting calendars, a little bunch of ducks, baldpates this time, swung in low and then towered when they saw us frozen at attention and knee-deep in cold water. It was snowing harder and they were simply absorbed into the sky in seconds.

"There aren't any bad days in a duck blind," Jack said again.

WHAT IS A DUCK HUNTER?

Charley Dickey

Charley Dickey's byline has never made The New York Times
*bestseller list, but it would not surprise me at all to wake up
some Sunday morning and find it perched there. He is an innovative
and talented writer who knows how to mix fact and emotion in
a way that holds a reader hard. Charley was a very successful
free-lancer before becoming President of the National Shooting
Sports Foundation, and since resigning that position he has resumed
his chores with typewriter and camera while living the good life in
Florida. Amwell Press wisely issued a collection of some of his
shorter pieces entitled* Backtrack. *It is a rich and rewarding work
that could become a classic. Charley's "What Is. . . . . " series first
appeared in* Field & Stream *and covered all those field sports closest
to our hearts. This one has always been particularly memorable
to me.*

BETWEEN A boy's first single barrel and a wistful old man, we find
an amazing creature called a duck hunter. They are found in patched
sweaters and cashmere, but all of them have the same idea: To enjoy every second of every minute of every hunting trip—and to protest violently at the slowness of the approaching shooting hour
and to give up reluctantly when the sun sets and the hunting ends
for the day.

Duck hunters are found nearly everywhere—on small creeks,
in great marshes, gun shops, pot holes, retriever trials, swamps,
slipping out of back doors, telling lies during working hours at
the office, and in the pin oaks. Mothers are patient with them,
young girls are suspicious of them, wives give up on them, brothers
and sisters think they are peculiar, the boss envies them, and
Artemis protects them. A duck hunter is Truth with freezing
feet, Beauty in long flannels, Wisdom during a gale, and the Hope
of the future with Nature as his God.

When you have work to do, a duck hunter is thinking of blocks, his Labrador pups, his newest shotgun, and rice paddies. When you want him to make a good impression, he may talk only of the nesting season in Canada, insulated boots, the best load for pass shooting at sprig, the honker he once bagged, and, regardless of where he is, he may demonstrate loudly the comeback call.

A duck hunter is a composite. At a camp breakfast he'll eat two pieces of country ham and six eggs for breakfast, but at home he gets by on coffee and cigarettes; he's always at the blinds before dawn, but he's been known to be late to see the banker; he has the energy of a Magnum shell as he slops through icy mud, but at home he's always too tired to help with the chores; he has the wind of a bellows as he blows the wrong notes on his call; he has the imagination of a politician as he explains why he missed his last five shots; he shows the courage of a polar bear as he gradually turns blue in the shivering dawn, but tells his buddy that he's quite comfortable; he has the enthusiasm of a kid at Christmas as he expects a scattered flock a mile away to decoy to his blocks, and, when they do come in and splash, he forgets to take the safety off.

He likes waterproof britches, all kinds of retrievers, slouchy hats, full-choked guns, smoggy mornings, frequent holidays, hidden ponds, hand-painted decoys, hunters he can outshoot, insulated underwear, nor-easters, and questionable characters who are also duck hunters. He is not much for dancing, duck hawks, posted land, loud clothes, shaving, bridge, weekend company, short seasons, dieting at camp, late sleepers, and bluebird days. Without thought of background, position or economic status, he likes people who hunt ducks two months a year and talk about it the rest of the time.

Nobody else is so early to rise, or drags home so tired and cold—during the duck season. Nobody else gets so much fun out of squeaky calls, frozen feet, leaky boots, muddy flats, and a thermos of hot coffee between flights. Nobody else suffers so silently with frostbitten hands, sleet dripping down his waders, and chapped lips. Nobody else can cram into one pocket a box of shells, a spare duck call, extra smokes, a squashed candy bar, a roll of string, a bottle opener, a plug of tobacco, a dog leash, and a busted dog whistle.

A duck hunter is a magical creature. You may get tired of him practicing on his call but you can't help liking him. He may be hard to locate at his desk during open season but you know he'll do his work with the best. He may stretch a weekend into five days but he'll do more than his share at the office the rest of the year. You soon learn that his calls to the marshes each Fall is as strong as the ducks he seeks.

You might as well give up. The duck hunter is a child of the wilds and no one can change him. He'll serve on community committees ten months a year but be careful how you schedule him the other two. When the ducks come whistling out of the north his soul won't rest until he gets mud on his feet and a blind full of hulls. He's earnest in his civic duties but he's just a little more sincere when he's giving a feed chuckle to a doubtful flock of mallards.

And though you lose patience with him in the Fall, you know you'll always like him. There's something about him that rings true as a shiny new barrel. He's an honest and kindly man who asks only of life that the ducks fly often and fast, that he give them a sporting chance, and that God will let him come back to the marshes again next year.

TWO

Myths or Mysteries

NORTH AGAIN

John Madson

Here is waterfowling's other migration, the great living tides of birds headed north in the spring. Even without the gunning we love, the event is one of the most compelling parts of the wildfowler's year. Here, in the finest word portrait of returning migration I have ever read, John Madson proves once again why he today is one of the country's most highly regarded writers on the outdoors. Few, very few, writers today can match Madson's talent for blending personal insight and emotion with reportorial skills. His pieces ring with truth and understanding. They do not bore or brag, nor are they marred by gaps of information and unconvincing twists of interpretation to fit some private goal. To me, Madson says: "Hey, got a minute? Let me tell you about something I saw and what I think it means to us all." Obviously, my respect for the man's work knows no bounds, so I will cease gushing and let the words speak for themselves. John is a writer, naturalist and wildlife biologist who until recently held the position of Assistant Director of Conservation for the Winchester-Western Division of the Olin Corporation. His work has appeared in virtually every nature and outdoor magazine, from Audubon *to* National Geographic. *This piece is from* Audubon *and was included in the marvelous collection of John's pieces,* Out Home, *published by Winchester Press in 1979.*

EARLY MARCH on the Canadian prairies is just another name for winter.

Oh, there's been some loose talk about spring coming, but not much to back it up. Cabin fever is rising. Vast numbers of small boys are getting whacked. Folks are edgy, and neighbors coming home from Mexican holidays are well advised to lie low and keep quiet until their suntans fade.

But now, for our old friends in Saskatoon, Moose Jaw, and Portage la Prairie, we're happy to verify that rumor of spring. Due south of you, the Cheyenne Bottoms of central Kansas are newly alive with ducks and geese. They're bringing spring up from the Gulf Coast and will be with you directly. Hang in there. The Grand Passage is under way. Spring is being delivered by our most dependable airline.

An excited, restless throng is coming up through the heart of North America—up from the wintering marshes and estuaries, from the Sabine and Aransas and Laguna Madre. Their impatience builds with each passing day, the hosts of wildfowl crowding behind the frost barrier of the 32-degree isotherm and pushing it steadily northward.

Most of them are being drawn to a vast arc of open land that sprawls through southeastern Alberta, southern Saskatchewan, and southwestern Manitoba, down into those parts of the Dakotas and Montana that lie east and north of the Missouri River. This is the prairie pothole region—the fabled Duck Factory—300,000 square miles of the richest duck-producing range in the New World.

It's a young landscape, no older than the retreat of the last lobes of the Wisconsin glaciation perhaps 10,000 years ago. Sheets, ridges, hills, and mounds of ground-up, heaved-up glacial junk were strewn over thousands of square miles—a rumpled landscape with a remarkable faculty for retaining surface waters. Lakes and ponds were dammed by countless glacial moraines; others were trapped in the ox-bows of Pleistocene rivers. Some resulted from ice lenses—the soil-covered chunks of ice left buried in the debris after the glacial retreat, later melting to leave water-filled depressions. It is a baby land, raw and new, still too young to have developed mature drainage systems. That will come, of course, when stream courses and river valleys deepen. The lakes and ponds not drained will eventually fill, choke, and die.

But that is long away, and now, in a wet year, the region may have eight million potholes, sloughs, lakes, and marshes that are enormously productive of waterfowl. Thousands of square miles of this region average an incredible density of over thirty-one breeding ducks per square mile—and although the prairie pothole region is only ten percent of the continent's total waterfowl breeding area, it produces at least half of the continent's ducks.

It's more than just abundance of water. The glacial tills, clays, and rock scourings that form the bed of this region are immensely rich in minerals. The young soils born of these parent materials have not been subjected to heavy precipitation nor efficient drainage, and the mineral wealth has not been leached out of the upper levels of soil. Much of it remains within reach of plant roots, to be recycled into standing plant parts. Water flowing over and through these prairie soils conveys a rich charge of nutrients to the prairie pond. The slightly alkaline water and warm summers of the prairie region promote rapid decomposition of plant materials in both soil and water, and filling of the ponds with plant debris is retarded. Even the occasional drought benefits these waters, for the organic stuff in their basins will break down even faster if aired and sunned.

The subhumid prairie climate not only built a deep grassland humus rich in nitrogen and phosphorus, charging the glacial wetlands with fertility, but made a prairie biome that is far more attractive to waterfowl than is forest.

The myriad potholes, ponds, and marshes of the northern prairie region offer waterfowl an incredible number of varied, interspersed habitats. No two potholes or marshes are alike. Their basic fertility provides lush vegetation and high production of plankton and insect life. They offer wildfowl escape cover, nesting cover, brood cover, loafing sites, and food in an abundance and variety that are incomparable, and between these richly varied waters there are fields and grasslands for feeding and nesting. Now, in early spring, this life-kettle is beginning to simmer.

They began pulling out of some wintering grounds in January, staging northward for as long as two and a half months with an urgency that grows with the strengthening sunlight. The vanguard of the waterfowl migration may reach the prairie potholes of southern Canada as early as mid-March, when Arctic owls are still adorning fenceposts like caps of snow and flocks of snow buntings whirl across the bleak fields. Any gains made during the day are lost at night, when newly thawed waters refreeze. Beneath a veneer of cold mud the ground is still frozen, and bitter winds sweep the openlands. But the ducks are not misled; they believe the zenith of the sun.

Mallards and pintails and Canada geese are the first to come, followed by gadwalls, shovellers, baldpates, teal, and scaup. Although the big marshes and lakes are closed with rotting ice, sheet water covers old wheat stubble fields and a few marsh edges are beginning to open. There may be no green foods for a month after the first migrants arrive, nor any new cover for nesting. The vanguards are content to eat seeds and nest in last year's dry vegetation.

Many of the prairie ducks begin pairing long before they reach the northern marshes. Prenuptial courtship was under way on the wintering grounds as early as January; most of the mallards are now paired, and many of the pintails. For these, the intense competition of prenuptial courting is almost over—most of the ducks have accepted their drakes, pair bonds have formed, and the mated birds fly low over the warming April marshes and ponds. Blue and snow geese have arrived at the prairie region, tarried briefly, and pressed northward to their nesting grounds. (And how can we forgive the taxonomists for discarding the old name of the snow goose, *Chen hyperborea*, "the goose from beyond the north wind?") The whistling swans have come and gone, keeping their tryst with the subarctic. Some Canada geese may nest in the prairie regions, but most of them, too, are drawn farther north. The prairie pothole country is left to the myriad ducks.

In spring mornings and evenings there are ducks everywhere in the prairie skies. Gadwalls are beginning to spark in earnest. So are the baldpates, those tardy lovers, among the last of the dabbling ducks to pair off. Canvasbacks perform their most breathtaking aerial rite—the drake closely pursuing the duck and seizing her tail with his bill in a game of crack-the-whip at nearly sixty miles per hour and only twenty feet above the yellowed marsh tules.

High over the prairie an echelon of pintails is in prenuptial courtship with several drakes pursuing an unmated duck. These bull sprigs are at their showiest and best—agile, swift, and ardent—but the duck gracefully outmaneuvers them. A highspeed ballet far above the greening prairies in the long April twilight, with the land in shadow below and courting wildfowl still in the sun above. The hen pintail glows like old gold in the late sun, and as the drakes wheel swiftly into the light their white neckstocks and upper breasts are suffused with salmon.

At last the ducks have made their choices. Unmated males go puttering off into idleness and bachelorhood. Mated pairs keep to themselves. Now the evening flights are searchflights, the paired birds examining the prairie waters and fields for nesting sites that fill their requirements.

For diving ducks such as redheads, canvasbacks, and ruddy ducks, such a site is emergent vegetation growing in water. In a band of cattails or hardstem bulrush a few yards from open water, the duck begins weaving stems into a strong, well-made basket platform that may rise a foot or more above the surface of the water—often complete with approach ramp leading up to the nest. The drake doesn't help. Not that the duck really needs him. Given good materials, she works fast and builds well. There may be times, during heavy spring rains, when a hen canvasback may race with rising floodwaters in an effort to raise her nest. In only a few hours she can raise her nest several inches, skillfully building beneath a clutch of eggs.

The puddle ducks—mallards, pintails, teal, and other dabblers—seek nesting sites on dry ground. This can be a haystack, in a field or meadow hundreds of yards from water, or in a patch of sedge only a few feet from the pond.

There the duck makes her "scrape"—the shallow nesting bowl in the earth that is unlined when she begins her clutch of eggs. She finishes the nest as her egg-laying proceeds, adding plantstuffs that are within reach while she's on the nest and pulling over any high grasses to form a canopy. She plucks feathers from her breast and belly, and the completed clutch of eggs will lie on a nest lining of dried grasses and starbursts of down—a mattress of great warmth and softness.

During the laying period the drakes still attend their mates, joining the ducks when they are not on the nest and flying and feeding with them. Some species, such as blue-winged teal, tend to stay together far into incubation time. But mallards and pintails leave their hens soon after laying is completed and incubation has begun. The drakes resort to loafing spots, joining the bachelors. They've been declared surplus, with nothing more exciting to do than sit around on muskrat houses and watch each other's feathers drop out in the summer molt.

Of all northern prairie marshes, the Delta Marsh is the most famous. Lying at the south end of Lake Manitoba about sixty miles from Winnipeg, it is one of the great continental magnets for waterfowl, which in turn draws hunters, scientists, naturalists, artists, writers, and photographers. This is the setting for H. Albert Hochbaum's classic, *The Canvasback on a Prairie Marsh* and *Travels and Traditions of Waterfowl*, and Lyle Sowls' *Prairie Ducks*. Delta has had a lot of good press, and deservedly.

I've never been sure whether Delta lies at the south end of Lake Manitoba or whether it *is* the south end of Lake Manitoba. For two thousand years, spring winds have driven ice packs onto shoals at the end of the vast, shallow lake, the grinding slabs overriding themselves and plowing into the lake bottom to bulldoze sand up into a long, narrow ridge. North of this natural levee is open lake. South of it is the great marsh itself—about 36,000 acres of plume-topped phragmites cane, bulrush, cattails, broad ponds and bays, and little secret potholes.

The marsh is connected to Lake Manitoba by several passes cut through the lake ridge, and its great open bays fluctuate with the lake levels and prevailing wind. Here are some of the most extensive stands of phragmites in the world—their ten-foot stems forming incredibly dense jungles that are analogs of African papyrus swamps. Through these jungles of huge grasses are waterways that may choke out and vanish, or open into great shining bays of clear water. The creeks and bays are essentially parts of the main lake itself, connected to it by the passes that break the lake ridge. Lying within the phragmite stands are isolated sloughs and little ponds that are born of snowmelt and rainfall and have no ties with the lake. These shallow, hidden waters are a wealth of submerged aquatic plants—sago pondweed, coontail, horned pondweed, and many more, with belts of cattails and bulrush that stand against the walls of phragmites. Sometimes, in high water, it is possible to drive a canoe back into some of these isolated sloughs. But during low water, when there are no routes through the depths of the phragmites, the only access is from the sky.

That wooded lake ridge abounds with birds. Thickly grown with ash, poplar, box elder, and some bur oak, the natural levee is never much more than a few hundred yards wide but stretches east and west for miles. In May it seems to be a stopover for about every songbird that is on its way to somewhere else, and many stay for nesting. I've never seen so many nesting northern orioles and yellow warblers; if there's another place with such oriole densities, I've not heard of it. Catbirds and warbling vireos abound in these lake-ridge thickets, and mourning doves—which were rare visitors in the 1930s —are nesting everywhere. Many of the transient passerines that kept going in May begin returning in July, their nesting completed, and the place teems with midsummer tree swallows.

In and around the lake-ridge thickets and out into the marsh are countless yellow-headed blackbirds and red-winged blackbirds. At the edges of the wet meadows are short-billed marsh wrens, and farther out in the hardstem bulrush and cattail edges are nests of long-billed marsh wrens. On islands of tules are noisy colonies of Franklin's gulls and Forster's terns, western grebes, and crowds of little eared grebes. Ease your canoe around a wall of phragmites and come upon one of these places unannounced. The marsh world tears itself into feathered fragments, with appropriate sound effects. Ears ringing, you retreat to a quiet, restful corner, only to run into a loose colony of black terns. If there's anything that can liven up a quiet moment on the marsh, it's nesting black terns. Cheeky little hellions. They've knocked my cap into the water and then combed my hair as I reached for it.

There are black-crowned night herons, American bitterns, pied-billed grebes, white pelicans, sora rails, and coots everywhere. And in the heart of the marsh—in the edges of sloughs and hardstem bulrush at the fringes of the great bays—are the divers: ruddy ducks, redheads, and the lordly canvasback. In a setting four miles wide and twenty miles long, there are more bays and channels and lost ponds than a strong paddler could explore in a summer, all set in a vast matrix of phragmites and tules. Al Hochbaum once said of it: "On calm, quiet mornings in May the prairie marsh floats lightly in a world of sky." It does indeed, and one's spirit floats with it. But in lowering weather the gray reaches of marshland can weigh heavy.

Strange, how the alchemy of open sunlight can transform a leaden marsh and lift and lighten the spirit.

For scientists, Delta is an infinitely complex organism whose value grows as the supply of such organisms dwindles. This is the site of the famous Delta Waterfowl Research Station and the nearby University of Manitoba Field Station. Delta is mainly concerned with waterfowl ecology and management; the Manitoba station deals with broader marsh ecology. Both are training grounds; at Delta alone there have been over a hundred masters' and doctoral degrees earned by graduate students from dozens of colleges and universities. It is a superbly organized field station with laboratories, living quarters, and an excellent library. The director of the Delta station today is Peter Ward—biologist, artist, advisor, and a marsh hand of vast personal mileage. No man knows Delta better than Pete Ward— unless it's Al Hochbaum himself. Al is retired director of the Delta station and one of North America's premier waterfowl authorities. He still lives at the station—his forty-year love affair with the Delta as ardent as ever.

Fifty miles west of Delta and the broad flats of the Portage Plains, the land begins to lift and fold. It rises into a plateau 1,500 feet above sea level—a lovely farmscape with clumps and groves of pale-barked aspen, neat farmsteads, and fields of cereal grains. And everywhere, jewel-like little potholes fringed with dark bulrush, the brighter greens of cattails, and the creamy green of whitetop grass. This is the famed Minnedosa pothole region, a rare meld of highly productive grainlands and equally productive ducklands.

One evening just at sundown we took a short flight over this country. To the east, the plateau fell away to the flatlands of Lake Manitoba. To the north it continued to rise, darkening and roughening into the bush of the huge Riding Mountain National Park. As far to the south and west as we could see from 3,000 feet, the country was a fortune in silver coins strewn over a rumpled green cover. Potholes, ponds, marshes and marshlets, lakes and lakelets by the thousands, by the tens of thousands. The shape and character of these little pockets of water are infinitely varied. Some are quite round, others are ovoid, angular, crescent-shaped, elongated. Some are hundreds of acres. Others can be measured in square yards. They are everywhere; the traveler is never out of sight of them. Just south of the town of Minnedosa is a hundred-square-mile study area being surveyed by a team of U.S. Fish and Wildlife Service biologists. The area has an average of eighty potholes per square mile, and there are square-mile sections that hold up to 140 potholes averaging one and a half acres in size.

The U.S. Fish and Wildlife team is studying canvasbacks in cooperation with the Canadian Wildlife Service. What is a good canvasback pond? What is its hydrology? What waterfowl foods does it produce, and how are the canvasbacks reproducing by age structure?

Which means censusing nesting canvasbacks in the potholes, a chore that consists of wading the edges and combing nesting cover without filling hip boots in the process—efforts that are wholly incompatible. It's a sweaty, leg-wearying business, wading thigh-deep through dense flooded vegetation, but never boring. Aside from the main feature of finding canvasback nests, there are endless short subjects. If I missed any of these, as I often did, biologist Jerry Serie would point them out to me. Jerry is a fieldman's fieldman, and a good one to prowl that country with.

In a biome simply boiling with life, there is always something to catch attention. While a nesting coot is having a hysterical collapse only a few yards away, a couple of black terns make a strafing run. There goes my cap again. And just beside the floating cap is a floating wad of bulrush stems and algae, its half-covered cavity filled with the tiny eggs of a horned grebe. A little farther, as we wade knee-deep through a dense stand of flooded whitetop grass, a hen mallard flushes beside me. Her nest is built over water, strong and substantial. It is well hidden, for whitetop stands are dense. Jerry submerges one of the eggs and judges it to be about eleven days into incubation. This is the first time I have ever seen a mallard nest built over water—which surprises Jerry far more than the nest itself, for it is a rather common thing in this country.

Mallards here in the Minnedosa potholes often build over water—a sharp departure from their usual tradition of nesting on dry land. Ron Gatti, a Wisconsin graduate student over in the East Meadows marshes on the other side of Lake Manitoba, tells me that as many as half of his mallards build nests over water. Such mallards are more likely to build over-water nests in bulrushes or cattails than in whitetop, but in any case it's a matter of emergency pioneering. On many of these waters, fields come almost to the edge, and a skimpy fringe of shoreline grass or sedge is heavily worked by predators. The mallards that build there often build out over water, à la canvasback. Ron doesn't think that they're as good at it as canvasbacks, but what the heck—I've never been much impressed by the few canvasback nests that I've seen built on dry land.

A little farther on, we check a canvasback nest that has been under surveillance for days. Big things happening. Yesterday there were nine eggs in the nest; now there are three. The others are newly hatched. One of the three remaining eggs is being pipped, and we can see draggled down feathers through an enlarging hole as the cap of the egg is cut away. The canvasback duck is close by with her other babies, and we get out of there.

The Minnedosa potholes seem hard-bottomed enough, lacking the soft flocculent muck that is known by such sobriquets as "loon puke" and other vivid terms you'll never find in the *Journal of Wildlife Management*. Yet, as we wade in the pothole edges and stir up bottom debris with our booted feet, there's that old familiar smell of marsh grass.

Our friend Paul Errington—who devoted his life to marshes and marsh doings—once took the urbane president of a great university to one of his research areas. Later, when asked what he thought of Paul's wild wetlands, the great man grimaced and said: "It stinks." Which it did, of course, and still does and always will. But it's all in the nose of the beholder. It tingles my sinuses like the devilish fumes of a Yellowstone geyser basin, or the pungent reek of skunk borne on fall wind and diluted with distance, and maybe laced with camp-smoke. And I know that the smells themselves aren't the important thing—it's the images they evoke. If I were a college president with no marsh memories, and no ken of wild wetlands and the vitality of these magnificent support systems, then I suppose they'd only stink for me, too.

The Delta Marsh is rich duck country. It produces many wildfowl —although its greater value may be as an arrival point for spring migrations, a summering area for bachelor puddle ducks, and as a staging area for the great fall flights. In terms of sheer production, however, it cannot match the Minnedosa.

There is an axiom of wildlife biology that the productivity of a wildlife habitat is largely contingent on the interspersion of types. Variety is the spice of life—and the Minnedosa potholes are infinitely varied. No two are the same in size, depth, vegetative composition, shorelines, or uplands. Some are almost entirely open water; others are nearly filled with floating and emergent aquatics. One shoreline is thickly grown; another is open, with prime loafing sites. Some potholes may offer sago pondweed tubers or smartweed seeds, or be richer in insect life than others, or have better escape cover for duck broods. Variety is enhanced by accessibility; no Minnedosa pothole is very far from another. Which counts for a lot, since a duck and her brood won't stay in a particular pothole if there's another within easy walking distance. Ducks ramble a lot, moving from one water area to another and relishing the change of scene. Ducks and their flightless broods may travel up to a mile from the original nest site. Pintail families are the most mobile; they rarely stay in a single pothole for more than two weeks. No mallard brood has been known to stay in one pothole for more than three weeks. Ruddy ducks are the least mobile of all—which isn't surprising, if you've ever seen a ruddy duck walk.

What with one thing and another, this is duck country supreme. The Minnedosa, in a good water year, may hold over a hundred breeding ducks per square mile and contribute at least a million ducks to the autumn flyways.

In a warm, light rain, my wife Dycie and I spent most of the June day out on the Delta Marsh, prowling down watery corridors between walls of phragmites and letting the breeze carry our canoe across the bays. There wasn't a whole lot going on. The gentlemen diving ducks had pulled out for their bachelor lakes, and the gentlemen puddle ducks still in residence were sulking because the lady puddle ducks wouldn't play—said ladies being off somewhere "with a loaf in the oven," as grandad used to say.

At about four o'clock we decided to hang it up. The rain had stopped, and the little breeze had died. We stripped off our rainshirts and rolled up our sleeves in the muggy air, and so we arrived at the last bay and headed up the narrow ditch to where the car was parked. There had been no insects out on the marsh, but when we entered that ditch, we entered banks of Delta mosquitoes.

In our ramblings around, we've known mosquitoes. On Mahogany Hammock in the Florida Everglades we once saw a skeeter so big that two wood ticks and a horseleech were attached to it. Another time, in the White River Bottoms in Arkansas, we were in clouds of mosquitoes so thick that you could reach out and grab and there'd be a sort of white place left hanging in the air. No josh.

But all that wasn't a patch on this narrow shoreline ditch in the Delta Marsh. We were using a Canadian repellent that's about as hot as any you can buy (95 percent N,N-diethyl-m-toluamide, the kind of stuff that can digest a watch crystal), and it was barely good enough. We made the landing in a gray, singing veil of insects, and set a new record for stowing gear and racking a canoe.

That evening Pete Ward stopped by our cabin. I sagely observed that it was a great night for bugs, and Pete replied seriously: "You know, most people regard this as tame country—safe and civilized. But out there tonight on the marsh edges, it's an incredibly hostile environment. I wonder if a lightly clad man could survive the night on one of those phragmite landings."

Which, in turn, caused me to wonder about the effects of this hostility on the creatures that are out there on such nights. Mosquitoes are active and voracious predators, and their collective effect is immense. They might not harm fully feathered birds, but what of newly hatched ducklings?

Waterfowl suffer heavy losses between hatching and feathering—a high-risk period when they are highly vulnerable to predation and all the sundry natural shocks that their tender flesh is heir to. Are mosquitoes an important cause of loss during this period? No one knows, although ducks have certainly coexisted with skeeters for a long time. They have, indeed, coexisted with a wide spectrum of predators and have adjusted well to a talon-and-fang world.

On the nesting prairies the three grades of waterfowl mortality are loss of eggs, loss of ducklings, and loss of adult ducks—in descending order of occurrence.

Crows are probably the most notorious egg predators. Originally uncommon in the northern prairies, they pioneered the pothole region with the first farmers and added a new dimension to the lives of northern waterfowl.

In his work at Delta, Lyle Sowls found that only 35 percent of 206 duck nests hatched successfully—and crows had destroyed 21 percent of the total. There were two types of crows involved. There were those nesting in trees near meadows where ducks nested, and whose predation on duck nests was usually in the immediate area. There were also crows wandering across the marshes for great distances, often in bands of a half-dozen birds or more. Such hunting crows are unmistakable; they fly with beaks pointed downward, heads twisting slightly, keen eyes searching. They are persistent and thorough—beating slowly into the wind and achieving maximum lift at a low speed, crossing marshes and meadows on efficient transects. Once across a marsh, they allow the wind to sweep them back to the far side again, and they begin crossing the marsh on a new course.

Hell hath no fury like that of a duck hunter being ripped off by Crow. Through the 1920s and 1930s, books and articles roundly condemned the black banditti, crying havoc and calling the brotherhood to arms. Elaborate campaigns were mounted. The Alberta game department set up a prize system in which hunting and fishing clubs competed for the largest numbers of crows and magpies killed. For a four-year period in the mid-1920s, there were from 45,000 to 107,000 crow eggs turned in annually in Alberta—and the adult crows and magpies tallied ranged from 22,000 to 45,000. Great works had been wrought. Or had they?

Alas, crows do not breed until the second spring after hatching, and unoccupied juvenile crows are likely to be among the most persistent duck predators. If the nests, eggs, and young of nesting adult crows are destroyed, these out-of-work birds may join the bands of juvenile egg-eaters that are out there working the marshes and meadows.

It is possible, too, that man may not only augment the number of crows hunting the marshes, but may unwittingly serve as bird dogs. Consider the eminent ornithologist who said: "The crow is the duck's worst enemy. I make this statement unreservedly . . . Exactly one week after I counted forty-two mallard nests, I found the crows had destroyed all but two of them."

I've little doubt that the good doctor had helped those crows. I know that I have, a few times. Crows watch lone men in marshes and shrewdly mark any effects of their presence—such as ducks flushed from nests. Much the same thing is true of certain mammals. I was once followed by a large striped skunk for a half-mile through low meadow and marsh edge. Tagging along thirty feet behind me, he seemed a healthy, normal animal, and my charm probably lay in the fact that I happened to be going in the direction that he wanted to go, and that I was breaking trail for him.

Skunks and Franklin ground squirrels both follow human trails through a marsh and will exploit any duck nests to which those trails are likely to lead. This is especially true in summer when grasses are green and lush and a man's trail is easily followed as he moves from nest to nest. As the nesting season wears on, and the marsh grows drier, skunks and ground squirrels tend to widen their cruising range as water barriers diminish. Not that a skunk needs dry ground for his work; Lyle Sowls and Pete Ward once found a skunk resting on a grassy couch ten inches high and two feet square in a wet meadow. Sudden encounters with skunks, by the way, are occupational hazards of marsh biology.

Until about forty years ago, the raccoon was almost nonexistent in the Delta and Minnedosa region. Since then it has come back from wherever it had gone (raccoons were there in the early times), and it has come back hungry. Raccoons are now abundant in some of the northern prairies that have been beyond the recent range of this species. Raccoons are rarely, if ever, mentioned in anything written about Delta or Minnedosa before 1945.

Today the raccoon may be the most serious of the nest predators —especially on canvasbacks and redheads. A water barrier that might deter most predatory mammals poses no problem for raccoons. A coon is fond of foraging around the edges of water, is an excellent swimmer, and relishes eggs. And after making a good meal of canvasback eggs, the rascal may curl up in the duck's nest and take a nap.

How serious is such predation? Again, no one is sure. There have been recent declines in the success of over-water nesters that might be attributed to a concurrent rise in raccoons. But with northern raccoon hides bringing $25 and more, the problem has a built-in solution.

If her nest is lost early in the season before incubation is well begun, there is a good chance that the duck will try again. Her renesting is a buffer against the special hazards of early spring, and she can often adjust to the raccoon that devours her eggs. She can never adjust to men who devour her marsh.

Lawrence King is a lean, weathered Manitoban who manages the East Meadows Ranch east of Delta. It includes thousands of acres of rich marshland, and King's job is to keep it that way. He is a professional marsh manager, and his is angry and worried.

"In this interlake country between Lake Manitoba and Lake Winnipeg," he told us, "they're tearing out aspen and draining potholes as fast as they can. The land is going into oats, barley, alfalfa. As far north as The Pas, they are draining, draining! Even up there, some people would like to see all the Ducks Unlimited levees and water control structures destroyed, the wetlands drained, new pastures made. Anyplace where grass can conceivably grow, they want to put in cattle. No thought of tomorrow. They just want to add to the glut!"

Pete Ward is also concerned. He fears for duck production on the Portage Plains south of Delta, and its effect on Delta itself, and talks grimly about the pernicious draining and filling of the little Minnedosa potholes. And although many American wildlifers don't share such pessimism, the disturbing fact remains that King and Ward have lifetimes of perspective, while the Yanks come from torn, drained regions that are likely to make even dying Canadian wetlands look pretty good.

And are the northern prairies' potholes and marshlands really doomed?

Well, it's a cinch that we won't get many new ones until the next interglacial period, and it's doubtful that astrophysical forces can move faster than a government drainage agency that smells pork barrel.

As a geologic agent, of course, man isn't always the omnipotent hotshot he thinks he is. It's true that his works can greatly accelerate the siltation of natural basins and prematurely drain wetlands long before maturing natural drainage would have done the job right, creating quality natural rivers in the process. But premature drainage is unlikely to be permanent unless carefully maintained. Drain tiles break and clog, ditches cave in and fill, and with just a little lucky neglect a natural marsh may reassert itself. The tragedy is not that we destroy a marsh for all time, which we may not do, but in the fact that we destroy it for our time. We do not deny the ages the wonders of a wild marshland; we deny only ourselves and our children.

But those are winter thoughts, the sort that have put this frost in my hair. Time to think spring.

Years ago, after an extended field trip to the marshes of the Gulf Coast, Paul Errington reflected: "The South was genuine, beautiful, and fascinating, but it was not home to one born and apprenticed in a country molded by ice sheets."

He spoke for all children of the northern prairies and glacial wetlands—people and wildfowl. Even though the prairie ducks have basked this winter in the Laguna Madre and other sunny resorts, it has been in forced exile. They were banished from their homeland by winter and are chafing to return. The North is where they belong, and for seven months, from ice to ice, they will be back in their prairie waters. The seven months are beginning; the fires of spring are kindled.

North again. Home again.

HAVE DUCKS THE POWER OF SCENT?

Ray P. Holland

Editorial skills and good judgment, combined with a strong sense of identity with an audience, are the crucibles of good editing. It is not necessary to be a writer to become a good editor, nor is it necessary to be an experienced expert on the subject matter. However, on the rare occasions when all of these credentials are embodied in one person, greatness can occur. That happened at Field & Stream *during the years it was edited by Ray P. Holland. Born and raised in the heart of the Mid-West's great game country and waterfowl funnels, Holland was tutored by market hunters during the turn-of-the-century halcyon years of shooting opportunity. By the time he retired from* Field & Stream *in 1941, he not only was an accomplished writer on all phases of field sports, but could look back on a stewardship of the magazine that had made it the most prestigious in the outdoor field at that time. Of all Holland's good works, the book,* Scattergunning *(Alfred A. Knopf, New York, 1951), looms in my mind as the greatest. Illustrated by the talented William J. Schaldach, the book is a massive triumph of combining information with action, with rich anecdotes and observations that make each chapter a classic statement on its particular subject. Whether writing about shooting skills, guns, waterfowl, or upland birds, Holland had a wealth of actual experience to prime the editorial pump. He was particularly fresh and inventive when tackling those arcane subjects that are so important to success in the field—weather, scenting conditions, unique characteristics of game, unusual tactics. This piece falls into that genre. You will find yourself thinking about it the next time a bunch of mallards veers away from your setup, just yards short and a split-second from the moment you were about to whisper, "Take 'em!" By the way, if you think I'm being over-zealous in my praise of the Holland years at* Field & Stream, *I suggest that you follow the advice of that great philosopher, Mr. C. Stengel, who said: "You could look it up!"*

CAN WILD ducks identify danger by scent? I don't believe that they can, yet I have met many men who insisted that certain species of ducks can smell a man and when they do are smart enough to get away from him. Some of these men were highly educated fellows, and others were wise in the ways of ducks even if their schooling had been neglected.

To survive, any wild animal must recognize man as an enemy. That seems easy for them, and they depend upon their eyes, their ears, and their olfactory nerves to tell them when danger is near. Game animals of high intelligence use all three of the senses for their protection, but there is usually one on which they depend. That one in big-game animals is scent. The eyesight of most wild animals is poor except where motion is involved.

At my home in Vermont we see wild deer around the farm almost every day at certain seasons. They know that we are not going to bother them, but when they get a good strong scent of man they take to the timber. I have often played with these deer and I know certain things about them.

Their eyesight is poor and they won't see me unless I move. I have stood perfectly still and watched deer feed down across the grass-lands near me. I have whistled or called without frightening them. They throw up their heads at the sound and look straight at me where I sit on a stone wall or stand in a thicket. In a few seconds they will go on grazing. Living around farms as they do, they are constantly hearing men's voices and other noises, and are not fright-ened. As they feed along, they come to the air stream blowing from me to them. That tells them things their eyes and ears have missed: there is a man close to them, and they get from there promptly and without ceremony in their leaving.

One fall I was grouse- and woodcock-shooting in New York State. My friend Harry Shedd was downhill in the heavy timber. A fast pointer with a sheep bell on his collar was working the cover while I skirted the woods along the side hill where a few little cedars grew, but where the country was mostly open. From my position I could see any bird that flushed wild before my friend or our dog.

Out of woods swamp came as beautiful a buck as I ever saw. He wasn't hurrying. He came straight at me in a slow lope, with his head turned back, apparently much interested in the bell on the dog. It was something new in his life. I wanted Shedd to see that buck and I began to shout and yell. I made no attempt to stand still and kept shouting and pointing. The deer had to keep turning his head to see where he was going and swinging it back to try to locate the dog and bell. He should have seen me. On he came straight up the hill. I wasn't sure he wasn't going to run me down.

The wind was blowing up the hill, so there was no chance for him to smell me. Shedd broke out of the cover, but that didn't bother the buck, for he didn't change his gait. That buck passed so close to me that I could have almost poked him with the gunbarrels. Then when he passed me he got my scent. He couldn't have started faster if he had been shot with a load of red pepper. He still remains in my mind as the fastest-moving deer I ever saw.

All big-game hunters know that if they want their game served up nicely to the gun, it must not get the man scent. This applies to all species, even the mountain sheep, which is credited with having the keenest eyesight of the lot. This ability to smell man and recognize him by his scent has not been given to game birds. At least, that is my opinion. Ruffed grouse and pheasants are credited with being the smartest of our game birds, yet I never heard their stanchest admirer contend that either could identify a man by scent.

The first man I ever ran across who claimed ducks could smell a hunter was an old guide on the Texas coast. As we came out on a large tidal flat, thousands of pintails left the water and circled. Many of them got up from a point and from the bare mud that ran alongside it. It was an ideal place to build a blind, but my guide said no. "It won't do you no good to set there. Wind would be directly behind you, and those long-necked rascals can smell a fellow a mighty long ways off."

We argued the question and I lost, because I have always believed that when in the other fellow's country you had better take his advice on hunting technique. That was many years ago; I have always wished I had made an exception in this case and put the decoys on that point to show this guide that pintails will decoy straight into the blind with the wind blowing over the hunters.

Ducks were very plentiful and we had good enough shooting

from his choice of location, which had the wind blowing across the face of the blind, so that the ducks coming in from the bay didn't get that terrible man scent. "Never give a pintail a chance to smell you, or you'll never get a chance to kill him," was his final word on the subject.

Since that day I have killed a great many pintails that came in against the wind with the breeze over my left shoulder, which has always been one of my favorite sets. Try it some time. It gives you a nice left swing on your second shot. I like it better than a left wind paralleling the face of the blind, as it usually pulls the birds in closer.

It was a long time before I again met a shooter who believed ducks could smell a man and hie themselves away from him. This Long Island duck-hunter insisted that black ducks could smell you every time, and he knew because he had been brought up hunting black ducks and he had seen them time and again flare from the scent. "Pintails can't smell you," he would say, "or none of the rest of 'em, but a black mallard can smell you, and don't you think he can't."

Not once but dozens of times I have had singles and pairs split from a flock when I was calling and light in the decoys. Wanting the flock to come in, I have paid little attention to them and kept on calling at the birds in the air. Those birds, quiet on the water, didn't smell the man in the blind, and that goes for pintails and blacks and greenheads.

Many Eastern gunners have a sort of fetish where black ducks are concerned. He is their duck of all ducks, and he is far smarter than any other species. Facts as I see them do not bear out this belief. I don't think a black is one bit smarter than his greenheaded cousin, if as smart. Harry Rogers, the daddy of New York's game farms, used to trap and band many wild ducks at the main farm at Sherburne, New York. He told me that he never caught a gray mallard a second time. He'd catch them and band them, and that settled it. No mallard would fool around that trap again. The black ducks with all their vaunted intelligence would go right back in and get caught time after time.

I once had the pleasure of discussing this question of scent with a scientific gentleman, one of those fellows who dissect all sorts of dead creatures and study them to see what they can find out. He said that a duck certainly had the power of scent, that their olfactory nerves were well developed. He believed that all birds could smell, and then he slipped. He suggested that vultures and buzzards locate the dead and putrid things on which they feed by their power of scent. He didn't say this was absolutely true, but he said he believed it possible.

I have heard or read that Darwin settled this for all time. He had some vultures in a cage. He put carrion in the cage with them and covered it with a thin piece of porous cloth. The birds tramped around on their food all day and didn't know it was there. This is good enough evidence that they locate their food by their marvelous eyesight.

Liking to know things first-hand, I did a little experimenting of my own. Florida has buzzards and black vultures to spare. Every time a car kills a raccoon, a snake, or a rabbit, the birds are right there to clean things up. I covered with a burlap bag a small coon that had been well run over. I dragged him to the side of the road and put stones on the sack to keep it from blowing off. Every day when I passed the spot going fishing, I looked at my sack. I didn't get out and examine it carefully because that was entirely unnecessary. I knew the coon was still there, even if the birds hadn't found him.

One morning on a California marsh I was shooting from a blind made out of large palm leaves. It was a dandy, and if advisable you could pull up the sharpened fronds and move your hide a little farther down the shore without delay. I was calling a large flock of widgeon with a few shovelers mixed in when one of the spoonbills lit inside the decoys and walked right up to the blind. As I kept on calling, she would turn her head sideways and listen. I was looking her right in the face, but she was listening, not looking, and I wasn't moving enough to attract her attention. Then she turned around and started calling the birds that were circling. She really put on a show. She was my friend.

When the flock scaled in with feet hanging and the pump gun began to rattle, I made certain that the little brown hen with the big voice didn't get tangled up with a load of shot. Now she must have smelled me, if ducks can smell. One thing I am sure of, if she did have the power of scent and smelled those gunners crouched in the palm-leaf blind, it didn't frighten her. It must have been a pleasant odor that inspired confidence and promoted co-operation.

Then there was a day down on Honga River. Shooting hadn't been too good, but we had killed all the ducks we wanted. At the time all blinds were baited heavily with corn. On fine days the ducks sat out on the open water until four o'clock, when the shooting for the day was over. Then they came in and ate the ten or twenty bushels of grain put around the blind that morning. They surely could tell the time of day almost to the minute. Or maybe it was the power-boat that visited the blinds at four o'clock and took off the hunters. Anyway, we often watched from the clubhouse dock until the huge rafts of ducks out in the bay had broken up and pitched in at the blinds to feed.

This day my companion and I told the boatman to go back with-out us and return in an hour, as we planned to stay and watch the feeding ducks at close range. He had no sooner reached the dock than in they came. Flock after flock of great canvasbacks pitched in to eat the corn until we were surrounded by an almost solid mass of feeding fowl, all scrambling and diving for the grain.

We watched them through peepholes in the blind. It was a sight worth seeing. We estimated that there were at least four thousand ducks within gun range. Almost all of them were canvas, but there were a few redheads in the raft. When we returned to the clubhouse, we found that the boys on shore had been watching with glasses. They estimated that there were at least five thousand birds feeding around us. One thing I know for a certainty: there were hundreds of them within twenty feet of us, and if they smelled us, they liked the smell.

No one ever heard a shooting man say that a quail smelled him, or that a woodcock or any other species of game bird had that power. Most of the boys know that you had better not talk to your companion when approaching a grouse, because he knows about the human voice. This is also true of pheasants, though few gunners real-ize it. If you want a pheasant to run away from your pointing dog, just carry on a friendly conversation with your companion as you come up. Unless a stanch dog has him pinned tight, he will slip away when he hears a human voice.

And a goose? Can geese smell you? I have seen them walk into the decoys with the wind blowing straight from the blind to the flock. It is not unusual, when shooting on a big river sandbar, to have geese alight before they reach the decoys and then walk in. Of course, they walk straight into the breeze that is blowing across the blind. Nothing makes a goose more uncomfortable than a tail wind ruffling up his feathers. On the Chesapeake and on Currituck I have often seen Canadas hit the water outside the stool and swim right up to the decoys. It is the same: they are facing the wind, which is blowing over the blind with the hunters inside.

All turkey-hunters know that the turkey is the smartest of game birds. Ask anyone who is enamored of wild turkey. Yet I have never heard anyone say that a turkey could scent a hunter from ten yards or ten feet. I have lain on my belly in the oak leaves and had a whole flock of turkeys walk up to the call, with the wind from me direct to them swirling the leaves around them every time they stepped.

Gene Howe, Amarillo, Texas, newspaper man, is a duckhunter of parts. We both apprenticed with men who made their living from the wildfowl. Most of Gene's shooting had been done on the Missouri River until he moved to Texas. In the Panhandle country he found thousands of ducks, but they posed a problem. He couldn't get them to come in properly to decoys.

The only duck waters in the country were the shallow rainwater lakes. The method local hunters used in those days to kill ducks was to dash downwind along the shore of these shallow lakes in an automobile, blasting the ducks when they rose against the wind. Naturally these ducks were gun-shy of all shorelines. They knew that they must keep away from the shores if they didn't want to get shot. The birds simply would not decoy to the orthodox set with the wind paralleling the shore. Then one day Howe set his decoys out in front of his blind with the wind coming in straight from behind him. The birds decoyed like chickens to the scratch feed.

Gene says that often when geese showed up he would let the mallards and pintails light until he had a mass of ducks covering the water in front of him, with the wind blowing right over the blind into them. They never knew he was there until the geese swung in and the shooting started.

Of course, a duck must have some use for its well-developed olfactory nerves. Gene Howe says they smell water and possibly food.

Often the Texas Panhandle makes a fine lake overnight. A young cloudburst may fill a basin that threatened to be a dust bowl the day before. The ducks like those new lakes, probably because they are filled with food in the form of grass seeds and tender roots.

Whenever Howe heard of a heavy rain nearby, he got there early next morning with his decoys. Always before noon the birds would start to arrive, in great flocks flying low to the ground and always into the wind, weaving and searching, following the wind stream to the new water. He says that often they would fly so low that their wing tips seemed to touch the sod. Until he had witnessed this procedure time after time, he had always thought that ducks located water from high in the air, with eyes that every gunner knows are keen.

One evening when talking over the day's sport at the Honga River Gun Club, I was surprised to hear Rodney Fiske say that black ducks could smell a man and identify him as such. Now, Dr. Fiske was one of the foremost medical men in New York City. Besides that he was a duck-hunter and a careful observer. Of course, I asked him why he thought as he did.

Rodney argued that countless times he had seen black ducks light outside the decoys and float away with the wind, and that always when they got downwind far enough to get the scent, they would leave the water and get away from there. There was no question in his mind that ducks can smell you—that is, black ducks, which were his favorites.

The argument won't hold water. Often single blacks, pairs, or even flocks of these cagey birds hit the water out of gun range and float away. I have seen it happen many times. When they get downwind they usually get up and leave, but it is my guess that scent has nothing to do with it. They were suspicious in the first place or they would have come on into the decoys. When they got down the breeze where they could catch every sound from the blind, they probably heard someone whisper: "Keep your head down!" or maybe a foot scraped along the floor of the blind. Possibly they saw that head! Anyway, I know from experience that a contented chuckle from a good call has frequently made them leave the water and come straight in.

In the past I have taken many photographs of flying ducks. I took the best of them before the days of telephoto lenses and extremely fast films. That meant the birds had to be in close. It is unbelievable what a man can do with ducks in the spring of the year with a good call. As the mating season progresses, the call becomes doubly effective, if you know what to say and how to say it. I have had ducks do almost everything but light on my head, and a goose came too close to doing that to be funny.

When a man is shooting, he goes into action the first time a flock passes in good range. When he is out with a camera, it is different. He keeps calling until the birds are where he wants them, and it is surprising how hard it is to frighten them if you keep well hidden. You can learn more about ducks in a few days taking pictures than in years of hunting with a gun.

Ducks have nostrils, and probably their first duty is to the bird's lungs. They have olfactory nerves, which they use to locate water and food. I'm willing to listen with an open mind to all arguments that a duck can smell a man and recognize him as such. To date, I don't believe that any duck ever smelled a man, turned over backward, and said to himself: "That was a close one, that man almost shot me."

WATERFOWL SPEEDS

Ray P. Holland

The next time you get the chance, watch one of those jumbo jets on its takeoff. They seem to waddle into the air, barely moving, while the smaller 727's and DC9's seem to cock their noses jauntily into the sky and zoom right out of the field. In actual fact, the small and large planes are flying at about the same speeds. You have been witnessing the kind of optical illusion that can have you shaking your head in a duck blind. One frosty mid-morning in Manitoba, Gene Hill and I thought for a minute that our cup had truly runneth over. We had enjoyed a fine shoot on a mixture of mallards, cans, and bluebills when a lovely flock of Canadas came right down the pike, yappping contentedly, looking slow as crows. Ensued: Blam! Blooie! Blam! Blam! Blooie Blooie! Followed by some harsh expletives that do not look good in print. We touched not a feather, for we failed to lead the big birds. We were out of synch with their actual speed. Incidents like that are the kind that made me appreciate this chapter by the great Ray P. Holland, previously introduced in "Have Ducks the Power of Scent." It's from Holland's Scattergunning, *Knopf, 1951, and will start you thinking about some of your own most frustrating moments when everything looked oh, so lovely and the bottom line came out empty.*

HARD-BITTEN SHOOTING men and beginners at the sport will probably always argue about the speed of wild ducks on the wing. When I was a young fellow and knew most things, I wrote a magazine article entitled "How Fast Can a Duck Fly?" From that point I proceeded to give explicit information on the subject. There was nothing haphazard about my methods or deductions. I had carefully checked the speed of flying waterfowl, and I knew things. The article was published in *Outing* and was widely quoted among wildfowlers for many years. My duck-hunting experience was wide even in those days, and the boys thought I knew what I was talking about. Me? I was sure of it!

Today if anyone asks me anything about the speed of a flying duck, I'm likely to up and say: "I don't know." I will go a lot farther than that: I don't believe anyone knows. You can't put an old hen mallard on a race-track and hold a stopwatch on her, and the more I worry about it, the surer I am that in no other way will man ever be able to say with authority just how fast any bird can move through the air.

Pick out a duck-hunter anywhere and he can probably tell you how fast he has seen ducks go. I am sure he can tell you which is the fastest flying duck, and maybe the slowest. I can't. I used to be an authority on the subject, but not any more. So that nothing hereinafter written or implied may be held against me, I want to go on record with one thing: my views on this important subject are open to revision at all times.

I haven't my former article before me, but I remember three instances recorded that I thought at the time were unimpeachable. Today I don't rate those records very highly. The science of aviation has taught us so much about flight through the air that until we strap a speedometer on an old hen mallard and get her assurance that she is going to do her best over a measured mile, I don't intend to enter my arguments.

Many years ago I saw an old slow gadwall jump from a prairie slough in western Nebraska and forge right ahead of the Burlington train I was riding on. Now here was something! I jumped right up and got hold of the conductor and asked him just how fast the train was going. He was very accommodating and went forward to get that valuable information for me. His report was that we were traveling at a speed of almost sixty miles an hour!

Of course, I put that record in the article. Here was the definite proof that a gadwall could fly better than sixty miles an hour. There are only two or three important screws loose in this reasoning. First, the train may have been curving toward the bird; but, more important, my guess of today is that the train was probably moving about forty miles an hour. Even if the conductor wasn't boosting his railroad, the speed I wanted was when the duck went ahead of the train, not when the conductor went forward to get the reading.

I was lucky enough to ride in an early-day airplane and live to tell of it. Now, here was the right way to check the speed of a duck. A friend owned an old Wright biplane. It was the first machine to cross the continent from east to west. The engine was almost directly over us when we took our seats and fastened the shawl straps around our middles. There was no windshield, and nothing but air underneath us. The propellers, for there were two of them, were turned by bicycle chains that ran from engine to sprocket wheels. Slender uprights went from wing to wing and I held on to a pair of these—while checking the flight of waterfowl.

My friend said the plane flew at sixty miles an hour or better. I don't know just how he arrived at this figure, but I took his word for it. Even if we were going better than sixty, it proved nothing. We didn't do any maneuvering. Ducks would leave the water long before we got to them and turn off when they got ready. There were pontoons on this plane, and we chased birds flying low over the water. Nice pastime for weak-minded duck-hunters.

My big moment in timing ducks came one day in Iowa when I shot on a long marsh that was spanned by two roads, one mile apart. At least, in that country, roads ran on the section lines and were usually one mile apart. It is possible that in making the fill for the road across the marsh the engineers may have shifted the roads closer together to take advantage of the higher ground. I didn't think of this possibility until twenty years later, at which time the marsh had been drained and I couldn't even find the places where I had shot.

Anyway, I had a swell time. Ducks would cross road number one, and hunters on that road would shoot at them. That was my cue to look at my watch and note the exact time. Then when the birds crossed my road, I would again note the time. It was simple to figure the speed in that way. No, I did not have my stop-watch, but I had a good timepiece and I was very careful. I got some great material for the first article, for all kinds of ducks were flying all over the place.

My best speed was well over a hundred miles an hour and had to do with shovelers, or spoonbill ducks. I recorded that there was a light breeze blowing with the ducks, but it wasn't heavy enough to make much difference. When the article appeared, I was amazed to find that the breeze was blowing against the ducks. I have always believed that the man who set the type for that article was a duck-hunter of experience and, like all good duck-hunters of that day, had often seen teal fly a hundred and twenty miles an hour; so he was sure I didn't mean "with," but "against."

With the perfection of airplanes and the knowledge gained by aviation, we first began to hear of air speed and ground speed and to learn that the breeze with or against, which is blowing along the ground, isn't necessarily the same as the air currents that are traveling up where high ducks are flying. Even if the roads were a measured mile apart and I was fairly accurate in my timing, those birds may have been taking advantage of a forty-mile wind.

A few years ago Charlie Cox phoned my New York office from Boston. He said he had flown a number of dignitaries from Ohio to Boston, and if I was going to be in, he would fly down and have lunch with me. Charlie got in about two in the afternoon. He said there was such a strong west wind blowing across New York City that he couldn't make it at the height he was supposed to cross, according to the law in the case. He was headed for the Newark airport, where New York planes landed at the time, and he either had to break the law or go up the river and across north of the city. There was only a slight breeze blowing by my office windows on the twenty-first floor, and on the street the air was practically dead.

I have often seen birds flying against a side wind that was not felt on the ground. At such a time, when shooting on a pass, your score won't be very high unless you allow for this in your lead and for the drift of shot that is sure to occur. For example, if there is a strong west wind blowing and the birds are moving straight south, their heads will be pointed southwest. To hit them, your follow-through must be along the body of the bird, and your lead ahead and to the west of the duck. With an apology, I believe I can say that I have had a wider experience in shooting waterfowl under different conditions and in different parts of the country than almost any man alive today. With ordinary powers of observation I have formed many opinions and then changed my mind—when the subject is the speed of flying ducks.

Whenever Glenn Curtiss was in New York and had the time, he used to drop into my office and we would argue about the speed of ducks. His pet contention was that the maximum speed of the different species didn't vary a great deal and that no duck that ever lived could fly through dead air at a speed of sixty miles an hour.

Curtiss had done about as much flying as most aviators of that period, and as he was a rabid duck-hunter and a keen observer, his opinion is not to be passed off lightly. Through the years I have found myself gradually leaning his way, although I think his speed limit of sixty miles is too low, and, of course, the top speeds of different species do vary, though not so much as most of us have been led to believe. All we really have to go on to date is what this man or that one thinks.

An argument was waxing strong among a group of duck-hunters along the Missouri River over which was the faster bird, a spoonbill duck or a lesser scaup. An old market hunter entered the room. This man had enjoyed an extremely wide experience with gun and ducks, and his judgment on such subjects was the best in the community. The question was put to him.

"Why," he replied, "an old spoonie can loaf along up the lake and bite a bluebill on the tail every third flap of his wings."

Like this old market gunner, I have always considered the shoveler a fast bird. Because he can loaf along slowly, many do not realize that the spoonbill duck has a wide change of pace and that he can move when he wants to. In build, the shoveler is nothing more than a large bluewinged teal, and no one claims a bluewing is slow.

Many believe that the greenwinged teal is one of the fastest ducks. I never rated him very high. He is small and does a lot of twisting and dodging, but he doesn't get out of my range nearly so soon as his slightly larger cousin the bluewing. Before magazine limitations, a good man with a magazine gun could lay down four or five greenwings when a flock came in fairly over the decoys. He couldn't do this with bluewings except on very rare occasions. I am, of course, talking about picking single birds, one to a shell, and not about cutting into any thick spots in the flock.

Many times in the West I have seen a single mallard flying with a flock of teal. It would be fair to conclude that when such a flock was fired at, the birds would put on all the steam they had in reserve. I have never seen greenwings fly away from the mallard, but I have seen bluewings leave the big fellow. For years I have used this argument to prove that the bluewings are much faster than the greenwings. But I am afraid the argument won't hold in the light of fact.

One fall in Saskatchewan we ran into a shallow prairie lake that was covered with teal, and much fun was had by all. Most of these birds were bluewings, and they could really step. There were four of us in the party, and we spread out far enough apart so that we kept the birds moving.

The sad part of this story is that there were a few greenwings mixed in with the bluewings, and I saw things I didn't want to believe. Along would come a dozen or more bluewings and one greenwing, and never once did I see a greenwing having any trouble keeping up with the crowd. I watched them right over my head and with powerful glasses when others were shooting.

The greenwing would flare more and dodge and whip around, but when the shooting was over, he would pull right up to his friends and ride along with them. I have always wished we had left that spot a little sooner than we did. I saw Harry Shedd shoot at a flock of birds and kill a large duck and a small one. As the flock came on, I saw there was a gadwall flying with a flock of bluewings. When they came over me, I killed that gadwall.

All my life I have belittled gadwalls as slow-moving ducks. I know they fly slow. I know they are easy to hit and easy to kill. Bluewings have been my "fastest duck." Yet here was a pair of gadwalls flying along with a flock of bluewings, showing that gadwalls can move up if they want to. I wouldn't know. All I can report is what I saw, and ask forgiveness for seeing it.

In trying to explain why bluewings have been able to leave mallards that fly away with greenwings, I have concluded that it is probably all due to the different methods of flight of the two species of teal. Both greenwings and mallards flare badly at the crack of the gun, while bluewings are more inclined to dip and dart and bore through. This difference in flight also explains why the man with a magazine gun can run up a better score on greenwings than on bluewings. The smaller birds explode and start to climb, and the gunner keeps pumping it to them. The bluewings go on off comparatively low and are soon out of range. It is much simpler to kill a forty-yard duck if he is up in the air over your head than if he is forty yards past you, streaking away level with the water.

Someone, many years ago, said the canvasback was the fastest flying duck, and that has been repeated down through the years until most people believe it. I don't. I don't have as much trouble hitting canvasbacks as I do certain other ducks with similar flight.

All deep-water ducks hold their flight without much flaring. In other words, they drive right on by the gun. Canvas and redheads often fly together, and I have never seen the slightest variation in speed. Not for one second do I wish to leave the impression that I do not think the canvasback is fast. He is very fast. But so are the scaups and the whistlers, and the ruddies and the buffleheads. They all buzz by fast enough to make you step up your swing if you are going to hit them.

Shallow-water ducks come into decoys and put on the brakes as they come, and in comparison a flock of canvas sweeping past seems the extreme in speed. Deep-water fowl all have some change of pace, but very little compared with the long-winged river and pond ducks. I know of no harder duck for me to hit than a ruddy flying thirty-five yards or more away at right angles to the gun. I know that this is partly due to the fact that he is flying close to the water. I also know that he is moving right along—especially when I see my shot drop behind him on the water.

Buffleheads and ruddy ducks are not considered fast by men whose chief experience with these birds has been following them with a boat and shooting the tame little fellows as they take off from the water. All I can say is, try these birds when they are passing you at a good stiff range, with no intention of stopping. It has always seemed to me that a golden-eye, or whistler, carried all the speed a duck was entitled to.

A number of years ago I was a guest at a swanky duck-shooting club in the Cheasapeake area. The first day, my friend and I shot black ducks. When we came in for lunch, we met Mr. Blank, a member, who had been shooting canvas from an offshore blind. He had has limit and was extremely well satisfied with the world in general. This man was an excellent shot, and on the day in question he had killed his ducks with a minimum of shells fired.

"You must get in that blind in the morning." he said. "Wonderful shooting! Wonderful! Tomorrow morning I am going up to number-three blind and shoot whistlers. There are thousands of them trading by. The next day I will go back in the marsh where you fellows were and shoot black ducks. Blacks are pretty tame after shooting cans, but I want a taste of all of it before I go back."

The next morning we shot cans and had royal sport. When we came in at noon, we asked about Mr. Blank, for we had heard him doing a lot of shooting early, and then, not hearing a single gun in the late morning, we concluded he had killed his limit again and gone in.

"He's gone home," the head guide told us. "He got all mixed up with those whifflers this mornin'. He couldn't get 'em to come down and lay on the water. Finally he just got sore and quit."

I repeat that this man is an excellent duck shot and that whistlers fly fast.

Any duck-hunter of experience has seen flocks of mixed ducks traveling together. A few mallards in a big flock of pintails never seem to have any difficulties in keeping up the pace. Gadwalls and widgeons fly together, and members of either species may fly with pintails.

An old friend of mine, Jay Kelsey, just walked into the room where I am writing. "How fast can a duck fly?" I asked him. He should know simple things like this, for he has spent most of his life protecting wild waterfowl for Uncle Sam.

"Sixty miles an hour is the limit a goose can go," he answered. "I know that because I once arrested a man in South Dakota for shooting geese from a plane and that is what he said, and, from the experience that fellow had, he should know."

That calls to mind a real effort to time ducks from a plane that perhaps comes nearer to cases than any other estimate that I know of. Colonel Edward L. Munson, U.S.A., is a duck-hunter. Occasionally he used to write for *Field & Stream* when I edited that magazine. I talked speed of waterfowl with him, as I did with all duck-minded men. Finally, when located on the west coast, Colonel Munson wrote me that he was going to settle this duck-speed question once and for all. He had the ducks, and he had the planes.

From then on he chased ducks whenever the opportunity offered. He would get in behind a flock of high birds and pull up on them. When the plane got too close, the flock would break up and dive or flare out of the way. Then, and not until then, did the Colonel read the speed at which the plane was traveling.

He made many notations. He clocked swans at forty-five miles per hour. He found that snow geese would give up the battle at fifty miles an hour, and his final conclusions were that no goose could fly faster than fifty miles an hour. He furthermore contended that the fastest goose could not equal the speed of the slowest duck. I must add right here that many times I have seen a few mallards flying with Canada geese. I don't recall ever seeing a lone goose flying with a flock of mallards; but I did see three geese traveling along with five mallards, and everyone seemed happy.

The most interesting notes made by Colonel Munson recorded canvasback at seventy-two miles per hour, pintails at sixty-five, and mallards at fifty-five. I don't know that these experiments were made on the same day. They probably were not. Birds clocked at different heights above the earth, going in the same direction on the same day, might have utterly different atmospheric conditions to contend with. Furthermore, I believe that a scared, wise old mallard would be inclined to dodge out of the way of a plane with much less cause for alarm than a bullheaded old canvasback whose every instinct would urge him to stay up in front and keep piling on more speed as long as he could.

I will quote a couple of paragraphs from a letter that I received from Captain Henry C. Morley, R.A.F., under date of September 2, 1944:

"Yesterday I had a chance to clock a flight of bluewinged teal—about thirty ducks. I was flying at 9,000 feet between Montreal, Que., and Megantic, Que., just on top of a flat layer of cloud—stratus cloud—when I saw the ducks about a half mile ahead of me. I was making 105 kts. and immediately slowed down to 75 kts. and came slowly up directly behind the birds. When about forty yards behind the flock I slowed down to 66 kts. (very near stalling speed) which was the speed the birds were making. I imagine they put on full steam when they saw me coming up behind. I stayed behind the birds five and a half minutes at 66 kts. indicated air speed. My air speed indicator has a correction of—15 kts. making the true indicated air speed 71 kts. which is 81½ M.P.H. Correcting this speed for altitude and temperature the birds were flying at a true air speed of 95½ M.P.H. I had a 26 kt. tail wind, so the birds were making a ground speed of 125½ M.P.H. Pretty fast for a duck.

"I imagine the birds were traveling about 40 M.P.H. before I scared them, which would have given them a ground speed of 77 M.P.H. at this altitude, temperature and wind. It looks like Mr. Duck can move his home in a hurry."

The one thing anyone can be certain of is that ducks fly fast—too fast for many of us. A sixty-mile bird with a sixty-mile gale behind him would do that old claim of a hundred and twenty miles per hour —maybe. He might just sit back and take it easy and let the wind do most of the work. I read a press dispatch to the effect that the Army had clocked a pigeon at 68.7 miles per hour. No duck-hunter wants to admit that a pigeon can fly faster than his favorite game bird. That is something we just won't believe.

Any hunter will tell you about ducks that flew so fast that it took two men to see them—one to watch them come and one to see them go.

The story I like best has to do with the two boys who were shooting ducks for the first time. A guide had placed them in the blind and cautioned them to stay down out of sight when birds were approaching.

A flock of forty or fifty bluewinged teal swept over the decoys with all the roar and swishing of air that such a happening can create. The birds were in and gone before either boy knew what it was all about. Then one boy dropped to the ground and hissed to the other: "Git down!"

"What do you want to get down now for?" asked the slower-witted of the two.

"Hell," said the first boy, "the world's round, ain't it? They'll pass us again in a minute."

MYSTERIES OF MIGRATION

Robert Elman

Where I live in New Jersey, the moment comes sometime in October. A new cold front pushes in, one without the tawny softness of Indian summer but with winds that show the beginning of the fangs of winter to come. Raking leaves, you think you hear them. No, you decide, it was only the wind. Then, suddenly, there it is: An unmistakable chorus of high yapping. You scan, squinting, and finally you see them in a ragged V, very high and fast on the wind. These are not local birds, trading between pond and fields. These geese hold express tickets for the Eastern Shore. They have come down from the wind-swept tundras hundreds of miles away, and the sight of them sends your spirit soaring with the thrill of seasonal renewal. What a strange and appealing event migration is to behold. We wait for the weather, we wait for the birds. In his book, The Atlantic Flyway, *Winchester Press, Bob Elman treats the subject with the respect and awe all wildfowlers can appreciate.*

SOUTHWARD BOUND, AND EASTWARD

IF WE CAN trust the maps of the United States Fish and Wildlife Service, four major flyways serve the migratory needs and mysterious whims of North American wildfowl.

Each of these corridors is more or less funnel-shaped. The widest at the top, spanning the greatest expanse of northern breeding grounds, are the Atlantic and Mississippi flyways, which are probably also largest in terms of total area covered. It may be that the Atlantic is both wider in the arctic regions and larger overall than the Mississippi, but one cannot be dogmatic in these matters because tremendous areas of the breeding region produce wildfowl for both flyways—in fact, for the Central and Pacific flyways, as well. Moreover, the migratory routes of many birds begin on the Mississippi Flyway and then, for reasons not fully understood, wheel eastward, to terminate on the Atlantic Flyway.

The blending, interlocking nature of the corridors, and the tributary lanes crossing from one to another, make it difficult to assign precise eastern and western limits to the courses of the aerial caravans. Though the Atlantic Flyway is bounded on the east by a vast oceanic expanse, the seaboard is sometimes visited by the European barnacle goose, which breeds on the Norwegian island of Svalbard, northeast of its other primary breeding site on Greenland, and is extremely common in winter along the west coast of Scotland. Even its name is purely European, having derived from an old Norse belief that the species hatched out of barnacle shells on water-soaked logs and driftwood.

The European widgeon also visits the Atlantic Flyway, from New England to Florida, and sometimes ventures far inland. It breeds in Iceland, and may be more common in North America than its name implies. A third visitor from the Old World is the European teal, a close relative of our greenwing. Since teal seem to have a propensity for incredibly long migratory journeys, it is perhaps not surprising that this "European" species also appears throughout Asia, breeds in the Aleutians, and visits North America's eastern seaboard from Greenland to North Carolina.

There are also migrants from the far Northwest, birds that touch all of the major flight corridors on their way to winter quarters. The Atlantic Coast receives some canvasbacks and scaup, for example, from Alaskan breeding grounds.

Still, if one bears in mind that the boundaries fade gradually and that migration patterns occasionally shift, it is possible to define the flyways geographically. The Atlantic Flyway gathers hordes of wildfowl from southern Greenland, the islands of Baffin Bay, Hudson Bay, Labrador, Quebec, the Gulf of St. Lawrence, and all the Maritime Provinces, Ontario, most of Manitoba, northern Saskatchewan, the northeastern corner of Alberta, and most of the Northwest Territories up to the northernmost segment of the Yukon border. The prairie provinces and eastern Canada are tremendously productive, but many of the birds breed as far south as New England and New York, Michigan, Wisconsin, and northeastern Minnesota.

Some species nest above or below this primary breeding range. The islands of the eastern Arctic are important hatcheries for Atlantic brant and snow geese. Mallards and black ducks are common nesters from Maryland northward. Wood ducks breed throughout the flyway.

The western limit of the flyway angles through the northeastern corners of Minnesota and Wisconsin, a large portion of northeastern Michigan, Ohio, and West Virginia, then turns sharply southward through Virginia, the Carolinas, Georgia, and Florida before sweeping southeastward again to the southernmost wintering grounds in the West Indies. Perhaps one cannot even classify the West Indies as the southernmost wintering grounds, because a few birds do fly on into South America. Since the ocean forms the corridor's eastern boundary, the Atlantic Flyway also encompasses Maine, New Hampshire, Vermont, Massachusetts, Connecticut, New York, New Jersey, Pennsylvania, Delaware, and Maryland.

For the Mississippi Flyway, the breeding grounds extend from Baffin Island and western Quebec westward through Ontario and the greater portion of the prairie provinces, all of the Northwest Territories, the northern Yukon and northeastern Alaska. The flyway proper covers most of the Midwest, from the amorphous edge of the Atlantic Flyway to the eastern Dakotas and Nebraska, and down through Arkansas and Louisiana to the shores of the Gulf. The upper part of this funnel heavily overlaps the Atlantic Flyway, but there are thinning stretches and even narrow gaps between the two corridors in eastern Kentucky, Tennessee, and Alabama, and in Florida's western panhandle where the shooting is generally not quite as good as it is slightly to the east and west.

The Central Flyway overlaps the Mississippi Flyway and continues much farther southward—through Mexico and all of Central America. It is fed not only by the prairie provinces (chiefly Saskatchewan and Alberta) but by most of the Northwest Territories and the Yukon, as well as northeastern Alaska. It should be noted that the breeding grounds for both the Mississippi and Central flyways are by no means confined to the regions above the forty-ninth parallel. Among the major nesting areas of the redhead, for example, are large prairie-slough tracts in Minnesota, both Dakotas, Nebraska, Montana, Idaho, Washington.

FURTHER MYSTERIES OF MIGRATION

The many factors of evolution—random mutation, natural selection, adaptation, survival of the fittest—have resulted in many wonderfully specialized creatures, but none more so than migratory birds. They are marvels of efficiency. It can be argued that the most efficient of all American species is the golden plover, a shorebird of the family *Charadriiae* whose annual journeys outdistance even those of teal.

This plover travels about eight thousand miles on its migration, chiefly using the Atlantic Flyway on its southward journey, though it returns by way of the Mississippi Flyway. The distance is known to be surpassed by only one other avian creature, the Arctic tern, which sometimes breeds within ten degrees of the North Pole and courses down the west coast of Europe and Africa to winter in the Antarctic.

The plover's autumnal flight is mystifyingly curcuitous. Upon leaving the arctic breeding grounds in late summer, it wends eastward to Labrador and follows the coastline down to Nova Scotia. But there it leaves the coast to strike out on a hazardous journey over the open ocean, not touching land again until it reaches South America. No one has yet discovered why this astoundingly difficult route has been established or why, in spring, the golden plover returns from Brazil or Argentina along an inland corridor, eventually flying northward along the Mississippi Valley.

Though the reasons for such migrations remain a mystery, biologists now understand some of the adaptations that make possible incredibly long flights. The metabolism of the plover, responding to seasonal hormonal changes, adjusts so exquisitely to the challenge of the long journey without food, without rest, that its forty-eight-hour nonstop oceanic flight of twenty-four hundred miles is fueled by two ounces of reserve body fat.

The golden plover is by no means the only species possessed of such metabolic efficiency or motivational caprice. Many ducks have been sighted flying over the Atlantic, two hundred miles offshore. Some of these birds are bound for Bermuda, the Bahamas, the Antilles. Bermuda does not offer much in the way of winter habitat, yet there have been casual island sightings of American golden-eyes, bufflehead, surf scoter, ruddy ducks, greater and lesser snow geese, Canada geese, whistling swans, hooded and red-breasted mergansers, black ducks, gadwalls, baldpates, bluewinged teal, shovelers, lesser scaup, canvasbacks, wood ducks—in fact, most of the Atlantic Flyway species.

The Bahama Islands provide breeding habitat for the Bahama pintail, of course, and winter habitat for pintails, shovelers, lesser scaup, bluewings (and greenwings!), ruddy ducks, redheads, and the ubiquitous mallard also winters here, as well as almost everywhere from New England southward. Moreover, just as the Atlantic Flyway is visited by European waterfowl, many ducks and geese of the eastern seaboard are occasionally found on European sojourns.

Still, none of this explains seemingly aimless flights that have been sighted far out on the Atlantic. Some observers have speculated that perhaps overpopulation of a given species in a small belt of habitat may, in unusual instances, produce a lemminglike flight to nowhere. This must occur rarely, however, for overpopulation is not a frequent problem. On the contrary, the problem is the maintenance of healthy numbers in spite of the attrition of habitat as man paves a continent, and in spite of nesting-season droughts, blights, and outbreaks of such diseases as botulism.

Hunting is important in controlling the populations of many waterfowl species, some of which would otherwise become an agricultural scourge. But there are other factors, good and bad. For example, New Jersey's Department of Environmental Protection has estimated that between 1950 and 1970 the state lost an acre of wetlands per hour. A strenuous effort is now being made to halt or even reserve that dismaying loss. Other estimates have put the total fall population of Canada geese at three million or more, with perhaps half that number heading toward the eastern flyways. But in spite of widespread habitat destruction, there are havens that support more geese now than formerly. For a decade and a half, the number of Canadas in the Chesapeake wetlands has increased at an annual average of six percent, primarily because of the Delmarva region's corn farming, plus the protection of the bay and the area's refuges.

It may be that some three million Canada geese embark on the southward journey each fall, headed for wintering grounds which, in all their vastness, cannot feed more than half that number. But no more than half that number need be fed, for no more than half will arrive. Some of the others die of natural causes, including age; some die in accidents. The relative safety of nocturnal flight may be shattered by an invisible power line, or by a metal roof glinting like water in the dim starlight when clouds smother the moon's surer illumination.

More are killed by predators. Man, most efficient of predators, too seldom realizes that his atavistic sport, his predatory instinct, is included in nature's balance. Were it not for the insanity of gunners who shiver away the dark in wind-lashed blinds, the geese would swarm like locusts over the southern wetlands in multitudes doomed to slow starvation. Yet a bird may run the continent-long gauntlet of shot for season after season until overtaken not by the reverberating crash of gunfire but by the silent death of the aged.

Each autumnal journey during the life of that bird is an achievement of puzzling magnitude. Even when buffeted by winds, both ducks and geese can cover vast distances at a steady, effortless speed of forty to fifty miles an hour. Canvasback ducks can attain an air speed of more than seventy miles an hour when pursued. The greater part of migratory flight takes place at altitudes below three thousand feet, but snow geese have been observed at twenty-six thousand feet. Such aerial prowess is made possible not only by a remarkable metabolism but by remarkable musculature. For example, a bird's pectoral muscles, contracting to move the wings, simultaneously push against the ribs to pump air into the lungs like an artificial respirator. It has been said that ducks cannot lose their breath because they fly into it.

The navigational ability of wildfowl is another mystery which is being slowly (and perhaps only partially) solved by the banding of trapped birds and the recording of where and when these birds are shot or recaptured. It is a relatively little-known fact that the first American banding experiments, perhaps the first of importance anywhere in the world, were performed on the Atlantic Flyway, near Philadelphia in 1804. The experimenter was none other than that avid gunner of the Atlantic and Mississippi Flyways, John James Audubon.

Unfortunately, no naturalist renewed the experiment until 1899, when a Danish schoolmaster named H.C.C. Mortensen began capturing and banding teal, storks, and starlings, evidently without knowing that his idea was antique. Three years later the research was taken up in this country by Dr. Paul Bartsch of the Smithsonian Institution, and in 1909 the American Bird Banding Association was organized. Its program was absorbed in 1920 by the United States Biological Survey, predecessor of the Fish and Wildlife Service, which still carries on the work. By now, literally millions of birds have been banded. The research is intensive and continually rewarding. It was the Service that published *Migration of Birds*, by Frederick C. Lincoln, whose pioneering investigations have been previously mentioned. Dr. Lincoln had charge of the Service's migratory studies, and his findings (based on band returns and since confirmed by additional returns) established the concept of flyways and helped to map them. As a direct result of his contribution, the flyways have been successfully used since 1948 as the basis for the annual review and setting of wildfowling regulations.

As to what has been discovered thus far regarding navigation, it is now known that birds navigate by the sun and stars, correcting course as the journey progresses to take into account the shift in star positions and the sun's path. They also employ landmarks both large and small. A mighty river may draw a flight forward for many miles, until a mere hillock of shoreline conformation signals the approach to a resting and feeding site. Along the densely settled stretches characteristic of the Atlantic Flyway, wildfowl have actually been observed to follow highways, and they seem to use city skylines and lights as beacons, too.

In 1966, an investigator named F.C. Bellrose reported on this use of landmarks in orientation and navigation, and the findings were confirmed in a 1970 report by Bellrose and Robert D. Crompton for the Illinois Natural History Survey. In emphasizing that "landscape features are important factors," the report relies on direct observation as well as banding: "We have frequently seen migrating ducks change directions upon sight of prominent landscape features."

This does not, of course, reveal how a duck or goose on its first migratory flight recognizes landmarks or translates the map of sun and stars. The miracle is, in part, a matter of instinct, interpreted lately by some animal behaviorists as analogous to Jung's theory of "racial" or "collective" human memory. According to this interpretation, migratory birds possess a vague, unconscious, inborn knowledge of ancestral routes and destinations, a physiological programming for the first long journey. In experiments with birds hatched and reared in captivity, then released to migrate without guidance from elders of their kind, wildfowl have managed to arrive on their ancestral wintering grounds. Still, what this may prove is no more than conjectural, for it is argued that such birds simply search for wetlands, where they inevitably find and join flocks of migrating wild birds. Moreover, studies such as that of Bellrose and Crompton prove conclusively that ducks become much more adept at homing with each repeated migratory experience.

Along the way they guide one another, reinforcing directional memory. And when visibility is poor, it is believed that they may chatter not only as a form of reciprocal encouragement but as a method of echo-location. The echoes bounce back to them from various terrain features and their sensitive hearing translates the messages of this natural radar system into directional instructions. Their voice apparatus seems to function without interfering with the breathing rhythm, so that it is always functional when needed. The man who hears the cries of geese far out over Delaware Bay on a foggy morning may be listening to birds probing an invisible map for a remembered cove.

A sudden early blizzard or a freeze that leaves too little open water in the north country will, of course, send throngs of wildfowl scurrying southward, but since they are likely to dally along the way, the migration schedule becomes a self-correcting process. It is the synchronization of the homing ability with this miraculous sense of timing that accounts for the entrance of ducks and geese upon the right stage in prompt response to nature's cues. Recent studies indicate that migratory birds are so sensitive to barometric pressures and other climatic indicators that they can "feel" changes in weather conditions about twelve hours in advance, and this weather-forecasting instinct helps them to arrive safely at various destination points along the flyway. The sense of timing is so acute among coastal birds that, after flying inland, they return to shore for feeding at just the hour when the tide is right.

A different and even more awesome timing ability governs the seasonal onset of migration so effectively that an early blizzard or freeze is merely a small variable in a centuries-old schedule.

It is possible to observe the birds making advance preparations for migration. Mel Evans, manager at the Santee National Wildlife Refuge in South Carolina, where large numbers of Atlantic Flyway ducks, geese, swans, and wading birds rest or winter, has remarked that he can tell about two weeks ahead of time when the spring migration northward will begin. Using the behavior of the birds, particularly Canada geese, as the key, he can predict almost to the day when the major exodus is to start. The geese feed less and less, and they become so restless that they are almost constantly on the wing. There is a great increase in aerial acrobatics, a tumbling activity that is especially marked among the younger birds. Evans refers to these antics as playing, but adds that the playing is of a sober nature. Canadas are not ordinarily among the most playful of wildfowl. Until migration becomes imminent, in fact, their behavior exhibits an almost haughty dignity and orderly discipline.

Evans and many other observers believe that the sudden indulgence in cavorting is a way of exercising by which the birds condition themselves for the migratory flight. It may also be a natural psychological preparation for the sustained activity to come.

But how do the birds sense the approach of migration time? It is no simple matter of warming or cooling weather. A snowfall in July will not send waves of ducks and geese down the Atlantic Flyway from James Bay or Hudson Bay, nor will an abnormally warm autumn significantly delay their departure. Only when the time is right do the multitudes converge along the tidewater flats of those bays as they have for countless autumns through aeons past. The skies and waters are then speckled with the thousands of blues and snows and Canadas. One can actually see the impatience take hold and surge through the flocks. Their chatter swells, becomes more raucous, until it is almost a palpable element of the air. Little bunches leave their comrades and make brief flights, still tentative but betraying the yearning to be gone. And then, on the environment's appointed day, heralds of the flight lift skyward, leading still scanty formations as they call urgently to the hesitant. As more birds heed the beckoning cries, the urgency subtly attains a purposeful quality. The tidal waters ooze over the flats as on every other day; nothing appears to have changed. Yet geese soon becloud the skies, formations blending with other formations, chevrons bulging into amorphous skeins.

For a little while the cries resound across the waters before melting away as imperceptibly as the tide itself. It is a seasonal farewell, and when the last echo finally subsides, an ineffable emptiness strikes the flats.

Patient observation and experiment have partially solved the mystery of this exquisite seasonal timing, for it has been proved that migratory birds possess a glandular specialization known as the biological clock. "Biological calendar" would perhaps be a more felicitous term for the seasonal phenomenon, but no matter. It is founded in the sexual drive which assures the perpetuation of species, and is powered by solar energy in the form of light. Among creatures that mate seasonally, there is a genital and hormonal shrinkage to the point of dormancy during the long nonbreeding period while all biological powers are concentrated on survival in a wild environment. Light governs the waxing and waning.

In describing the cycle, it is natural to begin with the spring awakening, when most wild forces come to life. Light stimulates the seasonal development of the bird's sex glands and hormones. As winter ends, there is a daily lengthening of the light over those Santee marshes, awakening the sexual drive, catalyzing the biochemistry of reproduction. As this primeval drive strengthens, the birds grow restless and the restlessness swells until it culminates when the birds strike out for their northern breeding grounds.

Scientists have confirmed this explanation by exposing captive wildfowl to increased hours of artificial light. From year to year, the variation in the hours of daylight during a given period at a given latitude are so slight that the biological clock of each species is superbly accurate. However, the clocks of all species are not set to the same increases and decreases of light. Evolution—nature, if you will—has meticulously staggered the timing of migrations so that overcrowding does not bring disaster along the corridors of flight and rest. This staggering applies to fall as well as spring, spreading the total migration over several months. It is why the gunning season can be satisfyingly long without devastation to the wildfowl populations.

As every hunter on the Atlantic Flyway has found, there is a considerable lapse of time between the first September skitters of teal and the waves of hardy scaup, among the latest of migrants. During the interval there is a steady flow of other species down the flyway. Pintails start early, often at about the time of the teal, but their journey is more protracted, as is that of other ducks that begin to wing southward in September—ruddies, mallards, blacks, redheads. These birds are followed or accompanied in September or October by wood ducks and shovelers, and October also sees the ringnecks, canvasbacks, and American golden-eyes leaving the north. The Barrow's golden-eye is headed for winter quarters in October or November, as are the old-squaws and the American and red-breasted mergansers. Scaup are not unique in their indifference to cold, for such ducks as the harlequin, bufflehead, and American eider remain in the upper latitudes until November and, on rare occasions, even a bit later.

The schedule is both complicated and eased by the fact that all birds of a single species do not migrate during one short period. In the fall, as the equinoctial control of the biological clock is reversed, the sexual and family-raising drives have abated, replaced by other urges. Though the adults of some species still exhibit a somewhat protective attitude toward the young, the immature birds are now strong flyers. The mature birds have regained flight feathers after the moult, and all are capable of extended flight, yet it is to their advantage to continue feeding and resting as long as possible before migration. The diminishing daylight seems to warn them of a coming scarcity of food, at the same time evidently working subtle changes in their biochemistry to prepare them metabolically for the efforts of the journey. But the effects of diminishing light are modified by other factors.

Generally speaking, the birds that subsist on molluscs and fish, and those that frequent the big waters migrate a little later than puddle ducks, and the reason seems obvious: their habitat is not soon frozen over, barring access to food. Similarly, mallards nesting about the eastern Great Lakes have no reason to leave as early as those on the windswept prairies of Manitoba.

Even the black duck, a species encountered in significant numbers only on the Atlantic and Mississippi Flyways and having a surprisingly limited breeding range, exhibits a diffused pattern of migratory timing. Since the black is of extreme importance to the gunners of the Atlantic Flyway, it merits special attention here. This duck nests only in the East, though pockets of the range extend into Manitoba. The breeding area sprawls from the upper shores of the Great Lakes northward and eastward through Ontario, Quebec, Labrador, Newfoundland, New Brunswick, and Nova Scotia, with some small coastal concentrations scattered as far south as the Middle Atlantic states.

The autumnal migration of those in the lower part of the range tends to begin substantially later than the procession from the North. Some of the southern black ducks, in fact, do not migrate at all. They have no need to—and the absence of migration is probably somewhat more common among wildfowl than is generally supposed. Occasionally a little group of Canada geese or mallards or other birds will gain the ability (for still unknown reasons) to ignore the nomadic urging of the biological clock if they have settled on some congenial slough. This probably occurs with greatest frequency where seasonal extremes of light and weather are not so pronounced as elsewhere—along the middle and lower stretches of the Atlantic Flyway, for example. On a Virginia estuary or a Delaware tidal flat, a little group of Canadas simply settles down to a lazily sedentary existence forevermore. There are also whole varieties of wildfowl that are virtually nonmigratory even in areas of greatly different habitat and climate: the white-cheeked goose of Alaska, a distinctly localized subspecies of the Canada; the mottled duck of Louisiana and Texas, the Florida duck which is common only on the lower tip of the Atlantic Flyway.

As to the blacks, they do have a strong migratory urge, whose timing is dictated in some degree by the nesting area. In spite of these variations, Arthur Cleveland Bent managed to amass the average departure and arrival dates for blacks and other major species in his *Life Histories of North American Wild Fowl*. Since the two volumes of this work were originally published as Smithsonian Institution *Bulletins* in 1923 and 1925, when banding on a large scale was still quite new, the accomplishment is outstanding. Bent states that September 30th is the average arrival date for black ducks in the area of Alexandria, Virginia. Those that continue southward first rest and feed for some time, and blacks aren't usually seen around Mount Pleasant, Charleston, the Carolina Bays until October 22nd. Later, some of them leave South Carolina for still warmer climes, and good numbers of black ducks, according to his compilations, are encountered in Wakulla County, Florida, in mid-November.

A bewildering complexity of patterns emerges as Bent then lists some average dates of major flight departures. Montreal, November 6 and 14; Ottawa, November 7 and 21; Prince Edward Island, November 13 and December 8. Many black ducks, then, are leaving the Canadian waters long after others of their kind have arrived in Virginia and the Carolinas. What seems to be a contradictory listing is further evidence of the connection between breeding area and migratory schedule for any single species, compounded by tarrying along the way even on the northern segment of the flyway. The complexity of pattern and behavior is underscored when, in a listing of egg dates, Bent includes for the period of April 20 to May 10 nesting sites as far south as Maryland and Virginia.

There is a tremendous need for a continuing accumulation and study of such data—as well as information concerning fluctuations in habitat, population, migratory routes, pollution, and the erosion of feeding and resting sites by coastal industry, shipping, marsh-draining land developers and the like. The importance of all this is made obvious by a few more statistics regarding the significance of the black duck to the Atlantic Flyway. Over 60 percent of the average total duck harvest in Rhode Island each year consists of blacks; over 50 percent of those bagged in Massachusetts and New Jersey are blacks; just under 50 percent of those shot in Maine and New Hampshire; more than 43 percent of the Delaware harvest; over 35 percent of the Connecticut and Vermont harvests; over 28 percent of the Maryland take; 26 percent in Virginia; just under 23 percent in New York; and more than 17 percent in Pennsylvania. Even as far down the flyway as North Carolina—the major wintering grounds for a great many other species—black ducks account for more than 12 percent of the annual crop.

As the case is stated in a Ducks Unlimited brochure, "The preservation of the black duck is critical to the Atlantic Flyway harvest." Ducks Unlimited must be credited with truly enormous achievements in the enlargement and maintenance of wetland habitat for the black ducks of the Atlantic Flyway (in fact, for all the major species on all four flyways). Funded solely by America's sportsmen, DU has contributed millions of dollars to securing or rehabilitating and preserving marshlands. A typical project is the Missaquash Marsh on the Nova Scotia—New Brunswick border, a drained wasteland until the organization built a dike and water-control system. There are now twenty-six miles of shoreline on this six-thousand-acre marsh, an important producer of blacks and other birds. The project was principally financed by DU's Delaware members, and another was made possible by the organization's Rhode Island members. This is on the Maccan River, ten miles south of Amherst, Nova Scotia, where a two-thousand foot levee has been built. The result is a small but important marshland, two hundred and ten acres with a long shoreline that contributes to the flights of black ducks heading down the flyway. In the spring of 1971, Ducks Unlimited opened a regional office in the Maritimes to coordinate new operations, initially costing well over $200,000, in the heart of the black-duck country. As this is being written, eight new projects are being maintained over ten thousand acres of wetlands which help to assure the future waterfowl population of the Atlantic Flyway.

Another species peculiar to this flyway—almost unique to it—is the American brant. This diminutive marine goose winters chiefly from New Jersey to North Carolina, with the greatest concentration in Virginia and North Carolina. In connection with the autumnal arrival of brant, one thinks immediately of such traditional gunning bays as Brigantine and Barnegat, or of the shores of the Delmarva Peninsula. Yet brant, like other migrants, can be capriciously nomadic. Although they don't often stray very far off course, Bent recorded (probably with some effort to restrain the delight of serendipity) that sightings had been recorded in Michigan, Nebraska, and Wisconsin. Once, in November of 1876, a brant was observed in Barbados. And the birds are occasionally seen on the Pacific Coast where a relative, the black brant, is alleged to be the exclusive representative of the clan.

Most northerly of all our geese, the American brant nests along the coast of Greenland and has more extensive breeding grounds on Ellesmere Island, well within the Arctic Circle. The short polar summer forces an early migration which descends into the Gulf of St. Lawrence before September ends. From that point on, however, progress is so leisurely that brant aficionados of the Atlantic Coast are assured of seeing the flights continue for a couple of months. Long, teetering lines of brant weave and undulate over the horizon, their quick wingbeats sometimes giving the impression of desperate escape from a sinking sky, a marked and touching contrast to the majestically effortless progress of the Canada geese as the brant sputter along toward wintering grounds that will not often be reached before mid-October or early November.

Apart from oddities of flight, the brant has other characteristics that are somehow touching. As with Canadas and other geese, the male stands guard close by while the female incubates the eggs. But a guardian brant lacks the imperious presence displayed by a guardian Canada. On the stark arctic tundra, it seems miraculous that a ground nest of moss and grasses, though lined with down of maternal breast, can sufficiently protect those three or four or five fragile, creamy white eggshells that hold the embryos of another generation.

Brant do not graze upon the dry land as do Canadas, snows, and many other geese but they, too, are essentially vegetarians and, unlike so many of the marine species, an epicurean delight. Their chief food is eelgrass (*Zostera marina*), which thrives in shallow bays and estuaries. This single staple is even more vital to the American brant than it is to the black brant of the West Coast. A hunting man on the Atlantic Flyway dwells upon the fact like that, for it demonstrates the fragility of a coastal ecosystem which, to the uninformed, appears too rugged to be gutted by any calamity short of technocracy's inclination to spread oil upon the waters.

Because brant have long been recognized as the most succulent of waterfowl, the batteries of the market gunners were trained on them; they survived even that. And then, in the early 1930s, a fungus struck the eelgrass.

The blight was severe along the entire Atlantic Coast and as far away as France. Starvation ensued. Before the famine, there had been more than a quarter of a million brant on the flyway. By 1935, there were perhaps twenty thousand left—about two percent of the former population. Birds more flexible in their migratory habits might have sought new habitat, as almost all species of wildfowl do in the event of catastrophes. But then, birds more flexible in their migratory habits would have to be more flexible in their dietary requirements—in which case there would be no need to seek out a new migration route.

What happened was a classic example of survival of the fittest, which in this case meant survival of the most adaptable. The few remaining brant, hardiest of their lineage, eked out an existence on substitute forage—sea lettuce and similar vegetation.

The eelgrass very slowly revived, and with it the American brant population. As recently as the summer of 1961, Van Campen Heilner, in an article appearing in *The American Gun*, said with some justification that "today the word 'brant' is almost forgotten in the lexicon of waterfowl gunners." The article was not, however, an epitaph; on the contrary, it was a paean to the miraculous return of brant to the Atlantic Flyway. Heilner continued, with regard to *Branta Bernicla hrota*:

> it is the name for a goose of diminutive size and succulent flavor that swept down the Atlantic coastal flyways in hordes each autumn to gladden the heart of every wildfowler with stamina enough to face the stinging winds and pelting rain of a wild northeaster. Good brant weather has always been bad weather, with curling crests of raging water smashing over sand bars, salt spray and stinging sleet driving into the blind. No fair weather bird is the brant, for it continues to fly or lies happily out to sea until the storms bring it into gun range. Then, flying low, it seeks shelter in the coves. . . . The greatest concentration of brant that I have ever seen was off Hatteras Inlet, North Carolina, in the days before the disappearance of the eelgrass. It was early November. . . . The bend of the beach near the inlet was black with them. . . . A steady stream of brant poured out of that bend for more than an hour.

Today, descendants of those birds still ply the Atlantic Coast, helplessly loyal to their ancestral foraging and migrating instincts. They are multiplying again, their numbers growing, their survival and renewed prosperity another beautiful mystery of this migratory corridor.

SECRET LIFE OF THE
SALT MARSH BARRENS

Robert Elman

Once again in a piece from his The Atlantic Flyway *(Winchester Press), destined to become a classic in my opinion, Bob Elman's prose is as engaging and knowledgeable as anything I've ever read. I pity the sky-busters and other fools and jackals to whom a day on the marsh is a limit of birds and nothing else. Can't these people read? Are they incapable of learning? I can't help but believe that a few minutes with a tale like this will make any person feel richer for living in the kind of world where there still are secret wild places we can enjoy and treasure.*

AFTER SEVERAL years of scrimping and cutting vacations short, a hunter from New York had finally managed to arrange his fall business schedule so that he could grant himself several week-long tours north and south on the coast he loved, exploring uplands and lowlands that he had never known well enough and probably never would know well enough to satisfy his curious yearning.

The season had begun inauspiciously in September, when he had accepted a weekend invitation from a Connecticut friend who wanted to introduce him to rail shooting on the marshlands sprinkled about the Connecticut River and Nells Island, near the mouth of the Housatonic. During the drive up, he had let his mind dwell on the somber and paradoxical combination of serenity and intensity in the Thomas Eakins' paintings of sportsmen and their guides "pushing for rail." He was under no illusion that the habitat or the hunt would be quite like the Eakins' milieu of 1874, but he hoped that the same palpably quiet atmosphere might prevail, and in this he was not disappointed. Neither was he disappointed in the suspense of waiting for the reluctant flush and short, erratic flight of the shy marsh birds, their legs dangling as they skittered over the tall grasses.

Other elements of the hunt were not, however, quite so perfect.

His own preparations had not been as meticulous as he might have wished. Though he was armed with a cylinder-bored 20-gauge gun and had managed to acquire some Number 10 and Number 11 shells, classic choices, business had prevented him from timing his hunt to take advantage of the highest flood tides on a day of the full moon or new moon. The guide had been reasonably competent, but with the water a bit low, poling was difficult. The art of the pusher has always been a demanding one. He must know the productive pockets of marshland, and he must pole the little shallow-draft boat along at just the right speed to prod unwilling birds into flight within range. Progress must be smooth and steady, for the gunner has to stand, ready to shoot fast over the tall reeds. Balance is essential. It is likely that truly great pushers have been in short supply ever since the sport reached its zenith of popularity in the last quarter of the nineteenth century.

Still, the New York hunter had managed to shoot a few of the whistling, whinnying sora rails, and had seen a couple of the larger clapper rails as well. Besides, he anticipated another try at clappers later on, near the mouth of the Cape Fear River in North Carolina, where the season stretches from the beginning of September through the first week in November. There, on the tidal marshes near Southport, one can find the king rail and the Virginia rail as well as the sora and the clapper, known locally as marsh hens. So he was not unhappy about his season's unimpressive beginning; it only whetted his appetite for longer coastal sojourns.

Early in October he shot woodcock in New Brunswick and Maine, and from a cramped sneakboat on Merrymeeting Bay he bagged a few teal. Then he wandered a bit on the chain of tidal marshes between Kittery and Portland before driving south to Portsmouth, below the New Hampshire line.

He walked the bleak barrier beaches which shield the marshes from the roaring surf, and even on the rustling sands where provender seemed scarce to his anthropocentric eye, the birds were plentiful—not just gulls, petrels, shearwaters, the expected ocean denizens, but grebes and shorebirds: plover, yellowlegs, sandpiper.

The Eskimo curlew and the Labrador duck were no more to be

seen, of course, having succumbed long ago to the rapacity of an un-lamented bygone era, but there were American coots and "sea coots" —scoter that he had gunned from sculls and gray double-ender lobster skiffs in the Maine coves and once from an unwieldy dinghy on Long Island Sound. He recalled how, during the early part of a past season, they had been so innocent as to decoy to lobster buoys and net corks. They would even toll in over an anchor-line float, though they did seem to acquire caution after a few volleys.

If succulent vegetation appears scant along the pebble beaches, breaker-smashed rubble, and cliffs, there is no mystery about the source of food for scoter. In one study, the stomach contents of 819 white-winged scoter yielded an analysis of 94 percent animal matter. Molluscs alone—rock clams, oysters, blue mussels, scallops—comprised 75 percent. Some crustaceans, with a few insects and fish, also provided a significant proportion of sustenance, while eelgrass, bur-reed, and miscellaneous plant foods made up only 6 percent. Yet Van Campen Heilner's excellent work, *A Book on Duck Shooting*, concludes a passage about hunting scoter with this declaration: "And when you take me home that night I want a big red-hot, steaming plateful of good old coot stew!"

There is no denying that even those waterfowl (or most of them) which rank low on epicurean lists because of a large intake of fish and shellfish can yield delightful table fare. Most connoisseurs utilize only the breasts, carefully marinating them; others combine the use of a marinade with a "throw-away" stuffing intended to draw off any trace of fishy flavor. By a number of means, man has elevated even the lowly among waterfowl to a significant rank in terms of his carnivorous appetites as well as his sport.

The surf scoter imbibes a bit less animal food than the white-winged variety, and a trifle more vegetation, including pondweeds—a reminder that even "marine" waterfowl are to some degree sustained by the sweet-water wealth of the inland marshes as well as the brack-ish and salt-water staples. The American scoter eats about as much animal food as the surf scoter, supplementing its diet with pond-weeds, muskgrass, and miscellaneous plant food.

Curiosity had led the New York hunter to delve into the reports of game biologists, and he knew enough about the foraging practices of coastal birds to understand that the stark shores, dark waters, and especially the flat, monochromatic ochre of lifeless looking salt marshes appear barren only to the unpracticed eye. They are delicate but rich ecosystems teeming with hidden resources, with life-giving life. Nevertheless, he felt a mild astonishment (or reverence, perhaps) at the ability of such birds as Canada geese, scaup, golden-eyes, and buffleheads to flourish on the coastal marshes and open waters as he prowled the estuary of New Hampshire's Great Bay.

Riffling through the pages of Kortright, he pondered on some revealing analyses of foods eaten by these birds. In an examination of 395 American golden-eyes, scientists had found that 74 percent of the diet consisted of animal matter, again consisting of molluscs, crustaceans, fish, and insects, supplemented by pondweeds, wild celery, spatterdocks, grains, and bulrushes. The percentages were not greatly different for 81 Barrow's golden-eyes. A sampling of 282 buffleheads revealed a slightly higher percentage of animal foods, particularly insects, similarly supplemented by various aquatic and terrestrial plants. Most of the diving ducks are either predominantly vegetable eaters or animal feeders, but the greater scaup is a border-line case whose diet consists of about 50 percent vegetation and 50 percent molluscs, insects, crustaceans, and so on. Among 752 birds examined, the vegetation consumed included significant percentages of pondweeds, muskgrass, water milfoils, sedges, wild rice and other grasses, and wild celery. The diet of the lesser scaup included more vegetation—about 60 percent. Over 1,000 of these birds were examined, and they had eaten significant percentages of pondweeds, wild rice and other grasses, sedges, bulrushes, wild celery, muskgrass, water lilies, coontail, water milfoils, smartweeds, and arrowheads. Samplings of this kind usually reveal puzzling exceptions: ducks which have been feeding exclusively on animal matter or exclusively on vegetation. However, such anomalies do not indicate a preference but merely the availability of one food or another in the most recently occupied habitat.

Some of the plants thrive best in or around fresh water, but others flourish in brackish or salt marshes. Such wetlands may often appear sterile except for reeds, high grasses, and occasional sedges, for they do not support luxuriant blankets of grains and shrubs. Their waters, too, appear relatively barren, the surface unadorned with lilies and duckweed, arrowheads and pondweeds. Nonetheless, those waters may harbor eelgrass, widgeongrass, wild celery and such (as well as sea lettuce and other aquatic weeds for the species of less fastidious dining habits).

Even the Canada goose, whose love of grain has ensconced the species in the gourmet's peerage, just as the bird's power and eerie intelligence have mythologized it among outdoorsmen—even this great wild goose can pluck sustenance from what seems barren.

Inland the living is easy as the flocks graze amid the stubble of prairie grainfields, glean the fallen grain in autumn, pick the lush green herbage of pasturelands. During spring migration, they may sometimes wreak considerable damage to young wheat, barley, corn, and oats. There is no doubt that on the easternmost flyway's great mid-Atlantic corn belt, with its mechanical pickers spewing kernels and chaff and half-denuded cobs as if the lumbering machines were giant robot poultrymen gone berserk in a sea of hungry birds, the migration pattern has been affected. Greater and greater multitudes of Canada geese, together with mallards and, to a lesser degree, other grain-loving wildfowl, have shortened their southward procession to pass the winter close by the corn stubble of Virginia, Maryland, and Delaware. It is probable that a larger wintering population of birds can be supported in these areas than could have survived prior to the advent of modern high-yield farming practices and the time-saving but grain-sacrificing mechanical harvesters.

There have been complaints from some wildfowlers to the south that their abundance of fowl has been preempted by the mid-flyway corn growers. Cotton and tobacco fields have little attraction for ducks and geese. Corn is the lodestone.

Still, it is unlikely that the more southerly wintering populations have been adversely affected to a perceptible degree. Each wintering haven absorbs the number of birds its habitat can support, just as it has for aeons past; the rest continue southward except for those harvested along the way. And corn is not the sole grain that magnetizes flocks; they can settle like a cloud amid the volunteer wheat sprouting in other stubble fields, or swarm like locusts where rice fields replace the miles of corn.

During midday, Canadas prefer to rest on open water, sandbars, or mudflats—fresh brackish, or salt. In the marshes there is no need to fast. Long before man's agriculture mowed the forests, filled the swamps, and covered the land with endless regiments of grain, the geese in the marshes fed well on wild rice, sedges, aquatic plants, insects, larvae, crustaceans, small molluscs. They still do. Though they are the most terrestrial of waterfowl and prefer to blanket the cornfields, they also forage as do the surface-feeding ducks, cruising about the shallows, tipping up their tails and feet as their long necks reach down while they pluck the riches from the bottom. The competition of other species is a small matter, for they do not seek the company of lesser wildfowl. And although a few intruders such as baldpates (aptly called thieving ducks or poachers in some locales) may hover about the fringes of a flock of Canadas to peek nervously at leavings, the great geese do not tolerate the intimate company of competitors.

Knowing of these things, the hunter could begin to understand how the birds waxed fat even during the arduous fall migration as they lingered upon the drab marshes and cold, inhospitable waters of New Hampshire's coast. He knew, too, that unlike an invasion of industry or concentrated settlement by man, an influx of wildfowl is more likely to replenish than impoverish a delicate ecosystem. The birds take only what the marsh can afford to give as nature balances itself. If foods are in short supply, the birds will move on, but before that happens a thickening, spreading crust of ice usually hampers feeding and prods the birds southward on their autumnal journey. Meanwhile, they have enriched the habitat with fertile droppings. Even shed feathers decompose and become constituents of a nourishing ecosystem supporting a complex chain of plant and animal life. Somewhere on an isolated marsh, a bird dies of age, disease, accident, or predation. Its flesh and bones enhance the nutrients of the wetlands; nothing is wasted, not even the dried bits of eggshells flicked about by the winds in the north.

One day the hunter tired of spreading huge rigs of decoys on the open New Hampshire waters—three or four times as many as needed on a small fresh-water marsh. While he did not much believe in the old "fish hook" or "crescent moon" spreads, he had expended much energy placing his decoys in a more or less pear-shaped arrangement —with his boat, camouflaged by a matting of bamboo and reeds, anchored at the pear's stem, on a known flight path. He carefully left an opening amid the decoys in front of the boat, a space where the birds could pitch in. And he situated the whole arrangement so that ducks would fly over the mass of stool, heading up wind toward the opening and the camouflaged boat, as they set their wings and attempted to alight.

Without a guide to perform the manual labor, this kind of water-fowling involves a great amount of heavy work even for two gunners. Small wonder that he tired of it after a week and, with a friend, went "cricking." The excitement of trying to anticipate the unexpected is a special joy of "cricking"—jump-shooting along the tidal creeks meandering through the marshes. Like almost every American wildfowling technique, it originated among the early settlers on the Atlantic Flyway and has since spread to all regions.

On this day, the hunter and his friend were not using a boat. It was low tide, the safest period for such a venture on a coastal marsh, and even chest-high waders seemed an unneccessary encumbrance, so the men chose to plod along in hip boots, crouching sometimes and creeping over hummocks to peer at potholes and creek openings where perhaps a few black ducks might be caught unawares.

The hunter from New York was thinking about various, perhaps trivial, bits of learning he had acquired along the flyway: how previously sterile manmade ponds had yielded sunfish and perch after they had been visited by migrating ducks for several seasons—ducks that must have carried fertile fish eggs on their feet, strengthening the ecological links of their migratory chain—and how a northeast storm brings the birds in close to a floating blind on the New Hampshire coast but a northwest wind is prayed for by the wildfowlers down on the Eastern Shore, along the Maryland wetlands where he would soon be hunting.

His mind was on such matters as he sloshed through ankle- and shin-deep marsh water, grasses hissing against his boots, while he looked for some perceptible demarcation in the reeds and blades, some line to reveal a tidal creek he knew to be close by. He wondered if perhaps it would have been wiser to don waders for this excursion.

Abruptly, his left boot plunged downward and found no support. Quickly but much too late he recalled a line in some outdoor magazine to the effect that "in unfamiliar territory you are likely to float your hat by stepping into a tide-hidden creek."

Afterward, as he watched the musky steam rise from his clothes before his friend's fireplace, he decided it was time to visit the warmer Eastern Shore.

A day in early November, colder than he had anticipated, found him in Maryland, just below the Delaware border, with another friend. They hunted quail that afternoon, ambling with a setter and a Brit down a large soybean field bordered by woods and a fallow pasture overgrown with high brush and scrubby pine saplings. On today's manicured farmlands the bobwhite quail is at best an impoverished tenant, scratching hard for a living and huddling in scant cover. But in areas where the farmers leave some of the land fallow, permit high, rough edges to grow, and keep some brushy woodlots in reserve, the quail covey still dominates the mid-Atlantic and Southern uplands.

The farm in this instance was admirably ramshackle. The very rows of soybeans wavered like sloping, broken lines of black ducks, and the gray-brown pods hanging heavily from the angular stalks were interspersed with jutting clumps of weeds. The setter bounded along an edge, brushed by tendrils of Virginia creeper, then checked his gait and walked a few stiff-legged paces, froze, dropped almost to his belly and gazed intently into a brushy corner. Before the Brittany spaniel could brake her run to honor the setter's point, a dozen quail erupted, feathered balls of shrapnel flung into the woods.

The Marylander brought down one bird and the setter fetched it to him, a plump, mottled cock with a very white chin patch. The New Yorker, not yet accustomed to such wild flushes, had failed to get off a shot. The next hour was spent in a quest for singles, scrambling over blowdowns, through little green hells of cat's-claw and holly and devil's club.

The yap and yelp of beagles could be heard to the east, where several farmers were rabbiting. On previous visits to this area, the hunter from New York had heard the bugling cries of foxhounds, and now he was only mildly startled when a fox stepped daintily from a tangle directly before him. For an instant the animal stood facing him, confused perhaps, momentarily stripped of the vital instinct to flee. Had it been a raccoon prowling in broad daylight, the hunter would have fired by now, but with a fox there was more to think about than a predator's villainous role as destroyer of eggs, fledglings, and even adult birds.

The men of this region liked to pursue the fox with hounds, but almost invariably after being run to ground the fox was permitted to live so that it might lead the chase again on some brisk morning. Many of the local farmers would be delighted to see a bird hunter kill a fox on their land but others would not take kindly to the final demise of their phoenixlike quarry. The owner of this acreage might well be a devotee of hound music; the New Yorker had met him but once and did not know.

As the fox wheeled, its dense coat rippled luxuriantly. This was no red fox, descended from English stock imported in the eighteenth century for the entertainment of the colonial gentry, but a gray fox, a native. For some ungrasped reason, not thought out, the recognition stretched the hunter's hesitation, as if the predator—together with the upland birds and mice and waterfowl on which it preyed —had more right to patrol this ancestral domain than man the newcomer had to intrude upon it. The animal streaked away, low to the ground, its brush straight out.

"Hey!" the hunter called to his companion. "There's a fox!"

"Shoot it!"

But of course the fox was gone.

Beyond a waist-high jungle of creepers, the decaying carpet of leaves took on a deeper brown hue where the earth sloped toward an intersection of two long-forgotten irrigation ditches. Here the hunter from New York slipped his third quail into his game pocket and was about to trudge on past a copse of swamp maples into a scraggly stand of alders when he heard a small, tentative, nasal chirp somewhere ahead. "Peent." Instinctively he raised his gun, seeing nothing but a brown clutter of foliage and sapling poles. He heard the woodcock rise before he spotted it, the whistle of air twittering through the three outer primaries of each wing as the bird dodged upward out of the twisted screen of branches.

Even as he pulled the trigger, the hunter knew that he had swung too late and was far behind the bird. As he walked on, he mentally toyed with his only alibi—that both dogs had been off to the left and had failed to scent the woodcock, so he had not been forewarned. As paltry an excuse, he reminded himself, as being caught off balance. He resolved to be more alert as he trudged on, and there were plenty of warnings now: the whitewash spatters dropped by woodcock, the borings where the birds were drilling for earthworms in the soft bottomlands.

"Nice to know they've arrived," his Maryland companion said. "I hunted here just yesterday and there wasn't a sign of woodcock. Might be a few natives around but these must be flight birds. Strange, isn't it, how they just show up one day? I mean, it seems like a tough way to migrate, even if they do take their time getting down here. Flying at night like that, you wonder how they find the good pockets to come into. You hit the woods one morning and they're all settled in."

"I don't know," the other hunter said, "I guess it's no stranger than how they manage to make all that distance on those stubby wings. It's like bumblebees. You'd think they'd never be able to get off the ground. Well, let's cover this woodlot."

Though woodcock give off a lighter scent than quail, the dogs were onto them now and pointing them well. Several bounced from the edges of an old orchard. When one rose, the hunters watched for a second bird, for they often seemed to feed or hide in pairs, and once the Marylander scored a double. Just as the whiter, brighter face of the male bobwhite differentiates it from the female, so does the longer bill of the female woodcock set it apart from the male, and the men found that they were shooting about equal numbers of cocks and hens. At dusk they had not quite bagged their limits but they were satisfied.

That evening, after the birds were cleaned and the drinks poured, talk flitted from woodcock to migration, alighting amid rafts of anticipated ducks, and it was decided to rise long before dawn. Only a few miles from the tumble-down farm with its quail and woodcock, the Transquacking River ("Yes," the Marylander said, "that's what it's called.") winds out into Fishing Bay.

On the side of the road was a small, mud-blanket parking area where the state had built a wood and concrete launching ramp. An electric torch danced in the dark as the New Yorker tried to play it on the trailer hitch and winch, wondering if he was furnishing any help at all. It took only a couple of minutes, however, for the Marylander to slide his flat-bottomed sixteen-footer into the water. The two men clattered aboard, stumbling over gear, knocking decoys out of their bushel baskets. On the third pull of the starter cord, the big forty-five horsepower outboard sparked to life and the Marylander climbed forward to kneel at the steering wheel.

At first the shoreline was no more than a low black-on-black silhouette and he seemed to feel his way rather than to see the familiar channel. The boat slapped and rolled against a steady surface chop where the river mouth opened onto Fishing Bay. Several miles down the windward side, on a ribbon of state-owned marshland open to the public for hunting, was a point where a slat-and-rush blind had been constructed. On the water in front of this the hunters trailed the decoys, some in tandem, out on their anchor lines, carefully avoiding the motor's propeller with the streaming cords. Nearest the blind and slightly to the right of it—aloof from the other decoys —a dozen plastic Canada geese rode the swells. Farther out and to the left were perhaps a dozen and a half plastic canvasbacks and scaup, and a few black-duck blocks bobbed on calmer water nearer to a crescent undercut of bank.

False dawn had snuffed itself out unnoticed during the labor of floating the blocks, and the sky was paling by the time the men had hidden the boat and settled themselves in the blind. The New Yorker glimpsed a scurrying dark form, just disappearing among the bases of the tall, thick grasses to the rear. A muskrat, he supposed.

Black coffee. A cigarette. Cold wind.

The sky cleared.

"Wind's in our faces, and the only other points around here are private," the Marylander said. "The birds'll have a hell of a time trying to come into this rig. Well, those are the breaks, I guess."

They could feel the tide-driven pulse of the waves, drumming steadily right under their feet, undercutting the bank, insatiably eating away this little point which would eventually crumble, retreat, reshape itself. It was cold and the time went slowly as the men peered at a cloudless, birdless sky. The New Yorker wondered aloud if the tide and wind didn't constantly erode the marshy shoreline.

It did, of course, his companion said. Some years ago there was farmland almost out to here, where they were sitting. But the bay's salt water ate away at it, in a slow but unyielding process that had been altering the shore for centuries, and seeped back into the land, raising the water table here, turning once dry and solid earth into a vast tidal marsh, creating small, brackish potholes where the prairie-like crust caved in. The undermining action of burrowing muskrats had probably enlarged some of those potholes, but weathering and the subterranean seep alone might replenish such wetlands almost eternally, cutting away, cutting away, as the rivers and tidal creeks brought fresh silt to maintain the delta's balanced fulcrum. Pile and crumble, build and cut, perpetual renewal, unchanging flux.

Still, thought the New Yorker, it appears so barren if the eye takes in only the wide waters before the blind and then, to the rear, what seems like an endless sea of cordgrass, saltgrass, reeds, and needlerush—just about worthless as fodder for the wildfowl. And, indeed, it is quite true that a salt or brackish marsh produces so little food per acre that its vastness is usually what counts.

But he knew there was more to it than that, much more. Just recently he had received a government booklet on the wild duck foods that can be propagated by a landowner who has a marsh or pond on his property. He recognized the salt marsh bulrush mixed in with the almost worthless growth, rush three or four feet high, with conelike heads bearing a heavy crop of brown seeds—salt marsh bulrush, self-renewing sustenance for ducks, a most important food. And where the fresh sloughs and streams were deep and still enough there was the wild celery. And where the saline current had some force there was the eelgrass rippling toward the surface.

In the fresh or brackish potholes, he knew, there was also likely to be a healthy growth of another important food plant, sago potamogeton. How odd that one thinks sooner of duckweed, which does not attract ducks and, in fact, may shade out submerged food plants.

There would also be dwarf spikerush in fresh, brackish, or even salty potholes. A remarkable example of self-perpetuation, it is sometimes pulled up in quantities by the ducks. They eat the roots, letting the tops float away, and rafted masses of these waste tops often float along the downwind edge of a pond. Yet the plant proliferates and the crop does not seem to have dwindled the following season.

Dwarf spikerush is only a moderately good duck food but it does not compete with the more important bulrush and widgeongrass. The waving widgeongrass grows from the bottom to the surface of sufficiently saline water, furnishing preferred food not for widgeon alone but for redheads, scaup, blacks, gadwalls, greenwinged teal, shovelers, old-squaws, ruddy ducks, and sometimes other species. The voracious birds devour the leaves, stems, seeds, and roots. But this plant, too, has a seemingly miraculous ability to replenish itself. When it appears to have been eaten out, the ducks have left enough so that the grass will reappear.

The real threat to widgeongrass is not the ravening of ducks but the smothering effect of filamentous algae. Fortunately, some fish—particularly mullet—thrive on this algae, thus controlling it. Mullet are frequently stocked in ponds for just this reason. The hunter wondered if their presence in some unstocked ponds might be explained in the same manner as the arrival of perch and sunfish eggs on the feet of waterfowl. Perhaps, but it is likely that most mullet fingerlings are carried by the tides and creeks. However they may arrive, they promptly add their service to the intricate, delicate ecological balance.

As the New Yorker and the Marylander huddled patiently in the cold, damp blind, there was little activity except for a skimming pair of red-winged blackbirds that plunged into the grasses to the right. Later, a Louisiana heron hovered momentarily above the Canada decoys, then flapped its wings ponderously and straightened its dangling legs like a kite tail as it sailed away. Several loons flitted over the water, to the surprise of the New Yorker, who always regarded loons as birds of the North. And an American merganser passed over the blind time and again, tauntingly. The men refrained from shooting it. A handsome bird, and legal to bag, it is a fish-eater not much sought for table fare. Its worst enemy may well be the fly fisherman, whose proprietary attitude toward trout has been fatal to many a gluttonish merganser.

"Broadbills," the Marylander whispered and hunched down in the blind, cupping his hand over his mouth and purring to them without need of a mechanical call. But the wind remained dead wrong. The scaup saw the decoys, circled in, traded to and fro beyond the rig, and could not pitch in close. Once the New Yorker imagined he could make out the jaunty broad blue bill of a duck in the vanguard of the tightly bunched flock, but he realized that wishful thinking would not bring the birds within range. They finally lit on the water, just beyond the outermost decoys, and there they remained, a bobbing invitation to additional small flocks which soon joined them.

At noon the New Yorker left the blind to ramble back across the marsh, hoping to jump-shoot any birds resting at the lee edges of the little potholes. He found none, but as he crossed a wide, prairie-like expanse he saw three black ducks speeding straight toward him. He was in the open, and could only crouch down and hope. They saw him, of course, and flared just as they nudged the edge of shotgun range.

On his way back to the boat he stepped into a muskrat hole, somehow lost his hat, and thought of the accidental dip he had taken in a New Hampshire tidal creek.

Picking up the decoys was a difficult, frustrating chore in the surface chop, but the hunters accepted the cold bite of misery that somehow adds to the joy of wildfowling.

"Skunked!" the Marylander exclaimed. "The little old ladies in tennis shoes would never believe a pair of hunters could be out here without massacring a pile of birds. They're supposed to hang over our heads and wait to get shot, you know."

"I guess nobody told them," the New Yorker said.

"Well, in fifteen years on the Eastern Shore I've only been skunked twice. If you'd been along the other time I'd figure you for a jinx."

That afternoon the Marylander put in a call to a Chincoteague friend, a decoy maker with the implausible name of Cigar Daisey. The incongruity of juxtaposition made the New Yorker wonder if the Marylander had invented that weed-and-blossom name as a joke, but he had read of early English settlers of the Chesapeake Bay area who had been encumbered with such names as Thomas Birdwhistle, John Halfheade, James Tendergrass, and James Wildgoose. Later, upon passing an old churchyard where the largest stone was graven with the family surname Daisey, he was glad he had kept his counsel.

He had also read that the islanders of Chincoteague Bay, steeped in the legacy of outlawed market gunning, could be as secretive and clannish as the descendants of New England's smugglers. The Marylander was telephoning Daisey to inquire about the best gunning prospects for the next day, and the New Yorker wondered if an islander would divulge such treasured information to an outsider. But the Marylander was a friend of Daisey's, and an islander—even an islander far less friendly than Cigar Daisey, who proved to be a most cordial gentleman—likes to accommodate a friend.

The drive to Virginia was short, nonresident licenses were readily available, and the next morning the Marylander and the New Yorker moored their boat at a small island—a "tump," in the Chincoteague vernacular—out on the wide and shallow bay. "It's a good point and public," Cigar had said, and so it was. "The brant're flying," Cigar had said, and so they were, as were buffleheads and oldsquaws and occasional cans and redheads and scaup.

Fifteen or sixteen Canada decoys were set out, with a trio of bald-pate blocks at the fringe of the rig, and to the left a dozen black-duck decoys. "Should've brought brant decoys," the Marylander said, but the New Yorker later wondered if any more brant could have possibly tolled in over decoys of their own kind. The island was fringed with clumps of myrtle bushes, high beach myrtle that would have offered almost adequate concealment even without the roll of cane fencing which the men unfurled and staked in an opening among the bushes to serve as an admirable portable blind.

In the distance a flock of snow geese passed, white dots across the sky, and then a "V" of five great white swans like aerial sails. Two godwits and later a dunlin flitted over the island. For awhile, a Wilson's snipe posed on the bank, a tiny and improbably misplaced lawn figurine. A little helldiver plummeted into a wave and the hunters did not see the bird again.

Though an inquisitive oldsquaw was disdained, there were birds in plenty to shoot at: scaup and redheads that would grace the table, two insistent buffleheads that were missed repeatedly amid squalls of self-derisive laughter—and brant.

Perhaps they are not so majestic as Canadas, nor even so majestic as less imposing geese. Perhaps there is a touch of diffidence in their uncertain strings barely worthy of the title "formation," perhaps their flight looks almost uncontrolled when viewed at a distance. Yet hen brant dive in low and fast over the decoys, directly toward the gunner, their curving wingspread commands respect and their purposeful demeanor seems to declare a wild, unconquerable will to survive. The black webbed feet of the leading bird abruptly reach downward, the flock dips, shots crash into the wind. Then there is silence. A man wades into the water, his rubber-cased legs plowing forward slowly, awkwardly. He lifts a limp bird from the surface.

It is vaguely like a miniature Canada though it lacks the white bib and has a short neck and small bill. The bill, head, neck, chest, and forward portion of the back are deep black, relieved only by a broken white crescent of slashings on each side of the upper neck. The back, scapulars and rump are dusty brown, the sides of the rump white, the underparts and sides ashy gray and white, the tail black above and white below. It is a goose only slightly larger than a mallard, and it is a creature of beauty.

The Marylander examined the area about the rectum of the fallen brant. If it had been tinged with green, the men would have shot no more brant that day, for a greenish tinge means the brant have been feeding on sea lettuce and other "trash food" which, though it saved them from extinction when the eelgrass was blighted, makes their flesh almost unfit for consumption. It took many years for the eelgrass and the brant to come back after the blight, but there was a turning point in the mid-'50s. After that, the population expanded quickly, and more and more of the birds returned to their ancestral diet of eelgrass. Occasionally, the flights that arrive on a given day have been feeding on the old poverty plants and are marked by the green tinge. But if the tinge is brownish or absent, the primary food has been eelgrass and the flesh will be as succulent as legend claims.

"No green," the Marylander said, and smiled. "They're fine." Heading landward at sunset, into an oncoming gale, the boat was laden heavily with decoys, ducks, brant, gear, guns, men. The craft shuddered with the impact of the waves, and the spray struck the men with a cold sting, like sheets of hail. The calls of the birds could not be heard above the motor, but a godwit flitted by and the ducks swarmed like black bees against the reddening sun.

Even with a powerful motor, progress was slow. The New Yorker thought of the old-time baymen who crossed in dirtier weather than this, propelled only by their own strength, stout oars, courage, and the strange drive that motivates men who lift "long ducking-guns . . . on bleak, wintry, distant shores."

THREE

Hunting Around

CANADA AND THE PROVINCES

Raymond R. Camp

The late Ray Camp's career was a galaxy of distinguished accomplishments—Outdoor Editor of The New York Times *for twenty-six years, author of scores of magazine pieces, editor of anthologies of hunting and fishing stories, and author of several books of his own. To me, however, one star in this array does shine brighter than the others. It is the book,* Duck Boats: Blinds: Decoys and Eastern Seaboard Wildfowling, *published by Alfred A. Knopf in 1952. With handsome and useful illustrations in line and color by G. Don Ray and an interesting collection of photographs, the work boasts Knopf's usual superb worksmanship and is one of those important works that belong on any serious collector's shelf. Camp wisely and effectively mixed the lode of information contained in the book with anecdotes and field experiences that make the book a fun narrative read. This piece on actual gunning experiences in the Maritimes begins the wildfowler's journey down the Atlantic coast.*

THERE ARE gunners who hold to theory that shooting accommodations, in order to provide a suitable background atmosphere, must verge on the primitive. On arriving at a shooting lodge or camp they expect, and almost welcome, musty beds, lumpy oatmeal, and muddy coffee. If the evening meal comprises anything more epicurean than meat, beans, and canned fruit they decide they have been deposited in a nest of sissy sports.

It is entirely possible that there was a time when I was inclined toward such views, but if so it was during a youthful phase. Experience, coupled with considerable rolling, scoured the moss of complaisance from my stone, and I began to associate discomfort with incompetence. Perhaps that is one reason why I contemplated the Manor with satisfaction. Planted firmly in a pleasant grove of towering elms and beeches, overlooking the long intervals of the St. John, the old manor house not only *looked* hospitable and comfortable—it was. A half hour after my first glance, drinking tea and munching hot buttered rolls in front of an open fire, I hoped the shooting would be half as good as the accommodations.

Tom Scovil, the young host at the Manor, started right in to banish any fears I might entertain on that score. Too often, upon arriving at a strange shooting-ground (or salmon river or trout stream), I have been greeted with the suggestion that I should have arrived "yesterday," or "last week." Tom's outlook was cheering.

"It looks as though you picked the right time," he said. "It's early in the season, but there seem to be quite a few whistlers on the river, and the blacks and mallards are unusually plentiful on the intervale marshes. What's more, they haven't been disturbed much by gunners since the opening."

The five-hundred-mile drive had been almost nonstop, so the lulling murmur of the river was wasted on me. I breakfasted early before a crackling fire, and not on cold cereal and a poached egg on burnt toast. There was real, old-fashioned oatmeal. Not the "hot-water-and-two-minutes" variety, but creamy porridge that had steamed all night on the back of the stove. Country ham, eggs from parents still cackling, and hot rolls were accompanied by coffee that had real body to it. I began to wonder if my luck was being pushed.

Tom joined me for the second cup, and his tidings were good.

"Mac, who is going to guide you on the river," he explained, "took a run downstream late yesterday. He thinks the cold snap in the north has pushed a lot of new whistlers this way. He put up several large bunches only a mile or two downriver, and insists there are twice as many birds in this area as there were last week.

"I suggest you try the whistlers first, and if things aren't right you can always have him put a few mallard decoys on one of the intervale potholes. You're certain to get plenty of mallards and blacks, and probably a few teal. Meanwhile, time's a-wasting."

Time was wasting and Mac was waiting, and there was a faint promise of daybreak in the east. Tom had sent my gun, shellbox, and lunch to the stoolboat, and when I climbed aboard the craft he performed hasty introductions from the dock and cast off the line that moored the ancient craft to the dock.

Mac, who had the name, appearance, and accent of a fugitive from the Highlands, had everything but the traditional dourness of the Scotch gillie. Nothing worried him and almost everything amused him. As a guide he had no peer. As a boatman he was the worst fraud who ever grasped a tiller, and the craft he had to work with would have constituted a full-time problem for an expert.

The stoolboat, a twenty-foot, clinker-built skiff, had not been designed for the purpose to which it was now devoted. The engine had, long, long before, supplied the motive power for that much-maligned vehicle known as the "Model T." It had been hastily, and far from thoroughly, "converted" to marine duty, and as a marine engineer, Mac had a knowledge of engines which could have been inscribed legibly upon a postage stamp with a dish mop.

He spun the flywheel several times without eliciting so much as an encouraging cough from Lizzie. A check of the assorted wires and coils apparently convinced him that everything was normal, so he tried again. Nothing happened. Refusing to admit defeat, Mac rooted around the bottom of the boat and came up with a grease-stained stick, which he thrust sharply into the gas tank. This vessel echoed tinnily.

"Just as I thought," Mac grunted.

He shook three large cans until one gurgled to suit him.

"Put oil in it once by mistake," he said. "Had a hell of a time getting it out."

He managed to pour about three gallons of gas into the tank and two gallons into the boat, which led me to a mental reservation to do no smoking until we were on shore. While this exertion, diagnosis, and cure were in progress we were drifting down the wind-ruffled bosom of the St. John. Our movement was not fast, nor was it smooth, for every few feet we grated over a rock or shoal, and occasionally the skiff, which was theoretically in tow, crashed solidly into the side or stern of the larger boat.

With the fuel shortage overcome, Lizzie chugged resoundingly at the first twist of the flywheel, and as Mac had unwittingly knocked down the speed lever, the starting lurch threw him to the floorboards.

"Damn all complicated boats," was his only comment.

The banks whizzed past at fully five miles per hour, and I took advantage of this period of comparative tranquility to examine one of the decoys which were racked up on the only seat the boat afforded.

This was my first gunning trip to the St. John, although I had done some salmon fishing on the upper reaches. Before leaving I had been advised to bring along my own decoys. Several friends who had tried the St. John duck-shooting had warned me about the local decoys, which were said to bear more resemblance to a tired seagull than any known species of waterfowl. Forewarned, I had loaded a couple dozen mallard and black-duck decoys in the back of the car, but to avoid the needless injuring of local sensibilities I had decided to look over the local products before bringing out my own. It was well that I had.

The decoy I examined was an excellent one, large, well-shaped, and apparently made of hollowed-out cedar or juniper.

"Pretty good decoys, huh?" Mac announced. "Come from the States. Quite a time back I guided an old man from Boston. He liked the gunnin' here and he liked my guidin', but he complained about my rig of decoys. Said they wouldn't toll in a sick coot that was dyin' for company.

"Next fall, before he come up, he sent me a lot of big boxes by freight. Paid the duty and all. These decoys were in the boxes, a hundred of them. Last winter the old man died, and nobody came for the decoys, so I'm still usin' them."

Mac paused to light his pipe and throw the still-smoldering match on the gas-soaked floor. I was prepared to jump overboard, but nothing happened.

With daylight, I began paying more attention to the passing scene. The St. John, in the Gagtown area, drains a flat, fertile valley that is fenced by rolling, wooded hills. It is almost continuously divided by a chain of long, pancake-flat islands or intervales. In the fall the river drops well below the rim of these grassy, sparsely timbered intervales, but the heavy rains and melting snows of spring flood them to a depth of a few inches or several feet, depending upon the volume of the freshet. This annual flooding is responsible for the great fertility of the intervales, and they provide lush pastures for the local farmers.

Dotted with potholes and grassy marshes, and cut by countless twisting drains and guzzles, they provide perfect nesting and rearing grounds for thousands of black ducks and mallards. They also form a natural habitat for several species of shorebirds, and our progress down the river was marked by the almost-incessant "skraake" of snipe.

We were following the left "course" downstream, and every few hundred yards a small bunch of whistlers were routed out ahead of us, most of them moving down the river. As we rounded the reedy point of a large intervale we saw that the river made a bulbous swelling a half mile ahead before swerving sharply eastward. High ground to the north and west provided a lee here, and several large rafts of whistlers were strung out along a wide stretch of open water.

Mac pointed with his pipestem toward a narrow point that sickled outward a few hundred yards above the turn.

"Looks like the whistlers are rafting up here," he announced. "There's a blind on that point, so we might as well rig out there."

When we arrived a hundred feet upstream from the point, Mac decided to beach the stoolboat and rig out the decoys with the skiff. His beaching method was as simple and direct as his character. He merely pointed the bow directly for the shore and ripped a wire from some vital part of the engine. The power plant ceased functioning immediately but the boat did not. We crashed up on the shingle with a force that would have ripped the bottom out of an ordinary boat. This shock was followed closely by another, as the skiff crashed into our stern. Mac treated this occurrence as though it were the normal, routine way of beaching a boat—and where he was concerned, undoubtedly it was.

"You relax here while I rig out the decoys," he suggested. "It won't take long."

It did not. What his system lacked in science it made up for in speed.

He poled the skiff to a stretch of water fifty yards upwind and twenty feet outside the point. Here he boated the pushpole and began tossing whistler decoys out of both sides of the boat while wind and current drifted him rapidly downstream. Directly opposite the point he ran out of whistler decoys. He then grabbed up the pushpole, jammed it into the river bottom to hold the skiff in place, and began tossing over black-duck decoys until he had fifteen of them in a small cluster. At this juncture he halted to examine his handiwork.

The whistlers were strung out in a sawtooth line; two or three which had the lines twisted around their necks were yawing and twisting in the current. Having surveyed his work and found it good, he nodded with apparent satisfaction at the grouping of the puddle-duck decoys, and wrenched the pushpole from the mud with a vigor that almost swamped the skiff.

"Just drop your gun, shells, and lunch in the skiff," he suggested. "If we don't get to the blind pretty quick we'll miss the early flight."

The so-called blind proved to be merely an extension of the point, and consisted of a double row of willow and alder saplings, now practically leafless. Into this slender, skeleton framework Mac thrust the skiff.

"Don't you think we might dress this blind up a bit with grass?" I suggested. "Any duck that couldn't see us behind these saplings ought to have contact lenses."

Being divers, the whistlers are not especially wary, but I couldn't see a mallard or black approaching within range of our hideout, even if it happened to be attracted by our decoys, which I thought doubtful.

Mac eyed the naked branches in deep thought.

"Maybe you're right," he admitted. "I'll gather up some water cucumber and string it through this stuff. It won't take much cover if we sit still and let them come in."

He splashed ashore through knee-deep water and returned with a great load of green vines that grew in profusion along the bank. While he draped this verdure through the stark branches on either side of the skiff I examined one of the tendrils. Each three- or four-foot length bore several cucumber-shaped pods two or three inches long. These pods had a skin somewhat similar to that of a bean pod and of about the same thickness. The hollow interior contained a few black seeds the size of a dime and as thick as a nickel. Mac noticed my interest and broke open one of the seeds to show me its white bean-like meat.

"We call them water cucumbers," he explained. "The blacks and mallards eat them until you'd think they would burst. They grow all along the river, and make the birds fat and tasty."

He paused to glance up the river.

"We've got company coming, and you haven't uncased your gun."

It took only a few seconds to unzip the case and load up, but the whistlers decided to move on to another part of the river.

"There's a boat coming down the river," Mac reported, after several moments had passed. "They'll stir up some birds."

He had hardly spoken when six whistlers spotted our decoys and swung in to pass over them downwind. They were moving too fast to swing and come in, but two of them cut off and passed directly over the blind. Had I been properly alert it would have provided a double, which is always a pleasant way to begin the day. As it was I had time to tumble only one, and was too much off balance to swing around for the second.

"I can wade out for that one," Mac announced, "so you sit tight."

The next visitor was a single mallard, a drake. Much to my surprise he not only approved of Mac's rig, but made a wide swing and was about to sit right down among the decoys. We added him to the score, but had to retrieve him with the boat.

"I suppose I should have brought the dog," Mac muttered, when we were back in our cover. "I use him for pothole shooting, but he has a bad habit that comes out when I use him on the river."

This seemed to have an angle, so we probed into the matter.

"Well," Mac continued, "he's a good retriever, but if a bird happens to fall outside the decoys he's as likely to bring in one of the decoys as the duck. I can't punish him for it, because I taught him to retrieve decoys at the potholes. Potholes are too deep to wade and you don't have a boat handy, so the dog has to retrieve the ducks while you're shooting, and the decoys when you're through."

I questioned Mac on his rather-unorthodox whistler rig, and he pointed out it was deliberate rather than hurried, as I had supposed.

"Whistlers don't fly in a tight bunch along the river," he explained. "They're strung out quite a bit. When I rig out fairly close to the shore, like this, I string out the decoys in a line. They seem to show up better, and the birds come in better. When I rig for whistlers out in the open water I make a V up front, then string out the singles inside it, in two lines. The birds are flying along the edge of the river today, in this wind, so I rigged them in a line."

The results of the morning seemed to prove his point, for we were through shooting at ten.

I have happy memories of snipe and plover shooting as a youngster, but while I was still in short britches these birds had so thinned out that we stopped shooting them. Occasionally a few birds would pass within gunshot while we were in a duck blind or goose pit, but you need more than a "few" snipe or plover if you are to enjoy them, so we merely followed them over the barrels and lowered the gun. Then they came on the "protected" list, and were forbidden even in the few areas where they still existed in fair numbers.

They are fair game in New Brunswick, however, and although the wind was quite strong we decided to try the intervale meadows after lunch. Snipe are close to the top of my list of "tough" birds, especially in any kind of wind. They are strange birds. If there is a dead calm they almost always seem to flush wild, often just out of gunshot. If there is a light wind, I have found, you can get quite close before they jump, but a strong wind seems to make them as cautious as they are in a calm. Also, the strength of the wind adds to their already marked tendencies to take an erratic course.

Just upriver from the bulge where we had done our duck shooting was a long narrow intervale with a crescent of tall willows at the upper end. In the center of this crescent there was a wide gap, and as we chugged upstream in the stoolboat Mac pointed his pipestem at this gap.

"There usually are quite a few snipe on this intervale," he explained, "and when they are put up they almost always cut through that gap in the willows to the next intervale. I'll drop you off at the head, and you can stand in the reeds at the gap. I'll walk up the meadow and flush them out."

I had come prepared, for once, and had a light twenty-gauge

and two boxes of No. 9 shot, so I stuffed plenty of shells in my coat and picked my way around bog holes to the gap in the willows while Mac turned the boat and sputtered off toward the base of the intervale.

As a beater he left nothing to be desired, and he managed to put up a snipe or two every fifty feet of his crisscross course up the soggy intervale. Almost every snipe he put up took a zigzag course up the meadow, but most of them passed through the gap that I was, theoretically, blocking with my gun. I made only two doubles, and a number of misses, but despite the ragged shooting I had a limit before he had moved halfway up the intervale. I could have accomplished this sooner, but experience had taught me to mark each downed bird carefully and retrieve it before shooting another, so a number of birds passed through the gap without being saluted by gunfire.

This is lazy shooting, but not as easy as it may sound, for frightened snipe have a flight pattern that calls for quick swinging on the part of the gunner. I have always found it more difficult than walk-up shooting, where the birds usually follow a straight course for a short distance before moving out of range.

The following morning I decided to try the so-called pothole shooting. For this we ran upriver several miles, finally beaching the stoolboat with the usual grating crash. The intervale selected was lower than any we had passed, the spongy soil rising only a few inches above the river level.

"This is one of the 'wild' intervales," Mac pointed out. "It's too swampy and full of sinkholes for pasture, but there are several pothole ponds, and the ducks like it here because no one disturbs them."

Each of us gathered up a half dozen large black-duck decoys, stuffed in a gunny sack. I took my gun and shellbag, and Mac carried a soapbox. After trudging a half mile through that spongy marsh, on parts of which you could feel the soil casing tremble underfoot, I began to feel the load. On such marshes the new collapsible rubber decoys would be worth many times their weight in gold. You could stuff a dozen of them in the back of your gunning coat without difficulty, and never know you had a load.

Mac finally came to a halt on the rim of a small pond, only seventy or eighty feet across, and roughly circular in shape. There was a small clump of dwarf willow near one shore, and Mac pointed to it.

"Dress that clump with a bit of grass, take this box along for a seat, and I'll be putting out the decoys. Make a little hide for the dog on the edge," he said, pointing to the grizzled Chesapeake that had accompanied us the expedition. "I just remembered I left the lunch in the boat, so I'll go on back once the decoys are out.

"And don't try to wade out into that pond. As far as I know there is no bottom to it. There's a sort of matting of roots about a foot under the water, but it won't hold your weight. Anyway, the dog will pick up the birds."

Our arrival had sent a dozen mallards and blacks and a pair of greenwing teal out of the pond, and it seemed reasonable to hope that some of them would return. Mac put out the decoys from the shore, throwing them as far as he could. Occasionally one would get a line around its neck and turn over; he would point to it and shout "Fetch" to the retriever. The dog would then plunge out, half swimming, half walking, and bring it back.

I went to work building up a screen of grass and reeds in the willows, and when I worked out a place for the soapbox in the center I understood why the box had been brought. The box sank halfway into the watery tangle when I sat down, and my boots sank in almost to the calf. Without the box I would have had a wet seat, and the willows were too low to shoot standing.

The first duck, a black, came in while I was patching some gaps in the screen; it sat down in the middle of the decoys. I tried to slip a shell into the magnum without excessive movement, but was unsuccessful. The black jumped and was out of range before I could close the breech.

A pair of greenwings came close on his heels, however, but since they whisked in low I did not see them until they were about to alight. At my movement they flared upward as though tossed by a spring, and the lucky first shot caught them both in the pattern.

Whisky, the Chesapeake, did not wait for my command to fetch.

When the teal splashed on the water he was off, and when halfway back with one he decided to get both on the same trip, so he paddled back, gathered up the other, and dropped them near his hide. He then plunged back into the pond, gathered up a decoy, and deposited it with the teal. Probably he would have kept up this process, but I pushed him down in his hide and tossed the decoy back with the others.

Later, when I related this to Mac, he thought a moment and then announced that Whisky undoubtedly brought in the decoy as a result of a faulty memory.

"He saw two teal fall, but forgot he brought in two the first trip, so he went out, gathered up the decoy, and brought it back to finish his job. He's like I am, I guess—forgets."

A pair of mallards came next. They circled to look the situation over, then swung wide and came in on a straight line. A perfect double! But I didn't make it. I shudder to think how wide my second shot was. I knew as I pulled that I was off, but it was too late to stop the reflex.

I tumbled the drake, but the hen winged off untouched, only to make two or three wide circles and come in to the decoys as straight as the proverbial die. This time I did not miss, but Whisky's plunge into the pond scared off a small bunch of teal that were headed our way. Unlike the mallard, they did not provide me with a second chance.

A lone black appeared next. He circled the pond several times, craning his neck toward the decoys. There was something he did not like, however, so he decided to find another pond. His mistake was in passing directly over the blind. It was a long, high shot, but the magnum was made for that kind. It was not made for the first load I touched off, but the second one caused him to fold in mid wingstroke. It took Whisky and me ten minutes to find him, for he had fallen in high grass, and hit the spongy ground with such force that he was almost buried.

As we returned to the blind, the only geese we had seen on the St. John were headed far out downriver. There was a close V of seven big honkers, with a squawking straggler a few hundred yards behind. They dropped lower as they reached the upper end of the intervale, and we crouched hopefully in the grass, holding Whisky quiet with one hand.

The geese wanted to come in, but seemed unable to find a place that suited them. They circled my position several times, but at a distance of several hundred yards, and on one occasion the straggler turned and headed straight for the pond, not veering until a strident honk from the old gander with the V called him back. Apparently the leader decided there was nothing about my intervale which appealed to him, so with one last swing he cut over to the river and headed downstream.

I finished out the limit well before noon, but as I had arranged for a shipment of dry ice to be sent from Montreal, I decided to forego a try at snipe in order to return and send off the ducks to some friends in the States.

On the return trip I asked Mac whether the shooting was always this good. He shook his head.

"Usually," he admitted, "but not always. Some years it's better, some worse, but I can't recall a day on the river with only one or two shooters that we didn't get a limit. This section is not too heavily gunned, and there is plenty of river and marsh. You can understand that, for right now there are four other parties staying in Gagetown, and we haven't run across one of them yet.

"Mostly, it's knowing where to go under different conditions, and at different times. The best shooting early in the season is on the intervale marshes, like the one we shot this morning. Later, when the whistlers are more plentiful and the scaup and canvasback come along, the river is best, and if it blows really hard, one of the lakes usually provides good shooting. There's no scarcity of ducks, but you can't always get the big ducks, like mallards and blacks."

As you move downstream on the St. John, the river widens, the valley spreads out, and there are more towns along its margin. The hunting pressure increases as you near the broad mouth of the river, and the number of puddle ducks decreases as the diving ducks increase.

The big redleg blacks do not arrive along the river until early November, unless there happens to be an early freeze-up in the north.

"Some years, when the redlegs arrive," Mac explained, "they really pour in. Two years ago I had a party out on one of the intervale potholes and it took us all day to get a limit of blacks and mallards. We did not see a single redleg during the three days. The afternoon of the third day it began to blow really hard from the north, with sleet beating us in the face on the way back to the Manor. That night the bottom fell out of the thermometer, and the next morning the river was loaded with redlegs. We broke the ice on a small pothole, put out a half-dozen decoys, and were all through shooting for the day exactly seventeen minutes after the decoys were out. The birds didn't like the river, and kept moving up and down. When they spotted that open water on the pothole they just poured in.

"But let me tell you, seventeen minutes was enough. I damn near froze, and I left the decoys right on the pothole. The wind blew the dead ducks in to the shore of the hole, and it's a good thing they did, for I would never have sent Whisky out into that water."

The Manor has a cook who can work magic with a few herbs, a pair of teal, and an oven. That night we dined on my favorite waterfowl, teal, washed down with a bottle of red Bordeaux. At the first taste and sip, I closed my eyes for a few seconds, and was back in a shell-torn villa on the rim of the Gaeta Marshes, while four teal sputtered on an improvised barbed-wire spit, and a mustachioed British Guards officer and a weary American infantry officer swallowed in anticipation of the feast to come. It is a compliment to the Manor cook when I admit that his teal were almost as ambrosial as those whose bones were picked that night.

Such is the typical St. John shooting. For many miles above and below Gagetown, the river and its margins repeat their pattern. You can find comfortable food and lodging at one of the small inns, or stay with one of the farmers whose lands fringe the stream. Compared to the shooting in many parts of the States, the prices are low, and considering the quality of both shooting and accommodations, the sport here is a "bargain."

BIG SKY

Charles F. Waterman

Back in my introduction of Charlie in "Duck Blinds," in the first section of this book, I mentioned that he winters in Florida after spending the summer in the Yellowstone area. Well, you can bet that he does not get so hasty about his departure from the high country that he misses the area's great duck hunting. As you will see here, he is right on top of things. The piece is from Gray's Sporting Journal, *Fall '73.*

FROM FARTHER south you look at the weather maps and think of the long way the birds must come, the alternate routes they have and the patches of bluebird weather that can entice them into periods of smug loafing. But waterfowl migration is more intimate when you are near the place where the flights begin.

In southern Montana the native gunners, somehow scornful of the resident "local ducks," keep an eye to the north, as if they could actually see and hear the restless staging movements in Alberta and Saskatchewan only a few hundred miles away. There is some southward drifting very early, the bluewinged teal and gadwalls puttering happily in the shallows of ranch ponds and irrigation ditches, their pointy, up-ended tails like floating villages of tiny wigwams.

They look remarkably like the despised "local ducks" that one gunner criticized me for shooting.

"We like to see those local ducks around," he said stiffly. "Real duck hunters wait for the big northerns."

Of course, when the Montana "locals" decide to move southward they become "big northerns" to Utah or Arizona or Texas. And although the Montana locals live on ribbons of water bordered by a patchwork of wheat and rye, resident hunters insist the northerns are "fat and grainfed."

One rebel who feels that a fat, roasted mallard from Montana is every bit as good as a fat, roasted mallard from Alberta explained the difference to me with a bit of gentle sarcasm.

"You can tell the local mallards," he confided. "They have green, muddy feet and smell bad."

In that spirit I once sent him a telegram from Fairbanks, Alaska.

"Lots of local ducks here," I wired, "but waiting for big northerns."

I still think it was kind of funny.

Although the fall movement has begun in rather disorganized fashion, there comes a day when the cracking cold strikes a thousand Canadian potholes, and the new ice stiffens bouquets of the emergent grass while the noisy flocks wheel raggedly, tighten their formations and bear south as they always have.

In southern Alberta the duck season opens on birds with blotchy, incomplete fall plumage, and although the shooting there must be early or not at all, I have always felt that the curtain went up before the stage was set.

There was the time when we had been hunting sharptail grouse near Esther and noted mallards and pintails hovering over a barely visible, grassy pond.

"I'll see if I can get a couple of greenheads to take home with us," I said as the sharptail quest ended.

So I put on a camouflaged jacket and hip boots and stoop-walked up a draw to the low earthen dam. When I straightened up there were two drake mallards almost at my feet, and for once I concentrated and felled them both within 35 yards, almost oblivious of the gabble and thunder farther out in the grass where the water barely showed.

But even if a pair of mallards had not been enough, my shooting for the day was over, for an overly-enthusiastic bird dog splattered about in the grass and brought in the rest of a limit: birds that had been struck behind my prime targets, unseen until the dog found them. It was exactly a limit and certainly not my fault that I had not broken Canadian law. And while the retrieving went on under my apprehensive eye, a procession of naive, young pintails and mallards swooped over the pond with set wings, eyeing me with more irritation than fear. Two months later and a thousand miles south they would act differently.

Red Monical and I hunted geese another year in the same vicinity, hosted by a local hunter who took us to high ground where we scanned 100 square miles of grain, grass and rosebush, pink in a warm dawn. And while our binoculars found the formal lines of geese going out to feed from their river resting places, our field of view was repeatedly crossed by fidgety wads of ducks.

"We'll dig pits over there," said our host. "It's only about five miles by road. Then after we get the pits dug we'll have a little duck shoot in some stubble I know of. This may be a new kind of duck business for you."

Red, who had been fondling three-inch goose loads since we crossed the border, confided to me that he wasn't exactly panting for a stubble duck shoot.

"I can shoot ducks at home," he said.

We drove our white camper to a field of rye stubble and the native selected a spot.

"I'll put out the decoys (we hadn't seen them yet) while you take the truck away," he said. "Put it about 100 yards over there."

Then he brought a small paper bag from his camouflaged jacket, doing it with the flourish of a magician under a spotlight. From the bag came little scraps of black cloth and he scattered them over the field, pulling each one into a little peaked triangle. From a distance they might have been the dark heads of drake mallards waddling about in the stubble.

Then we sat down, three men in dark green and brown camouflage against a background of yellow stubble, and I had the feeling of a kid with a burlap sack sent to wait for snipe on a dark night.

"It's about time," he said, and finally looked off into the windy prairie sky. That was when the blizzard of ducks arrived, fluttering down around us by dozens, and I fired wildly, missing too much and not certain the whole thing wasn't a pre-season dream. It was the first time those birds had been missed, I suppose, and it was good training for what would await them much farther south when the wind would be cold and carry a hint of snow.

Even before the great southward surge there are times when duck shooting is tough in southern Canada unless you have done a bit of homework. On one evening, not far from Taber, Johnny Bailey and I sat in a brushy fenceline and heard great flocks swinging down to darken a field, all of them a little out of range. We never fired a shot over that field, but sat there until long after shooting hours were over. By then the flights were indistinct against the sky, and the hiss of set wings had multiplied into a roar, the sound changing as hundreds of birds banked in swinging turns, and then changing again into the sputter of vertical landings.

But all of that is the prelude to storm-driven migrations when the birds probe for open water a little farther south. Then they follow big rivers like the Yellowstone and look for spring creeks among the cottonwoods and willows, spots that never freeze over; and a shooter hunched in a makeshift blind has no hope of a big flight attending his little clump of decoys. He watches for the confused split-up of a flock high between the mountains and waits for the straggling few birds to come in over the cottonwoods, looking for just the right patch of spring water with thick vegetation visible just below the surface.

When the first cold freezes the prairie potholes, there may be slush ice in the Yellowstone, coming down without the grating, cracking sounds of a hard-ice break-up, but making occasional sucking noises in the swift stretches. There will be clumps of ducks and Canada geese on some of the gravel bars, but those are more resting than feeding areas and the birds will go out to grainfields at morning and evening or seek the spring creeks where they can combine resting and feeding.

From early September on, the mountains have changed. There will have been reddish patches on the slopes and the aspen will have changed to gold and then faded into vertical, white trunks with most of their leaves gone. The cottonwoods along the spring creeks will have turned bright yellow and perhaps the real cold will strike before they are bare.

When there is sudden chill the spring creek becomes a gleaming route from above, its steam congealing into ice on the cottonwoods, willows and rosebushes. At dawn a man in waders with decoys and shotgun finds it a ghostly barrier of white vapor, shifting slightly with a faint air movement, and so opaque it is hard to believe that there is nothing more exotic than a strip of trees on the other side.

When the chill takes its hold on the prairie potholes, however briefly, it is also felt on the Yellowstone, and the flight from the north is not a matter of swirly weather-map designs, but a matter of hours. Four hundred, possibly 500 miles at 40 miles an hour becomes a fact rather than an estimate.

If they left this morning, I think, they will be here tonight, and tomorrow morning will be the time. They will have crossed the border high over a checkerboard of grainfields; they will have gone around the scattered mountain peaks; they will have been a bit uncertain over the Missouri Breaks and some of them will have stopped there, but many will have come on to the funnels where the rivers come down from the high mountains and the passes pinch in toward canyons. Ahead of them will be the white ranges themselves and they will look for open water where some will spend the entire winter.

There are other ducks, but I think mainly of the mallards—even more of the mallards than of the geese, because a farm kid from the Midwest, far from a real flight route, dreamed of glossy greenheads over his old shotgun barrel, and old thoughts cling to the minds of old men, richer in their antiquity. My first mallard was an enormous thing of matchless beauty.

But with that first cold will come the snow geese and the Canadas. The Canadas will be less resolute in their journey and might even hover over the spring creeks before landing, too often on river bars hard to reach. The snows will almost never come near the spring creeks, but their high formations are emblems of the entire migration.

Their night calls in the distance are bell-like, at first easily mistaken for distant hounds or coyotes, and once they are on their way they are truly southward bound. When cloud formations conceal the mountain passes, they will mill tirelessly, high over the confusing lights of small towns, lights that reflect from the park lagoon and from wet or snowy streets, and people stand in their yards to make out their ghostly waves, more and more of them as the flight is temporarily stalled. Then the leaders see the way, or think they do, change their calls and move on southward, the ranks closing quickly. But they will not stop at the spring creeks; it is still a long way to the Gulf of Mexico.

The spring creek shooting is a personal sport and perhaps it would not appeal to *real* duck hunters who scull a sneakboat, filled with a hundred decoys, across the endless flatness of great marshes fringed with rime along the cattail clumps and bullrushes. The spring creek business is reduced to miniature, and more than a dozen decoys will not help, being too much to carry anyway.

Go into the brush blind before daylight and possibly wade some sections of creek and slough on the way. If the steam is coming up heavily there may be birds on the water almost within arm's reach, and they startle me if they squawk off into the cotton batting. But I will not jump as far as if I am heralded by the incredible crash of a beaver's tail. I curse the damned beaver but it is my own nervous system that I really blame, and I know that I am a little afraid of the dark, a shred of primeval fear that makes mystery of a gurgling, little spring creek with nothing more dangerous than a corps of muskrats and a toothy woodcutter.

The two greenwinged teal come in with a swish just at shooting time, splatting down by the decoys while I search diligently for the safety and try to learn where they are. After incredulous study of the decoys they leave, and I give them a free pass. They swing by once, evidently to be certain they have really seen plastic ducks on tethers.

There are two especially good times on the spring creek. One comes just after dawn when some birds have left their resting places and are looking for food and at that time, too, hunters up and down the river may have stirred up loafers that will fiddle about at low altitude looking for peace and quiet. The other time of special activity comes around mid-morning. The grainfield addicts may be turning back toward water, their orderly flocks being chipped apart by individual preferences, often single drake mallards cruising over the spring creeks, their heads twisting warily at the complacent decoys.

I know from rueful experience that decoys will not pull many ducks to my little spring creek pool, but I expect them to drop down a bit for inspection, possibly within range, even though they have little thought of really pitching in.

The undecided, little flock in a mountain valley adds space and depth for puny human vision. It turns against the backdrop of enormous clouds and white peaks and makes it run at the ribbon of creek, coming fast and gaining speed as it loses altitude, driving upstream. When it is almost above my puddle there is a perceptible slowing for inspection of the decoys, the wingbeats a little slower, and one or two birds will actually set their wings momentarily to hold their positions. But they are too high, I think, and I assay a soft feeding gabble on my call, afraid to speak up with it for I am always unsure of my duck talk. But as they go on past, still losing a little altitude, I invariably decide that they were within range after all and tell myself that if they do that again I will damned well chop that leader out of the sky. It is pure bravado, for beyond 45 yards my occasional kills are things of personal wonder.

And then they pull up as if ending a strafing run, the scene changing dizzily. For one instant they are speeding images against nearby treetops, then against geometric benchlands and rimrock, then against the green steepness of distant mountainsides, and finally rising above snowy peaks. Caught by sunlight, they flicker briefly as they change direction to coast downward again and disappear on another run, this time over the river with its whispering slush ice.

Perhaps they are not of a single mind and there may be the rebel drake, a vision of the decoys evidently lodged in his adventurous brain, and he turns away alone and makes his own pass at the creek. I see him as a speck down the valley, growing in size, and he goes high overhead with a reedy quack, just outside my range, to turn and pass again.

He will not come in, I tell myself, but he is curious and this time he is low enough and he is below the tips of the cottonwoods. As he comes on he sets his wings briefly and teeters on them ever so slightly, and that is the exact instant, just before he goes over the decoys.

The decoys are only reassurance for birds that might come in anyway, and after a little bunch of mallards has inspected them from too high up, probably having had a glimpse of my face that was turned up just a little too much under my cap bill, they drop into the creek 300 yards away, and I fidget in the blind, knowing that eventually I will try to stalk them. Much of spring creek hunting is jump shooting anyway.

"You mean you just kick them up and blast them when they're trying to get out of that creek?" inquired a *real* duck hunter.

Well, yes.

It is almost noon, and I slip out of the blind and establish some landmarks. They will be in the wide place beyond the little sand bar where the widgeon rested last year. I'll stay well back from the creek until I come to the stray pine tree and then crawl up to the bank, crash through the thick rim of willows, land in a foot of water and swing my gun up while they're still staring in stretch-necked horror. Remember to hold just a little above them as they tower and be sure to check if there's lateral movement.

I walk to the stray pine tree, a little hunched over. Now the way to do it is to unload the gun, slide it into the old canvas case with the rope attached to one end and then drag it behind me as I crawl so it won't get stuffed with dirt or skinned-up on the rocks. But I do not have the old canvas case with me. In fact, I can't recall bringing it along since I rigged the rope with which to drag it.

At first I move toward the creek, just a little stooped over, and then I drop to my knees for a few feet. Then I begin to crawl with the shotgun in approved infantry position across my arms. The frozen ground is hard on my elbows especially where cattle have churned it up while it was muddy. A foot from my eyes is a feather that must have come from a ruffed grouse, and I find the dull brass head of an old shotgun shell, probably fired before they made the tubes out of plastic.

Deer track. Must have been a fawn. Rabbit foot. Something ate the owner. Someday, I think, I am going to find a valuable Indian artifact while thus crawling on my belly.

I can hear the mallard conversation now. Relaxed. Unsuspecting. Feeding gabble and one loud-mouthed hen. Wheezy drake talk.

Here's the row of willows. Check the gun, rise slowly, move in a little, and then step resolutely into the water. I think of the confident command, "Come out with your hands up!" There is a swish when I go through the willows and a plunk when I land in the water. Silence.

Then startled squawks and the mallards take off from a little indentation on my side, hidden by willows, and go off through the trees, giving me only one split-second view. I poke the gun toward them but there is no use shooting. It doesn't seem the little indentation was there last year. That was the time I caught them right in the middle, flat-footed with their wings down. I trudge back to the blind.

There is a greenwinged teal in with the decoys. He is darting about the shallow water the way teal do, tipping up in quick, jerky little movements. I have always felt that such teal hum to themselves like: "Tum-de-dum-dum—boy, that's juicy—tum-de-dum-dum."

To hell with him. I was after mallards.

ICE, DUCKS AND GOOD STRONG RYE

Martin Bovey

Currituck! The word has magic in it, for the Currituck Sound area of North Carolina occupies a front-row-center seat in the lore and legend of American waterfowling. Steeped in history and tradition, the area is the subject of many excellent works on waterfowling, and some of the best pieces can be found in Martin Bovey's Whistling Wings, *published by Doubleday & Company, Inc., in 1947. Martin Bovey was a conservationist and producer of wildlife films that are among the classics of the 40's. He is no slouch with a still-camera either. His photographs enrich both his books, as do the drawings of the celebrated Francis Lee Jaques. Besides* Whistling Wings, *Bovey wrote* The Saga of the Waterfowl *for the Wildlife Management Institute in 1949.*

ONE YEAR at Currituck, ice spoiled the shooting but produced adventures. Father and I reached the Poplar Branch to be met by long-faced guides. The Sound was half frozen and would probably freeze completely.

Next morning there was still a good deal of open water, so we started out with a battery—a double box from which Father and I could shoot together. There was ice to windward of where we wanted to shoot, and the men didn't like the situation, but finally we persuaded them to put the box overside.

"We'll keep a right smart eye on you," Sawyer said before leaving us. "That ice might start your way."

We got busy with the "cans" and redheads and forgot about the ice. It began to rain a bit, and fog settled down around us. After a while I became aware of a soft, grating noise to windward. I twisted around and looked out over the head of the stool. A sheet of ice was drifting slowly down on us, carrying the windward decoys with it.

Before I could call Father's attention to what was going on, I heard the muffled chug of an engine, and our boat shoved in through the curtain of fog.

The men exchanged a few excited words, then rammed into the ice, gave the motor full throttle, and smashed the sheet in half. With Grover at the helm and Green handling a boathook, they forced one piece to the left of us and the other to the right.

As the ice went drifting down outside the decoys, Grover cut off his engine. "Don't aim to be disagreeable," he said calmly, "but me and Green is takin' this outfit aboard. Next patch that comes might be a sure enough big one."

Late in the afternoon it cleared, and the wind went into the northwest. Next morning all the Sound that could be seen from the roof of the lodge was frozen except for two spots. There were more ducks jammed into those two holes than a fellow liked to think about.

For two days we sat in the lodge and tried to read. After every trip to the window to look at the thermometer, which was still falling, Father would utter some cheery platitude, but his voice was never convincing, and we both knew it. Finally I stopped smiling at his sunny remarks, and he gave them up. Then we settled down to being really sulky, and we both felt a lot better.

The third morning, soon after breakfast, I climbed to the roof with a pair of fieldglasses. The two holes had grown appreciably smaller. It looked as though the ducks were sitting on each other's backs, they were packed so tightly in those bits of open water.

Down by the landing I saw a small, flat-bottomed skiff and, lying not far away, some two-by-fours and miscellaneous boards. The germ of an idea began to sprout. I calculated the distance to the nearest water hole and started down the ladder. By the time I reached the ground my idea had blossomed into a plan.

Three or four of the guides were standing about, commenting on the injustice of the elements. "Who's got the nerve to go out over the ice with me and get some of those ducks?" I asked them.

No one accepted the challenge.

"We'll build a sled, load that skiff on it, pile in some stuff for a blind, shove until the ice breaks, then climb aboard, and cut the rest of the way with an axe," I explained. "With a little luck, we ought to have a hell of a good shoot."

Finally Carl Hubbard, my favorite goose-hunting guide, spoke up. "It's too risky," he said gravely. "The ice might break off from the shore and carry you plumb down the sound. It's startin' to warm up some."

Carl touched off a whole series of perfectly sound objections to the plan, but I was stubborn.

Finally the least experienced of the men declared that he was "game to have a try at it." His name was Jerry, a youngster about my own age with whom I had never gunned.

An hour later we were on our way. Bill Hunt, who managed the lodge, produced an old pair of skates and towed our sled until the ice began to crack. Then Jerry and I pushed until finally the ice broke, and we dove into the boat. We cut the sled loose, left it on the ice, and went to work with the axe, chopping our way toward the open water and those countless ducks.

It was infinitely harder work than I had expected, but at last we arrived. On one side of the hole, which was about three hundred yards long, the ice had shoved up over and old stake blind to form a solid mound perhaps six feet high and a dozen feet in diameter. Against this we tied the skiff, set up a screen of pine boughs as a blind, and tossed out a dozen decoys.

The ducks had all cleared out at our approach, and but a few of them returned. Those that did were distressingly suspicious of the pine grove that had suddenly sprung up in the center of the sound and gave us a wide berth.

Finally I grabbed the axe and my gun and climbed to the top of the ice mound. "Take that pine forest and yourself down to the far end of the hole." I told Jerry. "I'm going to fool these ducks yet."

By the time Jerry had paddled the boat away, I had backed out a hole in the ice big enough to lie down in.

Five minutes later I was chilled through and through. By the time I had extracted a flask from my pocket and got the top off, I was shaking all over. I remembered all too well a maxim to which Father had always subscribed: "Guns and alcohol don't mix." True enough, I told myself, but this was no time to be fussy!

I took a good-sized gulp and felt a pleasant warmth go through my body. It didn't last, however. Hardly had I got the flask stowed away before I was colder than ever. So now I took a really big shot of the rye. A lone redhead swung toward the decoys, and I gave him a couple of blasts. "That bird was a mile off," I said to myself as I settled down in the ice. "Are you maybe just a little tight, Bovey?"

During the next hour I took small, deliberate, frequent nips from the flask. With the earnestness of a laboratory research worker I attacked the problem of achieving the happy medium between miserable sobriety and comfortable intoxication. Perfect balance between the two had not been attained when I saw six canvasbacks coasting for the decoys. At that instant I was somewhere on the comfortable side of the happy medium. Quickly I rubbed a piece of ice over my forehead and eyebrows, jerked myself to my feet, and cut loose with the pump gun. I went to work on those ducks with the cool, confident precision of a great surgeon performing a critical operation. When the gun was empty, I felt that never before had I handled a pump gun so smoothly, never had I emptied the magazine more quickly or with more deadly accuracy. And there was not a duck left in the sky. I had done it at last! Six out of a flock.

I bellowed across the water to Jerry, but he was already paddling toward me.

"How was that for shooting?" I cried as he reached over the side of the skiff and picked up the first of my "cans." He held the big drake up for a moment for me to admire, then shoved the boat toward me through the decoys.

"Why not get the others?" I asked him as he neared my blind. Jerry grinned broadly as the bow of the boat crunched against the ice.

"Get the other five," I commanded, a trifle irritated.

For a moment Jerry merely smiled at me from the stern. Then he said quietly, "There was only one bird in that flock. You killed him dead with your first shot!"

Gun in hand I slid down the ice mound to the boat and climbed into the bow. "Let's pick up and head for home, Jerry," I said very humbly. "As long as a fellow sees only double the situation is still in hand. When he begins to see sixes he'd better get a new pair of glasses. Let's go!"

We had the devil's own time getting ashore. We reached our sled easily enough, but when we tried to get the boat onto the sled, our troubles began, for we didn't dare take all our weight off the boat for fear of breaking through. Finally, however, we accomplished the feat and got started. The boat seemed to weigh a ton, and the sled was hard to shove. Then the sled fell apart. We pulled the wreckage out from under the skiff and tried to push the boat over the ice, but our rubber boots slipped so that we couldn't really push. I found I could smash a hole through the ice with the heel of my boot and anchor myself, but Jerry was not heavy enough to do this. He had to chop holes. So I smashed while Jerry chopped. Then we anchored ourselves by our heels, lifted the boat, gave her a shove forward, and threw our weight on her just as the ice started to give way under us. Each time we did this we gained about a yard.

Before we knew it, it was pitch-dark.

"We won't get much sleep tonight if this ice breaks up and starts down the sound," Jerry said at one point.

"We got one duck, didn't we?" I reminded him. "Heave!"

We made shore at eight o'clock, having taken just under four hours to cover something less than a mile. Father and the guides had a big beacon fire burning long before we reached land. They were pretty worried about us.

"You fellows better have a good drink," Father said as we entered the lodge. We must have looked as "bushed" as we felt, for Father had no use for liquor, and I believe that is the only time he had ever urged me to take a drink.

"I had one out there on the ice," I confessed. "It wasn't very successful. Tell him about it, Jerry."

THERE WAS MAGIC IN HENRY'S JAVA

Henry was the tall, grinning Negro who rose at unholy hours to light the stoves and heap the breakfast table with fried eggs and bacon for the sportmen who patronized the shooting lodge at Currituck.

"Jes' one mo' cupful, Mist' Bobey," Henry would implore as he circled the table with his big pot of steaming coffee. "Ah want yo' eyes wide open w'en de boobies come rippin' ober yo' batt'ry."

Ruddies, always referred to on Currituck as "boobies," were the cream of the crop in Henry's opinion. Canvas and redheads were all right up North, where the host stood up at the head of the table and sliced the plump breasts with fine precision while he told of that magnificent double at fifty yards on the pair that had been too smart to decoy. But at a shooting lodge a guest is given a duck to himself, and the Lord planned things well when he fashioned the booby. He fits so nicely on the plate, and, surrounded by yams and creamed onions and supplemented by a cut of pie and a piece of cheese, he exactly satisfies the appetite of the average man. According to Henry, even a lady, if she's been all day on the water, can get through a booby. And now and then there came to the lodge a superman who could master two boobies when the long day was over. Who ever heard of a man—a real gentleman—who could eat two canvasbacks at a sitting and shoot straight the next morning? Yes, sir, the booby was the tenderest, sweetest, bestest duck on the Sound!

I was the last to leave the table one December morning, the last to get into rubber boots and start for the landing, buried under heavy clothing and laden with guns and shells.

As I headed for the door of the lodge Henry intercepted me.

"Please, Mist' Bobey," he implored, "git me some boobies today. Dey ain' nuthin' in de duck shed 'ceptin' a bunch o' redhead an' canvas. Ah sho hope de Lawd will sen' de boobies streamin' to you."

Henry's sad face and my lack of confidence in my ability to hit those plump speedsters prompted me to make a rash promise. "I'll turn over every booby I bring in today, Henry," I said glibly. "But if you really want boobies, you better ask the Lord to send them to Mr. Eaton's battery. Mr. Eaton can hit them."

Henry scooped up an armful of egg-stained plates and paused before turning to the kitchen.

"Ah's pinnin' mah hopes on you, Mist' Bobey," he said, beaming upon me. "You done drink three cups of mah Java dis mawnin'. Dey's magic in mah Java fo' sho."

I was out in the gray of a breathless dawn when he called after me. "Doan shoot too hasty w'en dem boobies come rippin' to you."

I promised I wouldn't and surrendered my two guns and five boxes of shells to Grover Sawyer and Lem Saunders and followed them down the duck boards to the wharf.

We tumbled aboard the battery boat, and Grover set to work on the flywheel of his temperamental engine. After a half dozen false promises she started, and we went chugging out of the bay.

Where the rushes bent away to the south and north and open water stretched indefinitely before us, Grover shut off the motor, and we floated with the other boats of the gunning fleet, waiting for sunrise to send us racing for the most favored shoals.

Gossip and gibes flew from boat to boat as the guides hailed each other across intervening water.

"Jed come down from Poplar Branch last evenin' an' 'lowed him an' Tom Green brung in fifty redhead Tuesday last."

"Uncle Willy went goosin' yesterday an' come home with nary a goose. Gentleman he was guidin' fer was shootin' one o' them 20-gauge popguns. Them kind don't more'n dust a goose."

"Sight safer'n shootin' a 10-gauge, though. Ain't that right, Jeff?"

Loud guffaws greeted this sally, for every man in the fleet had heard of young Jefferson Davis Sawyer's unfortunate experience. Shooting at a cripple with his father's 10-gauge, Jeff had touched off both barrels and been knocked over the side of the battery boat.

An engine wheezed, spat, and settled down to a steady deep-voiced chug-chug. The profanity of a half dozen marine motors mingled in a symphony of discords, for the sun was topping the sand dunes on the eastern shore of the Sound, and the race was on.

"Hope you get that old dishpan out an' back in 'fore midnight," a rival skipper yelled at us. "Don't envy your gentleman bein' served by sech an outfit."

Captain Sawyer made the appropriate reply, and we moved away to the southwest.

It was still and warm, and the sun rose blazing in a cloudless sky. The sound was as unruffled as a millpond.

"Doesn't look much like shooting weather, does it?" I remarked to Lem.

"Fair enough for quail an' doves," Lem replied. He took a generous bite out of a new plug of tobacco and settled the quid in his left cheek. "No, sir, this ain't my idea of duckin' weather, but you can't never tell 'bout duckin'. Things happen most unexpected like."

Then followed tales of limit kills under extraordinarily unpromising conditions. Lem is a profound optimist. When one is with Lem there is always the chance of a miracle.

Our talk veered to gunning strategy, of devices used by the old market gunners.

"Did you kill many of the birds on the water?" I asked.

Lem received the question calmly. It roused no indignation in him. "No, sir! Least of all not the gunners I worked with. We was gunnin' for business and couldn't 'ford to waste ammunition. Birds in the air is easier killin' than birds on the water."

Lem's answer surprised me, but it brought to my mind the many occasions on which I had fired two or three times at a swimming cripple before the shot penetrated the armor of folded wings or a pellet found its way to the bird's brain.

"That ain't sayin' we didn't let birds set down with the stool. We aimed to have plenty of birds in range 'fore we went to work on 'em. But we killed 'em in the air. Mind that bunch of canvas come to you jest 'fore we picked up last ev'nin'?"

As though I could have forgotten! They circled once beyond the outer edge of the stool, then came straight in over the foot of the stand—at least twenty of them—with the sun flashing on their breasts and the undersides of their wings as they put on the brakes. They looked as big as elephants, as though they were about to land on the wings of the battery. Yet when I came up on them I was amazed how far away they were and astonished at the speed with which they swung and hurtled down the wind.

"If you'd handled that bunch right, you'd of had time to pump your gun out and you'd have got maybe four or five 'stead of only two. Let the first of the bunch flop into the stool, an' when the tail-enders shove their feet out, take 'em. When you're done workin' on them, the others'll still be in killin' range. I know plenty old gunners who worked so fast they could shoot out two automatics an' still have birds in range. Got ten redheads meself once. Not a cripple in the lot. When a flock sets its mind on comin' to you, let 'em come."

Ten redheads out of a single flock! It made one's hair curl, it was such downright slaughter, and yet I was compelled to admit that for so mediocre a shot as myself it would be tremendously thrilling to see every shot go true, do its work cleanly and finally.

Ahead of us a small raft of birds rose from the water and faded away to the south. We chugged on for three or four hundred yards before Grover shut off the engine and Lem let the anchor go.

We got the battery over, the wings spread, and the weights placed. In a surprisingly short time the guides had surrounded the box with two hundred decoys. I arranged the iron decoys on the battery deck, hung my shell bag on the nail in the front of the pit, rammed shells into my pump gun, and settled down to wait for the first flock.

A few bunches of big birds, coming from the marshes to the north, passed down the Sound traveling high in wavering V's. Now and then a booby or two flashed by just outside my decoys. But not a bird came within range. At the end of two hours I was thoroughly cramped. The average sit-up battery was not designed for one who is six foot four.

I rose painfully to my feet, stretched luxuriously, and turned to see four canvas banking away from the head of the stool. How the devil had I missed seeing that quartette when I had twisted my neck completely around before standing up?

The wings of the battery lay still on the lifeless water, and the decks were baked dry. A pair of redheads or canvas came up from the south, sailed for the foot of the decoys, then flared and went on their way. A battery in dead calm water shows up like a dreadnought in a mud puddle.

Every ounce of iron in the battery boat had been stowed away in the slots, but still the box rode too high, so I took the bailing can and filled the pit with water until another canful would have flooded my seat. The water just reached the deck now, and I felt better about things. But still nothing came near me.

In rough weather a battery is a noisy thing, but today there was no slapping of wings, no hiss of water running along the deck. The peace and solitude were infinite, and the sunshine fell warmly on my face as I lay back in my seat looking dreamily off through the decoys, sitting so motionless on the still gray water. It was inevitable that I should doze off for an instant and equally inevitable that a dozen boobies should hurtle by not ten feet over my head. They did not stop, for boobies prefer to decoy to a small stand rather than to the many stools that one uses on Currituck for big ducks.

They did, however, get me wide awake in time to see a flock of birds coming up toward the foot of the decoys. They were low enough to make me think they meant business, and there was something determined about their approach. They came as straight and sure as an arrow from a longbow, and I waited tense and hopeful, eyes level with the rim of the battery, body doubled up over my feet, ready like a jack-in-the-box for the moment of release. Just beyond the edge of the stand their determination seemed for an instant to waver. The leader turned slightly as though to swing by on my left. But just as I caught the flash of sunlight on black head and neck, he banked my way and cut off the power. Once their minds are made up, bluebills come to decoys with the resoluteness of the Light Brigade.

There is something enormously exciting about those moments when you fear that the slightest movement of your head may end the wary approach of suspicious canvasbacks or that the flash of sunlight on your gun barrel will frighten a high-flying old black duck. But there is also something thoroughly splendid about those split seconds when bluebills are rushing in with the sheer bravado of youth. "To hell with the 'Keep off the ice' signs! Let's skate."

They looked tremendously big, those "blackheads" sideslipping into the decoys. I was already coming up on them when I remembered Lem's words: "Let the first ones flop!" I checked my rise and froze, until with a "wuuush" the leader and two others splashed among the nearest of the decoys.

Then tense muscles snapped me up into a world very full of startled birds. I felt completely surrounded by bluebills and missed with a vaguely aimed first shot. A bird cutting away to my left folded up at the second report, and the third shot dropped another on the same side. The gun barrel followed through and swung up on the track of a towering drake that fell like a stone as I squeezed the trigger. Three! Another shell in the barrel for a straight-away shot over the head of the stool. Four! Quick! That laggard climbing up on the left. Hold high! Bang! That's the way to see 'em fall; head flat against the back, wings folded, hitting the water, breast first with a mightly splash.

Five! And every one on his back among the decoys. What would Lem say about that performance?

The battery boat came up before long, and Lem hailed me from afar.

"How many out of that bunch? I see three from here."

"Five," I called back, trying to make my voice sound matter-of-fact.

"Good! You let that bunch come to you."

My watch said twelve o'clock.

"Take me aboard," I shouted, "I've had enough shooting for a while, and I could eat a horse."

We picked up the birds, dropped a quarter of a mile to leeward, and anchored while we wolfed down thick meat sandwiches and swallowed coffee that came piping hot from Thermos bottles.

When we had had a long smoke Lem said, "Better be gettin' back to the box. Got a notion you'll get some shootin' this afternoon."

"Hope you're right, Lem, but it isn't really necessary. Those five bluebills will hold me for awhile."

Lem grinned at me. I think he understood. But Grover said, "Maybe you can make it six this afternoon, if a bunch comes to you nice."

"Probably I'd get only two, or at the most three," I answered. "Even five would be an anticlimax. I'm going to shoot my double-barrel this afternoon."

The sound was just as calm as in the early morning, and the outlook for a good shoot just as unpromising. But a man has never settled himself in a blind or squeezed himself into a battery without hope in his heart. I felt sure that Lem, looking back at me as the battery boat moved away to the south, was about to produce a miracle. "We'll see if we can't stir up a flock or two," he had said as he handed me my gun. "Henry'll be right disappointed if you don't bring in a single booby."

The decoys looked as lifeless as ever; the battery rode just as high; the sky was as free of clouds as at sunrise. At the end of fifteen minutes I was ready to fall asleep, all hope of a miracle abandoned. Perhaps late in the afternoon a bird or two might come in, but for the present nothing would fly, much less come near enough to disturb my pleasant daydreams.

And just at that moment the miracle did happen!

I was conscious first of a vague and far-off sound as of honey-gathering bees, then of a strange moving haze rising above the water away to the south. For several moments I blinked, mildly curious, then rubbed my eyes and became instantly completely alert, vibrant with excitement. That droning sound could be made by nothing but an airplane motor, that haze was nothing less than a cloud of waterfowl. Already I could make out individual flocks. Big birds high in the air, boobies skimming the surface of the water. And all of them coming straight at me.

I have heard of the terrific pace at which driven grouse hurtle over the gunning stands on Scottish moors, and I have, of course, shot much on the Whittaker Pass over which canvas and redheads, teal and bluebills cross at astonishing speed. On that pass I have shot bluebills coming down on a northern gale, when an early freeze-up was at their heels. One led them an incredible distance and still killed birds flying in the wake of those at which one fired.

But never have I seen waterfowl travel faster than on that afternoon when Lem produced his miracle.

The canvas and redheads streamed by too high to be in range, but the boobies barely cleared the top of my hat. They came so fast and so low that once I actually ducked for fear of being hit in the face by a booby cannon ball. I had a very definite sensation of being not the marksman but the target, of being in the center of a barrage of boobies.

Once, when for a fleeting moment the air was free of them, I thought of Henry's parting words: "Doan shoot too hasty w'en dem boobies come rippin' to you."

Then they came at me again, and it was impossible to shoot too hasty, for one can only shoot when one's gun is loaded. I came to my feet when I shot, and I seldom had time to sink to my seat between shots, for there were nearly always birds in range when I had reloaded my double-barrel. They came without regard for me standing there in the midst of ducks that, strangely, showed no interest in their rout.

When at last no more ducks came, and the plane, which must have circled once or twice far down the Sound, hove in sight and passed low over my head, I found that I was wearing a heavy glove on my left hand. When the flight started I had been bare-handed. Never before or since have I shot ducks until my gun barrels were too hot to hold without a thick glove.

By the time the battery boat came up I had counted seventeen boobies floating among the decoys.

"You're three short of the limit," Grover called as Lem scooped the last bird into his long-handled net. "Guess you can pick them up before quittin' time."

"It's quitting time right now," I shouted back. "One more shot, and this gun barrel would melt. And besides, I want to make some arrangements with Henry."

He came down to the landing as we chugged into the bay, and we could see the white teeth flashing in his black face as he hailed us.

"Ah sho hope you got a pile of boobies fo' me, Mist' Bobey."

"Will you settle for ten?" I shouted back.

"Fo' ten honest to goodness, sweet-as-honey boobies? Why, Lawdie, fo' ten boobies Ah would sell mah soul to de debil. Ah would fo' sho."

Grover steered us alongside, and Lem and I tossed the boobies— ten of them, that is—onto the wharf.

"Lawdie!" Henry exploded. "De Lawd sho muster sent de boobies streamin' to you."

"He sure did, Henry, Lem pulled off one of his miracles today."

Henry straightened up, his hands full of boobies. "Doan know nuthin' 'bout Lem's miracles," he snorted. "Ah reckon mah Java done brung you dem boobies. Dey's magic in mah Java fo' sho!"

THE SUSQUEHANNA FLATS

Norris E. Pratt

The book, Chesapeake Bay Decoys: The Men Who Made and Used Them, *from which this piece was taken, was edited by R.H. Richardson and published by Crow Haven Publishers, Cambridge, Maryland. Each chapter is an individual contribution from hunters and conservationists who knew their particular area of the Eastern Shore intimately. In this piece you will find a great deal of charm and nostalgia as you read of the amazing halcyon days at the mouth of the Susquehanna River at the top of the Bay.*

PRESIDENT GROVER CLEVELAND will be remembered as one of our few sportsman Presidents. His was a familiar figure in Eastern sporting areas between 1885-1897. The type of game he preferred is unknown, but we do know he enjoyed shooting wildfowl at the head of the Chesapeake Bay. When he went to gun the Susquehanna Flats he stayed at the famous Wellwood Club at Charlestown, Maryland, on the North East River. The names of his guides and outfitters have been lost in time, nor do we know the name of his decoy maker, but the decoys known as Cleveland Canvasbacks remain to enhance a collector's rig. Pictures of Cleveland Canvasbacks appear on page 51 of the Shelburne Museum catalog. A few may be seen in private collections of owners living at the head of the Bay.

I have been told by some of the "old heads" that the basic design of decoys changed in the 1880's. Before this, decoys had been quite flat. I, for instance, have some about 2¾ inches thick and approximately 7 inches wide. Although weighted, they would not right themselves in heavy seas. I presume the hunter felt that if the decoys turned over it was time to get off the water himself. The older decoys have iron keels, made mostly from worn out horseshoes. The blacksmith would reshape them and point the ends so that they could be driven into the belly of the decoy. Decoys made this way are about one hundred years old. Mr. Evans McKinney of Elkton,

Maryland, has told me that he has examined old decoys that have been newly painted and weighted with a modern poured lead body weight. When he dug with an icepick at the rear of this weight he found an area which had long ago been filled with putty. This proved that the bird originally had an iron keel which had been lost or deliberately replaced. The modern decoy was developed at the end of the nineteenth century. The heads are not so high, and the body weights are sufficiently heavy to right a decoy if it rolls over. The body is made deeper. William "Snake" Heverin, of Charlestown, Maryland, made decoys that are 4½ and 5 inches deep. As far as I know, all the Flats' decoy bottoms were rounded, not flat.

My personal connection with the Flats began in 1922 while I was in high school at Oxford, Pennsylvania. I left my car in the Adams brothers' garage during the day, and I became interested in the piles of decoys stored there. I learned that the brothers operated a sink box rig on the Flats, barely twenty-five miles away. As I had learned to love gunning from my grandfather, I arranged to go with them.

In those days the cost of a non-resident license was $15.50, and the Adams' fee was $100.00 a day. This was for a party of four, and included overnight lodging and food. We were up at 2:00 a.m. and the whole rig left about 3:00 a.m. We went to an imaginary line drawn across the Upper Bay from Point Concord lighthouse at Havre de Grace to Carpenter's Point on the North East River. We were not allowed to cross this line with a rig before 3:15 a.m. After it was crossed, we were on the Flats. The box was put overboard in the darkness, and anchored fore and aft, up and down the wind. The decoys were put out in a long oval below the box. The outfitter placed long necked decoys close to the box to break up the outline to keep from flaring the approaching birds. Usually, about three hundred and fifty decoys were used in a single box rig; a double box rig might contain seven hundred decoys. Many times iron decoys with flat bottoms were arranged on the inner wing area of the box to provide enough weight to sink the box to the proper depth— just enough to keep it floatable. The amount of iron used depended on the weight of the man who was to go into the box to shoot. Flat bottomed wooden "wing ducks" were used on the outer wing areas of the box. These areas were constructed like large screen door frames, and were hinged to the outer edge of the inner wings. These were covered with old bed ticking, to blend with the color of the water. Small slits were cut in these wing covers to drop the weights through. These were used on the flat bottomed wooden ducks. All these decoys, both iron and wood, helped to camouflage the box, which was painted a dull grey to match the water. As daylight came, I had a chance to observe the shape and action of the various makers' decoys. Some rode the waves like real ducks; others rolled and pitched as the seas hit them. I learned the makers' names, and the characteristics of each maker. Each seemed to have a good reason for his pattern. Some were straight sided so the string would not fall off and become tangled while being wound around the decoy; others were concave behind the head so that the string would stay on when it was not in use. The Lockard decoys had individualistic nostrils. Some men carved the tails in the center of the rear end of the body. This is a truly North East River characteristic. Others made a slightly longer tail, as may be seen in a Scott Jackson decoy. Some carved the lower bill and throat area on a straight line. Early McGaw decoys were made this way. Another variation is found in the turned up tail of the Barnes' decoys. Another interesting example is the Ben "Daddy" Holly decoy, carved with the tail just above the center of the body, and turned up just a little. These have no shelf on the body to set the head on, as do the William Heverin's. Decoys carved by Jess Urie of Rock Hall, Maryland, had the bills the same width as the head was thick. He did not try to make them lifesize, but produced a grip area very handy to the hunter.

Since boats are a part of the gunning scene, I might add here that Jim Holly, Ben's son, who lived in Havre de Grace, Maryland, made "Bushwhack" boats, considered by many old heads to be the best designed of all the whack boats. Bushwhacking is an ingenious method of waterfowling that was practiced only on the upper reaches of the Chesapeake Bay. Several hundred decoys were rigged out in the water; the scull boat with its long rear mounted oar was taken upwind of the rig and anchored. When the ducks pitched into the rig, the boat was sculled downwind, usually by a Black man, with his "Sport" in the bow and only a canvas curtain between him and the vision of the stooled out decoys. The ducks would swim to the outer edge of the stool. Many times they would take off into the wind. This would put them in a position quite advantageous to the hunter. Perhaps the scull boat itself could be thought of as a decoy.

Most of the Flat's decoys were canvasbacks, but there were many Black heads and Red heads, a few Black ducks and Pintails, a scattering of Teal and Ruddies or "greasers" as they were called. Many years ago Captain Ralph Murphy of Charlestown, Maryland, told me that once when he was a "Duck police" he saw a big rig come up to the Flats in the late afternoon and lay off to gun the next day. Since he did not recognize the rig, he decided to go out and see who it was. When he came alongside he told the gunners who he was and discovered the rig of oddly shaped flat bottomed decoys belonged to Glen L. Martin of Baltimore. One can only guess what that load of Ward brothers' humpbacked Canvasbacks, Pintails, Widgeons and Whifflers might be worth today. At that time they were far from home, as the Ward brothers were way down the Bay at Crisfield, Maryland. On June 16, 1973, I mentioned the encounter to Steve Ward. He recalled that Martin's men had come to his shop on two different occasions and had picked up a truckload of decoys each time.

A list of the most famous decoy makers at the head of the Bay would include several names: John B. Graham, of Charlestown, Maryland, who specialized in Canvasbacks (his regular business was undertaking.); Leonard Pryor, of Chesapeake City, who made Canvasbacks and a few Pintails; Milton Watson, also of Chesapeake City, who made Canvasbacks; Scott Jackson of North East River, specialist in Canvasbacks; Henry and George Lockard, of Elk Neck, Maryland, who carved Canvasbacks, Red heads, and a few Black heads; William Heverin, of Charlestown, noted for Canvasbacks, Red heads, Black heads, and a few Black duck; Robert F. "Bob" McGaw, Havre de Grace, carver of Canvasbacks, Red heads, Black heads, Sprigtail, Bald pates, Black ducks and mallards; Samuel Barnes, Havre de Grace, who carved a few swans, possibly six or eight, Canvasbacks, Red heads, and Black heads; Madison Mitchell, of Havre de Grace, who made all species relative to the Flats; Paul Gibson, also from Havre de Grace, who also carved all species; Ben "Daddy" Holly, of Havre de Grace, who made Teal, Canvasbacks, and Red heads. A Holly Teal, in original condition and with the original paint, is just about priceless, as so few are in existence. (Ben had three sons: John, who carried on his work, Wilson, of whom little is known, and the Jim mentioned before in connection with his bushwhack designs.) Ben Dye, of Cecil County, Maryland, famous for his Canvasback (a rare Canvasback sink box wooden wing decoy in original condition may be seen in Norris E. Pratt's collection); Joseph Condon, of Aiken, Maryland, made folding decoys, and, in 1875, the wild pigeons which are now in the Shelburne Museum. He was also an artist, and did waterfowl pictures in wood in relief carving; Horace Graham, of Charlestown, did all species; J.F. McKenny of Chestertown, carved Canvasbacks and some other species; Charlie Joiner of Betterton and Chestertown, made all species. Incidentally, he learned to make decoys in Madison Mitchell's shop. Several little known gunners made their own decoys. Two of these were Bill and Bob Litzenberg of Elkton, who in 1933 carved some decoys. Their whack boat was made by Frank Murphy on a Holly pattern. Sometimes they teamed up with Ralph Murphy of Charlestown and double stooled for Canvasbacks and Red heads on the North East River.

Two of the most famous scullers on the eastern edge of the Flats were Alonzo and Harry Briscoe. Alonzo sculled Henry Mitchell of Elkton, but Harry free-lanced. Their brother Orrie sculled Jack Quiel of Kennett Square, Pennsylvania, among others. Another brother, Roy, gunned the sink box with Dick Armour of Wild Duck Cove. These East River Briscoes also market gunned. These men were colored. I have been told some colored scullers powdered their faces with flour so that they could not be seen when they peeped over the canvas curtains of the boat to watch the ducks during the scull down.

Leonard Pryor made several stools of bushwhack decoys, one of Canvasbacks for John Shaeffer, and another for Howard Brown. Shaeffer told Bill Litzenberg there were approximately forty sink boxes on the Flats in the 20's and 30's. In the 20's it was lawful to go out in the evening and attach a lantern to a pole so that one could claim that particular spot for the next day's shooting. Of course, there was nothing to prevent the unsporting from stealing the original lantern and replacing it with his own, thus setting up a second claim. Ernie Neiwig used to sit on his porch with a high powered rifle and announce to all the world what he would do to anyone who touched his lantern. I remember well the eerie lights twinkling in the dark all over the Flats. It was hard to realize these lights were 500 yards apart, as required by law. Although it was illegal even then, some people gunned after dark. Two old timers I know claim there are two kinds of Canvasbacks: one they call the night can, and they vow up and down he is never killed in daylight. They claim they are heavier, and would bring a dollar a pair more. Madison Mitchell explained this belief. He claims that some birds were older, bigger, and wiser than the rest. These flew in on the Flats at night. They fed, then flew back to deep water to raft up during the day, and did not appear during the daylight. These wise old birds would average 7 pounds, ranging up to 7½ or 8. John Shaeffer attests he has seen a group of fifteen dead canvasbacks that would weigh 8½ pounds a pair. These big ducks had an exceptionally long neck. This lead to the term "Bull Can."

In my time on the Flats I am sure some birds were shot to be used locally as food, and that the Sports who "shot the Flats" took their birds home to be divided between family and friends. Rigs were also used by their owners, who hired fellows who were good shots to shoot for them. These birds were taken to the railroad and shipped to markets in Baltimore and New York.

Horace Graham, of Charlestown, Maryland, who was born in 1893 and is still living in 1973, started gunning in 1910. He and Ernest Norman gunned one "box" for Charlie Biddle late in the season for market. Biddle gunned with a Mr. Gary and a Mr. Clark from New York the whole season. Graham said that on one occasion these two men had shot a case of 500 shells by 11:00 a.m., but had killed only 87 Canvasbacks. Biddle had to go back to the North East for more shells. Never was any impoliteness shown the Sports, but one can imagine that their ears burned on the trip back to New York, Philadelphia, or Baltimore after a day's shoot.

I remember hearing an old fellow saying to his two sons, "Well, boys, you'd better load them Canvasbacks and take 'em to the dump." These birds were tied in pairs and loaded into the back seat area of a Model T Ford touring car with no top. I'm sure they went to the train station in either Charlestown or Perryville, Maryland. There were about one hundred birds in that group, which had been shot from a sink box. I have no personal knowledge of big guns being used in my time. Most night gunning was done with automatics with extensions on the magazine tube. Blinds, both off shore and shore, were used in many areas, but the kill from them was negligible. About 1950 body booting became popular and legal on the Flats. A group of four men, maybe five, would work together. They would have a cabin boat, a bushwhack boat to haul the decoys in, and a smaller boat with a powerful outboard motor to tend the layout. The decoys at this time were usually geese. Their profile was arranged in groups of three. The few ducks flying would come to a goose rig. The hunter wore chest high Navy surplus waders and a white coat and hat. His blind was a giant swan decoy mounted on a long pole pushed down into the bottom of the Bay. This decoy had a rack on the back to lay the gun on, in case the hunter wanted to flap his arms to get warm. There was also a box attachment to hold fifty or more shells. The rig had to be placed so that the hunter could still stand up at high tide. Sometimes the tide would get so low the hunter would have to sit down. Nearby would be five or six floating swan decoys. These had metal waterproof boxes let into their backs to hold a box of shells. Sometimes there would be one hundred and fifty decoys put out, and two or three men would go into them to shoot. If the dead birds fell near enough for the men to retrieve them, they did so; if not, a man held his arms up as a signal. The men who stayed in the cabin boat, anchored some distance away, but who watched the rig constantly through glasses, would put out in the outboard motorboat to the set. It was their duty to chase all cripples and to pick up the dead birds that had fallen too far away for the shooter to collect. When "wet suits" were made available, the hunters wore these, and the profile swan and other swan decoys were no longer used. Now a large goose profile is used, as it matches the color of the wet suit. A man stays in the water as long as he can stand it, depending on the temperature. I have seen fellows stand in water so deep that when they shot at a bird overhead the water ran down their necks, but they refused to quit as the shooting was good. This is body booting. Shooting was good on the

Susquehanna Flats because the Canvasbacks wintered there. Ed Adams, of the rig I hunted with, was a short, chunky man. He used a Remington Automatic with the stock cut off to 7 inches long, and he wore heavy sheepskin clothing. Oilskins were used in foul weather. One of Howard Taylor's boys used a Model 1897 Winchester so badly worn he could hold the stock and bend the barrel and magazine tube from side to side in a four inch arc. Several Model 1912 Winchester pumps were used. Occasionally we saw a Sport with a nice Smith or Fox, but the work horse gun was the Remington Automatic. Once in a great while an old 10 bore hammer gun with 32 inch barrels will be offered at public sale. I have the good fortune now to own someone's pride and joy, an identically matched pair of 8 bore muzzle loaders with 34 inch barrels and back action locks. I think the highlight of my waterfowling career was the day I was told I could have the mammoth 4 bore percussion double from the Howard Taylor rig. This gun has 48 inch barrels, is a double, and weighs 33 pounds. It is 65½ inches tall over all, and the old box of wads came with it. It is a J.E. Evans of Philadelphia shoulder gun. Taylor himself got the gun in about 1900. It was given to him by a Sport from Philadelphia with whom he had gunned. I have seen this gun taken to the river and disassembled into two parts. Each part was put in a "Gun boot" and hung over a man's shoulder. In addition to Evans, other firms on the East Coast who made shoulder guns were Tonks, Snyder, McComas of Baltimore, Fetterman and Chase of Centerville, Maryland, and Parker and Smith. The only time I have seen a Punt or Swivel gun offered at public sale was in 1971. The gun was 9 feet, 6 inches long. It was a Pipe gun. The barrel was made of three sections of pipe welded together, three thicknesses at the breech, two in the middle, and one in the forward section. The stock was of oak, and a 4 inch by 8 inch timber had been used for it. The barrel was 7 feet 4 inches long, and it had been fitted with an old Musket lock. She had a 1½ inch bore. I have never seen a gun of this type used, nor have I ever heard one in the night touched off illegally.

Railbird shooting was an extra for gunners in early fall. The Litzenberg brothers told me that they gunned the Scotland Marsh in Elk River for railbirds. The limit was fifty birds to a boat at that time. Once four boats killed one hundred and seventy-five birds on one floodtide. Incidentally, some of those railbird rigs carried a few teal decoys, "just in case" there were some summer ducks or teal around.

Some little stories about my experiences in the 1920's might be interesting. After gunning that one season with the Adams brothers and Neiwig, of Oxford, Pennsylvania, my buddy, Joseph Mackey of Kemblesville, Pennsylvania, and I decided to get a rig together on the Flats. We built a small cabin in Wild Duck Farm Cove, where there were ten or twelve other cabins. Our lease cost us $7.00 a year. This allowed trespass rights from the main road across the farm to our cabin site at the water's edge. It also allowed us to gather firewood on the beach, but did not allow us to cut any trees in the nearby woods. We bought the last bushwhack boat that Clem Reeder built at North East. This boat was 18 feet long. It was complete with four rowing oars, four oar locks, a scull oar, an anchor, a rope, and a scoup. The total price was $75.00. The day we took possession of it we rowed from North East all the way down North East River, around Carpenter's Point, High Point, and up to Wild Duck Cove, about eight or nine miles. We bought fifty, second-hand decoys from Charlie Biddle of North East. As live decoys were legal then, we got ten or twelve mallards, also. We gunned the islands that lay to the southeast. We had a mud box, which is similar to a sink box except that it has no wing. It has one 12 inch board all the way around the area in which the hunter lies. A hole was dug to set the box in, out on the point of an island, then mud was piled on the sides to make it appear deeper. By night we were mud all over, after getting in and out of that box several times during the day. The decoys, both wooden and alive, were placed nearby, but when the tide rose quickly, we had to get out and move the box farther up the island. We didn't mind the mud, as we had plenty of shooting. The limit was twenty-five birds a day, but we never got our limit. Sometimes we got a goose or two. The next year I decided to try my hand at making decoys. I made six and took them to Buddy Reynolds at North East. He was was an outfitter who carried thousands of decoys on hand at all times. I had heard he would pay $1.00 each for new, unpainted decoys. He looked at mine and said, "Boy, those are no good, but I will buy them anyway. If you want to make decoys, come out on the wharf and I will show you some good ones." The building we went to held several hundred decoys. He selected one for me to copy. I made side and top patterns from an old shoe box, and established my individual pattern. I decided to make one thousand and sell them to Reynolds for $1,000.00. I wanted to buy a new Model T, and $1,000.00 was the asking price. I had the 4 inches by 7 inches white pine sawed in Mifflin County, Pennsylvania, one hundred and fifty miles away. I eventually got it home and sawed out the bodies on a band saw. About the time I had six hundred finished the gunning laws were changed. Maryland outlawed the use of boats under sixteen feet, and I had made a twelve foot model to be used in the Marsh! The Federal Government outlawed the killing of Canvasback and I was stuck for sure. I never got the Model T. Years later I painted those Canvasbacks into Black ducks and sold them in lower Delaware for forty cents each during the Great Depression. Somewhere along the line, I did make one hundred Canvasbacks for George Cairns. These were the same pattern, but were made of willow, which is similar to basswood. For these he paid me five $20.00 bills. To a country boy those $20.00 bills looked mighty big.

Facts From Friends—Madison Mitchell

There's a tale that circulates in hunting circles that may be appropriately told here. One day long ago a famous outfitter was startled when an acquaintance burst into his shop in an agitated manner with a long, sad tale of woe. He claimed he needed money desperately, and offered to sell one hundred fine decoys for sixty-five cents each. Suspecting that his desperation had been induced by a strong desire for whiskey, the outfitter tried to soothe him and talk him out of selling. What would he do for a living when the hunting season came in? But the man persisted, and the outfitter, knowing a bargain when he saw one, bought the decoys. Although they were excellent decoys, they showed use. He made the necessary repairs and painted them, readying them for a purchaser.

One day just before the season opened the local judge burst into his shop in an agitated manner with a long, sad tale of woe. All of his decoys had been stolen, and he would have to buy new ones.

Without so much as a blink, the outfitter showed the judge his new purchase.

"Those are my decoys. I can identify them even painted!"

"Are they? Tommy sold them to me several weeks ago."

"Tommy? He's my sculler, and the best dang sculler in the world!" Now the judge faced a dilemma. If he had Tommy arrested and allowed him to languish in jail, the judge would have to find another sculler, most likely one not nearly so skilled. There are two kinds of justice, legal and poetic. The judge waxed poetic. He bought back his decoys, and, when he was ready to hunt, he handed them over to Tommy without so much as a blink. Now Tommy knew the judge and the outfitter both knew—and were letting him "stew in his own juice."

This story can be verified, but the names were changed to protect the innocent.

The story is particularly interesting to collectors as the decoys in question had been made by Dick Howlett of Havre de Grace, who is documented in William Mackey's book.

A catalog of names of interest to collectors follows:

A Mr. Barnes made decoys, followed by his son, Samuel T., who made them from 1875 until he died in 1926. Mr. Mitchell worked with Barnes in 1924 and 25. Barnes made six or eight swans in his early years, but none after that. His daughter, Florence, painted many decoys for him.

Jim Currier of Havre de Grace made decoys for thirty-five years. Possibly he turned out 10,000 before he died in 1970.

Summerfield Wilson made four or five hundred before 1928.

Charles T. Wilson made three or four hundred before 1916.

Ed Sampson made thousands of heads for different makers.

Robert F. McGaw started making decoys in 1916. He made as many as fifteen hundred in some years. He died in 1963.

Herbert Gilbert made decoys before 1942.

Ben Dye made great numbers before he died in 1918 or 20.

"Daddy" Holly made many before he died in 1902.

Madison Mitchell was reluctant to say how many he has made, but he started in 1926. As many as ten men have worked in his shop at one time.

Evans McKinney

Madison Mitchell told Mr. McKinney that there were fourteen different decoy makers working in Havre de Grace at one time years ago. Mr. McKinney was born in Elkton, but in his early years he moved to the McCall Farm at High Point. When he was fourteen and his brother eleven, they had their own rig of 125 bushwhack decoys which they used on the Flats.

William Heverin box gunned with Charlie Biddle who owned the rig. Biddle would gun two single boxes in one stool of decoys, one for the Sports and one for Heverin. Incidentally, Heverin was as good a shooter as anyone in the Flats. He used two Remington Automatic shotguns. He also used the "Big Gun." Hired by Biddle, he saw to it that the Sports really had a load of ducks to take home. He was so skilled a marksman he could jump up very quickly, pivot, and shoot ducks flying by unhandily on the right side. He was born in 1860 and lived to be 91. McKinney bought the last decoys he made in 1941. These are all hand made, as Heverin did not use power tools.

Facts From Friends – Nelson H. McCall

Heis McCall of Charlestown, has filled me in on the story of his grandfather, Joseph H. Heisler, who gunned legally for the market in 1900. The Pennsylvania Railroad would send a one-car train up from Perryville each morning at 8:00 a.m. The hunters carried their ducks, tied in pairs and hung over long oars, two men to an oar, to the train to be shipped to the market. The fact that the railroad came to the Flats in the 1830-40 period gave the area its great popularity. Ducks were plentiful, and now the market hunter had a quick source of transportation at his back door. Also, the Sports could arrive by rail in the evening, shoot all the next day, and get a train to Philadelphia, Boston, Baltimore or Washington following the shoot. The market hunters here had an advantage over those who hunted lower down the Bay. There the hunter had to flag down a steamer headed for Baltimore. These steamer transported birds arrived at the market a day or two later than those that traveled by rail. There are tricks in all trades, and hunters have theirs. Since Canvasbacks were tied in pairs, a duck and a drake, a hunter short on hens might substitute a hen Red head, but buyers were alert to the stunt, and few got by.

Sink boxes used two guns in McCall's time: 8 bore doubles if the hunters were men enough to handle them, or a pair of 10 bore doubles if not. When the Sports came to gun, the Models 1887 and 1901 Winchesters were more in evidence.

On some occasions, when wind and tide were correct, Joe would sail his Bugeye down the Flats in late afternoon, taking along three small rowboats and a man for each. Upon reaching the proper location, he would lower all sails and soak them with water to make them as dark as possible. Then he would hoist and stretch them tightly across the boat from side to side. When all was in readiness, the rowboats would put out and circle a large flock of ducks and maneuver them in line with the Bugeye. At a given signal the men would pound the water with their oars to scare the frightened birds in the direction of the boat. In the darkness great numbers would fly against the darkened canvas, and fall crippled to the deck below, where strong hands waited to wring their necks.

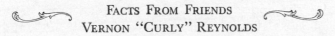

FACTS FROM FRIENDS
VERNON "CURLY" REYNOLDS

In the 1920's, men could live from the water the year round as they could do commercial fishing in the spring and early fall, then join the hunting crowd for the waterfowling season. My father, Andrew "Buddy" Reynolds, Clarence, my brother, and John Futty gunned the Flats. Whenever we had time off from school, John Futty, Junior, and I were allowed to go along on the hunting trips. It seemed like one big family, the Reynolds and the Futtys, all gunning the same sink rig. The rigs would come to the docks at North East with from fifty to one hundred and fifty canvasback hanging from the railing. The boats would go out in the afternoon toward Carpenter's Point, one of the line points for the Susquehanna Flats, and anchor along the line that prevented the rigs from entering the Flats before 3:15 a.m., so that no time would be wasted on a hunting day. The gunning police were very active, and kept at least the honest hunter within the law, but every one kept his motor in readiness at all times. Father gunned the Sports from Baltimore, Washington, Philadelphia, Wilmington, and New York. Mr. Charles Newcombe of Philadelphia, a salesman and demonstrator for Remington Arms, chartered the rig the first two weeks each season. Being an exceptional shot, he could throw his feet up, spin around in the sink box, and kill greasers going across the head of the box. Another hunter whose name I remember is Mr. George Connell, a councilman in Philadelphia, who was pleasant company, if not an expert marksman. He enjoyed bringing guests; one of the most popular was Alexander Murdock, public works director, and we also welcomed George Biles, city water director. The Sports enjoyed their visits on the Flats, even though they did not deplete the canvasback population very much, as from fifty to eighty ducks would be a good day's kill. I began as regular crew in 1930. Clarence, my older brother, took over the second rig then, and Mr. Frederick Lehman was among his Sports. I have a particularly fond memory of Mr. Lehman, for he gave me a practically new Winchester Automatic which I am still using, though one is allowed only three shots now. I still have the extension we used in sink boxes. As we wore heavy clothing, the gun stocks were cut short for ease in handling. Our double box was used mainly for the Sports, especially at Christmas time. Father once bought a boat at Tilghman Island that still had the mast and center board in it. These we removed and converted the boat to power by installing two Model T Ford motors with 14 inch weedless props, one on each side of the keel. We put in the usual necessities and comforts, such as a stove, cots, and a table to make our work as easy and pleasant as possible. This boat would run in 20 inches of water. We also had a 23 foot gilling skiff, the *Nora M*, on which we carried the sink box, and two bushwhacking boats that carried between five hundred and fifty and six hundred decoys. We distributed them over the boats in a way to keep an even balance. From twelve to fifteen flat wooden decoys were placed on the wings of the box to help hide it. Some rigs used old railroad car brake shoes as anchors, by the way, but we used a good double fluke anchor made by a blacksmith at the head of the box and a small anchor at the foot.

Back in the 1915-1918 period, my father and Frank Jackson gunned together for the market. These double stools, with two sink boxes and one thousand decoys were quite a sight to see. Once they killed enough birds to fill a 1917 Model T touring car, seats removed, completely level. Another time, they took 97 shells with them and came back with 100 canvasbacks. During this time bushwhacking and floating blinds were also popular methods of hunting ducks on the Flats and its many coves. Pleasurable hours were spent by local men shooting from both boat and blind. Many's the time I've stood on the after-deck of a small clinker-built, double-end marsh boat and pushed with a pole for miles as my father stood a-midship. We killed numbers of reed birds, Virginia rail and King rail. Blue Wing teal, and pretty little summer ducks were plentiful in Principio Marsh, and occasionally we shot them while rail bird hunting.

Some of the hours were not exactly pleasant, however. Once in the first part of December we noticed thin ice as the tide started to ebb. As we lay at anchor the ice kept getting thicker and thicker. My father and Mr. Futty decided to take up the small anchor which had a rope line and to drop the heavy anchor with the chain line, as we expected to stay there until daylight. In the cabin we could hear the ice running up the chain. The pull was so great we could scarcely keep our balance. About 5:45 a.m. there came a sheet of thinner ice and father decided to put the whacking boat ahead and to go back up the river to Carpenter's Point where we could find some shelter. Before reaching the Point we broke ice three inches thick. Because the cold kept increasing during the day, father took us to a more protected harbor at Baker's Cove. We were iced in for three weeks! We had, however, contact with home, as we could walk to Wild Duck Cove where hunters maintained cabins. Since someone from here went into town daily, we could keep in contact. We stayed on the boat in shifts, Clarence with a man or two while father and I went home, and then it would be their turn to leave.

Wild Duck Cove, located on the north end of the Susquehanna Flats between High Point and Stump's Point, was close to good hunting areas, and was popular with a number of people. One of the best gunners from here was Ralph Murphy of Charlestown, Maryland.

I am very glad I can remember these wonderful days of gunning the sink boxes. Future generations can never know the thrill of real gunning, especially on my beloved Susquehanna Flats.

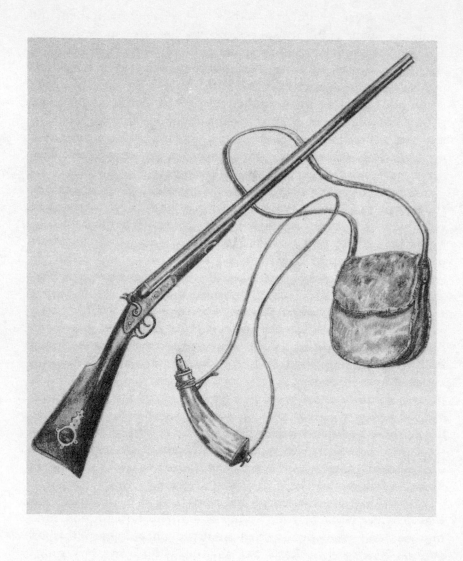

AND KEEP YOUR POWDER DRY

Colin Willcock

I knew that I wanted to include a look at wildfowling in the United Kingdom in The Duck Hunter's Book, *and when I ran across this piece in Willcock's book,* Landscape with Solitary Figure, *in the Princeton University Library, I knew that the search was over. Arrangements were made with his publisher, Longmans Green and Co. Ltd., London, but alas I can tell you nothing about the man himself. If there are more Willcock works like this lying around, American editors are missing a bet by not showcasing his work.*

IT ALL BEGAN with muzzle-loaders. Fill a muzzle-loader up with the right ingredients and it shoots as straight as a modern gun and in some respects a good deal more sweetly. It won't throw as tight a pattern because its barrels are innocent of those few vital inches of constriction towards the muzzle known as choke. That the barrels lack choke isn't surprising. The gunsmiths of a hundred years or more ago made their tubes in a relatively simple way. They took ribbons of soft iron, of which a vital component was said to be the heads of horseshoe nails, twisted these ribbons like sticks of curly liquorice, and then beat the results under cherry heat until it stuck together. The best Damascus barrels made in this way glimmered with a pattern like a mass of little metal roses preserved in a sleepy amber, the color of a well-smoked Meerschaum pipe. You didn't black barrels in those days: you browned them, and very beautiful it was. Add to those barrels a stock that shines like the rump of a thoroughbred chestnut, a lock that 'talks' with the confiding *tock* of a grandfather clock when you ease the hammers back, and you have something that must have looked like a fine antique the moment it was finished. A good muzzle-loader is not only a most handsome thing, it shoots hard and it shoots well. That's what the single mallard coming fast out of a November sunset discovered too late. It was important to me, that mallard. It was the bird that made me a wildfowler for the rest of my days.

I hadn't seen the duck coming, for the sun was low down over the muds which glowed like a red-hot plate whose farthest rim might have been Russia, or at least the fairway of the Medway estuary. All day I'd been nervous about firing the old gun. To tell the truth, I had my doubts about it, or me, being able to stand the shock of discharge. All day I had been spared the test. Nothing on wings had come my way. Now here was this mallard going inland to feed as if it had just been fired off a launching pad. I didn't have time to ponder the effects of those horsehoe nails coming unstuck after a hundred and a quarter years. I simply swung the gun at the fast disappearing duck and pulled. There was a gentle, gentlemanly *whoomp* quite unlike the nasty bad-tempered spat of a modern nitro-powdered gun. A leisurely cloud of white smoke billowed out accompanied by a stench of rotten eggs. There was little wind, so I had to take a pace to the right of the smoke cloud to observe the fall of shot. To my surprise I saw that the mallard was stone dead forty yards out in a creek that was fast filling with the tide. I collected both the duck and a waderful of water.

The fact that I was shooting with a muzzle-loader possibly needs a little explanation. At that time Jack Hargreaves and I were doing our best at least to postpone the demise of the magazine *Lilliput*. Whether we hastened or delayed its eventual, and probably inevitable, death I'm in no position to judge. It was in that post-war period when a ghastly falling sickness was beginning to attack the general magazines of Fleet Street. Our gambit for good or bad, or at least with the Management's cautious blessing, was to turn the gallant little monthly into a 'Man's Magazine.' Shooting and the outdoors, therefore, became a legitimate field of interest and, what was probably more important, one that delighted both of us. Jack Hargreaves has since come to the public eye as a television interviewer, though in his time he had been many more things than that: farmer's boy, trainee vet, dance-band promoter, writer, advertising man, magazine editor, advertising man again, and finally, though I hesitate to use the word finally about his career, a TV personality. Jack had a fine eye for the bizarre. That eye had now detected some especially bizarre correspondence in *The Shooting Times* between a group of sportsmen who shot regularly with muzzle-loading guns and were anxious to form an association of like spirits whose motto was to be 'Claret and Blackpowder.' One of the liveliest of these correspondents signed himself Richard Arnold. I was deputed to get in touch with him. Meantime, Hargreaves searched the junk shops of Edgeware Road and came back with a double-barreled 14-bore muzzle-loader complete with estuary rises in an archipelago of clay islands which are held together, but only just, by a carpet of scrub grass. The islands are topped here and there by wild rose bushes. To the south of the marsh there is a broken causeway that runs out half a mile or more towards the main river channel. Parallel to this, and about quarter of a mile distant, lies an ancient refueling jetty up which men cycle from time to time for no discernible purpose. Never mind why they cycle thus: when you are stranded on a lonely mud island with the tide flowing it is sometimes good to see another member of your race, even though he's half a mile away and can do nothing to help you, should the sea go mad and engulf you. On the northern side of the marsh there is a somewhat broader land-mass broken by deep creeks. The Isle of Grain oil refinery rises beyond this like the mirage of some inattainable, minareted eastern city. A slender tower rises among all the other shining aluminum temples. From this streams a long plume of yellow flame. The offering burns day and night. Its light is friendly powder and shot flasks and mahogany case fitted with all the original tools. Arnold turned out to be a little gnome of a man of hypermanic energy. He wore rimless octagonal glasses behind which his eyes shone with a frantic fanaticism. In a decrepit basement flat in Belsize Park, Arnold instructed me in the finer points of muzzle-loading. There, one winter's night, we poured out dollops of black powder before a roaring fire until three in the morning and then set off for the saltings of the North Kent coast.

These particular muds are a black, richly odorous morass of especially horrible viscosity. And yet, subsequently, I spent some of the most blissful hours of my life there. There are places in which the oozes are as soft as chocolate mousse and as tenacious as carpenter's glue. What is left of the land in this part of the Medway estuary rises in an archipelago of clay islands which are held together, but only just, by a carpet of scrub grass. The islands are topped here and there by wild rose bushes. To the south of the marsh there is a broken causeway that runs out half a mile or more towards the main river channel. Parallel to this, and about quarter of a mile distant, lies an ancient refueling jetty up which men cycle from time to time for no discernible purpose. Never mind why they cycle thus: when you are stranded on a lonely mud island with the tide flowing it is sometimes good to see another member of your race, even though he's half a mile away and can do nothing to help you, should the sea go mad and engulf you. On the northern side of the marsh there is a somewhat broader land-mass broken by deep creeks. The Isle of Grain oil refinery rises beyond this like the mirage of some inattainable, minareted eastern city. A slender tower rises among all the other shining aluminum temples. From this streams a long plume of yellow flame. The offering burns day and night. Its light is friendly and reassuring when slodging back to the sea wall in darkness after an evening flight with a quarter of a mile to go and the tide trying, as always, to win by outflanking.

To be far out on those grey muds is like wandering a world that man deserted long ago. Yet there are relics, often tragic relics, of his passing. Twisted pieces of tide sculpture reveal themselves as the bones of long dead aircraft. Above this wilderness were fought some of the bloodiest battles of the Few and the Many. Today it is no longer possible to tell whether the remains are those of Messerschmidt or Spitfire, Blenheim or Dornier. A wildfowling friend of mine did once find the skeleton of an airman, wearing, ten years after his final plunge, *Luftwaffe* identity tags. My friend dutifully reported his find to the police and promptly wished that he had left the German to lie in peace. The Constabulary called into action the whole rigmarole of inquest though there can, one would have thought, have been little doubt about the cause of death. Close by the unmarked grave of the dead flier lay scattered fragments of the very lives he came to destroy. Soon after the war causeways were built across the muds to the islands on the southern side of the estuary. The materials used were bricks smashed apart by German bombs during the London blitz. Among the mud-covered masonry: white shards of broken china, of prized best plates and Coronation mugs, tell you that this rubble was once the fabric of people's lives. On a chip of Royal Doulton I once found the perfect likeness of a flying snipe and, for no better reason than the strange appropriateness of its final resting place, put it in my pocket. I still have it.

Wartime associations apart, the muds at low water can be a grim place on a gray day. Then, as the tide flows, they are suddenly overwhelmed with life. Ducks begin to move in from the sea to find uncovered feeding grounds. Arrowheads of dunlin in close formation wing-whisper in along main channels and lilt over the sea walls. Wedges of curlew, with liquid bubbling call, flight in towards the land to feed where the tide cannot disturb them. Grey muds are at last drowned in blue water and the land, but for a few high points, have disappeared. Ships start to move upriver, seeming to slide across the land itself as some intervening island cuts them off from their natural element at the waterline.

The predominant thing about this marsh is its stench. I don't want to give the impression that the mud smelt evil. Far from it. Sometimes I can succeed in conjuring up that smell from memory. When I do, I experience almost total recall, remembering how a bunch of widgeon flew, the texture of a particular mussel scar, the way a certain red dawn broke. That marsh has one of the most evocative stenches I know. It should be easy to bring it back to the senses by sheer willpower of the imagination. But the blend is a subtle one. There is a touch of iodine, a hint of oysters, even of caviar about it. I suppose in the end it is just the smell of rich, stinking, estuarial mud. That mud when wet looks like something a beautician could sell in cartons as expensive skin tonic. In this respect only does it disappoint. Dry, it clings to the hands with the sandpapery clutch of a lizard. Whatever its delights and powers of evocation, it is certainly not the ideal compound in which to go muzzle-loading.

On a fine day on the marsh we muzzle-loaders were not at a great disadvantage. The drill took a bit more time than breech-loading, but then on a fine day, which is the worst possible day for wild-fowling, we did not get frequent opportunities to reload. There were, however, other drawbacks. The question of concealing ourselves from the fowl was one of them. You can slip a cartridge into a 12-bore easily enough when lying flat on your face in a creek, but just try pouring three drams of black down the spout in the same position. In ideal conditions it does not take more than twenty seconds a barrel to recharge a muzzle-loader, but then conditions on a salt marsh are seldom ideal. Whether in a downpour or on a useless, balmy day, the drill must be strictly observed if you want the gun to go off when the one chance at a duck presents itself. The drill goes like this:

Take powder flask set to the required measure for the gun. Invert with thumb over nozzle and flip back catch to release powder into measuring nozzle. Let catch fly back to trap powder. Turn flask right way up and then insert nozzle into muzzle pouring powder down. Tap butt against foot to insure powder has settled at base. Take felt wad, previously cut for purpose with plumber's punch, from pocket and stuff into muzzle. Ram it home with rod. Take shot flask, set to correct load. Place nozzle in muzzle and operate spring catch. Release, allowing correct shot load to fall down barrel. Take card wad from pocket and ram that. Repeat for second barrel. Rehouse ramrod, set hammers at half cock and put percussion caps on nipples. It sounds a lot, but I assure you that it can be done in the time, at least when standing up.

There are pitfalls to avoid, of course, and these are the same ones that trapped our ancestors. It is fairly easy in a moment of excitement to forget to withdraw the ramrod and to fire it out. Black powder being the gentle creature it is, the discharge does not usually blow up the gun. It does, however, end proceedings for the day unless you are very lucky. A ramrod will fly a surprising way, though, usually, with not sufficient accuracy to skewer a duck. In the wilderness of the muds it takes some finding. I know. Then again, when reloading after a single discharge there is the danger of forgetting which barrel you have fired, so you ram down a further charge on top of the one already in position. I saw this done once by a man who stood not much over five foot four. The gun held but the recoil laid the shooter flat on his back.

On howling wet days, no matter how much we trusted in God, it was almost impossible to keep our powder dry. The weak point was always the nipple on which the copper percussion cap perched ready for the moment of ignition. Water found its way down this pinprick orifice to the main charge. Once this had happened, no power on earth could send the gun off. The only course then was to insert the worm screw on the thin end of the ramrod, draw the charge painfully and start all over again. If you used lavatory paper for wadding as Arnold did this was a long and tricky process. Just the same, we became, in a perverted way, dedicated to our craft and I believe that if someone had offered us a brand-new Purdey each, we would have professed that there was nothing that shot quite like a muzzle-loader. And so we went on rolling our own and scoring a remarkable percentage of clean kills when our powder did ignite. And we persevered in a way that Colonel Hawker would have admired to perfect devices that might defeat the weather. As to the latter, the nearest we ever came to a solution was partially to encase a number of percussion caps in a short length of valve rubber. The rubber extended down onto the nipple when the cap was placed in position. If this didn't make the whole thing entirely waterproof, it did at least cut the chances of a misfire by about fifty per cent.

The eccentricity of muzzle-loading, of course, had its appeal but there was a stronger reason why I stuck to it long after the call of journalistic duty demanded. I was too broke to buy myself a modern gun and in those days soon after the war there were no cheap foreign imports on the market. In a theatrical costumer's I had found myself a beautiful single-barreled 10-bore by Hammond of Winchester, made about 1850. It cost me five pounds. I spent another thirty shillings on having it proved. For a long time I had to be content to shoot with that.

Despite the minor hazards of muzzle-loading, we never once got ourselves into trouble with our guns. The mud of that marsh was something else. It was a problem marsh. There was seldom any proper evening or morning flight. Rather, the birds were shifted around by the tide. The farther the tide ebbed out towards the main channel of the estuary a mile or two from the sea wall, the more the wigeon, mallard, teal, and waders retreated. This was natural and common enough. Obviously, freshly uncovered mud contains the richest feeding and the easiest pickings. When the tide 'made,' the reverse happened. The fowl were flooded off their feet and pushed in to find still dry muds where they could rest or feed. The tide, therefore, acted as our line of beaters. So far, so good, but the trick was to be in position when the tide moved the birds towards you. If you arrived too late, you'd find the whole marsh under ten feet of water with just the tops of a few mud islands showing. When the ebb came, it left behind strong rearguards in the form of filled gutters that were impossible to cross without a boat. By the time these had emptied, tide and birds had receded far beyond our reach. One answer was to plowter out through the mud at dead low water and allow yourself to be cut off on one of the islands. But this meant that you had to be out for twelve hours at least. The tide times, together with the demands of our domestic and working lives, did not often permit this. Such a tactic brought its moments of anxiety, too. It called for close study of the tide tables. On a Springer you were quite likely to find your nice dry island disappearing under a few feet of water.

We tried all manner of ways to defeat the tides. Some I remember vividly.

The second time I visited the marsh we took with us an eighteen stone, six-foot-six, press photographer called Tiny Bennett. Bennett, too, was a muzzle-loading man, though his real mission on this occasion was to take photographs of Arnold and myself for *Lilliput*. It was a long time short of daylight when the *Alvis* put us down behind the sea wall. In fact it was four a.m. on a windy, blistering, clear January morning.

Arnold, despite the fact that he had sat bolt upright and unprotected from the frost in the dickey seat throughout a two-hour journey, emerged brisk and eager to unfold his plan. For myself, I wondered, as I have wondered behind sea walls in spitting, hissing darkness many times since, just why on earth I had come.

In the distance the flaming plume of the refinery was spun out to twice its normal length by the icy gale. Arnold announced with genuine rapture that it was 'a lovely morning.'

A peep over the wall confirmed the fact that the tide had only just started to drop. We, said Arnold, would follow it out and be on the farthest knob of land, a mile offshore, by the time the dawn came up and the widgeon began to whistle as thick as a swarm of bees past our ears. He then produced from his shoulder-pack his surprise weapon, two coal shovels and a one-man R.A.F. rescue dinghy. With the aid of these, he explained, we would paddle our way across the bad gutters and thus be out ahead of the falling tide.

A night march through mud, even when you're used to it, is a depressing experience. We reached the first bad gutter after twenty sweating minutes. In that light, indeed in any light, it was an evil-looking chasm. Black water swept through it at a pace slightly below that of a mill race. Steep mud banks towered up from the primeval ooze. Arnold blew up his dinghy, seized his coal shovels and, declaring that he would show us how easy it was, launched himself on the ebb. The coal shovels never got a chance to take a grip. The tide, which went out through that gully like the last of the bath water, whisked him out of sight at once. The last I saw of him, and the last I expected to see of him, he was lying helplessly on his back like a man trapped in a narrow hip bath, staring livid-faced up at the moon. The sightless stars twinkled defiantly in his octagonal glasses, as he was swept, as far as I could tell, direct into the North Sea. Bennett and I sat down and waited for the tide to make the gutter wadeable. We did not see Dick Arnold again until well after daylight. By that time he had shot three wigeon, having, as he said, had a lovely ride. Tiny Bennett and I, behind the birds and behind the ebb, never got a shot.

Just as we were always advancing behind the tide, so we were constantly having to fall back just ahead of it. The retreat called for nice timing. Though the islands and the mud lagoons all around you might look safe and dry, it was only too easy to get cut off. The first of the tide came in and with a rush up the deep

mud gullies hidden in the main creeks. Quite early in the proceedings, these filled the treacherous gutters that lay in the rear
across our lines of communication. Perhaps because these places
were immersed for longer than the other parts of the muds, they
contained the most glutinous and dangerous ooze. The trick of
mud-walking is fairly easy once you have mastered it. In essence
it is to skate on the surface as much as possible and to keep moving.
Once you stop in a bad place, your troubles start. One late afternoon,
when it was nearly dark, Bennett stopped in the worst possible
place, in that same creek where Arnold had disappeared in his
rubber hip-bath. He stopped and at once began to sink. I came
upon him a few minutes later, floundering like one of those
mammoths caught in the Trinidad pitch lakes. A good deal of his
eighteen stone had already sunk from view. He was hull-down to
his thighs. The tide was already pointing a gray finger of scummy
water up the gully towards him. We had a good laugh about it,
and then suddenly realised that within an hour or so the water
would be well above his head. The first of the flow had already
filled in the morass made by his flounderings when Arnold arrived.
He had seen this sort of thing before and knew what we were too
green to know: that the best thing to do when you are trapped
like this is to lie down flat on your back and try to wriggle out of
your boots. We laid a gas cape down and started to tug at the
wallowing monster's armpits. We were fairly desperate by now,
for the mud was getting even tackier as the tide seeped up through
it. Maybe this loosening of its individual particles helped a little.
When we at last got Bennett out, his body was half awash. We
never saw his boots again.

The malevolent mud was waiting for Jack Hargreaves, too.
We took him down one February night and introduced him to
the marsh. Though he had shot all his life, he had never tried the
saltings before. We left the sea wall at four a.m. at dead low water,
intending to stay out on the islands and return about twelve the
next morning. It was very cold and wet. Jack stepped off dry land
on to his first stretch of mud and was instantly sucked out of both
boots. He was to stay in his mud-plastered stockings for much
longer than we had forecast. We didn't get off at midday the next

morning. It was dark the next night before we were able to regain the sea wall. We had hit a North Sea surge, a minor version of the disastrous 1953 flood. The tide, scheduled in the tables as a big one, rose eleven feet above its predicted level.

When dawn came there was nothing unusual about the scene except that the weather was perfect for a change with the sort of gale wildfowlers pray for howling in from the open sea. Already there were big packs of widgeon moving in from the tide line and black trips of waders skimming in along the fast-filling creeks. We thought that this was going to be a good one and for once we were right.

Jack and I began to shoot as soon as it was half light. I was confident in the invulnerability of our island. It had always ridden well out of the water even on a spring tide. Arnold had that day elected to experiment with a much lower and so far untried dot of land farther inshore. We heard his gun going and watched a couple of ducks fall out of the sky. The tide continued to build up at what looked like a normal pace throughout the morning. By eleven, when it should have been 'full,' it was still rising fast. By then we had done well, collecting ten widgeon, a pintail, and a mallard. I was now watching the line of floating driftwood for the turn, but the flotsam kept on moving up the grass towards us. To our rear Arnold's island had gone completely under. He now appeared as if walking rather inefficiently upon the water, a foreshortened figure cut off at the ankles. Arnold was still shooting from time to time though with no chance of picking what he shot. We decided that he must have been doing it to keep his spirits up. There were plenty to shoot at. Packs of widgeon zithered past us like volleys of arrows. Golden-eye, scaup, mallard, shoveler, pintail, teal, mobs of curlew, smoke clouds of knot, mixed formations of waders that included godwit, dunlin and redshank soared and piped around. By now the grass under our own feet was becoming soggy with sea water. Something had gone wrong. Because there wasn't any inch of mud in the estuary on which a bird could sit, everything on wings was airborne. At the height of it all, twenty-three whitefronted geese came cackling over our heads. But we had now given up shooting, for there was no sense in knocking something down if you couldn't collect it.

We could still see Arnold or rather about half of him. Just when it seemed that his time must have come, a broken box which had slowly been nudging its way up the grass towards my feet began to tilt and settle. Three hours behind time, the tide had decided to return the way it had come. At six o'clock the water was low enough for us to make a retreat. We had picked twelve duck and Arnold ten. We found him sitting on the sea wall, quite cheerful though wet to the navel. We asked him if he had thought he was going to drown that time. 'I got a little worried.' he said, 'when I saw a field mouse begin to climb the only bush on the island.'

Next season we took a boat. It was a marine-bonded plywood dinghy which Jack Hargreaves had built from a kit. Two fit men could lift and carry it fairly comfortably but we were seldom fit when we came in off the muds. Dragging it out to load was an oozy torture of considerable refinement. That boat was the direct cause of the one and only swim I have made in December. We had put the dinghy into a creek beside the sea wall in order to row out down the causeway as the tide began to flow. We had, however, forgotten the rowlocks. Foolishly, I volunteered to go back to the car for them. When I reached the foreshore, Arnold was well out down the main creek and apparently paddling hard away from me. What I didn't realize was that a brisk offshore wind had sprung up and made his return for me without the aid of rowlocks impossible. I stood on my mud-spit shouting and cursing until I looked round and found thirty yards of deep water had crept in between me and the shore. The situation plainly wasn't going to get any better. In fact it was rapidly getting a lot worse. The tide, held back by the wind, was now swinging in fast. Sadly I took off all my clothes, stuffed them into one wader, my gun and ammunition into the other, then I began the bitterest swim of my life. I made two trips, a wader at a time. I had never dreamed how inadequate a string vest is as substitute for a towel.

By the third season we had become a little less broke and a good deal more sophisticated. Muzzle-loaders only came out now on ceremonial occasions. We all had scraped together breech-loading

12-bores. In addition we were accumulating a sub-collection of curios. For some reason that now escapes me I had bought a double 6-bore muzzle-loader that was far too much metal to carry for its slender return in added distance and load. Jack Hargreaves had materialized with a single breech-loading 4-bore weighing sixteen pounds, which threatened to bury whoever carried it into the morass of the bad gutter. I did once trim out five teal from a bunch with this monster but, since flock shooting never appealed and I had learned to travel as light as possible on the muds, I never tried again with it. I had come to the conclusion early in that a three-inch 12-bore is as much gun as a wildfowler can use or needs. Nevertheless, these experiments with big gunnery coupled with the intractability of the dinghy were turning our thoughts in a quite different direction.

By next season we had built a light gunning punt and big gun. Hargreaves, a fine craftsman with wood, designed and built the little one-man boat. I was responsible for finding a serviceable half-pound muzzle-loading punt gun and converting it into a breech-loader. In the event, Hargreave's part of the operation was the more successful. His craft floated. My gun blew up in proof. But when the wigeon came in that year we were ready to go afloat for them. A gun shop in Cambridge had found us a double 4-bore whose barrels were said to be sound enough for simultaneous discharge. We tested them with a leather lanyard and found that the gunsmith had spoken the truth. The gun, an under-lever Reilly, hurled its combined double load of six ounces of BB with a heart-stopping thump and a fine tight pattern.

Never let people tell you that punting is an unsportsmanlike enterprise simply because it offers you a sitting shot. Punting is the least efficient way of harvesting duck that man ever invented. It is one of the most uncomfortable. It is also one of the most exciting.

Our marsh never provided us with large concentrations of water-borne duck. If I'd ever been faced with a raft of a thousand widgeon, as the old-time punters often were, my heart would probably have knocked the bottom boards out of the boat before I could pull the string. Little parties of ten or twenty were the best we could hope to find and then only in the early morning light when the tide was right and one could drift in with the land as a backdrop and catch them on the grass edge along the causeway or round one of the islands.

I don't suppose we were very expert at it and our punt was possibly a little too beamy. Our object had been to make it capable not only of taking punter but also transporting a shoulder gunner to some suitable vantage point where he could be dropped off. It was thus a dual-purpose craft and like most things with two objects in life it did neither one of them superbly well.

Its extra beam was apt to catch wind and tide just at the wrong moment. You'd be creeping up to a group of widgeon, paddling gently over the side with your wrists immersed in the icy sea and the little butter-pat paddles feathering softly beneath the surface, when the wind would catch you and just take the knife-edge off your bows so that the duck got a glimpse of one of your flanks. Then up would go their heads. You'd pray hard and give the boat just one last push. But they'd be up, catapulting themselves off the surface with that near vertical take-off that baffles the shoulder gunner with his feet planted on more or less firm earth, let alone the frozen, prone punter with his non-mobile siege artillery. Just occasionally you caught it right. Then there'd be a *whoompf* and a cloud of black-powder smoke and, if you were very lucky, half a dozen duck dead on the water. We seldom got more.

In the end we gave up punting. Our professed reason was that you needed more time than we could spare to make a go of it. There were so many days when the tides or the weather or the duck weren't right. In fact, very few indeed when they were. We told each other that one needed to live right on the sea wall to follow punting seriously. But there was more to it than that. Punting is sport all right, infuriating, thrilling sport, and I don't wish to say a word against anyone who likes it. But it does produce a lot of crippled birds and you cannot always dispatch or gather them all. I'm glad I've done it but I don't think that I want to do it again.

Nowadays I haven't much time for the hairy-shirted attitude of many wildfowlers. Their sport is a tough one, but then nobody asked them to join. On the whole it's probably tougher on the duck who may end up dead. So to me it doesn't seem appropriate to go around telling people how hard it all is, because you do it, after all, of your own free choice and presumably for pleasure. We did things the hard way those first four or five seasons on the marsh and I've never regretted it, though I'm a bit more cautious these days. I'm not denying that there can be a slight risk in coastal fowling, and in fog or gale more than a slight one, though you're a fool if you take it. Just the same, the thought that the risk is there does add a spice to things. That the tide is coming in sure as Doomsday keeps you on your toes and at times may even cause you to stand on them. The chance of ducking apart, the point which for me makes the saltings the most exciting place in the world is that for once in your overgrown, hothouse, automated life you are depending on your native wits. That, in this day, is an exalting feeling.

I don't believe that wildfowling has anything to do with shooting a lot of duck. I've very rarely done so and when I have succeeded I've usually regretted it. Nowadays, if things go right for me, which is very seldom, I stop when I've got enough and this can vary from four to a dozen depending on who wants to eat them. Wildfowling is the place, the smell, the cut-offness, the fact that people who *only* go ten-pin bowling can't really know that they're alive. It's also the ducks themselves and especially the widgeon. It's their hock bottle shapes hurtling through the darkness, their lost spirit cry, and their journeyings from such unimaginably far-off and cold places. Kamchatka, the Don, the Dnieper, Turkestan, and the open tundra. How did they ever manage to navigate to the Norfolk Coast or the Thames estuary? I hope that by the time I'm too rheumaticky to wade the bad gutter, someone will kindly carry me over and prop me up in the spartina grass so that I can at least watch the widgeon whistle over, for by then, I think, I shall have got over wanting to shoot at them. But not yet, not quite yet.

MAINE AND NEW ENGLAND

Raymond R. Camp

In this second piece from Duck Boats: Blinds: Decoys and Eastern Seaboard Wildfowling, *(Knopf), Ray Camp continues southward along the Atlantic Coast in the wildfowler's journey that began in the Maritimes. Now we enter the area where names like Merrymeeting Bay have created legends and lore dear to the hearts of all waterfowl lovers.*

IT HAS been said that the Maine waterfowl-resources have never been tapped, a statement that requires no explanation if a map is at hand, for one glance at the coastline stretching from Passamaquoddy to Cape Elizabeth provides the answer. A million duck-hunters could find a measure of solitude on the countless bays, coves, rivers, and island channels rimming this jigsaw fringe.

Maine has its full quota of waterfowl enthusiasts, and it never fails to attract a legion of visitors, but they have no excuse for getting in each other's way. From the opening of the scoter season in late September, until the last redleg has flared over the decoys in December, guns are booming along the tidewater. There are a few areas where gunners are rather concentrated, such as the margins of Merrymeeting, Penobscot, and Casco Bays, but for the most part you can sit in a blind for days without hearing the report of a gun other than your own.

Although the black ducks, whistlers, and scaup seem to be as plentiful as ever, and mergansers are literally a "dime a dozen," some of the species once common to many Maine marshes are no longer found in numbers. The teal, once an important bird to the Maine wildfowler, arrives too early for really good shooting, and the mallards, pintails, widgeon, redheads, and canvasbacks are less plentiful. Even the geese, which once thronged Merrymeeting, are less inclined to linger. Some of this decline is marked down to encroaching civilization and pollution, and while this might have some influence on the puddle-duck situation, the veteran duck-hunters are inclined to attribute it to a shift in the migration routes of these species. A few oldtimers, with some bitterness, attribute the poor gunning in some areas to the presence of the sanctuaries that have been created, and there is pressure to have some of these refuges opened to limited shooting, similar to that at the Mattamuskeet refuge in North Carolina.

Merrymeeting, like other popular waterfowl-areas, developed a duck boat to facilitate the various forms of shooting done on its marshes and open water, but the utility of this craft has been reduced by a shift in shooting practices, and perhaps even in the types of waterfowl. The Merrymeeting boat is a big one, compared to the scooter or the sneak box, or the universal "grass boat," and it was designed to be sculled rather than rowed or poled. The last three Maine guides with whom I hunted from one of these boats not only had no knowledge of sculling, but were not even equipped with one of the typical, crooked sculls. Although it has more freeboard and a longer, broader cockpit than the conventional duck-boat, it can be grassed up very effectively, and has the advantage of providing plenty of room for two shooters.

In the days of market gunning, the Merrymeeting boat had real utility. It offered safe passage across open water, even under rough weather-conditions, and when grassed up it could be sculled up to rafts of ducks without difficulty. Also, its shallow draft permitted passage up the tidal creeks and guzzles. Today, much of the Maine shooting is done from permanent blinds, or from boat-hides in the grass or rushes, and it is rare that a guide can be persuaded to scull up to rafted birds.

On most of the coastal areas the floating blind and the island blind, constructed of available rocks, is favored for black duck, whistler, and scaup shooting. The floating blind, while it is rather complex in architecture, is one of the most comfortable hides the wildfowler will ever encounter. It is large enough to permit a skiff to be drawn inside, and beneath the brush and grass exterior is a sheathing of canvas or wood which keeps out the bitter winds prevalent during the late season.

My first experience with these blinds was with Elmore Wallace, one of Maine's Sea and Shore Fishery wardens, who cannot understand any man who would not forego such elementary activities as eating or sleeping in order to hunt ducks. Elmore's blind sticks up like the proverbial sore thumb between two pine- and spruce-clad islands on the inner rim of Casco Bay. One of these islands harbors a tiny, shingled "shanty" theoretically designed for sleeping and eating, but as Elmore is constantly leaving this sanctuary to sniff the wind and listen, both meals and repose are haphazard in the extreme, for he likes company when he sniffs and listens.

Elmore is a firm believer in oversized decoys and, while making his watery rounds in an ancient but seaworthy cruiser aptly named the *Mackerel Cove Whizzer*, he gathers up all flotsam and jetsam in the form of composition cork. These blocks he whittles and rasps down in his spare time, and eventually they take the form of king-sized black ducks, whistlers, and broadbill. His decoy rig is an enviable one, and every decoy is set out with studied care. It must be admitted, in all justice, that the method and equipment pays off, for usually we manage a limit when others in that general area are dozing in their blinds and cursing the bluebird weather.

My first day in one of these floating islands was a memorable one. We were a bit late getting to the blind, as Elmore sheared a pin on the outboard motor on one of the few hidden rocks in that bay with which he was not familiar—or which he had forgotten in view of his anxiety to get rigged out. As I mentioned, decoy placement is a fetish with him, and he would not let me row to the "gates" of the blind until every block had been placed to his satisfaction, both from the point of pattern and distance.

"You sit on the left," he suggested. "Most of the birds will lead up from the left, and I want you to get some shooting. I can shoot here any day, but your time is limited."

Like many of the Maine wildfowlers, Elmore prefers the slide or "pump" action, and his was a magnum twelve. I then learned that he had the decoys so placed that any duck passing "inside" an outer decoy would be within range.

"You take the birds leading from the left," he advised, "and I'll take those coming in or over from the right. If a big bunch come in from your side you take the rear half, and I'll do the same if several come in my end."

As this was routine, I nodded my agreement.

A few seconds later three blacks winged our way, craning their necks at the decoys, but apparently they decided to swing to the right over the decoys and make a circle to come in upwind. Before I could move, Elmore rose to his feet and the magnum began to belch shot from one end and shells from the other. The three shots were almost as one, and the three blacks folded in that abrupt manner which indicated they were each right in the center of the pattern.

"I was afraid they weren't going to come around," he explained, "so I decided to take a chance."

While we were retrieving these three, two other bunches appeared but cut away at the sight of the skiff, and Elmore almost lifted the heavy boat out of the water at every thrust of the oars in order to get back to the blind.

We were no more than settled when seven more blacks appeared from downwind, flared up, made a high, wide circle, then set their wings to come in. I waited for Elmore's grunt, then rose to my feet and swung for the fourth bird, but before I could get lined up and touch the trigger there was a "brrrrp" on the right and the first four birds folded. I recovered just in time to get one of the remaining birds. Elmore had fired only twice, but two birds happened to be in the pattern of each load.

"Ain't that hell," my companion grumbled. "Those birds coming together that way cut down the fun of shooting. That's two less we can shoot at."

I decided that I would have to condition myself to quick shooting if I wanted to use any shells. The limit at that time was twenty birds, for two gunners, and with only a half hour gone we had eight ducks in the boat.

A half hour passed before any ducks came within range, although several small bunches of scaup swung our way and one bunch of whistlers tried to make up their collective minds about joining the decoys behind us. Then a long string of whistlers swept past low, made a sharp swing, and were almost over the decoys before I realized they were coming in.

"Whistlers behind," I whispered to Elmore, who had been concentrating on five hesitating black ducks. As I spoke I rose and swung to the rear. This time I had the pleasure of getting two down before Elmore unlimbered his gun, but he managed to drop the straggler.

Two wedges of geese came over, and we held our breaths while they cackled and gabbled at each other in a debate as to whether those ducks around that little brushy island were finding plenty to eat. One gosling broke away and dropped down to look the situation over at closer range, but he was not foolish enough to come within reach of Elmore's Long Tom. I could feel my companion tense as the big bird swept past, but the gosling apparently reported in the negative, for the two echelons finally appeared southward.

"I was tempted to strain the barrel on him," Elmore admitted, "but I thought there was a chance the others might come down for a closer look. Chances are these number fives wouldn't have reached him with enough punch to do any harm."

Elmore's only miss came next, when a lone black swept straight over the blind from behind, and caught him unawares. Even then he might have connected, had the duck not flared and towered just as he rose up.

The only redleg of the day then appeared on my side, and swept in low just inside the outside decoys. I under-led him on the first barrel, and saw the shot spatter one of Elmore's fancy decoys, but the second barrel tumbled the duck just as my companion brought his gun up.

I then proceeded to miss a lone, lonesome pintail, which caught me unprepared, but the bird flared to the right and passed within range of Elmore's lethal gaspipe. It was a beautiful drake, and only the second my companion had seen that season.

Three more blacks, two of which fell to Elmore, and four whistlers, three of them mine, finished our day, and when we returned to the island shanty for lunch it was exactly noon.

Elmore's only comment was that we should have been all through by ten o'clock.

Late in the season, when the redlegs have arrived, and the temperature has dropped down to a point that makes taking a deep breath a punishment, there is excellent shooting from the tiny rocky islets, especially if there is enough wind to drive the birds from the open water. Both blacks and whistlers decoy readily, and the gunner crouched in a makeshift rock-blind can usually get a quick limit if he is not too numbed by the cold to raise his gun. Two years ago Elmore wrote that he had his limit in a few minutes, and waited two hours for his companion to pick him up in the boat.

"During that time," he explained, "I could have killed more than 150 ducks without any trouble, and when the boat finally arrived there were at least fifty birds sitting right among the decoys. If only you could spread that kind of shooting over the season."

My first trip to Merrymeeting Bay was with another warden, John Perkins of the Inland Service, who was one of the oldest wardens in the state, both in years and service. John had spent more than sixty years on the bay, and had never killed a goose. As these birds were really plentiful during his younger days, he was inclined to mark the situation down to a perverse fate.

Although a wind sprang up at first light, while John was sculling the boat to the point he had decided on for the day, it faded out by sunup, and took on all the aspects of perfect bluebird-weather. After an hour the old warden shook his head.

"For all the shooting we're going to get we might as well be home in bed, but we're out here, so we might as well hope for the best."

For two hours I stretched out comfortably in the old Merrymeeting boat and listened to John's stories of the "old days," of the market gunners and their muzzle-loading four- and eight-gauge guns, and the toll a good sculler could take by grassing up his boat and drifting down on a big raft of ducks. He had just begun on his ill-fated experience with geese when he paused to listen.

A faint "Aaaahnk, aaahnk, aaahnk" drifted to us, and looking eastward we saw a long V of honkers crossing the bay about fifty feet off the water, and headed straight for our position.

"Maybe," John whispered, "just maybe, I'll get a goose before I die."

The leader of the flight apparently saw the half-dozen goose decoys John had placed to the left of the duck rig, for he emitted a few more "Aaahnks" and dropped still lower.

"For God's sake," John whispered, "don't even blink your eyes. I think they're going to sit right down with the decoys."

And there is every chance they would have done just that. But there are trigger-happy gunners even on Merrymeeting, and just as the big gander set his wings an idiot in a point blind fully two hundred yards to our left blasted away.

The geese gabbled wildly and made a climbing turn that took the them back toward the open bay.

John seemed to take it philosophically.

"Oh, well," he sighed, "I knew something would happen. It always has."

Shortly before eleven o'clock a half-dozen shelldrakes swung around the point, were serenaded by our goose-scaring friends, then made a circle and sat down among our decoys.

"Live decoys are illegal," my companion grunted, "but there's no law says we have to shoot a bunch of fish ducks if we don't want to. Let 'em swim around. They may attract an eatin' duck."

At the change of tide, a half hour later, several bunches of black began moving up the bay, and six circled our decoys, dropping in along the rim of the marsh out of gunshot to our left. Our trigger-happy friends decided to leave their blind and creep through the grass in an effort to get within range, but the ducks were alert, and jumped before they could get a shot. Fortunately they passed straight over us, not more than thirty feet high, and we dropped four of them almost within an oar's length of the boat. One of the pair made another swing to see what had happened to his friends, and we added him to the bag. In an hour we had twelve birds, and as the flight had stopped we decided to call it a day.

As we passed wide of the point on our way home, three geese appeared from the open bay, circled high, then dropped down to the very spot where we had been rigged out.

John watched them for several minutes, the crooked scull resting idly in its socket, then shrugged.

"I told you it's all a matter of fate,"

Some of the Maine shooters carry their love of creature comfort to the extreme. Not wanting to be subjected to the discomfort of a blind or boat, they have solidly built structures along the shore, only part of the "den" protruding from the soil, and with the roof well-camouflaged with sod and reeds. The decoys are fixed to triangle-and-T frames, and are hauled in and out by means of a windlass in the "blind," the ropes running to underwater pulleys set fifty yards out into the water.

Inside these warm shelters, equipped with stoves, chairs, and often a poker table, the gunners take their ease until the watching guide reports that a bunch of ducks or geese has dropped in among the decoys. Each man then languidly picks up his fowling piece, loads it, takes his appointed place, and prepares to shoot. The hinged upper portion of the shelter is then dropped, and the shooters pick their targets. When the guide has hauled the upper wall back in place he departs to pick up the dead birds, and the "gunners" return to their game, coffee, highball, or conversation. The rigors of an open boat, or a drafty blind, are not for this coterie. That, they point out, would be doing it the hard way.

The channels and guzzles of several of the bays, forming narrow, reed-fringed aisles at high water, provide good jump-shooting on occasion, and often a bluebird day is saved by this expedient. That is, of course, if you happen to have a guide who is not averse to the exercise involved. On some of the rivers the old market-gunner's method is still followed, although today the birds are not killed on the water as they were in those carefree days. A set of decoys will be rigged out along the fringe of a wide channel, and the duck boat will be sculled to a hide from two to three hundred yards distant. The shooters will wait until a few birds have dropped in on the decoys, then scull up to the rig and get their shooting when the birds jump.

I have found little wildfowling worth mentioning on the inland lakes of the state, except for shelldrakes, and few gunners are willing to travel any distance to shoot these birds. I did get several good days on blacks and teal many years ago on the big lakes near Princeton, but most of the birds were refugees from the St. Croix River.

The first day, as an experiment, we rigged out in a grassy cove about a mile from the junction of Grand Falls Lake and the St. Croix. The birds were trading up and down the river in good numbers, and some flights cut across the upper end of the lake, but not a duck that passed gave our decoys the corner of its eye. We were shooting with the late Levi Dow, later Warden Supervisor of Aroostook County. When you sat in a blind with Levi, duck shooting became secondary, for of all the tale-spinners in the world, none could approach him. Levi was never without a few pieces of soft, white pine and a sharp knife, and by noon the blind was knee-deep in shavings, for he never made anything—he just whittled.

After consuming some sandwiches and at least a gallon of strong, black tea, Levi regarded the larder with a frown.

"It's all well and good for you to sit here and gabble all morning," he announced (we had said probably ten words), "but unless one of us kills some ducks this afternoon we're going to eat potatoes and *withem* for supper. Potatoes are plentiful in this county, and there are none better, but no matter what kind of seasoning you put on *withem* it hasn't got any body to it. Looks like you'd better make some sort of noise on that gun of yours."

He regarded the upper end of the lake for several minutes.

"I've been watching that grassy point up there, and it looks to me as though a lot of ducks are flying straight over it, about fifty feet high. Think you might hit some of them if we went up there and sat in the grass?"

I ventured a guess that I might be able to get one or two, if they kept flying low and straight, so we picked up the decoys and departed for the point.

It was almost three o'clock when we burrowed into the grass, and a half hour later we loaded the limit of blacks and teal into the boat and headed for camp. The next day we slept late, for there was no point in turning out before daybreak to get that kind of pass shooting. By taking only the more difficult birds, we stretched out the shooting for more than an hour.

The following year we returned, and spent the entire day getting three ducks. Which, in the final analysis, is wildfowling in its typical form.

SKYFUL OF BRIGHT WINGS

Russell Annabel

Although his name is synonymous with Alaskan big game hunting, Russell Annabel's talent as a writer was evidenced in a wide range of subjects. The majority of his stories appeared in Sports Afield, *but many ran in* Field & Stream, True, *and other magazines. Annabel's stories have a strong narrative sense, good pace, powerful description, and compelling action. Ted Kesting, my predecessor at* Sports Afield, *felt that Annabel's regular appearances were one of the keys to the magazine's growth in the forties and fifties. After he moved to Mexico to live for the last thirty years of his life (he passed away there in the late seventies), Annabel continued to write about Alaska, as well as Mexican hunting and fishing. Little of Rusty's (as Ted called him) work has been anthologized. Copies of the huge and magnificent* Hunting and Fishing in Alaska, *published by Knopf and long out of print, today fetch hefty prices in the out-of-print sporting collection markets. Even though he was accused of too much "invention" in some of his later pieces, Annabel's early efforts from* Hunting and Fishing in Alaska *have not been diminished by time. They're still as fresh to me as a blast of wind off glacial ice.*

"GIT SET," Tex warned Doc. "Here comes the first bunch o' them big ice-bustin', blizzard-bangin' ducks ya been hollerin' fer."

"Qu-ACK, qu-ACK, qu-ACK, w-HUTT, w-HUTT, w-HUTT!" Doc called lustily.

They were mallards and they were coming in from the drab tidal flats, beating strongly into the hard offshore wind, their vividly patched wings flashing in the morning sunlight. They looked as large as geese as they began circling warily just out of range, turning their heads from side to side, staring down at our spread of decoys. You could see that they were northern ducks in full winter plumage, the heads, necks, and breasts of the drakes dark and gleaming, as if they'd had a copper-and-jet wash. When they had circled us three times, they swung back downwind and headed in, wings set for a landing outside the decoys, in true dipper duck fashion. At the last moment, as they were braking down to kill their speed, just starting to reach out with their orange feet, we stood up and opened fire. Doc and I got two apiece with our twin-bores, but Tex, strictly an automatic fancier, downed three.

Our Chesapeakes, Shot and Flaps, shuttled the birds in to us. Four of them were drakes, averaging about three and a half pounds apiece. Their crops were filled with frost-ripened brown saw-grass seeds and they were butter-fat, as these mallards from the high north always are. Doc stood admiring them and affectionately fondling his call.

"Worked like a charm," he said, all his two hundred and fifty pounds registering satisfaction. "From now on, duck hunting is gonna be twice as easy and three times as much fun. I shoulda learned how to call 'em years ago."

"They were comin' in anyhow," Tex said judgmatically. "They'd made up their minds. You couldn't of chased 'em off with a club. They prob'ly hadn't seen no sure-enough open water fer weeks afore they got here."

"I called 'em in," Doc said, his voice rising. "You know damned well I did."

Doc and Tex patently were started on another of their friendly but acrimonious arguments.

We were on the broad, October-tinted Matanuska Hay Flats, thirty-seven miles north of Anchorage, at the head of Knik Arm, a narrow branch of Cook Inlet. Six years had passed since we had last hunted here. In that time the countryside had undergone large and drastic changes. Land-hungry farmers and stockmen had pushed the birch and spruce forest back nearly to the snow-topped mountains, and in its place were roads, farmsteads, fields, and fences. Stock grazed where once Tex and I had hunted moose and trapped wolves and foxes. Out across the amber flats floated the sound of cowbells, of hammering, of tractor engines. Civilization had moved in. One thing here, however, hadn't been changed. There were still plenty of ducks and geese.

All about us the hazy sky was crisscrossed with cobwebby patterns of waterfowl. There was white weather from Point Barrow to the Yukon Basin, and ice was making on the lakes and streams, forcing the birds south. During the night, through the open upstairs window of the ranch house in which we were staying, we had heard the flights coming over—ducks, geese, swans, and cranes—the whistle of duck wings over the stubble fields and, high up against the misty stars, the wild, sweet clangor of great flocks of southbound geese. The ancient magic of this music had drawn hunters from fifty miles around. They had arrived by train and in trucks, Jeeps, and touring cars. It was the largest assembly of scattergun-toting, duck-happy hunters I had ever seen in the north. I hadn't heard such shooting since the last few desperate days in Okinawa.

"The boys're jest findin' out," Tex said, "that we got some birds up here." He shook his head and grinned. "Listen to that bombardment. They's anyhow six hunderd hunters out here on four square miles o' flats an' they'll shoot an average o' two boxes o' shells apiece. That's thirty thousand rounds, an' hit figgers out to about forty shots a minute. The ducks'll keep a-movin' today, all right."

A ragged fusillade of shots sounded three hundred yards upwind, and as we turned, here came a flock of about twenty pintails. They had a quarter-gale of wind behind them, they were scared, and they were pouring on the coal. Somebody once figured out that a pintail's top speed is sixty-two miles an hour, but he should have clocked this flock. I'll bet they were doing ninety. They were burning holes in the sky. But they wanted to come down. They saw our decoys and turned back to inspect them. They circled only once, then buzzed down in a dizzy, zigzagging dive, only to flare just out of gun range and climb for another look. The fact that we had mallard decoys out didn't make any difference. I don't know how it is elsewhere, but here in the north the mallards and pintails get along famously. Where you find one species, you usually find the other. They feed together, migrate together, and on occasion even interbreed. Doc hadn't learned how to call pintails, so he kept his call in his pocket. But Tex, who can call anything—bears, moose, foxes, wolves, hawks, and all sorts of waterfowl—whistled softly. The flock started down, talking confidently to him, and this time they meant it.

We opened up on them when they were at an angle of fifty degrees. I swung through with a handsome long-necked drake and dropped it, then turned and tried with the other barrel as they were going away from us. It was a waste of ammunition. I never do hit high-angle birds when they are going away from me. I always shoot too soon and the charge goes a yard or so behind the bird. Tex says my system is the opposite of what it should be. He says you shouldn't try to take ducks coming in at long range because then their feathers often will turn the shot; but when they are going away from you, he says, the shot goes in under the feathers and gets you something. I suppose he is right about it, but the method is not for me. I will take them coming in. They are my meat then, regardless of Tex's feather theory.

Tex and Doc had each killed two. The five ducks hurtled down the wind forty yards and thudded into a thicket of scarlet wolf-willows. Shot and Flaps streaked after them, and Tex followed to supervise the operation. Several minutes passed after Tex disappeared into the brush. Then both dogs began barking excitedly, and Tex came back out of the thicket. He had the ducks and was walking fast, looking back over his shoulder. The dogs continued to bark, and you could tell they were serious. I thought they probably had encountered a bear or some other large animal. During the hunting season bears, wolves, and coyotes haunt these flats, picking up dead and wounded birds lost by gunners, and also stuffing themselves on dead salmon that float down the creeks.

"You need any help over there?" I asked.

"I dunno if I do or not," Tex said. "There's a dang ol' billy goat in the bresh, an' he don't like me. What's the fine fer shootin' a nester's goat?"

"All you had to do," Doc chuckled, "was speak gently to him. Goats respond to kindness, like any other animal."

"Huh! I'd like to see you try hit on Ol' Whiskers in there. I spoke polite to the varmint an' he responded by tryin' to butt me up into a cottonwood tree. Snuck up behind me. Would of got me, too, dang his ugly picture, if'n hit hadn't been for the dogs. This country is gittin' too blamed civilized, with goats, cows, an' sech pokin' around ever'where."

As Tex returned to the blinds, a black Toggenburg billy goat—an evil-looking character with a mean set of horns—stepped out of the brush, followed by five white female goats, and all of them began browsing on sedge grass within fifty feet of us. Since the animals were out in the open, in plain view of any ducks that came over, it occurred to me that about all we lacked now was a brass band. I was looking for rocks to throw at them when Doc nudged me sharply and nodded toward the east. This time it was a flock of hooded mergansers, speed demons of the northern duck flats. No other duck in our country whizzes in so spectacularly, and Doc knows I get a tremendous kick out of watching them make a landing. These four came in like arrows, their wings making a swishing sound that rose swiftly to a thin whine. As always, it looked as if they were going to ball-up the landing and crash disastrously on the bottom of the slough. But at the last instant they leveled off and landed straight and sweetly, with never a bounce or an unseemly jib. I'll believe that aviation is here to stay when we have aircraft that will come in as neatly as the old hooded merganser does.

"Nothin' like a few live decoys," Tex said as the mergansers paddled into the sedge across the slough. "They'll help liven things up around here."

Doc had a book on how to call wild ducks, and he opened it and began leafing through it. He had been practicing with a call two weeks and had told us every day he could hardly wait to try his technique in the field. In his hotel apartment he had recordings of the various calls, and had played them over and over until a schoolteacher across the hall complained to the management that he was raising poultry in his bathroom. I had seldom seen him so determined about anything. He informed us that duck-calling was an art, and said he was going to master it no matter how much time and effort it took.

"What I wanta try next," he said, "is the greeting call. It says here you should give it in a happy, excited manner. It's like the feed call, but you've got to speed it up, sorta. Like this. Qu-ACK, qu-ACK, qu-ACK. Then if they don't come in, you argue with 'em. You tell 'em what the heck, everything's all right, they got old friends down here, it's a safe place, the water's just the right depth, and there's feed going to waste. Like this. Kwek, kwek, kwek, tic-a-tic-a-tic-a-tic. Oh boy, wait'll I give 'em that treatment."

"I'm waitin'," Tex said, "an' here's yer chance. Mallards headin' in high an' upwind."

The mallards up here normally are very wary birds. They don't come busting in to any small water without first looking it over carefully. If there is any little thing they don't like, they depart forthwith and don't return. Any movement or patch of off color in your blind is enough to cause them to veer away from your lay-out. These cloud-scrapers, however, made one tight circle at about six hundred feet, then slid down the wind and began their approach. I had forgotten about the six goats grazing behind us, but now I remembered them and would have wagered that the ducks would flare before they came in range. They didn't, though. They came right on in. Doc was talking to them, telling them every big lie he could think of. He was putting his heart into it. He was so interested he barely had time to exchange the call for his gun.

The next few seconds held the reason why grown men sit in cold, wet, windy blinds on forsaken swampy points hour after hour, neglecting their families and their business affairs, and getting chilblains, to take a few pounds of meat they could purchase with no hardship at all from almost any farmer. The ducks saw us and stood on their tails, scrambling for altitude. They were forty yards distant, and for a second or two, when their forward momentum was used up and the wind had stopped shooting them skyward, they were nearly motionless in the air. Then there was the ear-jarring multiple crash of seven shots, and the good smell of nitro in the blind, and the sudden warmth of the twin barrels in you hand. You could see shot spattering the far rim of the slough, and at the same instant five of the leading mallards crumpled, dropping out of formation to land with surprising softness on the water, bright wings trailing, the green heads of the drakes ashine in the sunlight.

"Well, I brought 'em in, didn't I?" Doc said triumphantly.

"I gotta admit hit," Tex said, scratching his head, a half-puzzled expression on his bearded face. "But hit's kinda queer about them goats. I was gonna work that billy over with a plank to chase 'em away, but I got a hunch now maybe we better let 'em stay awhile.

Seems to me them mallards was all-fired unspooky fer October frost-dusters out'n the Eskimo country. Maybe they're partial to sech barnyard stuff as goats 'n' cows."

I should explain here that for nonresident hunters looking for a place to get under some big flights of Alaska ducks with a scatter-gun, these Matanuska Hay Flats are just about ideal. There is good shooting throughout the season, and local hotel accommodations are excellent. At Palmer, the farming center a short drive north of the flats, there are two hotels, two restaurants, and two well-stocked general-merchandise stores. Meals and a room cost about six dollars a day. An Alaska Railroad mixed passenger and freight train makes six round trips daily between here and Anchorage. There is a taxi service that will take you from the settlement to the duck flats and return for you, at a reasonable rate. Most visiting sportsmen try to arrive on the opening day of the season. September 1, but in my opinion the best shooting is during the first two weeks in October, when the heavy, full-plumaged birds come streaming in ahead of the northern freeze-up, so happy to be out of ice and snow that they don't care where they pitch in.

Of course, there are hundreds of other shooting grounds. There are the Copper River Flats, the Beluga Flats, the Chickaloon Flats, the Redoubt Bay Flats, and the many gathering-places on the Alaska Peninsula and at the mouth of the Yukon. All of these hunting areas are accessible by airplane, and any bush pilot flying out of Anchorage can tell you all about them. But if I were a nonresident gunner yearning to bust some primers in a populous duck region, I would go up to the Matanuska Hay Flats. It doesn't cost as much as a hunt in any of the other places mentioned, and you'll find birds enough to satisfy anybody.

By far the greater number of ducks and geese that had come in during the past two days were out on the tidal mud flats. With my binoculars I could see thousands of them. I could distinguish Canadas, snow geese, specklebellies, brant, stilt-legged little brown cranes, and many, many ducks—mallards, pintails, bluebills, teal, baldpates, and such stuff as shovelers, golden-eyes, and buffleheads. Especially there were mallards, acres of them on the mud islands, along the waterline, and on the banks of the tidal washes. It was a sight to do a gunner's heart good. But there was no way you could get at the birds out there, because the tide flats are strewn with quicksand death-traps, and many of the steep-sided washes cannot be waded. A few flocks kept coming into water and to feed on the sedge, but the main body of them would not move until high tide forced them to. That would be in two hours.

Once in awhile a gunner finds himself unable to wait for the big flight to come in and goes out after them. Tex and I had such a chap with us in the autumn of 1928, an Englishman named Leslie. A huge flight had come in from the north, and the birds must have been wing-weary, for they dropped in recklessly, in some cases even ignoring gunfire. Leslie insisted on going out on the mud for pass-shooting, so we took him out there and he shot his gun hot in a few minutes. He said it was the finest shooting he had ever experienced. This was the reason, I suppose, why he refused to leave when we told him the tide had turned and it was time to get off the mud. He said he wanted a chance at some pintails. Then it was widgeons, then specklebellies because we had told him the specklebelly was our finest table bird. When at last we got him started toward higher ground we found the washes ahead of us and on both sides were nearly level full of water. We were cut off. In an hour the ground we were standing on would be submerged. We had previously explained to Leslie that the tides in this region are the second highest in the world, but his ears were so full of goose talk and the sound of wings that he hadn't paid any heed.

"We'll have to swim them guts," Tex said. "So take off yer shoes an' throw yer shells away. Stick yer gun up in the mud—we'll come back fer hit at low tide tomorrow."

"I'm afraid I'm in trouble—I can't swim," Leslie said. "It's my own fault, though. I never could resist ducks and geese, and I hadn't dreamt there were such flights in the world as this one."

"Don't matter a damn whether ye can swim or not," Tex said. "Take these geese. Tie their necks together an' use 'em like a life preserver. They'll keep ya afloat."

We crossed four of the bitterly cold washes before we climbed the bank and went in under a stand of cottonwoods to build a fire. By the time we had a fire going and the warmth of it had started to drive the chill from our bones, the mud flats were under water. Leslie picked up his largest snow goose and wiped mud from its feathers. His hands were shaking. He hadn't been visibly frightened when we were crossing the quicksand-bottomed washes, but he was getting a swell reaction now. He saw the rips boiling over the submerged flat like a fast river and knew that a man couldn't have lived three minutes in that icy, mud-laden conflict of waters. He wiped a drop of blood from the snow goose's red bill.

"Ironical, isn't it?" he said. "I killed this splendid old fellow, and then he helped save my life. I'm going to ship him to a taxidermist to be mounted. He's too fine for any man's pot. He goes on the mantel in my home, to stay there as long as the house stands."

So Tex, Doc, and I stayed off the mud flats, as did the other gunners that day, and waited for the tide to send the birds in to us. Meanwhile, as I said, flocks kept coming into the ponds and sloughs to water. And Doc talked to them, with wonderful results for an utter amateur. We discovered one secret of his newfound talent when a flock of bluebill—lesser scaup—came tearing in over the tree-tops and circled the decoys of some other hunters farther down the slough. Doc got out his book for a quick refresher on diver ducks and set about luring them away from those hunters. "Brrr, brrr, brrr, brrr, scaup, scaup," he trilled. The call sounded strange to me. It sounded as if he was trying to play a tune. The bluebills swung wide of the other hunters' decoys and made a fast power drag over ours. I know bluebills aren't supposed to hang around in timber, but these were doing so and I think they would have landed, too. Doc gave them the *brrr, brrr* business until he had to stop it to grab his gun. We took three of them.

"Wasn't there somethin' funny about that call o' yourn?" Tex said. "Hit sounded sorta like somethin' I've heard somewhere's afore, an' I don't mean on no duck flat, neither."

"Oh, that," Doc laughed. "Well, it says here on page ten that you shouldn't call in a monotone, and that the best way to avoid it is to play a tune while you're calling. I was playing the *Bluebells of Scotland*. It seemed appropriate. Bluebills, you know."

"Well, I'll be a—" Tex floundered. "Dang hit all, I started callin' ducks fifty years ago, down on the Rio Grande, an' I thought I knowed somethin' about hit. But now I s'pose I gotta start takin' music lessons. Fer snow geese I reckon ya'd play *Jingle Bells* or *White Christmas,* huh?"

Guns had been hammering so steadily out across the windy, golden flats that we were no longer conscious of hearing them. But now suddenly a particularly heavy bombardment began about five hundred yards inland. The reports were so close together they sounded like strings of firecrackers going off. In a moment we saw the reason for this—a flock of Canadas. Apparently they had been jumped out of a pond and were making for the tide flats. We were on their line of flight, and they didn't swerve. They knew where they were going and they came on steadily, maintaining an altitude of about sixty yards. There was a majesty in the slow beat of their broad wings, in their great size, and in the calm manner in which they held their course despite the gunfire, that made my scalp tingle. The Canada, of all our geese, has the most of that certain wonderful something that separates champions from runners-up. The brant is harder to hit, the emperor is handsomer, and the specklebelly is far better on the table, but I would pass up flocks of them all for a good shot at a Canada.

This flock of Canadas came over too high for Doc and me. We were shooting sixes, and we each gave them both barrels without interrupting a wing beat. Tex, however, was loaded with twos. He let the flock pass the blinds, then emptied his automatic. Two of the big gray birds spun down. I don't know how Doc felt, but I felt like a fourteen-carat chump. We both had twos in our shell boxes, but there hadn't been time to get them out and chamber them. If the birds had been any other kind of geese but Canadas, I wouldn't have felt so bad, but I hate to flub a chance at a Canada. Doc said he thought the goats had caused the geese to come over high, and looked about him for the plank Tex had mentioned, intending to belabor the billy with it and cause him to collect his harem and go away.

"Don't blame the goats," Tex said. "Blame yerse'f. Me, I don't shoot nothin' but twos, no matter what kind o' birds're flyin'. Fur's I'm concerned, anything smaller'n twos is jest sparrer dust. Hit's somethin' I decided on a long time ago."

I am aware that the argument of heavy shot versus light shot will never be settled. The gunners favoring the lighter shot contend it is better to catch a bird within range with a pattern of 5, 6, or 7½ shot and down it than to put one or two heavy shot into a bird at extreme range and merely wound it. I have long subscribed to this theory myself. Still, in our country the next bird to come over the treetops is as likely to be a goose as a duck, and the lighter sizes of shot are a severe handicap when you are trying to pull a big goose down from a height of fifty or sixty yards—unless you are a luckier or more expert gunner than most of the scattergun men up here. You are likely to defeat the purpose of light shot by wounding the goose and causing it to die somewhere over on another watershed. So I have concluded that next year I will use twos. Then the high-flying geese can watch out. I'll be ready for them.

While the dogs were bringing in Tex's Canadas we had a visit from a patrolling wildlife agent. He gave us some interesting intelligence.

"I see you've got the best decoys on the Hay Flats," he said, nodding toward the five goats.

"What!" Doc exclaimed. "Y' mean those beasts are an asset?" He surreptitiously dropped the plank with which he had been about to assault Ol' Whiskers.

The wildlife agent said it was a fact. He said on these flats any kind of stock near your blind was an aid. The ducks and geese that came in here, he said, were accustomed to feed in the Matanuska stubble fields both spring and fall and were used to alighting among horses, cows, sheep, and hogs. He said the presence of stock prevented the incoming birds from concentrating their attention on your blinds. In other words, stock was an attention-diverter. And the local hunters, he said, rated Ol' Whiskers and his gang as the best attention-diverters of them all. He said everyone tried to keep them around by feeding them cigarettes and candy bars.

"Well, I'll be doggoned," Tex said as the wildlife agent left. "First the *Bluebells of Scotland* as a call, an' now goats fer decoys. I dunno what duck huntin' is comin' to. I swear I don't." He glanced at Doc out of the corners of his eyes. "But I figgered them ducks was mighty trustin' an' unsuspicious to let you call 'em in thataway. Hit was goats fetchin' 'em all the time, huh?"

"That's a gross libel," Doc said loudly, getting red in the face.

"I called those birds in. The goats were just atmosphere. I even consider their value in that respect highly questionable. We'd probably do a lot better without them."

I couldn't decide which of them had won that round.

Today was the first time Tex and I had ever hunted in an area crowded with gunners. We had always shot in wilderness spots and hadn't had to resort to any of the refinements of the sport. For the most part, we had favored jump- or pass-shooting. When we did put out decoys we never considered such fine points, for instance, as the tendency of divers to land inside the spread and dippers outside. We just put out the blocks, silhouettes, or whatever we had and sat down to await results. On a few occasions, though, when birds were scarce or the terrain was against us, we had worked out stratagems, some of which were necessarily unique.

There was the scheme, for example, that Tex devised in the hope of getting within range of some geese in the Kuskokwim River country. These geese had consistently baffled everyone in the region. They had the exasperating habit of feeding at night and spending the daylight hours loafing on a low, barren sand island in the middle of the river. You could see them from our cabin window, a miscellaneous assortment of Canadas, snow geese and cackling geese together with sundry varieties of ducks, all of them sunning themselves at their favorite spot at the downstream tip of the island. They were out of gun range, and if you tried to approach them in a boat or canoe they would see you coming and fly back into the marshes. But on one particular morning Tex had a brilliant, scintillating idea.

"I've done figgered out a way to git some o' them geese," he announced. "Hit'll be easy as fallin' off a log. When you go down to the tradin' post today, git some sage, a can o' oysters, an' some yaller corn meal, because we're gonna have roast goose tonight."

Into our canoe after breakfast he loaded an axe, a saw, a hammer, nails, and a length of rope, stood his 12-bore against the thwart, and shoved off. I went with him because he said he needed help in the first phase of the operation. A mile above the village stood some small but very bushy white spruces. We put ashore here and Tex felled two of the bushiest trees and lashed them to the canoe, one on each side. He then added boughs here and there, nailing them to the tree trunks, until the canoe was completely concealed. It looked just like a couple of uprooted spruces floating in the muddy current.

"Don't fergit to buy them goose trimmin's," he said complacently as he got into the canoe and shoved off. "Might as well git the oven hotted up, too, 'cause I'll be back directly."

His scheme was now evident. He was going to float down to the island, and the geese wouldn't be alarmed because drift was always coming down on the current. I thought it was a wonderful plan. Unfortunately, however, things began going wrong with it at once. When he was floating past Lousetown, the native village above the island, an Eskimo put out in a little birch-bark canoe with the intention, as he explained later, of towing the trees ashore for fish-wheel pilings. He had a seal-hide tow-rope in his hand and was about to take a turn around the butt for one of the trees when Tex spoke to him wrathfully from behind the screening boughs:

"Git the hell outa here! What're ya tryin' to do, spile this project fer me? G'wan, beat hit back to shore."

The poor Eskimo was so astounded to hear a man speak from the mass of boughs that he nearly capsized in his panicky haste to turn the canoe around and get away from there. Tex drifted on, skulling against the thwart to keep the floating blind edged in toward the low island. He was doing all right until a magpie discovered him. Hundreds of these birds frequented the village refuse dump, and their curiosity was such that when any activity took place in the vicinity they were always on hand to witness it. The lone scouting magpie presumably sighted the top of Tex's muskrat cap through the spruce boughs and thought an animal was riding the trees. In any event, it set up a terrific squawking. Immediately a cloud of magpies rose from the refuse dump and hastened to the scene, each one endeavoring to outsquawk the others.

The geese took alarm while Tex was still a hundred and fifty yards from them. They couldn't have known what the trouble was, but they trusted the magpies. They took off with a thunder of wings and prudently headed away from the floating blind. Tex stood up, head and shoulders above the boughs, and fired a fruitless shot after them. Then he turned and emptied the gun at the departing magpies, and didn't hit any of them, either. The blind drifted three miles downriver before he succeeded in grounding it so he could cast loose the trees. When he arrived at the cabin toward midafternoon, he wore the expression of a man who had reached a momentous conclusion.

"All the good ways to hunt geese," he stated emphatically, "was invented a long time ago. So from now on I'm gonna be a old-fashioned hunter. The hell with these newfangled ideas. They git ya in trouble, an' they don't git ya no geese."

Nevertheless, despite his resolution—and over Doc's protests—after our talk with the wildlife agent he gave Ol' Whiskers and his harem our spare tobacco, two chocolate bars, some chewing gum, and a ham sandwich on rye to keep them with us. It was now ten o'clock and the tide was nearly at full flood. In a few minutes the mud flats would be covered. Doc began calling energetically: "Qu-HACK, qu-HACK, qu-HACK, W-HUTT, W-HUTT, W-HUTT." I saw a flight of widgeons lift from the mud, followed by some mallards and snow geese. The offshore wind now was sending wavelets over the last long line of mud and sand. The birds in the air circled, talking to the others. I kept my glasses on the diminishing bars, waiting for the exciting thing that was going to happen. Abruptly, as if a flight leader had flashed a command, every duck and goose on the bars took off. Along a three-mile front the air was filled with wings. It was a gorgeous sight. It was something every scatter-gun man ought to see. I am certain there were at least twenty thousand birds in the air.

The mallards and geese came highballing into the sloughs nearest the beach, while the other ducks fanned out over the yellow flats, heading for the water and feed that suited them best. Some widgeons—baldpates—came breezing in high, saw our decoys, and turned back for another look. Ol' Whiskers and his does behaved admirably. They were browsing on dwarf willow, facing away from us, which from the air must have given the place an innocent, pastoral appearance. Doc was blowing himself red in the face, and his quacks, trills and W-HUTT'S: certainly were given in a happy, excited manner. They sounded like a Cuban rumba to me. The widgeons were careful, shifty customers. They buzzed the far side of the slough, coming down fast on their sharp, trim little wings, their white breasts and large white wing patches clear and bright in the luminous blue air; then they banked away from us and went back upstairs for a second inspection. They started in again presently, and this time they were killing their speed. They had decided the place was all right. I slipped my safety latch and got my feet under me. Then something happened.

"Uh-oh," Tex said. "Lookit that!"

From somewhere, like feathered lightning bolts, came two duck hawks, diving on our widgeons. Probably they had been waiting here all morning for the big flight to come in. Perhaps they made a practice of ambushing the birds every time they moved inland. Their attack was so dazzlingly swift that it made even the fast widgeons seem almost stationary. The formation of ducks whiffled, some flaring, others pitching down to the water. It didn't do two of them any good. The lead hawk shot in beside a widgeon hen, and then suddenly hawk and duck were dropping out of the sky, first one on top, then the other. A moment passed before I realized the hawk had reached out a taloned foot and grabbed the hen by the head. The other hawk had struck a drake from above, apparently hitting it with clenched feet. The drake wavered, caught itself, and lurched on, losing altitude. All the birds were now in range. It seems Tex, Doc, and I all had the same idea. We held on the hawks. They came down like wash cloths tossed out of a five-story window. The flock of widgeons meanwhile had gone elsewhere in a hurry.

"Well, Ol' Whiskers done his best," Tex said. "Hit wasn't his fault them hawks cut in on the play."

"If you weren't so bullheaded," Doc said, "you'd break down and admit that I called those birds in too. You know confounded well the goats didn't have anything to do with it."

Tex grinned and began humming an off-key version of the *Bluebells of Scotland*.

There were so many birds on the flats now that there was no point in sitting in a blind waiting for a flock to come over us. So we took in the decoys, hung them in a tree, fed the goats the last of our sandwiches, and set out toward the highway. When the main flight is in, the jump-shooting here is marvelous. It is a lot like walk-

ing up spruce grouse in a blueberry thicket. The ducks feed in puddles of seepage water only a few inches deep, and the grass is so
high—five feet in some places—that you can approach within easy
range before they see or hear you. Up ahead of us a lonesome mallard hen was calling plaintively, and suddenly, fifty yards off to
her left, there was a chorus of answering quacks. We went toward
the latter sector. The wind covered the sound of our progress, so
that we were less than fifty feet from ducks before they heard us.
They obligingly sprang up two and three at a time, their vertical rise
taking them a good six feet above the grass before they flattened
out on the wind. This gave us the kind of shooting that hard-working
duck-hunters dream about. In about twenty seconds we had our
share of ducks for the day.

From the car you could look out over the tawny flats to the blue-
gray sweep of salt water, and everywhere in the sky above this beautiful vista wings were flashing.

"Hit's the same old shootin' grounds hit was forty years ago," Tex
said, "exceptin', o' course, fer a few more hunters an' a scatterin' o'
cows, goats an' sech. But they ain't hurt nothin'. In fact, fur's the
critters're concerned," he added with a perfectly straight face, "I
ain't never gonna hunt here again without I got me some goats to
take along. Look what them goats done fer us today—brought a
slew o' birds in to us in spite o' the noisy calls Doc kept makin'."

"The back of my hand to ye!" Doc said, but he said it happily.

BAIT: THE USE OF CORN

Harry M. Walsh

There is a man in Easton, Maryland, who sometimes leaves his house before dawn and goes to his goose blind nearby. He watches the dawn come, and sometimes the geese arrive with it and he shoots one. Mostly though, he simply looks at the water and sky and the day beginning and after a little while leaves for his workplace. Once there, he puts on his uniform and begins tasks that are at once beautiful, elemental, and exceedingly complex: He must prevent people from suffering pain and from dying. Harry Walsh, M.D., surgeon at Easton Memorial Hospital, is one of those amazing personalities who gets so much done that he makes ordinary mortals like yours truly appear to be lazy. One of the great historians of waterfowling on the Eastern Shore, Dr. Walsh has collected his years of research, interviews and photographs in the superb book, The Outlaw Gunner, *Tidewater Publishers, Cambridge, Maryland, 1971. "The Use of Corn" a look at the darker side of the under-belly of illegal waterfowling, is taken from Dr. Walsh's interesting and evocative chronicle. Walsh grew up near Chestertown on the shores of the Chesapeake Bay and served an apprenticeship under an old market gunner. By his teens, he was such a proficient guide that he partially paid for his education. He interned at the University of Maryland Medical School after having served as a Navy frogman in World War II. He is a wrestler, boat captain and active conservationist. He and his wife and six children live in the Easton area.*

A RAFT OF nearly 2,000 diving ducks, for the most part canvasbacks and redheads, rode like a flotilla of ships in the three-foot swells along the lee shore of the Bay. A lone fisherman sat close to the warmth of his wood stove watching their actions. His cabin, idyllically stiuated in the woods on the edge of a sheltered cove, had an unplugged automatic shotgun near an open window. Within easy range was a pile of corn whose location was well known to both the ducks and the fisherman. Soon the ducks would return and their numbers would be lessened by nearly a hundred.

Later that evening, only a short distance away, four men sat huddled against an overturned crab float as 200 canvasbacks swam in, never to leave. Across the river one gunning club shot over a case of shells daily for several weeks in the wild fever of duck hunting. In the seclusion of his private farm a retired New York stockbroker rode a golf buggy to the place where he enjoyed the hunting he had missed in his youth and his guide retrieved nearly a hundred ducks.

One common factor was present in these various violations . . . the use of corn to lure ducks into range. The technique of flock shooting with an automatic shotgun and the judicious use of corn constitute the deadliest method of duck destruction ever devised. The tremendous power of this tool (bait or corn) to concentrate waterfowl is well known. Given enough room and bait, all the waterfowl in one region, or even a so-called flyway, could be concentrated into one area. A poor habitat can be converted into a prime area with its holding or carrying capacity almost unlimited. For the duck, corn is the preferred food; for the hunter it is a real delight, but too powerful a medicine to be used—to the Wildlife Management Officer and the Game Warden it is a deadly poison.

The use of corn is so controversial and figures so prominently in gunning violations that it is difficult to confine the scope of its discussion. It is also a relative newcomer and cannot be discussed in the past tense. Though its use is now greatly restricted, it was once widespread; many gunning clubs used between 40 and 100 tons of corn every year. Near Rock Hall, one large club emptied 20 bags each day and enjoyed some of the world's best duck hunting. At nearby Cedar Point, 76 canvasbacks were killed in 15 minutes with a high day's total of 858. "Trash ducks" and cripples were not retrieved.

The plush Jefferson Island Club hosted three of our presidents and many of the nation's greats. Five to ten cases of shells were shot daily. After one successful hunt a special railroad refrigerator car was neccessary to transport the birds to Washington. On the marshes of the Chester River, 200 black ducks were killed by sportsmen in one day as an enterprising young guide proved his mettle.

The principle involved in baiting is relatively simple. Bait is placed in a convenient spot until it has been discovered by the waterfowl. Their numbers then become a simple ratio to the amount of bait. Once the flight and feeding pattern has been established, good hunting is assured. The ducks can then be conditioned to feed when and where hunters desire. A wide variety of substances has been used for bait, from crushed stone to weed and tomato seeds. Corn is most widely used, although milo seems to be preferred by ducks.

The various techniques of baiting, however, have reached highly sophisticated levels. Much ingenuity and imagination have been exercised in attempts to evade game wardens.

For baiting black ducks and other marsh ducks, it should be remembered that most waterfowl, with the possible exception of brant, prefer fresh water. Since a pond in the center of a marsh is an excellent place to start, one hunting lodge in a saltwater area has made such a pond with a 600-foot well. It is an excellent place to hunt, even without using corn.

Just enough corn (several cupfuls) is used, so that the ducks—but not the game wardens—can find it. Within a few days the first two or three ducks will have notified all of their friends and as many as fifty may be seen there. The corn is increased slowly as needed—never more corn than there are ducks. At no time are more than several bushels used. If possible, bait is put out daily to encourage feeding pattern.

The ducks are fed in the morning and a sanctuary of sorts is developed; all poachers and trespassers are kept away. After the ducks have fed, they are likely to remain and rest. In time, the pond becomes a duck haven.

After the black ducks have become accustomed to using the pond, there are several possibilities concerning its future. It can be maintained as a sanctuary and stragglers are shot as they trade to and from the nearby river shore. Shooting is done at a sufficient distance to avoid disturbing the pond and to allow time for crying "fowl" if the law should complain. This system is almost foolproof.

On the other hand, the pond itself can be shot several times a week. This is done when the tide is high and a strong northwest wind is blowing. The birds feed in the pond on high water and return there for food and refuge. This is a good situation for hunting, even without the aid of corn. Right at the edge of dark is, of course, the best time for hunting black ducks; more can be killed in the last hour between sunset and darkness than at any other time of the day. However, it has the disadvantage of attracting attention and scares away the ducks for several weeks.

For baiting along the river shore for marsh ducks, the procedure is different. Here, there is a great deal of traffic and the corn is more likely to be discovered. For this reason, corn is put out in the evening or at night. All bait should be gone by morning—just enough is used to hold the birds and have none left over to be seen by game wardens.

As the tide recedes, black ducks leave the marsh and feed along the river shore. With a low tide and a heavy wind, this is the place for the hunter to be. It is even better if the marshes become completely frozen. But one should never be so rash as to shoot on moderate days or when corn is still in the area.

Using this technique, a hundred black ducks can be killed in a few hours and no one is the wiser. Two men shooting flying black ducks killed 51 in fifteen minutes along a river shore. Using four shells, the same two men killed 55 black ducks sitting on a marsh pond.

It is not unusual for black ducks to dive ten or twelve feet for bait. A one-gallon can of corn each night is sufficient for 50 ducks. However, more corn is needed in cold weather.

There are many difficulties encountered in using bait. It can be spotted from great distances by an airplane. Muddy water helps, but in its absence, even if no corn is available, the birds soon wash away all of the silt from the bottom and a telltale bald spot develops. Unfortunately, bait also washes against rocks, roots and grass on the shore or the bottom where it is quickly covered with sand and can be retrieved by the law. Mixed with the corn, there is a great deal of chaff which tends to wash onto the shore as a giveaway. For this reason, it is best to put corn out to the leeward of the blind. One old-timer who has been baiting for more than fifty years and has never been caught, washes his corn in an outside bathtub before using it. Unlike diving ducks, black ducks will also eat the chaff and floating corn.

Immediately before and after feeding, all ducks "raft up" near each other. For this reason decoys should be placed as close together as possible.

"If you understand their feeding habits." said the old-timer, "you can make them sit on the end of your gun barrel." To attract diving ducks, one should start baiting in a known feeding area and gradually move the corn to the desired location. At times, a trail of corn (stringer) can be run to the desired site. Another method is to place a pine stake near the corn. Gradually the stake and corn are moved into the shooting area. The ducks will look for the stake and come directly to it. Corn is the best decoy anyone can use.

The feeding habits of diving ducks differ greatly from those of black ducks. They are constantly hungry. They feed, swim out and, five minutes later, return to feed again. The cycle is continued until all of the corn has disappeared. Then they raft up and sit within a half mile of the blind, waiting for more food and attracting game wardens. The law knows that these birds go from one spot to another in search of corn. The wardens simply watch their flight patterns and keep alert for concentrations of waterfowl.

Black ducks do not generally reveal their feeding areas; they feed and leave for several hours. As a black duck first approaches bait, he lands and cautiously looks about. He then slowly, preens himself and politely approaches the bait. If all is satisfactory, he gives a low-pitched quack and begins to feed. He, alone, is the king of ducks and well deserves his title.

With diving ducks, there is a lack of formality and a virtual absence of good manners. Their feeding habits leave little doubt as to the location of the bait. They fly hungrily toward a free meal and dive over each other in their haste.

Overfeeding, in addition to being dangerous, makes the ducks lazy. They sit nearby and, instead of flying, swim to the bait. They should be baited in the late afternoon when the wardens are not active and kept away from the area at other times. Two bushels a day can accommodate one thousand diving ducks.

The manner in which ducks are treated controls their actions. They should not be overfed or overshot. They should have a place for food, water and, especially, refuge. Birds like to feed early in the morning and late in the evening. Wise hunters feed them at these times so that all corn is removed from sight.

A good guide may have several locations baited so that he can gun anything, at any time, in any weather. Some hunting areas are rented and baited under an assumed name as a "decoy" to hold ducks in the vicinity; while the game warden is watching that particular site, the ducks are reaped in a neighboring location. Hunters dig a hole six feet in diameter and bait within its shadow. A tractor tire can be used in the same manner. The corn then cannot be spotted by plane. Another trick is to bait one-half mile or so on either side of the blind. The ducks are then shot as they work from one side to the other. The wilder the birds become, the closer to the blind the corn must be.

No corn should be set out when shooting takes place. The ducks are "starved-out" the day before a hunt; they fly about looking for corn and toll better.

A blind does not seem to frighten diving ducks. Frequently, the hunter actually stands and enjoys the hunt. After they are accustomed to feeding, it is difficult to keep them away.

Black ducks will go to a field at night when food is scarce; sprigtails, mallards and others will feed there during daylight hours.

Geese have been converted from waterfowl to upland fowl by their love of grain. If there is any trace of moonlight, they will feed at night and can be baited then. These birds are very susceptible to the "refuge" programs developed by some devotees. A pond is available and a place is provided for the geese to rest, water, and feed during their entire six-month stay. Proper crop manipulation can keep the entire operation within the framework of the law—or almost.

Geese can be baited in the water but habitually feed at low tide. Swans are attracted in short order and will eat all of the corn. The best place to bait geese, with the exception of a field, is at the head of a creek (again, fresh water). This is usually their resting place for the night or their haven in a storm. When it is raining they will go to a green field where the roots are easy to loosen. After a snowstorm, they can be killed with a broom in a cleared winter wheatfield. Geese will not come to a field when it is frozen or covered with heavy frost, preferring to wait for a thaw. At these times and on moonlit nights, a water blind is more satisfactory; careful observation of weather conditions helps to foretell the birds' subsequent reactions.

Recently, an old-timer named Lennie hung up his gun and all the birds left the area. "When Lennie quit, the ducks quit, too," said one of the hunters. The secret lay in Lennie's judicious use of corn.

Though baiting has some advantages, they are far outweighed by its devastating results. Waterfowl should always be wild and free from being pauperized by a hunter's corn. There is enough natural food for all and a healthy bird can find it. If baiting were legalized, the overkill would be disastrous and in a short time most of the birds would be concentrated only in the areas that could afford to support them.

It is with the aid of bait that the chronic "game hog" or lawbreaker can do so much damage. This man guns alone and never lets his right hand know what his left is doing. He picks his own time and place, baiting in a secluded grain or bags and is always moored in the same fashion. He guns only when the birds are "right"; with a windy day to fracture the sound of his shots. Ignoring cripples and game laws, he indulges in "flock shooting" and would shoot the last duck on earth if it came to that.

The sophisticated baiter is likely to be a respected member of his community and knows that too much bait is dangerous. He baits a mile or so away, and then guns along the flyway. The law may not be broken in any other fashion, except for occasionally exceeding the limit. To him there is nothing wrong in having a little sport. To appease his conscience he will give a yearly donation to conservation and, yet, be the first to condemn the game wardens and scream indignantly if arrested.

The significant game kill in this country is not due merely to the outlaw. The millions of little violations committed by honest people contribute to the problem, multiplied by the millions of times that they are committed.

Atley Lankford has gunned all his life on the famed Elliott Island Marshes. He gunned commercially from 1900 to 1918. The limiting factor in his daily kill of two hundred birds was, simply, carrying them off the marsh. Atley averaged better than 10,000 a year with a lifetime average of nearly half a million ducks. He has probably killed more ducks than any man alive and is still available for verification. The hard shooting would require a new gun each year. Around 1910, he acquired his first Remington Model 11 automatic and was able to shoot it for eight years. Each year a new wooden forearm was required. This gun has killed over 35,000 ducks—probably more than any gun in the world—and is still in his possession. Atley's father ran a store and sold him his shells; the receipts for his shells are also available.

Atley started baiting with acorns picked up from the church and camp-meeting yards. He switched to corn when it became available.

"There's no room for bait in today's gunning," said Atley. "What few ducks we have would soon be destroyed. Once," he continued, "the sky used to be black with ducks everywhere you looked. There appeared to be no end to their number. What a shame," he said sadly, "to see them go."

Gunning with an Outlaw

The sun set bleak and cold with the clouds outlined fiery red in its receding rays. Its beauty was wasted on the two outlaws who sat huddled together against the numbing cold. They knew full well that it prophesied more of the same bitter weather.

The sun had been fighting a losing battle for over a week, its efforts completely smothered by the clouds that had blanketed the sky. The land was locked in the frigid grip of winter and soon the river would be frozen solid. When this happened, the few ducks that were left would head for warmer climes and scant chance they would have of filling their orders.

The rich man had placed his yearly request of two hundred ducks and he was not one who would accept an excuse. His athletic club was holding its annual wild duck dinner. Only the freshest of ducks would be served. Usually there was plenty of notice, with the ducks aged for three days in the old smokehouse and even picked. Now, however, there was hardly time for the killing.

The 12-cylinder Packard had arrived without its owner and captained by his chauffeur. This pilot basked in his new-found glory of giving orders and had been "hypocriting" all over town. The women-folk were quite impressed but the only reason Eddie didn't have him hanging from a coathook somewhere was out of respect for the rich man.

For many years there had been a fond association between Eddie and these New York people. He had guided for them in sinkboxes on the flats, and, later, as chief guide at their gunning club. One of the guests had even given Eddie the diamond stickpin that had been his trademark. The friendship was deep and mortared together by that invisible masonry which binds most hunters.

Usually three days to fill such an order would have been more than enough. Now, however, no one had ducks. All the other mar-ket gunners were frozen out of business and only laughed at requests for help.

After five bags of corn and two days of hunting, there were less than fifty ducks hanging head-down in the old smokehouse. Things were bad—and it was tomorrow or never. Little wonder the sunset went unnoticed.

"Hope the birds have found that corn we put out at Possum Point two days ago," remarked Eddie. "It's our only chance and we will just have to try it tomorrow. Word has it," he continued, "that corn in Snake Creek has attracted more than just ducks. Man across the river said last night he'd seen the warden over that way."

This creek was a favorite haunt for black ducks and its properties were always enhanced by the judicious use of corn. In fact, Eddie had been baiting a secret spot there for nearly two months straight. It was now on the diner's tour of every black duck in the country.

It was a cold, dark, lifeless world at 3:00 A.M. the next morning as the two outlaws again began their labor. The boat was quickly and heavily laden with corn, decoys, guns and accessories. They broke windowpane ice all the way out of the harbor into open wa-ter at mid-channel. Running free, with a strong incoming tide, they proceeded upriver more by instinct than visual perception, as there were no landmarks available. Each man pulled hard on his oars as much to keep warm as to make headway.

"For some reason the tide always keeps a good hole open at Pos-sum Point," said Eddie, as they neared the end of their five-mile row.

"We ought to be in business if the birds have found our corn."

As they rounded the point, there was open water everywhere and they were greeted by the roar of a thousand wings as the ducks took flight.

"My Gawd," said Eddie, "we've got every duck in the country on our corn. Maybe we will make it, anyhow. The corn is all gone," he said jubilantly. "Let's make our stringers [two large strings of corn leading into the blind from midriver] and get going."

When the decoys had been set out, one bag of corn was dumped in a pile right in front of the blind at easy range. Out of the gray dawn with the rays of the sun came the first flight. As they "tolled over" for the third time, both men shot instinctively and six ducks were on the water. For awhile the shooting was nearly continuous and both men worked hard. Gunning for them was not a sport but an occupation.

As the sun grew higher, the day also grew in beauty. The ducks now no longer tolled but pitched into midriver and before long, there were ducks everywhere sitting comfortably out of range.

It became a typical bluebird day with the ducks preening themselves and feeding along the edge of the ice, as they do. One shot now and everything would leave for the day. By midafternoon, a few were feeding on the stringer of corn and slowly cutting it down as they approached the corn in front of the blind.

"Made that stringer too thick," said Eddie. "They won't get here before dark."

In another hour, however, a few had found the main pile and were feeding nervously.

"The only chance we have now," said Eddie, "is a good swim in. With all those ducks," he continued, "we ought to do it."

The main group, however, continued their vigil in midriver, unmindful of the pile of corn. A few ruddies and other "trash ducks" came in along with a few cans. They would work in slowly, nervously look around, dine, and then quickly fly back to safety. With such mild weather there would only be one shot and it had to be a good one.

With the shadows lengthening and an unfilled order, the outlaws were both worried and anxious. "They must see something they don't like," said the young boy.

"No," said Eddie, "they are wise and have been shot a lot. They know where the corn is and they will be there eventually."

Suddenly, as if ordered by some commanding general, an entire flock of several thousand birds began to work toward the corn. "This is going to be a good swim in," said Eddie, "Get ready."

Cautiously they came. The more rash swam up to the corn, then more and more, some flying and landing. Others dove over one another in their haste to get to the corn. The feeding was furious.

Then, without reason, they all flew out of range as though their invisible enemy had been seen.

"Don't worry," said Eddie, "that was just a trial run. Here they come again." Now they were even more bunched together. "Just as thick as they ever were in this world," said Eddie. "This is it!"

Suddenly, two guns spoke as one and then again, equally fast, both men shooting as fast as they could load. The fruits of their labor lay still on the water. The swing-in had been a good one.

"We're still short," said Eddie. "Only one thing to do and that is chance those black ducks. Probably the law didn't find our corn after all."

Snake Creek was a good eight-mile row away and the sun was falling fast. Both men knew that a night shot at black ducks was their only chance. In a few minutes the boat was loaded. All four oars flashed rhythmically in the rays of the setting sun. Each man was proud of his power and skill. They pulled quickly to the middle of the river to take advantage of the ebbing tide. With each power stroke, the boat leaped forward as though it had been whipped.

The young boy had eagerly grabbed the rowing harness and strapped himself to the oars. This instrument of torture consisted of leather straps crisscrossing the back and down the arms to the oars. Bracing his feet against a block, the boy could now pull with the strength of two men. They made good time—pausing only long enough to hide their ducks.

"Tide's the lowest I've ever seen it," whispered Eddie, as they approached their destination. "We've got a hundred yards of mud flat to get across." They dragged themselves and the corn across the flats to the marsh beyond.

The ice over the creek was quickly broken and shoved under the remaining ice to be carried away by the tide. An opening in the ice, about the size of a room, was made and baited. The outlaws made ready and settled back.

In the last few minutes before dark, the sky was full of ducks. There were hundreds of them looking like black specks against the sunset: the usual nocturnal flight of black ducks on their way to feed—the Achilles heel, their love for corn and tendency to feed at night. In the darkness only the swishing of their wings could be heard. Up and down the creek they flew, over and around the open water but never in it.

For an hour they waited in the total darkness. There was no sound save the constant beating of wings.

"Something is wrong," said the young boy.

"No," said Eddie, "they are afraid of that hole. Should have just dumped the corn on the ice. Soon as one gets down," he continued, "they'll all come. May have to wait half the night, though."

Finally, several hit right in the water and looked nervously about. Within a few minutes, another six or eight came in, and then another —soon the entire hole was filled with ducks. In they came, some slipping and sliding on the ice, others lowering over the hole and dropping in at the last second. It is unbelievable how thick they can get.

Eddie nudged his companion. He had a dime in his left hand. This would be tapped against the gun barrel just before they shot. The ducks were silhouetted against the ice and no aiming was necessary. The night was shattered by the sound of their shots. The flame-edged voice of death roared its lament across the marsh to the woods beyond, its echo reverberating again and again until it also died in a disgruntled roar, going down the river. It was as though nature herself was displeased at the deed now done.

"We can all have ducks tomorrow," said Eddie, as under the cloak of darkness they returned safely home.

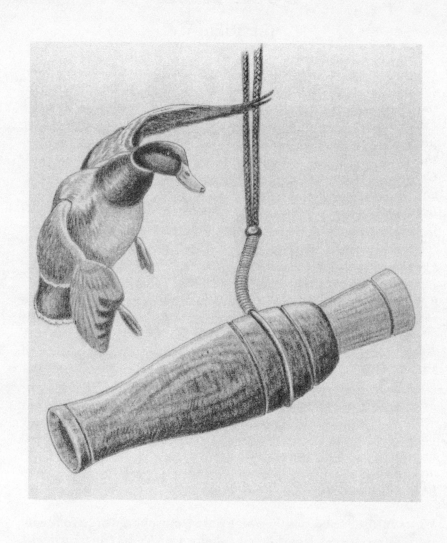

DUCK TALK

Jim Rikhoff

In a lifetime of waterfowling that I consider to be rich in experience, I must confess a couple of serious gaps. One of the most important that I still intend to do something about is to hunt the duck-rich Cajun country of south Louisiana. I love Cajun jokes, a lot of the literature produced by the region, and in particular I love to hear the tall tales of Cajun-swamp hunting spun by my friends Grits Gresham and Jim Rikhoff. Rikhoff is not known for being reticent and has spent so much Cajun time that he can talk-Cajun with the best. Lately, he has been turning his talented hand to writing about Cajun-country duck shooting, and some of that output is joyfully presented here. They're from Jim's monthly column on the last page of The American Rifleman *and are a sample of the tremendous job he's been doing for* Rifleman *readers since coming on board as a columnist in 1978. In his years with Winchester and since leaving there to found and run Amwell Press and the National Sporting Fraternity Ltd., the typewriter has always been an essential part of Jim's office. Publishing and editing have only been a partial outlet for the Rikhoff creative juices. His own writing has been a part of his considerable achievements, and it has been a pleasure to read his ever-growing skills over the years. Jim has written and sold hundreds of magazine articles, and the best of these have been included in his book,* Mixed Bag, *which Amwell published in 1979. Jim writes with energy and color, and with a special flair, and here is one of the most memorable I've ever heard. But like all Cajun stories, it's hard to recall—unless you're a Jim Rikhoff.*

WE HAVE received a number of letters from our devoted following in response to last November's column which was concerned with the unsolicited and, I felt unwarranted intrusion of George Martin's suggestion that I "write" like Ed Zern. The general tone seemed to be (one) "just who is this George Martin anyway?"—(a good question, I might add) and (two) "we know you can write like Ed What's-his-face if you really wanted to." All of which reminds me of an old story that Zern has always claimed, but one that I know to have been told in one form or another since Cro-Magnon man organized the first saber-toothed tiger hunt.

It seems that many years ago the late Nash Buckingham set out to make his yearly pilgrimage through the best duck clubs of the Mississippi Flyway. When he appeared at the old Horseshoe Bend Club, he was assigned his favorite guide, one Ephraim Turner, a somewhat elderly gentleman of the Old South who had attended to Marse Buckingham's needs for countless seasons. Among Eph's duties was the brewing of the mid-morning coffee. As Eph gathered together the "makin's"—a beat-up old coffee pot and a can of Louisiana dark-roast—Nash pointed out that there would be no need to load this equipment into the skiff as he had brought along one of those new "Thermos" jugs full of hot coffee. Eph stopped, somewhat perplexed by this revelation. After a moment he inquired of Nash just what was a "Thermos" jug, and what did it do? Nash thought for a moment and then, deciding he had best make the explanation as simple as possible, replied: "Why it kept cold things cold and hot things hot." Eph silently pondered this new knowledge as they loaded the boat, pushed off and poled for some minutes. Finally, he turned to Nash and asked one question: "Mr. Nash, that Thermos thing . . . You say it keeps the cold things cold and the hot things hot . . . Mr. Nash, how do it know?"

Which reminds me of the peculiar talents of a similar sporting folk, the Cajuns of south Louisiana, and a story Bill Simmons attributes to the late, great Nash. According to Bill, it seems Mr. Nash was making yet again one of his perennial pilgrimages through the better duck clubs of the Mississippi Delta and, as luck would have it, found himself being guided by one Jean Claude Thibidoux.

Early on, Jean Claude established "wan t'ing, dat for sure": namely, that he, Jean Claude, was nobody's man, and he would "shoot de duck too." Mr. Nash, being a prudent man who rarely started any argument outside his own turf, especially with one so renowned as a productive duck guide as Mr. Thibidoux, acquiesced to this statement with considerable grace and, it must be admitted, more than a little curiosity, for his Cajun companion carried a rather unusual fowling piece.

Of undetermined age and manufacture, Jean Claude's double barrel shotgun was rather more a hybrid than a firearm of single design and execution. While it was impossible to determine whether the barrels were of Damascus or nickel steel, as they were completely enshrouded in electrical tape and fine copper wire, the old dog-ear exposed hammers protruded with impressive authority from a massive action and trigger assembly joined to a homemade, club-like stock of solid swamp oak. Since Jean's gun was a muzzle-loader, there were no shotshells to give a hint to the barrel's gauge; and Jean Claude only shrugged when asked. Mr. Nash had to hazard the gun was probably a 10 gauge or close to it.

As they progressed down a bayou, Mr. Nash watched fascinated as, in between poling, Jean Claude would load his gun in stages. First, he loaded a huge measure of powder: then, snatching a clump of Spanish moss as they passed a tree, he rammed a glob of that down as wadding. Next he poured an assortment of shot, bits of iron and steel with a few tiny nails and other oddments, on top and rammed it all home with another patch of moss. At this point, it must be admitted that Mr. Nash viewed the upcoming first encounter with the local greenheads with mixed emotion. His curiosity and fears were soon to be rewarded, however, for as they rounded a bend in the bayou, they jumped a bunch of mallards swimming toward their pirogue. As the ducks flared up over them, straining to gain altitude and peel off and away from the boat, Mr. Nash was transfixed by first an incredible explosion, then a voluminous cloud of white smoke that enveloped him, and, lastly, the sensation of water pouring over the boat's sides as it thrust down and then heaved itself upward after the concussion.

When the dust settled and Mr. Nash once again regained his composure, he turned to witness his companion, with a look of benign satisfaction covering his features, scooping up four mallards from the water. There was about an inch of water in the bottom of the pirogue, but that skillfully designed craft seemed to have weathered the crisis quite well. As soon as Mr. Nash's hearing had returned somewhat to normal—he only heard a faint ringing—he gently inquired, simply as one dedicated shooter to another, how Jean Claude ever in the world knew when he had a proper load for his old cannon?

"Why, Mistaire Nash, I'ma tol' you, dat ver-ry simple t'ing . . . this lil' brother know he got a proper load when de ol' *bateau*, she swamp water!"

Both Bill Simmons and I have been looking for "the proper load" ever since.

Speaking of Cajuns, some years ago I was duck hunting with the late Gene Smith and that bard of the bayous, Grits Gresham, at Win Hawkins' Oak Grove Club in Louisiana. The Oak Grove is one of the finest traditional duck hunting clubs in the country and, under Mr. Win's serene supervision, things are done right. Early morning—like four a.m.—I was awakened, had quail on toast for breakfast (not all bad!) and was deposited in an airboat to be taken out to my blind. We swished through the narrow channels of the surrounding swamps, dropping off the various hunters with Cajun guides waiting in pirogues, which are long shallow-drafted wooden boats that were pushed through the reeds to blinds.

When it came my turn, I found a long lanky good ol' boy leaning on his pole like some sort of South Louisiana Ichabod Crane. After I managed to move my paraphernalia and creaking body into his pirogue with a minimum of clumsiness, we pushed off into the early mist as the sound of the retreating airboat gradually drifted away in the distance. In a few minutes we broke into a patch of open water of several hundred square feet in which a carefully constructed blind was perched on stilts. We tied up the pirogue, covered it with reeds and took our places, still silent, in the blind. My companion rearranged a few reeds in the front of the blind as all guides do to show how utterly helpless you would be without their expert eye and superior craftsmanship.

The first faint streaks of dawn were edging over the horizon, but it was still largely dark in the swamp. But it wasn't silent. The wings were starting to whistle past our heads, by our blinds, and occasionally we would hear a "plop" as one or another would drop into the open water about us. Then one would voice a tentative, sort of inquiring quack; another would plaintively quack-quack back; a more garrulous old-timer would vent his irritation with the younger set with a whole stream of indignant chortles, gurgles and quacks. The sun continued to fight its way through the Spanish moss, lush swamp grasses and reeds. Finally, some rays broke through to reflect over the face of the pond surrounding us just as a flight of green-winged teal swept through out of nowhere and dropping in among our decoys.

"It's just plain beautiful. Fantastic. You know, I don't have to shoot a duck today and I'd be perfectly satisfied. It's something just to be here seeing this dawn in the swamp." I rhapsodized to my Cajun friend, who was thoughtfully picking his nose.

"Wal, I'm-a-tol you wan ting, Lil' brother," were his first words, "Ol Jean Richard, me, take lotsa you dudes out here for shoot de duck and most of dem fellas speak to me just lak you. Yeah, so *trés bien*. So *trés belle*. Be-yu-tee-fool. But I gonna tell you wan more ting. Come day after de duck *saison* over, ain't wan dude come down here wit ol' Jean Richard at fo' clock any morning!"

Well, that says it all. Being a spectator isn't enough. You've got to be a piece of the action to want to get up at four o'clock in the morning for anything. And, oh yes, that just brought something else to mind. I know what to do in March now. If I can't go hunting or fishing and don't feel like reading about it, then I guess I'll just have to call up some of the boys, Davy, Joe, Hilly, Harry or maybe even George in Washington—and talk about it. I always could kill more ducks over a telephone or, better yet, a refreshment, than I could leaning over a blind anyway.

A CHRISTMAS PRESENT TO MYSELF

Robert C. Ruark

What would I give today to pick up a copy of Field & Stream *and find a new piece by this man gracing its pages? Or be able to buy a new book of Ruark's, its pages alive and bristling with his colorful and descriptive prose? Alas, that will never be; for he is gone, dead at the age of fifty in 1965, while at the peak of his abilities. For Ruark fans like myself, this piece will be a significant treat. For unless you have dug very deep into his works, you will have missed it altogether. It has never been anthologized since originally appearing in* Field & Stream *in December 1952. This article was one of several features that Ruark wrote for* Field & Stream *while still on an emotional high from a classic safari to Africa in 1950. That hunt led to the publication of* Horn of the Hunter. *The* Field & Stream *pieces in turn led to the creation and development of the "Old Man and the Boy" series and enabled Ruark to shuck his syndicated newspaper work—for which he was well known—and devote his time to a new safaris and the development of a massive book on Africa. That book turned out to be the best-seller,* Something of Value, *the first of a string of novels that included* Uhuru; Poor No More; *and* The Honey Badger. *The "Old Man and the Boy" pieces have been anthologized in two books published by Holt, Rinehart and Winston. Reading this, you will sense Ruark's personal rediscovery of his hunting heritage and the beginning of his turnback to the outdoors as the well-spring for his writing. God, do I miss being able to read fresh, appealing stuff like this.*

A CHRISTMAS PRESENT TO MYSELF

A STRANGER standing on the ramp at Moisant Airfield outside New Orleans might have observed a man with a silly grin on his face as he stepped off a Constellation, carrying a shotgun case in his hand. The stranger might have wondered briefly what could happen to any man, in this day and age, to make him look so pleased with himself. And if he had asked me, I would have told him.

I would have told him that I was in process of spending a Christmas present, and that I had opened it early. This was the middle of December, and I had already ripped off the seals and busted open the package. In this instance I had the right. This was a Christmas present to myself, given with the family's approval. It was a simple present, involving two weeks in which the recipient didn't have to do anything. I was free to shoot ducks, or not shoot ducks. If I shot them at all, I wasn't intending to work at it. There might be some quail later. Then again, there might not.

This is as nearly an ideal state as man is destined to live in, if you happen to love the city of New Orleans, admire ducks, and entertain no open enmity toward quail. It was a unique sensation for yours very sincerely, because in my business you are generally limited by time and somebody else's determination. I kept rolling the idea around in my head as the airport limousine sped toward Bourbon Street, a street which was very aptly named some hundreds of years ago. *Two weeks of free time,* I thought, *and a very Merry Christmas to you, old boy!*

A nice man I know with a sumptuous duck camp up at Lake Charles had said pray do come slay one of his greenheads. I took this under advisement. I took it under advisement while dining at the *Vieux Carré* restaurant, a procedure that was not complete until about 2 A.M. You eat slow in New Orleans when you're eating good, because you do not wish to hurry the wine, and garlic bread makes you fat if you eat it fast.

The night's flight was decoying in well on Bourbon Street, and seemed to be settling mostly around Monsieur Hip Guinle's Famous Door, where a fellow named Sharkey used a trumpet to call in the hens, which are legal shooting on Bourbon Street. There was also some activity in the neighborhood of Mr. Thomas Caplinger's Cafe LaFitte, where the late flight roosts. Somewhere before dawn I decided to go shoot a duck, it being a definitely ducky kind of morning.

This involved a hurried phone call to another friend, a rather dazzling fellow named Jimmy Moran—an ex-boxer and *bon vivant* who now runs a restaurant and the best duck camp in the world. What makes it so nice is that it is in Plaquemines Parish, less than an hour's drive from New Orleans, and a man may proceed there rather extemporaneously. Mr. Moran, an Italian by birth, whose name is really Brocato, loves two things. He loves diamonds and he loves ducks. He has a diamond zipper on his pants and a diamond bridge in his teeth, and he has the friendliest flock of mallards and pintails that you ever did see. They are evidently bemused by his flashing, 10-karat smile.

It is not true that a man must suffer to shoot ducks, not if he knows Jimmy. It is balmy in Louisiana, even in December, and the ducks down there have not been indoctrinated on lousy weather. They fly as happily in the sunshine as they do in a blizzard up north. And in Jimmy's camp a man may collect his limit while wearing a Homburg hat and a Chesterfield overcoat, and still be back in New Orleans in time for lunch. It so happened that when Mr. Moran picked me off the corner at about 4:30 A.M. I was wearing a Homburg hat and a Chesterfield overcoat, which did not cause Mr. Moran any concern. He was wearing a pearl gray derby himself.

You coast down the highway for about fifty minutes and you come to an oyster factory on a bayou, and there is Old Sam waiting for you in the speedboat. Twenty minutes more down the bayou, and you spy what appears to be a comfortable cottage smack in the middle of the marsh, or what Louisianians call "prairie." Old Sam, who is as black as a stovepipe, as old as time, and as ardent a duck admirer as you are apt to meet, already has the coffee bubbling happily on the hob. You gulp the coffee, unlimber the weapon, locate the duck stamp, and shove off in the pirogue. A pirogue is a water-going ashtray that will capsize if you shave more closely on one side of the face than on the other. Sam and I shoot together, because we are both lazy and our blind is only a couple of hundred yards from the house.

"Dey too many ducks aroun' this year," Sam says. "You got to shoot careful, or you gonna find yourse'f back in the camp in about twenty minutes. Don't shoot nothin' but them ol' bull pintails or them green-headed French ducks. Don't waste no time on trash."

It turns out Sam is right. The blind is attacked by ducks. Bluebills come along in squads of fifty and sixty, and seem determined to bash their brains out on the *roseaux,* the reeds that form the structure of the blind. The air is so full of golden-eyes and gray ducks and *poule d'eau* (coots) that you could stir them around with a stick. These you do not shoot because they have a limit on ducks, and in Louisiana anything that is not called "big duck" is not shot. Big duck is mallard. Big duck is pintail. Big duck is nothing else but.

"Big duck," Sam whispers, pointing and then delivering a few sexy-sounding quacks behind his hand.

Three mallards drift by, circle twice, and drop their flaps. The greenhead sits down, and then plunges straight up as I lurch onto my feet. A drake mallard, frightened and hunting cloud, is a sight that can be matched only by a cock pheasant in a squawking hurry. These are the times when you find it difficult to practice the ancient Cajun axiom: "If a duck he's come down, shoot hees tail. Eef he's go up, shoot hees nose." I shoot hees nose, and down he comes like a bag of bricks. The wind is our way, and he drifts slowly across the sweet-water pond and lodges behind the blind. Sam rakes him in with a push-pole. He is lovely to look at, with that vivid poison-green head and that flat blade of blinding yellow bill.

It was quite a morning. We had seven in the pirogue—four for Sam and three for me, all male mallards and pintails—when a black mallard passed high in the stratosphere. The big ducks had slowed down, and we were getting mostly trash business now; so I took a poke at the transient. I was shooting an ancient 32-inch full-choke double, and I think I led this baby a good thirty feet. It seemed to take him an hour to fall, and I will not brag of the fact that he had one pellet in him—thoughtfully, it seems, I had shot him through the right eye. Huge drake, he was nearly 5 pounds.

Over in the other blind, where Mr. Moran was making occasional sounds with his .410, the operation was observed. With the wind away, Jimmy couldn't hear our shots. He told me later the reaction of Cap, his companion.

"Lord bless and save us, Mister Jimmy," Cap said. "That black duck done had a heart attack."

It is indeed a shocking thing to see a black mallard collapse about seventy yards up and hear no shot to explain his plunge to the water. I was accountably smug when we got back to camp.

One of the things Mr. Moran can do is cook. He is an especially fine hand with a few teal and some button mushrooms and some broth of his own mixing, and breakfast in the little camp is always an event. I don't know whether you can better the sensation of blue sky, four people happy with twelve mallard and pintail drakes hanging on the line on the porch, swinging gently by their lovely necks in a stiff morning breeze, the scent of teal simmering in the pot. The sky full of ducks trading back and forth, the lonesome squawk of a lost blue goose, and red-winged blackbirds swinging on the rushes and tossing handfuls of silvery chirps on the morning, the smell of marsh and ooze and spent gunpowder, the quack of a hen mallard somewhere over in the prairie. Right then I decided that I didn't want to be anywhere else, because I was going to do it all over again tomorrow. I was as happy with my four big ducks as I might have been with sixty, because I had seen enough to shoot sixty and I had shot the ones I wanted the way I wanted to shoot them. With the exception of the big black, of course. That was pure dumb luck. Just show-offy stuff.

Then we went fishing. At a cut-off on the bayou Jimmy had built a sort of stage. When you chummed the swift water on the turn, the red drum and the trout made it boil. We caught fish. Then we took a nap. And we were back in New Orleans for lunch—this time at the *Restaurant Galatoire,* which does quite an artistic thing with trout Marguery and *rémoulade* shrimp and chicory salad and hot French bread. I concluded that even with taxes and the high cost of living life could be beautiful.

But, as always, there was a problem. Mine was whether to desert the cozy shooting of Mr. Moran's camp for a really elaborate operation at Lake Charles, operated by a collection of brothers who take ducks more seriously than money, and they take money very seriously. It was tough leaving New Orleans, but I could always come back. Airplanes run back and forth with alarming frequency. So a little later I am at Lake Charles.

They have lots of duck there, too. We had a three-day shoot, and of eight men only one failed to come in with his limit of big ducks. This gentleman, now passed to his feathers, was an extreme amateur. He went out with four boxes of shells, and came back with two ducks and no shells at all. He was chided somewhat ungently by his friends. Pulling himself up proudly, he uttered a disdainful line: "I came here," he said, "*to shoot.*"

We encountered a prime example of Cajun philosophy, I thought, on the second day. A mallard was coming straight into the blind, not decoying, but passing over. I stood up and walloped him, and he hurtled into the blind. He hit my friend and guide, Monsieur Lion Richard, smack in the face, knocking him backward out of the blind and into the pirogue. Monsieur Richard climbed back into the blind with the duck, his face full of mallard, his ribs sore, but his dignity intact.

"If you please," he said, "in the future will you please not shoot so good, you?"

One of the afternoons we went over to the flats to shoot geese, and you haven't seen geese until you see them there. Some hundreds of thousands rise, circle, yell and settle back down again, a little farther away. The Cajuns decoy them very simply. They take an old newspaper, fold it into the rough shape of a bird, prop it up with a stick, and the geese boil out of the sky like relatives to a will-reading. Those blue geese may have magnificent eyes, but for brains I rank them with dodo. In that country it is largely a matter of picking out the younger, tenderer ones and letting the grizzled white old squadron leaders pass by.

We shot geese. Then we went back to the swamp buggy, and I managed to fall in a hole. Water went into my boots, and I sopped and squizzled all the way back to camp. It was dinner-time, and I kicked off the boots and forgot to dry them. When they turned up sopping next morning, my room-mate regarded me with a jaundiced eye.

"Here is a fellow," he said in a pained voice, "who writes a syndicated column for a living. Five days a week he tells the world how to act. But he ain't got sense enough to pour water out of a boot." This seemed very humorous at the time, especially since this ignorant oaf had been clutching a water-turkey to his bosom for a whole day, under the erroneous idea that he had shot a rare species of black goose.

I don't know whether you've ever been on one of these expeditions where there are no game hogs, where the blinds are assigned by lot, where there are ducks enough for everybody, where the liquor consumption is mild, the poker stakes unsteep, the food constant, and the jokes tailored along childish but non-malicious lines. The sleep is sound, the weather beautiful and, while the sport is basically simple, you occasionally pause to pity all the rich millionaires on their yachts, with their ulcers and their taxes and their poor pinched faces. At the end of three days we had to go back to New Orleans. Poor us! We *had* to go back to New Orleans.

Again there was a dreadful choice. Would I stay in New Orleans, or would I go back to the little camp in Plaquemines and molest Moran's ducks some more? Master Robert Moran, aged 15 at that time, announced that insofar as he was concerned the Christmas holidays had started and he had decided to accept me as his partner. We shot ducks each day under a gentian-blue sky, in our shirt sleeves, with nobody out there but us, ducks and an occasional mosquito. Jimmy cooked. Bobby policed the camp. I supervised, generally from a supine position. Old Sam bragged about Bobby's prowess with a shotgun, which is natural, since Old Sam regards Bobby as his own child, despite a slight difference in color.

At the end of the eighth day I had reached a point I had not believed possible: I was weary of shooting ducks, especially big old green-headed mallards and big fat bull pintails. I was caught up on ducks. So I went back to New Orleans, and there was a telegram waiting for me. It said simply: "Why don't you come down to Hobcaw and miss a quail or so?" It was signed BMB, which means Bernard M. Baruch, a gentleman of some eighty summers who has the best quail shooting in the world on his vast acreage in South Carolina. I did not say no.

I expect I am a sucker for anything that occurs outdoors, and hence am apt to burble a bit, but if there is anything better than a duck-sky full of whistling wings it is an autumn wood in the warm country, the air just crisp enough to be non-sweaty but balmy enough to make a canvas shell jacket plenty of covering. The sun burns your nose gently, but the breeze cools you. The stodgy old pony picks his way delicately along the ridges, falling into an occasional stump-hole for laughs. The dogs flash here and there. The robins chuckle, the crows caw, and an occasional jay-bird gives an outraged scream. The pretty little bluebirds chirp, and the rabbits burst from under your feet. The smell is of sun-warmed broom-grass and crushed pine needles and sparkleberry bushes. Once in awhile a deer jumps and stands, startled but not really afraid. Over yonder somewhere one of the colored boys is out with a rabbit hound, and you can hear him yelp and then you hear his frenzied yap and the bang of an old single-barrel with a wired stock.

Then the quail dogs make feverish game, and finally the big buck pointer stiffens in the corner of a field and the little bitch falls stark on her stomach behind him. You get off the horse and pop a couple of shells into the little 16-gauge, and your heart stops somewhere between Adam's apple and mouth. Your hands sweat and your lips are dry and you walk up past the dogs and the woods explode. Somehow you have picked a bird out of the mass and the gun goes bang and the bird falls off the end of it—or not, as the case may be—and then you swing on another one by instinct.

At the end of the day you come in all full of excuses and falsehoods, and that first drink tastes like no drink ever tasted in a barroom. The food has an extra flavor and the fire some extra warmth. The beds are softer and the blankets woolier and the dreams sweeter, because you know that tomorrow you can get up and do it all over again. That is the full richness of a little time not governed by the necessity of producing a certain result before a deadline. Tomorrow's promise is always the best part of it.

I shot the last day the way a man dreams of shooting. The dogs worked faultlessly. The birds held perfectly. Taking no more than three from each covey, we had the limit in the bag by 4 P.M. And on the way back to the car, jogging down country roads, with the dogs working for fun on each side, we were forced to stop and flush thirteen coveys of quail! The enjoyment was in no sense lessened because the gun was in the scabbard under your leg and you kicked up birds just to see 'em fly.

It was Christmas eve when I caught the plane for Washington, to spend Christmas with the family. With me I had a gun and a bag and the legal limit of quail and ducks for possession. I was sunburned and slightly mosquito-chewed, and I had gained ten pounds off a combination of New Orleans-and-Baruch bill of fare. I had not seen a newspaper or heard a radio broadcast in two weeks. Maybe we were at war with Luxemburg; if we were, I didn't know it, and I doubt if I would have cared at that moment.

It was cold and crisp in Washington, with the sky full of stars and the Christmas trees all lit up and twinkling back at the stars. The bells were ringing and all the Congressmen had gone home and Washington had become the nice place it can be when the legislators leave. It is a very Christmasy town, clean and quiet, with practically no slums and the broadest population of reasonably happy middle-class people I know of.

I was wearing the same silly grin when I pushed open the door and said "Merry Christmas!" to the folks. My mother-in-law, who does not think I am entirely bad, handed me a holiday toddy and then asked, "And what do you want for Christmas this year?"

I took a moment to answer. I thought about two weeks with no work to worry about and early morning in duck blinds. I heard the teal whistle as they swooped into the decoys and the rustle and swish as they flopped down and the forlorn quack of a hen mallard away over yonder looking for her lost boyfriend. I remembered a vagrant yearling goose that we practically had to shoo out of the blind. I saw a composite picture of Old Sam the duck hunter and Ely the quail expert and Mr. Baruch, looking very much like a beardless Santa Claus. I smelt some woods and water and heard a quail explode under my feet. The silly grin remained.

"Polly," I said to my mother-in-law, "you may not believe this, but there is not one single, solitary thing I want for Christmas. I've had mine."

And I was right. For me, that year, Christmas was not over in a day. I managed to stretch it into two wonderful weeks.

FOUR

The Ropes and the Tools

ARE WE SHOOTING
8-GAUGE GUNS?

Nash Buckingham

By any measure of editorial judgment, this should be one of the most lavish introductions in our duck book. It will not be, simply because I have already fired both barrels in praise of The Main Man of waterfowling literature (see The Bobwhite Quail Book, *Amwell Press). In my love of Buckingham's works, I have a great deal of distinguished company, in particular, the outstanding upland-bird writer George Bird Evans, who has chronicled Buckingham's life and works in* The Best of Nash Buckingham, *published by Winchester Press in 1973. I highly recommend it as an adjunct to a full Buckingham library since Evans fills in biographical information and background details not available in the Buckingham text itself. If you have not seriously investigated the full works of Buckingham, I must say that I envy you. You have a treat in store that I can only partially duplicate in my rereading, which I do constantly. If anyone has ever written better about the halcyon days of waterfowling and quail shooting, I would like to know his name. Buckingham could write it because he was talented and because he* did *it! Until his death at age ninety-one—in his sleep on March 10, 1971—Buckingham used his days to the fullest and left behind a legacy of sharing what he saw and felt. One bit of news in the Buckingham story is that a very lovely set of his works has been republished by Delta Arms, Indianola, Mississippi. The collection is handsomely bound and boxed. My problem in including Mister Nash in this collection is obvious: What to choose? On any selection I make, someone is bound to complain, "Well, that's not the best Buckingham piece." Well, I'm going with my gut on the four choices that are included at various places in this book. My hunch is that for most readers, these Buckingham gems may be new reading experiences. This first piece is very much in the practice vein. The other three are warm and moving "fireside" stories. This is from* De Shootingest Gent'man and Other Hunting Tales—*not the original, but the expanded edition published by Thomas Nelson & Sons, New York, in 1961. The piece is late-Buckingham, having appeared originally in* Gun Digest *in 1960.*

In JULY, 1958, I was shooting at our venerable Memphis, Tennessee, gun club when my gifted gunsmith friend, Mr. H.L. Highsmith, one of the nation's top-bracket riflemen, shotgunners and stockmakers, arrived for a bit of skeet practice with a strange piece. Twelves, sixteen, twenty and four-ten gauges were already rapping on our four fields. Mr. Highsmith's weapon *du jour* was a 10-gauge Purdey hammer double, exquisitely engraved, with a deft, slide-slip opener beneath its trigger guard. Its stock, a thing of beauty and a joy forever to any gun collector's eye, couldn't have missed my own gun's measurements (14¼ x $^{19}/_{16}$ x 2¼) by more than a skeletal fraction anywhere along the line. The Purdey's 32-inch tubes of lovely flowered Damascus were, of all things, bored true cylinder. Probably made before chokeboring happened in Great Britain. Weighing 9½ pounds, it handled fast.

Mr. Highsmith had loaded himself a bagful of 10-gauge hulls with only 3¼ drams of black powder in some, semismokeless in others and the equivalent of smokeless for the rest. Using 1$^{1}/_{8}$ of 8's ahead of such propellents was almost too light for a 10-gauge. But Mr. Highsmith's was a crash investigation of a lot of gunning's adages and priorities ballistically. He was out to enjoy an afternoon's pleasant "boom-and-bust" on a shot-gunning Renaissance. He broke 23x25 at skeet, mixing the loads indiscriminately, to the amusement and amazement of his squadmates equipped with 12-bore doubles, over-unders, pumps and autoloaders. Some were using muzzle gadgets. Mr. Highsmith then turned the 10-bore Purdey over to Robert Sheffield, one of our region's summit all-around shotgunners, and he proceeded to shatter 25 x 25 skeet clays. Messrs. Highsmith and Sheffield are young, strong fellows, so the heavy Purdey was apparently no adverse factor even at station 8, which, in this scribe's opinion, is a silly trick shot. Birds shot at such ridiculous range would be pulped and ruined.

Everybody enjoyed the Highsmith-Sheffield exhibition and quite a few members tried the Purdey just to say that for once in their lives they'd fired a charge of ancient black powder. Mr. Highsmith, a student of Magnum shotguns (early and late vintages) has a gift for restoring "Grandpa's" old fowling pieces. Too, aside from his knowledge of ballistics, he can practice what he preaches, from duck blind, a goose pit or in the dove field. When it comes to stockmaking, he is an artist with a deep, keen knowledge, not only of woods and world models in stocks, but of what should be found in said wood; for perfect grains, burls and qualities of inlays that only perfect wood will allow. In short, in his chosen profession, Mr. Highsmith is a double-actioned, delicate and dedicated artist.

Watching him and Robert Sheffield shoot 96 per cent at skeet with that lovely, old-fashioned Purdey recalled for me a Father & Son Day in 1928 at the famous Camp Fire Club up the river from New York City. The late Captain Paul Curtis, then the famed gun editor of *Field & Stream* magazine, had invited me and the late and equally famous gun critic, Colonel Harold P. Sheldon (then Chief Conservation Officer of the United States Bureau of Biological Survey), to shoot the club's newly installed freshly discoverd shooting game called skeet. Having been Director of Game Restoration for the Western Cartridge Company, of East Alton, Illinois (now Olin Mathieson Chemical Corporation, Incorporated—division), I was in charge of its trapshooting activities when the originator of skeet, the late William Harnden Foster, of Andover, Massachusetts, brought it to Western and saw it adopted by them first. I had also served a term or two on the National Skeet Board. But I had had literally no experience at the game.

I had been live-pigeon shooting at the Philadelphia Gun Club with Eltinge Warner (then owner and publisher of *Field & Stream* magazine) and had with me a new 10-pound, 32-inch, overbored 12-gauge Magnum (with Askins-Sweeley type boring by the late Burt Becker) from which I had been firing Western's latest 3-inch case with copper-coated shot. In 1928 Burt Becker was acknowledged the world's master barrel-borer. Fox-Becker Magnums had been in production approximately five years and Western developed their first loads and copper-coated pellets. At the Camp Fire Club, however, I was using standard trap loads. Colonel Sheldon was firing a beautiful 20-gauge double just sent him by the late Bob Owen, the British gunmaker later employed by Winchester; with something to do with later development of their now famous Model 21. The Colonel and I were patiently briefed by "Cap" Curtis as to skeet's rigmarole; how to swing and lead and behave ourselves at each station; and followed it all with grave appreciation. Then, squadded with the Captain and two other members, we "lit out." There was covert eyebrow-lifting and subtle snickers at my Magnum and for the Colonel's 20-bore with quail loads. If I recall correctly, in those days, at station 8, instead of snapping at the incomers, you could wheel and fire at the target as it went away. I broke 98 x 100 and the Colonel (the first time he had ever shot skeet) shattered 97. Captain Curtis accounted for 95 x 100. We got bawled out as "ringers" and thieving ingrates, but we held it over Paul for many a day. Especially about how a Magnum 12-bore could be put to a good many uses, on the basis that you have to first hit something no matter what weapon you're using. It is a great satisfaction to me now to recall both Sheldon and Curtis as two of the soundest field and waterfowl shots I've ever encountered, and comradely, unselfish, high-grade sportsmen as well. In after years, I wrote a foreword for Paul's book on guns and shooting. And Harold Sheldon did, for me, an inspired foreword to the original Derrydale deluxe edition of *De Shooting'est Gent'man*.

From that pleasant yesterday at Camp Fire I was to shoot that 12-bore Becker Magnum at practically every species of continental wildfowl and upland game—except quail and snipe. I shot steadily for twenty-one years until, in 1948, December 1, an examining game agent just forgot to put it back where he found it in our automobile. He left it, lying 'twixt hood and fender; it was never recovered though engraved on both case and steel. With that gun I fired every 12-gauge combination from 3-dram 1-ounce loads to the heaviest charges in 3-inch cases. Long since, I have come to realize that while the good big guns will nearly always beat the good little ones, it is the gunner himself who must toe scratch and swing the weapon with effective timing—or be penalized. You either hit or miss, hit and kill, hit and cripple—and recover—maybe—provided you work hard or have a good retriever. The last named being the best Magnum load I've ever seen. When you discuss "long-range shotgunning" with Magnum guns and loads (neither is worth a hoot without the other), meaning anything past fifty yards for lethal falls, you had best have a good retriever at "sit" beside you in blind or boat. Or else go over your stock of alibis very carefully.

By the time I was fifteen (in 1895) I was no stranger to the Magnums. We didn't know 'em by that name then, such appellations applying to champagne bottles of greater capacities, vintages and voltage. The 20-gauge was practically nonexistent sportingly, 14-gauges were still around, and 16's frequently encountered. In fact, that was our first gun; a 16-gauge double, hammer gun by Parker, given to my older brother at Christmas, 1888. Twelve gauge was definitely standard, but for wildfowl there were still many 10 bores and quite a few 8's in use. My father used 12-bore hammer guns by E. Smith of England for quail, snipe, woodcock and doves and plains game. They were probably, as to boring, our today's improved cylinder and modified. For wildfowl, he shot a W.W. Greener side-bolt 11-pound, 32-inch, hammerless 12 bore—with 3¼-inch chambers. Its stock specifications would fit me today. Until a few years ago I had one of those long green Winchester cases he fired from the big Greener. Made with a reinforced base, it was loaded (according to its top-wad) with 44 grains of Du Pont powder but only one ounce of 6's. That was the load made famous by the late Fred (Old Fritz) Gilbert, of Spirit Lake, Iowa. Fred was employed by Du Pont as a professional trapshot, and I have a cup, won in 1915, celebrating his twentieth anniversary with that now empirical organization. My parent used many cases of those "Gilbert loads," so, naturally, I helped myself to them and fired 'em from my own double Bonehill. Taking a chance maybe, but what we didn't know fortunately didn't hurt us at that tender age. In those days the loading companies would put up for the ammunition jobbers the famous and favorite loads of "market hunters," duck clubs, and champion clay-target and flyer champions. A favorite load for the famous Wapanoca Duck Club at Turrell, Arkansas, was 3¼ drams with one ounce of chilled shot. Its members bought them lavishly. Duck bag limits were fifty a day, market hunting was strictly legal, and, with plenty of fowl around it was a pleasant load to shoot from both double guns and the new-fangled and increasingly popular repeating shotguns.

Four Wapanoca Club members used 10's and 8's by W. & C. Scott, of England; all sweetly handling, hammer doubles. I was permitted their use when their owners were absent. I was then five-foot ten and weighed 185 pounds, so recoil was no problem. And I had been taught how to mount a shotgun properly, too. There were worlds of swan and geese available and men didn't have to consider the word "Magnum." Big guns for wildfowling were simply a matter of course. There was no specialization for "long-range shooting" as such. There was little or no of what is known today as "skybusting." There were big bags to accumulate and the good shots and market hunters only "got 'em where they wanted 'em" before they fired, but everyone tried to make every shell count. There was no need to merely shoot on a chance of crippling.

Use of those 10- and 8-bore guns in my earlier years left me an experience that stood me in good stead in after years of controversial discussion about Federally legal aspects of their banning or regulation. There has never been a worse misunderstood nor more humorously garbed ballistic field, from the conversational or industrial slant, than the furored forensics by gun editors (some of whom never fired an 8 gauge and mighty few 10's) and official Washington, charged with such contentions under the Migratory Bird Act's rulings. One paragraph should cover that historical era of sham and pressures.

In the early 1890's first lever and then trombone-action repeaters by Spencer and Winchester, carrying six shells, made their appearance and quickly infiltrated the ranks of sportsmen and market hunters. About 1905 the first autoloading 12-bore appeared to further accelerate the pace of national waterfowl destruction. By 1912–13 when the Weeks McLean Bill and Lacy Act appeared, it had become obvious that wildfowl populations (whipsawed by upped firepower and first-noted agricultural attritions of northern breeding grounds) were doomed unless remedial measures were taken. Federal bag limits of 25 ducks a day and 8 geese, with 90 days open seasons (no "frameworks" or trading with the states—a bit of penny-ante wildlife management inflicted in recent years) were clapped on. To make assurance doubly sure, from the market-shooting slant, the good old 8 bore was banished. The lighter, faster-shooting pump-guns and autoloaders (putting more shot and powder under the trigger-fingers than the 8's) were not only allowed to continue, but made the watchword for advertising: "Shoot more, shoot faster and kill more." Putting away the 8 bore probably seemed the right thing to do to disenfranchised market gunners. But what swivel-chair Federals knew about real game management then was in swaddling clothes and there weren't many Conservationists around to raise a hue and cry.

The ballistic travesty, begun then, continues—and on a double-action basis of both too-large and too-small bores. A 3-shot Magnum 12, pump or autoloader, carrying three of today's maximum charges, gives the user as much if not more firepower than the old double-tubed 8's of my youth. (We'll get into that—later.) Nor, in those early times did we have the tiny .410 gauges with which to cripple game and lose it. Failure to ban those too-little guns on Federal migrants has for long pointed an accusing finger at the game management integrity of Washington. Gun editors and ballistic writers have for long panned this official deviation from Conservational common sense and principles. But there is where we stand today. Many preserve owners and duck clubs rightfully exclude .410's.

Nowadays, using "muzzle-gadgets" successfully designed to permit all degrees of barrel restriction, the gunner, by a mere twist of the wrist or a tiny wrench, can select the pellet density he deems best for wildfowl or uplanders. Or, for the type flushed game covert he's tramping; thick or wide-open walk-up. The mental processes channeled by such decisions constitute a fascination for hunters the nation over. If they miss, the alibi is "wrong choke selection"; not one's own faulty lead. Lakes of ink, mountains of papers, and earth-girdling typewriter ribbons have been dedicated to man's yearning for sporting weapons and their ballistic developments. I have listened by the hour to heated discussions on the "killing power" of guns of varying weights and chokes, on various loads of propellents and shot sizes. Lead and hitting, in such arguments, become rather vague inconsequentials. I have heard more simon-pure bunk spilled about Magnum shotguns and their loads then the law allows.

W.W. Greener (England) and Fred Kimble (U.S.) produced barrel restrictions or "choke-boring" in shotgun barrels a full decade before I was born (1880). According to Mr. Kimble's memoirs, it was not unusual for him during his market-gunning days along the Illinois, Mississippi and Little Rivers, to bag and boat as high as two hundred or more assorted ducks per day. He used his favorite, personally choked 6 gauge (Tonks, of Boston, finished up several such weapons for him) with a stiff charge of powder in the piece's single, muzzle-loading tube, and an ounce-and-a-half of what he called "St. Ouis 3's." In a delightful and voluminous correspondence with me during the mid and late 1920's, when, at an advanced age, he was living in retirement in California, Mr. Kimble described how he made his own powder. "It was," he wrote in an exquisite, copperplate hand, "of a slow-burning texture similar to today's progressive-burning powder. I cooked it up myself on the back of my kitchen stove, from personally compounded ingredients costing but a few cents per pound." (I would like to own that recipe today.) He had frequently, he said, made long runs on single mallards of 50 or 60 straight, flighting timber at 60 to 70 yards. "I came to realize," he wrote, "that to shoot a long way it takes a cannon, so, for my duck shooting, I tried to get the closest thing to one." (We are finding that true in shooting at the moon or more distant Mars?)

To really appreciate such bags and feats of marksmanship, think of the physical labor expended, not only to paddle or row a heavy boat all day and gather one's bag, but to muzzle-load for that many shots (many of which were undoubtedly missed) day in and week out. Such results were obtained, Mr. Kimble wrote, "by trial and error basis." That means, in effect, having to learn gun yardage the hard way.

Having sat at Mr. Kimble's knees for fifty years, I know that this means sizing up an approaching goose, duck or dove and saying to yourself, "The last time I saw a chance like you, I shot about, *yon-der*." And, suiting brain reflex to action, you try to swing ahead and hit, "Yonder." You're actually trying to hit a *moving spot* ahead of the quarry—just as you successfully tried before—at such a distance. Each try taxes your clearance of gun yardage. The quarry, meanwhile, is carried in your subconscious vision. You can't intercept it by firing at a fixed spot ahead—your gun must hit that *moving spot*. You know what happens to your distance off the tee at golf when your *swing* fails to follow through? In shotgunnery that means the same thing: follow on through—or else. And it takes many an "or else" to make a real, bang-up shot. It also takes absorbed energy to lethalize game and put it on your table. In a gunning way—never send a boy on man's errand. The use of a Magnum shotgun and loads means, simply enough, "Getting thar fustest with th' mostest—and big'uns at that." But get it out of your mind that simply because you buy a Magnum you have to shoot heavy loads out of it at everything. If your wildfowling's wild and rough select the maximum charge you personally prefer. If the shooting is in the woods—over decoys—the pigeon load of 3¼ x 1¼ x 7½ will knock mallards for loops. I've killed many a limit of doves with my Magnum, using that load or even 3 drams-one ounce. Magnum or no Magnum, the gunning law is, "You've got to hit 'em first—and hard." Absorbed energy means the knockdown and K.O. punch—remember *that*.

From a gunning and ballistic angle I am, as the old song goes, "right back where I started from," seventy years ago. I sometimes sit appalled and all but cringe at blue-sky advertising claiming that clean (worse) consistent kills can be made with certain 10-bore guns using a heavy powder charge and two ounces of No. 2 shot. That's the length of a football field. Have you ever paced off a real 100 yards and looked back? Would you try for a goose at such range unless you were starving and had but one shell left? Advertising can, and has taken shotgunnery from *ad astram* to *ad nauseam*.

During early day big bores and comparatively modern American Magnum shotguns lie two main differences in American wildfowling management. During the reign of the big bores (6, 8 and 10 gauge singles and doubles) there was so much game and populations so sparse that the wildlife hucksters rarely expended an unnecessary charge. They water-huddled or "flat-shot" fowl and boated as many as possible with one or two blasts. Seven-tubed muzzle-loaders hurled thousands of pellets into night-rafted concentrations. I saw the result of such a shot in the early morning of New Year's Day, 1930—when my host and I entered his shore blind near Washington, D.C.—of all places. A northwest gale was breaking up and sweeping ice floes downtide. Henry's binoculars revealed two men in a boat well out and upriver. He sent his helper out to aid them, figuring their decoys were being swept away—but they pulled away into the mist. Awhile later that big ice floe, crashed into the shore just below our blind. We picked up 187 dead black ducks. The "big gun" wasn't located for several months, but is now in captivity. Since then, in several states tremendous, organized rings of wildfowl thieves have been broken up by Federal undercover efforts—the only real way to accomplish it. Many of their duck slaughterers admitted using extension magazines on their autoloaders when firing into encircled night rafts. In the old days, however, when a market hunter fired at a single duck, "he had it where he wanted it."

Wildfowl market hunting stems from earliest shooting on New England's coastal fresh-water ponds. Village shoemakers built camouflaged shore blinds and cobbled footgear behind such brushed-up hides while crude goose decoys floated out front. When honkers dropped in, the cobblers let them huddle and then unleashed hails of hand-molded big pellets, cut-up horseshoe nails or gravel from their smoothbored, flintlocked muzzle-loaders. Their "Goodies" plucked the slain for feather beds and pillows and spread roast goose around the community.

Later, wealthy sportsmen fashioned elaborate lodges camouflaged seaward to match tidal levels; in adjoining watchtowers gamekeepers trained and released goslings to fly out as "greeters" to coastal migrants. With parent geese in restraint (the keepers having sighted flocks headed downcoast) the gaggle of "greeters" winged forth and vocalized welcome to safe harbor. When the visitors were "lit," the trained young stooges ducked under the gatepens and rejoined the old folks. Afront the clubhouse blind was a spring-latched window opening onto a big stool of floating lures. The keeper-lookout, pressing a buzzer, interrupted the card game and sent the players to the spring window with 8 and 10 bores. He then sprung the deadfall. Up lashed the window, and there, right under the sportsmen were the victims. The bigger the bags the bigger the sports! And I am now talking about what I have actually seen. By the time live decoys were banned, many autoloaders and pump-guns had found their way into these shore blinds—and displayed the big bores. Why not: they could throw more shot—and faster.

With pump-guns and autoloaders in use (despite the banned 8's) recession came with increasing speed to basic continental stocks. And, insidiously but inevitably, agricultural attritions on both our own and Canadian breeding grounds were gaining beachheads. But, even then, access to choice waterfowling centers was not too easy. Market hunters killed about as much game as they could carry, pack and ship. Some duck clubs, foreseeing an evil day, clapped on daily bag limits—usually 50 ducks—and as many geese as one could gun. In the light of today's emaciated bag limits—almost unbelievable.

Today, the sale of other than legally pen-reared and banded wildfowl for public use (in some states) is strictly forbidden. The fact remains that if, tomorrow, the United States suddenly found itself dependent upon the food values in quantity of its wildlife resources, there would be just about enough poundage for two square meals. As of now, however, we have not even approached, much less solved, the problem of combining decency afield with game production, on a controlled or managed basis. In this country, the public's first reaction to any game regulation is not how it can be best obeyed or enforced, but how it can be evaded, or worse, violated. An unhappy situation going hand in hand with crime increases of other fields.

Conservation, it its many fields and ramifications, made no move toward the curtailment of magazine gun capacities until the early 1920's. There had been mutterings through the years, but those were stifled by the gunmakers who had seen the big bores banned by the Migratory Bird Act and the Treaty Act with Great Britain. At the time, *Field & Stream* magazine (Eltinge Warner publisher) boldly challenged the autoloaders—only to emerge badly beaten. Soon, however, a new force arose which called magazine guns and their manufacturers to an accounting. Begun in 1929 by the American Wildfowlers, a small foundational group that eventually emerged as More Game Birds in America, and later still, as Ducks Unlimited, the battle terminated in 1934–35 when an Executive order by the late Franklin Delano Roosevelt restricted magazine shotguns to 3 shots. The various states then passed equivalent legislation, many of them outlawing guns of more than 3-shot capacity—on upland game birds. It is now freely admitted that had this not been done we would not, today, be shooting wildfowl. It is also worthy of note that practically every major benefit attained by this nation's wildfowl and upland-game-bird resources has been due to Conservationists' brains in not only conceiving such measures but being able and willing to stand up and fight for them against lethargic Congresses, faceless officials and villainously exploitative commercial interests.

Let's examine some of the old big bores, strictly from their own records, then compare them with today's 12-bore Magnums, in both doubles and magazined weapons. All targets used in these tests were one-foot square.

Fred Kimble's 6-gauge 36-inch barrel muzzle loading shotgun. Handchoked by Kimble himself.

6 drams, 1½ oz., #3's at 40 yards. 79 struck—or 44.7%
6 drams, 1½ oz., #2's at 40 yards. 55 struck—or 36.6%
J. Kelley's 8-gauge single-bored muzzle-loader. Rugh of Peoria, Illinois—builder; hand-choked by Fred Kimble.

5 drams, 1½ oz., #1's at 60 yards. 40 struck—or 33.75%
Long's 10-gauge double, 32-inch barrels, breechloader. Maker—Schaeffer.

5 drams, 1½ oz., #2's at 40 yards. 58 struck—or 38.6%
4½ drams, 1½ oz., #2's at 40 yards. 59 struck—or 39.2%. Only one pellet struck outside of 25 inches.

These, then, were the guns that made history in the art of choke-boring, a restriction that permitted powerful charges of powder and heavy-shot loads for lengthened kills. They were about as close as Fred Kimble could come to a cannon. They, or their likes, endured until 1912–13, when a well-meaning Federal assumption of water-fowl protection banned gauges larger than 10's. Now, nearly 50 years later, let's appraise the situation. My own wildfowl and field artillery will suffice.

Model 21 Winchester Magnum 12 bore with 32- and 26-inch tubes. 3-inch cases.

Model 50 Winchester autoloader with 30- and 26-inch ventilated ribs. 2¾-inch cases.

Model 59 Winchester (Win-Lite glass tubes) 28- and 26-weight 6.4. 2¾-inch cases.

Burt Becker handmade 10-pound 12-gauge Magnum—32 inch. 3-inch cases, coneless.

> This is the last Magnum ever built by the late Burt Becker; described by the late Colonel H.P. Sheldon as "the finest barrel borer the world has ever seen." It will shoot consistently better than 90 per cent patterns with 4's coppered.

It is possible from a 3-inch chambered autoloader to fire three Magnum shells, each containing almost five drams of powder and as high as one and seven eighths ounces of shot. Thus giving the user almost 15 drams of propellent and almost six ounces of shot under his trigger finger. If the old big-bore users had had such devastating machines, chances are our waterfowl populations might have been wiped out earlier.

Today, with Federal bag limits running from three to five ducks a day in the four flyways, and "goose management" down to one honker a day in some areas, it matters nothing what type of gun or load the fowler uses. Provided it is of sufficient gauge and load to not cripple wildfowl and upland game like the "too little" .410's and 28's. The more (and bigger) shot, the more penetration, the more lethal absorbed energy; the less chance to cripple (provided the Government slackens its decimating practice of permitting too-early and too-late wildfowling). The Magnum shotgun trouble is this: the American gunning public has, as unusal, been "overexposed," as the advertising trade puts it, rather than "overgunned." The novice hunter (and they not unnaturally increase nowadays) hearing about fantastic "long kills" buys himself a Magnum and the heaviest charges available. Expecting, by merely pointing his great gun in the quarry's general direction, to see it collapse, fall from great heights and completely vindicate the copy-writer's claims. If these latter would but stress the fact that a Magnum isn't a special weapon shooting 3-inch cases *only*, but can handle any length hull and bag its fair share of close or distant game—if it's hit—the shooting field would be a better place in which to live. That's the one big important piece of business. You've got to connect—first.

CALLING DUCKS

Gene Hill

The Sight of Gene Hill with a duck call in his hand makes me cringe as badly as when my piece of marsh has been invaded by a sky-buster. Over the years I've witnessed Hilly take on all kinds of ambitious feats—sixty-yard mallards, three-foot putts—the fact that he was incapable of achieving, and blowing a duck call tops the list. The sounds that have come out of the chain of calls Hill is constantly fooling with have done more to protect ducks than bag limits. Now, writing about duck calls is something else. I enjoy reading Hill on any subject he cares to tackle. At Sports Afield, *I ran Hill columns on everything from chewing tobacco to handling your wife, and the readers loved them all. He's at* Field & Stream now, *still slaving over a hot typewriter, and he has gotten around to collecting many of his best pieces in books. If you've never met in person an author whose works you have admired, take my word that the experience may be a disappointing one. In the flesh, many wordslingers do not seem to match the image that was spawned by the printed page. Not so with Hill. In a duck blind or on a trout stream, you would find him to be exactly what you expected—warm, generous and friendly. Despite the fact that he went to Harvard. Wait a minute— so did Nash Buckingham! Something must have lingered in the air up there. This piece of Hill's is from* Sports Afield and Mostly Tail-feathers, *Winchester Press.*

ULYSSES S. GRANT once remarked that he only knew two tunes. One of them was *The Star Spangled Banner* and the other one wasn't. And compared to me, General Grant was a musical prodigy. Be that as it may, I am getting my hands on as many duck and goose calls as I can. I intend to learn to call waterfowl even if in the process I offend every ear in the country—and I just might. Even my Labradors have started to slink into the dark recesses of their kennel, and the rest of the world around the farm becomes dumb and silent as I turn up my "highball" and "feeding chatter" out behind the barn.

I thought I had a goose call working pretty good—and I did except the one I had down to an acoustical fine point was the danger call, a single, piercing *honk* that I can reproduce with such fidelity that no goose ever hearing it has stopped climbing until he has reached his maximum altitude, which I believe is somewhere in the neighborhood of 28,000 feet.

My duck calls, on the other hand, are such a curious combination of unnatural sharps and flats that more than one mallard has succumbed and warily circled over my blind, no doubt only out of an incredible aural curiosity rather than what I hoped would be a verbal promise of feathered companionship, great food or a torrid love affair.

Like most of us, I tend to quickly shift any of my own personal shortcomings over to the era of blaming them on faulty equipment and go out and buy something new. Right now I have four different calls, two duck and two geese—and a pintail and widgeon whistle that I won't count, because I haven't gotten around to working on that yet. I'm not sure if anyone makes an instrument that can begin to compensate for the fact that I'm about as tone deaf as a post— but I'm trying them all. And to give myself the pat on the back that I truly deserve, without out-and-out bragging, after only a few months of practice I have come up with a very recognizable version of both *Mary Had a Little Lamb* and *Silent Night* on the harmonica.

There are few things I enjoy more than waterfowling and all that goes with it. The deep envy that I radiate when the weather-tanned guide nonchalantly hauls some birds down within range with a few casual notes on his call is becoming more than I can control. When I'm out behind the barn practicing to the sheep I constantly have this mental image of myself, dressed in hip boots, my old and battered but very distinguished ducking cap pulled just slighty down over my eyes, my three-inch Magnum 1100 casually tucked in the crook of my left arm and about four assorted calls strung around my neck. My weather-tanned face warily scans the cold and shallow light of just dawn on a real weather-making morning. My experienced eyes pick out a small flock of ducks—still so far away that the other men in the blind have no idea of their presence.

"Blacks," I say casually. "About two miles off, twelve hundred feet high, at eleven o'clock."

"How can you tell?" Ask the greenhorns with me in the blind.

"Count the wingbeats," I whisper, and start to finger the Olt call I favor for distance work.

"He thinks he can call those birds in," followed by not too muffled laughter, comes from behind me in the blind. I turn, silence the chattering with a scowl and put my call to my lips. In spite of the incredible volume, there issues forth a sound so ancient, so pure, so wild, so magically entrancing that even before the lead black starts to turn I can hear the quick snapping as the gunners check the safeties and the rustling of heavy gunning clothes as the men instinctively crouch lower in the blind.

I smile to myself and shift to another call, a gleaming masterpiece made from soft glowing Osage orange. A subtle series of chuckles follows what sounds like a hen mallard reading the menu of a duck's version of the 21 Club. The flock is swiftly closing in and is about to turn upwind and scatter in the blocks. I give the signal for the other guns to stand and take their shots. And after all have missed, I rise and pull a pair of drakes, stone cold, at 55 or 60 yards. Then without a word, I send my perfectly trained retriever into the bay. My weather-tanned face permits itself a slight but manly grin of satisfaction as I turn to the other men and promise that I'll call the next bunch in a little closer—if they'd like. I bring out my pintail whistle and start to work a flock that they have yet to spot, as the Labrador brings in the second duck and puts it in my hand.

So this fall if you should happen to see a weathered ducker in hip boots, a nicely flavored cap pulled down just slightly over his eyes, an automatic Magnum tucked in the crease of his left arm, a perfectly mannered Lab at his side and enough calls strung around his neck to make him look like a pipe organ, stop and say "Hello." It's me imitating a duck hunter.

PAINTING DECOYS

Eugene V. Connett, III

The visionary Eugene V. Connett founded Derrydale Press in 1926, and during the years until the publication of its last book in 1942, Derrydale produced the most magnificent collection of sporting literature ever published. After Derrydale, Connett turned his talents as an editor to the huge books, Duck Shooting Along the Atlantic Tidewater *(Morrow, 1947) and* Wildfowling in the Mississippi Flyway *(Van Nostrand, 1949). He also edited Joel Barber's* Wildfowl Decoys. *Connett, who shot his first duck in 1908 and made his first decoy in 1915, was destined to write a book of practical waterfowling of his own. In 1953, Morrow published* Duck Decoys, *from which this piece is taken. The achievement of detail that is the hallmark of Derrydale books is very evident here as Connett reveals himself as a man who knew that small things are important.*

SOME MEN have the knack with brushes and paints, and other men don't. I have friends who can turn out a beautiful decoy up to the point of painting it. Then they just don't seem to be able to carry on. I have other friends who can paint a decoy nicely but simply can't turn out a decent body and head, nor put them together so that they will stay put. Fortunately there are two styles of painting decoys and for many long years the birds have been coming to both of them.

The first style we will call the bayman's painting. Thousands of decoys have been painted with sash brush and house paints—the way most baymen did it, and these decoys have probably accounted for more dead birds than all the more modern and carefully painted decoys ever will. That is because there used to be so many more ducks. I suggest that you make a real effort to achieve the more modern and careful painting that the best decoys now have; but if you simply can't do a decent job in that style, you can still adopt the simpler style that will bring in ducks—although not quite as readily.

First we will take up the bayman's style of painting, and with the help of our series of illustrations I will indicate the colors that go on the various areas of the different species, with information on how to mix the colors.

Starting with the black duck: the body color is a brownish black made by mixing black with burnt umber until a dusky color—like burnt cork—is obtained. Flat paints are an absolute requirement, and in thinning them turpentine should be used but not linseed oil. Use only "outside" paints, except for such small details as the wing speculums; these bright colors can be artist's colors which come in small tubes. These may be used with house paint in mixing certain colors. Many old time decoy makers believed that leaving freshly painted stool outdoors at night to become covered with dew tended to reduce the shine of the paint. I think it helps. The finished decoy must be as lacking in shine as possible. The base color for the black duck head is made by mixing a trifle of yellow ochre with some white and burnt umber. The safest plan is to start adding the light colors a bit at a time until the umber has been reduced to a sort of tannish putty color. Some black duck heads are grayish, others more yellowish. In my rig there are several shades of base color on the heads. The feather markings are burnt umber with some black—but not pure black by any means. The body color is right for the head feathering. There are two ways of feathering out the black duck heads. 1) Paint the head the same color as the body. When this is dry put on a coat of the putty color, quite thick in substance so that it won't run, and then with a nail or other sharp instrument, scratch off little lines of the putty color, allowing the dark under coat to show through. This is an easier method for those who aren't accustomed to using fine brushes than 2), which involves painting the putty color on and letting it dry. Then with a fine sable artist's brush painting little lines of burnt umber mixed with black all over the head, with the heavier concentration of streaks that run over each eye and over the top of the head and down the back of the neck. A purple wing speculum can be added, but it is not really necessary on a decoy painted à la bayman. As noted elsewhere, solid cork black duck bodies are not painted but burnt with a blow torch. Wood and pressed cork must both be painted, the latter with a number of priming coats to fill in the surface of the cork. Then the final body color is put on. USE FLAT BURNT UMBER and LAMP BLACK; AVOID SHINY FINISH. There is no difference between the coloration of the male and female black duck. The bill is olive green and the nail at the end of the bill is black.

Now let's do a broadbill in the simplified manner. The head and breast and tail section are dead black, the back is gray made by mixing black into white until it makes a medium gray. The sides are white. The bill is light bluish gray, made by adding a trace of blue to the white and black. The nail is black.

The female broadbill is brown except for a yellowish patch back of the bill, with a white speculum, as shown. The head and body color is straight burnt umber, but the lower sides should have a little white mixed in to make them a lighter shade. The bill is dark slate blue, made by adding some black to the color used for the male bird's bill.

The male canvasback's head is a sort of brick color made by mixing burnt umber, burnt sienna and white. The head, just back of the bill, is blackish, best gotten by smearing some black with your finger on the half dry base color of the head. Carry the black over the head and down the back of the neck. The bill is solid black. The breast and tail sections are black, and the center section is white.

The female canvasback head is a yellowish brown—burnt umber, white and yellow ochre—with a lighter area just back of the bill. The breast is burnt umber, as is the tail end. The back and sides are grayish brown—burnt umber, white and black. The bill is black.

The male mallard's head is a greenish black. First put on the black and when it is half dry stroke a little bright green over the cheeks and with a dry brush fade the edges into the black. The breast is a maroon color made by mixing burnt sienna, a trifle of purple and some white; don't make this too light. The back is a medium gray and the sides a lighter shade of gray. Before these two colors have dried run a line of burnt sienna between them and blend it into the upper one as evenly as you can with a dry brush. The under part of the tail is black, and the tail feathers show as a rim of white around the edges of the top of the tail. The speculum is purple bordered at either side by a stripe of white. The ends of the wing feathers on the after end of the back can be indicated with some burnt sienna, and there is a patch of white just forward of the black patch under the tail. The bill is greenish yellow made by mixing a little white and a trace of blue with yellow. The nail is black.

The female mallard's body color is mixed by adding a little burnt sienna to white; then add a little burnt umber, and then a trace of yellow ochre. The effect you want is a lighter color than a black duck, but still a dullish shade—not bright reddish or yellowish. The speculum is purple with a white stripe on each side. The head is similar to a black duck, but add more yellow ochre. The line of dark feathers over the eye is made with black and burnt umber. The bill is orange (yellow, red, plus a little white), with a smudge of black on the upper ridge. Go easy with the black; put a little on your finger and rub it in a bit while the orange is still half wet. Make the edge of this smudge soft, not sharp. The nail is black.

The male pintail's head is about the same color as the mallard's breast—mix burnt umber, white, and a touch of burnt sienna. The back and sides are gray. The lower sides are very light gray, almost white. Down each side of the head and neck runs a pure white streak which runs into the white breast. The rear end of the under body is light tan, with black beyond it and a white stripe around the end of the tail. The top of the tail feathers are black. The bill is black with a light blue patch on each side. When this much painting has thoroughly dried, sharply paint a few long pointed feathers on the after end of the back in black; when dry add a thin line of white on each side of these feathers. These tertiary feathers of the pintail are very characteristic and well worth bothering with. If there are black ducks or female mallards in your rig, don't bother with she pintails; in fact, I don't think they are worth bothering with anyway, as the males are the birds that will be noticed by the live birds.

The male widgeon has a white head with a black-bordered green streak running from around the eye to the base of the neck. The breast is a lighter shade of maroon than the mallard and the color can be mixed by adding more white to the mallard mixture. The back is brownish gray, made by mixing black, white and a bit of burnt umber. Don't get it too dark or too brown. The side is a lighter shade of the breast color, with a shoulder patch of pure white, fol-

lowed by a stripe of black, in turn followed by a speculum patch
of bright green, ended off with a stripe of black. The under tail is
white, with black above. A white stripe can be painted around the
edge of the tail. The bill is pale blue, with a black nail. I see no reason for making female widgeon as the males will do the attracting in
the rig of stool.

The Canada goose has a black head with a pure white chin patch
which runs up almost to the eye. The neck is black and the breast
light gray. The back and sides are brownish gray made by adding
some burnt umber to black and white. There is a big pure white patch
at the after underend of the body, and the top of the tail is outlined
in black. Both sexes are the same. The bill is black. The eye is dark
brown, by the way.

So much for painting decoys *à la* bayman. Now let's see what
it takes to paint a really fine decoy. First of all you must have an
assortment of artist's brushes—some flat ones for the larger surfaces
and some pointed sable ones for the feathering and other fine lines.
The main body colors have been described, and the greater care
that you use in painting these on, the better the job will be. The addition of feather markings can be carried just as far as your patience
will permit. It recently took me one whole day, really sticking to
the job, to feather out nine wooden black ducks. They looked like
a million dollars when I finished, and I think black ducks appreciate
million dollar decoys!

First of all, always do the complete body painting first, as the
head will make a good hand hold for turning the decoy this way
and that as you paint in the detail. When the body is completely dry,
tackle the head, and the bill, holding the decoy by the body.

Don't have your paints too thin for most of the work, but those
used for feathering must not be too thick or you will never finish
the job, as the small brushes you use won't hold much paint. Have
the paint so that it flows from the brush without running or spreading beyond the area covered by your brush point. You will appreciate what I mean when you start to paint feathers with a small brush!

It is utterly impossible for me to explain minutely all the detail
work that must be done on each species; I can only show several
methods of feathering used on different birds, and then you must

try to obtain a superbly painted specimen of the decoy you wish to paint. If you are a much better artist than I am you can work from a dead bird; but that really requires unusual skill, which probably could be more profitably employed in painting pictures on canvas rather than counterfeit wildfowl.

Naturally I don't mean that you should actually paint every feather that may be on a duck, but you can do enough of them to cover the desired areas to give a perfectly lovely effect. And I can assure you that the wild birds appreciate such work, for I have many times seen them drop in with birds so painted, and immediately ruffle their feathers and settle down as peacefully as though I hadn't been within a mile of them. I have also seen birds drop in to crudely painted decoys and take five minutes to settle down; they just knew something wasn't exactly right.

In feathering out a black duck the feathers on the breast are quite small and are indicated by little wavy lines, more or less feather shaped. As you go around the side of the breast, begin to form individual feathers. The feathers on the back are larger, becoming even larger along the sides, and these large feathers are carried aft under and to the rear end of the speculum; then they become smaller again around under the tail. The wings, of which the speculums form a part, consist of long overlapping quills that start about halfway down the length of the decoy, on top of the back, separated at the center by about an inch at the forward and end coming to within half an inch of each other at the rear end. Small feathers are shown between the wings. These primary wing feathers end a couple of inches from the tail end of the body, with about half an inch of small feathers between them and the tail feathers, which radiate out to the end of the tail. With some of the thinned out feather paint on your finger smudge light colored overpainting from the forward end of the primaries down to the last four primaries, making the overpainting sharp along the center edges and fading out along the outer sides. This represents the shiny surface of the primaries and gives a very striking appearance of reality. The color used for feathering a black duck is the same as that used on the head, which I have referred to as putty color for want of a better term. It is really a tan shade, rather than a gray putty color. I have told how to mix it. The speculum is deep blue—not too bright—with a black border fore and aft. If you succeed in doing a first class job of feathering, be careful your friend doesn't take a pot shot at the decoy; it will look like a live black duck!

I don't think that this form of feathering can be accomplished on either a solid cork or pressed cork body; it will require the smooth surface of the wooden body to get this fine detail. However, I have done a cruder form of feather painting on my pressed cork decoys and it is very satisfactory. Simply paint thin, rounded lines indicating the curved ends of the feathers.

To answer a question that I have been asked: yes, this fine feathering is entirely practical. I first painted my hollow wood black ducks four years ago, and am still using some of them without repainting. Others have had new coats of body color and new feathering, which should be good for another three or four years.

When light fowl—broadbill, canvasback, etc.—are resting in the water, they snuggle down so that their body feathers on the sides come up over the lower edges of the wings to some degree. On the broadbill, for instance, this results in the white side feathers forming a convex curve along the side of the body. Above this curve will be the wings, and then the back is covered with gray feathers reticulated with white. The most beautiful broadbill stool I ever saw sits on my mantelpiece. The reticulation on the back was superbly achieved by a thick layer of heavy, half dry white paint, which finally dried out with little irregular ridges all through it. You may have noticed this effect around the bottom of an old paint can, where the thick paint had dried. Then dark gray paint was wiped over the rough surface, and wiped down so that the raised ridges in the white paint were cleaned off, leaving the gray in the hollows.

A simpler, but very effective way to reticulate is to give the back a coat of white and let it dry. Then put on a coat of gray, using thick paint that will not run. With a comb moving back and forth to make wavy lines as you draw it over the surface of the back, remove the gray to leave the white showing through where the teeth of the comb have passed over it. This makes a beautiful finish. Use a coarse comb.

But the back of a broadbill, male or female, can be reticulated by painting very thin, wavy little lines of white on the back. This same effect can be produced on the back of a canvasback, whose back is really pale gray with white reticulation. In our canvasback painted *à la* bayman, we simply left the back white. I doubt very much whether it would pay to try to indicate the reticulation on a canvasback. Far more important would be to get the sooty color on the forehead, crown and chin nicely blended around the edges with the rufous color of the head.

To go back to the broadbill again: the head of the lesser scaup is black with a purplish sheen; that of the greater scaup, black with a green sheen. I have found it easier—and perhaps more profitable— to imitate the greenish tinge. It is quite an art to apply the bright green paint to the cheeks and then blend it into the black with a dry brush. You will just have to experiment until you get the knack, and it is well worth getting.

There are two points about doing a good job on the pintail drake that will pay dividends: the correct shape and sweep of the white neck line, and the important tertiary feathers on the afterend of the back. The pintail is the most stylish of all wildfowl, and much of this impression is due to the graceful way in which it carries its head, and the way in which its perky tail sits up. It is hardly practical to build the long sharp tail on a decoy. I have seen it done with a metal strip, but heavy usage would soon demolish this. So by correctly painting the after end of the bird we must try to give the stylish impression. This can be heightened greatly by using care in painting the beautiful tertiary feathers, which lay over the end of the wings. The color of these is made by mixing a trifle of yellow ochre with white. These feathers should not be done until the decoy has completely dried, and they must be sharply defined. They run from fore to aft, but those on the outer sides droop downwards. The paint must be thin enough to flow easily from the brush, but not so thin as to run. They are best painted with a sweeping motion, coming to a sharp point at the after end. When this has thoroughly dried, the central feather shafts are painted in a black line down the center of each feather, in such a way that the light color forms a border all around the black quill in the center. In other words, the black does not extend to the end of the feather, which should show as a long sharp, light-colored point. Another important feature of the pintail decoy is the lovely speculum, a greenish bronze—or better yet a bronzy green. The forward end of the speculum is light brown, then a broad band of the green, with a little brown overlayed in light, soft streaks—not too many, and carefully! Blend them in. Then a jet black band and behind this a pure white band. I believe in making this speculum quite showy, as it is an important characteristic. The underneath part of the afterend of the body is the same buff color that was used for the tertiaries. Aft of this is black, with a pure white streak along each side of the tail. For basic body colors please refer to the earlier description of this (and the other) species.

An old cock widgeon will have a pure white crown on his head; the younger birds have a yellowish tinge to the white. I suggest that the crown be pure white and the cheeks and neck yellowish white, made by adding a trifle of yellow ochre. Always go easy when adding yellow ochre to anything; it is a powerful color, as is burnt sienna; treat them both with respect. Then put the delicate little black feather marks over the cheeks and neck when the head is perfectly dry. The speculum on the widgeon is a brilliant feature, and should be brightly and boldly painted in: first a white shoulder patch several inches long and rounded at the forward end, then a black stripe at the afterend.

Feathering on a Canada goose is important and easy to accomplish due to the bird's size. The breast is a much lighter brownish gray than the back; some gunners paint the breast white to produce a more showy decoy. In any event it may be quite light. The back color, made with burnt umber, white and black, can be considerably lightened with additional white for the feather markings. These may be rather boldly indicated—not as delicate as duck feathering, as we want them to show; but they must not be startling. Pay a good deal of attention to getting the chin patch of white in just the right position. It starts at the lower afterend of the bill and slants upwards and backwards under the eye, rounded off and back to the afterend of the chin—where the head meets the neck. This and the pure white under the tail are the two important characterisitics of the goose. The primary wing feathers may be indicated at the afterend of the body much as those of the black duck were.

The following is a short summary of the colors required for the various species; the methods of mixing them have been covered in this chapter.

Black duck
    Body—Flat black, burnt umber
    Head—White, yellow ochre, burnt umber
    Bill—White, blue, yellow, black, burnt umber
    Speculum—Purple, blue, black, white

Mallard drake
    Body—Burnt sienna, purple, white, black
    Head—Black, green
    Bill—White, blue, yellow, black
    Speculum—Purple, white

Mallard duck
    Body—Burnt sienna, white, burnt umber, yellow ochre
    Head—Burnt umber, yellow ochre, white
    Bill—Yellow, red, white, black
    Speculum—Purple, white

Pintail drake
    Body—Black, white, yellow ochre
    Head—Burnt umber, white, burnt sienna
    Bill—White, blue, black
    Speculum—White, burnt umber, green, black

Broadbill drake
    Body—White, black
    Head—Black, green
    Bill—Blue, black, white
    Speculum—White

Broadbill duck
    Body—Burnt umber, white
    Head—Burnt umber, yellow ochre, white
    Bill—Blue, black, white
    Speculum—White

Canvasback drake
    Body—Black, white
    Head—Burnt umber, burnt sienna, white, black

Bill—Black
Speculum—None

Canvasback duck

Body—Burnt umber, white, black
Head—Burnt umber, white, yellow ochre
Bill—Black
Speculum—None

Widgeon drake

Body—White, burnt sienna, purple, black, burnt umber
Head—White, black, green, yellow ochre
Bill—Blue, white, black
Speculum—Green, black

Canada Goose

Body—Black, white, burnt umber
Head—Black, white
Bill—Black
Speculum—None

The black, white, burnt umber, yellow ochre, burnt sienna should all be flat house paints. The green, blue, yellow and purple are artist's colors in tubes. Wherever possible, mix the latter colors with some white or other flat house paint; but this is not always possible for brilliant speculum colors.

Before closing this chapter on painting, it might be well to mention that some decoy makers believe in giving the bodies of wooden decoys a good priming coat of lead and oil paint, letting this dry thoroughly, and then painting on the plumage colors. I have never considered this necessary, and I believe that it has certain disadvantages. In use decoys get some pretty rough treatment, and more or less of the paint is rubbed off here and there. I have found that without a priming coat, which, of course, must be a solid color of some kind, there is no paint to show through when the plumage coat is worn down in places, and the bare wood under the plumage coat is sufficiently stained by it to be inconspicuous. Furthermore, I believe that a plumage coat painted directly on the bare wood will be much duller in finish than one applied on top of a priming coat.

THE CRAFT OF THE BLIND

Raymond R. Camp

When we previously introduced Ray Camp in "New Brunswick to Main," we were quite lavish in our praise of his book, Duck Boats: Blinds: Decoys and Eastern Seaboard Wildfowling, *published by Knopf in 1952. This additional presentation from that book can only add power and shot to our claim that* Duck Boats: *is one of the true musts for the library shelf of the serious waterfowler. We cannot show you the book's rich array of photographs and drawings, but this look into waterfowling hideaways will convince you that the late Mr. Camp was a man who knew what he was talking about before he put words into print. Like good camps, duck blinds stay with you long after you've left them. You can always stir the ashes of your memory and find all the dawns and skies, good friends and dogs, and the moments of suspense when time seemed to stand still.*

WILDFOWLERS FROM a score of shooting areas, if called upon to define a blind, would describe twenty different structures. Many blinds, especially those in northern areas, are not primarily "hides," but combine concealment with shelter.

What many hunters do not seem to realize is that a good blind is not necessarily an elaborate one. I am speaking now in terms of true blinds, not shelters designed to hide the hunter *and* protect him from the elements. If it is possible to rig out decoys and attract waterfowl to an area adjacent to tall grass, reeds, or brush, the smart hunter will do nothing to improve on the natural concealment at hand, but will merely worm himself into this natural cover. If it is necessary for the shooter to wear weatherproof clothing in order to do this, the improved shooting normally will compensate for the increased discomfort.

If the shooting position must be in the area where the vegetation is scarce, the construction of an elaborate hide will often defeat its very purpose. All the wildfowler requires is enough background material to break up his outline. Surprisingly enough, this can often be accomplished through the use of clothing that blends reasonably well into the background, and by a wisp or two of the neutral cover. This, of course, presupposes that the shooter can remain absolutely still while the birds are approaching. And by "still" I mean completely *immobile;* no turning of the head to follow birds that cut behind, no readying of the gun for the shot, no shifting of the feet or legs to get in a better shooting-position. Do all of these things immediately before or coincidental with the raising of the gun for the shot.

There are three species of duck, I have found, that are especially wary, and seem to be able to detect the slighest movement on the part of the gunner—the pintail, the black duck, and the teal. I spent one morning in a "reef" blind, in an area where pintails were really plentiful, but we never had an opportunity for a shot. My shooting companion just could not sit still. He was constantly shifting to look around, lighting a cigarette, flicking the ashes from a cigarette, adjusting his cap or his coat, or rearranging the shells on the shelf in front of him. Even when a bunch of birds cut around the decoys with the possibility of coming in, he could not remain immobile. As a result, not a pintail came within 150 yards of the blind. That afternoon—I spoke to the head guide at lunch—I turned the blind over to my companion and went to another blind by myself. I had my limit of pintails, plus two geese, by three o'clock, and there had still been no shooting from my partner of the morning. After three days of lone shooting, which had produced one blackhead, apparently suffering from myopia, this gunner complained to the head guide that he had been consistently relegated to a blind that provided no shooting, while "the rest of the gunners get blinds that offer limit bags every day."

The guide suggested that if the shooter would push himself firmly against the back of the blind and not move a muscle, even in his eyes, until the ducks were about to sit down in the decoys, he would get a limit without any trouble, if he could shoot. The man took the advice, and proved he could shoot. He merely had to learn the hard way.

In some areas, where temperatures are extremely low and winds are strong, a blind must provide shelter as well as concealment, and normally a permanent blind is the only answer to the problem. By "permanent" we mean that the blind should be constructed *before* the waterfowl begin to arrive in the fall. Not before the season opens—that is often too late—but *before they arrive*. The blind, if possible, should be dug out, at least partially, and the shelter material, whether canvas or wood, should be screened with vegetation *natural* to the immediate area. If it is in willows, the screen should be of willow; if it is evergreens, the screen should be of evergreens—and in this case the screen must be replenished occasionally with live branches. A screen of dead evergreens, which have changed color, will attract the immediate attention of the waterfowl. If the screen is of reeds or grasses, replenishment will not need to be made as often, for this vegetation turns color as the fall season progresses. By digging to a foot or even two feet below the surface, the shooter normally will get a better wind-break and can keep the silhouette of the blind lower and therefore less conspicuous.

The best blind in the world will not be of any value if the hunter tosses shiny plastic cushions, gleaming Thermos jugs, brightly colored blankets, or similar things inside, nor will it be effective if he wears brightly colored blankets, or similar things inside, nor will it be effective if he wears brightly colored or light clothing while shooting from it. Every item of my own equipment that goes into a blind, including shellboxes, seats, cushion life-preservers, Thermos jugs, and other incidentals, are painted a dull greenish-brown color, with occasional streaks of dark brown. This equipment is not pretty, but when seen forty or fifty feet away it merges with the background and loses its identity of outline. I have seen some shooters who have spent considerable effort in camouflaging their duck boats, and done an excellent job, only to forget the oars completely.

The camouflage sheeting used by the Army during World War II is still available, and a crude, hooded parka of this material can be contrived without difficulty, even by a man who has never before threaded a needle. This material is reversible, having light figuring on a light background on the other side, so it can be turned inside-out to merge with the background of almost any normal duck-hunting area. It accomplishes one thing, even if it does not merge with your background—it destroys outline.

The effectiveness of the finest blind ever constructed can be destroyed by carelessness in approaching and leaving it. The blind with a "path" leading to it may look well from a man's eye-level, but from a point fifty feet in the air it has all the aspects of a trap. Where a blind is located in fairly thick natural cover, the gunner should approach it from a different angle each time, and should *never* destroy the natural cover directly in front of it. I have seen gunners bring down a duck, then thrust their way right through the front of the blind. Another shooter will take every other precaution to preserve the natural aspect of the blind and its immediate vicinity, then leave his duck boat or skiff on the edge of the shore twenty feet distant. The outline of the boat must be broken as well as the outline of the shooter.

When a permanent blind is constructed, it can be "natural" when built prior to the arrival of the ducks, for they see it and come to associate it with the natural background, even though it may protrude like the proverbial sore thumb. An example of this can be found in areas where the tall "stake" or "reef" blind is used. This structure resembles nothing so much as a large pianobox on stilts; often the bottom of the blind is from six to ten feet from the surface of the water. Why ducks and geese approach within a hundred yards of this is something of a puzzle, but the chances are they associate it with a buoy or channel marker, and since it is there the year round they accept it merely as an obstacle to low flight if it happens to be on their course. Even the wary pintails come in to decoys within fifteen yards of these blinds.

Often the sun glinting on gun barrels or stocks will frighten approaching birds, and some hunters who take their duck shooting really seriously take care that these surfaces are dulled. Often they will not be a problem if kept low in the blind or duck boat, and are not moved. It is movement that often causes the telltale flash, blinking DANGER to the approaching ducks.

Constant use of the same blind is another factor that often results in disappointing shooting. The man who can afford the time and effort to build one blind can put in the bit of extra effort required to build two or three. No blind should be shot more than three days a week and, if possible, a shooter should alternate in the blinds in a manner that will not put him in the same blind more than once every four days. This may seem a small matter, but often it spells the difference between a successful or a disappointing day.

In constructing a blind, old and weathered boards are far preferable to new ones, unless the builder is willing to dabble at mixing paint until he gets a color that will merge with the blind material. And the color should be applied both *inside* and *out,* not just outside. In building a blind with a wooden base, especially if the blind is below ground level, a well that is six or eight inches square and of the same depth should be inleted in the bottom, especially if a pump is to be used in eliminating the water that is certain to get in. The floor of such blinds should be at least an inch lower at one end, and the box-well should be installed at the low end. Even if a pump is not used, in which case the well should be large enough to permit the insertion of a bucket, such wells are the only means of insuring a dry blind.

The type of heater to be used in a blind also has more importance than many realize. In some really cold areas, a heater spells the difference between comfort and discomfort. The most satisfactory kind, although not the most simple, is the old-fashioned charcoal brazier. This gives off no odor—an important factor under some conditions. Some species of waterfowl, and this includes scaup and scoters, do not seem to mind the scent drifting downwind from a kerosene heater, but some others are definitely allergic to this. Many shooters have discovered that such heaters are fine in a goose pit or blind, provided you would rather be comfortable than shoot geese. I have seen this demonstrated on several occasions, so I know it is not another gunning fable. If you have ever approached upwind on a blind equipped with one of these heaters you will not need much of a "smeller" to get the acrid odor.

Blinds can be roughly classified in two general categories—"fixed" and "floating," and each of these has several subdivisions.

In the fixed class there are "point" blinds, which in turn have several forms. The sunken box is used in many areas, and unquestionably it is the most productive and also the most comfortable of them all and is especially effective in an area where the natural vegetation is either extremely sparse or nonexistent. It should have a cover, to keep out precipitation in various forms, and in an area where other gunners are inclined to go on the "first come, first served" basis, and object strenuously when ejected, it should have a cover that may be locked. This cover can be of waterproof plywood, painted to merge with the background, and should be removed some distance from the blind and draped with some natural grasses, weeds, or even mud to break its outline.

This blind is used extensively on Barnegat Bay, especially on the small mud-islands, and forms a perfect hide and a really comfortable shelter even on the most bitter day. The blinds are built to handle from two or four persons, but the majority accommodate two gunners and the guide.

The sunken-box blind is also very satisfactory for the man who uses a retriever, and does not like to think of the dog being exposed to the elements on a really cold day.

Similar to the sunken box is the sunken barrel, which is equally comfortable under all weather conditions, and has no construction problem. Like the box, it should have a well for the removal of water, and if possible should have a few rocks under the bottom. In placing either of these blinds, especially in areas where the bottom is well below the water level, a few crosspieces should be nailed or bolted to the bottom and allowed to protrude, which will keep the blind "rising" after the fill has been tamped in. On the sunken box, a few cleats or strips of four-by-four can be bolted outside to accomplish the same purpose.

The brush or grass blind on a point should, where possible, be sunk at least a foot below the ground level, but this often brings the bottom below water, and not too many are willing to take the necessary effort to make the base waterproof. Galvanized chicken-wire with one-inch mesh, painted a dull, neutral color, should be stapled around the outer perimeter of the blind; this mesh makes the task of replenishing the screen very easy, and often gives a more casual appearance to the screen. In placing the screening material, be sure it is ragged rather than even at the top, for obvious reasons.

On many marshes, a permanent point-blind has many advantages, and usually provides better shooting than temporary structures, for birds trading in the area tend to cut around points, and they soon notice any drastic change in contour or silhouette. This is especially true of black ducks, which seem to become extremely blind-shy after the first few days of the season.

In rocky areas, a rock or stone blind is both effective and comfortable, but care should be taken that the blind does not have a sharp outline. This can be eliminated by running off an occasional short wing and having the top or rim extremely irregular. The chinks between the rocks of the blind itself can be stuffed with moss, seaweed, or stones, and some shooters even hold the rocks with cement to avoid having to rebuild it after storms.

Many years ago another gunner and myself built a fine rock-blind on a point, and for two seasons enjoyed unusually fine shooting. Later I moved, and did not hunt that particular area for seven or eight years. When I returned I found that another pair of enthusiasts had a blind on almost the exact spot, but they had built a framework and laced it with bayberry bushes. It merged with the natural background as subtly as a silk hat on a ditchdigger. I spoke with the two gunners crouched behind this silly screen and discovered that they had managed to get three ducks during the first five days of the season, all three of them scoters. Black ducks, they explained, seemed to be very shy of that point, and they were at a loss to explain this phenomenon. I decided it was not my prerogative to solve the mystery.

On many rocky points it is not necessary to construct a blind, but merely to remove a few boulders from a natural hollow, and arrange a few rocks for a seat. Such a blind usually provides a perfect shooting point, provided the clothing and equipment conform with the general coloration, or at least do not clash sharply with it.

In some areas a slight swelling on a shoreline can be extended by means of stakes, rocks, or forms, and enough earth to bring it just above water level. By transplanting some of the natural vegetation from the shoreline (but dig it out of an area a few hundred yards distant) this artificial point can be made very natural after a year, and a point blind at its tip will usually provide exceptional shooting. Ray Adams, at the Whalehead Club on Currituck Sound, has several such points, and they cannot be told from the real thing except after careful investigation. Such projects call for considerable effort on the part of the shooter, but as permanent installations they pay off in results year after year. In areas where permanent blinds can be licensed, and thus be safe from trespass, such points are an excellent wildfowling investment.

The boat cove is another form of point blind that is used in many areas, and many of them are found on Barnegat, where they form a tiny but snug harbor for two or three sneakboxes. The diagram shows the method of construction; they are particularly effective in areas where there is little or no vegetation, or where the vegetation is low or stunted. In tidal waters they are especially effective, for they keep the duck boat well below the ground level at the low-tide phase.

Even in areas where there are good growths of grasses or reeds, these are often beaten down by midseason, either as the result of high winds or by a combination of winds and snow. In such areas the gunner may find a single-boat cove very effective, especially for salt-pond shooting, where the duck boat is left without adequate cover during the low-tide phase. For this cove it is merely necessary to dig out an area the size of the boat and of sufficient depth to bring the deck level with the ground at low tide. By grassing the boat over, the gunner has a dry and comfortable blind that merges perfectly with the background.

For use in this type of cove I normally make flexible mats of grass or reeds, for they not only save time but usually offer a better screen. In making these mats the novice is often inclined to make them too heavy. A bundle of reeds or grass one inch in diameter is adequate, for the mat does not need to be thick to be effective. Either wire or heavy twine can be used, but I prefer wire; it is easier to handle and cuts the preparation time almost in half.

Similar mats can be used for constructing temporary blinds, and with them, plus a half-dozen three-foot stakes, an excellent blind can be thrown up in five minutes or less. It is important, however, to make the mats of the type of reeds or grasses indigenous to the area in which they are to be used. These mats, when rolled up, can be carried in the duck boat, for they take up very little room. With them I usually carry along a "spike seat," which any man can make if he is capable of driving a nail without losing a thumb. With such a seat, at least one important part of the anatomy is off the cold, and often wet, ground. Some shooters go to extremes and have the seat revolve on the spindle, which permits them to swing right to left with ease. This tends to complicate the carpentry somewhat, and I have found the simple form adequate.

Included among the fixed blinds is the "reef" or "stake" blind, previously described. This blind calls for more work and material and is not nearly so widely used. You find numbers of them on Currituck, Albemarle, Croatan, and Pamlico Sounds and, as they are normally placed out in open water areas, they often produce action when shore blinds are ineffectual, especially on bright, windless days. While they appear to be simple structures, the placing on the piles or supports often constitutes something of a problem. Unless the supports are firmly placed, this blind can be dangerous as well as unsteady, and the rule of thumb seems to be that the piling should be sunk into the bottom to a depth one half the height of the blind itself. For example, if the top of the blind is eight feet off the water, the pile should be four feet into the mud.

The observation slots in these blinds are extremely important, for the birds will readily spot any head that appears above the rim. The height of the boards depends upon the shooter; the top of the blind should come to the elbow of the shooter with the arm held flat against the side. This insures enough height to hide the shooter while he is seated, and gives him freedom of movement when he rises to shoot. When more than one gunner is shooting from a reef blind, it should be arranged in advance which shooter is to give the signal to rise. Except in the instance of passing singles or pairs that apparently are not going to decoy, the shooter stands to shoot.

My friend Ray Trullinger had an interesting experience in one of these blinds at Pamlico. We were shooting with Tom Eaton, known locally as the "King of Hatteras," and we drew not only for blinds but for shooting companions. Ray drew an elderly gentleman, about five foot two inches tall, who might have tipped the scales at a hundred pounds, provided he had first been immersed in water.

When they had taken their place in a reef blind near Green Island, a fabulous pintail-area, Ray's miniature companion un-zipped his gun cases and withdrew two immense shotguns, one a ten-gauge magnum, the other a twelve-gauge magnum. The shell for the former resembled a stick of blasting powder, and had about the same punch. Ray did a double take at the sight of this armament but, being a quiet individual, he made no comment.

A few moments after the guide had completed setting out the decoys and had departed for a nearby island to await activity, a pair of pintails approached from the south. The rest is best explained in Ray's words.

"Those pintails were so high they looked like bees, but that did not dismay my friend," Ray said. "He grabbed up the ten-gauge magnum, pushed off the safety, and announced that they appeared to be within range of this bit of ack-ack ordnance. To me, they appeared to be safe, but I've learned to keep my mouth shut in a duck blind. Well, my small friend reared up and touched off both barrels.

"My jaw dropped until it rested on my Adam's apple when I saw the two birds fold, and right after that I thought the damned blind was going over backward. My friend bounced off the back-board three or four times as a result of the recoil of that magnum, and to my recollection he was still bouncing when the two ducks smacked the water.

" 'Raymond,' I told myself, 'you are going to have to do some plain and fancy shooting to keep up with your present gunning-companion. Any man who can comb out a pair of birds that high was teethed on a shotgun.'

"Well, to make a long story brief, those were the only birds my friend touched that day. I'd wait until he touched off before shooting, and when I shot nothing was on its way down. He would put up that big gun, close both eyes, wince and shiver in anticipation of the mule's kick to come, then yank the triggers. Naturally nothing fell after the explosion. The double boom of his big cannon apparently confused the ducks, for I managed to get one or two every time the birds came in.

"Around noon he turned to me and wanted to know what he was doing wrong.

"Now, I've hunted ducks quite awhile, and it has been my experience that a man who asks that kind of question doesn't really want an answer. He's just making conversation and hoping someone else will provide him with an alibi. I'm not the bird for that job, so I'd just shake my head and admit I couldn't understand it.

"Finally, after I'd managed to gather in a double limit, except for his initial success, the guide came along with the boat and picked us up. In climbing down the ladder from the blind I noticed my companion put most of the strain on his left arm. The right one was not working too well.

"He seemed like a nice little guy, and it seemed a shame that he should continue to take that beating, so I suggested that the answer might be that he was 'overgunned.' I pointed out that while I was twice his poundage I would hesitate to shoot a ten-gauge magnum for any length of time. I suggested that the next time he raised it he pause and take stock of his position just before he touched the trigger.

"My friend didn't say anything until we had returned to the dock, but when we arrived he handed the oversized magnum to Tom Eaton and suggested he might be big enough to handle it. The next day the little man took a regulation twelve to the blind, and did all right."

Another popular fixed blind is the brush or "offshore" blind. This is also on pilings, but, as the base board of the blind is close to the water, it is not so important to sink the piles deeply into the bottom. Normally the weight of the blind itself will be sufficient to keep it steady. Like other blinds, these are boarded up, but not so high, and then are screened by brush or reeds similar to those found on the adjacent shores. In appearance they resemble tiny islands and, as they are permanent structures, the birds normally are accustomed to their presence before the season opens and are not inclined to swing wide. In the majority of them, the floor boards are high enough off the water to permit a skiff or duck boat to be concealed underneath, and in this case a "gate" is provided at one end which can be opened to permit the boat to enter.

I have seen these blinds in a score of states, and although they vary slightly in size and screening material, the general construction is similar. In positioning one of these blinds, it is important to spend some time determining the normal flight-line of the waterfowl in the area. Some states have laws limiting the distance from shore at which these blinds can be placed, which calls for a more lengthy reconnaissance. Once you have located a flight line that is followed by most of the birds, the blind should be constructed somewhere along that line. Also, it should be constructed early in the season, for this will give the local birds an opportunity to grow accustomed to it, and to assume that there is no reason to be frightened of it. At first they may tend to swing wide of it, but usually they will have returned to their initial flight-line by the time the season is open.

If you have ever hunted driven snipe, in an area where there is a row of willows or other trees, you will notice that the birds seem to pass over a gap in such trees. The reason for this is obscure, for normally they are much higher than the tallest tree along this line, yet they seem to prefer passing over the gap. Waterfowl apparently have a somewhat similar tendency that is regulated by shore-lines. In moving from one area to another they will often fly a mile or even more off their actual course to follow an invisible flight line. It is this tendency that helps the wildfowler in selecting the location of any offshore blind. Even if the blind location is a hundred yards to either side of this line, the decoys, occasionally aided by a duck call, will pull the birds within gunshot.

Which brings up the somewhat touchy subject of duck calls, for such lures are part and parcel of the blind. Unless you have practiced for some time with a call, and have mastered the tone and timing to a point where you can attract rather than repel the ducks, a call is a handicap rather than an aid.

Many hunters do not seem to realize that some species of ducks are practically mute, others whistle, purr, or chirp rather than "quack," and some are repelled by any sound whatever. I have seen, or rather heard, hunters emitting mallard calls while rigged out for broadbill, and have heard them emit a goose call in an effort to entice brant.

If you want to hear duck calling at its best, take a trip to the flooded oak-flats of Stuttgart, Arkansas, and you will soon realize that the successful use of a call is an accomplishment reached only after considerable study and a tremendous amount of practice. Those callers can speak in duck language, and you will never have a better opportunity of proving that the improper use of a call can repel ducks as readily as the proper use attracts them. In puddle-duck shooting, a call can be a distinct asset, if correctly used, but I cannot overemphasize the importance of proper calling.

Many years ago I hunted geese every year with old Uncle Ike, who had his base at Poplar Branch on Currituck Sound. If a bunch of ducks appeared to be passing our rig without giving it a glance, Uncle Ike let them pass. But if one or a dozen geese approached within three hundred yards of the blind, Uncle Ike had an uncanny ability for getting them to pass within reasonable gunshot if not to decoy. The shrill call he emitted bore no resemblance whatsoever to the "aaahnk" of a goose, and the first time I heard it I thought he was in pain. That is, until the lead gander of the passing flock swung his long neck our way, then turned to see where this noise came from. Another scream from Uncle Ike and the echelon set their wings, and a final scream brought them low enough for a shot. I have never known Uncle Ike to give his call more than four times, and the call rarely failed to attract birds that were within range of his voice. I have spent hours in an attempt to duplicate it, but have never succeeded, with the result that I remain mute except on occasions when a flight of geese are going to pass wide, and I figure that a call can do no harm even if it fails to do good. Occasionally I seem to get the right pitch, and manage to turn a few birds, but in most instances they keep right on in the direction they were headed.

Immediately after the war I hunted several times on the Gaeta Marshes in Italy, with Brigadier D.E.P. Hodgson of the Welsh Guards, who was not only a caller of symphonic caliber but one of the finest wing-shots I have ever seen in action. With an empty twelve-gauge shell from which the primer had been removed, the Brigadier could bring widgeon and pochards within easy gunshot, and he could "purr" the fast-flying garganey (similar to our teal) to within twenty yards of his position. His mallard call did not sound too much like a mallard, but it had all the efficacy of a magnet. I asked him how he had learned these calls, and he looked at me as though I had suddenly taken leave of my senses.

"Why," he explained, "listening to waterfowl, of course."

The Brigadier had another accomplishment that, to me, appeared to be sheer magic. There was no such thing as a duck limit, and when we went to the marsh it was with the idea of getting enough birds to give the officer's mess a treat. It would be impossible to estimate the number of ducks on that twenty-mile belt of marsh, but certainly there were in the tens of thousands. It was all pass shooting, and our procedure was to wade out in the knee-deep water until we found a small patch of head-high reeds. We would take up our position, in clumps a hundred yards apart, and take the ducks as they passed. To avoid losing birds, I would immediately wade out and recover mine after each shot. Not so the Brigadier. I have known him to have from 18 to 25 birds down before he moved out to retrieve them, and I have seldom known him to hunt for these birds, despite the clumps of grass. He seemed to be able to mark down every bird, and would walk with assurance from one to the other.

A few local farmers were inclined to poach this marsh, but they devoted their powder to gathering in coots, with which the marsh abounded. They would sneak along in tiny eight-foot boats that resembled kayaks without the decking, which they poled along with two sticks after the manner of a man on skis. While primarily interested in coots, they were not averse to grabbing up any good duck we had shot that happened to be on their course, and they could flick a duck in their boat without pausing and with hardly a noticeable movement. After the Brigadier had lost a number of ducks to these boatmen he would step from his screen of reeds when he saw one of them approaching a point where he had marked down a bird. He would then wave an arm in a dispersing gesture and shout his one word of Italian.

"Avanti!"

If this failed to divert the boatman the Brigadier would raise his gun and blast away in the general direction of the boat. After a few such experiences, one of these poachers would send his boat through the water in a flurry of foam at the sound of this word.

But to return to fixed blinds.

In this category we can include another form of the brush blind, probably the simplest one to construct. This comprises merely a score of small trees, willows, poplars, or evergreens, depending upon the local verdure, their butts whittled to a point and thrust into the bottom to form an outline similar in size and shape to the boat used. These blinds are widely used, and will be seen on many of the Canadian rivers and lakes, principally because they are easy to construct and serve their purpose well.

Some are placed close to the bank of the stream, others well out in the water; while they do not form a dense screen, they serve to destroy the outline of the boat and shooters. Along the St. John River in New Brunswick, where some of the shooting is done from canoes, the experienced shooter will lash the gunwale of the canoe to a half dozen of these stakes on either side in order to insure a firmer shooting-platform. A duck shooter is not always in perfect balance when he touches off at a duck, and this lack of balance can be disastrous in a light, short canoe. Some of these blinds are employed as an artificial extension of a point, and others, dressed with brush, will stick out several hundred yards from shore. When not in use, these blinds appear impenetrable, but two or three of the trees at one end are driven only lightly into the bottom, and can be removed for the entrance of the boat and replaced after it is inside.

Floating blinds, although illegal in some areas, are widely used in others, and they have the advantage of mobility, which is important in the event birds begin following a different flight-line. The most elaborate such structure I ever encountered was in Maine, and was the handiwork of my friend Elmore Wallace. The diagram shows the structural features, and should be self-explanatory. In an area where small islands are plentiful, these blinds are extremely satisfactory, for the boat can be hauled inside, and the wooden sides offer shelter from the cold wind.

This blind, while it calls for quite a bit of material and the expenditure of considerable time in construction, has a life expectancy of from ten to fifteen years, although it must be screened two or three times during the season if evergreens are used. It may be necessary to replace the underwater logs or kegs, but the main structure is stout and gives long service. The dimensions of the blind depend upon the size of the skiff to be hidden inside, and since many of the blinds are used on open water that, during a blow, is not navigable in a small boat, the tendency is to build large ones. The visibility from these blinds is not the best in the world, but the gunners usually take turns at watching, and with reasonable care the watcher will not alert the approaching birds.

Another form of the floating brush-blind is much easier to build, and costs less for materials. Under normal conditions it is extremely effective and, as shown by the diagram, it is not at all difficult to assemble. It is much easier to move from place to place, and in some areas these blinds are towed to a different shooting-area each day. Before building one of these structures, however, check with your state game-department to make certain they are not illegal. The laws of some states call for fixed blinds, and in other states stipulate that blinds must be within a given distance of the shore.

There are many variations of both these blinds, and the man who is at all handy with tools can vary his to suit his requirements. The basic structure is similar to those shown, and variations in length, width, or height can be effected with ease.

The most popular form of floating blind—and it was certainly more in the nature of a blind than a boat, considering its immobility except when towed—was the battery. This contraption, which resembled a coffin with three and sometimes four wings protruding from its sides, probably resulted in the gathering in of more canvasbacks, redheads, and scaup than any other shooting platform of any type. The battery had four general forms, the double (designed for two shooters), the single, and either of these in a lie-down or sit-up model. When rigged, with the wings weighted down to the surface of the water by heavy cast-iron decoys, and the battery itself weighted until it had barely an inch of freeboard, diving ducks were inclined to pass within easy gunshot without the slightest appearance of fright. To supplement it, from two to five hundred decoys were rigged around the battery; a set of that size pulled passing birds like a veritable magnet.

This rig was normally set out in shallow water, although occasionally an intrepid shooter was willing to risk deep water if he had insurance in the form of an adequate life-preserver. Once the weather began to blow up, the battery had to be taken in without loss of time, for it took only a light chop to slosh water over the sides and cause the thing to sink like a stone. The Chesapeake was the real home of the battery, and some amazing kills were made during the days when waterfowl were considered to be an inexhaustible resource, and many market gunners resorted to this device during the days when such hunting was legal.

It is now a violation of federal law to use a battery, and although some oldtimers still hold out hopes that it will be legalized in the future, the chances of this are very slender. The battery had to be towed or hoisted bodily aboard a large boat, and to get it in position and put out the normal set of decoys called for the united effort of several men. Even were it legal, a day in a battery would be far beyond the financial reach of more than ninety per cent of wildfowlers. The average price for a day of battery shooting was forty dollars back in 1880, when a dollar was a nice, round sum, so I leave it to your own conservative estimate what the charge would be today. When you consider that the law says you have "had it" after you have gathered in four (six in the West) ducks, the price of roast duck would be about similar to that of an equal weight in lark's tongues.

Duck shooting, regardless of where you practice it, can be expensive if a guide is employed. Many shooters, a large percentage of them financially able to hire an expensive guide every day of the season if they wish, have discovered that by doing their own work, handling the boat, rigging out and picking up, they get much more out of the sport.

The shooter who serves as his own guide enjoys more of the challenge of wildfowling. He must select his shooting site after studying the wind, weather, and temperature. He must know how to rig out the decoys under varying conditions, and where to rig them. To a large extent, the success of the shoot depends upon his personal knowledge and skill, and this brings an added thrill to the sport. If the shooter carries his activity a bit further, making his own decoys and selecting the site and building his own blind, he will multiply his satisfaction.

The majority carry on these activities not by preference but by necessity, simply because they are unable to afford participation under any other circumstances. Such shooters do not wait until the day before the opening of the waterfowl season to build blinds and get the necessary equipment in order. Like many human activities, the return received from duck shooting is relative to the effort and thought put in it. The smart shooter will check the shooting area several times during the three weeks preceding opening day, learning the location of the waterfowl concentrations, at what time and where they trade, where they are feeding, and where they are likely to fly under hunting pressure. Some of these matters can be determined, others must be estimated, but the shooter who takes the trouble to make such sorties in advance of the opening usually has more success when the big day arrives.

In addition to such permanent blinds as he may put up, the shooter should be informed of sites that might be productive, with temporary blinds, when there happens to be a radical shift in wind and weather. As for his permanent blinds, their relation to other blinds is extremely important. In every area there is a prevailing wind, and the blind location must be selected with this in mind. The man who puts his blind on a point to the eastward of another blind, in an area where the prevailing wind is an easterly, may find the blind to the west is right in his "lead," and that birds swinging down to come in to his decoys may decide to drop in on his neighbor instead. Also, it often proves sound to know something of the shooting habits of the man in the next blind. It is amazing how many duck hunters, some of them experienced, have an exaggerated idea as to the killing range of a shotgun, and a blind spot when it comes to range estimation. Such neighbors can spoil the shooting of every other shooter within a half-mile radius, for they will strain their barrels in an effort to reach high or wide ducks that otherwise would have come in to another rig.

A few years ago I was shooting on a rather narrow river. My guide, a young man but one who had spent his life on the river and knew the "form," rigged out on a slender point near a sharp bend. An hour after we had taken our places in the reeds, a group of three shooters moved up the river in a rowboat, passed downwind of our point about sixty yards, then hauled their boat into the reeds and got ready to bring down the ducks. In order to get in to our decoys, the ducks had to pass almost over their position, and during the succeeding hour at least twenty birds that would have come up to us were blasted at by this group. They did not bring down a single bird, but they effectively spoiled our shooting.

My guide finally stood up, his lips pressed in a thin line and his eyes wild.

"I'm going over to have a word with them," he announced.

A few minutes later he returned, and by the time he had seated himself in his old position, the three "sports" across the way had thrust their boat into the river and moved downstream out of sight. Apparently his few words had been effective, so I did no questioning.

I met one of this trio at the inn that night and he explained the substance of the few words. He repeated them.

"We were here and rigged out before you left the dock," he stated. "You came along and deliberately stopped in our lead, a procedure that not even a skunk follows in this neck of woods. I'm willing to admit I can't force you to be sportsmen, but I'm going to tell you what I can do. I am shooting a magnum, and back in the boat I have six loads of single-ought buckshot. The next ducks that pass you I am going to consider within range, and I'm going to try for them with buckshot. If I happen to hold a bit low that is going to be your tough luck."

The member of the trio who was on the receiving end of this conversation explained that the guide looked as though he meant every word he said, so they decided to move on downriver. I recall that the guide did pause at the boat and fumble in his shellbag, so there is every chance that he was serious. While I do not recommend such drastic action, I must admit that there have been many occasions when the idea found favor with me. Wildfowlers are essentially sportsmen, but there are renegades in every activity, so you must expect to encounter a reasonable number among the two million who take to the marshes. But there is no point in cultivating them, and under conditions such as those we encountered on that occasion, it is often sound to pick up the decoys and find another shooting site. But not in the "lead" of another shooter.

SETTING DECOYS

Norman Strung

I had been buying Norm Strung's magazine pieces for Sports Afield *for some time when I first heard of his plans to do a practical book on waterfowl hunting. My heart sank. I knew the book would be packed with information, for Norm was an outstanding wildfowler, but I honestly did not see it as part of my future fireside reading for pleasure. Then the book arrived. Not to worry! The title was* Misty Mornings and Moonless Nights, *and it was apparent from the first page that Norm knew how to make good reading out of a presentation of solid how-to advice. The book, Macmillan Publishing Co., Inc., New York, 1974, is one of the best guides to wildfowling ever done, and this particular segment on decoys is clearly my favorite on the subject. Norm is a prolific freelancer in the outdoor field who divides his time between Montana (where he has a guiding service), Florida (when the action gets cranked up on the flats), and New York (where he learned the art of waterfowling on Long Island and still loves to keep his hand in every winter).*

THE WATERFOWLER who lures birds to decoys is like a painter, working his canvas in the half-light of morning to create an illusion of nature and life. His raw materials are water, marsh, blocks of wood, and a sense of proportion.

"This decoy goes here," is the unspoken decision, born of careful observation and past experience.

Line, anchor, and hand-hewn block of cork or wood sing through the chill air like the broad stroke of a brush, landing with a splash. The decoy bobs upright, then swings into place as it's snubbed short by the tightened line. It yaws in a puff of breeze, suddenly alive.

"Now another over there, and one by my feet."

Slowly the picture takes shape. The placid gray water gains dimension and depth as decoy after decoy is placed, carefully gauged to complement the whole.

Hummocked tufts of marsh grass mark the borders; the rich golds and soft reds of dawn begin to creep across the sky and are mirrored in the calm. The last ripple from the last decoy drifts outward and dies.

"Not quite right," is the critical judgment. A decoy just beyond good gun range is pulled in a bit closer, and another that has lost its balance weight and rides awry is retired for the day.

A soft breeze again stirs the incredible stillness of the marsh. You smile, suspecting it will blow the rest of the day, and watch as it sets the stool to motion, swinging on their lines. It is so like a flock of real birds that you do a double take, just to make sure a black didn't sneak into the rig when you weren't looking.

Not to shoot—it's still before gunning hours. But a bird coming in while you were still in the rig would be the finishing touch, and a good omen.

You go back to the blind to admire your creation over a cup of coffee; a few puffs on a smoke, and the cold muzzle of your Lab nudging your hand. The dawn explodes in rainbow hues. It's the prettiest time of all; those last few introspective moments before the gun.

In the final analysis, setting a rig of decoys is an expression of personal style, taste, and experience. There's a hunch factor that operates among decoy hunters: that if you put a certain decoy over here or two way out there, the rig will draw birds more effectively. Balancing the configuration of your stool against things like locale, weather, wind velocity, and waterfowl behavior creates more possibilities of design. Consequently, no two sets are ever exactly alike.

There are, however, some rules that apply to all decoy rigs, rules that provide at least a frame for the picture you paint.

Waterfowl will be attracted most readily to their own kind. One of the few constants of decoy hunting is that you must use diving-duck decoys if you're after divers, and puddle-duck decoys if you're after puddlers. This *caveat* has further subtleties of individual species too; a black duck will come to black-duck stool more readily than mallard stool, though because of similarities in habit and food preference, both feel rather free to drop in on one another. Chances get slimmer, however, when you try to lure a black to pintail decoys or, less likely, woody or widgeon stool. This same tendency is exhibited by diving species, but I haven't found it quite so critical as with puddlers.

Diving ducks want a lot of open water for a landing spot, open water that should be engineered into your decoy pattern. Puddle ducks will be glad to flutter down into a rather tight space right among the decoys. Generally, you'll find you can anticipate the spot where a diver will land; puddlers will be less predictable.

Spacing of individual blocks are dependent on the weather. During pleasant weather, spread them out. In bad weather, bunch them up.

On bluebird days, ducks and geese are at their leisure. They feed at will and bask in the warm temperatures. As a consequence, birds tend to spread out—not individuals equidistant from their partners, but in loose groups of two to five birds, one group here, one group there, the entire configuration of scattered individuals making up the flock. Placement of decoys should reflect this tendency.

In cold blustery weather you should pull your decoys into a tight knot. This copies the behavior of the real birds, who develop a sense of urgency about them. They become agitated and nervous, feeding amid the protection from wind and waves provided by their partners.

How close is close? I've seen rigs with some blocks no more than six inches apart, though a foot or two is more my idea of right. This close proximity seems to violate a universal *caveat* about decoy hunting, that no block should touch another; but that rule is misunderstood.

When a decoy hangs up with another—gets its anchor line entwined or otherwise remains glued to a neighboring block for minutes at a time—that's bad, and a detriment to your rig. But when decoys bump into each other as they yaw on their lines, then quickly disengage, that's perfectly natural and even desirable. Real birds in real flocks are doing this all the time. They get into fights or they try to steal another's food. I once watched a black duck get into a fight with, of all things, a decoy!

John Kouchinsky and I were rigged out in the spring, shooting with a camera, and an incoming black tolled the tail end of the stool, then started preening. With his head buried in his back feathers, he didn't see the approach of a decoy as it swung on its anchor line. He very nearly shot out of the water as he was bumped. It looked like the duck had been goosed. He turned in fury, pecked at the decoy's head and back and, apparently satisfied that he'd won, indignantly swam another ten feet toward the head of the rig before he resumed preening.

Bunching up your blocks occasionally will be in order even on bluebird days. If there are plenty of ducks in the air and they're ignoring your well-distributed spread, pull your blocks in a little closer. No matter the weather, ducks always sleep and rest in close proximity, and you might be hunting during a resting rather than a feeding period.

Oversized blocks. These are decoys larger than life-size. Because they're so visible, ducks can see them from far off and they have good drawing power. But there's a fine line to tread when choosing to use or not to use oversize stool. Ducks also feel there's safety in numbers; so the more oversized blocks you use, the more room they require for transport and the smaller total number of decoys you'll be able to carry and rig.

When I'm limited in the bulk of decoys I can lug around, I usually bring a half dozen or so oversized decoys, and keep the rest of my blocks natural size. The oversized stool then provides maximum visibility when waterfowl pass at a distance. As they come in for a closer look, they then pick out the smaller blocks and, lured by their numbers, decoy freely.

When rigging mixed-sized blocks, always place your oversized decoys where they can most easily be seen by waterfowl on the wing.

"Confidence" decoys are imitations of species that you don't necessarily wish to shoot but that are normally found among a contented flock of waterfowl. I've occasionally seen seagull decoys used as confidence stool, but coot and, especially, geese are more commonly used. Geese have two attractive features as confidence stool: they're wise birds, so their presence in a rig indicates all is A-O.K., and their large size allows them to function as an oversized decoy.

Confidence decoys have another function. Because they're plainly different from your other blocks, you can use them to mark distance from your blind or boat, thereby providing an accurate gauge of ranges.

LOCATING THE SET

You'll get the most birds to decoy if the wind is blowing across the blind, slightly quartering your back.

This is one of the most common mistakes I've seen on the part of waterfowlers; they set their rig in relation to their blind so the wind blows directly from them to their stool. Waterfowl decoy right into the wind, and such a blind location then has incoming birds looking right down your gun barrel.

If they don't spot you before touching down, they'll flare as you rise to shoot. Waterfowl coming straight at you also give the illusion of taking the entire season to get into gun range, tempting the unknowing hunter to shoot early. And they'll often sit down on the far edge of the rig, rather than coming in close.

In terms of divers, there's also a "safety" factor inherent with a crosswind. Open water, to a diving duck, is the same as safety. When your rig is engineered to draw a bird directly to shore, his approach zeros him on land, a thing he likely associates with danger. A wind blowing parallel to land, on the other hand, gives the illusion of plenty of water ahead of the spread. Even though land might be quite close to the bird's left or right, that open water ahead is a persuasive hint at a safe harbor.

But these pragmatics aren't without their price. Even though they cost you shots, a straight-on toll holds a reward all its own. In this set, waterfowl come in breast exposed, wings fanning the air, and legs extended in anticipation of touchdown.

The looking is far more important than the killing when you're hunting with decoys, and a bird tolling directly to you is one of the most beautiful sights in the out-of-doors.

A wind blowing toward you is unworkable in most situations since incoming birds must swing over land and you to approach the decoys. As a matter of fact, there's an old saying about the man who hunts ducks with the wind on his face: he should be hunting with someone else.

WATERFOWL VISION

Knowing something about what and how waterfowl see is of immeasurable help when decoy hunting. The visual acuity of ducks and geese is an old subject of controversy and myth-making. I can remember reading an article where a guy painted "fake" and "traitor" in bright red all over his decoys, and supposedly brought birds in. Yet you hear so much about the necessity of camouflage. Where, then, lies the truth?

In fact, waterfowl have poor eyesight by one set of human standards. They lack our degree of binocular vision.

The close-set position of human eyes allows us to focus on an object using both eyes at once. The triangulationlike view we get of that object, coupled with the blurred areas in front of and behind the focal point, allow us to perceive depth and distances rather accurately. Put a pencil in the ground five feet away and an identical pencil twenty feet away and we can quickly judge both to be about the same size; though if you measured them with a yardstick held at arm's length, the distant pencil would appear far smaller than the near one.

Waterfowl, on the other hand, have their eyes set in the sides of their heads. If you look at a duck's profile, the entire eye, pupil and iris, appears nearly on a flat plane. Look at the same bird fullfaced, and very little but the cornea is evident.

This difference constitutes an evolutionary adaptation for protection. With this type of sight system, waterfowl literally can see from the back of their heads. Sitting on a pond or lake, or in a close-cropped grainfield, any predator would be quickly discovered. But it also limits waterfowl to looking out of one eye at a time, which robs them of binocular vision.

Think back to the last duck you saw pass overhead. When waterfowl want to examine something, they cock their heads to one side, viewing it with one eye rather than looking straight ahead. Now you try the same. You'll note that you now view the world on a single plane—two-dimensional instead of three.

Without the ability to judge depth, the ability to judge speed and distance is also altered, explaining, in part, why waterfowl so regularly have collisions with telephone wires, buildings, and aircraft. They simply don't have the mechanisms needed to determine how fast these things are looming up. The same limitations will be revealed if you carefully watch a duck land. Waterfowl bumble into a landing, with much hovering and a slow descent as the ground comes up to meet them. At the last moment they simply abandon flight and splash down. This will be most obvious if you're ever fortunate enough to witness the circus that occurs when a flock of ducks or geese attempt a landing on ice. They'll skid, slide, lose their balance, and, more often than not, end up flat on their stomachs, wings askew, like some portly squire's first adventure on ice skates.

Contrast this, then, with a bird of prey: a hawk or an eagle. The latter, are capable of pulling out of a hundred-mile-an-hour dive to skim over land closely enough to snare a mouse that is surely hugging the ground in the bargain. Birds of prey are masters at judging distance, and their eyes are set quite close together.

Granting a waterfowl's characteristically poor depth perception, then, the relative size of things and their spatial relationships aren't too important. An oversized decoy can be seen from afar more readily than a normal-sized block, but, as the bird approaches, any difference in proportion makes little impression because it isn't that perceptible. The same is essentially true of your rig's distance from your blind or boat. Some gunners I've hunted with have theorized that birds weren't coming in because their rig was too close to shore, and moved the whole set out five yards.

While it's certainly true that heavily gunned birds will get shore-shy, jackassing the rig out a few feet isn't going to do any good because the birds are incapable of determining or assessing such a critical "safe" distance.

There is, however, another side to the coin. Look again at that one eye that will be looking at you. The pupil is quite large, and the eye itself is, in proportion to the duck's head, far larger than the ratio that exists in humans. It's a good bet that a duck does a better job of perceiving detail than a human. He lacks depth perception, but on that flat-plane view of the world around him he's better equipped than you to pick out a spent shell casing, a badly painted decoy, or the sunlight glinting off an upturned face.

RIGGING DECOYS FROM SHORE

Puddle ducks are creatures tied equally to land and water. Their legs are set close to the middle of their body, for walking on dry land as well as paddling, and their broad wings allow for slow, precise flight. They can thread their way between towering trees to flutter down on a quiet pond, or follow a twisting riverbed with swallow-like grace.

Coves, cuts, backwaters, sloughs, and small ponds are the places to locate a puddle-duck decoy spread. It's there the birds go for feed and sanctuary.

Coves and river backwaters that open onto big water are generally my first choice when choosing a place to set puddler decoys. These places not only afford the natural protection puddle ducks normally seek—they open onto probable flyways where birds trading over open water can see the rig.

The most popular configuration for hunting a cove is the C. This was the first pattern I ever learned, shown to me by a kindly old gent who used to walk the marshes every morning.

After passing by my blind a half dozen mornings or so, he stopped to chat one day and, in the course of our conversation, informed me that my black-duck decoys, set off Hollins Point, could be complemented by "steamrolled corn and oats, advertised on an electric caller," and I still wouldn't get any respectable black within gun range.

It was a tough decision to make; the location of my blind faced seaward on a long spit of land, and there were so many birds trading back and forth out there! But I tried his advice, pulling my blocks back from open water and into a small cove the next morning.

I didn't see how the rig would work; hell, passing birds could barely see me in this spot. But I cleaned house that morning with my three-bird limit, sweet success indeed for a fourteen-year-old kid and a bolt-action shotgun.

There are two variations on the C rig: one for pleasant weather, one for bad weather. On bluebird days, open the letter way up, with your farthest stool just inside gun range, and blocks arranged in loose groups of three to five birds. If trading waterfowl don't respond, or you're hunting a storm, tighten up the rig so the majority of decoys lie to one side of the letter—the side closest to your blind. The C then begins to assume a J shape.

In the C configuration, incoming birds should toll to the center, to the open-water portion of the letter. As you pull stool closer together, they'll tend to fly directly over the bulk of the stool, and will look to land toward the upwind half of the main concentration.

Drainage sloughs and natural cuts in a marsh are my second choice as a place to rig out. Puddlers often follow these riverlike ribbons of water for miles, like a hiker follows a trail. In most circumstances your rig won't be visible from afar due to obscuring vegetation. The duck will suddenly find himself on it, and won't have a lot of time to decide if he wants in or not.

For this reason, I like to prepare incoming birds for what lies ahead by rigging one or two oversized stool between one hundred and one hundred fifty yards downwind. Don't set out more than this or you might find birds landing there. Place these decoys close to the shore you'll be hunting.

The type of rig you set in front of your blind should be largely a function of the width of the cut. If the opposite shore is within gun range, run your decoys in a half-moon pattern, with the bulk of the blocks close to your blind. This will have a braking effect. Even if the bird doesn't particularly want to drop in, he will slow up, affording a good pass shot. If he does choose to drop in, he'll probably do so at the very head of the stool.

Because birds will happen on this decoy spread quite suddenly, even the presence of those decoys one hundred yards downwind might not be enough to prepare them for touchdown. They might want to make a second pass before setting in. If, however, they still fiddle and fidget around on the second pass, dump them at the first opportunity; they probably won't toll right anyway.

Wide expanses of water, where the opposite shore is outside of gun range, require a decoy configuration that assumes a tadpole shape. Arrange your blocks so the head and body of the tadpole are in front of your blind, with the tail curving slightly out from shore. This should result in a corralling effect, with the incoming bird picking up the tail and sticking to the inshore side of it. The landing area will be between shore and the tail, or in the very middle of the bulk of the blocks; so it's wise to leave a landing hole in the head of the tadpole.

 PONDS

This category can be the least productive or most productive place you'll ever set a decoy. If a pond is merely one of many in an area, without any special food or attraction, or if it's close to lakes, bays, or rivers and the weather's pleasant, chances are it will be a poor place to put a blind.

But if it's the only water around in an area rich in grain or other foods, or if it provides a haven from churning waves on larger bodies of water, a pond can provide the fastest gunning of your life.

Placing a decoy spread in a pond involves essentially the same patterns and precepts as those you'd use in a cove: a C configuration set somewhere near the leeward shore. Scatter your decoys when the pond is used for water and rest after feeding periods, and tighten them up into the J when the storm chases birds off big water.

One exception to this rule involves larger ponds that are surrounded by obscuring cover. Make every effort to determine the direction from which the majority of birds will be approaching, and place your decoys so the rig is the first thing incoming birds see.

One of my most frustrating experiences involved my failure to do just that. Bob Yaskulski and I were hunting a marshy cove that faced into Moriches Bay. A sudden storm came up, blowing hard from the north, and we lost our lee. Lousy luck, but we theorized that, if the blow continued, ducks would soon tire of fighting the weather and pour into a fresh-water pond we knew of a half mile behind us.

Although we were correct in our prediction, we failed to recognize that the ducks would take the shortest route to the pond rather than approaching the place by flying into the wind. That shortest route found them flying over the tallest stands of vegetation around the pond—vegetation that obscured our spread from that direction. As a result, the birds plopped down in open water, *then* they noticed our stool. A few ducks made a half-hearted attempt to swim over, then started building into a raft, remaining at the opposite end of the pothole.

One of the toughest decisions in the world is to start messing and moving around, changing your rig when there are birds in the air. You always hope, and half expect, at least a few birds will choose you to drop in on. So we elected to wait it out—and didn't get a shot.

The combination of long-range visibility and the undeniable pulling power of live "decoys" brought every bird into that real raft. By rights, we should have moved the whole rig near to where they were resting, even though we would have had the wind in our face and spooked birds in the bargain.

RIGGING PUDDLERS FROM A POINT

While puddle ducks are ordinarily attracted to marshy inland areas, this rule has exceptions like any other. When birds are so heavily gunned that they become shore-shy, you can occasionally get good shooting if you'll rig off a point. Open water is the reason: like divers the puddlers become accustomed to its safety, and decoys rigged off a point jutting out into a bay or lake create that safe illusion of open water.

When setting out stool in this situation, the I formation usually draws the best. This pattern is nothing more than a long, narrow grouping of closely spaced stool. I favor bunching up the blocks whenever shooting off a point, nice weather or not, and I like to use lots of decoys—thirty to forty if possible.

The placement of the configuration is rather important. On any point, whether it's in a lake, river, or salt water, there's going to be a lee, an area where wind, waves, and currents are cut off by the jutting land. Rig that I right along the line of the lee, the place where large waves or strong currents sweep by the calmer protected waters.

Place your decoys remembering that birds will swing over this spread from tail to head and, if they are sufficiently fooled, that they'll land toward the middle of the configuration. If they hopscotch across this portion of your set without dropping in, the odds say they'll pass by the front half entirely, and either make a second pass or head for other climes.

RIGGING DIVERS FROM SHORE

Although points are good for puddler species only sometimes, they are the only place you'll regularly be able to lure diving species within range of a shore blind. Divers are extremely reluctant to pass over land or come into the tight surroundings of coves and cuts so favored by mallards and blacks. When hunting off a point there're good odds that you'll be able to engineer their characteristic overwater approach to your decoys, no matter the wind.

The pattern to use when point-shooting divers is the fishhook. This classic configuration, also known as the stovepipe, finds a half-moon of decoys set in front of the blind. The inner portion of the half-moon should be within good gun range, for this is the place tolling birds will look to land.

Once the half-moon is set, run a tail or line of decoys off the inshore side, curving it out toward open water. Space decoys on the tail wider and wider apart as you move away from the blind.

This tail functions like a path to lead birds into the main part of your decoys. Ducks trading back and forth over open water will pick the tail up and show interest in it from a mile out; so it pays to have readily visible oversized decoys there.

Set the fishhook so it lies along the rough-water/calm-water point of lee, and use a lot of decoys. I'd say thirty is a bare minimum, with forty-five better still, and the outside limit being set only by the numbers of blocks you can handle. I've hunted over fishhook rigs of more than one hundred fifty decoys, with a tail that stretched for a quarter of a mile; and, in this case at least, the more the decoys, the merrier I've found the shooting.

Rigging mixed species is probably the most popular set, but only because, as in any endeavor, there will be more amateurs than experts. Setting out thirty broadbill, a dozen blacks, and a half dozen geese would appear to be the panacea—the ultimate rig that would draw birds of all varieties.

In practice, however, I haven't found this to be the case. And I've surely made enough trial runs, having gone through the mixed-species stage of rigging decoys myself. I feel there are comparisons to be made with other forms of outdoor sport—like the nimrod who shoulders a shotgun and simply goes "hunting." He seldom bags the game that the fellow who centers on quail or pheasant does. Similarly, an angler who outfits himself for walleye or bass or trout, and actively pursues just one type of fish at a time, usually is considerably more successful than the tyro who grabs rod, reel, and line and goes "fishing."

If, however, going "duck hunting" appeals to you, the mixed-species rig is virtually always a point-shooting proposition.

Rig your divers first, using the fishhook described previously. Set the configuration downwind from your blind but close enough so that the inner half-moon area falls within good gun range.

Although logic would seem to dictate otherwise, set your puddle ducks well in front of the divers, and well defined from them by open water. Set your geese inside the puddlers, closest to shore.

I realize that this puts your geese and puddlers—two calm, shallow-water-loving species—out in the brunt of any wave or wind activity, that the big geese should rightly go out in front to act as oversized decoys, and that any sane duck or goose should rightly stool to the quiet water of the lee; but I've hunted over just that kind of "sensible" setup and done nothing on puddlers (though divers came in pretty well).

Ever since a seventy-five-year-young guide on Shinnecock Bay named Captain Downs showed me this perfectly unnatural and ridiculous way to rig for mixed species, I've persuaded my gunning buddies who insist on going for everything that flies to try it. Doggoned if it hasn't worked better than any other, though personally I'm still a fan of outfoxing one type of waterfowl at a time.

RIGGING ON OPEN WATER

Location

Setting up a lay-out boat and placing a rig of open-water decoys has subtleties on a par with shore gunning. Just choosing a spot at random seldom produces shooting worthy of note because diving species establish feeding lanes and flying patterns that render portions of a bay, lake or estuary barren of activity.

As I grew into my late teens and began to earn money—primarily as a clam-digger—I decided that part of that income just had to be invested in a lay-out rig. I ran into the deal of a lifetime one fall: a punty and fifty decoys for $150.

When the divers arrived on the scene later that year, I spent morning after morning rigging out in the darkness of predawn, each day expecting action and adventure to reward my investment and effort. It never came.

Broadbill by the thousands passed within sight, amoeba-like bunches on the horizon. But, except for a few bufflehead that blundered into the rig, my gunbarrel remained as cold as the salt ice that began to build on the bills of my stool as the end of the season approached.

I was simply out of their flight pattern. The places I chose to rig neither offered food for the birds nor functioned as a resting spot. What's more, it didn't lie on a path between these two areas.

When the birds you're after travel in the thousands, or are familiar companions to flocks of that number, trying to interest individuals to break what is essentially a habit with a piddling rig of 50 to 100 stool is futile. They're simply not going to alter their daily pattern to swing over you. If you had 1,000 decoys, you *might* pull it off, but it would take an army of gunners to maintain that kind of rig.

The cardinal rule of open-water gunning, then, is to spend a lot of time looking first. Forget about being set up by daybreak, and don't be seduced by a handful of birds passing by a particular place. Get a good set of binoculars and watch carefully. When you see flight after flight tolling to a well-defined area, or passing by it, *that* is the place and time to rig out.

Easily the best open-water gunner I know is Joe Arata, a friend since boyhood, and I still hunt with him and his buddies whenever I visit the East during duck season. We kid Joe a lot. We even bought him a bus driver's hat for his "tours," because a typical day of gunning with Joe involves about five hours in a car, visiting different spots along the shores of Long Island. Joe will stop along some sandy beach or marshy point, gaze out to sea for five minutes, then say, "Not here—let's try the Sore Thumb," or, "Maybe they're tending to Oak Neck," and we drive some more.

Sometimes we don't have our rig in the water until two or three in the afternoon. But when Joe says, "This is the place," we always get more than good shooting; we get great shooting. Joe really understands the importance of, and how to identify, the flight patterns of diving ducks.

Beyond the powers of observation, there are a few other things that hint at good places to rig for divers. First, they tend to fly along the "edge" of anything.

During a fog, they'll often follow the shore. If there's a partial sheet of ice on a body of water, they'll follow the edge of it. Should that ice be broken into slush, or the water be "making ice," and it's pushed into a slushy broken line by wind, currents, and tides, divers will follow that too.

If a shoal, shelf, or drop-off is visible from the air—even if it's

no more than a matter of a slight difference in water coloration—
they'll follow that line. Likewise for a line created by the conflict
of wind or bottom contours with moving water.

Note again the effectiveness of a long tail of decoys stretching
out into open water when you're gunning divers; you're creating
that path, that line, that "edge" they love to follow.

Food is another drawing card. If you know a lake or bay contains
extensive clam or mussel flats, or beds of wild celery, eel grass, or
any other type of favored food, the chances are better than good
that spot will be visited by ducks sometime during the day.

When you can find those things occurring simultaneously—a flight
path that follows some sort of an "edge" near feeding grounds—a
lay-out boat with fifty decoys will still produce the kind of gunning
that makes bag limits more than mere pipe dreams.

The V rig is the setup I've seen Joe Arata use most often. It's
nothing more than arranging fifty to eighty stool in a V configuration with the boat at the crotch of the letter.

The V is easy to set because up to ten decoys can be put on
one long line for quick handling, without appearing unnatural and
soldier-straight on the water. This is a probalem with some of the
other rigging patterns because of their graceful curves and S's.

Another plus to the V is that it's perfect for two shooters. Other
designs find the boat lying to the side of the landing area and one
hunter shooting across the other.

One disadvantage of the V is that decoying birds tend to the head
of the rig, and suddenly discover you're there. You seldom get a
perfect, classic toll. But you do get easy wing shots as decoying
divers will pick up one wing of the letter and slow way down as
they look for a place to land.

The fishhook draws ducks over open water as well as it does near
shore, though it creates some problems when you're setting it up
or bringing it in.

When your decoy configuration involves essentially straight lines
like the V, setting them out and picking them up is easy—nothing
more than a matter of drifting with the wind.

Curved patterns like the fishhook require a lot of jockeying
around to set them, and aside from the extra work involved, there's

always the chance that you'll wind an anchor line around your prop —cussed luck at best, and conceivably a very dangerous situation in heavy seas and frigid water.

Fishhook configurations and patterns like it are particularly effective over open water because of the tail. If you find you've misjudged flight patterns, you can extend a line of decoys to the right or left to intercept the passing birds.

Mixing divers and puddlers is seldom done in open-water shooting. It just isn't that productive.

Occasionally goose or brant decoys are included with a diver rig when these birds happen to be in that area. These decoys are set apart from the main configuration of blocks, up toward the head of the pattern and within gun range of the lay-out boat.

They should be placed with some sort of design in mind, the simplest, and the one I most often use, being a half-moon configuration.

SETTING FIELD DECOYS

Setting out decoys in a field largely involves goose stool. Puddle ducks will freely decoy to a flock of geese; so aside from a few confidence mallards or pintail there's no real need for lots of field duck decoys.

Choose a place to set the decoys that has low or virtually no cover. Geese are reluctant to land anywhere that could hide a hunter.

The same caution is true of a field surrounded by tall timber or thick brush; set your stool in the middle of such a field. If you rig too close to the borders, birds will come in sky-high and will be reluctant to land.

The best blind location in relation to the decoy configuration is among the decoys at the head of the spread. The presence of decoys in close proximity to the pit helps break up revealing outlines, and you have the "peep-hole" option of a slit-sided hollow-bodied stool on your hatch cover.

The only disadvantage to this pit location is that birds will occasionally land behind you, making for a tough shot. But all in all, I think the credits far outweigh the debits here.

Geese generally want a much bigger landing spot than ducks. If there are none provided, they'll land outside of the stool, usually toward the front half of the flock. Like water decoys, field decoys should face into the wind. Be very aware of wind shifts, too. A drifting decoy will align itself naturally, but a field decoy can't.

Another pitfall common to field hunting is frost. Just before sun-up on cool mornings, check for frost on the backs of your decoys. If you find it has formed, take the time to dust it off with a whisk broom; even the lightest touch of frost appears white and unnatural from the air, and when it melts, the wet decoy backs will shine like polished glass.

The V formation is the field rig I usually set for Canadas and their subspecies.

This configuration requires between fifteen and fifty decoys, with the pit located in the crotch of the V. The open end of the V affords plenty of landing room, and birds will tend to this spot, offering the best shot in the business.

It is common practice to set a gander in the alert posture, ahead of and slightly off to one side of the V configuration, as all real flocks of feeding geese post at least one sentry.

Occasionally, goose hunters like to set five or six more stool in a separate block to the side of the main body of decoys, but I find this practice questionable.

It is designed to give the illusion of a newly arrived knot of birds that haven't yet had time to join the main flock—sort of a confidence setup—but I've found it serves to encourage incoming birds to land in back of the pit. Jumping up, swinging around, locating and tracking birds behind you adds up to tough shooting.

If you have trouble with high-flying geese that don't want to come down, set a small bunch of stool one hundred yards or more downwind of the main spread. Approaching birds see these decoys first and are encouraged to drop down for a closer look at what lies ahead. This then puts them in a more willing position to decoy.

Be careful about the head positions on your stool; too many sentries will give indication of a nervous flock. In a rig of forty decoys, set no more than nine heads in the alert position, an equal number of sleepers, and the rest feeders.

Field duck decoys, if you choose to use a few, should be bunched together and distinct from the main body of geese. Geese will harass smaller waterfowl in a feeding area; so the twain seldom meet. I generally set four or five ducks off to one side of the crotch of the V.

The I formation is mostly commonly employed in goose hunting when decoys numbering in the hundreds are used. This is often the case in snow-goose country; newspapers or diapers are set up on dowels to complement full-bodied stool, and the rig often stretches from one end of a field to the other. Snow geese seem impressed with numbers, not details.

When setting out the I, the length of the letter should follow the drift of the wind. Several sentries may set out along the I, but keep most of them around the upwind half of the letter, and locate the blind in the middle of the letter.

DECOY PROBLEMS

No matter the species of waterfowl you're hunting or the terrain where you've rigged your blocks, one of the few certainties of the sport is that ducks and geese will come to an appealing set of decoys. If they don't, you've done or are doing something wrong, and the birds will tell you what.

When there's no activity whatsoever, no birds in the air or waterfowl passing too far away to see your decoys, you're out of flight patterns. Find a different location for your blind—one that's closer to established passes, resting spots, and feeding areas.

When birds pass you at closer ranges where they surely can see your decoys (two hundred to four hundred yards out), watch their movements aloft very carefully. If they follow an arrow-straight path with purpose and dedication, again you're in the wrong place with your decoy spread. There's something about the area that simply is unattractive to ducks. Although I have no idea why, I have seen broadbill refuse to cross a sandy-colored submerged shoal to come to my decoys, and blacks flare from a telephone pole behind my blind. The puzzling thing is that this doesn't always happen; so you can't make any rules about shoals or telephone poles. But be aware that certain features of the terrain on certain days occasionally add up to places where ducks refuse to go. When you think you're in such a spot, move.

If, however, you note fly-bys tipping toward your rig, rising up for a better look, banking as if to come in, or otherwise altering their course of flight, the chances are good you're in the right spot but that there's something wrong with the way you've put your spread together.

Check your blind for good camouflage, and check those inside too. Occasionally a strong sun will find faces inside literally shining.

If the blind fits in well, look next at your decoy spread and the way you've set it, with an eye to the type of duck that's passing you by. I once changed my shooting from poor to excellent by pulling my rig of mallards off a point and changing it to a C in a nearby cove. It was a move of less than twenty yards; we didn't even have to change the location of the blind. But where birds had flown by before, they now banked around the point and decoyed perfectly to the cove.

Another way to tempt fly-bys to come in closer is by extending the tail of a fishhook out farther. This is particularly successful on divers, but I have persuaded puddlers using a tail too.

Ducks flaring at close ranges means some detail is out of whack. The first thing to consider is your blind location: is it eyeball to eyeball with incoming birds? If so, that's your problem.

Next, check your decoys. Are any hung up with each other; is one overturned or riding awry? Perhaps they're just poor stool or poorly painted. It doesn't take much to frighten waterfowl when they're getting ready to sit in.

Note, too, where they're trying to sit down. If there's no room for them to get in—decoys packed too tightly where there should be a hole—open up a landing area.

If all these things check out, look again at your blind and the surrounding area. Shiny objects like spent casings, the jetsam of washed-up tin cans, even your gun barrel, will flare birds. Remember that those shiny or otherwise alarming objects could be under water. As birds come in, watch and mark exactly where they flare, and try to estimate where they're looking when they do.

There was a day on the Moriches marshes when the black duck were thick and willing, but just as they got within gun range they flared wildly. I spent a half hour examining the beach and the water and, by a process of elimination as each bird flared, finally discovered they were frightened of an old sunken rubber tire that had totally escaped my notice. I pulled the tire up from the bottom, hid it under some seaweed on the shore, and the birds decoyed without blinking an eye.

Admittedly, there are no hard-and-fast rules about what draws or flares waterfowl around decoys—just an interminable bunch of variables that it's up to you to assess. But that's what's so damned intriguing and absorbing about the sport; if you're really waterfowling, you've got no time for the mundane cares of bills, work, wives, or lovers.

And when you put decoys, days, marshes, and blinds together so well that birds decoy into your lap, you know you've done something right, and all the cussing, work, waiting, and past frustration pale in the reflection of that glorious day.

MAKE THE DUCKS COME TO YOU

Ted Trueblood

Among the many strengths that I admire about Ted Trueblood as a writer is his considerable ability to turn to the practical side of sport and present his experiences and observations without being didactic. Trueblood has always taught me a lot, and at the end of each session I feel as though I've had a chat with a friend—not a lesson. This one originally appeared in True *and is included in the anthology, the* Ted Trueblood Hunting Treasury, *published by David MacKay Company, Inc., New York, 1978.*

ANYBODY CAN kill ducks early in the season and again, later, on those days when unusual weather makes the birds forget all caution. But normally by late season some ducks in every flock have been shot at. Then they are blind-shy, call-shy, decoy-shy, and always suspicious. This is the kind of duck hunting that separates the men from the boys. It sometimes makes me appear downright juvenile. But during many years of trying I've picked up some tricks from older and smarter duck hunters, and I'm going to pass them on.

The most important thing, always, is to find the right location. Not being a duck, I don't know why they like some spots and don't like others that look similar to me, but that's the way they are. Careful observation is your best guide here, though sometimes luck can help.

One day four of us put out two dozen decoys on a little puddle at noon and crouched in the reeds around it. About the same time, a fellow who has the reputation of being one of the finest duck callers in this part of the country put out his stool 250 yards away.

We had shot twenty-four mallards and four or five pintails and baldpates and were picking up by 2 o'clock. We did no calling. Meanwhile the other hunter blew his heart out and killed one duck.

Unfortunately, you can't always be in the one best spot. There may be a dozen equally good, with ducks willing to light in any of them, and plenty of competition. It's then that a good stool, a suitable blind, the ability to talk duck language, and attention to details can bring them in to the man who knows how.

Let's consider decoys first. The most important thing is the overall impression created by the stool. Even the best decoy, taken by itself, resembles a real duck about as much as an artificial fly looks like a natural insect. But the entire spread can create the illusion of a flock of feeding, loafing, or resting birds, and the more successfully it does that, the more birds it will bring within range. A few little touches can make a big difference.

You need only a few decoys on a pond or a small stream. Ducks trading among such places are usually in small flocks, and a little bunch of decoys will bring them in. A dozen is frequently enough, and I can't recall when I needed more than twice that number.

On big water, however, I like a big stool. I use about five dozen most of the time, and I'd probably use more if setting them out and picking them up didn't run into so much work. A big flock of ducks ordinarily won't pay any attention to a little wad of blocks.

About fifty of these decoys are mallards and the rest are pintails. Their purpose is not to bring in sprigs, which, like all other shallow-water ducks, will come to a mallard stool. They provide eye-catching splashes of white and help to attract the attention of passing birds.

There is another eye-catcher that works well when some of the decoys are set on the shore of a pond or on a river bar. I save a few duck wings early in the season and lean them against four or five decoys, with the white underside out. In any flock of loafing ducks, one or two always have a wing up, stretching or searching for bugs. The white wings are perfectly natural as well as attention-getting.

A few drakes usually have their necks erect, looking around. On a bar, you can add one more detail to your illusion by propping up a few ducks—after you shoot them, of course—among your stool. I think real ducks set in a natural position, their heads held up by 15-inch wires, are the best decoys. The trouble is, with the current limits, by the time you have enough decoys out you're through shooting.

I skin out the necks of the first half dozen I kill each year. Then I pour borax into them and work it well up into the head, and they stay in the freezer until hunting begins to get tough. With a little care they last the season.

I carry my heads, wings, and a dozen pieces of No. 6 wire, 15 inches long, in a little bag with my decoys. When I set up, I put a wire inside each skinned-out neck and stick it into the head. I shove the other end into the ground. Then I set a decoy close against it so that the decoy head won't show, and the deception is complete.

It is amazing what the heads and wings do for a decoy spread, even when you know what they are. I discover hopeful hunters stalking my stool every season. When I make the setup in a stubble, I can hardly resist stalking it myself.

About three dozen of my decoys have strings a little less than 2 feet long. There are three reasons for the short strings: First, puddle ducks don't like deep water; so this usually is long enough. Second, short strings don't tangle so badly as long ones. Third, and most important, decoys on short strings are far more active in a breeze. They swing steadily back and forth.

Most of my remaining decoys have strings 4 feet long. In some places where I hunt there's no choice but to set out in deep water and then, of course, I need the longer cords. Fortunately these places are small pockets surrounded by willows where I don't need so many decoys.

Five of my decoys are rigged with heavy anchors and strings 6 feet long. On the big river where I do most of my hunting, I set them way out in the current, as much as 50 yards from the remainder of the stool. Their purpose is to catch the attention of high, passing ducks. They're supposed to be taken for a little bunch swimming in to those already clustered along the bar. Apparently they are, because they seem to help.

Loafing, resting, or feeding mallards are always tightly bunched. Therefore, I group my decoys tight—as close together as they can be without touching. Ducks never attempt to light among them, just as they never pitch into the middle of a raft of their fellows. They always light on open water nearby and swim in. So I divide the bulk of my decoys into two bunches with a patch of open water 25 or 30 feet wide between. All the ducks that decoy head for that.

A lot of factors enter into the arrangement of decoys: the wind, the current (if you're on a stream), their relation to the spot from which you have to shoot, and the direction the ducks are flying. Usually it's impossible to have everything just right, and what is a good stool one day may not work the next.

The ideal, of course, is to have the wind coming from behind the blind with the decoys in front of it. This gives you one shot as they're coming in and a second as they flare up toward you. With a wind from right or left, you get crossing shots; I find it helps to locate the blind toward the downwind end of the decoys, if possible. A wind blowing from the decoys toward the blind means tough shooting with your back toward the stool. If there's room. I move a little farther away and take the ducks as they come to me, just before they're directly overhead. With this one exception, I like to have the blind as close to the decoys as I can.

All of these things, from the pintail blocks to the location of the stool in relation to the blind, help to bring ducks into range. There is one remaining thing that helps more than any of them—possibly more than all the others together—when the going is tough. This is what Clayton Davidson called his "worker decoy," "jumper duck," or "diver." He "invented" it, as he did many other tricks of duck hunting.

Everybody knows how lifeless a spread of decoys looks on a flat-calm day, and they look even more artificial to ducks in the air than they do to the hunter in his blind. Clayton's jumper duck animates all of the other decoys within 10 yards by sending waves among them. It also provides movement that attracts the attention of ducks overhead.

He simply attaches a 2-foot strip of rubber—six or eight heavy rubber bands looped together will do—to the keel of a decoy. He ties a piece of cord to the end of the rubber and a second cord, about 50 feet long, to the keel. The short cord is tied to a stake; the long one goes to the blind. When the water is flat, he begins working the cord while approaching ducks are still mere specks in the sky. Each time he pulls and releases it, the rubber jerks the decoy back toward the stake. This makes the jumper tip up, bob, splash, and dart back and forth.

Clayton believed that the jumper was worth more than a call for bringing in skeptical ducks. I think he was right, but it's a wonderful help with a call, too. Everybody who uses one has seen ducks overhead looking for the old girl that's talking to them. The jumper attracts their attention and keeps it away from the blind.

The cord from the worker to the blind should be an inconspicuous color. It should be kept fairly tight, so that you need move only your hand to make the worker bob around. This hand, of course, will be down in the corner of the blind where the ducks can't see it.

The thing that makes the jumper so valuable should be the tipoff for the hunter in his blind. Nothing catches a duck's eye like movement. One day last winter I had a single mallard coming to the decoys. She made a couple of passes and finally was satisfied, dropping in against the wind with wings cupped and feet down.

I had been chuckling to her through the call, which was in my left hand, and I was watching her through a hole in the reeds. When she was about 60 yards away, I dropped the call and lowered my left hand to the fore end of my gun. She flared off and bounced 30 feet with the aid of the breeze, and I never did get a shot at her. Just the movement of my hand was enough!

You don't need much cover if you can hold still. If you can't hold still, you can hardly build a blind that will hide you. Every winter I see blinds that might pass for two-car garages. They're probably necessary for men who can't hold still. But I've seen good duck hunters kill limits while crouching in a few sparse reeds or lying flat in open stubble.

There is nothing to be gained by turning your head to follow circling ducks. If they're going to come in, they'll come into the wind and you'll be looking right at them. A white face surrounded by the dark shadows of a blind looms up like a neon sign. And if you twist around the chances are they'll see you and won't come in at all.

I like to get all set, with my back to the wind, while approaching ducks are still a long way off. My call is in position in my left hand, and my gun across my lap with my right hand on the grip. I lower my face so that I can barely peek under my cap over the edge of the blind. Then I don't move a muscle until the ducks are in range. When they're close enough, I drop the call and come up ready to shoot.

Since my hunting covers quite a stretch of country as I follow the ducks in their feeding and loafing, the advantages of a portable blind are obvious. A good many years ago, Sam Davis showed me his. It was the best I had ever seen, and I made one like it. Later I made another. They weigh only nine pounds apiece and roll up into bundles 10 inches in diameter. I can carry both under one arm and set them up in five minutes. They can be used separately, with a hunter in each, or together, in which case they will conceal two men side by side.

Best of all, there is no place they can't be used. They are practically invisible in typical marsh surroundings or along the reed-bordered edge of a slough or a pond. I have used one successfully by setting it up in front of a cut bank or beside a puddle on a mud flat. They can even be used in an open stubble field or on a bare river bar. A little tuft of cattails is inconspicuous anywhere.

Sam made his blind—and I copied him—by stretching two ropes tight on the ground, 26 inches apart, fastened to stakes at each end. The ropes were 7½ feet long, including the loops at the ends through which the stakes were driven. Next we tied to the ropes cattails cut 44 to 48 inches long, keeping them parallel, like the pickets of a fence. The butts must be kept even, but the tops should be irregular. Tan cord and ¼-inch hemp rope are best. The leaves on each stem are tied in, but the fuzzy tops are cut off. The whole job can be done in about an hour.

Each blind is complete with four 48-inch stakes made from old broom handles or the like. One stake stays in the loop at each end. The other two stakes are rolled up inside.

To set up a blind for one person, I drive the loose stakes a few inches into the ground about 30 inches apart, pull the blind around them with the rope inside, and drive the two end stakes, pulling the blind tight as I do. This makes a U-shaped shelter. You sit with your back to the open, upwind end on an empty shell box, or kneel, and lean forward, hiding your face.

There is only one blind less likely to flare ducks than a little clump of cattails, and that is none at all. If your setup is close to brush or reeds, you're better off to kneel or sit on a low box in them than to make a blind of any kind. Camouflage clothing, especially a face net, helps.

I suppose every duck hunter in grain- or corn-raising country has a sheet to hide under when there's snow and the ducks are feeding in the fields. The trouble with a sheet is that it's so awkward. Cover yourself well enough and you can't get out from under the thing to shoot. Remain partly exposed, and the ducks see you long before they get near enough for shooting.

Another old duck hunter showed me the obvious solution: A pair of white coveralls, such as dairy workers wear, big enough to go on over your other duck-hunting clothes. Crawl into them, pin a piece of white cloth to your hunting cap with some hanging down in the back like a bobtailed burnoose, put on white cotton gloves, hide your gun with another strip of cloth, and you're practically invisible when there's snow on the ground.

This getup is perfect in stubble. It works well even on open mud flats when there's snow. You don't need any blind at all. Just tip your face down. And hold still!

FIVE

Mallards, Pintails and Some Other Puddlers

DUSKY DUCKS IN
THE WILDERNESS

Bert Claflin

There can be little argument that in terms of numbers of birds and shooting opportunity, West Coast gunners enjoy a large advantage over their Eastern counterparts. Additionally, the Western marshes hold abundant pintail populations, while the meager pintail flocks in the East are likely to whip through before opening day. The Eastern waterfowler can, however, lay generally exclusive claim to one segment of the art of duck hunting seldom experienced by Westerners—the uppers and downers of messing around with black ducks. Unless you've actually experienced the hunting, it is hard to believe how skittish the average flock of black ducks can be. Blind shy, decoy shy, call shy—the black duck becomes one of the most prized ducks to bag because he is so difficult. Through the blurred stalks of marsh-grass brown, you watch the knot of birds turn into the wind, heading your way. Your face is down; still you roll your eyes upward and try to peek. They're coming! Don't move now! Don't breathe! Don't even think! Suddenly, ten yards from the outer perimeter of the decoys, the birds flare, bouncing upwards as though an explosive charge has been detonated under their tails, the underside of their wings flashing silver. What went wrong? You will think a lot about that while the skies are empty. Right now, you don't know whether to cry or to salute a worthy adversary. In this chapter from his book, American Waterfowl *(Knopf, 1952), Bert Claflin aims to ambush his black ducks far to the north, near their breeding grounds, figuring to crack down on a few before they become such wisenheimers. As a book,* American Waterfowl *is a handsome, eminently readable work, typical of the Knopf excellence of the period, though not quite as over-all superlative as Ray Camp's* Duck Boats: Blinds: Decoys *and* Eastern Seaboard Wildfowling, *also published by Knopf in 1952.*

WHEN THE subject of waterfowl hunting comes up, or when I am alone in my lodge with nothing to do, which is seldom, my mind wanders to a spot far off in the wilderness of Ontario where three years ago, all by myself, during the first week in October, I enjoyed some highly unusual duck shooting. It was not hunting that only I could enjoy. Anybody can do the same who is not afraid of solitude. There are times when I crave it, although, generally speaking, I derive much pleasure from having about me sympathetic friends who speak my language.

There is something about being alone, particularly in wild places, that is very difficult to describe. Do not attempt it if you are subject to nostalgia, for when night comes even the leaves of the trees whisper to you. They bring messages from friends far away, and you feel that you must answer them, and you cannot, except in spirit. The best way to overcome this feeling of uneasiness is to busy yourself with something, anything, such as sweeping the floor if you are in a cabin; or dressing some fish or game for the ensuing day; or reading, if you have a book.

When the urge assailed me to get away by myself I lost no time assembling my paraphernalia and heading for Canada. I went directly to Winnepeg and looked up my old guide, Perot. I explained to him that I wished to hunt and loaf for a few days where nobody would bother me.

The little Canuck seemed to be somewhat nonplussed by my unusual idea. He mulled the matter over in his mind for several minutes. Then he spoke: "Let me see—I know of a river that comes into the upper end of Lake Winnepeg. There's a cabin on it. Some fellows built it a couple of years ago. They were going to live in it; so far as I know, they never lived there. We can use it and nobody will bother us."

"That will be fine," I said. "But you're not going to stay there with me. This is once that I want to be by myself."

"How long do you want to stay?" he asked.

"That will depend upon circumstances," I replied. "I'd like to be alone up there about four days. Then you can come up after me. Do you think I might get some good shooting there?"

"Yes. Black mallards. The cabin is really on a small lake. It's part of the river. The ducks come down that river and stay there to feed up before they go south. It's all woods around there, and nobody hunts there that I know of."

I went home with my guide and remained with him overnight. The following morning he put some blankets in a bag, borrowed a few simple cooking utensils from his wife, cleaned and filled an old but serviceable lantern and put it in his car, and then hooked up a trailer with a light boat on it, in which there were some decoys. We started. In Winnepeg I purchased the food I would need, and we were off for what proved to be a very rare experience for me. The fact that a cabin awaited me in this hidden-away spot may have been a rare coincidence, but it was there, and I hope to use it again when the urge strikes me to be alone.

We managed to get within a half mile of our destination in Perot's car; but that was the end of what had at least resembled a trail. From there we hiked the rest of the way, carrying the loose impedimenta. Then we went back and fetched the boat on our shoulders.

The cabin was clean, although it smelled a bit musty. We opened the two windows, performed some strenuous house-cleaning, and built a fire in the fairly good-looking stove that stood in a corner. Soon the place was livable. Perot and I now went down to where we had deposited the boat in the cattails. Alarmed by our talking, a big flock of dusky ducks burst from the weeds not far from us and took off down the lake.

It was late in the afternoon when my guide left. I told him when to come back. Now I was on my own resources. I entered the cabin, replenished the fire, and made up my bed in an empty bunk. Then I proceeded to boil some spuds and fry a few slices of bacon before the java pot started to sing. An hour later, with the lantern doing its best to liven things up, I had not an enemy in the world. In a swamp along the river bottom I heard the "Who-who-whooo" of an owl; a chipmunk ran up and down the roof; and from out on the lake came the faint quacks of feeding ducks.

I stepped outside to have a look at the weather. In the clear air the stars appeared to be unusually large and bright. They presaged lower temperature. But I had plenty of warm clothing with me.

When I rolled out of my bunk in the morning the cabin was like an icebox. It had grown much colder during the night. I warmed it up very soon, however, and prepared a hearty breakfast. Then I was ready to interview the ducks.

In all the years I had hunted, in both well-known and unfrequented places, I had never seen as many dusky ducks in one restricted area as greeted my eyes when I cautiously approached the shore of the lake and peered through the brush. Literally thousands of the kingly birds were in sight on the water, and, as I learned when I showed myself, fully as many more were puddling around and feeding among the dense cattails and other vegetation.

Now that I had been treated to this unprecedented sight there was no reason to remain hidden. I knew that once these ducks were frightened into leaving the immediate neighborhood without a shot being fired at them, they would return, not all at once but a few at a time. I stepped boldly out into the open. Such a scrambling, quacking, and fluttering of wings I had never seen or heard before. They rose from the water with a roar, and for some time without letup were joined by thousands of others from the surrounding weeds. The air was full of them, moving in all directions to escape the supposed danger.

I stepped into the boat with my gun, and poled out a few rods from the shore. I set my six decoys in a clear spot, and then shoved back into a thick bunch of cattails, loaded my gun, and sat down to await the return of the birds. Soon I saw four of them winging their way against the wind that had sprung up, and heading directly toward me. Their black bodies and the white underparts of their wings formed a striking contrast against the clear sky. When they saw my decoys, undoubtedly the first frauds of this kind they had ever seen, they swung over them about forty yards high.

There was no reason to "strain my gun," so I let them go. They came back with a rush, sailed over the blocks, and then turned back toward them. When they were within thirty yards of me I rose and dropped the nearest one. That was all I wanted. I anticipated no difficulty in getting my limit at any time during the ensuing days before Perot returned. Besides, it was not solely for the purpose of shooting ducks that I had exiled myself on this occasion. If I never killed another duck I had, undoubtedly, taken more than my share during the many years I had hunted. Of course, I wanted the ducks to be there—lots of them—where I could see them. But chiefly I desired to be alone, to rough it in a limited way, to commune with nature all by myself.

I retrieved my bird and returned to my hiding-place among the cattails. There was no hurry about doing that, but I wished to have my victim where I could examine and admire it and heft it.

From then on, there paraded before, above, and behind me by far the greatest assembly of dusky ducks that I had ever witnessed. They came from all directions, from the opposite side of the lake and from over the tall spruce trees that bordered its shores. I knew from experience that the eyes of dusky ducks are very sharp, so I had broken the weeds so that they leaned over my boat and hid it completely. Presently individuals and small flocks of the birds began coming back along the surface of the lake. Some of them alighted beside my decoys, even though they were crudely made. For a few moments the graceful duskies, with their necks stretched to full length, looked suspiciously at the clumsy blocks, and then they leaped into the air, to settle down again in the weeds not far away.

I remained there two hours just watching them mill around over the weed-infested lake, cautiously looking for good feeding grounds. I am not exaggerating when I say that during that time I believe I saw not less than ten thousand ducks, and every one, so far as I could tell, was a dusky. I concluded that many of them had hatched and matured in the immediate neighborhood, and Perot later agreed with me. But after I had told him about the great number I had seen he hazarded the belief that the majority of them had been brought forth in the heavily forested region of Ontario miles north, and also as far away as the western shore of Hudson's Bay.

"They probably drifted down to the lake we are on to feed and get fat before they start southward," he explained.

Finally I picked up the decoys and went back to the cabin, where I prepared and ate a lunch and then dressed the duck I had shot. The weather had turned much colder by this time, so I hung the duck outside the cabin. It would make me a fine meal later on. It was midafternoon when I completed my "housework." Then, by way of diversion, I took my gun—in case I ran across a "b'ar" you understand—and walked along the shore of the lake for about a mile. Rushes grew thickly along the edges of the sand bars, and what from a distance looked to me like wapato flourished in profusion where the bottom was muddy.

At intervals of perhaps a hundred yards I stopped and whistled or shouted. It sent clouds of ducks into the air. I cannot adequately describe the show that was put on for my entertainment. I had not thought there were that many dusky ducks in existence. Some distance out from the shore, disturbed by the noise I made, a flock of fully a thousand—or perhaps many more; I am only estimating the number—rose lazily and flew down the lake.

I had struck it just right to see these grand birds in unbelievable numbers. In a short time they would be gone, many of them heading for the ponds of the New England states, and thence southward to the ricefields and other extensive feeding grounds in Virginia and the Carolinas, where they would spend the winter months. Others would forge down the Mississippi River Flyway, finding their way eventually to their winter homes in Louisiana and other southern states.

I turned in early that night and was up at daybreak. For me the hour before sunrise is the most interesting one of the entire twenty-four. A hush of expectancy in the air, accompanied at times by the whisper of a breeze in the tops of the tall trees, lends mystery to the surroundings. The guttural note of a feeding dusky duck, and then the sharp quacks of incoming birds, brought me to a realization that another day would soon unfold its attractions.

I shivered as I walked down to where the boat was moored. At the water's edge ice had formed during the night. It crunched as I trod on it. Today I would shoot my limit of the big, fat, dusky beauties, and the low temperature would preserve them. Tomorrow I would repeat the performance. I had told Perot to come for me at the end of the third day. Then, if he wanted some ducks, there would be more shooting.

This day I decided to do my shooting at another part of the lake. Accordingly, I poled the boat from one open spot to another until I was about a half mile from where I started. Finally I came to a point of vegetation which extended well out into a rather large, open spot free of all weeds. I immediately decided that it was an ideal place. I set out the six decoys belonging to my guide, and pushed my boat into the thick grass.

The fact that there were no other hunters in this region gave me a big advantage. Had there been, the ducks would not have come to my decoys so readily, since they were duskies, a naturally wary species. As it was, they soon started coming back to the open spots from which I had chased them. I do not recall ever having better or easier shooting. I brought down a bird from every small bunch of less than a half dozen, shooting only at those so close to me that regularly I killed them in the air. Before an hour had passed I had my limit, and it was a bird for every shell that I fired, save one that was used to prevent one of the ducks from escaping in the weeds with only a broken wing.

I do not speak of this shooting in a boastful way. As I have intimated, it was very easy. The big birds, at no time extremely fast flyers, simply saw my blocks, swung in over them, and slowed up preparatory to alighting near them. It was much different from pass shooting, which at times calls for leads of twenty feet or more.

It was too cold to stay out on the lake with any degree of comfort after I stopped shooting. Therefore I recovered the decoys and returned to the cabin. There I dressed my ducks and hung them on the low limb of a tree, where they soon stiffened in the now frosty air.

It was much colder the following morning when I turned out. Intermittent, fine snow accompanied the strong northeast wind. I did not need to go far from the boat landing this morning. The air was full of the big, black birds, flying in every direction. They seemed to be very uneasy, no doubt sensing the approach of weather that would lock the lake with an icy cover. I worked fast and soon bagged my limit. I had visions of a nice warm fire in the cabin.

About four o'clock in the afternoon my guide showed up at the cabin. I had not expected him to come until the next day, but, considering the fact that winter seemed imminent, he was welcome. I had had my fling at the dusky ducks and I was satisfied; also, I had enjoyed being alone for a short period. Had it been earlier, say the first part of September, I would have remained isolated much longer. Perot did not care to do any hunting, so we pulled out for Winnepeg that same afternoon.

Right now is an opportune time to speak briefly about guides. It is understood, of course, that on waters with which you are well acquainted it is not necessary for you to have one. In fact, knowing where and how to hunt anywhere means that you yourself have the qualifications of a professional guide. But when you hunt in the Canadian provinces, or in any other region that is strange to you, to be successful—that is, to get the most out of it—you must engage a guide.

Those you will find in Canada are in a class by themselves. It has often appeared remarkable to me how they can find their way to the countless different regions and back again. They have not necessarily been there before; there is always a first time.

A great many of the Canadian guides are not literate. They have practically no book learning. They do not need it. They are highly educated in their own profession. Most of them were taught the ways of the woods and waters by their fathers. Wild game is an open book to them. A competent guide is not talkative, yet will answer any question you may ask him relating to his stamping ground and its inhabitants.

When you approach a guide of the provinces with a view to engaging him, you will usually find him inclined to be hesitant in extolling the possibilities for good hunting in any locality, particularly if he is rather old and highly experienced. But if you leave it to him to select the place you will rarely, if indeed ever, be disappointed.

How to select the right kind of a guide? Frankly, unless you have been advised just whom to select by competent and honest persons, you will have to take your chances. And here is a tip: If his charge for services strikes you as being somewhat exhorbitant, *that is the man to engage.* If you have to figure the cost of a hunting trip in the Canadian provinces down to dollars and cents, I suggest that you go to Uncle Hiram's farm in your own county and hunt blackbirds.

Guides in Canada will charge you from ten to twenty dollars a day, depending upon the services they have to give you. And such amounts are not exhorbitant. You pay for the sport shown you, and you *get the game*. It is up there. All you have to do is take the necessary steps to find it.

Canadian guides are, as a rule, temperamental. If you fail to have the kind of shooting you want the first day out be very careful how you speak about it to your guide. Do not upbraid him for it. Far better to pass it off lightly when you come in at night, perhaps wet, and undoubtedly tired, and your guide attempts to explain the situation. Do that and he will put you down as a good sport, and extend himself in every way to earn his money as long as he is with you.

Always remember that your guide knows the woods and waters of his native land as you know the streets of the city in which you live. He meets with all kinds of people, some good, some bad. It never takes him long to learn whether or not the man he is guiding knows anything about hunting. And he much prefers to work with those who do know something, although he will never show it. If you are an experienced hunter, the best way to convince him of that is to act and not talk about it. One thing to bear in mind is that, particularly if you have had a successful hunt, you may want to come back again. If you have made a friend of your guide he will want you; if not, he "won't be home," and you will have to secure another one, *if you can*. You know the old saying: "The evil that men do lives after them. . . . "

The right kind of a guide will never shoot at game unless you tell him to, even though it should happen that you are missing badly. He will carry on hour after hour without faltering; he will hunt with you as long as you want him to, and he works under no eight-hour-a-day rule; he never needs to be called in the morning. When you crawl out you can wade into the flapjacks, bacon, and coffee—they'll be ready for you.

Some of the guides I have met in the north country were crack shots, but many of them would not take chances on a long shot. The game had to be very close before they would pull the trigger, and then they did not always hit the target. Certain gunners demand good shooting ability in the guides they hire. But they have to be assured of that by persons other than the guides, whom I have found to be very reticent in this respect.

It has been stated by an authority on Atlantic coast duck-hunting that the guides in Back Bay, Virginia, are the best shots one will find in a long travel. He states further that many of them expect—and get—twenty-five birds out of twenty-five shots. He says they are much disgruntled by a miss, and when one of them misses a bird, which is only very rarely, his companions taunt him. Missing a bird is not a matter of vanity with them; this authority claims that they consider it an act of negligence, and are much distressed.

I have traveled widely and hunted very extensively, and my experience forces me to say that I doubt these extravagant claims. I have yet to meet the hunter who can kill a bird with every shot. Indeed, I consider the gunner who can average one duck for every three shots an expert of high caliber. I am, of course, referring to an extended period—a month of steady shooting, perhaps, or a season.

There are occasions when an experienced gunner makes a long run of kills. I have done it myself many times. Once I killed twenty-five scaups with that many consecutive shots, then missed one, but wound up the day with thirty-two of the birds for thrirty-three shots. This shooting was done over decoys. Again, while jumping mallards in a marsh, I dropped nineteen of them without a miss, but it was a very windy day and they did not hear me until I was so close to them that I could have killed them very easily with a 28-gauge gun.

It must be understood that those were the days when ducks were extremely plentiful and hunters scarce, and bag limits had not yet been restricted. Nor do I submit those feats as something to brag about. I am confident that many gunners have greatly exceeded them.

HUNTING THE POTHOLE DUCKS

Hart Stillwell

The many excellent magazine pieces that Texas outdoor writer Hart Stillwell produced were collected by the venerable Knopf organization in two fine additions to the company's esteemed library of hunting and fishing books. Hunting and Fishing in Texas, *from which this piece was taken, was published in 1946.* Hunting and Fishing in Mexico *was also a Knopf offering. Both books contain the gritty, colorful prose that made Stillwell a favorite with editors and readers during his career. He knew sport in Texas and Mexico as few others have lived it—and even fewer have told it.*

WILD WILLIAM LONGINO and I got off to a bad start, and from then on things degenerated rapidly. Bill had lent his decoys to a friend, a thing no man should ever do, and the friend had returned them in a cluster. We didn't discover this until Bill dumped the decoys out of the gunny sack after we had waded out into the icy water of the pond.

There they were, with all those strings with pyramid sinkers on them wound together in a hopeless maze. I stood holding the guns and Wild William hovered over those decoys, cussing until his ordinarily red face turned a light blue, then purple, then black. In the meantime ducks we had scared up as we waded out into the pond wheeled overhead, and this made things worse.

We finally had to give up any thought of separating the decoys, so we dragged them over near shore and left them huddled there together, figuring maybe any passing ducks would think they had bunched up that way to keep warm. We waded into the tule, or cattails, and started waiting. By that time the ducks that had been milling around had gone, and no others showed any indication of moving in.

The little pond was only four or five miles from the Gulf, way down the coast of Texas, and it was an ideal spot for early-season pothole shooting. I had been there the opening day and had some good shooting even though the lake was practically surrounded by hunters. The tule made an ideal blind, and the entire layout was good, with a big ridge with heavy mesquite on it to the east of the lake, and a resaca where the ducks watered still farther east, then a big bay, and then the Gulf. Ducks flew to the resaca to water, but they didn't stay there—they moved back to the little pond, or to a larger one nearby, to feed.

We had gone out about the middle of the afternoon, figuring on getting into the afternoon flight. But nothing came our way—not even black mallards, which we can almost always depend on to move around now and then in twos and threes. As the sun neared the horizon Bill and I were about ready to call it a bad bet. Then a flock of ducks suddenly whizzed in over us from the mesquite brush on the ridge to the east, and we cut loose on them. They were widgeons, or baldpates, and we got two of them. Then as we were settling back in the tule after retrieving the ducks, there came another flock. The widgeon flight was on.

The widgeon is a duck that intrigues me, and I don't care if the market hunters of the Mississippi Valley, who valued only the canvasback and the redhead and the mallard and the teal, did list him as a trash duck. He is a clever duck, and I have always had a secret admiration for the manner in which he will hang around the deep-diving redhead and steal food away from that duck when it comes up from the bottom too weary to defend itself against the widgeon.

Then I like the way the widgeon looks in flight, businesslike and neat with his sharp little wings cutting the air and his clear markings showing. And on top of that I like to eat widgeons—their meat is a little lighter-colored than that of most ducks, and that gives it a special appeal to me.

In fact, I like few things better than getting in a good flight of widgeons, although it is something that I seldom run into, since the widgeon is a shy, shifty fellow who changes his watering place and feeding place often. And he thinks nothing of changing his habits and feeding at night if the hunting begins to annoy him. That was evidently what those widgeons moving in on Bill and me were doing —feeding at night.

The flight was fast and furious and we shot until our gun barrels got hot. We were taking them as they came whizzing in with the wind, and it was fast, hard shooting. Maybe it would have been better if we had let them fly over and bagged them coming back in against the wind. I suggested it, but just then another flight came over and I beat Bill to the draw. We simply couldn't let them go by.

The widgeons were still flying when the sun went down and we gathered in our ducks and decoys and left. We could hardly wait to get back out among them the next afternoon. But nary a widgeon showed up that next day, and all we got for our trouble was two black mallards and an old shoveler that I would just as soon have passed up entirely. The widgeons had changed their feeding place.

It isn't often that you get into a good widgeon flight hunting the little potholes along the Texas coast, or even inland, but you do get a wide variety of good shooting at these places. You can bag green-head mallards and the old long-necked pintail, or sprig, and gadwalls now and then, and teal, and such stuff as butterballs and shovelers. Then at times you get black mallards and pretty fair shooting at some of the diving ducks, particularly the bluebills. Near the coast you get redheads occasionally, but we prefer pass shooting on the redheads.

It makes me sad that the kingpin of them all, the big old greenhead mallard, doesn't like my own stomping ground down around the Rio Grande, but shows a weakness for the ricefield country farther up the state, and the potholes on across the state northwest toward the Panhandle. This duck, with his brilliant coloring, his fine flavor, his size as the largest of the ducks, and his habit of decoying nicely to a neat spread nestling up near the shore of some little pond, is the odds-on favorite of the pothole hunter.

But even though he will decoy about as well as any duck, the mallard is no set-up, wherever you find him, as proved by his relatively large numbers. He is almost as shifty as the widgeon in the matter of changing habits to fit the occasion, for he can also take a hint that's thrown at him with a load of No. 7½ shot. For instance, he will change to night feeding, particularly in the ricefields, and you frequently get your shooting, when you get any at all, just before sundown.

But you can trick the greenheads at times just as you can trick other ducks, and I got quite a kick out of working them over once, although it took a regular squad, working in a sort of relay, to do it. There had been an unusual amount of rain that year, and water had overflowed on one big ranch near the coast, enlarging the small water holes on the ranch and making several new ones, so that there were seven ponds, or sloughs, on the ranch.

I went up there once, at the invitation of the ranch-owner, and managed to bag three or four greenheads, but the trouble was they would move away from a pond and wouldn't come back. I saw that I needed more hunters.

So seven of us, one for each water hole, went the next time. We tried to arrange it so we would move in on the ponds at the same moment, and pretty soon the air was full of ducks, as plenty of mallards were feeding on those lakes. But within ten minutes all the ducks had left the ranch, and they didn't come back.

The third time we tried a different bit of strategy. The seven of us made the trip, but we took stands at only four of the seven ponds, leaving the other three for the ducks to settle on and feed. After the first burst of shooting we waited half an hour or so, then moved in on one of the three ponds where the ducks were.

By the time the greenheads had finally figured out that none of the ponds was really safe, and left for good, we had a nice collection of them, along with some pintails and a few bluebills.

But hunters who don't get greenheads can usually console themselves with the pintail, and I don't find anything wrong with him even though he is classed below the mallard on the table. The pintail probably decoys as readily as any other duck, although he is more cautious about it than most of them. Even a big flock of pintails flying over fairly high are quite likely to turn and carefully inspect decoys, whereas redheads in such a flight won't even give the decoys a glance.

But you never have your pintail until he is absolutely convinced everything is all right—until he circles and turns his head from side to side to stare down at the decoys, and at the last minute, when you figure he's coming in to settle, he's likely to move on. Redheads don't do that. Once they start to decoy it's hard to scare them off.

The best way to get pintails is to call them, and I envy those hunters who can really do this. I call pintails myself, but evidently I don't speak the right language. When they come in, softly talking to the decoys as pintails usually do, I am afraid to open up for fear of scaring them, and then when they have completed the inspection and have turned to fly away, I start calling, but they ignore me.

Wild William can call them, along with hogs and horses and other such animals that would lead a quieter, more pleasant life if he wouldn't. And it is an amusing experience to sit and watch and listen as he and a lonely old drake pintail carry on a lot of banter as Wild William lures the pintail in to its doom. That's one of the reasons I like to hunt with Wild William—I figure there is small point in acquiring rare ability at something like calling drake pintails when you can take along some other hunter who already has the trick mastered.

They give us plenty of action along the Texas coast, these long-necked pintails, and you get by far the fastest action when you set out a spread of decoys right along the edge of some big bay, if you can get far enough out from shore.

The fastest and in many ways the most entertaining of all hunting in Texas is teal shooting, and we get both the greenwing and the blue-wing in our country, although it is seldom that we bag a cinnamon teal come early in the fall, and as the season moves along, many of them continue on south into Mexico. Still there are enough hanging around to furnish fair shooting.

The teal is usually the first duck to move in the morning and the last to move in the evening, and back in the old days, when there were no regulations, or when nobody bothered with regulations if there were any, many hunters along the Texas coast skylighted their teal after the sun had gone down. That's when the big flights usually moved. Many Texas hunters have told me about skylighting teal, about listening for the whir of the wings, then snap shooting during that instant when the vague outline of the ducks loomed overhead, listening for the thud of the falling duck, and rushing to the spot where he landed. Of course many ducks were lost in hunting like that, and it's fortunate that skylighting ducks has gone the way of headlighting deer.

But you still get some nice late afternoon shooting now and then on teal and other pothole ducks, and some of the finest teal shooting

I have experienced in a long time occurred only recently on a trip into Mexico.

This was a sort of combination trip, as Wild William and I were mainly interested in hunting ducks, while our host, Manuel Garcia Gomez, owner of a ranch near the coast in Mexico, wanted to hunt geese. We took off from the ranch early in the morning, and Manuel took us first to a resaca not far from the ranch house. There was heavy brush all around the resaca, and as we sneaked through this we could see thousands of ducks on the water in front of us.

A flock of wild-eyed widgeons sounded the alarm, and within five seconds the air was full of ducks, flying over us and around us and away from us, most of them low enough to be in range when they came over. We bagged some pintails and gadwalls and a bluebill and one redhead and a teal—quite a combination.

Then farther along we did some black-mallard shooting, or rather Manuel did, for Bill and I were saving our hunting for a spot near the coast—a spot we had been watching longingly for many months. Hunting black mallards is a little like walking up quail. These ducks, which I am told should really be called black ducks and not black mallards, feed in tiny puddles of water, in drain ditches, borrow pits, and any place where the ground is wet. And if you are careful you can ease up to them and get shooting on the rise.

Bill and I flushed them, and Manuel bagged five of them on the way to the coast.

About halfway to our duck-hunting spot and Manuel's goos-hunting pit, we stopped at a ranch and picked up our cook and our lunch. The lunch consisted of a live *borrego,* and in case you don't know what a *borrego* is I'll tell you: it's an animal that would be a young steer except for the fact that it was a lamb instead of a calf when tragedy struck in its early youth.

At a spot about five miles from the Gulf we let Manuel out so he could go down to a goose pit he had dug near a big lagoon, and we also let the cook and the *borrego* out so they could attend to the business of getting grub in shape while we hunted. Then Bill and I drove on to that great mass of tule we had been watching from the north side of the Rio Grande—a mass of tule covering perhaps forty acres of ground.

It seemed like a million ducks got up from that tule as we slopped through the mud at the edge of it, but we got no shooting on the rise. We pushed our way on through the high, thick mats of tule at the edge of the pond and then worked on across a narrow channel of open water until we found a fine place to take a stand, right in the middle, where a sort of ridge of tule grew with channels on each side of it.

That day we got the kind of duck shooting I'd travel many a mile for—not too fast, not too slow, just a single or a double or a small flock now and then, with time in between to build up your anticipation. First a flock of bluebills—lesser scaups, if you insist—came breezing along, whizzing over one corner of the lake and flying parallel to our ridge. We downed three of them.

Then we waited until we were just beginning to get impatient, when here came a lone pintail, and Bill started talking to them. The pintail moved right on in and I got even with the fellows who shoot my hawks out from under me when I'm calling—I shot the duck. Bill didn't mind; he was used to it.

Then without any warning four gadwalls showed up from behind us and we blazed away, but got only one duck out of the four. They were a little high and were past us when we saw them. Immediately afterward a small flock of redheads, splitting off from the great flight that was moving high across the river to the west of us, which we could only stand and watch, came tearing in low over the tule.

After another fairly long wait three shovelers showed up, but we passed them. I can pass a shoveler if other ducks are moving. Then a dumpy little butterball came in low and lit out in front of us and we let him alone. He could be our decoy, since we had brought none. We didn't need decoys there.

Thus it went until along early in the afternoon, when we decided we would call it a day and move back in to see how fate and the cook had dealt with the *borrego*. Manuel got out of his pit and came over to the campfire on the bank of the Rio Grande as he saw us driving up. He had three geese—a specklebelly and two snows.

Our lunch was spread out around the fire, stuck on little green willow twigs thrust into the ground beside the coals. We ate it right from the stick, drank black coffee out of a tin can, and started back toward the ranch to get a little late afternoon shooting—maybe on teal, more likely on bluebills.

We counted up and found that I had five ducks to go, Bill had four, and Manuel had seven. We stopped at a long resaca that wound through the farmland at the ranch, and took stands about three hundred yards apart, so we would keep the ducks moving. Several bunches of them got up when we took our stands, but Manuel sent one of his ranch hands to scare up the ducks farther along the resaca.

It was almost sundown when ducks really started in, and they came tearing along with the wind, bluebills and teal, just as I had expected. Manuel had crossed the resaca and taken a stand in some brush on the far side, and Bill had a stand at a bend where the ducks swung wide and came near him. But where I was standing in the edge of some brush, the ducks were flying too far from me.

Finally I walked over to a fenceline that ran right down into the resaca and waded out and stood leaning against one of the posts. A fenceline makes about as good a blind as I know of. The ducks simply figure you're a post that happened to take root and grow, and they breeze right over you.

That's when I got my teal. I passed up the bluebills, for the teal were really moving in then, and bagged my five, but it was getting so late that I almost had to skylight them by the time I managed to pick off the fifth duck.

It was a nice trip, and I've had many more like it, both south of the Rio Grande and north of it, although I admit I don't get *borrego* on the north side of the river. But I do get greenwings and bluewings and greenheads and all the other pothole ducks now and then. I even get into a flight of shy little widgeons on rare occasions, and that is something worth remembering.

All over the huge state of Texas my fellow hunters seek out and bag the pothole ducks, and each man has his own system—his own way of spotting his decoys, his own idea about the number of decoys he should put out. Some hunters insist that a man ought not spread more than half a dozen decoys hunting on little ponds, and I like that theory myself because a half-dozen decoys don't weigh as much as two or three dozen.

Each potholer has his own favorite duck, and his own theory

about calling it in. And when the hunters who insist on going to the coast, where they can see thousands and thousands of ducks in the air and stand under impressive flights of redheads and pintails—when these men who insist on pass shooting start gently ribbing the potholer because he will sit for hour after hour and never see a duck, why, the potholer has his answer, even though he may choose not to give it—just keep it to himself.

He has his answer when that flock of big old greenhead mallards finally move over, wing on to the far end of his little pond, circle there, and then come back toward him, beating strongly into the wind with their brightly colored wings. He has his answer in the thrill that comes as he crouches there waiting for them, in the still greater thrill as they flare up suddenly when he raises his gun, and the final answer when he bags three of them in rapid succession before they can get out of gun range.

BLACK DUCKS HERE AND THERE

Van Campen Heilner

I can't remember where I first obtained a copy of Van Campen Heilner's classic, A Book On Duck Shooting, *as a young man, but I am certain that it was not from the Public Library. Unfortunately, such beautiful books do not survive long in most libraries; they are stolen! Originally published by the Penn Publishing Company, Philadelphia, in 1939 and later republished by Knopf in New York,* A Book On Duck Shooting *is one of the big-bore magnums of waterfowling literature. With marvelous paintings and illustrations by Lynn Bogue Hunt, plus a forty-six-page section of photographs, the total volume of 540 pages is a massive testament of the comings and goings of a dedicated wildfowler. Heilner's reputation for the book is only over-shadowed by his achievements in saltwater fishing, which are legendary. His book,* Salt Water Fishing, *illustrated with fine-art paintings by William Goadby Lawrence, was first published by Penn in 1937, went through several printings, and was regarded as a classic by the time it was updated and reprinted by Knopf in 1953, with preface by Ernest Hemingway. Heilner did his first book,* The Call of the Surf, *with artist Frank Stick at the ripe old age of twenty-one. At that time he was already a prodigy, selling articles to most major outdoor magazines. Heilner was born of wealthy parents from the Philadelphia Main Line and began his outdoor experiences on the nearby Jersey Shore, the setting of many of his pieces. Heilner was an associate editor of* Field & Stream *and a field representative in ichthyology for the American Museum of Natural History. Heilner maintained several residences, says author George Reiger, who profiled Heilner in his superb book,* Profiles in Saltwater Angling, *Prentice-Hall, but until the day he died his mailing address remained simply care of* Field & Stream, *New York City. The New Jersey Shore beaches and marshes were the scenes of many of Heilner's most memorable experiences in hunting and fishing, and his special affection for the area comes across well in this effort. However, the article does move farther afield, since it is not an area-oriented piece but a celebration of those wily dusky ducks that have confounded and delighted East Coast hunters since Day One.*

CHANNEL BASS and fluke have always been my favorite fish to catch, due I suppose to the fact that they were the first saltwater fish I angled for as a youngster. Youthful memories are the strongest and carry the greatest affection.

So it is with the black duck. The first time I ever raised a shotgun to my shoulder I looked down its broad beam to the form of a black duck pitching into the salt marshes near Barnegat Light. I can never forget that black duck. In every black duck I have shot at since, I can see him. I see him hanging there in the air, feet extended, wings raised above his head, preparatory to lighting, and the thrill of that first sight of him comes down across the years every time I pull the trigger.

They're a wary bird, those black ducks. The encroachments of civilization seem not to have affected them at all. In fact they only grow wiser and warier. Along the Jersey marshes it is a common thing in late summer to flush black ducks right out of the back yards of the natives who live along the Bay. You see he is accustomed to man and knows how to avoid him. And for that reason he'll be around long after other species of ducks have disappeared. Only the Emperor Goose in the far off Aleutian Islands have I found warier, but what the advent of civilization would do to him, I do not know. For the black duck I have no fears.

My earliest recollections of "blackduckin'" are of the Jersey marshes. I was raised along the Jersey coast, hardly a stone's throw from the sea. In early autumn the long lines of cormorants winding their way south along the surf line was always a sight to stir the blood, for it meant the fowl were starting on their way. Our home was right in the line of migration and I must be one of very few persons in the world who has shot a duck from the roof of his house. The top of my father's home had a look-out reached by stairs from the attic and this overlooked everything in the immediate vicinity. One fall I noticed a number of flocks of Canada geese passing apparently within range of the top of the house each evening around sunset. I knew they were bound for Barnegat Bay about fifteen miles south of us and it occurred to me that if I kept a watch up there I might be able to intercept one as he came by.

I took my gun and sat up there for three evenings in succession. The geese came by all right but they were much higher than I had thought and entirely out of range. It was useless even to shoot at them. On the third evening I had about given up in despair when I heard a whisper of wings and a small company of duck sped swiftly over. I let fly with both barrels and one fell out and went hurtling into the road below. I dashed down the steps, through the attic and down through the house and out the back door. As I arrived breathless in the street, the butcher's boy had just descended from his wagon and was picking up my duck.

"That's my duck!" I panted, "I just shot it off the roof of my house!" He looked at me rather queerly but as I still had the shotgun in my hand he seemed disinclined to argue and with a shrug of his shoulders departed. It was a black duck and no duck ever tasted better before or since.

But it was in the pond holes of the marshes that stretch from Bay Head to Cape May that was the real home of the black duck. When the yellowleg season used to open around the 16th of August we could see the clouds of young black ducks winging across the marshes and knew that we were in for a good year.

The opening day of the season, and I haven't missed it for twenty-five years, always found me concealed in the marsh-elders near the border of some salt pond, a pair or two of decoys in front and perhaps a live "quanker" tethered close in under the bank, all set for the opening bell.

Just about sunset the first scout of the black duck legions would be seen coming in over the dunes from the sea. He would head straight for the pond, then make a wide swing, round once more, and then coming up into the wind put on the brakes and sail right in. Then others would follow, thicker and faster until the sunset sky would be laced with strings of black ducks settling down all over the great marshes. The shooting didn't last long, but while it did it was fast and furious.

One of the most terrific shoots I ever had on black ducks a friend and myself enjoyed in a small pond on the Carolina "Banks." All the conditions were just right. There was a big spring tide reaching its highest about dark, no moon, and a howling northwester whipping out of Pamlico Sound. Nothing could live out in that sound, even if the tide wasn't covering everything. Those black ducks had only one thought in mind, to reach the shelter of that pond and get in out of that storm.

They started in early and by five they came with a rush. Some of the flocks were so large they scared us. One must have contained two hundred birds. The rush of their wings as they backed and filled in the air above the pond sounded like a train crossing a trestle. We shot until our gun barrels were hot to the touch and our shoulders sore from the recoil. The main shoot didn't last over twenty-five minutes but it was terrific while it lasted. When we picked up, we had forty-six birds and had fired 117 shells from two double-barreled guns. Let not the sentimentalists gnash their teeth and tear their hair—only twice in a lifetime of shooting have I had conditions like that. Once I spent ten days on an island in the middle of Barnegat Bay towards the end of January, every one of those days lying in a sneak-box alongside of an airhole in the ice, so cold I could hardly move my fingers, and never got *one* shot during the entire time! I would like to put some of those long-haired boys out in the ice for ten days and then let them tell me they care more for the perpetuation of ducks than I do!

I remember a black duck, must have been a young one, that came and hovered right over the top of my coot decoys one autumn off Cape Cod. I was so astonished that I fired both barrels at him and missed.

There was a cove in the marshes back of a Jersey inlet that was always good for a shoot if the Coast Guards hadn't cleaned it out before the season opened. And later in the season, too, after the first blush was off, you were almost sure of picking up a few red-legs. One evening in December I got eight of those big Canadians there that must have weighed nearly five pounds apiece. Some ornithologists won't recognize that there is such a thing as a red-legged black duck but to them I suggest a little more field experience.

The black duck is gradually extending its range west of the Mississippi. There is a mounted specimen in the Bear River Club in Utah and I observed a pair in the Peace River country of northwestern Alberta. Out there he's the black mallard or dusky mallard and some day he might be seen in numbers clear to the Pacific Coast. Dusky is the right name for him, not alone for his color but because just at dusk he really comes into his own.

One January down the bay there came a wild southeaster. All the ponds in the marsh were frozen up tight. There'd been a small airhole in the north pond but it had closed up the night before. I figured that they might come back, ice or no ice, so went up in the late afternoon and put a half dozen wooden decoys on the ice where the airhole had been. The weather got dirtier and dirtier, and just before dusk in they came and lit right down on the ice. I let a few of them light to see how they'd act and when they hit the frozen surface they'd skid right across it. That was a nice shoot too. All shooting in the ice is nice shooting, if you can take it.

One time Julio and I were up in Quebec. It had rained by the bucketful for two days and the lowlands along the St. Lawrence were all flooded. The black ducks were on passage and we could see them coming in high from the north and coasting into the flooded fields.

The next day my guide and I set out in a galvanized tin boat, the damndest thing I've ever seen, and went down the irrigation ditches and across the fields in it. When we came to a fence I'd lie flat in the bottom and he'd push the boat right under the wire. The boat had no thwarts in it, no nothin', and was soldered together. Made it himself, he said.

At long last we came to a big haystack right out in the middle of a huge field. There was a pool of flood water out in front of the stack and it was full of black ducks. We tried to sneak up on the far side but they saw us and all got out with a rush. But there were more coming all the time and we hid in the stack and had a beautiful shoot. There was an old barn over on the far side of the field and the ducks coming in from the north would raise when they reached it and then start a long coast right down to our pool. Never saw anything prettier in my life. I found out you could only get this kind of shooting at certain times of the year, when it rained and the river flooded.

My guide seemed to understand my French but I couldn't understand a single word he said. French Canada is a picturesque country and they've got swell duck shooting up there.

Every state has a state flag and a state flower. Some of them should have state ducks; a canvasback for Maryland for instance, a coot for Massachusetts, a Canada goose for North Carolina and so on. Long Island isn't a state but I always like to think of it as the 49th State and its state duck should certainly be the black duck and nothin' else but.

I've never seen so many black ducks in my life as I've seen on Long Island. Of course you have to look in the right places. And some of the places are far from the bays and sounds, right down in the middle of the woods where you'd never in the world expect to find so many black ducks.

The famous Flanders Club near Riverhead not only attracts thousands of black ducks to its ponds and marsh but by careful cross breeding has developed a duck which it can raise in large quantities and is 80% wild black duck. This club raises and releases each year three times as many ducks as it shoots and is an example for every duck club in the country to follow. Their banded birds have been reported from all over the eastern part of the Continent.

Another friend of mine has always had an average of from ten to fifteen thousand black ducks on his sanctuary at the opening of every gunning season. It stands to reason that ducks do not congregate in such large numbers in places where they are heavily shot. No matter how much food there is they will not stand for hard shooting and no one can convince me otherwise.

Along the outer beaches from Fire Island to Montauk the bays and ponds literally swarm with black ducks in the autumn. With the right weather and tides it's no trouble to get a shoot most anywhere along there. Before Great Pond at Montauk was cut through to the ocean, the black ducks used to pour in there. They still do, in bad weather, but nothing like the old days. There are plenty of ponds left though.

We were in a blind on a little pond along the Peconic River. It had been a still dull day and nothing had flown. There were lots of black duck about but they'd been sitting still all day and hadn't moved a feather.

We were just about to pick up and call it quits when Wooly looked up and hissed a quick "Down!" High over the tops of the trees six black ducks were pitching in to our little ambush. Winston and I gripped our .410's and waited, tense. At the word we all three rose as one and the staccato bark of the guns echoed through the woods. Six shots, six black ducks, and with .410's. Something to remember.

The wind had been northeast for three days and suddenly it shifted into the northwest and blew a living gale. The bay was a smoking mass of white-caps and nothing could live out there. It was cold, too, for it was December and you needed your warmest clothes.

Down by the ponds the black ducks would be coming in early. You would too, if you knew there was a quiet sheltered pond waiting for you full of lush widgeon grass and a bunch of your own kind to gabble and splash about with.

When they started to come in you were there waiting for them. The sun had gone down and the horizon was a blaze of crimson, cold though, with the biting December northwester howling across the marsh and the sedge grass bending and hissing before the blast.

Then the whisper of wings and three silhouettes coming up from out the sunset, nearer and nearer. They don't hesitate but come right in with a rush and when they're right over the pond you raise and let them have it. One falls with a splash, the other two mount high in air, but at the top of their rise you cut down another one and he falls in the tall grass on the other side of the pond with a terrific thump.

More coming now. The sky is full of them. It's getting darker by the minute and you have to strain your eyes to see. Wings are whispering all about, above and behind you. You can hear them settling into holes all through the marsh, the muffled quacks of the ducks and the faint mews of the drakes.

Suddenly right over your head appear two dark shadows, beating time it seems against the wind. If you had a stick you think you could crack one down. But you raise your gun and let fly. You can hear the shot, *chack! chack!* striking against them as they pay off

backwards with the wind and down they come, one-two-*splash!*
thump! Too dark to see any more now and you get out your flashlight and start to pick up.

By the time you've gotten in your decoys your fingers are numb
from the cold and the freezing water but when you look at your
game you see that they're all big Canadian redlegs.

You wish you could spend the rest of your life crouched beside
a little pond in the marsh with a northwester howling across the
sedge and the black ducks coming in against a sunset sky.

BAYMAN'S SOLSTICE

Norman Strung

I introduced Norm back in our "Setting Decoys" selection when I singled out his practical waterfowling book, Misty Mornings and Moonless Nights, *as being particularly outstanding in the how-to genre. I mentioned also that he spends summers and autumns in Montana but returns to his favorite waterfowling haunts on New York's Long Island every winter to see if the skills he honed in that area are still operative. This piece, from* Gray's Sporting Journal, *Fall, 1980, grew out of his Long Island experiences. It's about an incredible hunting shack that will, perhaps, remind you of some similar havens you've known—and the people you liked to have there with you.*

"A LITTLE bit of heaven." That's how John and Ray described the shack. The roof leaked; and when the north wind blew, you sat on the south side of the stove. But it was lonely and free and part of the marsh, and they wanted it to be a part of me as well.

"We'd better do it this season, though, before somebody torches it, or the town pulls it down."

So in mid-December we loaded the stool and the supplies in Ray's old Pacemaker, snubbed the two duckboats up close to the stern, and threaded our way through the creeks of Baldwin Harbor on our way to the shack and the wetlands.

An anachronism. We knew it, but never spoke it, for to do so would have been a partial admission of defeat. We were ten miles from the New York City limits. Launching ramps, super highways and solid suburbia encircled the shack. If all we wanted were black-duck, it would have made more sense to trailer the boats and hunt by the day, and then be warm and sensible and secure at home by the night. But such pragmatics exact a compromise. You lose the richness of truly being there. Of being part of the thing you are hunting.

The creek opened to the bay, and you could feel the freedom. One moment we were prisoners of a narrow waterway, and the next we were on the marsh—open and salty and wild. The hundred-thousand-dollar homes stacked up like standing dominoes, the black and foreboding bulkheads, the forest of pilings and the fiberglass cabin cruisers all ended at the beach head and marshlands. No easy transition; it was like a time warp, or perhaps it was more like a battlefront.

"Drop the boats back, John. I'm gonna take her up to 15 revs."

Outside, beyond the canvas curtain, a nor'wester was freshening; cold, clean air tumbling down from Canada. Inside, it was warm and moist with the heat of the engines and the dampness of the bilge, thick with the elusive yet distinctive odor of an old wooden boat—mold and gas and oil and salty, wet wood.

John payed out the painter on the starboard duckboat, then the port, as Ray eased the throttles forward. The bow rose, and the motors pitched an octave higher, a trifle out of sync but relaxing in their throaty, rhythmic thrumming. The boats found their place just beyond the crest of the second stern wave and planed smoothly in the flat water of the wake.

I glanced astern as John entered the cabin. The houses on shore had become indistinguishable individually, melting into a solid white wall that encircled the bay. Ray was absorbed in the intricacies of the twisting, winding channel. John poured a cup of coffee and watched the wake and the duckboats.

The shack . . . its status was hard to define. It was legally owned by George Combs, who has eeled and clammed and run a line of killie pots for as long as anyone can remember. He built it as a kind of line shack, a place of shelter and food in the days when the run from his pots to his house was often complicated by fierce nor'-easters and cranky outboards and ice making up. It was always stocked with food and blankets, and the coal bin and kerosene lamps filled, but it was never locked. If anyone was in trouble, they could always count on the shack. That's what it was there for. And if you knew George, or knew someone who knew George, it was yours for the asking when the blackduck flew. You just had to keep the lamps and the coal bin full, and put a few bucks in the kitty for what you used.

But George didn't own the marsh and mud where the pilings were sunk 60 years ago. He never dreamed of owning it, of filing deeds and such, for it was of the sea, and what fool would lay claim to that? The Town of Hempstead asserted its ownership of the marsh-lands and now leases the right to the mud that lies under the shack. There were other such shelters on the bay, but one by one they fell to the match and the stone and the scavenger and the bureaucracy. The shack is one of two left on the marsh—proud and defiant.

We rounded the bend of a narrow neck in the bay, and a small frame building broke the straight horizon. The network of islands and water stretched before us—crooked checkerboards of golden meadows laced by whitecapped creeks and channels.

We were laying off the shack in a half-hour, two hooks in the muddy bottom to hold the 30-foot cruiser against the wind and the tide. We loaded the duckboats with coal, water and grub, stool, shot-guns and decoys. Ray battened down the canvas drop and jumped into his bouncing boat. Then we were off across the channel.

The wind had risen to plus-30, and it was whipping up a stiff chop—nothing dangerous on those protected waters, just a staccato beat against the thin hulls as we ran into the teeth of the blow. The shack loomed ahead, and a dozen black duck leaped out of a calm lee, struggling against the wind, then wheeling gracefully to run with it, becoming mere specks against the gold of the marsh in a matter of seconds.

John's boat bumped the floating dock in front of the shack and six more birds rose and wheeled two hundred yards away.

"Lookin' good," he announced, more to himself than us. "The tide's dropping and they're moving out of the Sanctuary to feed. We'll have some good gunning this afternoon."

We hustled the provisions into the shack, each of us glancing over his shoulder to watch the birds aloft. The staples and gear were simply plopped down. Order would come later. Birds were moving, and that was the priority.

In a matter of minutes we were skipping down the creek in front of the shack, bound for Huckleberry Lead. The place was a dead-end creek, a backwater, where the black duck could find water right for feeding, no matter the tide. John pointed to two fresh cuts in the shoreline: eroded channels from when a nor'easter had coincided with a high tide. The islands were covered waist-deep then, and the flood of water that moved on the ebb had carved the cuts into the face of the marsh.

"Right there, Ray. Inside the hook."

. . . A room-sized nick in the shoreline surrounded by high grass. Easy hiding, where the boats would conform to the contours of the marsh. Decoys were set quickly, nothing fancy or extensive. Seven oversized, handmade cork black duck stool, four in one bunch, three in another, with a hole in the middle. John and Ray were of the mobility school, which holds you are better off to move with the moods of the black duck than to try to change their minds with a huge spread of decoys. The boats were tucked into the bank, pinned with a stake, and they disappeared.

" . . . Meeep . . . meep . . . meep." A burnt umber apparition appeared at the periphery of vision, coming from behind, gliding into the wind. John replied by mouth. "Meeep . . . Meep," not a loud quack, but a reassuring, low grunt. The bird dropped low on the water, wanting to land outside the rig. John's assurance drew him nearer; he rose on the wind, slapped his wings three times, and continued to glide.

No words were spoken nor signals given, but simultaneously, as the black reached a point predetermined by 70 collective years in the marsh, both men rose from the waist, and John shot. There were no adjustments of lead, no tracking; John was up and on the bird the instant the stock was nestled against his shoulder. The black duck crumpled, fell and was stone dead before it hit the water.

" . . . Better get him. I usually let them blow into a bank, but the tide and the wind are working together and he'll drift fast and far.

John stepped out of the boat and struggled through the soft sand and mud of Huckleberry Lead. He reached the bird, and halfway back two more blacks approached.

"Down!" Ray hissed.

John curled into a ball, hugging gun and dead bird to his breast, crouched low on the water, watching the pair from under his hat-brim. It didn't work. The birds hovered on sky hooks just out of gun range for 15 seconds, then they were gone with the wind.

" . . . Happens every time you get out of the boat," John grinned. The black landed on the afterdeck with a thud, John climbed aboard, and we closed the grassboards around us again.

Four birds approached from the northeast. Wind drift vectored them well outside the rig. John called, but the blacks showed no interest. Instead, they landed 300 yards away, in the lee of a large hummock.

"Keep your eye on them. They might swim into the rig."

We settled back and talked in hushed voices, watching hopeful birds trade across the sky. John recounted other days on the marsh—when the black duck were more plentiful and limits more liberal; a week at the shack when they were locked in by ice; gunning mentors who are dead and gone.

John Magnus, 51. A 30-year man with Ma Bell. Thirty years of wires and poles and telephones and The Public. On call 24 hours a day for ice storms, accidents or poor service. But a bayman at heart, who shot his first duck at age eight when Long Island was rich with game and open lands.

Ray Milek, 64. Salesman, draftsman, engineer. He works with figures, but his deft fingers belie that calling. I have never seen a rope more lovingly handled nor more deftly coiled, a knot more swiftly tied. Like John, he is a bayman at heart. But there was just so much work for baymen, so they succumbed to sad reality, and dreamed of their days at the shack.

"Quack . . . Quack . . . ." A fat mallard hovered over the stool, dropping in like a chicken to cracked corn. He was the product of some freshwater pond on the mainland, raised on white bread and birdseed, and dumb. No need to call him. He was an obvious sucker.

He crossed the threshold and Ray snapped up like a jack-in-the-box. The mallard, too, was dead before he hit the water.

"Boys, I hate to say this, but we'd better scoot." The water was ankle deep as John retrieved the bird. "This nor'wester is blowing all the water out of the bay, and this whole creek is gonna be dry in an hour."

Just as the wild storms from the east flood the marshes on a high tide, a strong wind from the west empties them at low: the workings of wind and tide and water. Adjust to the rhythms or stay on the marsh until nine? Too cold. A salt marsh at 35 degrees feels like Montana at 20 below. The tips of my fingers and toes were getting numb, my sinuses swollen.

"Let's go then."

John was right. The creek was already too shallow for the outboard, and the boat had to be poled to the shack, but we were running with the wind and the tide, and the poling was easy.

Ray moored the boats, I hung the birds, and John laid a fire in the pot-bellied stove. By the time the sashweight fell and the door closed snug behind me, the cabin was tainted with the sour, sulfury smell of burning coal. Coal crackling and hissing, red and glowing behind the ash box.

At first, we stood and sipped sherry, feeling the warmth of the fire grow without and the warmth of the wine grow from within. They met each other somewhere beneath our first layer of clothes, and the heavy jackets came off, then the sweaters and then the heavy boots, until we were seated around the oilcloth-covered table in wool shirts and pants. Then the warmth drew out another odor— the boat-smell but now with kerosene instead of equal parts of gas and oil. Old, salty, damp wood. A meadow mouse scurried across the floor.

John stretched, took another sip of sherry, and leaned back in his chair. "A little bit of heaven," he announced to his glass. And he was right once more.

The dining area was its biggest room, and obviously the first. Two bedrooms angled west and north as an afterthought. The paint on the cabinets was at least an eighth of an inch thick, flecked and stippled with the peeling remnants of preceding layers. On the walls were dozens of yellowing prints: "Calling Mallards," "Greenwing Teal Buzz," "A Black duck Set," "A Turnback Whistler," "The Brant Are Back," "Canvasbacks and Redheads on a Tidal Flat," "Bluebills in a Snowstorm," and boatman's charts of Gloucester, New Bedford Harbor, and the Great South Bay.

I walked over to the dirty, dusty windows, and looked beyond the boardwalks and the collected driftwood, the eel and the killie pots, and saw that black duck were now pouring into Huckleberry Lead. The water was only inches deep, and draining down from the shoreline to expose mud flats and sea cabbage and all the creatures large and small upon which black duck dine. If we could be out there, we would all limit out; but the tide had dictated otherwise, and so be it. We had a place to eat, to sleep, to keep warm and to dream—satisfaction of the most basic needs without the complications of social living. The shack was our retreat.

We bagged three more birds in the morning. The wind had swung to the southwest overnight, and water poured into the bay at the turn of the tide. By nine it was clear that the black duck wouldn't fly until the ebb; they were now dipping and gabbling, preening and paddling, in the Sanctuary by Jones Beach.

"Wanna take a run west and see George?"

"Sure. Maybe he's got a line on where the black duck are tending."

In half an hour we entered one of the hundred-odd mainland creeks that fed into the bay. Four clapboard buildings stood on pilings clustered at the end of a dock and boardwalk. Two Garvey skiffs, a Maine Lobsterman, and a half-dozen grassed duckboats tugged at their moorings. Ray's air horn bellowed twice, and a figure appeared on the dock.

I was introduced, and immediately forgot the man's name, for he had far more memorable attributes—hard, outsized hands, a shock of white, tousled hair, eyes blue and deep as the sea, and a face the color and texture of raw roast beef. A bayman. And with no more to go on than a how-do-you-do, I was aware by the touch of that bucket of a hand that I was surely among friends, and welcome.

We hobbled down the rickety boardwalk, heads bowed to the bite of the wind, turned a corner, and went through a door. The room beyond was a wealthy cousin to the shack, but undeniably of the same blood, and alive with warmth and conversation and rough laughter.

I shook hands with old George and young George and Fred and five other people whose names I cannot remember either, for they all seemed cast from the same mold: hands as hard as horn, beefsteak faces, wool pants and the knee-high rubber boots that are symbol and sustenence of their trade; they are baymen all.

Ushered to a place next to the stove, a fresh cup of coffee in hand, I listened to the conversation, and watched the comings and goings through the heavy, black door, its seal against the gnawing, searching wind assured by the same pull of sashweight, rope and pulley that closed the door of the shack to the weather, yet left it open for all who wished to enter.

"Hell, it's the weather that's ruining the black ducking. Fred's still catching striped bass down by the bridge, that's how warm this fall's been."

"There's a pile of birds in the Sanctuary, but they're natives. No redlegs down yet, and that little nip we had last night was like a fart in a hurricane. It'll take more than that to move the blacks down from Canada."

"George had a party out last week, and they had 11 birds toll inside Huckleberry Lead, but the sports couldn't hit 'em."

A young teenager wearing wool pants and black rubber boots burst through the door with a lone bird. "Missed the other half of my limit," he said, proud that he'd hit his first half. "He landed right next to me as I was picking up the stool."

I finished a second cup of coffee, then it was time to go. The tide was dropping, and the shack lay on a creek that was too shallow for an outboard at low water.

"Good luck, boys, and if the birds fly, let your conscience be your guide."

The tide . . . the comings and goings of the tide, and how it orders your life on the sea. Lunar time, a different rhythm. If the world clocked itself by lunar time, eight-to-five jobs would be one hour and 23 minutes later each day—a natural way out of the bondage of the regular and the ordinary. I suspect that is one of half of the reasons why people become baymen—to heed that different-tolling bell.

We killed two more black duck that evening. One was a pass shot that was no more of an accomplishment than hitting a thrown tin can, but the second bird tolled from 300 yards up, and with such cupped-wing grace and confidence that you could hear the wind whistle through his feathers as he descended. We feasted on roast duck that night. and raw hard clams and steamed soft clams.

Before bed, I went outside. The lights of suburbia twinkled from every direction. The bay and the marsh were a soft, black velvet, waves gently lapping on the shore. A jet approaching Kennedy passed overhead, gliding into the light west wind. I felt as if I were in a black hole, the center of a tiny universe.

In the morning, a thousand brant with their coarse, gutteral prattling, flew over the shack as we made the boats ready. Brant season had been closed for three years, so the birds continued to trade all day long, coming into our black duck stool like flies to sugar. It was particularly frustrating because the black duck didn't. We saw them on the horizon, miles distant, and they swarmed like bees over the Sanctuary, but it was a bright, warm day, with only enough south wind to riffle the water.

We hunted from sunup to three, and Ray finally managed to scratch down a black who came too close to the rig. He didn't have the slightest intention of decoying, and Ray's shot was satisfying for that reason.

We packed it in well before sundown. Loading the boats, transferring the gear to the Pacemaker and cleaning up the shack were chores that would be complicated by darkness. By the time we were done it was nearly sunset . . . the last day of autumn, the longest night of the year.

The sashweight fell behind me, and I walked to the end of the dock for one last look at the shack. The sun was gorged fat and sped doubly on its way by heat mirage, moving so fast that I could witness the ebbing toward the horizon. Behind me, a full moon was rising. Standing there, on the jellied and quivering marsh, I thought I could feel the earth spinning.

BEYOND THE LIMIT

Nelson Bryant

Even though he writes the "Woods, Field and Stream" column for
The New York Times, *Nelson Bryant maintains his permanent residence on Martha's Vineyard Island, the setting of this warm and
evocative piece. Nelson is a Dartmouth-educated, ex-paratrooper
who has hunted and fished from Alaska and Nova Scotia to Costa
Rica and from Scotland to Yucatan. His first book was* Fresh Air,
Bright Water *(McGraw-Hill, 1971); and in his next he teamed up with
my* Sports Afield *staff photographer at the time, Hanson Carroll,
to produce* The Wildfowler's World, *published by Winchester Press
in 1973. Nelson's only problem with his writing is the lack of space*
The Times *gives him, a difficulty he did not have to contend with
when he wrote this for* Gray's Sporting Journal, *Fall, 1976.*

TO MOST New England waterfowlers, the black duck is everything.
Whether huddled against the stinging rain out on the edge of a salt
marsh, or crouched down among bare, black, hardwood branches
beside some inland beaver pond, give a grizzled, old Yankee gunner a
grey November day and a brace of black ducks wheeling down out
of the wind-tattered clouds, and his soul will know no hunger.

If a gunner lives along the seacoast, he may also pursue greater
scaup—or bluebill—as well as mergansers, eider, scoters and old
squaw. If he lives inland, mallards and wood ducks may be more
the common fare than blacks, and in both areas there will be several
days each season when the sweet-sad cries of Canada geese, their
great wings winnowing the air toward the decoys, instantly erase
all cold and fatigue.

Few hunters are able to express fully their love for the game they
pursue, but sometimes the preoccupation of New Englanders with
the black duck crops up in an interesting manner.

Nearly 30 years ago when I worked summers as a carpenter on
the island of Martha's Vineyard, one of the crew was an old-time

gunning guide. One afternoon as he and I were shingling the roof of a house in Lambert's Cove, a well-shaped girl walked by. My companion put down his hatchet, put a white cedar shaving from a shingle in his mouth and chewed on it as he watched the young lady pass. Finally, he removed the shaving from his mouth and tendered the lass what I am sure he considered the ultimate accolade. "She's got an ass like a black duck," he said.

My fascination with black ducks began over 40 years ago—before I started to hunt them—when I ran a trapline for muskrats in the streams and salt marshes of the Vineyard, where I still live.

Winters were colder then, and there were a few days in late December when I could not set my traps because nearly everything was frozen over. But then the January thaw would come, and from the window of my bedroom I could hear the surf moaning on the outer beach, and the warm southwest wind carried with it the smell of the sea and the rich, black mud of the marshes.

Going forth at such a time was a delight, and always when I reached the point on Mill Brook where there is a long pool and a graveled, sandy shore that continues to produce a good crop of watercress each year, a brace of black ducks would vault skyward from the water, sounding cries of alarm. Downstream, where the brook widens into Town Cove, there were always a few more birds, and I marveled at their wildness, for they invariably took flight when I became visible to them even if I was over 100 yards away.

The blacks were usually in groups of less than half a dozen. One bitter February, however, the temperature dropped far below zero and the only open water on Tisbury Great Pond was where Mill Brook entered, and I watched them come in by twos and threes on a brilliant, starry night until the half-acre of water before me seemed filled with birds.

This was the same location where, a year later, one of my boyhood companions, Albion Alley, Jr., and I attempted to bag ducks with air rifles.

My aunt had had a piano shipped to her home, and Albion and I laboriously transported the crate in which it had arrived to Town Cove on two hand-drawn wagons. There we set it up on the shore under an old chokecherry tree. We equipped it with two seats, a table and sliding window, and spent many happy hours in it looking down on the water, waiting for the ducks to arrive. We had no decoys to lure the ducks, but we knew that sooner or later something would land.

Such an endeavor was against the law, of course, but that was a time when such illegalities by small boys were overlooked.

Our golden chance came one evening after the post-sunset flight of black-crowned night herons had lumbered by on their way to a roosting area just north of us where the brook enters the cove, and just after we had fired up our tiny oil lamp.

From the west, a pair of black ducks dropped in on the dark water, gabbling softly to each other. We carefully slid the window aside and were squinting down our gun barrels when, with the air hissing through their wings, five Canada geese joined the ducks.

It was almost more than we could bear, and we trembled as we discussed in whispers which birds to shoot at. I settled for the nearest duck and Albion chose the closest goose. The birds did not jump at the soft coughs of our air rifles, and the night was so still we could plainly hear the shot striking feathers. There was, of course, no penetration and the BBs dropped harmlessly into the water. Reloading, we repeated the performance with the same result but by that time one of the ducks sensed that something was awry and departed, taking the other birds with him.

That ended our attempt at waterfowling with air rifles, but I am sure that those few, intense moments were responsible in large part for my interest in the sport.

About ten years ago, six of us—five men and a woman—made a car-train-canoe journey to the western shore of James Bay, Ontario to hunt blue geese. Somewhere along the line we mislaid two boxes of provisions, and once settled in our huge umbrella tent on the edge of vast, desolate tidal flats we didn't want to waste the time to take a canoe south to Moosonee for supplies. Although I always eat the birds I shoot, this was to be the only time during the past decade when I would have gone hungry without them.

The first morning a few geese fell to our guns, but during the remainder of our stay, shots at them were rare. By the evening of the second day, however, we found that black ducks were tumbling into a pot hole at dusk about a quarter of a mile from our tent, and it was never difficult for two of us to limit out on them on a given night. Near one edge of that pot hole was a clump of marsh grass that had been woven and tied into the vague silhouette of a duck—a creation, we believed, of the Cree Indians who often hunted there. We had no duck decoys, but that never seemed to make a difference. Perhaps the crude grass replica was doing the job.

The mornings were gradually taken over with flight shooting of snipe, no mean trick with tightly-choked guns loaded with number four or six shot. We were always sufficiently successful at both the snipe and duck shooting to dine on the former for breakfast and the latter for supper.

I also learned to be aware of my advancing years on that excursion.

The one female among us was an attractive girl, the friend of the only unmarried male of the group. One gloomy afternoon toward the end of our week, I ventured back to the tent early and found her alone. Her long blonde hair and shining eyes suddenly seemed singularly appealing, and she apparently sensed my shift in mood, for, out of the blue as we were sharing a small bottle of wine, she said: "Mr. Bryant, didn't you say you were Dartmouth '46?"

Receiving my reply in the affirmative, she piped, "Oh, that's nice! That was my Daddy's class. You must have known him."

Incipient desire fled, and I picked up my shotgun and went out into the cold rain.

As I grow older I am bedeviled by the ambivalence involved in shooting a bird I love so dearly. It is (and, dear God, how I have wrestled with it!) a riddle beyond solution. With it, as with any other form of hunting I do, the ritual and trappings and literature of the endeavor have me in their embrace and I do not enjoy a trip afield with camera half so much.

And yet, the kill is not all-important although well-prepared game seems to close an ancient and necessary circle—for there have been times when I have not pulled the trigger when the opportunity was present.

One such occasion came a few years ago at the end of a long day spent sitting with a companion on a rise of land overlooking a salt marsh. The day had been cold and dark, but the wind, although strong, was not strong enough to move the birds. It slammed the surf against the beach at our backs less than a mile away, kept the cattails and salt hay before us in constant flowing motion, combed the sparse brown grass of the meadow beyond and whined through our makeshift blind of bushes draped with eelgrass. Talk, when we indulged in it, was sparse. We were at once together and apart, each hearing the wind's song and needing few words.

Over the years I have learned that when I am outdoors, whether on bonefish flats in the Bahamas, fishing for salmon in Labrador, or waiting for ducks along the Connecticut River, that I cannot concentrate on anything but the subject at hand. A twist of wind across the water, a hawk riding thermals over the river valley, even an ant struggling away with a crust from my sandwich, are infinitely more compelling than either the wrenching strains of great music that often fill my head when silence is about, or the lovely poems I committed to memory in my salad days. It is as if the river, the sea, and the wind in the trees are moving through me, and all the man created beauty I so cherish is immersed in that primal current. I become an observer, to be sure, but a passionate observer, an observer aware that the forces working on the ant laboring under its huge burden are also my inheritance. This awareness and the ability to even remotely understand it is man's glory, to deny it is his despair.

But I cannot talk about these things when afield. The summing up comes later, when, at my desk, I try to tell of the wondrous world I glimpsed and felt.

Throughout most of that day beside the salt marsh, all we saw were distant geese, an occasional great blue heron stalking the shallows in search of mummichogs, or herring gulls wheeling over us, then slicing away.

Then, when only little shooting time was left—when marsh and pond and sky and land were blending into one—five black ducks appeared against the failing light from the west and headed for our decoys. When they were 35 yards away and setting their wings I raised my gun and swung past the lead bird, already thinking of the one that would fall to the second shot.

But I didn't shoot, for the day had been complete and the hunger to gather game had been replaced by an overwhelming sense of peace and pleasure that grew as the birds clawed desperately for altitude —knowing the depth of their error—then hurtled downwind over the dark land to safety.

In the early days I learned that black ducks do not usually move into secluded coves, ponds or streams before sundown unless a storm drives them from open water. It is for this reason that the black duck hunter greets a wild dawn with delight. It is best if snow, hail or rain is driven before the wind, but wind alone is enough if it approaches gale force, for under such conditions blacks seem to become confused and almost nothing will stop them from seeking shelter.

It was on such a day that my brother Dan, my brother-in-law Bob Morgan, and I set forth for some duck hunting on Chappaquiddick, the eastern portion of the Vineyard.

Heavy snow had been falling for three hours when we stepped off the ferry onto Chappaquiddick, and by the time we reached the outer beach near Cape Pogue lighthouse, Bob's Wagoneer was bogging down in hub-deep snow. Several times Dan and I got out to push, and eventually we realized that even if we did reach our destination, a tidal pool near Cape Pogue Gut, we would probably not be able to drive back.

With great difficulty, we turned the car around and were nearly back to the ferry landing when the snow stopped and the sun glinted through a rift in the clouds.

It was nearly mid-afternoon by then, but we retraced our route and finally reached the aforementioned pool. By then, the temperature had dropped 20 degrees and the sky was scrubbed clean of clouds by a bitter northerly wind that approached 50 miles-an-hour. It was blowing so hard that the wind's load of stinging sand, picked up from bare spots on the beach, actually etched the soft glass of the Jeep's windshield.

Inching out of the car on the leeward side, we made our way to some wild rose bushes, where, after putting out three decoys—more than enough for black ducks—Dan and I sat huddled in one clump and Bob in another. Spray torn from the surf beating on the windward side of the narrow strip of land we occupied whipped past, and the moaning of the wind and waves filled our ears.

It was then that four black ducks materialized over Cape Pogue Pond, flying directly toward us. They were about 200 yards away when we first saw them, but so strong was the wind they battled, it seemed several minutes before they were over our decoys.

Dan and I had shot together for many years, and because he was on my left I knew he would take the lead bird first, concentrating on those still aloft on his second shot. The ducks came from my right, heads outstretched and searching from side to side. When they were so close I could clearly see their eyes I swung on the second bird and fired. The first and second bird fell less than 30 yards away, but at the instant I shot I knew I had nothing to do with their demise, for Dan had fired a split second earlier and even as I pulled the trigger on the number two duck it was falling. Dan had taken both birds with one shot.

I was so nonplussed by the event that I lowered my gun, one barrel still unfired, and watched the two remaining birds flare, and fall away down the wind at an incredible speed.

With Dan having taken his limit of two, Bob and I soon filled out also, and we sat watching blacks come into the deepening tidal pool until nearly 50 of them were gathered there, while overhead— so high that the light of the sun which we could no longer see glinted on them—small flights of goldeneyes streamed south.

SIX

The Divers

CANVASBACKS FROM NORTH TO SOUTH

Van Campen Heilner

In another selection from the venerable A Book on Duck Shooting *(see introduction to "Black Ducks Here and There"), Van Campen Heilner shows us that the good old days of the canvasback were sweet indeed. Enjoy them in print, for they are gone, gone. Canvasback limit on the Chesapeake Bay last year: one bird per day!*

IT WAS WONDERFUL in the old days on the Chesapeake. You'd drive down to Havre de Grace in the afternoon from Philadelphia so's to be on hand for the Opening.

Everywhere you looked you'd see gunners. The air even felt "ducky."

The cans were there, too. Everybody said so. More than had been seen for years. They looked like plumes of smoke when they got up. And red heads! Man alive! They'd almost take the top of your head off if you stuck it out of the battery. There'd be some powder burnt on the Flats in the morning.

We'd get aboard our houseboat that night and go down to the "Line" and anchor so's we'd be on the grounds at daylight. Others had the same idea, too, it seemed, and we could see the anchor lights of other boats twinkling in the dark across the water.

"Blowin' up boys! Listen to that old nor'wester comin' down! They'll fly in the morning!"

Morning would come all too soon. Not much sleep. Too excited. And it was necessary to be up by three because by the time you had breakfast and then got the battery rig out another two hours would have gone by.

We could only shoot Mondays, Wednesdays and Fridays in those days and then not before an hour before sunrise and until a half hour after sun down. It took three men to run the rig and we had about four hundred decoys.

As a rule, if there were two of us, we would use a single battery and take turns, maybe two hours in and two out with a toss-up of course as to who went first. If, as occasionally happened, there were three of us, we would use a double battery and one fellow would change off every hour, which gave each man two hours in the sink box.

These were lie-down batteries and I taught myself to shoot left-handed when I drew the right-hand side of a double battery. In Currituck I've often shot out of sit-up batteries, where the water was deeper, and this is far more comfortable. One of the worst cases of "battery back" or whatever you want to call it, I got from a lie-down battery and I reached the point where I couldn't raise up when fowl came to us. My companion had to put one arm behind my back and raise me up, then grab his gun and shoot.

After you've lain for hours on your back in the bottom of a battery with maybe a little water slopping in on you every once in a while you get so you never complain at home any more about whether your mattress has been turned recently or not. In later years when I began to think about making duck shooting more comfortable, I had a kapok mattress made for our batteries in the Carolinas and from then on had many a delightful snooze when the fowl weren't flying!

But those days on the Chesapeake are the ones I will always remember. The Sassafras River, Kent Island Narrows, Spesutia, Carroll's Island, the Choptank and others were all places where you could load a boat with cans and red heads if you were so inclined.

I've seen the cans, and red heads too, strung out over the flats until it looked as if there never was an end to them. It was that way sometimes also on Back Bay and Currituck before the saltwater came through from Norfolk and spoiled all the feed. But then they put the locks back in the Albermarle and Chesapeake Canal, thanks to Messrs. Knapp and Corey, and the food's coming back. What with one thing and another the good old days are on the way back, let no one tell you to the contrary.

There were two big bodies of red heads that came every year to

Pamlico Sound. There were about five thousand in one raft and about half that number in the other. You couldn't get at them though because they always sat way out in the open and all got up together and settled together. It was only when a big blow came along and broke 'em up that you could get any shooting out of them.

There were quite a few cans with them too and I remember one day in December, it was the day they dedicated the Wright Memorial at Kitty Hawk if I'm not mistaken, it stormed and blew a living gale. Hi and I were down in the ponds trying to get a shot at a black duck when the cans started to fly. Never expected to see cans way in there, you understand, lighting in pot holes like black ducks, but I guess it was too tough for them outside because they sure piled in in great style. In less time, almost, than it takes to write this, we had our limit, and never expected it. Just one of those things that make duck shooting so fascinating.

And there was the day that the battery foundered on Linc and me. We were up on the Cape Reef and hadn't done much in the early morning and then the wind shifted and started to get up and the ducks began to fly. First they were mostly red heads and then a lot of cans and we were banging away at them and never noticing that the water was coming in every time we jumped out to pick up game.

And then it got rougher and rougher. We turned the lead edging all the way up but it didn't do any good. We hated to wave for our boat because the shooting was so good and yet the waves were breaking right into the battery now and it was one thing or the other.

At last we waved for the boat, but before it got half way to us the battery sank and we had to hop out and stand in water up to our waists until they could get to us. Even at that I killed a can that flew right over us just before the boat came.

The days of batteries are over for the moment and maybe they'll never come back. But who can tell? John J. Audubon, writing in 1845 states that in 1838 a law was passed in the state of New York prohibiting batteries. For a short time it was respected, but the gunners who depended upon waterfowl shooting for a great part of their living, considered it such an invasion of their rights that they defied it; at first shooting with masks, at the same time threatening to shoot the informer, should one be found. They finally laid aside their masks, and the law became a dead letter and was later repealed. That was over a hundred years ago, which gives some idea how long these contraptions have been used. Undoubtedly they are one of the most deceptive and most destructive devices used in fowling. But like so many other gadgets used in our sport, the mechanics of the thing is fascinating and the mind that conceived it probably did so out of necessity.

One early Autumn, Hi Blauvelt and I decided to go up into the Lake Winnepegosis region of Manitoba where we heard there really *were* some canvasbacks. On our way west we had some time to kill in Chicago and were taking a ride on Lake Michigan with Jack Clay in his cruiser before it became time to depart for the Northwest.

About an hour before train time, while we were thinking of turning shoreward, Jack suddenly announced he was going with us. The next hour I remember as somewhat of a blur. The boat put us ashore and we made a wild dash in a taxi for Jack's apartment. About this time Hi remembered he'd left his overcoat on the boat and took another taxi north to the boat basin to try and recover it while I helped Jack dig his gunning clothes out of moth balls and stomp them into a suitcase.

We caught the train by the skin of our teeth, a man from Jack's office appearing at the *nth* moment with money, which he handed to him in the manner of a relay team passing the baton, and we were off. After Minneapolis and St. Paul we recovered our breath and from there on enjoyed the rest of the ride to Winnipeg immensely.

Winnipeg is one of the nicest cities in Canada and before proceeding further north we did some shopping to pick up what we'd forgotten. From here our trail lay northwestward and when we arrived at Dauphin, our destination, we were in fine form. Our host, Joe Allard, met us at the station and hustled us into the car for we still had fifty miles to camp.

The camp at Cucumber Point was on the shores of Lake Winnepegosis. The lake is nearly a hundred and twenty-five miles long, an astounding thing for a fresh water lake when you come to think of it, and simply loaded with duck food and ducks.

In the morning we walked out on a long rocky point jutting into the lake, piled up some stones as a sort of blind and went to work.

We were right in the center of a big flight of cans. They kept getting off the lake and flying straight over the point towards a little bay in behind. All pass shooting, no decoys. The prettiest kind of shooting. There were a few bluebills but the majority were all big ducks. Hi was in good form that day and was knocking them over like ten pins. How those big cans would come down and how the Chesapeake we had with us would gather them in! By noon we all had our limits and decided to go up the lake to Kettle Bay on Red Deer Point where Allard had another camp which he said ought to be pretty "hot," as it hadn't been shot that season.

On the way up the lake I gathered some local information. The big flight of cans, Joe told me, always left between October 10th and 12th. As they arrive on Lake Erie around the 16th and 18th it must take them about a week to make the passage. As I had noticed a flock of blue geese southward bound, Joe told me something about them. In the Spring, around the early part of April, the blue geese arrive from Louisiana and stop for two weeks at a place called Grant's Lake near Portage la Prairie. It is one of the greatest sights on the continent. The birds come in about two million strong and people drive out for miles around to see them. This is their one main stopping place before they take off for their nesting grounds in Fox Basin north of Hudson's Bay. Like the swallows of the California Mission, the birds can be counted upon to arrive on the same date every year.

It has often been said, especially of late when shooting hours have been so strictly regulated, that ducks carry watches. Not only am I convinced that they carry watches, but surely barometers and calendars as well. I know this is especially true of geese, the first outposts of which will arrive on their wintering grounds within a day or so of the same date every year. Regardless of the weather, when the time comes for them to arrive, they will be there. It is only in the case of large mass migrations that the fowl can be clocked with any certainty. If complete records were available for all species I doubt not that they would be found to move on migration with the regulation of a time table.

When we arrived at the camp at Kettel Bay we put up thousands of canvasback ahead of the boat. They had torn the wild celery roots out of the bottom in such quantity that it had drifted along the shore in regular beds. I saw as many cans at one look at Kettle Bay as I've seen on the Susquehannah Flats at Northeast or Havre de Grace.

It was cold that night and we sat around the roaring camp fire in front of the shack and swapped yarns. A camp fire does something to you. You can't explain what it is, but it does it just the same. Maybe it strips off the superficiality that we all have and makes you *yourself*. Whatever it is, when you sit down in front of a camp fire and it dies down and you look at the glowing embers you feel that after all there isn't much else in the world that really matters.

It was a good camp fire that night. We sat on the ground with a great big log for our backs and watched the embers and every once in a while someone would get up and throw another log on the fire and we talked of this and that but mostly the conversation was of ducks. How they seemed to *know* when bad weather was coming and when the ice was out and how there were times when you just *couldn't* fool 'em and at other times they'd come right in and sit on the end of your gun barrel. Of the days when everything was just *right* and you'd have a hell of a shoot and other days no matter what you did you couldn't get a bird. There just *wasn't* another sport like duck shooting on the whole face of the world. There *couldn't* be! If anyone said there was, he was a liar.

The cook had a little beagle named Joe and when we turned in he went to sleep with him but sometime in the night I woke up and there was Joey in my bed. I got up and put him in Hi's and it seems that after a while that Hi put him in with Jack and by the time morning came he'd been passed around to every bunk in the camp. We decided we'd invented a new game called "Pass the beagle." He was a cute dog and it didn't seem to matter where he was or in whose bed he found himself, he was perfectly happy.

Daylight found us down on a long marshy neck of land between two bodies of water. You couldn't see the ground but you could see the sky when they started coming. Flock after flock they were coming and when I could see the wedge of them outlined against the sky, I let go. It got light fast and all the canvasbacks in Manitoba were coming at us and over us. We lay in the grass only a couple of hundred yards apart and if one didn't get a shot the others did. There wasn't a minute that ducks weren't in sight and every bunch of them crossed right where we were!

And then they started coming from the other direction! You needed a swivel on you neck in order to watch them all. It just couldn't be done. The dog was nearly crazy. First a duck would fall on one side of the neck o' land, then on the other. He was busier than the proverbial paper hanger.

Suddenly there came the chickens. I was watching a flock of ducks when I heard a *ca-ca-ca* and here they came! Fifteen prairie chickens flying from the woods straight across our point and over to the woods on the other side. The first ones passed directly over my head, so close that if I'd had a crab net I could have scooped one down. They went right over Hi and then over Jack and Joe. It sounded like the battle of Bunker Hill. We *could* see the whites of their eyes but we must have been aiming in the other direction for they all reached the further shore in safety. We didn't dare look at each other.

We went back to camp for lunch and repaired to the point again for the evening flight. It was shorter than the morning but just as good. And then, just as we were about to call it quits, back again came the chickens! Believe it or not, we, who had been making all sorts of fancy shots on cans, even to the point where I believe we could have done it with mirrors, never touched a feather!

I've thought a lot about this since and have come to only one conclusion. It must have been a matter of *tempo*. We had been shooting so much at cans and judging our lead accordingly, that when it came to the slower flying chickens our judgment was bad. Still, that is no excuse, and it remains one of those inexplicable things that make the great game of shooting so fascinating.

But on our last day we redeemed ourselves in a big way. The chickens had become so disdainful of our marksmanship that they had even posted a sentinel in the tip top of a tall tree to let them know when the coast was clear. At Hi's by now familiar cry of "Here come the chickens!" we raised our guns, more as a matter of habit than with any hope of success. But this time things took a turn considerably for the better. Everyone of us made a double and

Hi got three, killing two with one shot! Boy! were those chickens surprised! We decided to quit, right then and there, and write *finis* to a perfect day.

We started back to camp, Joe's Chesapeake carrying across his back, panier fashion, a duck strap festooned with cans and chickens. Halfway to the shack a red head jumped out of the reeds and made off, but not far, for Hi dropped him. The dog made one leap after the duck and had it not been for some thick reeds through which he passed that scraped the duck strap and its load off his back, we would have had to swim for a large portion of our day's bag.

Thus the end of a perfect trip. There was a day back at the home camp when Pete Bilenduke and I sat out in the rain and I had to shoot my gun up in the air to scare off the bluebills that tried to drive us out of the blind, and there was the afternoon we watched Pete's bob-tailed mongrel Collie retrieve ducks as well as any Chesapeake or Labrador I've ever seen.

Altogether we'd killed twelve different species of ducks, seen more canvasbacks than we thought existed, eaten a lot of good grub, slept under the stars and the vast silence of Lake Winnepegosis and had just about as good an all round duck hunt as anyone could wish.

There was a little pond in the vast marshes of Louisiana that Ned McIlhenny told me about and it was just about the best canvasback hole in the South. It was full of them when we got there and after we chased them out they kept coming back in most all day.

When an animal or a bird has got a name that's so old that most people forget what it means, you can bet it's been coming there for a long time. Well, *coacoxtle* is what they call them down in Mexico, or I should say *up*, because it's nearly 8,000 feet above the sea, and that's an Aztec word so figure it out for yourself. Juan Zinser told me that at least twenty percent of the ducks wintering in Mexico were cans and when I saw the first one coming in with the silhouette of old Popocatepetl against the pink of the coming sunrise I thought of Lake Winnepegosis and Long Point and the Finger Lakes and the Susquehannah Flats and Currituck and mostly I guess of the Eastern Shore and Baltimore and diamondback terrapin and soft shell crabs and a bottle of Port and a canvasback duck!

REDHEAD RIDGE

Hart Stillwell

I introduced Hart back in "Pothole Ducks," and I'm happy to have him on board again with a piece that has always been a favorite of mine. Redhead Ridge was obviously the place to be. The piece is from Hart's Hunting and Fishing In Texas, *published by Knopf in 1946.*

THE OTHER day I went down and stood on Redhead Ridge and watched the redheads fly over. It was a sight a man ought not miss, especially any man who was on that ridge ten years ago. He ought to go back and stand on it and watch the redheads fly over in neverending waves—watch that fascinating network of weaving lines crisscross the sky—just to remind him that the redhead is back in such numbers as even the most optimistic among us did not think was possible.

He ought to go and watch the redheads so he can realize how fully he is being repaid for those years when he passed them up entirely, and for those years when he could take only three, or maybe four, a day.

And, disregarding the practical aspect of the situation, he should go watch these redheads on Redhead Ridge for the plain and simple reason that there are few other places where he will find so impressive a flight of these birds. The situation is entirely different today from the sad one of ten years ago. And it is entirely different from what it was twenty years ago. Twenty years ago the ducks flew over in hundreds of thousands and you could shoot until your gun got hot; today the flight is about as impressive, but you're lucky if you get any ducks.

Redhead Ridge is a long finger of clay rising from ten to twenty feet above the salt flats and shallow lagoons near the Gulf of Mexico just north of the Rio Grande at its mouth. Through this strip of coastline redheads funnel, and biologists who have studied them tell me that one of the greatest concentrations in the nation is found right at this southern tip of Texas. That was why it was so hard to convince the people of South Texas that the redhead was a vanishing breed ten years ago.

Redheads from the two main flyways in the middle section of the country, the Mississippi Flyway and the Central Flyway, merge in this area. Biologists believe that the majority of the redheads here are those of the Central Flyway, even though some of the ducks from this flyway migrate right down the coastline while others come across Texas from the Panhandle region, furnishing good shooting along the path of their migration.

After the redheads move on across the Rio Grande, they begin fanning out over Mexico.

But in this strip of coast from Port Aransas to the Rio Grande the ducks are really concentrated, and in those early days of the glory of Redhead Ridge it seemed that all of them—in fact, all the redheads in the world—flew over that ridge every day. At that time there was a large shallow lagoon of saltwater on the east side of the ridge and an equally big shallow lake of fresh water on the west side, with that narrow finger of clay separating them. It was an ideal set-up for the ducks, and for the hunter. The redheads would feed on the wild celery in the bay, lift from the tremendous raft there that looked for all the world like an island, clear the ridge, and drop to the fresh water to the west.

That's where the hunter got in his work. Here was a spot where there was only a short distance between freshwater and saltwater, and when you find that situation you are likely to find good flight shooting for redheads, for this duck doesn't fly high if he is going only a short distance. The redheads came over the ridge low in those days, and the take was tremendous.

But those days are gone. A ship channel was dredged through the ridge, the lakes were drained, and the redhead changed his ways. You can still stand there and see him—but usually that's the crop. Now he's headed for Mexico, where the big fresh-water lakes near the coast haven't been drained. And when the redhead is traveling a long distance he usually gets up out of gun range.

This is a fascinating duck, the redhead, and he is our favorite, because of his big flights and his quality on the table. The redhead is best early in the season, when he has just come across the plains of northwest Texas and hasn't acquired any fishy taste from feeding in the bays. Along the coast we hunt mainly the redhead and his fellow traveler, the pintail, or sprig. These two ducks are just about as different as two ducks can be, and this fact adds a lot of interest to our hunting. They feed in more or less the same areas, and follow about the same flyways to fresh water along the coast country of Texas, although you can get greater variety in pintail hunting because you'll find more of them some distance from the coast.

But let me give you an illustration of what I'm talking about by relating some of the things that happened to us on a recent hunting trip. We had been driving along near the coast early in the season, hunting for a place where we could take a stand and get some shooting. We saw hundreds of redheads and pintails flying across the river at one spot, but they were all too high.

Finally we found a better flight. At this place the ducks were coming back to the American side of the river after watering in Mexico. They were flying over the river out of gunshot, but as they neared a big lagoon about half a mile from the river, they would drop down and barely skim over the edge of the land there near the lake.

So we walked out to the lake and took a stand. The ground there was covered with wild cranberry bushes, but they were too small to furnish any cover, so we simply squatted in the open. We figured we'd get some shooting in spite of having no blinds, for there was a cold north wind at our backs and a little mist blew in with it now and then, holding the ducks down.

We got set and waited for them. We could tell the redheads from the pintails as far away as we could see them. The redheads bunch up closer and have less formation, and they have a faster wingbeat. And, of course, they have a much shorter wing span.

When we saw redheads coming we simply froze where we were, even if we were standing. The redheads would bore on in, swing across the river a little above gunshot, then start coming down. Some flocks would whiffle, breaking formation entirely and buzzing down, then re-forming nearer the ground. Other flocks would just start down gradually.

As they neared the edge of the water they would put on an extra burst of speed and sweep on over the shoreline. And when a redhead puts on his last burst of speed in reaching for the water, he is as bull headed a duck as the Lord ever made. I have actually stood up and waved my hat and yelled at them trying to scare them off, back in the days when I couldn't shoot them, but they would bore right on in. When you fire into a flock of redheads they seldom climb; they usually head downward, putting on an extra burst of speed. I took advantage of this fact one day to get some shooting at redheads, although I have to admit I got mighty few ducks, for it was without any doubt the roughest shooting I ever got into. Redheads were coming over out of range, but hunters were shooting at them any-way, as many hunters do. I eased on back to the edge of the water behind the other hunters and got my shots after they had fired into the flocks. My redheads were in range all right, but a redhead diving for water after he's been shot at is something that baffles many a gunner, including me, as I proved quite conclusively when I swung on one duck and managed to down another one about six feet be-hind him. Still, I got shooting.

But out on that flat ground near the Rio Grande we got set for our redheads, and for pintails, which were also flying. As I say, we would freeze up when we saw redheads coming. The redhead has a keen eye for movement at a distance and will veer away quicker when he's some distance off if you try to change position than he will if you stand your ground. So we squatted there in the open and got some shooting. The only reason we didn't get more was that they were flying in to the lake over about a half-mile stretch of land, and only a flock now and then was in range of us.

But we had a tough time with the pintails, which were also flying. The pintail is the wariest of all the ducks we shoot along the Texas coast with the possible exception of the widgeon. He is suspicious of everything, even of the other sprigs flying with him, as is demon-strated by the fact that he insists on flying in formation so he can see that every other pintail in the flock is accounted for.

But the pintail has some habits that endear him to the man with the gun. The hunter knows that pintails coming in high aren't going to whiffle and drop to the ground before they reach the water, the way redheads will, so he doesn't pay much attention to the high fliers in the pintail family. But for some unaccountable reason pintails will at times get right down on the ground and go skimming along not more than ten or fifteen feet high for a quarter of a mile or so before they get to the water; then they flare up in the air before settling on the water. This is probably a trick of some kind, although to this good day I have never figured out the purpose of it—that is, looking at it from the pintail's point of view.

Once in a while a flock of those low-fliers would come boring in toward us. Then we would lie flat on the ground. We had to, for the old pintail is a keen-eyed customer who veers away from anything suspicious. We would lie there, guns gripped tightly, peering carefully over the little cranberry bushes out of the corner of one eye, wondering just when was the best second to get up off the ground and start shooting.

We would wait until the pintails were almost on us—until we knew they would suddenly veer upward and off to one side even if we didn't move. Then we would bound up off the ground and start pouring lead at them. But it takes more time to get up from a prone position and start shooting than you think, and during that time the pintail gets in his work. I don't know of any faster-climbing duck than the pintail. He uses his wide wing-spread and relatively light weight to full advantage. He flattens himself against the wind and while it's pushing him backward he's poking his long neck straight up, reaching for the sky.

We got some pintails, but hitting those climbing ducks is one of life's little problems that I have never yet figured out exactly to my liking, and I note with interest that even the best of wing shots have trouble with this bird.

You should not conclude from the events of this one hunting trip that the redhead is a creature so dumb that all you need do is get close to water and he's your duck. The redhead is a creature of habit, and he changes his habits reluctantly; but once he changes them, he is equally reluctant to go back to his old habits, you may as well give up hope of getting him again with the old tricks.

Redheads in flight follow almost exactly the same path through the air, and once that path has been clearly outlined as one of perfect safety for the duck, it's seldom that the redheads leave it. The way one flock will get up from a raft and follow the exact path of another flock that has already gone is an interesting phenomenon to me.

I was sitting one day in a blind on a point of land jutting out into a bay where redheads were feeding. The redheads were watering in a lake several miles away, and there was a fairly steady flight. A flock of redheads would lift from the raft, circle to get their bearings, then head for me. They would buzz right at me, and I would crouch there in the pit, clutching my gun, sure of getting some shooting. Then when they were about a hundred yards away one of them would make a little dip with his wings, and the others acted just as though it were a signal from the lead plane in a formation. They would all swing to one side and the whole flock would buzz on around the point of land, barely out of gun range. The next flock would do exactly the same. I never even got a shot, and I left there convinced that the redhead can be the most tantalizing duck in the world, because I was certain those ducks flew in close to me just for the sport of it. They learn to know gunshot range, and they fly just above it, or just beyond it. They had learned about that pit there on the point.

But while they are learning you can at times get in some spectacular work. I believe one of the wildest flights I ever saw took place at a little reservoir a short distance from a big bay on the Texas coast. It was an ideal duck day, and we seldom get ideal days for duck hunting. What I mean by an ideal duck day is one with a cold north wind, low clouds, and maybe a fine drizzle. What we usually get is clear, warm weather when a man ought to be fishing instead of shooting. And we have been known to take our tackle along on some of our trips for redheads and come back with more trout than ducks.

But on the trip to the little tank, as Texas people call small lakes or reservoirs, we ran into a combination of good weather and plenty of redheads. The ducks were getting up off a nearby bay and coming in just above the tops of the mesquite trees. Then as they saw the tank they would bore down on it, going in about eight or ten feet above the bank at one corner.

A man could have moved off twenty yards or so from the corner of that tank and blasted maybe five or six ducks out of the air in one shot as they wadded up together and sped over the levee. We had to move some distance from the tank and carefully pick our shots, for that was in the days when the limit was three.

Those redheads were flying only a short distance, and conditions were right. We had remarkable shooting for a few minutes, although we soon got our limit and spent the next hour or so just watching, and hoping for a pintail, but the next time I went to that tank there were no redheads flying to it. They had abandoned it, as they will quickly any small body of water if there is heavy shooting.

He isn't so dumb, after all, this redhead, and you can't blame him for the way he let hunters bag him on Redhead Ridge, for that ridge is about five miles long, and it seemed that there were millions of ducks flying over it. The redhead would abandon one part of it and fly over another part, only to run into hunters there also.

Although most of our hunting for redheads and sprigs right along this coast country is pass, or flight, shooting, we hunt them there at times with decoys; and when we do, we get mostly pintails. It's a tough job to pull redheads out of a big flight unless you have a huge spread of decoys and are out in the middle of them, whereas the pintails, even in big flights, will swing down to decoys now and then.

But there are hundreds of little back bays, little protected spots, where redheads, especially when they scatter here and there in cold weather, will move in on the decoys—even on a little spread of them. And it's a good thing for the redhead that the big flights don't decoy much, for these little scattered bunches, once they start in for decoys, are just as pig-headed as redheads sweeping down to water after a long overland flight. I've actually seen a flock move steadily in to the decoys, keep right on coming after I shot once, and some of them settle there, as though to defy the gunner. And I've seen the time when a flock, after they had been shot at, would circle the lake and come back to be shot at again.

So it's fortunate for the redhead that he gathers in huge flocks and pretty much ignores the small spreads of decoys most of the time, for when he does decide to decoy, nothing is going to change his mind.

You find big flights of redheads and pintails all along the coast country of Texas, and equally large flights along the coast of Mexico.

And you find that, as with most other game, the hunting is much better in Mexico than it is in Texas. The reason for this is simply that there are about a hundred hunters in Texas to one in Mexico.

I go into that Mexico country now and then in pursuit of the redhead and the pintail—yes, and the widgeon and the gadwall and the teal and the black duck and other ducks. And every time I go there I am thrilled with the remarkable shooting. On my last trip I found a place that reminded me of the glory of the Redhead Ridge of old. I took a stand between two big lakes—one of them fresh water, the other salt water.

There was a steady flight of ducks, mostly redheads and pintails. And I noticed once more the sharp contrast that these two ducks make in flight, just as in most other respects. The pintail is, in my opinion, the only duck that really has grace in the air. For one thing, he has a long tail and this adds symmetry to his form as he wings overhead, whereas the redhead and most other ducks look bob-tailed in comparison. And the pintail has a slower, more graceful wingbeat and carries himself well. A single pintail is impressive in his flight, whereas the redhead doesn't move you until he begins to form those networks in the sky.

We had them both flying over that day, and we soon got our birds. Then we stood and watched awhile longer, and as we watched I realized that this country to the south of the Rio Grande is, in a way, a sanctuary for the redhead and other ducks. Even though commercial shooting of ducks is a common practice in some parts of Mexico, it is doubtful if the annual take equals the take of birds on the opening day of the season in the United States.

Yes, Mexico is a sort of duck sanctuary. But it is a sanctuary simply because it's too difficult right now for my fellow Americans to get to the ducks. And that situation is fast changing. Roads are being built into that remarkable duck-hunting country along the north-eastern coast of Mexico, and the day is not far off when the American hunter will be there in large numbers.

I merely mention this in passing, for it is possible that a change will take place in the supply of redheads when that vast feeding ground is opened to the American hunter. I mention it because I don't want the U.S. Fish and Wildlife Service to get caught short—

I don't want anything to happen to the redhead, now that he's back with us in large numbers and doing quite nicely.

For he is a noble duck, this redhead. Along our Texas coast, where there are mighty few canvasbacks, he is the noblest of them all. He has made a remarkable recovery in recent years, and I want to see him keep on increasing. I want him to be on hand, flying overhead and making those moving networks against the sky, now that our sons have put away their Garands and will pick up the old double gun to join us some cold morning on some redhead ridge near the coast.

THE MEANING OF CANVASBACK

Gene Hill

In his columns and books, Gene Hill has written lovingly and well of the Chesapeake Bay region in so many pieces that selecting one from the lot isn't easy. This short look at the canvasback, however, is one of my favorites. Its from Norman Strung's The Complete Hunter's Catalog, published by J.B. Lippincott Company, New York, in 1977.

THE CANVASBACK is a now-diminishing duck that was originally created to inspire exquisite decoys and, when it was legal to take them in numbers, gluttony.

The undoing of the canvasback was a combination of many circumstances. One is the whim of nature, which brings forth more males than females and creates a lot of arguing about double-dating and poor jokes like "Who was that lady I saw you with last flight?" Another is that the artistry of the decoy proved as irresistible to the duck as it is to duck hunters. No matter how pathetic a wing shot was, and I personally know how pathetic that can be, if you had enough patience, northeast winds, and shells you could count on a duck dinner.

And canvasback was *the* duck dinner! Even the most indifferent Eastern Shore bride could toss a brace in a roasting pan and come back in a half hour and serve up a meal that grown men would fight over. But put into the hands of a sensitive chef, the canvasback took on the aura of sacredness. Take a fine establishment like the old Eager House in Baltimore; thick damask napkins a yard square tucked into the hard, starched collar of a serious trencherman; a bottle of Maryland rye whiskey close at hand; a variety of exquisite local or imported German beer that, unfortunately for us, bears not the slightest resemblance to what now passes for a similar beverage; heavy-bodied Bordeaux and Burgundies rich with the threat of gout; tureens of terrapin soup; several dozen musky-salty Chincoteague oysters, platters of cornbread and yeast biscuits; a small saddle of hare; perhaps a woodcock or two—and then, with the appetite slightly edged for its full delectation, came the canvasback! With wild rice, of course, a variety of berry sauces, pan gravy for those who chose or a thin sauce redolent of brandy, wine, orange bitters, and wild plum jelly for those who really cared. And afterward a glass of port or perhaps Madeira and, with certainty, a hand-rolled, pure Havana cigar as thick as a sash weight. This was the picture a gentleman was once delighted to envision at the mention of canvasback.

The men who provided the canvasbacks for such as the Eager House knew port only as a nautical position and believed that Madeira was the capital of Spain. Their concern with the canvasback was as exotic as the gourmet's but the utensils were different. Their talk was of ten-gauge Lefevers and Smiths. Semiautomatic Remingtons with magazine extensions that ran right up to the end of the barrel. Pungeys, deadeyes, sneak skiffs, and sinkboxes that were as cold and deadly as coffins.

They gunned by lantern light, moonlight, and ice-shrouded fogs so thick that the only direction they knew for sure was straight down. They gunned for money, they said. But as long as the canvasback swept down to the celery-covered Susquehanna flats of the Chesapeake, they spoke of them with a tone in their voice and a wild light in their eyes that had little to do with cash. They called themselves baymen, with a soft pride that is bought with the copper taste of fear and crippling frostbite—it was a way of life a lot more than a way of making a living.

And then the wild celery was gone, smothered by industrial waste, and the canvasback almost all gone with it as well . . . and a way of life . . . and the decoys and the silver tureens . . . and men who should know better—and who really do—asking, "Where did we go wrong?"

Canvasback was also the trade name of a very good, very reasonable hunting coat—also, like so many good and reasonable things, almost extinct. We seem to be still wrong.

TO RIDE THE WIND

Albert Hochbaum

When Al Hochbaum steps out the front door of his house, he looks across an expanse of marsh grass and open water that is more often than not crowned by some superb vision of waterfowl. There may be skeins of Canada's, yapping like dogs as they tumble and sideslip toward a clamorous patch of their brethren; knots of canvasbacks boring straight-lined and purposeful just above the reeds; high wedges of mallards, beating against the wind, heading for distant farm fields. These and hundreds of other images of waterfowl have been as close to Hochbaum as a man can possibly immerse himself, and he has captured them in words and paintings in the magnificent book, To Ride the Wind, *A Richard Bonnycastle Book, published and copyrighted by Harlequin Enterprises Limited in Toronto, Canada, and London, England, in 1973. If you do not have a copy in your waterfowling library, you're not as well off as you thought you were. With a foreword by Sir Peter Scott, the world-famous painter and naturalist, the book's text, paintings, and drawings— superbly reproduced in large format—are the crowning achievement of Hochbaum's life as a naturalist, author and painter at the Delta Marsh Waterfowl Research Station in Manitoba. Born in Greeley, Colorado, and educated in ornithology and wildlife management at Cornell and the University of Wisconsin, Hochbaum was Director of the Wildlife Station from 1938 to 1970. Since then, he has re-mained there as Writer-in-Residence. Hochbaum had written two highly-regarded waterfowl books—*The Canvasback on the Prairie Marsh *and* Travels and Traditions of Waterfowl—*when I first visited him at his home in 1970. Along with Jimmy Robinson, I had the rare chance to get a peek at a work-in-progress that was destined to become a classic. I can tell you that Jimmy Robinson is not ex-actly given to reticence, but when Al showed us some of the paint-ings he was working on for* To Ride the Wind, *even Jimmy could only stand in awe-struck silence. This piece is from two chapters of the book. Enjoy!*

Here Am I

BEHIND MUSCRAT COVE, just north of the meadow and beyond the slough, a sandy lane passed a neat little square of clipped lawn behind a low barbed wire fence. There was an old decoy nailed to each fence post and a Canada Goose weathervane on a poplar pole. A gravel walk led to a green cottage with a front screen porch running its full width. Over the door was a home-painted sign: *Bluebill Lodge*. In the shade at the rear, a canoe rested on two saw horses, drying after its coat of lead-gray paint. In the northeast corner of the yard, close to the fence, was a shed with gable roof and middle door. On the west side, were two canoe racks with another canoe; and on the east, a work bench with a few broken decoys. Between the bench and the back wall were shelves holding several dozen duck decoys and twenty goose decoys each neatly in place.

The wildfowler was at the bench tightening keels, putting on new heads and tying anchors. He glanced out the door to the bright mid-September afternoon. It was still summer; but gunning would start in five days. There was a heavy movement of Canvasback drifting steadily eastward—at least 40 flocks had passed during the last hour. They were low, just over the reed tops, sometimes a flock only partially in view. Probably, they were on their way to Simpson Bay or to Blackfox Bay or somewhere beyond. There was plenty of sago out front, but the ducks had to keep busy, to find greener beds. It was their way; they must be moving, flying about to gain strength.

A Canvasback has a heavy wingloading compared with many other migratory birds. To get someplace, a Canvasback must keep beating those wings hard and fast—200 to 250 strokes a minute. Not simply a fluttering of feathers; each stroke must bite into the air strongly enough to keep three pounds of dead weight aloft and with enough push to move the bird ahead at 50 to 60 miles an hour.

The cans were on the move along the edge of the bay. They would pass the point of the cove, fly across a mile of open water, dash over a narrow wall of reeds across President's Point to Simpson Bay. Old timers called the reed narrows the *Hole-in-the-wall* because when Canvasback were going to feed on an east wind they came over the pass like flies through a hole in the wall.

The wildfowler gave a practice Canvasback growl, then looked around sheepishly to see if anyone had heard. He was in camp by himself but Tim was roused from his snooze in the sun to amble over. He tried again, breathing in hard, his vocal cords tightened, making a loud, rasping sound like a child with the croup. The dog picked up his ears and looked out toward the bay. Many hunters used factory-made, walnut duck calls; the sound was produced by blowing on a reed. But, most native guides called with their own voices and so did he. This was not simply a matter of pride; he was forever losing his store-bought calls, or the reed kept clogging, resulting in a squeak or silence when it was most needed.

Calling takes a lot of practice—and throat conditioning. It is easy enough to growl like a Canvasback but then, after three or four times, one has to cough and after that the sound does not come out right. The best thing to do is to practice until you can call all afternoon without coughing.

Redhead come to a Canvasback growl. In fact, the hen voices of the two species are hard to tell apart. On the other hand, one has to do it just right or the birds will get wise and bend away. Bluebills are easy to call by trilling the tongue while at the same time pronouncing a long, high-pitched *R*. Mallards—are not easy to call— always tough until the middle of October.

There are two Mallard calls that work: the *hail call* and the *feed call*. The hail call is also known as the *decrescendo*—a loud series of quacks offered on a descending scale. It is, indeed, just that: a hail that can be heard a mile or more away, farther if the wind is right. Essentially, it is an invitation to join—a solicitation with sexual overtones. The old suzie has finished moulting, or the young hen has just come of age, traded her juvenile tail for adult feathers and is ready to tell the whole world of her availability. While the hail may be heard by late August, most hens do not come into full voice until after the middle of September. Nor is there much response by males until they are green-headed and curly-tailed in October.

The hail call brings potent drakes and hens together on fine autumn days when they court on sand bars or shallows, sometimes to form pairs that will last until spring. Even now, six months before nesting, the pairs copulate. This is what makes the hail call irresistible: it is a hope and a promise for a lonely male who may have just pulled in from the Northwest Territories. There is the bare possibility, too, that the hail call may reunite old partners. Once a drake lives through an April on his mate's home range, there is evidence, from banded birds, that he sometimes returns there after the moulting season. If he does and she is around, there may be a reunion.

Hens of the other dabbling ducks also have their own hail call. In each, the *decrescendo* is much like that of the Mallard, loud quacks on a descending scale, but of a different timbre. The voices of teal are much higher pitched. On warm September evenings, the *decrescendo* calls of hen bluewings give the typical early fall sound of the marsh—old biddies, back in shape again, calling out for handsome friends to escort them south.

The *decrescendo* call can be imitated either with an inbreath or an outbreath. The former gives far and away the best results but is much harder on the throat.

The other Mallard call, the so-called *feed call*, actually has nothing to do with feeding. To be sure, the birds are in shallow water or on mud bars and some may be eating. The main thing is that they are secure and contented enough to let themselves be distracted by courtship activities. The call is the female's sexual incitement, the preliminary pitch she makes toward the drake of her choice. She sidles up to him, bends her head to his side, over her shoulder, rapidly rattles her bill up and down. All the while she utters a course *tuckata . . . tuckata . . . tuckata . . . tuck . . . tuck . . . tuckata* over and over again. From time to time, she turns to threaten another drake, stepping spritely back to the side of her love-to-be, repeating her *tuckata . . . tuckata* call. On warm autumn days, many hens are inciting drakes, here, there and everywhere about the edge of the flock. This call carries only a short distance, 200 yards under the best of conditions. Hunters depend upon the hail call to draw the attention of ducks at a distance, enticing them closer with the *tuckata, tuckata* call after the strangers sight the decoys.

The response to either call may not reflect sexual interest. Mallards and other dabbling ducks associate the *decrescendo* and incitement calls with safe situations. No frightened or wary hen would call out this way so these voices clearly say "all is well."

In ducks, it is almost always the female who has the resonant, far-reaching voice. This results from the vibration of membranes within her trachea; the hail call of the Mallard or the growl of the Canvasback are vocal. In the male there is quite a different arrangement. Instead of having a simple trachea that splits like a Y, there is a large, bony bulb where the tube divides. This, essentially, is a musical instrument, similar to a flute.

This vocal difference between male and female ducks is related to their interrupted sexual life, the annual separation of the sexes and the requirement to find a new mate each year. The hen calls out loud and clear when she is ready to entertain. It is she who gathers others around, builds the balanced flock that eventually holds eligible suitors. The drake quietly goes about his business, not advertising himself but responding to the loud female proclamations. His high-pitched notes serve their function within the limited range of the courtship party; but they do not advertise this behavior to the world beyond the nearest reeds. The high-pitched, musical calls of the male are much more specifically characteristic than the voices of the females. Thus, it is not always easy to distinguish the *decrescendos* of Mallard, Pintail or Gadwall hens. But, the courting notes of the drakes are unmistakable. Some wildfowlers can imitate the Pintail's whistle or the preep of Green-winged Teal or Baldpate, luring drakes within gunshot, though never before mid-October.

The gentleman with the paint brush was sanding the back of a small Canvasback decoy, one that had been given to his father nearly 50 years ago. It had been used on the marsh every year since. It was a Heron Lake decoy: small, 11 inches breast to tail. The angular head and long bill were set saucily up on a two-inch neck. It was built like a boat beneath, fluted with a weighted keel. It rode the water as a live bird. Its eyes were round brass tacks, originally painted vermilion, but long since blackened. The body was dull grey-brown. White-backed, black-chested, brick-headed, bright-eyed Canvasback decoys simply did not work on the Delta Marsh; juveniles and old hens would not give them the time of day. And yet, up on the moulting lakes, a rig had to be mostly white-backed drakes or you could not pull anything in except stray hens and juveniles.

When hunting Canvasback, you had to set your decoys in a spot which the Canvasback were using if you wanted a good shoot. You

could set up near a pass or a point or along an edge which was followed to or from their feeding places. But if you wanted the decoys
to work, you had to be near feed. Since the feed beds often were
wide spread, the birds could come in at their leisure without paying any attention to the decoys. In fine weather, you might have
to pick up several times before locating exactly the right spot, a
place where the Canvasback felt they would like to join. On other
days, in a heavy wind, you could read the situation easily, figure
out exactly where the birds had to come in and then fill out your
limit almost before you were settled down.

Bluebills and Redheads came easily to Canvasback decoys, especially the small flocks. But, only two's and three's of Canvasback would come to a set-up of Redheads or Lesser Scaup blocks.
Indeed, almost any duck would come in to Canvasback decoys, if
only to take a look. This would be early in the season, of course;
later on, all ducks became decoy-wise and great skill was required
to set out properly for a decent shoot even when there were lots
of ducks around.

The flight along the bayside had thinned down a bit. From all
about came the calls of Lesser Yellowlegs, *shey-shee-shup* the Cree
called them after their mellow whistle. Jacksnipe were underfoot
nearly everywhere; and every once in a while a band of Long-billed
Dowitchers sifted past on their way to a better mud-bar. The wildfowler stepped from the shed door as he heard the voices of wild
geese. Seventeen were approaching over the ridge trees from the
northeast. He laughed to himself—some of the East Meadows Ranch
birds over for a snack. He let out a call, partly closing his nose with
his hand to get a break in his voice. Then another call. The flock
turned to come directly over his cottage, then bent out toward the
bay, setting wings to more genuine invitations.

Canada Geese—all geese for that matter—are the easiest waterfowl
to call. They depend so much on their voices to maintain flock unity
and to arrange their various comings-together. The easiest of all to
bring in are the loners, the two's and three's that are lost from their
families. A goose announces itself every time it calls out. *"Here am
I,"* it says. In its next breath it requests response: *"Where are you?"*
If it is a lost bird or in a small flock, it turns at once to other geese

calling in reply, sometimes to be greeted by men who have learned to talk like geese.

In flight, the members of the flock call back and forth even though they see each other. Flying is a dangerous business under the best conditions and, for wild geese, calling is a part of flying. When there is a storm or if it is a cloudy night in the dark of the moon, the flock is held together by the flight calls; these enable each member to arrive at its destination in flock companionship.

There is no great difference between the vocal organs of goose and gander; in each sex the trachea forms a simple Y without a bony bulb. Gander and goose voices are essentially the same, although in any pair, the voice of the male is louder, more resonant and higher pitched than that of his mate. There is some individual variation in all voices. A man living near a breeding clan of Canada Geese soon learns to distinguish certain individuals by their voices, just as the geese themselves must recognize friends, neighbors, enemies and relatives by their calls.

Another flock of geese, some 40 birds, came across the ridge, following the trail of the first wedge, more mothers and fathers showing their youngsters around. They cut across one corner of the old wildfowler's lot, less than a gunshot high. They were above protected land and knew it—or at least the elders were confident and the young behaved accordingly. There were a few old timers around 24 or 25 years old, still guiding their families about and, in due course, showing the youngsters the way south. There was no doubt about these elders; their age was identified by colored leg bands they had received from a naturalist when they were young birds.

There must be many other members of the clan over ten years old and perhaps a few over 25 or 30. In captivity, Canada Geese have been known to breed and raise families each season until they were 45 or 50 years old. Dog men like to say that one year for a man equals seven for a dog—a ten-year-old dog is 70 years old, relatively speaking. Nobody has figured this out for Canada Geese. But, if 30 years equals a human generation, certainly three years is one generation for Canada Geese. This being so, the 20-year-old leader of a flock of Canada Geese is, relatively speaking, a contemporary of George Washington in the goose world. The wildfowler wondered about such an old timer. What experience must be stored in that head! The senior bird has raised 17 or 18 families, more than 70 offspring, each reared and held within the family circle until it was ready to go out on its own. In such a life span, there would be literally hundreds of aunts, uncles, cousins, grandchildren. A twenty-year-old goose might have an acquaintance with its grandparents twenty times removed and with grandchildren way down the line to the abundant progeny of its first family, hatched and reared almost two decades earlier. If one lead-gander became lost in migration, there were always other oldsters in the flock to find the way.

It was almost supper time. No Canvasback had gone along the edge for half an hour. They'd all be feeding by now, busy over their broad shallows in hundreds and thousands, with here and there a Coot pretending that it had just happened by.

There were all those Canvasback out there with nothing more important to do than to take their fill of rich food. Most were young. A larger proportion of experienced old drakes were still in the lake country. Thus they could not hand down their wisdom to the new class. There were some old females on the marsh, to be sure, and a few old drakes. Could these be the guides leading the juveniles when it was time to migrate?

The wildfowler wiped his hands on a cloth, went to the kitchen to start the stove and put on the kettle. Then, after rewarding himself with a tall amber drink, he went to the table in the front room where the Journal, its pencil attached with a string, had rested for 64 years. He thumbed through the pages from the beginning, reminiscing at first—there was the first hunting license, 1911. He put on his glasses and sat down to the business of checking the Canvasback bags, holding his tongue in the corner of his mouth as he made his entries on a scrap of paper. The kettle had almost boiled dry when he totalled up the figures. There was one old bird bagged for about every ten young. You could give or take a few mistakes but Canvasback were easy to age by their wings—at least, it was simple to tell all birds-of-the-year (with their scant wing-covert vermiculations) from all birds older than one year (their lighter pencilings bold on old females as well as on the old males).

One in ten; he replenished his drink and refilled the kettle. He thought back over the years. You could take two or three, four or five, sometimes run up a string of seven or eight young birds, but, sooner or later, that old hen came along, or, less often, an old drake. They were pretty well spread among the flock in autumn. A traveling bank of twenty birds without one or several oldsters must be very uncommon, indeed.

As he stood up, he turned to read a note for October 12, 1946:

> At the cove, Russ and I bagged two limits of Canvas in an hour and a quarter before sundown. There was a nice northwest breeze when we rounded the point. They came out of there in one great rush, running a long way across the water with the wind on their backs, some stalling out at first. There must have been three hundred birds, all Canvas. We slipped around the point up to the northwest wall of the cove. They were coming back in before we had all the decoys out, were landing in the decoys before we were tied down. 1 ad. male, 4 ad. female, 6 juv. male, 9 juv. female.

There had been lean days and there had been big days and they were all good days. He got out his steak. From the kitchen window he could see the Mallards on their way to the fields. The juveniles had the abundant companionship of old drakes. It was the same with Blue-winged Teal—old drakes in early September, then the hens; there were always some adults in company with the young. The relationship was not the same with ducks as it was with geese; mother and father were long gone; but other experienced birds took their place. Maybe that was one of the functions of the old hens' *decrescendo*; it induced the inexperienced to gather close to the wise old members of the race.

Even if there was a flock that lacked the company of experienced adults, random flying in juvenile explorations would inevitably carry them in the direction of the main flow of wind—from northwest to southeast. Once below the frost line, they'd surely run up against birds that knew the side trails to special wintering places.

After dinner, he tested the paint on his decoys, wiped his finger on his pants and reached to the nail for Tim's dummy. Tim was dancing the moment he saw the arm moved to that special place;

then he raced to the landing where the roll of canvas fell again and again into the bay. No living animal on earth has so much downright fun as a wildfowler's dog.

 FALL FLIGHT

The wildfowler sat in the bow seat of his 18-foot Canoe. He had pushed into the bulrush by way of a muskrat clearing on the right, so that the border remained pristine. He was on the north side of Dandy Island 300 yards south of the reedy shore of the bay. Before him, twenty-four Canvasback decoys seemed alive as they danced in the light southeast breeze. The day dawned behind light layers of cloud, tiered in rose and gold until the sun climbed above the overcast. Cottonwoods along the lakeshore ridge were golden against the darker bronze of box elder and ash. Bulrush had changed to burnt umber, the yellow reeds were brilliant. It was the 14th day of October.

Amidships sat old Tim, elder specialist in marshology. At each thwart was a yard of stout clothesline rope with which the wildfowler had tied the canoe to hand-grasps of rushes, making it nearly as firm as a platform. On the bottom of the canoe was a carpet of freshly-cut yellow reeds, a dry floor above the water which Tim inevitably shook from his coat after each retrieve. Laid out on the reeds behind his seat, feathers carefully stroked in place, was a brace of Gadwall which had sought the friendship of the decoys at daybreak, his first double of the year. Tim had made a nice retrieve, going first after the farthest bird. Beside the Gadwall was a young Redhead. Its presence saddened the wildfowler; it was a flabby little juvenile just on the wing. But it had come in boldly with five others and he was not aware of his mistake until Tim's retrieve. Its quills were still soft, its breast thin. There were four Canvasback, each taken from small bands that had stooled in nicely. The first two were young hens; the second a young drake still in dull juvenile plumage, perhaps a July-hatched bird. The fourth, the day's prize, he had taken at first to be an old male. It had the silver back, shiny head and jet breast of an adult in full spring plumage and it hefted about three pounds. But when he spread the wing, it was gray, showing none of the heavy white pencilings that an adult wears. He examined the bird again, pressed the breast feathers to his face to savor the dry smell that reminded him of his first trip to the marsh, of his first duck.

Across his knees was an English double, a Westley Richards 12 gauge, his father's gun. He rubbed the stock with the palm of his hand, ran his thumb over the scroll engraving on the frame. There was a brace of Mallard within the oval on the left, three Red Grouse on the right. Underneath was a setter stiffly pointing a tiny Woodcock. The engraver had carved the Woodcock with only four or five strokes; it had been the delight of his boyhood to find the bird squatting under the engraver's alders.

The Mallard flight was nearly finished. All were high, well out of gun range. Now as a late flock passed over, sixty-odd birds in a wedged line, he could hear the whisper of their wings, the low voices of the males. From deep within the rushes to his right came the hail call of the hen Mallard, a loud series of quacks on a descending scale. She was speaking out to the stubble birds: *I'm lonely. Come join me, especially if you are male.* From the bay shore, a hen replied, but the greenheads overhead gave no heed.

The big water of the bay was littered with Canvasback, their numbers bolstered by occasional arrivals of small bands from the east. These darts crossed further south; only the few daybreak bands had acknowledged his decoys. He had thought of moving to a position where he might intercept their return but the flight was nearly finished and he did not wish to break the pleasure of the moment with the rustle and bustle of picking up and going elsewhere. Besides, the wind had dropped to a dead calm.

As he gazed upwards, a thin line of birds crossed his vision, moving southeast. They were so high they appeared as a thread in the sky. Then came another and another followed by a regiment of flocks, some almost beyond vision, some so low that he could easily distinguish individual birds and catch the rhythm of their wing-beats. "Divers," he said to himself, reaching for his binocular. "Canvasback!"

He lowered himself in the bottom of his canoe, his back against the seat, his elbows braced on the gunwales for steady holding. The birds were traveling in tiers. Some were as low as 1,000 feet. His glasses soon found other flocks invisible to the naked eye. He guessed that most were between 2,000 and 3,000 feet. They came in an unbroken flow. He ranged his glasses east and west. As far as he could see there were traveling flocks, always at least one wedge in the sky no matter where he looked, sometimes 10, 12 or more within a glance. All traveled toward the same point in the southeast, their lines in arcs that wavered slightly as they crossed over the marsh. There were Canvasback, Lesser Scaup and Redheads. The flight was mainly of these diving ducks, but there were Mallards and Pintails, Gadwall and Baldpate and, as far as he could make out, some few Green-winged Teal. For an hour, there was an avalanche of migrants, never once was the sky completely vacant.

The highest went swiftly on their way. Many of the lower flocks bunched up as they crossed over the marsh, rising and falling, some turning east or west, a few even swinging around to fly north for a short way. Each flock, after its apparent confusion, soon reformed its orderly line and continued on into the southeast. A few bands of bluebills dropped out of the sky in power dives, the sound of their wings ripping the air like the tearing of a sheet. They caught their dives just above the water, then began to dash about the marsh at low level. These would settle down and stay for awhile.

At about nine-thirty, two hours after sunup, the flight dwindled, then petered out entirely. He remained seated where he was, shifting slightly to relieve the tension on his legs, still scanning the sky. In twenty minutes or so there was another rush of birds, some Canvasback, many of other species.

There came a *swish* close by; he lifted his head to see nine juvenile Redheads sitting amongst his decoys. Tim was on his haunches, ears cocked, on alert, puzzled. *"We've had our share of those, old boy."* He chuckled to himself as the visitors, becoming wary of the wooden stools, swam toward open water. With his eyes on the sky, he exercised some mental arithmetic. The flocks were moving as far as he could see east and west. Probably the passage was as wide as the whole breadth of the south end of Lake Manitoba: thirty miles. At least three thousand ducks had passed over the width of Wendigo

Bay, perhaps 100,000 had crossed southward over the Delta Marsh in little more than an hour!

At eleven, there had not been a migrant in view for half an hour. He took his bow seat again, scanning the marsh. There was little movement. The calm held but there was a wedge of blue sky breaking the clouds in the northwest. Just offshore, nearly a hundred Canvasback had gathered during his quiet watch, looking more than twice as big as life as they sat on their perfect reflections. They started to swim alertly away as he rose to his seat and skittered off to alight on big waters amidst many others of their kind. Hardly a bird was in the air. Many bluebills and a few Redheads were on the bay in rafts of their own, not with the Canvasback. Most were asleep. It was warm for October 14th. He moved his birds, laid his hunting coat on the reeds, urged Tim toward the stern and rested on the bottom for a nap.

He was awakened by the gentle rocking of the canoe, the lapping of water on its side. He lay for a moment with his hands behind his head. The tops of the rushes were bending against a wind coming out of the northwest. He pulled himself up on his seat. There was a small chop on the bay. The chill in the wind prompted him to put on his sweater before getting into his hunting coat. It was 2:30 in the afternoon. Birds were on the move, mostly bluebills in small bands dashing east, west, some north, flying low. He turned suddenly at a roar of wings behind him, a dozen bluebills swinging over his decoys. Unable to join the blocks because of the wind, they scooted away, just above the water. He would have to shift, set his decoys to the south side of the island.

He untied the thwart ropes; now free, the canoe heaved and rocked with the swell of the waves. On his knees, amidships, he paddled backward to the muskrat clearing, then out to open water. The wind was now blowing at least 18-20 miles per hour. Unless he held the bow constantly into the wind, he would be forced back to the island. One by one he picked up his decoys, wishing all the while he had put out only 15.

With all aboard, he turned, letting the wind rush him back to the rushes west of his first stand. Now he could manage a good shoot to fill out his limit; but it was clearly pointless for one man. He couldn't risk letting Tim go downwind after birds that might drop more than 30 yards offshore. Nor could one man make it home against the storm if the wind picked up any stronger. With the bulrush holding his craft in place, he wound each block with its anchor string, then piled them neatly under and behind the stern seat. He cased his gun, placing it and the rest of his gear behind the decoys. Then he moved back until his rump touched the bow seat. Tim, who knew the scheme, went forward, climbing over the decoys to snuggle down in the prow. With decoys, this put some 125 pounds in the stern. Paddling the canoe stern forward, kneeling just behind the middle, he could balance his ship against the wind. It took him three-quarters of an hour to fight his way to the north shore. There he rested to catch his breath, feeling good that he could still make it alone. Then he straightened his cap, spit on his hands and started to paddle westward under the lee of the tall reeds. He had a tough pull to get around a small point of reeds to reach the cove in the corner of the bay. There followed a five-minute fight to gain the northwest edge of the cove. Finally, he pulled into a clearing, passed a muskrat house, turned into the rushes and again was in calm water.

He tied down and tossed out fifteen decoys; it was too much to paddle forth to drop them properly. He and Tim took their places. It was ten minutes after five.

A great arc of blue sky was pushing the clouds to the southeast. The wind must have risen to 25 miles per hour, gusting to 35 or more. He hunched his shoulders in the chill while Tim rattled the reed floor in spasms of shiver.

Out over the bay, there was a constant movement of birds in eights, twelves and twenties, most bluebills. Many were new birds that had come down from the morning flights. With his glasses, he could see Canvasback facing into the wind, riding it out where they were. They were restless, some preening despite the wind. Overhead there was a steady passage of stubble Mallards, high as always with a strong wind on their backs. East and west as far as he could see, Mallards were moving southward. For sure, they were traveling to feed, not to migrate.

Some of the Lesser Scaup and a few Redheads were flying west along the north shore, but they cut across the point, beyond gun range. Then suddenly there were Canvasback in the air, moving north in twenties and thirties. He watched with his glasses; first one, then another band took off into the wind, gaining altitude, some crossing to the lake, some only to the north shore of the bay. Each flock then turned to disappear at a breakneck pace into the southeast. Several darts came right for him, but they remained high, not heeding his decoys, turned and vanished with the others.

He took a bluebill from a flock which swung past within range, then another. The wind caught the second bird which dropped far out. Old Tim found it easily, but was hard pressed in the return against wind and wave. Except for Mallards, none of the local dabblers were moving; they had found shelter when the wind changed and were staying put behind protecting reeds and bulrush.

The movement of Canvasback was steady; they arose endlessly from the bay only to turn on the wind and sweep southward. He saw that Redheads were following the same pattern but no bluebills were leaving. Now birds were getting out of the slough beyond the reeds behind him—Gadwall, Baldpate, a flock of about twenty Shovelers. They were barely in the air before the wind caught them, sending them on their way south. He turned in his seat to try for a double as another dart of Gadwall swept past, but he shot behind. He laughed to himself and repeated the old doggeral that came to mind: *to hit is history; to miss is mystery.* No mystery about that shot! They were just moving too fast! There was a croak on his left and he saw a bittern rise from the edge of weeds, to be taken instantly downwind. The bird dangled its legs as it tried to keep balance in the gale, yet it rose all the while for a free ride to Minneapolis and beyond.

Against the bright sunset, there came a steady flight of wildfowl out of the northwest, all lower than in the morning passage. He held a paddle to steady himself as he stood to look into the west. Ducks, ducks, ducks, all the way to the horizon, all moving twice as fast as the wind, in lines and threads. Some of these, he guessed, must be leaving the open lake. Others, perhaps were coming from Sandy Bay and other marshes along Lake Manitoba's west shore. They were mostly divers but he could no longer identify species.

All the while, the local Canvasback kept moving out as if their supply was inexhaustible. Thirty-nine Whistling Swans went over, the voices of the adults changing pitch as they passed, the squeals of the young carrying above the wind.

He looked at his watch; 20 minutes to legal closing time—and only one bird to go to fill his limit. He decided to pick up, but as he had done for as long as he could remember, he started to count to a hundred first, crouched now on his seat. At fifty-six, three Canvasback cross the point. Unlike the others, they turned abruptly and came directly for his stool. They had seen the decoys silhouetted against the bright water. He bent forward, freed the safety, straightened. One of the birds crumpled in the air, dropped dead among the decoys, kicked its feet for only a moment and then was still. Old gentle-mouthed Tim came snorting to the canoe to present him with a hen. He bit his lip as he examined his reward in the evening light. She was an old female, with heavy gray markings on her wing coverts. Her breastbone was sharp against this thumb. When he spread her wings, they were short, their quills gorged with blood.

Next morning, he walked down to the landing to scan the bay with his glasses. The Canvasback were gone, and so, too, were the Redheads. There were many bluebills. Mallards had made their morning stubble flight, undiminished. But the multitude of cannies had left. It was this way every year. They built up their numbers through late September and early October. They traded back and forth across the marsh at their chosen passes, behaved as if they had settled down for good. Then, sometime in mid-October, a strong cold front moved down from Lake Athabaska. Under its favorable winds and on its clear sunset, the Canvasback, all but a handful, departed. The beds of sago were still lush. There would be another two or three weeks of open water. The Mallards, the Lesser Scaup and the Green-winged Teal stayed on along with the big Canada Geese and Whistling Swans. But come mid-October, the Canvasback were gone, not only from the Delta Marsh but also from all marshes across the prairies as far as the Rocky Mountains. All of the young birds, all of the old ladies, all of the marsh birds. Meanwhile on their lakes, the old drakes sat tight, safe, fat and happy where they were.

All along the way south, at Lake Christina and Heron Lake, on Mendota and Koshkanong, the word soon would get around. *The cans are down.* Their arrival prompted a mid-October festival of wildfowlers who close their office doors to spend a few precious days in their blinds. Heron Lake: the Chesapeake of the west because of its Canvasback. Christina: the best Canvasback Lake in Minnesota. Ten Mile Lake, near Dalton, where in mid-October there is an endless flow of Canvasback across the pass. Mendota, with its rich rewards in sight of the Capital dome. They would tarry for a week or ten days at the top of the Mississippi Flyway, then they were on their way again, some down the big river, some cross-country to the Great Lakes, to Lake St. Clair, to Long Point, to Winous Point, on to Cayuga and then to the Susquehanna, the Choptank and the Nantikoke. Some, from Alberta and Yukon marshes cut down across Montana, then followed up the Yellowstone or other mountain passes to Utah and then to California. The whole passage from nesting grounds to wintering waters seldom consumed more than a month.

And still the old Canvasback and Redhead drakes sit tight.

Why do most of the Blue-winged Teal leave in September? Why is October the greenwings month? Why do the marsh Canvasback leave while autumn is still mild? Why do bluebills and Mallards stay on? These questions are presently beyond answer. But one thing is clear: early or late, in mild weather or in frost, every major flight south takes place during the same weather pattern. The Canvasback, like the Blue-winged Teal before them and the Mallards which follow, all move south under the influence of high pressure weather; usually departing with clear sky in the west and north winds on their tails.

High pressure cells usually form deep in the northwestern Arctic, traveling diagonally across Canada to the southeast. Almost always at sundown, as the high moves along, waterfowl take flight from lakes and marshes that have come within the weather's influence during that day. These travelers, flying at air speeds of 50 and 60 miles an hour, cover the ground at 75 to 100 or more miles per hour, depending upon the speed of the wind they are riding. Traveling faster than the weather, they are soon well ahead of the front. This accounts for overflights on the Delta Marsh hours or days in advance of local departures. It also explains sudden mass arrivals of ducks that come down short of their destinations because they have run into impassable weather. Occasionally, this over-running of the weather results in mass accidents; sometimes, hundreds of migrant Mallards or Lesser Scaup crash into large buildings or come down on wet roads and fields when they strike fog or heavy rain.

The high pressure weather influences waterfowl everywhere within its realm. When there is a mass migration of Blue-winged Teal or of Canvasback from the Delta Marsh, these same species are moving out of the country as far west in Saskatchewan and Alberta as the front extends. Wildfowlers on the Netley-Libau Marsh and on marshes near Regina see the aerial spectacle as watched by gunners at Delta on the same evening. The extent of the exodus is apparent next day from Wisconsin to Nebraska.

The most spectacular of all migrations is the frost flight of early November. Then, the northwind sweeps the country clean of waterfowl. The advance regiments cross the Delta Marsh three days before the cold front arrives. Then the sky finally clears and the north wind pounds on the lakeshore ridge. The temperature drops below freezing. At sundown, the local Mallards and Lesser Scaup, and all that are left of other species, fly south in massive departure. Next morning, the marshes are frozen from Delta south to Minneapolis. The travelers move all night and part of the next day until they reach Iowa, Illinois, Michigan or beyond.

Old Bullneck and his crowd took off from their moulting refuge on the evening of November 5, flew down the east side of Long Island just above the reeds. They lifted gradually higher as they reached big lake water. There were forty in his flock, two juvenile males, three old hens, and the rest, all silver-winged drakes like himself. They cut southeast across Michalot's hay field, struck Lake Manitoba just north of Meadow Portage, then headed SSE, on their line of flight slightly east of the 40-mile wind. The sky was still bright when they crossed over the Delta Marsh; there was some light when they passed the border. They had struck an altitude of about 2,000 feet over Lake Manitoba and were holding this when darkness overtook them as they crossed Red Lake, Minnesota. Right and left, ahead and behind, were other flocks of old drakes, Redhead and Canvasback, each species traveling in their own tribes. On through the night they continued, breaking more to the east after leaving northern Minnesota, on over land and lake until, in the faint light of pre-dawn, they came down on the open water of Long Point Bay on Lake Erie's Ontario shore. They all were sleeping by sunrise, continuing their rest until almost noon, when old Bullneck and his crew had their first taste of wild celery since March.

The Long Island Bay Canvasback could stay awhile at Long Point. From here, it was but a short hop to Cayuga where some drakes had wintered for seventeen years. Or they could continue on down to the Susquehanna. There were many ten-year olds or older in Bullneck's crowd; could there be a hen more than five years old in the whole State of Maryland?

The wintering down of old Bullneck and his companions brought to a close the annual reproductive cycle of the wildfowl of the Delta Marsh. Such was the story of these prairie waterfowl in their abundance that held strong until the middle of the 1950's.

SEVEN

The Fireside Stories

A SHIFT IN THE WIND

Sigurd Olson

I had this private little fantasy about Sig Olson: Some day on one of my canoe trips to the Quetico-Superior region, I would ask to see him at his home in Ely, Minnesota, gateway to the great wilderness area spreading north into Canada. We would talk of his books, pieces remembered and treasured, his experiences and insights. I waited too long. Among the other bad news waiting for me in The New York Times *one day this year was the headline that the venerable figure of north-country literature was gone, at age 83. What I miss now is that I never took the time to tell him how much pleasure his books had brought me over the years. Angus Cameron, his editor at Knopf, is a personal friend, and I suppose that in my constant praise of Olson's work to Angus, I somehow was diverted from writing to the author himself. Anyway, Olson's books—*The Singing Wilderness, The Lonely Land, Runes of the North, *etc.—look somewhat worn and scruffy on my library shelves, for they have been much-used over a lifetime of reading and rereading about the northern canoe country. When I first began reading Olson as a young man, I became convinced that some of my own outdoor trails had to lead to the Quetico country. Thank God, that has come to be, and I treasure every moment I've spent out there, fishing and camping on the lakes and streams of the* voyageurs. *As much as I've enjoyed my experiences, I have not written much about them. One of the reasons is that I have not wanted to get into the ring with Mr. Olson. This piece is not canoe-trip Olson, but one of his magazine hunting pieces that you should find no less compelling than the selections in his books. The article originally appeared in* Sports Afield *and was anthologized in the splendid collection of stories,* Outdoors Unlimited, *edited by J. Hammond Brown, sponsored by the Outdoor Writers' Association of America, and published by A. S. Barnes and Company in 1947. It is a classic look at the kind of "bluebird" day we all know too well.*

] 437 [

MY MIND was made up. I would work all day Saturday and might even go to church on Sunday morning. The more I thought about it, the more decisive and masterful I became. My old gypsy ways were over. I was beginning to see that there was infinitely more satisfaction in getting a host of long-neglected jobs out of the way than in heading for the rice beds to what I knew would be just another fiasco as far as ducks were concerned. I felt virtuous and substantial. This weekend I'd stay home.

But as the days passed and Friday night was only a matter of hours away, a strange excitement filled my being. I had a feeling that something unusual was going to happen and I was never one to take my hunches lightly. There was, I began to sense, just the barest ghost of a chance that the wind might shift for perhaps an hour, just long enough to make them uneasy. One shot would be enough, one last flock careening over the decoys.

Another thing, it was getting late. October was getting well along and though the weather wasn't ripe, it was the time of year when anything might happen and wouldn't it be criminal to be caught with a shovel in one's hand or pushing a wheelbarrow with the flight coming down? And this I knew, too, that when the ducks did come, they would come with a rush. All they needed was a jittery temperature and a shift of the breeze to send them hurtling down out of the north.

And though the days for a month had been warm, I knew the snow soon would be flying and then it would be all over, portages covered with yellowing leaves, the rice beds blue and gold. There was just a chance something might happen and it wouldn't hurt to take a little swing around to look things over. If there was nothing doing, I would turn right around and come back, finish that perennial bed, the storm windows and the other things that had been waiting all fall.

"Thought you were staying home this weekend," queried Elizabeth, as she watched me stack the tools. "You know there isn't a chance of a flight this weekend any more than last. The weather report says there will be no change and you know yourself the barometer is steady."

I tried to explain that I had been having a feeling that most barometers couldn't register, a sort of a hunch that something might happen which would redeem the past barren month, that to play safe I'd decided to look things over once more, a sort of final reconnaissance, so to speak.

Two hours later, I was in my old blind looking at the same old duckless skyline, watching the slowly drifting haze of forest smoke and a coppery sun working its way over the northern Minnesota wild rice beds. A lone mallard took to the air far down shore, winged its way leisurely toward the horizon. I followed its slow, almost tired flight until it was a mere speck drifting over the trees. For a moment it disappeared and then I saw it again, now steadily holding one position. Suddenly, I realized that it was larger, that it had changed the direction of flight and was coming toward me.

The bird was dropping fast toward the rice bed it had left, then rose once more high above the trees; another low flying circle close to the water and then to my delighted eyes there were two heading swiftly toward my blind. No chance of that pair decoying to a hunch of bluebills off a point. They were looking for some quiet, shallow bay down the lake. There was just a chance, however, that they might come within range.

I slipped off my safety, got set—no use even trying to call that pair—a chance for a double if they were close—hold dead on and pull ahead. Another few seconds and they would be in range. Big birds they were and slow, heavy with the rice they'd been feeding on all fall; not too much of a lead. One was slightly ahead. I held to the point of its bill, followed through and fired, turned quickly and caught the second as it was climbing for the clouds. Both birds were falling now, fell almost together in twin water spouts in the midst of the decoys.

In a moment I had them back in the blind, a greenhead and his mate, laid them close beside me where I could watch the changing colors of their plumage and where I could feel them once in awhile just to know my luck had changed. We would have them for Sunday dinner stuffed with wild rice, some cranberries and all the trimmings, concrete evidence of my excellent judgment. I was almost happy as I stood there congratulating myself, almost forgot that my good fortune wasn't due to a shifting of the wind or a change of weather;

almost forgot that what I really hoped would happen, that the flight of northern bluebills would somehow get under way, seemed no nearer to materialization.

A raven wheeled high in the still smoky blue, circling, floating on the light breeze. One wing, I noticed, had lost a feather. It was a rather ragged looking pinion and the bird seemed to favor that side more than the other.

The great bird swung toward me, spiraled sharply downward and lit in a pine tree back of the blind. Then and there it proceeded to tell the world what it thought and watched me with a mind, I was sure, to the potential carrion it hoped I might become. While watching the raven and marveling at the superb scratchiness of its voice, I suddenly became conscious of a difference in the behavior of the blocks. For hours they had bobbed steadily, sedately, never changing position; but now they were bouncing around frantically, pulling their anchor strings, getting together in peculiar and undignified formations; all that, in spite of the fact that there had been no apparent change of wind. I had been so busy visiting with the raven that I had failed to notice what was going on, but now I watched the sky, the decoys and the water with new excitement.

Long experience had taught me that decoys can be as good barometers of weather change as the waves themselves. Now they were riding quietly for the first time since I came and the water was dead calm. Then a long series of riffles started out from shore and the rice bent and swayed beyond the decoys, swayed toward the south in a distinct breeze from the hills behind me. In half an hour the air began to clear as the wind out of the north steadied and I knew my hunch had been correct. At least for the moment, things were different.

If it would only hold, the ducks back in the innumerable pot holes and beaver flowages would get restless and begin to move. I watched those new riffles and prayed. If they stayed, my weekends of waiting would not have been in vain, my sacrifice of the perennials would be more than justified and everything else answered for.

The sky began to darken with real clouds, not smoke this time, and the shores changed from their old sunny gray and red to a somber dullness. The coppery sun disappeared entirely and the air grew appreciably colder. If I were a mallard or even a bluebill, I thought excitedly, and saw what was in the wind, I would pick right up, no matter where I happened to be, and streak straight for the south.

But the mallards did not share my excitement, or the bluebills, and two long hours went by before anything happened. Then came a swift hurricane of wings that almost took my breath away, one closely packed, lonesome bunch of bluebills streaking it down the channel with the speed that only miles of flying can give. Far out of range, the flock bore steadily for the west end of the rice bed with a surety of purpose that bespoke no interest in me, the decoys, or the wonderful stand of rice along my side of the shore. I watched desperately as they grew smaller and smaller, faded at last against the rocks and trees of the far end of the lake. Then, for a panicky moment, I thought I had lost them entirely, that drifting patch of black dots soaring for a moment into the blue only to fuse an instant later with the haze. Then, miracle of miracles, the dots suddenly grew more distinct again, swung swiftly into the wind and came once more down the center of the channel, this time directly toward my point. I crouched, got under cover, prayed with all my soul once more. This was the moment, this the realization of the hunch I had had all week. All I asked was one short chance.

They were getting larger, swinging toward shore, would surely be in range if they held their present course. Still too high, but as they went over I called steadily, seductively, saw them hesitate, then veer. They had heard and were coming over. This time it would be different.

I shifted my stance, parted the brush in front of me, braced myself in good shooting position, got set.

They were swinging in now, a matter of seconds and they would be in range. Perennials, storm windows, fertilizer and shrubbery, what piddling, mediocre stuff. This was worth dying for.

My safety was off, a new shell in the chamber. A split second and they were in—over the decoys—pandemonium—whistling wings—outstretched necks—tails and feet braced for the landing—consternation as I rose.

"Pick your bird and hold dead on; don't shoot at the bunch; always pick a single." The old admonitions flashed into mind. I drew hastily on a big black and white drake, fired and watched with joy as he crumpled neatly and lit. Turning, I drew speedily on another quartering away, saw him skate on the water, bounce with his momentum. And they were gone as swiftly as they had come.

But what was that? A lone single had separated himself from the flock and was tearing back along the shoreline as though possessed. He was coming high, just at the limit of range, would pass right over my point, a perfect overhead shot. Once again I held at the end of a bill boring into space, this time with a feeling that I could not miss, followed an instant as the extremity of the angle swept just ahead and fired. At the report, he folded his wings, did a somersault dive for the rice bed, struck in a funnel of spray. It was the sort of shot one remembers all winter long and I yelled for the sheer joy that was mine. That alone was worth the whole season of waiting, days of standing around with nothing to while away the hours but the chickadees and whiskey jacks, the long empty days with not a wing moving. This was more than compensation; it was double proof that my judgment was infallible.

Pushing the canoe out into the rice, I picked up my ducks almost reverently, two drakes and a hen, all well feathered and plump, the first of the northerns. Back on shore, I hung them carefully in the crotch of an aspen, hung my two mallards just below, admired them to my heart's content. No ordinary birds those, each one a thrilling shot, a story in itself.

I watched the horizon an hour longer, but not another duck swung into view. The shifting of the wind had unsettled one lone flock or perhaps it was just my luck. In any case, the rest of the blue-bills knew and to prove that contention, the sun came out once more and the clouds evaporated into the same old hazy sky I had known for a month. Gradually, the wind shifted back to its accustomed corner in the southwest and the flight was over.

Tomorrow, I reflected, was Sunday. Chances were that after this lone heaven-sent flurry, nothing would stir for another week. I decided to pick up my outfit, my five beautiful ducks, and go home. In the morning, I thought righteously, I would go to church as a substantial citizen should. I might even get up early and attack that perennial bed or take off the screens. Here was a chance to redeem myself in the eyes of the world.

As I paddled down the lake that afternoon, my mind was at peace and I was happy, happy with the knowledge that I was doing right and that all was well. But at the portage I did an unforgivable thing for a man who has made up his mind. I turned to have one last look at the rice beds against the sunset, stood there athrill with their beauty, watching and wondering. Suddenly against the rosy sky was a long V of black dots and the peace that was mine a moment before vanished swiftly. There must have been a hundred and they were settling into the rice near the blind I had left. And there were more, flock after flock in silhouette against the sky. The rice was alive with wings. These ducks, I knew, were riding in ahead of a storm. The flight was on.

For a long time I stood without moving, watched the incoming flocks until it grew too dark to see, wondering what to do. And then I knew, for after all I had promised no one but myself. Almost stealthily, I cached the decoys where I could find them easily in the dark of the morning, threw on the canoe, plodded up the portage toward home.

A DUCK LOOKS DIFFERENT
TO ANOTHER DUCK

Robert C. Ruark

*I've never seen a better case of editorial judgment and courage earn-
ing rewards for a magazine and its readers than the launching of
Ruark's "The Old Man and the Boy" series in* Field & Stream *in
1953. Editor Hugh Grey and publisher Ben Wright went out on a
considerable editorial limb in giving the column a home. Ruark was
well known as a newspaper columnist and magazine feature writer.
Therefore, he was expensive. Secondly, he was clearly looking for
a way to reduce his newspaper chores while moving ahead with his
other writing projects on Africa. Would he do the series with his left
hand? (See the introduction to "A Christmas Present to Myself.")
As things turned out, Messrs. Grey and Wright and* Field & Stream's
*readers came up winners. The series had warmth and charm seldom
matched by anything in the outdoor genre. Ever notice that Ruark's
stuff is fairly packed with how-to, without being didactic or boring
like most of today's magazine hacks aspiring to be known as* writers?
Ruark set the style for having the action itself become the how-to
*in the very opening sentences that launched the series. I've always
loved them: "The Old Man knows pretty near close to everything.
And mostly he ain't painful with it." You will find no pain at all in
this beautiful duck-shooting piece from* The Old Man and The Boy.

IT WAS ONE of those November weeks when the skies were about
the color of putty and the wind bored holes in you, and even down
South there was a little feeling of snow in the air. The clouds were
very low and the gray river was chopping straight up and down.
One night after supper the Old Man checked his barometer and said
it was dropping some.

"I guess you don't know much about ducks," he said. "Tomorrow
looks like it's going to be real nasty. Some sleet and mebbe a little

] 445 [

snow flurry. Stiff north wind and a choppy river. They'll be flying, and they'll be flying low. Maybe we better get up early and break you in on ducks, now you're a quail expert."

The Old Man grinned at me and I grinned back. I was a very chesty young fellow since yesterday afternoon. It was the first time I had ever got a limit on quail. It had been one of those wet days with the birds holding good for the dogs and the singles scattering just right in the broom grass. I was shooting the new 16-gauge double the Old Man had given me and taking my time. I got two sets of doubles on the covey rises and only missed with both barrels once. When I shot the fifteenth bird, even the dogs looked pleased, but they didn't look as pleased as I did.

"Just because you know about this quail business now," the Old Man said, "don't go thinking that the same thing applies to ducks. Quail are reflexes, like I told you. There isn't time to do any figuring. But ducks are ballistics."

"What's a ballistic?" I asked him.

The Old Man had a lot of big words he liked to spring with no explanation, just waiting for me to ask him. He said curiosity was necessary to intelligence, and that curiosity never killed the cat. The cat died from stupidity, he said, or mebbe an overdose of mice.

"A ballistic," he said, "is sort of hard to explain. Let's see can I. Suppose you take the speed of a bird and the angle of flight and the speed of wind and the direction of the wind and the height of the bird and the size of the shot pattern and the speed of the shot or the strength of the powder, and then you grind them all up in one mill and the right answer comes out. Maybe that ain't the book definition, but it's my definition. I can explain it easier to you after you've missed a few ducks."

We got up the next morning away before dawn, and it was so cold your breath was standing out in front of you and your ears felt like they'd drop off if anybody touched 'em. Getting out of that warm bed and into ice-cold long drawers and into your pants and your ice-cold hip boots was torture.

When I got downstairs, the Old Man was in the kitchen. He had a fire going in the stove—one of those old, big, square wood burners that lit up rosy when she really got to jumping, and warmed up the room like a furnace. The Old Man had his pipe going, and he was busting some eggs into the skillet over pieces of bread that were already sizzling in bacon fat. He had some strips of fried bacon laid out on a tin plate, and the coffeepot was talking on the back of the stove.

"Ain't nothing quite as cold as a cold duck hunter," he said, "unless maybe it's a cold, *hungry* duck hunter. You can build a fire in your belly with some hot vittles that'll spread all through you and keep your insides warm even if your ears and hands are cold. I allus say if a man eats a big breakfast he don't have to worry about dinner. Come and git it."

The Old Man laid out the eggs on the fried bread, and the yolks broken and soaked down into and bubbling up from the bread, which wasn't crunchy like toast but was part of the egg and the bacon grease, and he put the bacon strips across the eggs and poured the coffee. We ate about six eggs apiece, and I don't know of anything that tastes as good as eggs cooked that way when it's cold as sin outside but warm inside the room. They don't make that kind of coffee any more, either, coffee percolated in a tin percolator until it's got some body to it and you can smell it all over the house.

After we finished, the Old Man went over to the crockery cookie jar, winked at me, and stole about two dozen of Miss Lottie's yesterday's baking off the top, picked up two apples and two oranges, and made a little package of them. He took down a Thermos jug and poured the rest of the coffee in it, and filled a quart milk bottle with water from the pump on the back porch. He put on his mackinaw and his old wool cap with the ear flaps and reached for his pump gun and announced that we were ready to go duckin'.

We walked down through the cold night, with the stars still bright when you could see them through the racing clouds and the little bit of moon just starting to die, down through the dead streets to the river. The roosters were just beginning to crow and the dogs beginning to stir and bark without much heart in it. It was cold down by the river, cold and black.

We went to where the Old Man kept the skiff, and he sent me up to the bow and then untied her painter and kicked her off the bank. He said he would row her; it kept his circulation up. He said I could row her back when we came home in the sunshine, if there was any to come home in. The breeze was stiff on my back as the Old Man rowed the skiff along, her nose bouncing on the little waves and sending spray up on my neck, the spray standing like dewdrops on the stiff, hairy wool of my mackinaw. But I was warm inside me from the breakfast, just like he said I'd be.

I looked at the back of the Old Man's neck as he hunched his shoulders over the oars, and I could see his big ears standing out from the side of his head and the pipe stuck out of the corner of his mouth and the ends of his mustache blowing in the morning wind. He rowed about two miles, and then he ooched the boat around a corner of marsh grass and rested his oars. "Hand me the push pole," he said as he shipped his oars and stood up.

I reached him the push pole, which I had helped him whittle out of a piece of the toughest hickory I ever laid a barlow knife to. It was just a little limber, and you couldn't break it even if you were strong enough to bend it in a half-circle. We had sanded her down until even the bumps were smooth as glass, with not a splinter to come off in your hand.

The Old Man stood facing me in the back of the skiff, and he shoved her along until we came up into a little, shallow, sweet-water pond, with lily pads on it and all sorts of curious snaky-looking roots growing down into the black mucky bottom, where the push pole roiled up the water and made muddy puffs. The skiff sort of bubbled along on the surface. She was flat-bottomed and didn't draw much, and she just slid along. We went all the way across the pond to a little headland where the grass grew five or six feet high.

"This is as good as any," the Old Man said.

He got out, with his hip boots pulled high and hooked into his belt with string. He braced his feet and pushed the skiff with me in it, all the way into the grass. The grass finally jammed her bow, and he wedged her stern in with an oar, the blade sunk down deep into the ooze. "Throw me the decoys," he said.

I threw him the decoys. We didn't have more than a dozen. The Old Man had whittled them out of cork, sitting on the back steps by the fig tree and whittling very carefully. Then he had got some paints and painted them. They didn't look very much like ducks to me. I told him so. He was pretty short when he answered me.

"They look like ducks to a duck," he said. "Trouble with most people is that they always think about everything selfish. You ain't going duck hunting to shoot you. You're going to shoot ducks. From up in the sky these things will look like ducks to a duck."

The Old Man waded out, with decoys strung all over him, hanging from his hands and over his shoulders by the strings with the lead weights on the ends. He started throwing the ducks out sort of haphazard, about twenty-five yards from where I was, with one out there by itself, two or three together in one clump, a couple here and a couple there. All together they made a little half-circle around the point of grass. The wind was blowing from behind us, I noticed, and the decoys were bobbing and dancing on the water, with the wind mostly in their faces.

"Bend them reeds down over the boat so's to cover most of it from the sky," he shouted at me. "Leave us a couple of peepholes to see through without raising up. I'll be through directly."

I cramped the reeds down so that when I was sitting down you couldn't see there was a boat or a boy in the grass, and made a couple of holes in the front and sat back. The Old Man was wading back now, and it was just coming a little light. The stars were gone, and the clouds had gathered and were very low. The wind had picked up considerably. It seemed to be getting colder.

You could hear the soft brush of the wings in the dark sky, and occasionally a whistle as some teal passed low, chuckling. A hen mallard quarreled at a passing flock from her feeding place in a mud-hole in the marsh, and the drake answered her from away high up in the sky. The rush of the wings was all around us now, and occasionally you could see a small flash of black against the lighter sky. You could hear splashes in the marsh, too, as the mallards began to sit down like motorboats in the pools where the water was shallow.

"How long before——" I started to say to the Old Man, and he cut me off.

"Might's well learn not to talk too much in a duck blind," he said. "Maybe it don't make any difference, but it takes your mind off watching. And four-fifths of shooting ducks is watching. *Shhh.* Sun's beginning to come a little now. It'll be shooting light in a minute. When you start to shoot, do it your way."

There is something about waiting just before dawn in a duck blind that makes you forget everything but the slow passage of time. Seemed to me like it never was going to get light enough to shoot. The whole sky was full of noise, and you could see the long strings of ducks, flying away high, it seemed like, but not very high because you could hear the whistle of their wings. Out on the water the decoys were bumping and rocking and making little noises in the water. One seemed to be standing on its head. Another was looking under its wing. In the half-light they looked an awful lot like ducks now. If I was a duck, I would think they were ducks too, I said to myself.

I forgot it was cold. I was looking through my peephole, trying to see ducks. The red-winged blackbirds had started to sing all over the marsh, and the bitterns began to croak and the marsh hens to rattle and the bullfrogs to growl and the ducks everywhere to quack. There was a hiss in front of us, and a swarm of teal dipped and passed low over the water, to get away, long gone. It was very light now, not even very gray any more, and a little more pink was showing on the horizon.

"You can shoot now," the Old Man said, "whenever you see anything to shoot."

I loaded up my 16-gauge with No. 6's and shoved her nose away from the Old Man, pointing the barrel over the stern. The clouds were dropping even more, and the strings of ducks had lowered in their flight until you could hear the wing beats very plainly. You could see the flicker of light on white bellies as one string wheeled over us.

"Pintails," the Old Man said. "Big ones."

In a minute he reached over and clamped my shoulder with his big, knotted hand. He nodded his head and looked straight ahead. "Mallards," he said. "Coming this way."

I looked and looked and I couldn't see anything, but in a few seconds I made out a string of dots. How he knew what they were or which way they were coming I couldn't say, but they kept getting closer and closer and I tensed up and half-raised my gun, but the Old Man said, "No," just as they wheeled around us and passed to the left. "They'll be back," he said, and began to gurgle and chuckle softly, like mallards do in the mud puddle in the back yard. Then he nodded to the right, and I could see the birds pass. The Old Man now began to cackle like his life depended on it. *"Gack-gack-chuckle-gurgle-gack,"* he was saying around his pipe.

The birds swung and came in to us fast. There were about twenty, with a big greenhead out in front. They set their wings, put on brakes, and, coming low over the water, dropped their feet at the outer edge of the decoys.

"Now," the Old Man said, and I lurched to my feet, bringing the gun up under my chin, with my eyes never off the big greenhead that was coming in for a landing.

As he saw me he turned and went straight up. I covered him and pulled, and he kept going. I pulled again, and he still kept going. I turned to the Old Man, shaking, pale, and sick.

"There'll always be more," the Old Man said.

I was baffled out of my mind and sick to my stomach when the big duck went off and took the other ducks with him. Those big mallards had come roaring into the decoys as though they planned to live there all their lives. The drake was as big as a goose, and so close you could make out all the gray and blue and green and yellow on him. You could see even the close-barred markings on his sides and the blue feathers on his wings, he was that close.

Once again I was wanting to cry, because I felt as if I had let the Old Man down, but then I figured I was a pretty big boy now and big boys that cry generally get their guns taken away from them; so I played it tough.

"Okay," I said. "Okay. I did it wrong again. I missed him clean and I ain't glad, but I musta done something wrong, and you might as well tell me what it was. What was it?"

The Old Man grinned, very happy. He took a lot of time lighting the big redheaded match and shielding it from the breeze as he cupped his hand around the pipe. The Old Man had times when he enjoyed cruelty.

"You did it all right," he told me. "You missed that big duck as clean as a whistle. The reason you missed him was ballistics. You remember yesterday we were talking about ballistics?"

"Yessir," I said. "But I remember that you weren't too sure about ballistics, either. Gimme some more ballistics."

All this time I was thinking: *Damn ballistics! I missed that duck, that duck as big as a turkey, as big as a house, and I don't know why. So now I get a lecture from the Old Man.*

The Old Man snickered a little more. "I think I got this ballistics drawed down to where you can understand it. I got it what they call reduced to its component parts.

"Let's say you are watering the lawn. Your Cousin Roy runs through the back yard and you got the hose in your hand and all of a sudden you would like to wet down your Cousin Roy. He could probably use a bath, but let's don't get personal.

"If the kid is running against the wind and you got a hose in your hand and you want to wet him, you got to do several different things. One, you are pointing the hose. Two, you are figuring the wind. Three, you are figuring how fast is Roy running.

"So you know that a hose will squirt only so far before it bends backward in the wind. You know that Roy can run only so fast. So if you're as smart as I think you are, you point the hose somewhere ahead of Roy, let the wind take the water stream backward, and then let Roy and the stream collide at a point you've already figured out.

"That's duck shooting. That's ballistics. Shots go from a gun like water out of a hose. The duck comes on like Roy is running. The shot goes one way, like the water goes one way. The ducks go one way, like Roy goes one way. And the wind adjusts the relationship between Roy and the water, between the shot and the ducks. Because shots always string out like water from a hose."

The Old Man settled back with that any-questions look. I had one to throw at him. "Sure, that's fine, this hose and Cousin Roy business. But the one I missed a minute ago was coming down fast and going up fast. Gimme one of them ballistics on this, that rule of thumb you're always talking about."

"It's really a shame," the Old Man said. "I hate to spoil you so early, but there was once aponst a time when I shot ducks down in Louisiana with a Cajun guide, and he told me a very wise thing. I will tell you now. When a duck is coming down, you aim at his tail. When a duck is coming up, you aim at his nose. When he is doing either one of those things but crosswise, lead him. Lead him twice as far as you think you need to lead him. That won't be far enough, but you'll probably hit him in the tail and slow him down, anyhow."

"How far is a lead, a real good lead on a duck?" I asked him. "Golly, I mean how can you make a rule out of it?"

"A lead is as far as you can swing a gun ahead of the bird," the Old Man answered. "You'll never be able to lead one far enough, because you can't pull the gun that far ahead of him in the time you've got to do it. There are all sorts of ducks that fly all sorts of speeds. Teal go off on a level line faster than most of the others. But under certain circumstances a mallard will be faster than a teal. Bluebill coming in low give you a bigger ballistic, because they look faster than they are and mostly you are shooting down at them, which means you'll shoot over 'em unless you're careful. Hell," the Old Man said, "I can't tell you how to do it. You just got to miss enough to make you automatic. And there will be enough for you to miss. Like now. Get down, boy! We got pintails in the breeze!"

The pins came in like pins almost always come in, which is fast and undecided and not wishing to tarry unless somebody asks them. The Old Man asked them, using his pleading pintail voice this time. They swirled in a big circle and slanted low, and then they shot up in a hard, smooth skid from the water they didn't want much of anyhow. I was standing straight up in the boat when they zoomed, and when I shot I was bending backward. The pintail I was pointing at hit the water about the same time I did, because the discharge of the gun sent me tail over tip into the mucky water, mashing the reeds backtilting the boat. The Old Man seemed pleased at both results.

"If you can retrieve yourself," he said, "I'll go out and pick up a fine drake that you must have killed by accident. Very fine bird, the pintail. He doesn't cheat, which is more than you can say of some people. He won't eat fish on you, like a mallard will, or even like a canvasback will. And he's the best-looking duck in the business, unless you like 'em lead-colored like the French ducks, the big greenheads."

I climbed, dripping, back into the boat, scraped off some of the awful-smelling ooze, and watched the Old Man retrieve my first duck. Did you look at your first duck, or your first pheasant, real close? Ever see a bull pintail at close range?

Maybe this wasn't a very special pintail, but the gray on him was like a fine herringbone suit, and his belly was white, and the crest on his head was still ruffled. His open eye was white rimmed, and his head was dull red-golden brown, and his tail was sharp as a dart. He was as big as a mallard and would taste just as sweet, because he was an honest duck that wouldn't cheat on you and go gormandize himself on fish.

And he was *my* pintail, my first duck, my first big duck. Sometime later I might shoot a goose or a wild turkey or almost anything, but this was my first real big duck. I hated to think that he would stiffen up and his glossy feathers would get soggy and his fine open eyes would glaze. A man's first duck is an adventure.

I still didn't know how I had shot him, except that whatever I did sent me backward, overboard. I swore I would try to do better. In the meantime I would admire my pintail. The Old Man stopped my reverie in full bloom.

"If you ain't so caught up in your own importance," he whispered, "you might be interested in the fact that there's a hull passel of mallards about to decoy in your front yard. Maybe you better figger it out for yourself."

I came out of the fog, and there among the decoys were a double dozen mallards, in the water already, two drakes out ahead, swimming into the blind, some brown-flecked hens behind, already chuckling happily and standing on their heads. Some more drakes and some more hens behind them settled down into the decoys as if they'd found friends and relatives with money. I looked at the old boy. He broke a rule and talked.

"There's three or four in line," he said. "If you were hungry, you could loose off at the lot and fill up the boat. But if you're wondering how good you can shoot, I'd recommend that you stand up and holler, 'Shoo!' and see how good you can do. It's up to you, bud."

It seemed that the Old Man was looking very intently at me, and I decided I'd better stand up and holler, "Shoo!" Which is what I did. The two drakes went out of the water in a vertical climb, and I never saw at all what the rest did. My eyes were full of mallard drakes.

I pointed the gun at the first drake's nose, as the Old Man had said. Then I pushed her ahead a couple of feet and pulled on the trigger, and the first drake came down like a sack of meal. The other one had got up high enough and had squared off and was heading for elsewhere. I led him as far as I could and pulled again, and down he came like another sack, and all of a sudden there were two big green-headed, blue-winged, yellow-billed and yellow-footed, curled-tail mallard drakes floating belly up on the pond. And they belonged to me.

"Easy, aint it?" the Old Man said. "Once you know how, I mean."

"I think it's pretty simple," I agreed. "You make it awful easy the way you say it."

"I wouldn't get awful cocky about it, if I were you," the Old Man warned. "Not just because you got three ducks in the boat and they're all good big ducks. You'll miss a lot of ducks before you get as old as I am. You'll very likely miss some ducks today."

The Old Man was right. Some more pins came in a little later and decoyed to the Old Man's pretty-please talk as tame as bluebills. I made the same shot I had killed the mallards with, and as far as I know I never pulled a feather. Some teal came in and squished down in the decoys, and I led one a mile and he dropped like a rock. I led another the same mile, and he went on to Mexico.

There were a lot of ducks around in those days, and not much of a limit to worry about. The weather got better as the morning wore on. The clouds massed low and solid, keeping the ducks down. The open water was rough and the ducks were looking for still-water ponds.

I burned powder until my arm was black on the muscle, but I could have shot a 10-gauge off my nose that day and never noticed the difference. The Old Man didn't coach me too much. He would just nod when I killed a hard one and shake his head when I missed an easy one. He didn't shoot anything flying. I had a lot of cripples, and he shot their heads off with his creaky old pump gun. Every time he turned a cripple over he looked sort of sad and disapproving, as if a man shouldn't go around crippling ducks because of the cost of gunpowder.

Along toward the end of the morning, when the ducks stopped about nine-thirty, as they usually do, I figured I had a pretty good grasp on the Old Man's idea of ballistics. At least I knew one thing for sure: you can't aim at it and hit it unless it's coming straight at you or going straight away, and this never really happens. A duck coming is either dipping down or slanting up, and a duck going is always heading up a little. You got to aim at where you think it'll be when the shot gets there.

It began to snow a little at ten, when the Old Man counted the ducks in the boat and said, "That's enough. We got more than we can eat at the house and give to the neighbors. Let's save some for next week, or maybe next fall."

We sat there in the marsh, with the marsh smell coming strong on the breeze and the soft flakes of snow falling, drinking what was left of the coffee and eating the apples and Miss Lottie's cookies we had stolen out of the crock. The red-winged blackbirds had shut up, and there was only an occasional string of ducks flying low under the solid clouds. It was getting colder all the time.

"We had a pretty good morning," the Old Man said. "I thought you did pretty good for an amateur. I guess you feel like celebrating some; so I suggest you row the boat home. It'll calm you down."

TIMES PAST ON THE EASTERN SHORE

Gene Hill

When Gene Hill first handed me this piece at Sports Afield, *I knew without reservation that he created one of the warmest essays ever written on waterfowling. Later, in 1975, he included the article in his collection,* Mostly Tailfeathers, *published by Winchester Press. Now I'm grateful to have this opportunity to bring it to all who missed its other outings and to urge its rereading by those who saw it before. The Eastern Shore is not far from Gene's New Jersey home, and he is down there with guns, gear, and labs as often as time permits. But no trip in reality is like the one he takes in this look back through times gone but never forgotten.*

MY DAYS SPENT on the Eastern Shore are all too few. And no matter how good the gunning ever is, the memory of how it used to be makes my "three dead in the air" seem a mockery of what the word "waterfowling" used to mean to the men of the Chesapeake Bay.

I've listened to the old-timers wistfully recalling the nights they took ducks outlined in flight against the full of an ice-white moon. I've heard them talk about the sinkboxes surrounded by more than three hundred decoys and how they would lie there wet, frozen and often frightened of a running sea and a ten-knot wind. I've heard the baymen talk softly among themselves about the live tollers, blacks and mallards and Canadas, that they used to train. I've seen their guns from "0" bores to the "little" 10-gauge side-by-side. Yes, I've listened to the talk and seen their boats and held their guns, but I know nothing of the meaning of their words.

I will never see the thousands upon thousands of canvasbacks on opening day along the Susquehanna flats. I will never thread a boat, shipping water from the weight of mallards, with a sculling oar at one end and a gunning light at the other.

I will never know the bellow of a half-pound of sixes tamped down in front of black powder and oakum. I'll not likely take in my lifetime as many as some of these men have often taken in a single day.

They tell of the nights so filled with music; the whistling of pintails, the grunting of geese, and tuk-tuk of mallards that two men in a blind had to talk to each other by kicking and poking.

They let me hear their words, but it is really to each other that they talk of another time—and not to me.

I will never know their Currituck, their Pamlico, their Nags Head, their Smith and Tangiers islands.

But the one thing I know is their mind. I can imagine what it must have been like to set out with a case of handmade shells and expect, on a very good day, to use the whole batch up. And I wish I could have done it—just one time.

They—the old gunners and baymen—talk about the hardness. They talk about the cold and the wet and the days that came and went without sleep, and I see their hands and I understand. Hands that lived in ice and around oars and push-poles and rope and frozen netting and hatchets, draw knives and files. Hands that brought canvasbacks and ruddies and brant alive from cedar logs. Hands that crafted deadeyes, and sneak-skiffs and pungeys. Hands that tell me more of what they're saying than the words.

But it's the eyes that give them away. It's the looking backward to the day they stared down the barrel of an old Remington Model 11 with a ten-shot extension on the magazine more than five hundred times a day—on more days than one. And I see an excitement there that I wish I'd known firsthand—just once.

We are the same, these old men and me. Separated a bit by time and fortune, but imagination stirs my gunning blood the same—and when I close my eyes I can see it all . . . I can feel the cold, duck-riding wind on the back of my neck. My hands, still frozen from helping set out more than a hundred blocks, are tucked up in my armpits for warmth. I would have had my 10-gauge hammer gun reamed out about to almost cylinder bore for the first shot, and a touch more choke for the second. It is still night, the reluctant winter sun imperceptible yet behind the heavy banks of scudding clouds that promise snow before noon. But I can hear them overhead pouring through the dark from sheltered bays on the first flights to the flats where wild celery grows. And I wait—not for any legal shooting time, but just for light enough to silhouette the sculpture of the canvasback over a gun barrel.

And at last, as it always must, it happens. I have heard the cans dropping in among the decoys for the last half-hour and now with light, I stand and shoot. Three fall with the first barrel as they blossom up from the water and then a pair of drakes tumble with the second. (I always shoot beautifully in my imagination.)

And as fast as I can load and shoot they drive in to the stool. My pick-up man is standing by until I'm done—and by the time the other working men are at their jobs, I'm through.

Ducks of all sorts nearly brush our caps as we retrieve and pick up the handmade decoys from the freezing chop. Who could have ever stood there then and guess that in less than thirty years these skies would be near silent and a box of shells would last the average gunner for a month? Who would then have ever said that his great-grandchildren would likely never know the smell of roasting canvasback and a daily limit of other ducks could be carried in just one hand?

I can't find it in myself to condemn the old-time gunners. It is indeed a tragedy that they did not realize the havoc that they wrought—but a tragedy born of ignorance rather than intent. And lest we too hastily blame them for being ignorant, let me remind you of the atomic clouds that still circle the atmostphere, DDT, thalidomide, leaded gasoline, mercury wastes, phosphates, just to name a few—that in the last years have done more to affect our living environment than the short span of time that was the heyday of the commercial gunner.

And what about you? I'd like to bet that I could find you any morning of the gunning season dressing in your union suit of scratchy wool by the light of a smoky kerosene lantern. Your good wife downstairs in the kitchen making oatmeal, some fried home-cured ham and a blue enamel pot of boiled coffee, and maybe a buttermilk biscuit or two to tamp the whole thing down. Along about half-past three, with the second cup of coffee in your hand, you'd be out on the porch smelling the wind like an eager hound. Your wife sees the timeless excitement in your face and takes pleasure in the fact there's still a lot of boy that's living in the man she married years ago. I hope she'll be the one to hear my horse's hooves striking sparks from the frozen road and come out to say hello when I stop to pick you up—with a hot cup and maybe a biscuit or two.

You take the reins while I light my pipe and tuck Old Maude's blanket in a little tighter around my knees; seems the mornings are a little brisker than they used to be. The horse forces herself into a trot, pretending she's as excited as we are, and we just sit there staring at the cold blue sky—not saying much, just sort of puffing our pipes at each other as certain men are apt to do when they know for sure that there's no place in the world they'd rather be.

Give Maude a little flick of the reins; it won't do much good, but it flatters her.

Tom Hennessey—

PINTAIL POINT

Kendrick Kimball

This story is an outstanding example of the kind of literature that flourished in the outdoor magazines until the 1960's, when most editors and publishers became enamored with service pieces—which they called "how-to"—and embraced the formula as though it would be a magic carpet to the hearts of multitudinous readers. The change was especially welcomed on Madison Avenue, where the czars of advertising had already researched and decreed the fact that reading skills and interest were diminishing in the electronic age (think: video games weren't even here yet!) and that short-and-snappy was the way to go—with lots of "pix" (photos to you and me). Madison Avenue could not then, and still cannot to this day, fathom the emotions and commitment of the outdoorsman. It can, however, understand outdoor magazines better when their over-all format— the "look" as it is called—is similar to other magazines thought to be in the mainstream of public acceptance. When Cosmopolitan *magazine publishes a piece called "Ten Ways You Turn Off Your Man Without Even Knowing It." Madison Avenue can dig it. If the article is good enough, it may even inspire some immortal lines of advertising copy, since it will obviously be very product-oriented. An article called "Pintail Point" in an outdoor magazine—even when presented with the art of Bob Kuhn, or Dave Maass or Chet Renenson or Tom Hennessey—would be a total dud to such thinking, however. The reason:* It would have to actually be read to be understood. *The Madison Avenue editor/publisher would say: "got to jerk that pintail piece, baby. It's 'way too long—goes nowwhere. Two old geezers on a hunt. Yak! Yak! Yak! So who gives a* bleep*! If we have to have ducks in this issue, let's go with something solid. Like: 'Ten Ways to Rig Your Decoys to Fool Ducks in Every Kind of Weather.' Give each tip a hundred words and a drawing to show how to set the ducks. Take two pages at most. No four-color art. Meat-and-potatoes . . . . . give 'em what they want!" "Pintail Point" ap-*

peared originally in Field & Stream *and was reprinted in the anthology,* The Field & Stream Reader, *published by Doubleday in 1946. The book, not to be confused with the* Field & StreamTreasury, *published in the 1950's, is one of the toughest "oldies" to get your hands on. Reading this (and other pieces in this book), you will be reminded of the kind of writing and story-telling the price of a magazine would once bring into your home and is now being rejected, revised and generally scorned by the power brokers of outdoor magazines. Somewhere out there, I have to believe a new generation of Gene Hill, Ed Zern, Russell Annabel, Jack O'Connor, Ted Trueblood, Nash Buckingham, Havilah Babcock, Robert Ruark (to name a few), is working, learning, trying to break into national print. I hope that some of them will make it. We need them now as much as we always have.*

WIB MET me at the lane—the same old Wib, unshaved, dressed in a torn hunting coat and a pair of tarry pants. Old Maggie, his Chesapeake, padded at his heels with a litter of solemn, yellow-eyed pups which added a series of distracting yaps to his greeting.

The leathery features of my host broke into a smile, but not the polite, formal kind worn for guests at his shooting lodge. It was a smile inspired by some circumstance of unusual omen—one that bubbled from the very wellsprings of his being.

"It's goin' to blow," he announced in a voice like the roar of waves against the headlands of Lake Huron. "Out of the nor'west, too. And them mallards will come bustin' off the bay for shelter."

Wib's state of mind was both logical and understandable, for he had dedicated his life to the pursuit of "them mallards." They were a contrary lot, refusing to move into the pot-holes until sunset and departing when the first grayness filtered from the east. At least once a season, however, when storm routed them from their sanctuary, they drove into the marsh in long, straggling files, accompanied by widgeons, pintails and knots of green-winged teal.

In recent years misfortune conspired to busy Wib elsewhere on the red-letter days. When a "whopper" piled up the bay the previous fall, his cheek was puffed twice its normal size by an ulcerated tooth. Another opportunity found him in bed with a wrenched back, result of a tumble from a bee-tree, and on a third occasion he was one of a jury whose deliberations on a fence-line suit were both quickened and confused by a parade of ducks past the county court-house.

"This time I'm goin' to clean up on them big bottle-necked lunkers," he promised. "In the mornin' the bay will be whinin' like a sick cat. They'll buck the storm into Pintail Point before swingin' into the marsh, and we'll be settin' there to nail 'em."

A glance toward the rice beds disclosed nothing prophetic of good shooting. October was in her most indolent mood. Bees droned in the pale sunlight; frogs stirred in the sedge, and over the hay meadow a few butterflies danced against the frosted sumac bobs. On a nearby reef a flock of waders in gleaming salt-and-pepper plumage picked up crustaceans under the bills of a score of dozing gulls.

"I'll admit it don't look much like a weather change," confessed my host as he swabbed his brow with a bandanna. "But my information never fails. That's why I wired you to come."

"Your information?" I echoed.

Knowing Wib's failing, my spirits collapsed. Like many a son of the open spaces, he was somewhat of a mystic. He was rational enough in his everyday affairs, but when ducks were the object of his endeavors he became prey to an outrageous set of hunches and superstitions.

"I suppose you mean that goose bone over the kitchen stove?" I asked fearfully.

Grunting a denial, Wib drew a grimy and yellowed almanac from his pocket. He turned page after page of testimonials and sketches of the digestive apparatus, pausing with a flush of pleasure at a calendar illustrated by signs of the zodiac.

"Look here," he demanded triumphantly, shoving the torn page under my nose. "Professor Zeno's weather forecast," he read. " 'Compiled by the celebrated Arabian seer and astrologer.' Tomorrow's October 23, ain't it? Wal, here it is in black and white: 'severe gales from the nor'west.' "

"And you had me drive two hundred miles on the strength of

that?" I gasped. Attempting to be patient, I showed him the official Government forecast in my newspaper. " 'Fair and calm with slowly rising temperature,' " I quoted.

Wib regarded me with pity. "The weatherman is just a guesser."

"Anyhow, he doesn't try to predict a year in advance," I countered. "That almanac you depend on was printed last fall. It's silly, ridiculous."

"That's what you think," Wib snapped back, eyes alight with fanaticism. "The weather, every schoolboy knows, is caused by position of the sun, moon and stars in relation to each other. A feller like this here Zeno can dope it out a long time ahead. The weatherman wouldn't dare, even if he knew how, because he'd kick himself out of a job. Simple as skinnin' a mud-hen."

I turned away, disbelief confirmed by the cloudless sky and perpendicular columns of smoke from the village. Everywhere I saw evidence of Wib's preparations. A freshly caulked skiff, a pair of oars against the boat house and a heap of decoys with new swivels and anchor ropes awaited our pleasure.

"Maybe we can find a few woodcock in those tag alders by the river," I proposed. "There's no use in our getting up before daylight. We'll sleep late, of course, and—"

"We won't do no such thing," Wib expostulated. "Oil up that gun! Get out them boots! Fill up the shell box! The perfessor has been 100 per cent right all fall, and he ain't goin' to let us down now!"

Awakening at midnight, I groped to the window. The quiet was so pronounced that I heard the rustling of uneasy wings over the shoals. A mallard lifted its feeding call to a moon looming through the stars like a blob of butter. Teal also raised their voices as they splashed in the weed beds and waddled about the bars. Then a shadow fell across the yard, and through the inert leaves of the willows I saw Maggie on a round of the premises.

Not a vestige of hope. A cloudy sky or even a touch of dampness would have been encouraging. I resented Wib's untroubled sleep below, but consoled myself by picturing his chagrin in face of a clear dawn and my comments at the breakfast table.

I was awakened, however, by a sharp pounding. Other noises beat their way into my consciousness: those of pots and pans, someone struggling to put on a pair of boots and a dog pattering excitedly over the floor. Yet the house seemed filled with additional sound which I could not identify.

"Daylight in the swamp—roll out!" Wib yelled briskly from the foot of the stairs.

I sat up in bed, heart beating wildly. A draught of cold, raw air sluiced through the screen as the wind tore under the eaves with a howl. The roof creaked and groaned under a pelting rain. Trees tossed their limbs in torment, lashing the side of the house and releasing branches which whirred through the blackness with every gust. Through the symphony a low, throbbing note beat like a drum.

Wib, a steaming platter in his hand, accepted the storm as a natural and logical consequence.

"Seas are breakin' over the reefs," he declared. "No duck can stand it on the bay today. The wind will take the tail feathers off those blacks and greenheads if they try to ride it out."

I glowed with elation at the prospect of matching wits again with the mallard. One does well to select it as his favorite duck. It furnishes sport on the season opening to gunners in shirt sleeves, and to the muffled, blue-faced veterans who peer through the bleakness at the close. A few, of heroic mold, winter in the northern tier of states, foraging along icy creeks and gleaning in the fields rather than surrender to frost.

There are faster ducks and those less reluctant to decoy. The mallard lacks some of the patrician qualities of the canvasback, the bluebill's dash and the brilliant flight performance of the teals. But its intelligence seldom sleeps. When it spills from the skies, wing-bars flashing iridescently, a feather or two floating in the wake of the charge that struck it down, no gunner, no matter how often he has centered such a target, fails to respond to a feeling of satisfaction and achievement.

Breakfast was a formality, for we were both too anxious to be on our way. Groping through the inkiness, I followed Wib to a pen where he gathered a half dozen live decoys and thrust them into sacks.

"Punt's a half mile 'cross the flat," he shouted back at me as he set forth.

I plodded after him as best I could, thankful for the dry footing on the ridges. We sloshed through a series of shallow ponds, barely able to distinguish the grasses twining about our legs. More than once a black object, bounding from some sheltered pocket, hung momentarily against the pewter tones of the cast before it vanished with a reedy whistle.

"Teal," Wib proclaimed amid the gabbled complaints of the decoys. "Lot of 'em in here. Better watch out for the soft spots where they've dug up the sago."

I slumped wearily into the narrow punt. We nosed into a channel through a bed of rushes where blackbirds clucked a sleepy protest over our invasion. The darkness lifted rapidly, and through the misty half light we discerned the bay, convulsed by combers, over which masses of ducks rolled downwind like smoke.

"Point's just aroun' the bend," yelled the dripping Wib as he heaved with the punt stick. "Unwind the anchor ropes on them wooden decoys. Clouds are liftin' in the nor'west—blow's comin' harder."

The live birds regained their composure after a preliminary splashing and ducking. Eighty feet beyond them, a scattered flock of redheads and convasbacks tugged at their moorings. We crouched behind a screen of cattails on a mucky promontory, posted at opposite ends of the punt, thereby enjoying the important comfort, a firm, dry seat.

Dawn was filled with testimony of the fury of the storm. The wind flung streamers of spray over the reefs, where yellowlegs and plover huddled disconsolately. Jack-snipe flitted about us like bats. A gallinule, or "rice hen," fluttered above the vegetation, but the gale proved too much for its comparatively feeble wings, and it plumped with undignified haste into the muck, disappearing with the rapidity of all members of the rail family.

I shivered abjectly. The rain drummed a tattoo upon my back and trickled in widening streams down my sleeves. Our shells were in a hard pail, the humblest and most serviceable of waterproof containers. Gulls streamed overhead in gray battalions, melting into the horizon that promised nought but further unpleasantness. But Wib's sight was keener than mine. He nudged me as three wavering dots broke through the murkiness and threshed to a precipitate landing among the live decoys.

"Mallards," he whispered. "Five minutes before shootin' time. If we keep quiet, they might stay."

His voice sounded dubious, for five minutes is a long while for mallards to remain deceived. Through the cattails I glimpsed the newcomers, stiff as grenadiers on parade. I was not surprised when they edged away, suspicious of the wooden stool and fearful of what the dark, shifting background of vegetation might contain. Stooping to remove my gloves, I launched them into space with a bound when I accidentally knocked over a can used for bailing.

Wib eyed me reproachfully, but the neccessities of the moment were to urgent for speech. Masking his disappointment with a smile, he cut an armful of grass to patch our blind in the rear. As I rose to assist him a cluster of scurrying, shadowy bodies emerged from the grayness. They whisked down to the stool, extended their legs and fanned their wings while I stood as if paralyzed.

The next instant I clutched desperately for my gun. The ducks found none of their kind in the puttied and shot-scarred array beneath them. Perhaps they saw me against the vegetation, for they scattered like a pile of leaves struck by a gust. Two of the mounting forms were suspended above the mud-daubed rib of my barrel. When they slithered to the water, I swung on to a third, half expecting to blast the atmosphere beneath it. But my snap shot sent the target spinning, for, struggling in an air pocket, it was almost stationary when I pressed the trigger.

"Bluebills," grunted Wib, still working on the blind.

I knew he was mistaken—no sea duck is capable of quitting the surface at a sharp angle. Regretting the absence of Maggie, at home with her puppies, I left my companion to his labors. Before I had proceeded ten feet in the punt, I bewailed my awkward use of the long, ungainly paddle with which such craft is propelled on Saginaw Bay. Three specks were floating into an arm of rushes where a possibility of disaster was presented by a reef frothing with whitecaps.

I gathered the bag with an ineptitude that must have been amusing. They were drake greenwings in winter plumage and not much larger than a jack-snipe that tacked across the channel. On my return I squinted through the mist at my companion, whose gun, hitherto unnoticed, was still in the punt. He was a sorry spectacle, crouched in ooze within an inch of his boot tops, his dejected gaze on another band of teal bouncing from the decoys like so many rubber balls.

When the blind-patching job was completed, ducks shuttled down the channel without interruption. The majority were too low to see the stool in the shadow of the vegetation. Mergansers were among them, long-bodied and rakish; redheads, ringbills flying in reckless formation; canvasbacks in geometrical pattern, and a scattering of pintails, bluebills and widgeons. A line of ruddies went past, racing pell-mell a few inches above the surface.

Our attention was distracted by a clamor from the decoys. A lone mallard about to drop among them reversed himself with surprising celerity. He was so near that we noted the curled feather on his tail, the yellow leg and the ring of white around his neck. It was well we fired quickly, for he had rocketed to the limit of range when he crumpled.

I had waded no more than a few yards when Wib's hoarse command sent me tumbling back into the punt. Several hundred pintails poured over the marsh in a disorganized column. They wheeled in desultory fashion, intent on returning to their meal of sago and water potatoes after a brief tour of the skies. But a group of the adventurous broke away from the rear guard and sailed alongside in a sweeping curve—six big, long-necked ducks, buffeted by the gale.

True to pintail tradition, they were deliberate in their curiosity. Boring upwind, they strung over the vegetation in the same leisurely fashion to appraise a half dozen pot-holes in the rice. But these refuges, tenanted only by coots, were not to their liking, and they bunched for a sharp turn down the channel.

"Crack 'em on the first swing," Wib whispered as their wing-beats expressed indecision. "Can't wait on those fellers." He shifted his chew to his right cheek with ease born on long practice. "Still com'n. Now!"

When he poked his muzzle over the top of the blind, the formation broke into six speeding fragments. Wib's drake faltered when the charge raked it. A pinion curled at the second explosion, and the bird, stone-dead, thwacked the water with such violence that the feathers were stripped from the breast-bone. The mark I selected seemed too high for sane shooting. But the wings folded, the neck dropped limply onto the back and a twisting bundle of feathers terminated its plunge by a splash and a smother of bubbles.

Wiping the water from his face, Wib discoursed on the psychology of the species. "Most of the time you can count on 'em bein' pretty leery," he asserted. "If they saw a few pintails among the decoys, they'd come in better. Take a few dead birds, put their necks in forked sticks, lay 'em out natural like, and an awful lot is added to the drawin' power of your flock.

"But like all ducks, they have their dumb brethren too," he ruminated. "A bunch of forty dropped into bluebill decoys when I was settin' on Sand Point one day. Flopped right into a rummy-lookin' outfit of blocks that weren't entitled to fool a butterball. They were tired and hungry, and had come a long distance. Funny bird, the pintail."

We sat back, lost in retrospection. The air became colder, the wind more biting. Our circulation was restored by a flight of teal dislodged from the reef by a redoubled assault of waves. They darted down to pot-holes, flared up for a mad circle of the locality, and dashed away in the aimless and erratic manner of snipe. When they hurtled over us from behind, the most frequent method of approach, they seemed as elusive as a wisp of thistle-down. One had no time to calculate leads, to line up the sights on the bill and jerk them ahead the required distance.

My eagerness spoiled several chances at mallards. Misled by their size, particularly that of the red-legged Canadian blacks, I made the common error of firing too quickly. As they circled behind us, I committed another mistake: that of bobbing my head to follow their progress. Several small flocks shied off abruptly, having seen the motion of my hunting cap or my tense face pressed against the cattails.

Other discouraging factors arose. The decoys nearly burst their throats with invitations to crows stringing to the uplands. But when ducks hove in sight, they tippled for delicacies or floated in silent contemplation of their lot. The most aggravating incident occurred when a pair of pintails glided from the heavens at an angle that indicated a willingness to dispense with maneuvers. Just when we were about to shoot, a hen among the decoys flailed the water in a panic, her bill caught in the neck ring at which she had been picking all morning. The pintails banked suddenly and twinkled away.

Then, to exasperate us further, a wedge of canvasbacks bowed their wings, but swept on without satisfying their curiosity. They were followed by a troop of redheads. The latter veered toward the bay at the instant it seemed they would upend their broad, chunky bodies above the outer edge of the fleet.

Wib's theory for the conduct of the last two flocks seemed plausible. "They know it ain't more than a foot deep here," he grumbled. "Been through the channel in calm weather and seen the bottom. Or else they're wised up by the reefs." He sighed wearily. "Butterballs and mergansers hang out in water like this, but the big divers want depth and plenty of room."

As if in contradiction, two bluebills, tired of fighting the gale, broke from the van of a flock. With that lack of wariness so characteristic of the species they sailed to the stool in a graceful curve. Though they were heavy birds, not the underdeveloped youngsters one so often encounters in October, their deportment was that of novices. We gathered them in.

The next visitors were hooded mergansers, a duck with better qualities than the name implies. They weaved about us confusedly before their swift descent to the stool. Their crested heads and bristly tails lent oddity to their appearance as they stretched their feet to cushion their contact with the surface. Their leave-taking was as impetuous as their arrival, for they slanted broadside into the wind at our bombardment and tore wildly across the channel, leaving two drakes, whose crops were filled with vegetable food, as a penalty for their ill judgment.

A widgeon whizzed past a quartering angle. Then, cupping the air with their tails, three mallards swooshed into the live decoys after a short turn into the wind. Two dropped at our salvo, but the third, a bit wary of the layout, was well on his way to safety when our sights found him against the clouds. He slopped into the water and swam for the rushes with his head up and neck extended.

My companion acted with characteristic decision. A dash through the decoys brought him within questionable range. It was a graphic picture: the man silhouetted against the sky, whipped by wind and rain but rigid as a statue, his legs braced against the current, his piece to his shoulder. And then the mallard slipped through the waves to the yellowed vegetation, where it would lie flat as a shingle until a favorable opportunity to skulk away.

Wib's muzzle jerked upward, and a strong of shot splashed behind the target. He had failed to account for the wind. Again the pellets ripped into the waves, but this time the charge was too high. He pressed trigger again when the mallard rose on top of a comber, where it hung momentarily within a yard of its objective. But the bird was not destined to die miserably of its wounds or be picked to pieces by gulls. Through the curtain of spray lifted by the charge I saw an inanimate patch of black drifting toward the channel, then Maggie plunging through the water on her way to get what otherwise would have been a lost bird.

"Thought I told you to stay home with them pups!" Wib shouted, but the Chesapeake had reached the deep water by this time and with powerful strokes was on her way to the drifting mallard.

She had probably listened to our shooting all morning and finally decided the pups could take care of themselves for awhile.

"We've got enough," Wib declared after checking the bag. "We can afford to let a few go for next year's breedin' stock." His eye twinkled. Then his reddened features broke into a grin, and I knew what was coming. "Next time don't believe what you see in the paper," he chided. "Git your weather dope from headquarters— from me and the professor."

"Hit it lucky, eh?" asked the gasoline-station attendant, peeping into the back of my automobile. "Down at Wib Sawyer's place, I suppose. He's the blamedest cuss I ever knew. Smells a storm a week in advance."

"He lays it to a patent-medicine almanac he got some place," I revealed. "Says it predicted every blow this fall."

"That thing?" The attendant asked disgustedly. "It came out in 1923, but the days fell on the same dates as 1934; so I ripped off the year and gave the danged book to Wib as a joke!"

Tom Hennessey—

GREAT DAY IN THE MORNING

Nash Buckingham

This has always been one of my favorite Buckingham tales. I find the beginning particularly enchanting: dusk coming on, gathering at the duck camp, the meal, anticipation and preparation for the 'morrow. It appeared originally in Field & Stream *in 1941 and was included in* Tattered Coat, *G.P. Putnam's Sons, New York, 1944. The "Hal" of the story, by the way, was Hal Bowen Howard, Buckingham's closest friend and shooting and fishing companion.*

WHEN OUR automobile slowed to enter the road turning westward toward Beaver Dam Lake, I told Johnny to stop and let me look around a bit. It was coming dusk.

Across the dimming cotton fields I saw lights springing up in tenant cabins and winking through vague sails of low-hanging wood smoke from fall burnings. Eastward, I could just make out the black rampart of the vast Owen cypress brake—thousands of forest monarchs towering just as God grew 'em. Beyond and without blemish of axe or saw lay the Dooley and Savage Woods with Walnut Lake winding through them. Ample stocks of deer, wild turkey, and bear harbored there, and I figured on contacting some of them, too, before winter wore out. South of us lay clearings crosscut by a wide bayou winding luxuriantly through second growth. Westward, stars brimmed above sundown's afterglow. A jagged skyline of timber stood clear-cut against a belt of dull, smoldering amber.

Just then the rattley "Limb Dodger," evening accommodation train from Memphis, pulled out of the hamlet of Evansville and whistled sharply for Beaver Dam's lonesome, uncovered stop sign amid the tall and uncut. Hal, I told myself, would be getting off it, with old Horace on hand to assist him in unloading the bird dogs, pointers Ticket and Flash, from the baggage car. I could even spot the gigantic pecan tree lording it over the moss-shingled clubhouse. Many's the rough night I had been able to locate the boat dock by glimpsing that patriarch's bulk through an opening in the willows.

Then I told Johnny to pull on down the lane and over the ramp to the home close. And sure enough, there were Hal and Horace and Aunt Molly and the dogs.

As usual, any number of delightful presupper chores confronted us. The pointers were allowed to ramble before feeding time. This included a visit to the boat dock to observe the water stage and listen to roosting geese raise sand in the saw grass sloughs of the far South End. For early December the water was still pretty low and the moss heavy. Those honking geese were music to our ears, for we planned a long hunt at the goose camp over on the river. Our tent there was on an Indian mound just off Ship Island sand bar, and we itched to get in behind the denizens of that game pocket.

Then we retraced our steps to the clubhouse for those puttings away and settings about that are, to all intents and purposes, ritual with any long-organized and convivial wildfowling outfit. Ticket and Flash made themselves strictly at home. When Hal and I go shooting, those bullies never step out of character as home folks. This includes bunking on our beds if they so elect. As Hal used to say, "What are a few fleas among pals?"

The club ledger revealed that only two members had hunted at Beaver Dam during the week previous. This was rather surprising in view of Horace's report that there was a "worl' o' ducks."

Came supper, and what a meal! Nothing but smothered mallard, rice and giblet gravy, grilled tomatoes and savory bacon for snack garnishment with the hot biscuits. Hal and I are notorious one-dish men.

Aunt Molly, expecting us, had quite thrown herself away in getting those ducks to just that right stage of juicy succulence no other cook or chef in my lifetime has ever even tried. And I've done trencherman's fatigue behind some of the allegedly top-flight saucepan and spider artists of terra firma's kitchens. From Cajun concoctions to *salle à mangers* where the help wear fancy pants and bumblebee weskits, and the carpets are so thick that you need snowshoes to stay on top. Let me give you Aunt Molly's recipe for smothered mallard just as she told it to me that evening in her own kitchen.

"Whin I heahs you an' Mist' Hal is comin', I teks 'bout fo' mallats whut's bin hangin' out in de col' fo' two-three days, an' dresses dem ve'y keerful. I don' nevah put no watah on my ducks. No, suh! I jes' wipes 'em dry wid er rag an' lets 'em set awhile. Den I gits me er stew pot an' puts in some red pippers, vinegar, an' fine yarbs outa de gyarden, an' den I adds er li'l watah an' lays in de mallets.

"I brings all dis to er slow bile fo' 'bout tin minutes. Den I teks out de mallets an' dries 'em off an' sets 'em out in de col' air fo' 'bout er hour. But I saves de watah dey done bin biled in. Nex', I gits my ol' deep skillet hotter 'n de hinges o' hades an' swinges of de mallets quick on bofe sides. O' cose, dey done bin split wide open up dey backs.

"Atta dat, I sets de skillet onto de back side o' de stove an' po's in some melted butter an' some o' de bile watah. I puts de ducks back into de skillet wid dey breasts dow'ud, an' covers 'em wid er flat top an' lays er smoothin' iron on top o' dat. Ev'y now an' den I adds er sluicin' o' elderberry cordial an' er li'l mo' bile watah. Den I draps in er few bay leaves an' er mite o' Tabasco. O' cose, I keeps de baste po'hd ovah de mallets all de meanstwhile.

"Whin I heahs de Limb Dodger blow fo' de flatform, I sets dem mallets in de oven to jes' sorter brown 'em er li'l bit mo'. I meks my gravy an' stirs de hot bile watah an' some mo' elderberry wine into hit. Den, when I sees you-all is really heah, I finishes wid de tomatoes, rice an' buscuit. Dat's de way I cooks dem mallets, suh!"

Ah, me! Aunt Molly of marvelous culinary attainments! Cooks have gone to Heaven for far less than those "mallets."

After supper we sat around in the snug clubroom with its prints and antlers looking down on us from walls and rafters that began accumulating grime in the late seventies. Then began preparations for the morrow.

An English friend had just presented me with a trim, handsomely engraved sixteen-gauge autoloading shotgun with two sets of tubes: improved cylinder for upland birds, and a full-choked one for wild-fowling. I decided, however, to use it only on quail next day, for I was headed for some tall timber gunning and never believed in sending a boy on a man's errand. I can hear some reader sniff and allow as how he can kill as many high ducks with his sixteen-bore as I can with my ten-gauge and hand-loads of five drams of powder and an ounce and a half of hard 4's. I've been trying, unsuccessfully, for a great many years to see the color of such money.

I put the shorter tube on the sixteen-gauge autoloader, however, and false-swung it a bit to get the hang and feel. The stock specifications were just about right. Then I readied my tin shell box with ammunition, water bottle, camera, emergency kit, and strong cord. That is about all I ever pack except when I'm out for all day. Iron rations are then included.

Hal and I never shake the dice box or draw for stands and paddlers when no other members are at Beaver Dam. Horace just naturally takes charge of my boat, and burly Jesse Taylor looks after Hal's interests. Hal likes to jump-shoot ducks in the North End trails, for big Jesse is particularly adept at squirming the sneak float noiselessly through button willows and elbow brush. But of course we have an understanding that if the shooting turns out poor for either of us, the other fellow comes at once where the sport sounds good.

When bedtime came, Hal took the walnut couch in the northwest corner by his locker, and I always favored the feather bed in my southwest niche. Horace left the clubhouse door wide open; and when frost cooled the stove, the dogs each crawled aboard a bed. Breakfast was, as usual, informal; we never bothered going to Aunt Molly's dining room unless a crowd was down.

Stirrings-about in Horace's quarters, and wood chopping, generally awakened us. Then Horace entered, got the stove going, and lit the center lamp. Returning with the white china coffee dripper, he tinkled on a cup with a spoon. That meant the end of extra snoozing and to come alive. And by the time that eye-opener and ablutions were over, Horace was back with eggs and battercakes.

That particular morning, the five-thirty Y & M V express had just rumbled northward when we parted at the dock. The last thing Hal said to me was: "If I'm not in by nine o'clock, don't wait for me. Take the dogs and kill a mess of quail—Irma and Marion want them for their dinner party."

Then he and Jesse disappeared in the swallow-ups of misty predawn.

Horace yanked our little duckboat's nose southward and paused to take bearings off a big white star. I knew that by holding it true aft we would hit the trail opening into the South End right on the nose. But before hitting that mark, we had to pole across a quarter mile of willow stumpage.

Masses of mallard, gadwall, and widgeon thundered into flight and we could hear them resettling nearer the woods. The geese we had heard the evening before had moved westward during the night; I could hear them cackling and grunting over in the Teal Pond. Horace and I decided to wade and sled the boat rather than push through the top moss. We entered an aisle through the forest and, though walking as noiselessly as possible, raised clouds of birds ahead.

It was breaking day when we rounded the bole of a huge stunted cypress with our destination—the Clover Leaf Hole—in front of us. Hundreds of mallards roared out of it. Their strident alarm set the whole marsh a-spout with ducks. Through lacelike boughs the heavens were atwinkle with milling *Anatidæ*.

Suddenly a bunch of perhaps fifty widgeon lowered delicately into the pool just across the buckbrush from us. Quietly they settled to feed and preen. They were perfectly safe, too, for what Horace and I had in mind was a shot at those geese in the Teal Pond. He knew without my telling him that his next job was to wade a circle around those honkers and, if possible, send them over the woods my way. Leaving me seated on the end of the duckboat, he picked up his gun and faded from sight up the trail.

Distant goose agitation soon told a story of suspicion. Rasping cackles and guttural conversation became more and more confused. Then a muffled beating of wings told me that the flotilla of *Branta canadensis* was getting under way. In stalking game, Horace had the past master's super sixth sense. I heard him shouting, and knew that he was on the outside of the gaggle and trying to shoo them against the bank timber and more nearly over me. By then I saw them too, gaining altitude over the willows and headed my way in a swinging loop. I sat perfectly still; that was no time to flush the unsuspecting widgeon and have them flaring skyward in alarm.

Then the geese were over me. I turned the heavy ten-bore ahead of their veering mass formation and scored a double kill with its first tube. At the report the widgeon leaped and almost obscured my second blast, which downed another bird. I heard Horace's yell of congratulation. There were ducks every way I looked. Now was my time to start scoring.

By the time Horace rejoined me, he had quite some retrieving to do. But I delayed this and stationed him across from me about fifty yards. The ducks were crossing heavily, and our combined calls lowered them to just above the tree-tops. The ten-gauge cracked regularly and successfully. It was one of those mornings when a fellow doesn't let many get away. So heavy was the flight that I shot only greenheads. It was just eight o'clock when Horace, sloshing through the woods, called out: "Dat's d' las' un, Cap'n. You got d' limit."

Laying aside my gun, I helped him pick up, and we waded up the now sunlit trail. Out across Stumpy Opening and into paddling water, and the lake became a picture. Its deep, unmolested coves, rimmed with yellow saw grass, were packed with ducks. Its broad bosom flashed with color off the white and black of concentrated scaups. Great patches of greenish moss seed swung with the wind drift, and I thought of summer and fall days when a bass fly tossed to the edges of such scum fetched heavy strikes and battles royal.

At the club I cleaned up a bit, changed to field boots, unleashed Flash and Ticket, and shoved the sixteen-gauge autoloader into my gun scabbard. By then Horace had the mules saddled. We heard Hal's gun working in the North End; so I knew it was all right for me to begin accumulating those bobwhites for the girls.

Hardly had we crossed the railroad and skirted new ground east of the club before Flash found, and rugged Ticket honored the point. When the bevy flushed, I repressed the inclination to empty the piece, and downed two birds with three shots. The gift gun handled superbly.

Horace marked the escaping singles beyond some mutton cane and briars separating the new ground from a cornfield. Emerging there, I dismounted hurriedly, for, almost side by side, Ticket and Flash were pointing stanchly in opposite directions. Off to the right a bit, two Negroes pulling corn stood watching the scene.

I walked in ahead of Ticket, and a cock bird buzzed to my left. The two dogs stood shot like statues. I clucked softly, and Ticket pussy-footed to the fetch. Dilating with intensity, Flash's gaze was still "eyes right." I swung into firing balance just as a jack snipe floated from the muck. Flash's optics popped, but he held his ground. Over went *Scolopax,* and the big pointer retrieved at command.

Then, happening to look down, I noticed that my gun was empty and open. I had failed to reload after firing at the bevy rise; so now the weapon needed refueling. I dropped a shell into the carrier and pushed the release pin. Down went the action with a sharp clang. Horace cried out in amazement, for up from a wet corner of the mutton cane and briar patch flapped a mallard drake. What that lone duck was doing in that out-of-the-way spot will forever remain a mystery. Almost by instinct I bowled over the fellow, and Ticket fetched at a lope, head high with pride at this unusual package.

I made a present of the mallard to one of the corn pullers.

"Cap'n," he said in thanking me, "whut kinda funny li'l ol' long-billed bird wuz dat you jes' kilt?"

I told him it was a snipe.

"Shucks, Cap'n," he replied, "ef you laks to shoot dem things, dey's er whole passel of 'em uses not fur from heah. Whin you an' Ho'ace comes roun' de lane pas' Aun' Molly's cabin, why jes' look in dat wet place out in her cotton fiel'—hit's plumb packed wid dem fellers."

I thanked him kindly for the information, but with the mental reservation that he had merely noticed a lot of killdeer.

For two hours or more Horace and I rode through cornfields, sedgy new-ground tangles and weedy bays. The work of Flash and Ticket was superb. Conditions couldn't have been better, and by eleven-thirty Horace's pouch was puffy. We turned homeward across the corn and, by sheer accident, found ourselves passing Aunt Molly's domicile.

Remembering what our colored friend had said, we dismounted, put Flash and Ticket at heel, and went over to have a look at that wet place in the cotton patch. A hundred yards from the house we struck it, just a jelly-textured depression among the bare brown stalks. But out of it whizzed clouds of snipe. I sent Horace scurrying to its far end to keep the birds from pitching there, and hunkered down in the scant cover.

Ticket and Flash, flat on their bellies, looked on in amazement.

Snipe hung over the area like a locust swarm in Egypt—a sight I shall always remember.

I fired away as fast as I could cram quail loads into the new fowling piece. Had that gun jammed, I would have gone stark mad; but it functioned perfectly. Hal said later he never heard such a bombardment. And before very long Horace and I and the dogs gathered up twenty-five snipe that further heavied the sack.

Hal hadn't been in very long, with a limit of ducks and three geese to show for his forenoon. He hadn't taken a stand and put out decoys; had just eased along, shooting at leaping or overhead birds. Horace strung up the entire bag for a snapshot just as Aunt Molly came out on the porch to ring her dinner bell. I can see her standing there right now and hear her admiring cry of, "Great day in de mawnin'!" There were seventy ducks, six geese, twenty-five quail, and twenty-five snipe.

But hold! Hold! Don't bawl Hal and me out for a pair of law violators or unmitigated bristle-backs. Don't wire Federal and State enforcement agents to hop on our trails and track us down. I began this by telling Johnny to stop the car and let me look around a bit. Well, so I did, not long ago. But the old club's record book and my private shooting diary of decades' standing remind me that our bag of seventy ducks, six geese, twenty-five snipe, and the same number of bobwhites was made one rare morning in early December of 1909, just thirty-five years ago, come next gunning season.

I can even tell you exactly where all that wild game went, too. Three honkers went to the Old Men's Home, and the other three went into cold storage for the Christmas quail hunt at Hal's home in Aberdeen. Most of the ducks went to the Church Home and St. Agnes Hospital. And Hal and I worked on the quail and snipe aplenty when Marion and Irma gave their big dinner party. It came just before the debutantes' ball at the old Chickasaw Guards' Club, and I can shut my eyes and see those two lovely girls who later became our "missuses" standing on the grand staircase with their arms full of long-stemmed American beauty roses and the stags in windrows at their feet. Ah, me!

In 1909 there was no Migratory Bird Law; and in the state where Beaver Dam lay, there were only county game laws, and those wholly uninterested in waterfowl. In fact, most of the duck clubs of that region were shooting daily limits of from forty to fifty birds. But at Beaver Dam there was a self-imposed one of thirty-five ducks.

There was no limit, for instance, on wild turkey. But those fellows were none too plentiful by 1909, nothing like the late eighties and early nineties, when I first began hunting the big gobblers. We had a rule against more than twenty-five quail, snipe, or woodcock per day per gun.

Our hotels and restaurants served wild game openly and legally. And be it remembered that when the Migratory Bird Law did set a Government limit of twenty-five ducks and eight geese per day (a very generous one, if you're asking me) it was, to all intents and purposes, eighteen years before obvious impairment of basic stocks necessitated the lowering of those figures.

So when I had Johnny stop our automobile for me to look around, I figured, in surveying the landscape, that where we sat was just about in the middle of that patch of snipe bog in Aunt Molly's cotton field. But there was no distant Owen cypress brake in sight, and I guess the bear and deer and wild turkey that we used to hound and dog through the big woods are about things of the past. Maybe there are a few here and there on over into the Tallahatchie country. And that clear, deep bayou overhung with cypress and full of game fish is now a silted and muddy drainage ditch.

Today, everything is pretty much cotton, and the country-side, from the farming angle, is almost manicured. Rarely do you sight a real specimen of the old-time log cabin like Aunt Molly's sturdy structure. But there are any number of elegant, electrically equipped residents, with radios wide open. Laundry, bakery, grocery, and soft drink trucks supply their every want. All of which, no doubt, is as it should be.

Mighty little smoke drifts off new-ground burnings, and the homey smells and sounds of a pioneering backwoods country are missing. But strange to relate, there are fallow fields and woods pastures where some pretty fair quail shooting can still be had if the cornfields and pea patches help out. The farmers collect for not planting some grounds, and such lands lie out or are planted to lespedeza and non-shatter beans. But most plantations are now posted, and their owners co-operate with the State Game and Fish Commission to restore and maintain well-fooded habitats for wildlife.

The younger generation of plantation owners is just as hospitable as their forebears, but they are a sight wiser as to the value of game crops. These, they realize, have become an integral and valuable part of the farm's yield and the county weal. Quail, duck, and fish bootleggers are beginning to fear fines and jail sentences. Town and country sportsmen are frowning upon and turning up the chiselers. Not alone as good citizenry, but because, as a basis of sound sportsmanship and justice to others, it is the right thing to do.

Beaver Dam Lake still has a goodly skyline of timber. Even some of its saw grass rim is intact. But drainage and varying water levels have hurt its once magnificent fishing, and at times endangered duck shooting because of drought. Gone are the coontail moss, duckmeat, yonquapins and other aquatic naturals which once fed the migrations. For many years the old club baited the lake, but a Federal edict stopped that and hurt the gunning to some extent. The members shot over live decoys, too; something we of the older times didn't have to worry with particularly.

Somehow they still have pretty good shooting at old Beaver Dam, and occasionally, on a right water stage, the bream, crappie, and bass fishing picks up. But there is no huge pecan tree sheltering a moss-shingled clubhouse. A cyclone bowled over the patriarch and crushed the building. All I salvaged were some English sporting prints, deer antlers, pictures of the club's founders, and the historic log-book.

In 1909 there were probably not more than half a million pioneers and less than ten million acres going out of circulation in the duck factories of the waterfowl-producing Canadian provinces. In much of that area the beaver was still the chief hydraulic engineer in charge of water levels. Chances are, the plains country we used to gun outproduced more northern breeding grounds. There was plenty of water, and only casual drought. Offhand, I'd guess the supply of 1909's waterfowl was two and a half times that of today. And to think what has happened to wildfowl habitat in our own and the Canadian country is to heave a long sigh.

How do I approximate such matters? Purely from memory. I shot

ducks on the Canadian prairies and the plains of our own Northwest just after entering my teens. The other evening I came across a
hunting license issued in South Dakota (1902) to Young Buckingham. I wasn't out of college, but a veteran at wildfowl, chickens,
and big game. We had grand sport at prairie chickens, but I have an
idea that the ring-necked pheasant has rather displaced the glamour
boy of the old wheatlands as the major target for South Dakota's
sportsmen.

In fact, barring a few states in the Union, I have gunned waterfowl pretty much wherever they use. Black ducks in eastern Canada
and coastal flights from New England's goose stands to the rice
paddies of South Carolina. I've tumbled velour-headed canvasbacks
from Currituck batteries and taken like toll at shore blinds along
Potomac broadwaters and Virginia's rushy ponds.

The "bluffs" and duck ponds of Saskatchewan, Manitoba, and
Alberta were friends these many years agone. In September, 1938,
judging the Saskatchewan Field Trials, I rode a week over the southern plains country—recently made a shambles for wildfowl by eight
well-nigh rainless years. Shades of Nebraska's sand hills and bird
dogs statuesque on chickens of the wheaty Dakotas! Colorado's
plateaus! My tawny Chesapeake crouching in the rushes! Ribbons
of weaving, flashing teal!

From Minnesota to the Gulf of Mexico are moored memories of
houseboat days and nights along "Ol' Miss." I'm remembering stately
cypress, dismal stumpage of the delta's sunklands, the "limberjacks"
of Reelfoot, and flooded pinoak bottoms in the heart of ricelands
once grand, lush prairie. Across those prairies we drove in approaching springtime, when snipe hosts swung their long-billed migration
homeward via the vast Mississippi Valley and we shot our guns hot
when *Scolopax* fled the slashes. Too, Louisiana's tidal rims of sere
grass and, in far-gone times, acres of redheads rafting off the Texas
coast. Lullabies from drifting flights of blue geese and deeper-
throated honkers lowering to winter-graze off the bays of Lafitte.
Add fifteen years' prowling with gun, camera, and binoculars, and
my waterfowling saga is brought rapidly to date.

All in all, old Beaver Dam is typical of those duck shooting properties that have weathered the storms of encroaching civilization

because of sporting idealism that cares for and protects them. Down the years, its membership refused to quit for hell and high—or low—water. That is what tradition and the will to hunt will do for a bunch of gentlemen.

There are probably two thousand "Beaver Dam Clubs" in this country today, exclusive of the fine guides who operate on public waters and the strictly commercial gunning places. Mighty few, however, have been steadily shot over for more than sixty years and survived to offer sport. Some of the largest have been sold to the Government for wildfowl refuges; others couldn't stand the pressure of drought and restrictions, and folded up.

One thing is definite. If, during the droughts from 1929 through 1934, the majority of the worthwhile duck shooting clubs of this country hadn't stuck to their guns and, at great expense, co-operated by hoarding water and feeding highly concentrated migrations, we would have closed seasons quite awhile ago. And last but not least, the most wretched move that ever impeached the integrity of conservation was that propaganda which branded all duck club members as wealthy game hogs and, in setting class against class, dismembered our union of sportsmanship and set back the clock of wildlife restoration at least two decades.

There is good, sound restoration work going forward. But one major waterfowl problem remains, and that is the adjustment of commercial shooting's status.

It's a far cry back from my telling Johnny to stop and let me look around after we turned off the concrete highway. We could stand out there nights in the long ago and hear the swish and gentle whir of duck wings overhead. But now the only swish is that of car tires whizzing endlessly north and south. Why, that strip of concrete runs from the very breeding grounds of the North into wintering grounds of Louisiana and Mexico.

It's still farther back to that lovely forenoon of December, 1909, when Hal and I had our pleasant yesterday and our great-day-in-the-morning at old Beaver Dam. Writing this, there is a true prayer in my heart that the old club's members of today and their sons, too, will in some measure relive Hal's and my good times there.

What wouldn't I give to see those gorgeous mallards floating over the lacy cypress tops and hear Aunt Molly ringing her dinner bell and calling: "Great day in de mawnin'! Come an' git it!"

Tom Hennessey —

POTHOLE GUYS, FRIZ OUT

Gordon MacQuarrie

In his magnificent collection of Gordon MacQuarrie stories, Stories of the Old Duck Hunters & Other Drivel *(Stackpole),* Zack Taylor *describes the popular magazine writer and twenty-year Outdoor Editor of the* Milwaukee Journal: *"Physically, he was a wiry, red-headed man with a down-to-earth attitude and a quick, salty wit. He entered the field of outdoor writing when it was at a low point; most stories were poorly written, with little or no imagination. With his light humor, careful character delineation, story sense, and descriptive ability he helped raise the level of the entire field. He was a pioneer, and a dedicated conservationist when it was neither fashionable nor politic to be one." Zack's book of MacQuarrie pieces is a joy to read and a tribute to the man who wrote about hunting and fishing in the upper mid-West with style and warmth. The book's single flaw is that it missed this story, which originally appeared in* Outdoorsman *magazine and was later reprinted in the rich anthology of stories,* Outdoors Unlimited, *edited by J. Hammond Brown, sponsored by the Outdoor Writers' Association of America, and published by A.S. Barnes and Company in 1947. By the time he wrote "Pothole Guys," one of two MacQuarrie gems we are privileged to present in this collection, the author had fully developed the fictitious Old Duck Hunters' Association. The members were himself and his father-in-law, The President. In this piece the device is in its full glory. I enjoy both The President's wisdom and his wisecracks; the feel of weather coming on, bringing down the ducks; the gathering at the cabin in preparation for the hunt. What Zack said about outdoor writing then is still true today: a lot of it is poor and unimaginative. Not so, our man MacQuarrie! Here's a little tease from the piece you're about to read: "The lake in the darkness held an ominous quiet, like a creature which had threshed itself to exhaustion." What do you call that if not good and imaginative writing? Dick and Jane?*

THE PRESIDENT of the Old Duck Hunters' Association, Inc., hauled up in front of my house in the newest, gaudiest automobile which had to that date, turned west off Lake Drive onto East Lexington Boulevard.

It seemed that even the gray squirrels among the boulevard beeches were impressed by the streamlined vehicle, if not by the inelegant driver, Hizzoner himself, in a flannel shirt and battered brown hat.

I saw him coming for two blocks for I had been expecting him. The village hall and police station are his landmarks. He made a horse-shoe turn around the end of the boulevard, slid into the curb and yelled for all to hear:

"The minute I saw the jail I knew where to find you!"

Leaf raking brethren of the chase leaned on their implements and yipped. The Old Man freed himself from his imposing machine and studied a Schnauzer dog which had arrived with a band of kids to investigate the new automotive device. Anent the dog, Mister President demanded:

"Is that a dog or a bundle of oakum?" He is congenitally allergic to all but the hunting breeds.

In due course he came inside. He'd driven the dealer's super duper model up from the factory and was stopping on the way by pre-arrangement to rescue me from the city's toils.

"Going through Chicago," he explained, "every cop on Michigan Avenue made the same mental note as I drove by—'roughly dressed man in brand new auto.' If the police come, my identification papers are in the glove compartment."

He had climbed into his old hunting clothes for comfort in the long drive.

Later in the evening we loaded the car with decoys, shell boxes, duffel bags and in the early morning while the household slept the Old Duck Hunters' Association crept away.

The elements had descended. Streets were semi-granite with frozen sleet.

"Just what the doctor ordered," Mister President exulted. "If it's freezing down here, it's frozen up there."

Daylight came on the feet of snails but long before then the Old

Man bade me halt on the slippery road. With the tire gauge in one hand and a flashlight in the other he let 10 pounds of air out of each tire. After that we got along faster.

At Portage, Wis., the President was happier than ever, for snow was falling. We had breakfast and went on. North of Tomah the sleet was gone from the road and dry snow was whipping across the concrete. We re-inflated the tires and pushed on. At Chippewa Falls, crossing the big bridge, visibility up and down the Chippewa River was 200 yards.

Hizzoner nodded in the seat beside me. He was asleep and snoring at Spooner. The snow and the wind increased. The footing for tires was perfect, thanks to the built-up highway over which dry flakes rolled in sheets. Mister President awoke at Minong while a man by the name of Andy Gorud filled the tank.

"Is this it, Andy?" the Old Man asked. For an answer Andy took us to his back porch and exhibited a possession limit of snow-sprinkled redheads. Andy said indeed this was it, but if the weather kept up it might drive every duck out of the country before morning.

"Bosh!" said Mister President. "Only the shallow lakes and potholes will freeze. The ducks'll have to wet their feet in big water tomorrow morning."

Such a man, that Andy. Once he walked two miles in the rain with a heavy jack to hoist us up and put on our chains.

The snow kept up. At Gordon we turned off. The Old Man was wide awake now.

"She's a good un," he said, watching the country trunk. "Come so quick they haven't got all the snow fences up. If you see a drift, back up and give 'er tarpaper."

Tarpaper was required in several places. I complimented him on the power under the hood of his newest contraption but he was not enthusiastic—"They're all too low, no good in a two-rut road. They're making them so low pretty soon you can use a gopher hole for a garage."

It grew dark. The driving flakes stabbed at the windshield. By the time I was ready to turn off the county trunk onto the town road the Old Man had demanded the driver's seat. He knew that the in-road would be well filled with snow. I protested but he said I could drive "the day you learn your driving brains are in the seat of your pants."

There were a few spots on that narrow road between the jack pines where we barely got over the rises. The car was pushing snow 12 inches deep when we stopped at the top of the last hill.

We went ahead and got a fire going. When I got to the cabin with the first load the fireplace was roaring and he was coaxing the kitchen range to life. By the time I had hauled in the last of the gear and shoveled the snow off the stoop he had water hot enough for tea. While we ate supper the temperature slid from 28 to 24.

We hauled in wood, broke out blankets and took a hooded motor from the shed down through the snow to the lake. We took a boat off its winter roost and set it handy by the edge of the tossing lake. We brought down guns and decoys, put them in the boat and covered everything with a canvas tarp. Then there was time to size up the night.

It was a daisy. There was snow halfway to the knees on the beach. The flashlight's circle revealed a black, tossing lake. From the hill at our backs the wind screamed down through the pine trees.

"How'd you like to be a field mouse on a night like this?" Hizzoner reflected.

We went back up the hill. The last thing Mister President did was study the thermometer. I heard him say, "She's dropped to 22 and it's only 8 o'clock." After that the fireplace crackled, the wind cried, the blankets felt awfully good...

In the morning there wasn't a breath of wind. Of course he was up before me, useful and belligerent. Everything was ready, including the country smoked bacon. I started to open the door to inspect the thermometer and he announced, "Fifteen about half an hour ago."

I studied him jealously as I have often. There he was, 30 years older than I, tough as a goat, alert as a weasel. He'd just finished an exhausting business trip. Forty-eight hours before he had been 600 miles from this place. He ate six eggs to my four, eyeing me with the indulgent authority a bird dog man feels for a new pup.

"The hell with the dishes and put on all the clothes you've got," he directed.

The lake in the darkness held an ominous quiet, like a creature which had threshed itself to exhaustion. We flung off the tarp with one flip to keep snow off gear, slid in the boat, screwed on the motor and roared out.

We were afloat on blackness, rimmed with the faint white of snow on the shores. Mister President huddled in the bow in the copious brown mackinaw, its collar inches above his ears. He fished in pockets and drew on mittens and when his hands were warmed he fished again and presently a match glowed over the bowl of his crooked little pipe. I saw that he was grinning, so throttled the motor and yelled, "What's the joke?"

"No joke," he came back. "Just a morning for the books."

The run to this place requires about 30 minutes. Dim landmarks on shore were illuminated just enough by the snow. We cut wide around the shallow point bar and went south for the shallow end of the lake. The Old Man has bet that he can, blindfold, land an outboard within 100 yards of the shallow bay point from our beach. There are no takers.

A little daylight was making as I cut the speed and turned toward the shore. The President said, "Go back down the shore farther from the blind. The boat'll stand out against the snow like a silo." We beached 200 yards from the point.

There was plenty of time. When the Old Man is master of ceremonies you get up early enough to savor the taste of morning. And what a morning! Just once in a coon's age do the elements conspire with latitude to douse North Wisconsin with snow of mid-winter depth in October. It is a very lovely thing. We toted up the gear to the blind. I was impatient to get out in the shallows in my waders and spread decoys. The Old Man detained me.

"I suppose," he said, "that when a man quits liking this it's time to bury him."

He was determined to size up the morning, and he did size it up. Between hauls on the blackened briar he continued, "Once before I saw this point just as pretty. Back in 1919. Just about the same depth of snow, same old lake black as ink, trees ag'in the sky..."

I had paused to honor his rhapsody, so he snorted, "Get them boosters out there, dang yuh, while I rebuild the blind!"

Rebuild it he did, pausing now and then in the growing light to tell me where to place the next decoy. In the blind I found he had the rough bench swept off, the blind repaired and a Thermos of coffee at hand. He sat on the right side of the bench and both our guns, his automatic and my double, were held away from the snowy wall of the blind by forked sticks. It was unmercifully cold for sitting. He explained his thesis for the day—

"The potholes chilled over in the night. The ice crep' out from shore. The ducks huddled up, getting closer and closer as the ice reached for 'em. First good daylight they'll look around at each other and say, 'Let's go. This place is getting too crowded'."

"You don't suppose they've all left the country?" I ventured. There was scorn in his reply.

"The best ducks stay 'til the last dog's hung."

A burst of bluebills went over and planed into the lake, far out.

"They were up awfully high for cold weather ducks," I said. "I'm afraid if they move they'll go a long ways today—if there are any left around."

"They'll be lower," He said.

A pair dropped in from in back of us. It was apparent they'd come in from any quarter in the absence of wind. I reached for the gun and slid out a toe to kick my shellbox. The Old Man put a mittened hand on my right knee. I could feel his fingers squeeze through leather and wool. Following his eyes I saw what he saw.

They were at the left, about a hundred ducks, an embroidery of ducks, skeined out in a long line with a knot at the head. We crouched down and the Old Man whispered:

"Pothole guys, friz out. Might be from Minnesota. Maybe Ontario. They'll swing and size 'er up and the whole dang bundle will——."

Swi-i-i-ish!

While we had watched the mid-lake flock fifty or so had slid into the decoys, bluebills everyone. The President from his corner eyed me and whispered, "Flyin' high did you say? No, don't shoot! We're gonna have fun."

The mid-lake flock swung in, decoyed by their confident cousins. The President of the Old Duck Hunters grinned like a school boy.

He was on his knees in the trampled snow, close against the front wall of the blind. So was I and he was laughing at me. Fifty ducks sat in the decoys, another hundred were coming in, and the Old Man said to me:

"Hold out your hand so I can see if you're steady."

At the moment that the landed birds were flailing out the incomers were tobogganing in with their wing flaps down. The Old Man arose and shouted:

"Hello, kids!"

His deliberateness was maddening. I emptied the double before he brought up his automatic. I reloaded and fired again and he still had a shell to go. He spent it expertly on a drake.

Then the ducks were gone and I was trying to stuff a round brass match safe into the breech and the Old Man was collapsed on the bench, laughing.

"Up high for cold weather ducks!" he howled.

There were seven down, two far out, and as I raced back for the boat Mister President heckled, "Wish I had that East Lexington Boulevard Snootzer here and I'd learn him to be a dog!"

As I rowed out for the pick-up he shouted across the water, "Do you get a bottle of turpentine with every Snootzer you buy?"

As he had predicted, it was a day for the books. The clouds pressed down. They leaned against the earth. No snow fell but you knew it might any minute. There were not just clouds but layers of clouds, and ramparts and bastions and lumps of clouds in between the layers.

We sat and drank coffee. We let bluebills sit among the decoys. That was after Hizzoner decreed, "No more 'bills. Pick the redheads if you can. If you miss a mallard I'll kill yuh."

The quick dark day sped by. To have killed a hundred diving ducks apiece would have been child's play. Canvasback, whistlers, mergansers, redheads, and bluebills by the hundreds trouped over the hundred-year old decoys which are the sole property of the Old Duck Hunters' Association.

"I'd give a lot for a brace of mallards to color up the bag," he said.

The Lady Who Waits for Mister President likes mallards.

Be assured, mallards were present, as well as those dusky wise men, black ducks. They would swing in high over the open water and look it over. They did not care for any part of our point blind in the snow.

"Wise guys," Mister President said. "They see the point and two dark objects against the snow in the blind, and one of the objects wiggling all over the place. That'll be you."

We went back to the boat and fetched the white tarpaulin. He threw it over the top of the blind and propped up the front of it with cut poles. The tarp erased us from above and seven laboring mallards swung closer. Before throwing off the tarp, Mister President whispered: "Slow down sos'te to nail 'em."

Back went the tarp. I missed a climber, then crumpled him. Hizzoner collected three. He just spattered them. Because these were for the Lady Who Waits.

We picked up and hauled out, raising rafted diving ducks in the long run back.

We hoisted the boat onto its winter trestles, upside down, to let it drain and dry. We put the gear beneath it and slung the tarp over it. We went up the hill and stirred the fires.

I got supper. I worried about the super-duper on the hilltop at the road's end but he said he had drained it. I lugged in more wood and heaped up the fireplace.

He said in the morning we might have to break ice to get out from shore. He said, "we might not see much more than whistlers." He said to steep the tea good. He said not to forget to climb down the well and open the bleeder on the pump "because she's going to really drop tonight." He said he thought he'd "take a little nap 'fore supper." And finally he said:

"Draw them mallards will yuh, son? She likes 'em drawed."

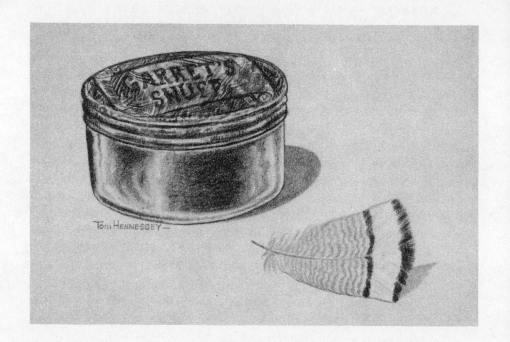

MOSS, MALLARDS AND MULES

Bob Brister

This is the title piece from Bob Brister's marvelous collection of stories published by Winchester Press in 1973. Brister has few peers as an outdoorsman who can do it all—and that includes writing lively and convincing prose that is rich in scene, character and action. Although you may have read him mostly in his shooting pieces in Field & Stream, *Bob has been published on a variety of subjects in leading magazines. As Outdoor Editor of the Houston* Chronicle *in 1961, he received a Pulitzer Prize nomination for his coverage of Hurricane Carla. Renowned as the top shot with the scattergun, he is a confirmed Southwesterner whose worldwide experiences have taught him that he's got the best right there at home.*

THE ACORNS had begun to fall around Uncle William's shack at the edge of the Trinity River bottoms, and cold rain had moistened the red and brown leaves and left the air fresh and crisp in the early mornings.

Uncle William was behind the barn, hitching up the wood wagon, and I was waiting to go with him because not even the old Ford pickup with the mud-grip tires could get down into that black-gumbo bottom after a rain.

In those days Uncle William and I had a sort of unwritten agreement; certain staples such as Blue Ribbon Malt Extract, empty gallon jugs, and occasionally a length of copper tubing were quietly brought to him from town.

In exchange, he took along and tolerated a somewhat precocious white boy in the throes of learning about hunting, fishing, girls and hound dogs. And he did so with the total discipline of age and authority.

"You jess as well leave thet shotgun to the house," he warned. "Today is wood-cuttin' an' line-settin' day, an' you know duck season don't open till Sattidy."

A finger-in-nose delegation of jet-black small fry poured out of the shack to look me over, stairstepped proof of prolificacy for an old man in his seventies who had children as young as some of his grandchildren.

Two or three of them were jumping up and down, pointing toward the barn and what was obviously a developing conflict between Uncle William and a mule named Rodney.

"Lookit ole Roahd-nay go," they chanted in glee. "He sho gonna git hainted now!"

Rodney's mind was apparently made. He reared, backed up, kicked the barn . . . stirring out a cackling procession of setting hens, pigeons, and squealing hogs . . . and with his ears laid back defied Uncle William to force the bit into his mouth.

"Haint him!" the rooting section chanted. "Haint him now, wheah we kin watch!"

I had heard the word "haint" used by colored folk referring to ghosts or spirits. After all, the logical thing to haunt something would be a "haint." But I didn't grasp this usage.

"You ain't never seen Uncle William haint nothin'?" one of the older boys whooped gleefully. "He kin put haints in anythin', bad haints. Las' summer he hainted a lizard fo' us, an' dat lizard clumb straight up de chimney an' jumped off lak' a flyin' squirul!"

About that time Uncle William began making some strange sounds, in a tongue unknown to me, and suddenly he jumped back and raised both hands high over his head.

Rodney stood there a minute. He sneezed mightily. He lay down in the corral mud and rolled over twice, kicking all four legs straight up into the air as if trying to run upside down, braying and bawling at the top of his lungs. Then he rolled over, shook himself, and stood placidly while Uncle William harnessed him to the wagon.

We climbed in and rattled off toward the timber, no questions asked, because Uncle William would discuss haints only if he wanted to anyway, and Rodney had become a paragon of pulling power.

In the foreboding darkness of the moss-draped cypress, mists were rising from the brown current of the river. Giant alligator gars rolled, and the overhanding willows, vines and semitropical vegetation might as well have been the Amazon. I would not have gone in that bottom on a dark day without Uncle William.

He cut through the woods, dodging the low places, and finally stopped the wagon a long way off as he always did when he was coming to his "cookin' place," I had to sit in the wagon and wait; he didn't want any witnesses nor wagon tracks to his "kitchen."

He came back presently, rolling a big oaken barrel. He never dumped the mash near the still for several reasons, one being that he always had something else to do with it.

"I ought to put dis heah in de perch hole wheah we cut dem new willows," he said. "Perch likes it moah'n people. But you's got youself in such a fizz to go duck huntin' we maybe better take it over to de slough."

"Will ducks eat that stuff?"

"Will dey eat it? Boy, once dey gets a taste of it, dey all but starves lookin' fo' mo'. Dem mallets gits high as a minister in a hoah house on a little of dis 'stuff,' as you calls it."

Without looking at him, I knew Uncle William had finally decided I was old enough for man talk, because it was the first time he had ever mentioned a minister in a whorehouse, and also the way he said it meant he was ready to answer some of the questions I had been asking for a long time.

"How old is yoah runnin' buddy, Richard, now?"

"Fifteen, I think."

"An' you keep botherin' me wantin' to know what wrong wid him an' how come he won't go coon huntin' wid us no mo'. You don't notice him hangin' 'round dat li'l Smith girl?"

"What's that got to do with coon hunting?"

"Enough dat he ain't got time fo' no coons rat now. Ain't nothin' wrong wid ole Dick; he jess cockstruck."

"How can you keep that from happening to you?"

"Well, you kin not ever git to be mo' than foteen, or you could try an' jump a bobwire fence an' not quite make it, or you could get youself some li'l ole girl just because she a girl an' not git sweet on her. But since you ain't gonna do none o' dem things, best way is to stay outa town till you know what to do 'bout dat problem."

"I know already."

"Uh huh; you thinks you knows. No man knows nothin' 'bout thet till he git thirty-five, an' after that he just find out how little he do know."

"Well then, why do I have to learn it all the hard way, why can't you just tell me what is the best kind of girl to have and all that? You've had enough of 'em."

He grunted, belly bobbing in the overalls, and spit a stream of snuff. "You jess looks fo' de one dat make you think you really doin' somethin' to her; if dat be good enough, she likely git to believin' it, too."

He reached beneath the wagon seat, pulled out the clear, half-gallon jug with the handle on it, and threw up his left arm to cradle the jug, pulling three deliberate, sucking swallows around the dip of snuff.

Then he screwed the lid back on, ignoring the request I had already made a hundred times.

"You gits a sip o' dat when you gits old enough to handle it an' know what to do wid it. The very devil in dat jug, boy, an' he git out if you ain't ready fo' him."

The mules bogged down to their bellies a couple of times crossing the river end of the duck slough, and half a dozen mallards exploded out of the button willows well within shotgun range. I wished mightily for the .410.

He got out of the wagon, picked up the crosscut saw, and motioned for me to take the other end. As we worked, I couldn't help but ask why he had to pick a great big pecan of a squirrel tree, right by the edge of the bottom, not doing anybody any good.

"Fo' one thing, pecan wood happen to be de best fo' several purposes, one bein' to smoke sausages, an' fo' another thing, dis heah tree dead anyway, if you didn't notice, 'cause the moss choke it to death, an' fo' another thing we is rat now making' a li'l white boy a cinch place to kill hisself a mallet duck next Sattidy, lessen he don't keep on pesterin' de brains o' dis outfit.

"You notice a quail or duck in de bresh; very fust thing he think 'bout before he jump is how he gonna git outta der widout gettin' tangled up in de limbs. He pick out de best openin' an' go right out it every time. We jess made ourselves de best openin' on dis slough, an' every duck on it gonna come out clost 'nough wheah even a white boy wid a .410 can worry one to death as dey goes by. Now come help me roll dis bar'l o' mash."

The next Saturday was a drizzling, dreary day, fitting for revelations of haints or mallards, and when we stopped the wagon in the wet underbrush Uncle William sent two of his older boys around the slough.

"Go all de way aroun' now, long way out in de bottom from de slough, an' come back up thisaway slow an' quiet. Jess play lak you all got guns staid o' sticks. Dem mallets need a chance to swim up thisaway before dey jumps."

Uncle William sauntered his girth down through the bushes without getting wet, not making a sound, and stopped beside the big downed pecan. He backed up against a tree, dropped two shells into his old 12-gauge hammer gun with the copper wire wrapped around the stock, and told me to keep still.

Our drivers weren't making a sound. Thirty minutes passed, and a woodpecker worked diligently on the downed trunk of the dead pecan. Then suddenly a wood duck squealed, there was a muffled roar of wings, and a beautiful pair of mallard drakes were heading straight for us, wings beating, heavy necks straining to clear the trees.

Uncle William got them both, and with his shots the air was full of ducks. A beautiful wood duck drake passed, not fifteen feet from the end of the gun, but I wanted more than all else a mallard, a big greenhead.

Three hens passed and I heard Uncle William's double speak twice more, and then there was the greenhead coming straight to me through the hole and I pulled the little .410 barrel out in front of him, jerked the trigger, and he dropped like a rock.

Some of the ducks were still circling, and one mallard hen was hanging right over the trees, even after all that gunfire, quacking her heart out. I started up with the gun, and Uncle William grabbed the barrel.

"She's jess a l'il tite on dat mash," he chuckled. "Someday you be tite an' maybe somebody won't kill you fo' talkin' too much."

His boys came running up excitedly, wading out in the cold water to pick up the ducks, and I stroked the green head of the biggest drake and announced that he was mine.

"No suh," Uncle William said firmly, "thass yo duck." He pointed to a scraggly little bird of a species I had never seen, with a high green topknot on his head, a narrow beak for a bill, and less than half the size of the fat mallards. But I knew I had shot a mallard; he had looked as big as a goose up there, white breast shining against the dark cypress trees.

I turned over the little duck, and his breast was white, and under his wings was white. But he was not a mallard.

The little boys gathered around. "Did you haint dat duck, pappa? Look how he done drawed up to wheah his head don't fit his feathers no mo'; pappa done shrunk dat duck!"

Uncle William's belly was bouncing inside the overalls, but he didn't say anything until we were halfway home, and the boys had picked the ducks as we went, talking among themselves but afraid to pick the "hainted" one.

"Ain't much to haintin' things fo' dem younguns," he said, speaking low and watching to see, the boys didn't hear.

He produced the brown bottle of Garrett's Snuff from his overalls.

"Jess put a l'il pinch o' dis in a lizard's mouf, an' he plumb go wild. An' a dog dat barks at night, pshaw, one dip an' de devil got his tongue. But ole Rodney, now dat mule he takes half a handful to do right. Some powerful haints in dis one l'il jar," he grinned, "but don't you go tellin' dem younguns. Dat duck you kilt is a l'il ole trash duck, dey calls 'um mergansers o' somethin', an' dey ain't fit to eat noway; tastes lak spoilt fish."

I pondered this hainting business.

"If one of your boys wouldn't mind you sometime, you wouldn't haint him, would you?"

Uncle William looked at me sidewise. "Man carryin' a big pistol," he philosophized, "most likely never have to use it . . .

"Naw, boy, I ain't givin' no stuff to no chillun . . . all I kin do to keep in it fo' me an' ole Rodney. Dat old mule," he chuckled, slapping the wide, bluish back lightly with the reins. "He sumptin. Dat mule ain't really been mean nor bad in three o' fo' years. He too old now. But he jess have dat tough act he go through every now an' den when he need a dip o' snuff."

POT LUCK

Roland Clark

*Students of outdoor literature will already know that Roland Clark was a star in the Derrydale lineup, producing two books of stories and paintings—*Stray Shots *(1931) and* Gunner's Dawn *(1937). He also did* Roland Clark's Etchings *for Derrydale in 1938, and some now-famous prints.* Pot Luck *would have made a Derrydale-triple for Clark, but alas this third book of stories and pictures was not ready when the Derrydale dream ended in 1942. The book was published by A.S. Barnes, New York, as a Countryman Press Book in 1945. Introducing the book* Pot Luck—*our selection here is the title story, one of six in the book—John Holman says of Clark: "We who have known him long and loved him well have come to consider Clark and wildfowl as one and the same word. It is impossible to think of one without the other. This has come about because he has not only written so delightfully about ducks—his favorite theme—and the men who hunt them, but he has also been drawing, painting and etching them with masterful technique for many years. This combination of author-artist has made him great among all others of wildfowling." We'll go along with that!*

HE WAS affectionately known as "the doctor" in our county, although I doubt whether he had ever qualified, professionally, for the title thus bestowed upon him.

However, Doc Airlee could set a bone when necessary, or "break" a stubborn fever. When a horse ran afoul of a stray barbwire, he could stitch the wound with the skill of a practiced surgeon. The most efficacious treatment for stone bruise, sore throat, and such minor afflictions was at his fingers' ends. No malady, however trifling, failed to receive his care.

He used to ride into town astride a rangy thoroughbred and he never missed a Court Day, let it come rain or shine. Just behind his horse's heels a gaunt old hound kept a difficult pace, stopping from time to time to scratch in a languid sort of way as though it wasn't worthwhile after all.

Inseparable was this trio. You never saw the one without the other, and you might meet them at all times, night or day, and in unexpected places. Distances were long in our county. "Neighbors" lived far apart. Just what section of the county the doctor hailed from, I hadn't the faintest idea. That a fondness for sport, moreover, had any part in his life I never suspected until several years after I had come to live in Virginia.

For two successive days I had miscalculated the weather. The blow I looked for failed to blow. The sun shone out of a cloudless sky. No slightest breeze blew over the marsh, and by the same token the ducks, which I had hoped to find in plenty, continued to drowse in the open water, and be damned to all my plans. And so I kicked my heels in a stuffy blind, cussing the luck and Solda, my Pamunkey guide, and thinking dismally of the thirty-mile drive back home.

"No ducks come. Better tomorrow," Solda grunted—the optimistic "tomorrow" of all educated guides. "Solda," I said, "you underrate my intelligence. Home, sweet home, for me and *now*. Your cabin needs much airing. Your food is vile. Ducks are on a holiday. Only the weather is beautiful—so beautiful that it gives me pain." Then I hit the road, resolved to strain old Jezebel to the limit on the long trip that lay before me.

If I had paid proper attention to my driving, I wouldn't have struck the stump. I wouldn't have hurled my car into the ditch, nor would I have gained a friendship which has lasted through the years. Standing over my half-buried car, I debated whether I could establish sleeping quarters within her angling body. Already miles from Solda's camp, on an unfrequented road, I saw little chance of a helping hand to pull me out of the ditch. Then I saw the doctor ride out of the swamp a hundred yards ahead. He was mounted as usual, the hound at his heels, and across his saddle dangled two great bronze gobblers, their heads almost touching the ground.

"Spoiled a mighty nice shot for me," he growled. "Called a flock almost up to the blind when you raised this confounded racket."

I was mildly apologetic, thinking, none the less, that his misfortune was far less important than mine and that he already had a bag that should satisfy anyone.

"Well," he said at length, "what's the matter? Broken steering-gear? Bent axle? Um'm—both, I reckon. Damned poor contraptions anyway. Let's see. We've got to do something."

I was glad of the "we." He was mollified, interested, apparently, in getting me out of a mess. It was a desperate case from the first. Pushing and hauling, with Airlee's nag pressed into service at one period, we continued our efforts till the sun had set and shadows had deepened about us.

"Whew! I give up," he said at last. "We've tried everything. Get what traps you have, and let's go home. Pot luck, understand. But Wash will dig up something for supper, and at least I can give you a bed."

"Home" proved to be a full three miles away, over a narrow trail and through thickset pinelands, now dark as Egypt with the near approach of night. But I was glad enough to accept the doctor's hospitality, and I made this clear to him as we rode and walked, by turns, through the somber forest.

A little daylight remained as we emerged from the high bluff of pines and looked down on the lower ground. I could just make out a rambling structure with outbuildings scattered about it, and a giant cottonwood towering high in the fading dusk. The Rappahannock stretched away in the distance and a full moon rising above its banks lent a glamorous air to a picture that I have remembered to this day.

I seemed to see this land below me as strangely aloof from the world; an isolated principality over which my host, alone, ruled with a lordly hand.

I was soon to find verification of the mental picture I had drawn. As we reached the house an old Darky stepped from the shadows, ready to take the horse.

"Well, here we are," the Doctor said, dismounting. "The place has always been called 'Kenjockety,' an Indian name. It means a quiet, restful spot. Perhaps you'll find it so."

Dogs were barking, children shouting, and an indistinct sound of music underlay all—an air of gay and splendid confusion dominated the entire premises. "All part of my family," the doctor laughed. "I take care of them; they look after me. An excellent arrangement." Then we were in the house, a house strongly suggestive of the hubbub that reigned outdoors. Nothing seemed in its proper place. A piano served as a resting spot for saddles, guns, mounted birds, and a miscellany of other things. Pictures hung askew on the walls. A ship model stood on a broken chair, and two setter puppies romped from room to room quite oblivious of our presence.

The doctor, standing beside me, evidently saw nothing amiss in all this. No doubt it was the customary order in which he lived his life. "A quiet, restful spot," he had said, and I remembered a glint of humor in his eye as he explained the Indian name.

"Wash! O, Wash!" Airlee shouted. "Asleep, I'll bet. And that's for huntin' coons all night.

"Naw suh. Wash, he op'nin' eysters. Must I tell him yo' 'all is come?"

The voice came from some remote quarter, but Airlee was off without a reply and for a time I was left to delve deeper into the oddities of that room.

My years in Virginia have taught me that a 'supper' may mean a feast. Larders appear to be at all times supplied from an inexhaustible source. I shan't elaborate over old Wash's menu that evening, only to remark in passing that Chesapeake oysters and roasted black duck furnished a fair foundation for a sumptuous repast. Lingering over the table, I learned something of the doctor's "family" and his philosophy of life.

"Work and play. A proper balance between the two gives the best assurance of contentment and leaves little time for worry, or the harboring of regrets. That sums up my code. Simple, sensible," he laughed. "I've never found a better. I work to make my play a success. Those turkeys, now. You'll hardly know the patience it takes to fool a wise old gobbler. I watched their range for a week or more; then I threw up a blind on the edge of the swamp. Today was the first time that I managed to call them within range. Tomorrow, the next day perhaps, I'll be off to the end of the county, and I call this a working day. Lad down there with a fever. Fisherman's son, *and* a cripple. Right poor folk they are, too, but I reckon I've helped them one way or another to get over a few rough spots."

"Yes," he continued, "first and last, there's a lot of fun in life. Patchin' people up is one thing, seein' them get along afterwards is what really counts. Many you'll see at Kenjockety have had their troubles. White and black, I took 'em in, gave them land to farm on shares, seed and tools—all the rest. They have boats to work my oyster beds, and they can get lumber out of the woods. Old Carter's boy takes care of the stock, and Wash has a couple of husky boys who look after my duck blinds every year, stick new ones when I need them, and keep decoys in shape. I think they're all contented. Certainly I have no complaint."

I slept that night in an old four-poster—high, wide and comfortable, after my stay at Solda's camp. I thought of the successive Airlees who, through the years, must have sunk, like myself, into the depths of that mammoth bed. And I thought of my poor deserted car, piled up in the roadside ditch. What could I do about that? I must . . . Oh, pshaw! Let the morrow . . . .

Surely, something was wrong. I knew, now! It was the rattling of the shutters. Wind! Wind that blew in angry gusts, tearing at flimsy sashes and moaning dismally about the eaves. The blow which I had earlier looked for was on us now in all its strength. Strange noises, sounding apart from the wind, came to me from the house itself. Voices. The doctor's, clearly heard above the general din. He was at my door now, a candle in his hand.

"What is it?" I asked, bouncing out of bed.

"It's mainly black duck, I reckon. There's usually a scattering of sprig in the pond and maybe a goose or two for good measure. Want to try 'em? The wind ought to drive a lot of ducks in!"

He spoke a little apologetically, as though loath to rouse me from my slumbers. But I was already out of the blankets. Did I want to try them! Hell, yes! Where were my boots—my gun and shells?

"Take it easy," Airlee chuckled, "plenty of time for a bite of breakfast. It's barely six o'clock and we haven't far to go!"

Outdoors, the sleet was driving, each particle a steely barb that struck with merciless force. Three sturdy colored boys toted our traps: guns, cartridges, and a charcoal stove which the doctor insisted was indispensable to his comfort in a frigid, wind-swept blind.

A fifteen-minute walk through stubble fields and marsh brought us to a broad creek, and we poled across to the opposite bank, not without some difficulty, for our boat was small and unadapted to the carrying of heavy loads.

A faint light showed in the east as we waded ashore and pushed through the heavy sedge grass bordering the stream.

"Move as quietly as you can," Airlee whispered. "Our pond is just inside this grass and I hope to show you a raft of ducks when it lightens up a bit."

"All right," I answered—and promptly stumbled noisily over a sunken log.

Instantly came the beating of wings. At our feet—to the right and left of us—rose squads of startled ducks faintly outlined against the dim screen of dawn.

"Just as well to put them up. They'll be back before we are well set out." The doctor was in high spirits, and I shared in his enthusiasm, despite a soggy boot.

"We'd better split up this morning," he said. "Sam will rig you in the north blind, and I'll take a chance across from you. That way we'll keep them from settling in any part of the pond!"

Sam and his dusky partner were hauling our skiff across the bank. All was hurry and bustle now. My gun and shell box, rubber poncho and blanket were quickly tossed into a second skiff, and we were off in the teeth of the wind.

Day was breaking through the clouds and I could now see that Airlee's pond was really a sizeable lake in the woods, with thick pines on three of its sides. I saw, moreover, a legion of ducks spread over the water before me.

Sam was all excitement. "Great Day," he exploded, "I ain't know so many ducks been bo'n. Must be de sky done rain 'em down!"

Our decoys looked rather messy when, at length, we had them out. But ducks were over us most of the time while we dropped the blocks, and those that fouled or dragged their weights we left just as they were. *I wanted to get in that blind!*

Airlee had beaten me to it. The bark of his gun every minute or two assured me that he was keeping busy at the farther end of the pond.

How dark they looked, yet illusive, through the blanket of pelting sleet! They sped down the wind like bullets, then turned in an ever narrowing arc to breast up to the decoys. Fifty yards? No, forty! Now! Whang! Whang! I watched them tower into the murk with a lively sense of shame. "Dub!" I said to myself. "How long have you been shooting black duck? Yes, seventy yards, possibly more. You *thought*—oh, quit your grousing!"

A pintail drake was over the stool, widespread wings now motionless. Ah, easy did it that time! A clean right to the target. Boy, you're pretty good, after all! More blacks. A pair of widgeon now driving to the rig. Which would get in first? Widgeon. All right. Remember the light—the lead—the wind. I was concentrating on those widgeon with devastating zeal. Now they were almost over the blind, my twisted neck refusing to allow me to see them farther. Quickly, I turned to catch them while still within decent range. I centered one with my first shot, and the second went down with a resounding splash to windward of the decoys. When later he washed ashore with the seas, I counted myself quite lucky. There could be no fun in attending to cripples on such a day as this.

Once or twice I heard the call of flying geese, but they sounded high above the pond and seemed to be travel-bent.

It was, after all, the blacks and the mallard that furnished the best shooting on that long-remembered day. A lull in the flight, shortly after full daylight, gave way to the greatest movement of ducks I have ever seen in a like constricted area. As the clouds shifted, and clearing weather promised, long lines of black duck, sprig, and widgeon streamed in from the Rappahannock to find comparative shelter in Doc Airlee's pond. The business of the day was really started by the lifting of those clouds. A wing-tipped mallard contributed largely toward the making of my bag. Now a crippled mallard in heavy seas is something to regret and forget, a conclusion which many a gunner has arrived at long ago.

But Sam was not of their persuasion.

"Doctor Airlee he say yo'all ain't do right to leave no ducks for de hawks an' owl to pick on. Naw, suh, I don' need no gun," he answered when I spoke of this small detail. "I goin' to git her with dis yere paddle." And Sam put out from shore.

Ducks that had rafted below us were instantly on the wing. His noisy paddle was constantly stirring them up to lee'ard, when I was sure of a shot from the blind. I must have been engrossed in Sam's operations, for I never saw a bunch of mallards until they had pitched to the decoys. Twenty or more were in the flock, and they seemed to accept my jumbled stool as bona fide pals.

Suddenly they discovered their mistake and, rising as one bird, swept directly over the blind. I picked a big old greenhead, to my eyes well in the van, and mentally counted him in the bag before I had pulled the trigger. But who can time the rapidity with which ducks shift position? Who has completely mastered the vexing problem of "lead?" My greenhead, unscathed, was climbing to the skies, while below him it was raining mallard. Again I had misjudged that damnable lead and had driven my load into "the brown." Sam, returning from his futile mission, managed to retrieve five ducks from my late barrage; I am afraid he left several others for the hawks and owls to "pick on."

In spite of his vehement protests (Sam was having a wonderful time), I decided to call it a day. The bag limit which, I regret to say, was not too scrupulously observed in that era, had been reached. The doctor's gun had been silent for a long while, and it was time to make for the house.

Airlee was picking over our pile of ducks with evident satisfaction. Pintail, mallard, widgeon, black ducks—all were spread before us, their varied colors fusing in an alluring pattern that continued to hold our eyes.

"And you didn't get a goose," he said. "I'm mighty disappointed. They were right high-minded today."

"Doctor," I said, "what is a goose, either here or there? I've had a tiptop, bang-up day. All unexpected, I won't say out of a clear sky exactly, but every sky has a silver lining and this one produced the goods. Blessings on the ugly stump that threw me into your hands."

Once returned to the house, a fresh surprise awaited me. Jezebel, polished until her old face glittered, stood solidly in the doctor's roadway. Her bones seemed whole, her frame intact. Her salvage, none the less, remained to be explained.

"The boys managed it," Airlee chuckled. "I left word this morning to take a yoke of oxen and haul it over here. But I didn't mention the polish. They thought of that themselves.

She moaned and groaned, wheezed and sputtered, in her customary way. Nothing appeared to have gone amiss from a night spent in the open, and she certainly looked much better than I had remember her for years.

The skies had cleared and bright sunlight shone on Kenjockety as I took my leave of the doctor and of the "family" group assembled to see me off. At the last moment a small Darky scuttled up with one of my host's fine turkeys and thrust it into the car.

"Don't forget to hang him awhile," the doctor admonished. "The big ones are sometimes tough."

ONE TO GET READY ....
AND TWO TO GO

Harold P. Sheldon

This matched-pair of stories, presented here as one selection, appeared originally as back-to-back chapters in Sheldon's third book of Tranquillity stories, Tranquillity Regained. *Sheldon wrote* Tranquillity *for Derrydale in 1936. Countyman Press printed three volumes in 1945:* Tranquillity, Tranquillity Revisited, *and* Tranquillity Regained. *In 1973, Winchester Press published all three volumes combined into one book,* The Tranquillity Stories. *It is hard to think of the Tranquillity series without conjuring up images of grouse and woodcock shooting, for the books are packed with classic tales of the New England uplands. Among the other diverse pieces that make the books so memorable to me, this duck hunting sequence ranks as my favorite. The familiar characters are in full fig here, the Colonel and the Judge, and we see them as they fidget through preparations for the opening day of duck season. The day arrives, and we go with them out onto the marsh. The story is as simple as that, but boy does it work! The magic of getting ready—fiddling with gear, plotting a strategy, even the celebration of a pre-hunt meal—all combine to make this tale feel like something lived, rather than merely read. Wounded at the Meuse-Argonne in World War I, Sheldon returned to civilian life in his beloved Vermont in 1919. He was Game Commissioner of Vermont from 1921 to 1926, and worked with the Fish and Wildlife Service, Department of the Interior, until his retirement in 1943. He wrote many magazine articles in addition to the Tranquillity books and was well known as a gun collector. Sheldon became a close friend of Nash Buckingham during his stint in Washington and appears in several of Buckingham's stories. Despite his varied career, Sheldon the writer is most remembered for his evocative treatment of New England sporting life. In* The Tranquillity Stories, *the Colonel was in his element, at home, and truly at his best.*

ONE TO GET READY —

THE NARROW southern extremity of the Lake which leads from Fort Ticonderoga to the village that was called Skenesboro on the old colonial maps is a region of singular beauty and charm. From the rugged cliffs of gray limestone which rise abruptly from the eastern shore it is no more than a long rifle shot to the foothills of the Adirondacks on the opposite bank. Between these massive barriers lie great marshes, the haunt of wildfowl and muskrat and also, in due and proper season, of the fraternity of gunners, fishermen and trappers who go there seeking sport or profit.

It was nearly sunset of a quiet September day when two men descended a steep wooded bluff on the eastern shore and after briefly surveying their surroundings found seats for themselves on the exposed roots of a great butternut tree which grew at the water's edge.

They were dressed in worn and faded shooting clothes, and their long boots were splashed with mud, but, other than a pair of hatchets, they bore no weapons.

One of them, a lean and grizzled individual, fished out a package of cigarettes and offered it to his companion.

"No, thank you, my boy," said the Judge, "I believe I'll fill my pipe." Which he proceeded to do, and when the tobacco was well lighted he rested his thick shoulders against the gray bark of the butternut and lifted his gaze in owlish contemplation of the scene before them.

There was a curious unwonted atmosphere of complacency and virtue about the pair. They grinned at each other and the Judge between puffs emitted a low and happy sound. Had it issued from any throat other than that of a dignified Justice of the Supreme Court it could only have been described as a purr.

"When it comes to the business of duck shooting," he remarked sententiously, "there's nothing like being forehanded, my boy. I'm good an' tired of leaving things to the last minute an' having to flounder around in the dark trying to locate a place to shoot from and building blinds in places where no ducks come, and, like as not, if they *do* come, the dawn's early light discloses that the dang blind is wrong side to or something. A blind ain't worth much, you see, if you can't see the ducks and the ducks can see you. That ought to be apparent even to a person of your questionable intelligence."

The Captain snorted.

"I've heard that song before, you old, fat, slothful devil. But who's responsible for our present very favorable prospects? Who was it that found you drowsing at your desk and forced you to come out here and engage in a little unwonted activity? I'll tell you who it was; it was—"

The Judge interrupted. "I *know* who it was! I wasn't asleep, I was just momentarily relaxing from my labors," he declared, "but let it pass. The main thing is that the day after tomorrow we can arise at a reasonable hour, partake of a satisfactory breakfast, pick up Cam at his house and proceed without heat, discomfiture, or undue haste to the Big Slough. Once here we will, or *I* will, wet my right forefinger and hold it aloft. Having by this means determined the direction of the wind we'll know which blinds to occupy and from then on it will be merely a matter of shooting ducks."

"The easiest thing in the world," agreed the Captain.

Before them spread the flat alluvial marshes covered, at this season, with rippling banks of wild oats and rushes as yet untouched by frost. A winding channel of open water divided the green morass. In times past this narrow waterway had been a link in the principal line of communication between the Province of Quebec and the settlements of the Hudson River Valley. But for a thousand years before that, these verdant shores had known the light ripple of the canoes of Iroquois and Algonquin war parties. The Jesuits, too, had passed this way on the grim path to martyrdom. Afterward, for a century and a half, the cliffs echoed again and again to the roll of drums and the squeal of pipes, the crash of musketry and the thunder of heavy ordnance as the reverberations of an Old World quarrel rose and fell and finally died away in the forests and mountains of the New.

Then, following Burgoyne's disastrous invasion, for many peaceful years, barges laden with tea, salt, soft iron billets, gunpowder and other necessities and luxuries had voyaged northward to the settlements and landings to return with cargoes made up of the rude products of the frontier.

When the coming of the railways finally ended the romantic bois-terous heyday of the "canal boaters," the craft continued in dimin-ished numbers and dingier aspect to carry burdens of lumber, coal, oil and other supplies, accepting these humble tasks without complaint.

Our friends beneath the butternut tree were made aware that they were about to witness the passage of a group of these burthen-bearers, for the valley echoed the slow rhythmical thud of an en-gine, and presently a tug swam into view around Maple Bend trailing three long barges under its plume of smoke. As it proceeded, the silent reaches of the marsh came to noisy life. The slow waves spread-ing from blunt bows raised the vegetation in long, hissing undula-tions which brought acute dismay to the rails and bitterns hiding in the rushes. Great pickerel darted from their ambuscades; startled black ducks and teal sprang aloft from the suddenly agitated pools where they had been basking and preening, countless frogs and tur-tles felt the mounting panic and plopped incontinently overboard from the mudbanks and bits of water-logged driftwood along the shore. A kingfisher, who had learned long since how he might reap profit from these alarms, sat quietly upon a willow stub until a school of nervous minnows darted into view and then, with a triumphant rattle and a downright plunge, snatched a silvery fish for his supper.

All these signs and activities were observed with profound interest by the two friends as the boats drew slowly past in single file. The dark-skinned men who made up the scanty crews seemed as drab and weatherworn as their barges, but they returned the salutes of the two spectators with an air of grave condescension as befitted courtesies shown mere landlubbers by those whose noble lot is to ride the mighty deep. Their laundries of frayed shirts and overalls fluttered dejectedly from lines stretched amidships, like the sorrow-ful battle signals of a fight already lost.

"Canucks," said the Judge, disparagingly, as he observed the darken and sullen visages of the men. "I can smell shag tobacco and onions."

And that may well have been partly true, for a man with a clay pipe between his teeth sat on the stern of the last barge holding a trol-ling line with which he alternately released and retrieved the trailing spoon which spun and glittered far to the rear of the procession.

Even as they watched the line suddenly jerked taut in the fisherman's hands. That worthy instantly leaped to his feet and released a flood of shouted epithets and instructions in French. His pipe fell to the deck unnoticed while he hauled away at his heavy tackle. A fat woman in a faded red wrapper appeared at the cabin door, adding her shrill commentary to the hubbub as she ran to the assistance of her man, whose pipe now lay in shattered fragments beneath his prancing feet. The entire fleet came to life. Men, women and swarms of children appeared magically at every vantage point on the preceding craft to give aid and counsel to their valiant comrade.

It was evident that not all of the onlookers were in strict agreement as to the best method of dealing with a ten-pound pickerel, for there were shouts of *"Doucement, doucement! Nom de Dieu!"* rendered in falsetto, and others at the extreme opposite, both in vocal register and counsel, bawled, *"Hardi! 'on gar!"* and "Pool heem een, Jacques, ma frien'!"

But Jacques, obviously a sensible angler, had a well proved method of his own and gave no attention whatsoever to the shower of admonition raining upon him. His first powerful tug had lifted his fish half-way out of the water, and there, by rapid manipulation of the line assisted in no small way by the four-knot speed of his vessel, he kept it. The pickerel skittered helplessly along the surface completely deprived of any means to resist either in its natural element or in the fatal rarefied atmosphere above it.

So, swiftly and ignominiously, the fish was brought alongside. The fat woman retrieved it with a boat hook.

As the stern of the barge slid from the view of the two men on the shore, they heard a final tragic declamation from Jacques. It was clear and distinct in the brooding twilight.

"Marie! Marie! I get de feesh, ho kay, but I'll was be bust mah sacre goddam peep all to Hell!"

The two men on the shore exchanged glances.

"Well, 'Jacques, mah frien' '" said the Captain, rising to his feet, "in the words of the poet, 'there is no joy unmixed with woe'."

The Honorable Justice also rose and tapped his pipe bowl against the tree while his glance ranged again over the green watery meadows to the towering ramparts of the mountains beyond. The muted throb of the tugboat now turning the angle of the narrows above came pleasantly to his ears.

"I wish," said he, "that I'd gone in for canal boating. Let's try it a whack sometime and hire passage on one o' 'em to Montreal. We can take our guns and fishing tackle and see the sights and have fun."

"Have you ever *been* in one o' those cabins?" inquired his friend. "No? Well I have, and thought myself lucky to get out again before the bugs ate me up. Also there were certain antique fragrances in there that I knew were all of a hundred years old. The pea-soupers don't seem to mind it, bein' brought up on it. But the idea in general is a good one and maybe someday we could charter a cleaner craft of some sort and make a trip of it. We'll get Cam and the Doctor to come along. Ralf, too, if he can get away, and we'll load up with supplies and go where we please." Still dwelling upon the engaging prospects of such a voyage, he set out along a dim grass-grown path that led to the top of the bluff. The other followed.

The Big Slough, where they had built their blinds and where they proposed to establish themselves on the opening day of the wildfowl season, was one of a score of shallow irregular bays which are characteristic of the area. At some prehistoric period these sloughs had been deep fissures battered into the great limestone barrier to the east. The tempest-tossed waves of an inland ocean had dashed in thunder against the castellated cliffs, and monstrous creatures had fought and bellowed where today the gentle woodduck rear their broods and one will hear no sound more terrifying than the drums of the grouse, the chatter of the squirrel and the gasping bark of the red fox.

As the great waters receded they brought down as tribute deposits of rich silt from the hills and this as it settled in the depressions of the emergent shore formed the typical slough, which is in fact a tributary of the Lake rather than an integral part of it. The marshes are moistened by spring-fed brooks, which spread their waters over the flat expanses of silt and drain away at last into Champlain through a maze of winding creeks and channels moving imperceptibly beneath a canopy of oaks, elms and buttonwood trees.

The ducks against whose safety and well being our friends conspired were almost without exception natives of the locality, born and reared in the pleasant backwaters and grown fat and succulent upon a rich and varied diet. There were blackduck, bluewinged and greenwinged teal, with an occasional rare cinnamon. There have also been noted in recent years increasing numbers of widgeon, pintail and the gray mallard. Inasmuch as these latter species had been almost entirely absent for many years, their return is hailed by the local gunners as a significant and happy sign. And then there are the woodduck, hordes of them, to delight the eye and ear of the wild-fowler even while they exasperate him by continually offering fair shots that can only be taken at the risk of inviting legal vengeance administered at the hands of a rural Justice of the Peace.

None of the great flocks of migrants which in October and November sweep southward along the Lake ever visits or tarries in the sloughs. These environs remain forever secured to the uses and enjoyments of the puddle ducks, the rails, bitterns and the statuesque herons, and to the frogs and the frog-hunting raccoons, the muskrat and the mink, the partridge that feeds upon the wild grapes and the beechnut mast, and the woodcock that loves the moist banks.

Twice each twelve months the somnolent tranquillity of the sloughs is disturbed. The first of these noisy invasions is that of the wildfowlers who, on opening day, and intermittently thereafter until the marshes freeze, occupy every pot-hole and point. They do a prodigious amount of shooting and bag an amazingly disproportionate number of ducks. Again in the spring, for a week or two, the light skiffs of the muskrat trappers plow their dim trails through the sodden waste and floating debris that was midsummer's lovely mantle. Woe betide the muskrat who thinks at this season to enjoy his nocturnal supper at his accustomed dining-place on a half-submerged log, for there will be set a snare for his undoing. Woe to him also if, on his way to visit his lady love, he crosses open water, for his journey is more likely to end with a tiny bullet from the trapper's rifle in his brain than in the delights of amorous dalliance.

As far as the Judge, the Captain, Cam, and a dozen other male residents of Tranquillity were concerned, the last day of the closed season was one of intense industry, but not one of profit.

The Judge gazed upon a lengthy petition of sorts bound in blue paper covers and came to no conclusion whatsoever except that the profession of Law is a dull and wordy business at best. At eleven o'clock in the forenoon he gave it up and phoned the Captain, to ask him to lunch at the Tavern.

The Captain accepted with alacrity, for all morning long he had been interrupted by discouraged voices inquiring if he knew of *any* place where a man could lay hands on a box of 12 gauge 6's, or 2's or 4's or even 8's. It was a source of great satisfaction to him that he could do so and that he did. Thanks to the recent and timely benovolence of a nameless Christian, a whole case of 12 gauge 6's reposed in the basement. It was enough to get him elected to the United States Senate if he ever wanted to run for that office, but what with trips to and from the basement his manuscript suffered. Immediately after the Judge called he pushed his pages aside and made a final descent to the basement. He returned with five boxes of 12 gauge 6's, and addressed the Dark-Haired Lady.

"One box for Bill Reed's boy. One box for Jim Gamble. One box for Frank Sheville. One box for the Superintendent of Schools, and one box for the little Parson who lives down the lane. They will call for 'em, and they will ask 'how much.' Tell 'em to go to Hell, particularly the Parson. The Lord giveth and the Lord taketh away."

He was gone and the Dark-Haired Lady realized that nothing could be done about it even if she had wished to do anything. She picked up a dust mop and listened for the doorbell.

Cam, meanwhile, was in no better case. Nancy, who was his wife, and far above his desserts, had come down to the office to straighten out the scratches and scrawls that recorded her husband's business transactions. She brought to order such items as "P. Douglas, welding seat, $2.50." "Jake Goodrich, removing carbon, grinding valves, $6.80." "Starting motor for B. Daniels, $.25. Damn fool didn't have ignition on."

She was dutifully entering cogent information in the ledger and chuckling occasionally at her husband's whimsies, while Cam and his helper assembled their tools and advanced upon a mud-spattered Ford truck. But before a blow could be struck, Al Wilson stuck his red head in at the door to inquire whereabouts did Cam intend to go tomorrow, and did he know by any chance where a man could lay hands on a box of 12 gauge sixes? These and such as these are questions that can't be answered in one or two sentences, and considerable time passed while Cam elaborated and Al agreed.

"But, don't, for Pete's sake, tell the Cap'n I sent ye," he admonished, as Al set forth with a gleam of hope in his eyes.

He had scarcely vanished when Rick Davis came in on identical business. Following Rick came the little Jones boy, the one with the twisted leg. He'd gotton hold of a 20 bore single barrel and kind-hearted Cam found a box of shells which he gave to the eager-eyed lad along with some top secret advice as to where to go and what to do.

Then the phone rang, and he heard Nancy say, "I'll tell him. He'll be along right away."

She spoke to her husband.

"That was the Judge, Cameron. He wants you to come up for lunch at the Tavern." There was a twinkle in her gray eyes. "I told him you'd come right along. You might as well. All you've done this whole enduring morning has been to pick up that hammer and put it down again. Run along now, little man, and have a good time."

"By Crimus, Ma'am. I b'lieve you're right! Duck huntin' generally takes three days if a man's lucky—one to get ready, two to go, and three to pick ducks. There ain't any use tryin' to go against Nature."

He laid the hammer gently down on the bench.

"You'll be there," said he to the hammer, "when I get back."

At the Tavern the host welcomed the Judge and led him furtively away to the big kitchen, where, with a reverent gesture, he lifted the cover from a battered hamper.

It was filled with oysters, fresh and cold and bedded in seaweed. The old sportsman reached for a knife. The opening shell released a breath of brine, fog and the winds of the sea, and then the oyster, a creature of humble aspirations, which only yesterday had believed that it was firmly and permanently cemented to a rock some three fathoms down in the Atlantic Ocean, entered the legal profession.

The host beamed upon his guest.

"Now, sir, ain't they prime eyesters? I declare, I'm as praoud o' 'em almost as if I'd raised 'em myself. 'Git 'em fresh,' sez I, 'or leave 'em be.' Dang these poor washed aout things thet hev been shucked an' froze an' thawed out an' froze agin. *I* won't tech 'em. They ain't bigger'n a shotgun wad, an' they taste much the same. 'Course these here prime eyesters cost ye a leetle extra, but who wants to feed his purse an' starve his stomach?"

"You never spoke a truer word," said the Judge solemnly. He could eat hardtack and singed bacon when necessary, and relish the fare; but he was a sensible man with a taste for chops, steaks, venison, bullheads, brook trout, game and seafood.

"Now then, Cameron and the Captain will have lunch with me and I believe we can handle three or four dozen of these fellows among us, and somewhere near a gallon of ale. Yes, and a modicum of horse radish and vinegar and a good store of those butter rolls your Missus makes."

The host flipped a pad from his pocket and made some entries with a pencil.

"Yes, sir, Jedge. You shall hev it right on the dot." Then, the business secured, he put the pad away. "Goin' duck huntin' tomorrow, I s'pose? Well, sir, I'd dearly love to go myself. Would too, if I had any ca'tridges for my gun. Prob'ly you wouldn't know where a man could lay his hands on a box o' 12 gauge sixes?"

◖ ◞◠◝ And Two to Go ◟◞ ◗

DURING THE night the Lake had drawn over it a thick blanket of white wool as a protection against the threat of frost in the upper air. Every familiar aspect and landmark had been swallowed up in the silent opacity which concealed from the occupants of the car first, the presence, and then the identity of all objects up to the very moment of imminent collision. The fact the Cam and the Captain were anxiously endeavoring to penetrate the deceptive curtain gave the Judge, who was driving, little comfort and no help whatever, for when something monstrous and menacing swam down upon them in the ocean of mist he saw it as quickly as did his passengers, and if it had not been so, their warning cries would have been too late to stop him from plunging the chariot into the creek, or folding it up accordion-fashion against the base of a sturdy elm. Nothing was what it seemed to be in the swirling phantasmagoria. The creek resembled the road and the road resembled the creek. A late wandering 'coon, when suddenly confronted by the glaring headlights, looked like a grizzly bear for an instant before the animal reassumed its proper proportions and vanished in the murk. A plot of cropped alfalfa into which the Judge turned in order to get away from the dangerous proximity of the creek turned out to be a field of standing corn, and the Judge drove strongly across a dozen rows before the thump of roasting ears against the windwhield and the yelps of his companions made him aware of his error.

Thereupon he stopped the car and the engine and addressed the fog-bound universe.

"A back-seat driver is a damned fool to begin with," he announced, giving expression to an idea that he had been entertaining for some time. "I believe that I can see as far into this soup as either of you fellers—a mite farther, perhaps, to judge from your reactions. If I'd waited for you to holler we'd been halfway up that 'coon tree back there. But let that pass. The point is that if I hear another yip out of you we'll leave the car where she sits and walk the rest of the way. It ain't much more than four miles farther. What do you say to that?"

"Nothin', Your Honor, and we're both sorry that you misunderstood us. We weren't finding fault with your driving. We like the way you do it, don't we, Cam?"

"Why certainly," agreed Cam with much heartiness. "I ain't had such a nice time since the pigs ate my little brother."

The Judge appeared to be mollified, and in the absence of further suggestions from his passengers he steered a precarious course onward to their destination.

The jurist's wet forefinger, when he exposed it upon arrival, gave no indication of a breeze from any direction. In the pre-dawn darkness the world about them lay hushed and breathless. Far away a farm dog chivvying his cows yapped like a sergeant major, and near at hand there was the slow drip of water from the saturated foliage, the plop of a feeding fish or a diving muskrat and then, and best of all, the throaty *reveille* of a black duck, "Quaaa-quaa-qua," as he summoned his dusky company to salute the dawn, never dreaming that it would usher in a day of fright and death-from-ambush for the Clan of the Webbed Foot.

They were three merciful men, but the voice of the wildfowl sounding through the mist roused in them wild echoes from the dim ages, long before men had learned to till the soil or practice law for their daily bread.

"Hear that old fellow," muttered Cam, and there was a predatory gleam in the Judge's normally kindly eyes as he drew his famous old hammer gun from its case and assembled it.

Unlike his two friends, the old sportsman never had to undergo the pleasant agony of choosing from an arsenal of weapons a special gun to suit the occasion. Not he. Let others spend small fortunes on duck guns, goose guns, partridge guns, and woodcock guns. He scorned such nonsense. Except for a pair of beautiful muzzle-loaders inherited from a sporting ancestor who had died on the field of battle, our friend had only one shotgun to his name, and for two score years he had used it with great and equal success upon all manner of flying game from woodcock and snipe to the lordly turkey and the Canada goose. It was a nobly proportioned piece of 12 bore, and the Captain, who as a connoisseur admired it greatly, had once determined that the left barrel had been bored half choke while the right was no more than a strong improved clyinder. According to the highest authorities on the ballistics of the shotgun, the Judge therefore had a weapon that was nearly ideal for the shooting of light-feathered upland game birds, but which would be practically worthless for anything else. Yet its owner, who knew little and cared less about the intricacies and exactitudes of the science of ballistics, could with an ounce of nines and the same gun, tip a woodcock into birches at fifteen paces without ruffling a feather, or stop a goose dead with an ounce and an eighth of twos at four times that distance.

Nor would the Judge have anything to do with the heavily charged modern cartridges, after having tried a couple of them. In his light gun they jarred him painfully.

"By the Lord Harry," he remarked, rubbing his jaw, "if I've got to stand up to that sort of thing every time I shoot a duck, I'll quit shooting ducks. I don't give a darn if they'll shoot a mile, which they feel as if they would. The fact remains that I can't hit a duck that far, and anyway, you don't need to eviscerate the poor critters if all you want to do is to kill 'em."

So, forswearing the doubtful benefits of progress, he continued to use his favorite brand of shell loaded with three drams of good Dupont powder, and to use them with such consummate skill that his companions were confounded and often made to wonder if they knew as much as they thought they did about these vital matters.

Cam was armed, surprisingly enough, with a fine new double barrel of 12 bore, which, until recently, had been dedicated by the War Department to the savage business of shooting Nazi paratroopers and spies. When none of these unsavory scoundrels appeared to violate the peace of the neighborhood, a remote authority allowed Cam to purchase from the Ordnance Department for the sum of fifteen dollars and fifty cents a notable fowling piece. In those strange days when the clouds never discharged upon the earth and its inhabitants anything but lightning, rain, hail and snow, it would have cost him five times that amount at Pingree's Hardware Store.

"The feller that had this gun in the State Guard told me that it shot slugs fine an' that with buckshot he thought a man might maybe hit a mule once in ten shots at four rod," said the proud owner, "but it did all right with number sixes when I tried her on crows."

By the time the three had assembled their gear the fog had lifted somewhat, and a wan light was about them.

"I believe," said one, "that daylight'll bring a breeze from the south. In that case, a couple of us should be on the Point and t'other one in the little blind near the muskrat house."

"I'll take the muskrat blind since I know where it is, and you and Cam go to the Point," the Captain volunteered, "and let us pray that the far-shooters and spoil-sports all overslept and stayed at home."

"I ain't hoping too much," remarked Cam, "for there is generally at least one of the danged fools to every marsh on opening day, tryin' hard to kill ducks so far away that if he *did* kill one, it would spoil long 'fore he could get it."

The Captain's blind was nothing more than a low clump of tangled buttonwood brush which thrust its crooked arms and twisted fingers from the ooze, grasping for its humble share of air and sunshine from a footing too unstable to support the weight of its loftier neighbors on the shore. He had added a few sprigs and cuttings here and there in an attempt to heighten the illusory quality of the pattern created by the confusion of broken lines and deceptive shadows. Neither he nor his companions just across on the Point had decoys, for they needed none this early in the season. The wildfowl, bewildered by the shooting on the neighboring sloughs, could be expected to seek refuge from the unwonted tumult in these hitherto peaceful fens without further inducement in the way of wooden effigies.

The gunner hung his leather cartridge bag on a convenient sapling, and opened its flap. Then, with his gun loaded and all preparations made, he seated himself on a root and gave himself up to the contemplation of his surroundings. It still lacked a few minutes of the zero hour, but he did not need to consult his watch, for a salvo from a dozen guns would inform him promptly when the time came.

The light strengthened and the mist, warned of the near approach of the Lord of the Day, began to loosen its clammy hold upon the woods and waters. It formed its silent legions into diaphanous columns which rolled and twisted slowly above the trees. Now the shore line beyond the narrow waterway was visible, enabling the watcher to see his companions making their final preparations. Even as he looked, their heads and shoulders disappeared from view and the slight sounds of their furtive activities ceased.

More even than the sharp excitement and action which was soon to come, the Captain relished these last moments of anticipation. It is at this time that Man, the Hunter, is able to free himself from the irksome swadling-clothes of conventional society. For a little space he finds himself repossessed of an ancient heritage. In some degree, he experiences a physical regeneration, also. The rank fragrance of the marsh strikes more sharply in his nostrils; his vision is magically cleared; the dull scales of habit fall from his eyes, so that he no longer looks without also seeing; the slightest sounds from fen, and forest suddenly become as distinct and significant to him as they had been in the ears of hairy Esau and of all other mighty hunters of the ages past.

These were the thoughts that occupied the Captain's mind that morning, as he sat with his ready gun in his hands and realized that two score years of wildfowling had not taught him how to suppress the convulsive shivers that ran through him.

The Doctor had once explained that the whole business was the result of a glandular activity, "more adrenalin pumped into the blood stream," said he, and the Captain received this scientific information with a respect that approached reverence. He also observed on more than one occasion, that despite his knowledge of the cause, the gruff old healer evidently had no cure for it, since he himself shook like a wet spaniel whenever a flock of black ducks set their wings to his decoys. Moreover, the Doctor hadn't been able to name the thing that started the adrenalin pump.

"Just as well, too," thought the Captain, "for if we ever manage to find out everything about everything it will be an exceedingly dull existence. If I ever get to the point that I don't quiver in a duck blind at zero minus five, I shall sell the best fowling piece in the world and devote the proceeds to the advancement of the cause of temperance, for the delights and amenities of good drinking, eating, and of more or less ribald talk will also have been lopped off by the same cruel stroke, and we shall find ourselves in a pallid world indeed."

These philosophical reflections were interrupted by the sound of a shot somewhere to the south, and then came an uneven fusillade as other skirmishers opened fire. A double report near at hand roused the marsh before him, and in an instant the place was noisy with the quackings and spatterings as, flock after flock, the startled host of wildfowl took wing.

A gaunt blue heron stumbled aloft, discharging a copious ballast as it rose, together with a stream of hoarse-voiced curses upon the ill-mannered folk who had spoiled his fishing. The panic spread throughout the marsh as alarum followed alarum. A partridge making a breakfast upon the wild blue grapes in a vine-draped tree nearby added to the mounting tumult by taking off with a thunder of wings louder by far than the sounds made by the flock of teal which at that moment swept over the Captain's blind like a flight of arrows. Now, in all directions, ducks were moving restlessly. Several small flocks passed within a few yards of the hidden gunners, who were hard put to it to hold their fire.

"If we shoot at 'em while they're going out," Cam whispered with his eyes following a pair of black duck, "they won't want to come back, but if we let the big bunches go they'll come back later in singles and pairs, just the way we like 'em."

The sound of firing increased on all sides. It seemed possible to trace the passage of a single flock of birds as it swung to and fro above the neighboring marshes from the volleying that greeted it from a score of ambuscades near and far.

"Now you know there's a devil of a lot more ammunition around here than I've been led to suppose," the Judge remarked.

"And most of it's being wasted," the other observed. "See that flock flare over yonder! Somebody shot at 'em away up there. Didn't want 'em to get too close prob'ly. If that's what he's scared of he could save money by bringing along a dishpan an' whangin' on it with a rock. But he's turned 'em, an' if they're left alone I b'lieve they'll come in."

The small flock of black duck swept overhead. They were out of range but the thrilling sound of their flight came clearly to the ears. It died away as the birds passed from view behind a distant wooded hill.

Cam and the Judge crouched motionless with heads bowed as in prayer. One spoke in low tones:

"They're makin' a turn. They're makin' a turn."

There was a long minute of tense immobility in both blinds, for the Captain was also alert and from his vantage point had been better able to observe the aerial maneuverings which would have seemed vague and without purpose to eyes untrained in plotting the shifting, evasive tactics of a leader drake whose squadron has heard the whistle of shot. He had seen the turn and the deceptive spiral dip that the old drake executed a half-mile beyond the slough, which meant that he had decided to bring his family into this peaceful-seeming cove. The Captain slipped the safety button on his gun to the "off" position.

"That old feller is going to bring 'em in past the point, turn 'em downwind, bring 'em back over Cam and the Judge, turn 'em again and land the whole lot right in front of me. Only he won't land 'em and there won't be so many of 'em, either, if the boys are awake and do their duty."

There is no wildfowler worthy of the title who is not convinced of his ability to predict what a flock of ducks will do once it has taken wing. It is a harmless foible. The fact that the prophet is nearly always completely wrong causes him no dismay, nor does it lessen his confidence in his perspicuousness.

The Captain shared his delusion, and was greatly encouraged when the flock reappeared beyond the point flying some thirty yards above the water. It turned into the wind in precise accordance with his prediction and swung back. As it passed, the hidden guns spoke and three of the birds pitched down to float lifelessly among the wild oat stalks. The survivors flared toward the Captain, who felt that the day had begun auspiciously when a single well-aimed shot brought a lofty straggler crashing into the buttonwood almost within reach of his hand.

He had scarcely reloaded when a plump little teal coming from nowhere popped over the blind. The first hasty shot was a clean miss at fifteen yards, but the second charge tumbled the saucy little duck into the willows.

Presently the Judge won the unqualified admiration of his friends by executing a perfectly timed double on a pair of gray ducks that came over so high that the Captain thought them to be out of range until his sharpshooting friend proved otherwise.

And now the ducks driven off the neighboring marshes began dropping in, and the gunners were busy. For an hour the shooting reminded the Judge of red-letter days he had enjoyed on the great waterfowl marshes of the Gulf Coast and in Arkansas.

So far they had not been annoyed by over-eager gunners, but they were not to escape one disagreeable experience. It came when a pothunter sneaking along the wooded shore fired a load of shot into the blind where Cam and the Judge were crouching. Cam was badly stung and also thoroughly aroused.

He shouted a warning and rose to his feet.

The offender bore a striking resemblance to the late Italian dictator, and his response was in keeping with his appearance.

"Why de Hell you fellas no git where somebody see you! Huh?" adding a ferocious curse and a menacing gesture.

Cam took a single cartridge from a pocket of his jacket and held it up to view.

"Listen, Mister Mussolini, this one is loaded with buckshot, an' if you shoot into us again you're goin' to get it!"

He spoke with the calm authority of a man who intends to execute his promises.

"To Hell wit' you!" said the careless one bitterly, but it was only a token of defiance for he turned and stumbled off in the direction whence he came.

"Just as well *that* brother wasn't using buckshot," Cam remarked, "he'd have killed the pair of us deader'n a hammer."

"I believe, Cameron, that you *would* have shot him."

Cam grinned, and rubbed his sore spots.

"Maybe I would," said he.

A lone mallard drake now appeared high above the trees on a scouting mission apparently, for he showed no sign of making a landing. The greenhead is rare in the locality, and therefore it is highly prized. The Captain was sorely tempted. Though high, the big bird was coming straight over him at the best angle for a long shot. The gunner yielded and had the intense satisfaction of seeing the drake crumple at the shot. It hit far back on the slope with a solid thud.

"Gosh!" exclaimed Cam. "Did you see that one! And he's shooting that little sixteen gauge gun, too."

The Judge explained. "That little sixteen ain't just an ordinary sixteen. One of the best gunmakers in the world made three of 'em before he satisfied our long-legged friend over yonder. When the brother is in the groove, as he was just then, that gun'll kill ducks even higher than that."

He continued.

"We were shooting down on Mattamuskeet, let me see, two, no, three years ago. The old boy was in good trim. He was revelling in one of those 'can't-miss-'em-if-you-want-to'; 'shoot-the-head-off-a-pin' spells which come to us occasionally and make us realize that we're but a little lower than the angels. All the guides on the Lake came up to our room the first evening to look at 'the big ten gauge magnum' we'd had in our blind that day. They couldn't believe it when he handed 'em a little six-and-a-half-pound double barrel.

"The second day there went even better, and he pulled off a double on a pair of geese that I'll swear weren't less than seventy yards up. Both of 'em stone dead, too. It was one of the prettiest shots I ever saw. Everybody on the Lake saw it, too, and *that* night we had more beverages proffered us than we could manage. It's quite a gun and he knows it, for he's kept it for twenty years or more."

The sound of footsteps announced a second visitor.

"Maybe Mussolini's coming back to see if I meant it," remarked the younger sportsman. Then his eye caught a glimpse of a uniform. "No, it ain't Mussy. It's the Game Warden making his rounds."

The Warden was an old and highly respected friend, and he paused to give them news of how the day had gone on the other marshes.

Cam seized an opportunity.

"Tom," said he, "there was a fat, dirty-lookin' cuss came along here an hour or so ago pot hunting. He stung me good with a load of shot. It just came to me that he might not have a license even to shoot ducks."

Tom grinned. "He didn't, and he did have three woodducks. Bill

Pickett got him, and he's on his way right now to tell the Justice how come."

The Warden stopped to chat with the Captain, and then went his way satisfied that no high crimes or misdemeanors had been committed here.

Save for an occasional shot, there was nothing now to disturb the customary quietude of the marshes, for the greater part of the wildfowl had discovered that enemies noisier and more dangerous and terrifying than the duck hawk and the mink had invaded their summer homes. Their flocks were now resting safely on the open waters of the Lake and, it may be, counting their casualties of the morning.

The mudhens were comforted by the pervading silence and timorously emerged from seclusion to swim jerkily here and there while with increasing boldness they snatched their breakfasts from the brown water. The heron, too, came sailing in on set and silent wings and made an awkward landing on his long stilts. Thereafter for some minutes he stood tense and erect while he examined the familiar scenes for any sign of danger. Finding none, he relaxed his vigilance and resumed the unending effort to satisfy an appetite as sharp as his gaunt form suggested.

"The trouble with Old Beak and Legs," said Cam in low tones to his companion as they watched the big bird impale and swallow a six-inch dace without visibly increasing its meager bulk, "is that he don't hang on to his rations long enough to take any nourishment from 'em. If he had three, four loops in his insides to slow down his digestion, that feller would be fat as butter an' wouldn't have to work so steady at his fishin'."

This critical analysis of the heron's internal deficiencies apparently had the effect of reminding the speaker of his own, for he offered a suggestion that was received favorably by his companion and which was promptly endorsed by the Captain when they mentioned it to him.

So they withdrew to the vicinity of the car and while one built an "Indian fire" to broil a rack of the spicy little sausages for which Tranquillity was famous, another laid out the bread and cheese and the Judge pried the caps off the ale bottles which he had thoughtfully provided.

The ale was cool and sweet and mildly bitter on their tongues.

Cam lowered his mug.

"Better than swamp water," he said.

" 'Much has been said in praise of ale'," remarked the Captain. "That's a quotation, and here's another. My good friend Pitkin called it to my attention and it pleased me so much that I memorized it. It's by George Borrow, who wrote a book some ninety-odd years ago. The speaker has just given a pitcher of ale to some poor disconsolate people at the English tavern.

" 'They could have found water in the road,' says George, 'but they wanted no water. Meat and bread? Go to, they were not hungry. Money? What right had I to insult them by offering them money? Advice? Words, words, words. Friends, there is a time for everything: There is a time for a cup of cold water: There is a time for strong meat and bread: There is a time for advice, and there is a time for ale—and I have generally found that the time for advice is after a cup of ale'."

His audience expressed their unlimited approval of the Borrow sentiment and the Judge added:

"Very good, indeed, my boy, but I don't seem to require your advice, as maybe I shall after another mug of ale."

While he was finishing it, the chef pronounced the sausages at the proper state of crisp, fat-spurting succulency, the lid of the battered coffee pot was clicking gently and the three friends began their leisurely meal.

As they ruminated, their glances roamed over the fields and hills and marshes. They spoke or were silent in their companionship. One noted the tell-tale crimson thread of an ivy vine woven through the untouched greenery of the elms and reflected that the ivy and the water maple are the first of the forest sentinels to tell of the coming glory and splendors of autumn. Cam, a fox hunter, traced a wooded notch above a distant sheep pasture, and concluded it would be a fox-crossing when his old hound took up his patient musical profession in bleak November. Another's thoughts were of a lonelier character, for he was recalling days like this when they had shared the wildfowl and the beauty of this scene with an eager smiling boy who was at that moment somewhere on the high seas bound for old battlefields that were still fresh in his own memory despite the passage of the years.

The Judge must have read these thoughts, for he gave his friend the gentle compassionate smile that had power to make the heart glow.

Cam broke the silence.

"Wasn't something said around here about 'farshooters' an' what about the wicked practice," agreed that worthy. "Why do you ask?"

"Oh, I suppose the cuss is talking about my mallard drake," said the Captain. "I've been expecting it from one or the other of you. But I earned that bird, my friends, for I bet a life-long reputation on that shot. If I'd missed him, you'd be reminding me of it from now on. But I didn't miss him, as you can very well see if you examine the *corpus deliciti*. And note that there's at least six shot in it."

He picked the mallard out of a row of dead ducks and passed it to Cam.

Cam grinned and handed it back.

They lacked not many birds for their limit bag, and since no one cared greatly if it happened that the bag might be a few short at the end of the day, they decided to utilize only the last hour of the legal shooting day, that time when the skeins of returning wildfowl could be viewed against the sunset skies, and the Slough and its surroundings would gather a swiftly-changing beauty from the glowing firmament.

Cam went off to confirm his suspicion of the fox crossing; the Judge dozed, and the Captain, taking his gun along, in case he should jump a flock of ducks in the course of his wanderings, set out to explore the upper reaches of the little creek that fed the Slough and to make a census of the local partridge population.

The sun was well down when he returned. He had added a single black duck to his bag and had found encouragement to hope for other holidays to come in the presence of two goodly flocks of full-grown grouse. Cam had proved his knowledge of the habits of the resident foxes, and the Judge, between naps, had thought of something that he wanted to communicate to the Governor.

They returned to their blinds and if, now and again, ducks swung past without receiving the salute to which their rank entitled them, it might have been because a gunner had been absorbed at the moment in watching a flight of ten thousand blackbirds passing to their roosts in the cattails and rushes below Fiddler's Elbow. Another might have been too much engrossed in observing how the light of the passing day wrought its magic upon the ancient ramparts that enclosed the valley.

With the last shot of the day, Cam dispatched a crippled bird and was glad that he had been able to administer a merciful end to the unfortunate creature.

Then they gathered their ducks and in the twilight crossed the field to the car, but having arrived there, they did not immediately enter the chariot, but instead they sat for half an hour watching the scene while night came striding down the distant flank of Bald Mountain.

The Judge produced a flagon, the contents of which, when the stopper had been removed, gave off the fragrance of burning heather, and the three friends in great contentment proceeded to fortify themselves against the chills and vapors.

Cam regarded his share of the game with a satisfaction somewhat tempered by the realization of grievous labor yet to come.

"Dang it!" said he, finally, "I love to shoot 'em an' I hate to pick 'em. I'll be up half the night wrastling with those birds. I've tried to make Nancy understand that pickin' ducks, skinnin' squirrels an' cleanin' fish are her proper responsibilities, but she can't seem to get it through her head. Yet she's a smart girl, too, in some ways."

"Smart in *all* ways," remarked the Captain by way of amendment.

WHAT RARER DAY

Nash Buckingham

*Consider the assignment Mister Nash set for himself when he started
this piece. It is simply the story of a single day's hunting, from begin-
ing to end: the weather, the action, the things he felt and remembered as the day unfolded. I give him the highest marks on achieving
his goal. "What Rarer Day?" is the right blend of action and senti-
mental reflection. It is from the original* De Shootinest Gent'man,
published by The Derrydale Press *in 1934.*

THE PLANTATION'S great bell suddenly crashes the portals of sleep.
Protestingly I snuggle deeper into *reveille* to cottonland. From his
kennel an old pointer chimes in with dismal howlings.

Lying cozily, I compare my laziness to the alacrity in many a
lowly shack and cabin. Lamplight will begin to wink through rag-
stuffed window panes. I catch the ring of axes biting into chop-logs,
and sniff smoke from revived ash beds. There will be muffled voices
and stable stir; the rattle and clink of agriculture's army going into
action. Then it comes to me that for fully forty years I have listened
to this same bell "ring out and ring in," as the black folks say.
Others, too, from neighboring plantations, have hailed me as I poled
an early trail across Big Lake.

Fifteen minutes of stolen doze. Footfalls on veranda steps. A
latch turns gently. The guest's presence is respected. I peep as my
door opens gently. A huddled scuttle-bearer darts to the hearth and
applies fire-magic.

"Pomp!"

"Yaas, suh, boss."

"That you?"

"Yaas, suh. Da' me."

"What's it doing out?"

"Kind o' brief lak!"

"How brief?"

"Jes' tol'able."

"Going to rain?"

"Naw, suh, not 'ginst it cloud up."

"It's clear, then?"

"It's clear now, but—"

"But what?"

Pomp falters. "Ol' Zeb say de moon tips down too far. Say he gwine lay off killin' hawgs till de sign git right."

"Pomp?"

"Yaas, suh, boss."

"Put the coffee pot on the stove and those cold rolls in the oven. Don't monkey with that sausage. Wait till I get there—understand?"

"Yaas, suh."

Another fifteen minutes. I tiptoe, gumbooted, into the warm, spacious kitchen. To Java fragrance I soon add the stimulating reek of frying sausage. Heavy backstair clumpings announce huge Ab, my Negro paddler. After making deep inroads upon the provender, I abandon rich picking to the onslaught of Pomp and Ab. Soon I return with shell box and big double gun. Dousing manor lights, Ab and I strike along an orchard path leading down the bayou bank to Arthur's duck boat. Pomp trails, in case of last-moment forgetfulness on my part. He hums a love ditty, the refrain of which is interesting—"Whar's you goin', Adam? I'se Eve."

"Pomp isn't courting, is he, Ab?"

Ab sniffs. "He call hisse'f."

Ab fills the frail craft aft, and my own bulk forward sags a doubtful freeboard. We nose gingerly through a strip of open channel in the arrow-grass.

"How much water under us, Ab? About four feet?"

"Better'n dat, boss; mo' lak twenty foot. Don't rock de boat, please, suh. Dis ain't no mawnin' to dive!" Then Ab whispers, "Ol' Simmons seed two big al'gators down below Life Boat Chapel dis summer. All dem Darkies down dataway scared mos' to death o' de bayou."

I rearrange even mental ballast. "Run the trails lately, Ab?"

"Me an' Cap'n done so las' Friday."

"Jump many ducks?"

"Dey was right smart plentiful—yaas, suh."

"What kind mostly?"

"Most gin'ally mallets, suh."

"Can the Cap'n still hit 'em?"

"Well, suh, co'se Cap'n he ain't so spry lak; but when dey gives him a fair shot, de ol' gent'man he's jes' as pizenous as ever he was."

The bayou slips its high banks and narrows to an opening in the beetling cypress.

" 'Bout a foot o' watah in de woods," whispers Ab.

We slow down for readjustment before serious business. Eleven years have skimmed by since the last well-remembered day I heaved my own duck boat through this South End muck. Forty years of such swamp scuffling! Ab's paddle jabs us noiselessly up the narrow cut. Speed yields to tense silence. It is legally safe to shoot, but we are jump-shooting. Against the dim background of low visibility, it is futile to grant a leaping mallard overly much leeway. In scant light, once he beats you to the skyline, the chances are in the green-head's favor.

To our right, from a seldom penetrated morass, rises a mallard chorus. But a sudden, frog-like "me-yamp—me-yamp" to our left makes Ab sink his paddle and hold hard. The call is answered—here, there, beyond! Then I get the talk—of course, gadwalls! Now, I see a black bed of them, crossing trail twenty yards ahead.

"Gawd A'mighty!" breathes Ab. "Now's de chosen moment. Flat-shoot 'em, boss! Flat-shoot 'em!"

My shoulders heave, but there we crouch, with Ab, I know, bleeding internally. The gadwall raft drifts round a bend. Dawn flicks into day. A startling flight of grizzly buzzards skims overhead. Ab gets the pirogue stealthily underway. At the trail's crook, I signal him to stop and rap sharply against the boat rail. A roar from the buck-brush! I have miscalculated and been beaten to the punch—too far over! I glimpse fugitives scattering across timber tops. But a party of confused stragglers pinches off and lurches too close. The big gun mauls down a pair of drakes! Visions of baconed bosoms, corn-meal dressing and giblet gravy.

Ab chuckles as he hefts the prizes appraisingly. "Dese bullies is fat fo' goodness' sake; but, boss, why didn't you slam dem rascals back yondah? Us could've done had de limit wid one bust."

Realizing that an extended discussion of shooting ethics will end at the impasse of Ab's conviction that "a duck in the boat is worth two in the bush," I decline the issue.

"Yaas, suh," agrees Ab solemnly. "Yaas, suh, Da's right; da's right; but mos' o' de gent'mens up at de club dey don't shoot lak you an' Major Ensley does. Dey 'ranges so de ducks lights 'mongst d' m'coys, an' when dey do—Great I am! Sometimes dey does say 'Shoo,' but dey says it not very loud, an' it has sho' got to be a swift duck to leave dar 'twixt de shoo an' de shoot!"

By now the run widens into linked ponds. These open spaces are covered with a scum of seedy duck meat and bordered with button willow. A second smothered roar from around the corner! Ab steadies the boat. I pick them up through interlacing covert, a bunch of suspicious mallards driving for safety. But they must pass our way to clear! I "hunker" down and blaze away. Two birds tumble all awry from among the leaders. My second blast bites off a dismayed climber. Pandemonium! The marsh is in riot! Alarm calls! The surge of zooming pinions! Teal, mallard, widgeon and sprig hover singly and in bunches overhead.

It is, somehow, not easy to avoid shoving shells wrong end first into one's gun. But I manage finally to concentrate, find the combination, and center a pair of easy sprigs. Ab retrieves with mumbles of wonder when the hubbub ceases. "Sho' was some votes in dis district!"

We head up-trail. Tree tops ahead are mazed with circling birds. I am tempted to stop off awhile and call. But the charm of idle jump-shooting is far too potent.

Every shove of Ab's paddle reveals familiar territory. I part the viny overhang of a pond hole hidden amid lofty cypress giants and pause in spellbound reflection. Here, these forty years come November, I saw my first duck brought down. Morning of youth! A shaver, warm beneath the folds of a buffalo robe. Black Jackson is bringing lunch, and me along with it, to a certain gallant gentleman. Jackson thrills me with panther stories, and shows me hawks and eagles as the lazy *bateau* slips from open water into the brake's somber labyrinth. Closer and closer comes the occasional boom of black powder. We creep to where I now sit wrapped in thought. The screen of life lights in vivid memory. A lone mallard swerves into the picture. The drake's hissed greeting to silent, scattered forms; sunlight glinting from a green velvet head. Faith in Nature poised for its rendezvous with fate. A jet of smoke! A crash that sets the crispness dancing! Blue and reddish gray plunging headlong in a crumpled heap.

From a deftly woven hide at the bole of that lightning-struck cypress yonder, a great brown dog challenges watchfully. Out steps a tall, thick-shouldered, dark-haired fellow. Loblolly clings to the calves of his rubber boots. The soft brown of his velveteen shooting coat blends in deadly camouflage with his hiding place.

"Daddy!" I cry, springing crazily to my feet and setting the boat atilt. "Daddy, lemme shoot a duck!"

"I'm as hungry as a wolf!" he shouts. "Bring that rascal here to me, Jackson, an' I'll eat him." Then, as now, I would have died for him.

As we swing about, the picture fades, and in its place I see a youth reading by lamplight in an old log clubhouse his first treatise on duck shooting. That worn volume, than which he has since read nothing better, is still a priceless possession. How he longed and vowed to follow like trails!

"Watch dat bunch yondah!" warns Ab. "Dey's circlin' disaway!"

Shielded by a fallen pin-oak top, I unlimber my call. Around and around they go. Then, just as conversation peters out from lack of breath, they veer abruptly out of line to investigate my racket. "Now!" I say to myself, pitching up the gun and loosening its starboard charge at that charmed spot out ahead. Rapped head over heels, number one bird hurtles down through splintering branches. Swinging off at a flaring hen, however, I am reminded that pride goeth before a fall. Not a feather!

As we glide through weaving aisles I calculate that I have dropped ducks on well-nigh every square yard of this time-worn shooting ground. We have shared—still share—glorious years. The two of us are still hard at it. The reason? Because it has been left just as it was. Because of sporting unselfishness and pride in its maintenance. Because the beauty of Nature and wildlife meant much to a family of real sportsmen.

Thinking all this, I tell myself that any proper visualization of duck shooting must include a background of reminiscence, a foreground of its modern administration, and an estimate thereby of its future, as affecting recreation, industry and national character.

Morale in shooting has become superficial. The flavor and romance which graced old-time shooting standards and companionships among gentlefolk are being forced to wave the white flag to protuberant boorishness. Natural resources in both birds and habitats are being wasted through the rape of ill-devised drainage and delay by haggled interests of research and appropriations. We vaporize amid unsolved weather cycles; we temporize with raw political expediency. Hunters increase. Dizzy transportation facilities give access to remote sectors.

We are drifting faster than we even dream toward a sterility in wildlife of the marsh and upland, from which there will be no returning. The pace must slacken! How truly has it been said that "as a nation allows itself to lapse into a condition of sophistication, irresponsibility, materialism and other resultants of luxury and wealth, it loses its place in the sun. Slowly it is supplanted by other nations, hardier, more vigorous and more moral."

But by now our prow strakes are asplash. Big Lake, stretching away northward into the fog, gives off only the wrangle of distant, rafting coots. My eyes travel the winter-stricken circle of forest. Recollection grips again. Yonder, a husky of twenty, home for Christmas holidays, I had a narrow squeak.

One bitter dawn I managed, by some lucky maneuvering through the ice, to outstalk a gang of roosting geese. Glowing with the excitement of a successful right and left, I jammed my boat in the stumps and waded off across an open pocket. Retrieving the first honker, I flung it behind me and made for my second victim. The water, first calf- and then knee-deep, began sloshing my thighs. It was no morning for wet feet, but youth rarely kens restraint. With stunning abruptness, I stepped off into space. The water, so cold it actually burned, closed over my head.

Emerging in a paroxysm of anger and fear, with shell-laden coat dragging me down, I grabbed at some drooping willow strands. The slender withes tore through my fingers—broke! I saw them whip upward as I sank! Coming up, I seemed to time their lashback. My lunge caught firmer strands and held. There I clung until a careful knee-hold eventually enabled a crafty wiggle from the death trap. Then I stood up and, with clothes stiffening, loudly reviled such luck. On a platform stand nearby I built a rousing blaze, stripped, and dried out as best I could. Then I resumed, without ill effect, the serious business of the day.

But scarcely have Ab and I re-entered the trail when two dainty duck shapes whir into the air! In the ensuing millionth of a second's trigger pause, it flashes over me how many times hereabout I have had this same opportunity to score double on teal. The straight, thick gun comb shoves both eyes beyond a tilting guide-sight, wilts the escaping right-hand bundle of green and brown, and levels off in search of number two. It is a patchy scratch, but we find him, stone-dead.

On the home stretch we take our time, "turning" a squirrel or two while accumulating an easy limit. And so we come, about mid-morning, to the end of a perfect jump-shoot. Carefully, with decks awash, we negotiate the alligator water.

Ab cocks an eye at the sun. 'Whut you say us rides ovah to de rivah, boss, an' try dem geeses? Mister Arthur says he seed a whole passel o' dem over dar las' week."

A second attack upon hot coffee and country sausage. Some pony-express mule saddling by Pomp. High noon finds us breasting the great levee's ramp and dropping down again into the black gold of riparian wilds.

Landmarks crowd up for greeting. The old commissary is a flood-swept, jack-strawed ruin. Even the road has changed. We are forced to circle a quarter-section of sloughed woodland—mighty trees gone the way of all grandeur. But a tottery log cabin still clings to the bank. What a change in the sand bar itself! In earlier days its white expanse cut sharply from the caving escarpment of Harbert's Bend. Thence it bellied north a full three miles toward the Harding light.

Across, behind the bar's loftiest plateau, lay a cutoff section of the old riverbed. What black mallard shooting we used to have in there on windy days with a rising river!

Westward hissed the furious main channel, the rise and fall of its insatiable gnaw spitting spume and drift over gravel and reefs. Bar change is an old story to the veteran goose hunter. Old Man River has a way of not letting his right bank know what his left doeth—that is, until he gets good and ready. First he coats a lower bar tip with silt, gradually building fields of soft, treacherous mud blocks sprouting grand goose feed in the form of tender young switch willows. Then, all at once, some flood scours out a whole bar, tumbling it downriver, to be reorganized miles below. Thus, a plantation owner gains or loses hundreds or even thousands of acres of fast-growing cottonwoods, revetting willows and crop lands, to say nothing, incidentally, of goose bars and duck sloughs.

Ab shoulders decoy pack and shovel. We thread Arthur's path, slashed through half a mile of slender willow stalks. "A school marster sho' would be in de Promised Land wid all dese switches to grab from," ruminates my companion. There is something reminiscently callous in Ab's simile.

We emerge upon a wide bar. The distant river, lower than I have ever seen it, is a mere gash. Barely audible from far below lilts a high goose note. Ab grins as he lowers the profiles and begins spading. "Dey done give deyselves away, an'," shading his hands to peer across the river, "yonner's some mo' struttin' roun' on dat long p'int."

I am soon correctly dug in and stooled. We confer on the stalk.

"I'll ease into de willers, boss," plots Ab, "an' sneak to de low end o' de bar. Den I'll slip out an' git below de geeses an' try to start 'em disaway. You know, boss, sorter rounst aroun' wid 'em."

If agreeable to the "geeses," the plan is quite clear and has my hearty endorsement.

Shouldering his one-hammered double-barrel, in case, as he puts it, "sumpin' mout rise up outa de bushes an' flounce onto him," Ab soon disappears beyond the dunes. Mid-afternoon sunshine hangs in surrender to the chill of expectant waiting.

My eyes travel a panorama of dun shoreline. Where I now stand was mid-current of the Mississippi five years ago. Those tree tops away off there mark the Indian mound's magnificent oaks. The chances are they saw empires change hands. Beneath them, year after year and with Horace to help, my wife and I pitched the goose camp. In memory, the gleam of our fire beckons. We slog toward it, heavily laden and in biting darkness. I strain to lift the heavy yawl upcurrent. I feel the rip of whirlpools, the smother of heavy chop with its sickening sense of disaster left just behind. I hear the patter of rain on our canvas; the frantic bluster of night winds; the clanging din of voyaging goose music trailing into the maw of starlight. I live again the days around our stew kettle with its savors of duck, goose, quail, fish and what-not. Jimmy and Don find bevy after bevy amid the corn and wild peas. The jungles yield tribute of muscadine and persimmon. Whimpering hound pups catch primer scent from "varmint" spoor in the night tangles.

Back talk from the goose precinct arouses me from reverie. Excited gabbling joins the watchman's higher flutings. Suddenly I fancy I catch the thump of lifting pinions. Righto! A black mass winks over the bar parapet. By George, Ab's stalk may bear fruit! They'll hardly take to the river this late. The dark spot writhes into a dotted line against the sky. By the tin ear of the great jinx, they're fixing to cross out my way! Something inside me as old as life and younger than youth zigzags from spine to hair roots.

On they work! A slit 'twixt pit rim and a decoy belly shows that our set is spotted. With my back to the breeze, I am concerned only with the big moment. Is it a straight decoy or just a veer? To do business, or a hasty look-over and fare-thee-well? My eyes read sign through the peep-hole. Excited chatter is suddenly hushed. That has a meaning all its own. No decoy! Their flight is too strong and steady for a slide-in, but they're not disturbed and will cross over me not twenty yards high.

A great black and white shape fills my upturning eyes. The masked muzzle slips evenly past it and erupts. *Wha—am*! The victim blurs as I leap to my feet and swing on to a frantic climber. Reeling under the heavy impact, he slants out of control and crashes in a flurry of sand. It is fast coming sundown. From a distant speck Ab materializes, waves congratulations and retires knowingly beneath a snag root. Flocks of ducks, lazily spending the day on the river, strike course to roosting lakes inland. I decide to gamble fifteen minutes against picking-up time.

Ab whistles shrilly. Good Ab! My eyes devour the Bend, high—low. Ah-ha! Five geese from off the cross-river point! I shiver, wet my lips and stare in almost unbelieving gratitude. They are over our bar now—rising, sinking. Yes, they've seen our profiles! Guttural "alunks" break out! I understand that kind of talk, too!

"Lay off them guys!" the squad sergeant is saying. "I don't like their looks. Step on it, File Closer, an' no back talk! We've five miles to do to Kirby's cornfield."

"Give us a break!" grunts File Closer. "I think I know a gal in that outfit. Gee, but you're tough! Have a heart, Sarge!"

"Oh, all right, buddy, but not too close," growls Sarge, winging a slight left oblique that is really very much against his seasoned judgment.

I hurl both tubes of fours out across space. Good-natured, gruff old Sarge, his canny neck gone suddenly limp, has led his last detail across the cleanest highway.

Ab comes running. We sack the shadows. I am thinking, while we backtrack and board our patient mules, that another rarer day has been vouchsafed me. Such, I reflect, is divided into anticipation, participation and, best of all, memories. Fire-log and impending grub call are vanguard to dreams. To rig decoys, tune one's call or stow plunder against the clock's urge is wine to the blood. To mush fair going or foul, to gauge wind or lead, is to reach as fine a skirmish line as God's outdoors affords.

We top the levee. Wrapping my weather-beaten old mackinaw more closely, I settle deeper into the saddle and turn in fervent blessing and *au revoir*. The west is a melee of brilliance. Far-flung ensembles of pink and purple expire against an ice-blue east. And as it all sinks gradually from view, some unseen hand repaints life's dearest picture. Fire-glow and student lamplight tussle the shadows of a book-lined chamber. A sweet-faced lady reads *Oliver Twist* to a sleepy lad at her knee. Beside the boy, dreaming his own dreams, is stretched a great brown dog. And close by, busily engaged in polishing the chaste side locks of a beautiful gun, sits Brown Velveteens!

Aye, what rarer day?

Tom Hennessey —

TRASH DUCKS

Harold P. Sheldon

In case you did not know it, Sheldon's abilities as a writer ranged beyond his classic "Tranquillity" stories. This gem is from Field & Stream *and the* Field & Stream Reader, *published by Doubleday in 1946. (Not to be confused with the* Field & Stream Treasury *published by Holt in the 50's.)*

OUTSIDE, IN the icy blackness, a blustering wind roared across the open water of the lake. It made ghostly furrows of white water straight across from the Island Point Lighthouse to the bay; it whipped spouts of sand from the rim of the high bluff above the beach and shot hissing volleys of dead leaves along the bare and flinty upland fields.

Inside the cabin the fires roared. The lamps beamed a yellow, comfortable radiance. A tremendous steak just browning nicely on the hot griddle exploded tiny drops of gravy at the bubbling coffee pot. The Baritone and the Sniper, renegades for three days from any useful form of human endeavor, were in high spirits, for the weather, so unpleasant for any Christian undertaking, was just the sort of stuff that whistlers and bluebills glory in.

The steak was evenly divided into two juicy halves, and then for a time the wind and the fire had the argument to themselves.

"Whuff!" said the Baritone finally. "That was a three-pound steak, wasn't it? An' look at it now! I swear it doesn't seem possible that we'll survive the night! But I s'pose we will, an' if we do there'll be whistlers—green, sappy, unsophisticated whistlers just in from points north, so ignorant that they'll be fooled by the awful mess of blocks that Old Gabe calls his decoys. Trash ducks—whistlers and bluebills—*trash* ducks! My Lord! So they call 'em down Currituck, but it ain't so! No, sir! It ain't so! They're good fowl!"

Now it is a fact that whistlers are viewed with scorn by some wild-fowlers, but game species really ought to be, and in some instances are, valued according to the skill and endurance required of one who would take them. On such a basis the golden-eye is an aristocrat, even though the savory flesh that pads his ribs is not so thick, for instance, as that found on the mallard. His jacket is beautiful, and he is a fast and tricky flier. Above all else, he is a rough-weather bird, and one may—and will—get precisely as cold and windbeaten in the legitimate pursuit of whistlers as he will when gunning for canvasback.

Rap! Rap! Rap! Some hand at the door panel sought the refuge of the cabin.

The Sniper and his friend quietly exchanged a quick, understanding look.

"Ol' Cost-Ye-a-Little-Extry!" muttered the Sniper, and he opened the door to admit a mean-looking person in untidy clothes, whose sharp black eyes peered avariciously about the room as if appraising the cash value of the equipment which the gunners had unpacked.

A huge hawk nose gave the face a terrific predatory cast, and to the initiated all these signs marked the man a horsetrader. He was that, and he also owned the two rough ducking blinds down on the jut of sand and rocks that ran out into the waters of the bay. The revenue that he collected from this source and the additional increment derived from such unwary wildfowlers as would play poker with him in the cabin at night made up in total a considerable sum.

Tonight he carried in one hand an earthen jug that bumped against his boot as he shuffled to a seat and gave off deep liquid sounds when he put it down. He pushed his cap back off his low forehead.

"Fetched ye a little mite o' cider," he remarked. "Course, it'll cost ye a little extry, but it's mighty heartenin' on a cold night. Sweet, too, jest as sweet as sugar. No, tain't hard. No, sir. I put a puservative into it, an' it's kept nice. Goin' to be a good day for whistlers. Yes, sir! The bay's full o' duck. Fifty thousand of 'em, an' more coming in. Yes, sir. If the wind holds, the south blind'll be good; an' if it turns, as it may, the north blind will fetch 'em. You'll prob'ly want to hire both blinds, won't ye? Course, it'll cost ye a little extry, but what's money when you're shootin' ducks!"

His scornful laugh indicated that no real gunner ever thought in such mercenary terms.

Presently he proposed a little game of cards, with his jug chortling an accompaniment. The stuff tasted sweet and bland as milk to the palate, but was really as potent as a burst of machine-gun fire.

Now the "old" Army taught two things well—poker and due caution with treacherous beverages—so it happened that after an hour or two Gabe announced his decision to quit and go home. He had sustained alarming losses—two dollars and thirty-five cents, in fact—and his progress to the door was a marvel of high and solemn dignity. With his hand on the knob, he remarked disconsolately, "Certainly spread that puservative with a liberal hand," and vanished into the howling night.

The wind swung about during the night and blew more gently from the south when the two gunners slid down the sandy bluff to the beach a half hour before dawn. A few inches of water slipped uneasily to and fro across the bar as they made their way to the blind.

Such duck blinds are possibly seen nowhere else in the world but on Lake Champlain. They are a source of awe and wonder to every visiting sportsman, who, if he has shot ducks at other resorts, regards these monstrous, evergreen-laced shacks with frank suspicion and speculates as to the mental equipment of any duck that would approach such a flagrant device—and that of any man who would expect any duck to do so.

The blind is really a small cabin equipped with bunks, stove, cooking utensils and two or three old chairs. The single door opens upon a narrow sort of porch with walls shoulder-high and a raised plank platform which the gunner mounts in order to fire over the decoys. The whole structure is covered with evergreen boughs— though no evergreen grows within half a mile of the stand.

The whole affair is as obvious as a lobster on a platter. As a matter of fact, these blinds are fishing huts, used by the sporting shore-dwellers for smelt and pickerel fishing on the ice in the winter months, and made to do duty as shooting boxes when the cold winds of autumn bring the hosts of winged migrants hustling down the old Iroquois war trail.

And the ducks do really come in to those blinds—even the cautious blacks. Possibly they feel that so obvious an ambush can't possibly be an ambush. Yet in other waters these same birds will laugh at the most skillfully arranged rigs in the world and flare off from a muskrat house, unless the rat himself is visible on his porch as evidence of verity.

Old Gabe's sack of disreputable decoys was dragged out—a most woebegone, battered and mismated set of blacks. The riggings of some had been shot away, accidentally, perhaps, or maliciously, by previous gunners. Here and there one showed a ragged hole at the water-line, where a fair load of sixes had landed.

"Looks like the Constitution and the Guerriere," observed the Sniper. "Pickups, every one of 'em. The old scoundrel never brought a decoy in his life—he waits for 'em to get adrift from some other stool. But fasten 'em good, my lad! If you lose one, it'll cost ye——"

"Shut up!" growled the other savagely. "All this chat about money makes me nervous! Just hear the ducks!"

Across the water came the strange, faint roaring sound made by thousands of diving ducks feeding. Now and then they heard the querying "When? When? When?" of bluebills above the murmurous chorus, and once a soft, wild gabble of sound that thrilled them both like a bugle.

"Geese, by ginger!" said one, and hastily they placed the last of the decrepit stool and beached the boat behind the blind.

A faint luminosity lay across the upper air. The beam from the lighthouse on the farther point had lost its earlier brilliance, and winked palely and wan. With a ringing of tiny bells a flock of whistlers, early astir, went down the bay, passing like specters just outside the decoys. The gray and white of their regimentals were nearly invisible against the vague background of sky, far shore and water.

The lighthouse gleamed again, and finally, daylight was suddenly upon the waters, and simultaneously there came the whipping rush of heavy wings from somewhere above the blind. Too late the Sniper spied the five big birds hastening southward and already eighty tantalizing yards away.

"There go the geese!" he exclaimed. "Gosh! They must have passed us in range, too! If I could get one good crack at those fellows, I'd be willing to hang up the fiddle!"

The Baritone moaned. "Me, too! I never did see one of 'em closer than half a mile before. Lord! Aren't they beauties?"

While they gazed, entranced at the vanishing geese, a whistler, coming close under the lee of the spit, dropped quietly among the decoys and sat there, as wooden as the worst of them.

The Baritone looked northward toward the raft of feeding fowl. None were moving yet; or if they were, the faint haze that blew gently along the water effectually masked these distant maneuvers. He occupied himself in a bitter contemplation of Old Gabe's stool.

"Ain't that a hell of an outfit, now it's light enough to see 'em?" said he. "The dowdy-looking, leprous gargoyles! Look at the one on the near corner! Gosh! We ought to go out and set his head on straight. He'll scare a duck to death—sittin' cock-eyed that way. Hell fire! He doesn't look any more like a whistler than my aunt's hat! I've a notion to——"

The derided decoy at this point set his bill toward the lighthouse, and took off in a flurry of foam and flickering wingbeats.

"That's funny, I s'pose," said the Baritone.

On this water, bluebills are loath to come to a point set; but a long curl of them, coming up the lake in perfectly drilled squadrons, suddenly tilted and came straight in—a disciplined van of birds that swept across the decoys and wheeled and swung not twenty yards above the blind. A particularly fat and attractive duck caught the Sniper's seeking eye, and his 16-gauge began to erupt. The duck, among the countless scores that hissed past on all sides, looked as big as a buzzard, but the gun refused to get to that deadly spot six inches in front of the broad bill. Load after load went fruitlessly aloft until the edge of the blind blocked further effort.

The Baritone, humped over his weapon like a machine gunner, was cleaning ducks. Four of them fell in and around the blind before the cavalcade swept out of range.

Afterward, the Sniper stirred a heap of smoking cases with his toe. "Dog-gone, boy! Look here!"

Five shell cases lay on the floor at his feet, and of the five only two were empty!

"Pumped 'em through without shootin' 'em," he declared wonderingly.

And so he had—but he never knew how he did it, for it was supposed to be a mechanical impossibility.

The shooting stirred the rafting fowl. Thousands of birds were in the air—compact flocks of six to a dozen birds and skeins made up of hundreds of fowl swinging and weaving low across the water or twisting in loose curves and spirals above the horizon. The gunners gave little heed to the larger flocks, but watched eagerly the smaller bunches that moved like swallows just above the water. These stragglers would furnish most of the shooting, while the larger congregations would pass wide and high off the point.

The whistler is admirably colored to harmonize with the slaty blue and dense white of rough water. Even with two good pairs of eyes on watch, whistlers will again and again sneak into the decoys unseen until the long splash of their normally tumultuous landing warns the gunners. Someone—an Indian, probably—named these birds ghost ducks, or spirit ducks, and so is qualified to rank with those immortals who knew the priceless value of the right word.

"There's a bunch coming on the inside track!" whispered the Baritone, his forehead pressed against the prickly evergreen screen as he strove to follow the driving flock.

"Can't see 'em!" muttered the other. "Say the word when they're in!"

They're coming! They're coming! Right over the corner! Now!"

Both men lunged upward on the shooting bench. Thirty yards out, eight whistlers, six hens and two cock birds, were slanted into the decoys. Three alighted and sat among the wooden ducks, while the others, alarmed, lifted their paddles and with furiously beating pinions bore straight out into the open lake. Three of these went down, to strike the water like plunging shells and float breasts upward amid the decoys. Thereupon, the birds that had alighted looked at one another in a shocked and horrified manner, and essayed to leave the unholy congregation without words and at once.

The Baritone's big 12 boomed twice, while the Sniper swung with deadly intent on a black and white drake. The bird collapsed, but went under water the instant it struck in a single continuous motion and without interrupting its fall, apparently. It did not show again until it was seventy yards out.

The Sniper dashed out, leaped into the skiff and started off in pursuit, for if a wing-tipped whistler is not retrieved at once he is not retrieved at all. Driving the skiff with all his strength, the gunner gave the bird no attention until he was over the area where it had vanished. Lifting his oars, he watched the surface, and presently, fifty yards away, a black head showed momentarily and vanished. After him went the Sniper, repeating the performance half a dozen times.

By now the duck was tiring, and its brief appearances were at shorter intervals and within a few yards of the boat. Now the Sniper dropped his oars and seized his gun. Twice the quick black head rose and vanished before he could bring the gun to bear, but at last the chance came. A load of shot exactly timed caught the target fairly, and a plump duck bobbed to the surface.

"Glad of that," muttered the gunner. "I'd rather a darned sight miss 'em clean than hit 'em and lose 'em." He was astonished to observe that he was half a mile from the blind.

The Baritone slew a pair while the other was rowing in, and there was joy in his face as he looked down at the Sniper from the high wall of the ridiculously effective ambush. "A flight must have come in last night," he announced. "They're all decoying. Get in here quick!"

A lone bluebill, following the shoreline on hissing wings, came to the Sniper's side, and was dropped and gathered with all the acclaim due his rank, for though whistlers are not to be scorned, the plump scaup rates an extra flourish and ruffles.

Another highlight came when the Sniper, seated comfortably before the oil stove in the blind with a smoking cup of coffee in one fist and a huge sandwich in the other, saw, through the tiny window, a shadow that flashed past the stool. At high speed and with perfect economy of motion, he placed his viands on the bench, seized his gun, dashed back to the door, and nailed a whistler just a yard inside the extreme range limit of an ounce of chilled sixes!

Soon after lunch the two gunners observed various flocks of bluebills that came from far down the lake. The first of these dropped to the surface of the bay half a mile away and were instantly lost to view against the neutral background. But presently, as other flocks decoyed to the small original colony, the living raft grew until it was visible as a deep, black line that stretched for a mile across the water.

"Must be ten thousand of 'em," the Baritone estimated.

"Yes! And might little good they'll do us. They'll sit there until sundown and never get nearer than they are now. I'm going up to the cabin and get a box of 2's. There'll be a lot of birds passing outside the stool just at sunset, and with the right prescription you can trip one up at sixty yards once in awhile."

The speaker left the blind, crossed the bar and climbed the bluff. At this point he paused. A deep, rolling thunder came from the bay, and turning he saw the whole tremendous raft of bluebills on the wing. With the perfect precision of flight so characteristic of the scaup, the whole division swung against the breeze, dipped and flowed—exactly like masses of maneuvering cavalry—and then, to the Sniper's amazement, came swiftly and certainly toward the blind. He prayed that his friend was on the alert to profit by this phenomenon.

Just as the front ranks were breaking and flaring twenty yards above the blind, a gun barrel rose behind the cedar fringe and he saw the light vapor of the explosions and stricken fowl collapsing. After an appreciable time the sound of the shots came to his ears. The leading ducks spun off to the right and left, but the rearward squadrons swept on, heedless of the Baritone, who now dropped his empty gun and seized the one the Sniper had left. This he emptied also, and still the stream of ducks swept on and over until the last filed closer in the uttermost rank had sped over the decoys and slanted away after his fellows.

Six birds bobbed about among the decoys when the astonishing visitation had vanished. The Baritone, reluctant to spoil the flavor of the experience by further shooting at strays and stragglers, collected his birds and retired to his corner for the afternoon to meditate, no doubt, upon the infinite powers of a telepathy that could call ten thousand bluebills to him from the safety of the open bay. Having accomplished the incomprehensible stunt, the entire raft swung back and alighted precisely on the spot from which it had recently risen. Nor, so far as the human eye could measure, had the raft moved a yard from its position at sundown.

The Sniper, who warmed a hope that the miracle would be repeated for his benefit, was compelled to make up his score from the smaller bunches of whistlers that scouted continuously up and down the shoreline. At sunset he climaxed his day by doubling on a pair of fat, red-legged black ducks that came silently down over the bar. So heavy with luscious fat were these birds that one of them, hurtling down upon the hard sand, split like a ripe plum!

That night the cabin stove was stuffed until it roared. A pair of ducks, neatly trussed, lay ready for the bed of broiling coals. The Baritone, kicking off his boots from numbed feet, held his cramped fingers to the heat and remarked:

"Trash ducks? No, sir! It's a rough, tough sport, and I'd as soon have whistlers as canvasback—'specially when I can't get the canvasback. Ho, hum! How about opening a couple cans of beans and some corned beef to sort of go with those ducks you're fixing?"

MEDITATIONS IN A DUCK BLIND

A. Starker Leopold

Whether in solitude or shared, the time spent in a duck blind is made richer by private moments in which feelings and observations become intense. This piece by A. Starker Leopold stirs my own memories of dawn on marshes past and renews my anticipation for the season ahead. A. Starker Leopold, himself one of America's most effective voices for conservation and responsible wildlife management, is Aldo Leopold's son. His father was one of the nation's greatest conservationists and author of the classic, A Sand County Almanac. *This essay first appeared in* Gray's Sporting Journal, *Volume Two, Issue Six.*

THE WARMTH of the sun finally penetrates the chill in the barrel, and the numbness begins to leave my toes. I have noticed often that the coldest period in a barrel blind is the half hour or so after sunrise. Cold air trapped in the barrel seems to persist after the marsh itself is steaming with warmth. But now, with physical comfort being restored, I have no complaints with the world.

The duck pond surrounding my barrel is calm—really much too calm for duck hunting. From the vantage point of eye level just above the waterline, I see each decoy mirrored upside down on the still surface. A promising north breeze diminished at daylight, and with it the chance of a good morning flight. But I have two fat sprigs in hand, taken in the flurry of activity at daylight, and it really is not important that I kill any more. Why then will I sit on the blind through the long hours of the morning? The ostensible reason is the outside chance of another shot at a duck. But the real reason I suppose is that tranquility of being alone in the marsh, untroubled by the banalities of human society—the frets and frustrations of home, the office, the highway—all completely out of mind for a few refreshing hours. Only the marsh and its life claim my attention.

There are still a few high flocks of ducks passing overhead, perhaps on the move from Suisun Bay to some of the refuges farther up the Sacramento Valley. They hold their travel formation without showing the least interest in my little pond. A flock of about 40 geese trails along the same route—mostly snows but with a few dark white-fronts scattered through the ranks. Such mixed flocks always bring to mind some smile about integration, but the idea passes quickly for I have no time in the marsh to worry about social affairs.

A dozen dowitchers, skimming the water in close rank, swish a few feet overhead, startling both me and my dog. Of all the shorebirds that grace the Valley marshes in winter, the dowitchers are the most lively and most interesting. Sometimes a flock will alight in shallow water near the blind and immediately each bird starts probing the mud with its long beak, seeking insects or invertebrates of kinds unknown to me. A low warbling of plaintive notes signifies some sort of social communication as the group moves slowly along. A passing marsh hawk often is the stimulus that sends the flock on its busy way again with a shrill chorus of farewells.

The marsh hawk also stirs up the jacksnipe that frequent the more heavily vegetated fringes of the marsh. They fly about singly or in little "wisps," and I keep hoping for an overhead pass shot, since snipe are among the most appreciated trophies of the hunt. When I leave the duck barrel I will spend half an hour trying to take a few on jump shots. But they do not often come over the blind, or if they do, it is from behind with no warning. I recall vividly the jacksnipe winnowing and courtship display in June near Bethel, in western Alaska, and wonder how many of these seemingly frail little birds came all that distance to winter in California. When the first big wave of snipe reaches our pond in early November, the birds have little subcutaneous fat—they have used it en route apparently. But by early December they are roly-poly again.

A dozen sprigs appear directly overhead with wings cupped and showing definite interest in our pond. I duck my head and watch under the brim of my hat as they cut a wide circle, dropping down but not very rapidly, inspecting the situation with all the caution of ducks that have been shot at more than once this season. Still I am hopeful that they may come down, until far in the distance some other hunter shoots once, and my flock flares up wildly as though the shot were directed at them. So much for that opportunity. It occurs to me that I have not heard a shot for at least half an hour, but this one had to come at the precise moment of decision when I have birds dropping overhead.

My attention is drawn to a white-tailed kite, hovering motionless over the nearby pasture—its eye doubtless glued on a meadow mouse runway, looking for the slightest movement of the owner and occupant. Kites have increased spectacularly in California in the past 25 years. At one time they were reduced to the verge of oblivion, presumably by thoughtless shooting. So scarce did this handsome little hawk become that the California legislature placed it on the list of completely protected species, along with the condor, the sea otter and some others. Now with protection and the termination of the frontier prejudice against birds of prey, the kite has again become the most numerous resident hawk in the Central Valley. Its recovery is a tribute to the conservation endeavor. As I watch the little fellow hover, he suddenly stops his wing beat and floats gracefully to earth with wings held rigidly upward. Since he does not reappear I am led to hope that he is enjoying a meal of fresh mouse.

I re-examine the two sprigs laid out with care and ceremony on the lath platform beside my barrel—a cock and a hen. Both seem to be fat, judging from the heft as I lift one and then the other. Likewise the keel of the sternum is scarcely discernible above the level of the breast muscles. They ought to be fat, for both came out of flocks milling about over the pond at daylight. Skinny sprigs usually fly alone, unable to keep up with a flock because of some past gunshot wound or illness. Mentally, I go back over both daylight shots— a flock of a dozen coming straight overhead just at 6:40, shooting time, 30 yards high and set-up double. I killed a drake with the right barrel and inexplicably missed another drake with the left. There is lots of time to think about those mysterious misses. Twenty minutes later three hen sprigs came by a bit wide for a twenty gauge but I pulled one out dead with a left barrel and did not try for a second. Two birds, three shells—I am ready to settle for that. Moreover, the dawn brought with it the usual mystique—whispering wings overhead before there was enough light to see, then the ghostly shadows that come and go in the dimness of pre-dawn. Soon there are clearer views of ducks passing in easy shotgun range, some clearly identifiable as sprigs, others just ducks (maybe spoonies—watch out now!). The watch is checked with increasing frequency—four minutes 'til legal shooting time, then two, one minute—NOW. As gunfire begins to reverberate over the marsh, I have first chance and score, as I have said. I know of no situation that raises the adrenalin level like daylight on a duck marsh.

But that was hours ago. Adrenalin is long since expended, and as the warmth of the sun penetrates the back and my hunting coat, attention wanders and I indulge in various displacement activities. A careful search of all the pockets in my hunting coat reveals a single stick of gum which is unwrapped with considerable ceremony. The flavor is cheering and I carefully wad up the wrappings and spend some time deciding how to dispose of them (they are shoved into an empty shell case ultimately, and pushed deep into the mud). A spider sways on his trapeze between two grass blades, and I think of Robert Bruce and the inspiration he derived from a swinging spider that impelled him onward to victory over the English at Bannockburn. A flight of long-billed curlews passes nearby in stately array— they frightened me at first for I thought they were ducks. We do not see as many curlews now as in the years past when more of the countryside around our pond was in pasture. Now most of it is in row crops—corn, sugarbeets, or tomatoes—of less attraction to curlews.

Without forewarning I look up directly into the face of a pair of sprigs coming straight at me in easy shooting range. How they arrived without my seeing them I do not know. I snatch up my gun, fumble for the safety, and bring the sight to bear on the flaring drake to my left. The swing is jerky and by no means precise, but I shoot anyway and see the bird flinch heavily but keeping flying. So I have to use the second barrel on the same bird, and this time I connect solidly. The bird folds convincingly and falls in a long arc toward the pond.

My fine little setter is going blind, unfortunately (the vet calls it "retinal atrophy"), and he no longer can see ducks overhead or mark a fall. But he does a fair job of retrieving with his ears and nose. At the shooting he sits up very straight and listens intently. When the heavy drake sprig hits the water with a resounding "splat" the dog takes off in the general direction of the noise. Usually he drifts downwind to cut the lee of the bird. Today there is no wind, so he zig-zags about the pond until he finally catches the scent, then proudly picks up the duck and looks about for some clue as to the whereabouts of the blind. A little blast on the dog whistle orients him for the retrieve. I receive the prize with warm expressions of gratitude and then turn my head as the dog shakes a curtain of water before returning to his small barrel beside mine.

Before laying out the drake with the other two birds, I admire the sheen of its plumage and the long pintail feathers which signify more surely than the calendar the end of the season is approaching. Early fall sprigs do not have the long pins. There is a purplish iridescence on the head of a male pintail that is best seen on a fresh bird before the feathers are pressed down. I check his weight and he feels fat, too—three dandy birds in hand. It will be a pleasure to clean them and manicure the white skin under the breast plumage. Christmas is coming and I will need a good number of prime ducks to dispense among favored friends—two fat sprigs and a good bottle of red wine have long seemed to me a proper holiday gift.

I settle back comfortably in the blind and resume my reflections. I am increasingly distressed to meet young people who know nothing about hunting—little or nothing about the outdoor-life, in fact—but who take violent exception to the propriety of shooting wild game. They envision hunters as wanton killers marching about the countryside "shooting as they come" to quote from *Peter and the Wolf*. I wonder if they could possibly understand the spiritual and inspirational experience that constitutes real hunting, as I know it. I wonder, too, what these youngsters do themselves for a calm escape from the pressure of 20th century living. I find this escape in the precious hours or days that I am afield with gun and dog. Presumably, non-hunters have some alternative escape from reality, hopefully as effective and restorative as mine.

A tree swallow swoops into view beside the blind and startles me to reach for my gun, until I have identified the source. From the flight of the swallows it is clear that they are finding flying insects to eat, and when I look very closely at the water surface near my barrel I can see tiny midgets emerging and popping directly into the air. A swallow must have to consume myriads of those little bugs to find the energy for its graceful flight. Where do the swallows roost, I wonder? Where were they at daylight when there was heavy frost on the marsh? To what mountain aspen patch will they return to nest? These are intriguing questions, but I must keep alert, lest another sprig surprise me in my musing.

But no ducks appear. I finally acknowledge, regretfully, that the flight is over. It is time to leave the blind, to try for a few shots of jacksnipe, and then to walk to the automobile and face the world again.

THE DUCKS AT TRANQUILLITY

Archibald Rutledge

In reading and enjoying the works of Archibald Rutledge over the years, one impression that has held fast in my thoughts is that the Rutledge plantation, Hampton, appeared to be a slice of pure heaven that had inadvertently been placed in South Carolina. Imagine that sprawling, mighty acreage of croplands, ragged edges, tall and uncut forests of pine, oak, cypress, and sweet gum, the whole layout dotted with jewel-like, sweet-water ponds and laced with hidden creeks of black water that led eventually down to the mighty Santee River and thence on to the ocean. Imagine also the feelings that stirred through Rutledge as every Christmas vacation neared its end. For, alas, despite his great land holdings Rutledge was a dedicated teacher whose duties took him away from his beloved Hampton for most of the year. While serving as Professor of English at Mercersburg Academy in Pennsylvania, Rutledge furthered his vast hunting and wildlife experiences in the rugged, rock-ribbed Alleghenies, and he wrote well of what he saw and felt there. But it is his Hampton-inspired South Carolina material that has formed the basis of most of his voluminous books of hunting stories, wildlife and nature essays, and poems. (He was Poet Laureate of South Carolina.) The best two hunting books are the anthologies, Hunter's Choice *and* An American Hunter. *If they are not on your library shelf, you are missing two classics. After serving at Mercersburg from 1904 to 1937, Rutledge retired and then lived full-time at Hampton for thirty-six years, hunting and writing until he passed away at the age of eighty-nine, early in the 1970's. He was never better than in this charming tale of the region's great duck shooting opportunities. It's from* An American Hunter.

THE SEA-ISLANDS off the Carolina coast are, I suppose, as primeval in their abundance of game as any other places in America. Deer, wild turkeys, shore birds of all kinds, and wild ducks abound. The

deer and turkeys are permanent residents; most of the shore birds
are seasonal migrants; and the ducks are occasional winter visitors.
On stormy days they love the utter peace and security of the ponds
on the islands that are sheltered by the dense semi-tropical forests.
But on calm fair days they roam far up the deltas of the coastal
rivers, finding in the old ricefields there ample food, and in many of
the winding creeks and straight canals shelter, solitude, and security.

My place is ten miles up the Santee River; and on the delta both
above me and below me wild ducks have always wintered in myriads:
mallards, black ducks, teal, sprigs, widgeons, blackheads, and occasionally a few canvasbacks. About fourteen miles from its mouth the
river divides; and its waters are borne to the ocean and two parallel
channels, approximately a mile apart. This country between them
is the Santee Delta, one of the really great wildfowl rivieras of our
country. Ever since that part of the world was settled in 1986, it
has afforded almost unfailing sport to generations of hunters. I too
have had good times there.

The thought of going down the river to Tranquillity came to me
about noon one December day, after I had returned from the pinelands where we had been hunting deer. Just before reaching home,
riding along with my Negro driver, I had seen a big flock of mallards
passing low over the yellow pines, heading eastward.

"I wonder where they're going," I said half to myself.

"Dem's gwine Stramfittity."

The Negro spoke as one having authority. I knew that he meant
Tranquility, one of the strangest places on all the wide and lonely
delta.

Reaching home, a Tranquillity feeling took possession of me. I
thought of the solitary sand-hill amid the wild wastelands of the
South Carolina coast; I thought of the snug cabin there; I thought
of the clouds of wildfowl that loved that place. When a hunter begins to entertain such seductive thought, his moral resistance is as
good as gone. It was so with me. After I had taken one look at the
river, I yielded. And before an hour had passed, I was on our old
wharf, my things in a dugout cypress canoe, and my sturdy paddler
waiting for me to get in.

With some ruefulness I eyed the ancient craft. It had an indefinable air of weariness. It seemed to me that its spirit was sinking. I told my dusky navigator so.

"She is all right," he reassured me. "My preacher," he went on, "done already tole me that Gawd loves a gunner-man; and Gawd will keep him safe even if he ain't got no sense hisself."

Comforted by this speech, I took my seat in the canoe, the gunwales of which were just about awash; and merrily we dropped down the yellow Santee tide. Like the ducks that I had gazed at longingly, we were "gwine Stramfittity."

A seven-mile paddle brought us into the creek that leads far into the heart of the delta country. A wide, placid stream it was, overhung by many tall reeds, by whispering marshes, by elders and willows. After a time we came within sight of an ancient circular brick tower, standing weirdly up in the desolate marsh. I knew that it was on Wicklow, the place next to Tranquillity, and that it was a "slave tower."

A century ago, when rice-growing and slaves were the great crops in my country, these towers were built as refuges for the slaves and their overseers when sudden West Indian hurricanes swept the delta. In the great gale of 1922, at Murphy's Island, only about three miles from Tranquillity, almost a hundred Negroes were drowned in one of these storms.

Soon I saw two gnarled live-oaks amid the marshy wastes; then a humble cottage, from the chimney of which smoke curled. Beside the cottage was a tiny shack that I used as a clubhouse when gunning.

London Legree, a Negro, lived on Tranquillity, and whenever I went down he looked after me. He lived like a prince on his little island in the delta; but he spent much of his time on the adjacent mainland, where, it was rumored, he practiced among the other Negroes all kinds of occult wizardry. I think this was chiefly financial, for he was President of the Good Centurion Society and the treasurer of the Come and Go Burial Association.

London saw us coming down the creek in the full, placid sunlight of the late afternoon. When we reached the wharf, he was there to meet us and to welcome us.

"Plenty of duck is here for you, Cap'n," were London's words. "They been in my garden last night."

If you can visualize Tranquillity, you can appreciate what London meant. The highland of Tranquillity is not over three or four acres in area, a strange sandy plateau in the very heart of the whispering wilderness of marsh. On all sides are flooded fields were ducks spend the night, and sometimes the day as well.

To this elevation, when the waters are high, incredible numbers of Wilson's snipe throng. It is the only place where I have actually seen flocks of several hundred of these fine game birds. Here, too, ducks would occasionally come at night, waddling about on the swampy edges or even, as London had said, invading his humble garden. Even while we were going up to the clubhouse I saw the first flocks of the evening flight coming in.

In almost any kind of hunting there is always a certain place of which the sportsman says, "if I could only be there." Tranquillity is that place, as far as the ducks of the Santee Delta are concerned. After the mallards and black ducks, the widgeons and the teal have spent the day in the warm offshore waters and on the sunny off-shore banks, they are hungry; and here are silent overflowed fields that offer duck-oats, waterlily roots, lotus seeds, and other duck delicacies. Of course, they come to spend the night.

"You gwine shoot this evening, Cap'n?" London asked me. "I notice they is flying over a little oak."

Taking my gun and a pocketful of shells, I went with him to the smaller of the two live-oaks, over which, even then, a good many ducks were passing. The ducks were coming from the southeast. We stood just northwest of the oak, and partly sheltered. For an hour, while the sun sank and a gorgeous sunset flamed and faded, I watched the mighty host of wildfowl streaming in over the lonely sedgefield country.

I had some shooting; in fact, bagged seven mallards. Two of them fell straight through the oak. All of them fell on the highland. It gives one peculiar satisfaction to bag these splendid birds "in the dry." After it was too late to shoot, I stood on the sandy plateau listening to the thousands of ducks beating overhead, calling from the old fields, feeding in vast squadrons with a noise that made me think of the rushing of a distant waterfall. Then I went indoors to the good supper that London's wife had prepared, after which I told him that we would leave at daylight for the real shooting.

I turned in, expecting to go speedily to sleep; but a man who loves wildlife can hardly be wooed to dreamland when the mysterious night-air is full of those very sounds which he likes best to hear. I lay with my head close to an open window which overlooked a northward stretch of the glimmering country. A misty moon shot long lances of light into the reeds. I could not only hear the ducks; I could actually see them as they entered certain pools in the reedy morasses.

As for hearing them, they were literally beleaguering the place, and their talk was intimate, confidential, trustful. I heard more actual domestic duck-gossip that night than I had ever listened to before. Far into the night I listened, fascinated; then I drowsed off to the thin sweet music of winnowing wings, splashing waters, faint dreamy wild voices. I slept soundly until London called me the next morning at six o'clock.

After our breakfast and just as the first hints of day were showing in the east, we went down to the wharf and climbed into my boat. London had offered to paddle me; and I was glad to have him do so, for he knew every ditch and creek of the delta. He also knew where we were most likely to find sport that was worthwhile. I asked him if he had faith that Providence always would look out for the welfare of a hunter. London laughed with high good humor.

"I done hear dat St. Paul been a hunter hisself," he told me.

"What makes you think so?" I asked.

"The Bible done say," London told me, "dat Paul p'int his pistol at the Fesians."

Somebody had been telling London about St. Paul's Epistle to the Ephesians; he had slightly misinterpreted the business. As a theologian, London is a cracking fine ducker.

This particular kind of ducking that we were about to enjoy is, I think, of a rather rare variety, and it has a charm all its own. The idea is that while many of the ducks repair to the sea with the coming of day, many more do not, preferring to spend the daylight hours in the old canals, on sheltered mudbanks in the lazy creeks, and in the sunny privacy of the flooded marshes.

A man paddling about these old watercourses can, in the course of a morning, flush at close range a great many single ducks and not a few pairs. Any shooting done from a boat is fairly difficult; and when one does not know exactly when his game is going to rise before him, the sporting chance is heightened.

Down the misty creek we dropped. There was hardly light enough to shoot. I could hear and faintly see many ducks passing overhead. Suddenly I felt London check and slightly veer the canoe. I knew what he meant. A moment later a big mallard drake rose from the marsh-edge with a lordly outcry. My gun gave answer to his hail, and he plunged downward on the brightening waters of the creek. I have always felt that a good start in shooting is like a good start in anything else; it takes a man a long way in the right direction.

At my shot, which reverberated far across the solitary fields, thousands of ducks arose. My paddler, knowing that some of these would pass us, guided the boat inshore as soon as we had retrieved our first bird. A flock of perhaps forty greenwinged teal came zipping by. A teal never has any regard for speed limits and other traffic regulations. I shot into the flock, and we picked up three.

Then down the creek we stole noiselessly, watching the bends and the little coves and the lee-stretches. By the time we reached the river, we had altogether a bag of eleven ducks. London was in high spirits.

"This next Sunday, I'se gwine acclaim myself a Christian of the Church," he told me earnestly.

I asked him what reason he had for doing so.

"Nobody could have the luck we is having unless his soul is right with his Maker."

Being no authority on such matters, I forebore to answer, but his philosophy was a pleasing one.

We cruised down the river's edge for two miles, until indeed we could see the ocean ahead. On this long stretch we jumped perhaps a hundred ducks, most of them from little estuaries in the rugged banks. By no means did all ducks that rose offer us shots. But we had good sport and, ere we made a turn, we had almost the limit.

London now took me into an old canal that cut into the very heart of the delta. Though originally artificial, it has long since reverted to Nature, and is deepened and widened by the constant dredging of the tides. In this dim backwater and in the smaller feeding-ditches running into it, there were a good many ducks in singles and pairs. Occasionally these would hear us coming and would rise out of range. Again, we might come within twenty yards of them.

I have found that in jumping ducks the art of killing apparently consists, as it does in all shooting, in keeping one's nerve and then holding fire until the bird has completed his first mad upward leap. There is great danger, otherwise, of undershooting. A frightened duck, spasmodically propelled by wings and feet, will often leap seven or eight feet straight up, after which he will start away in standard fashion. As in grouse shooting, the height of the rise often offers the best chance.

At the head of the canal we entered a tortuous creek that, after windings of three miles, led us serenely back to Tranquillity. It was now midday. We had the limit of ducks. The sport had been fast and clean. My guide had been cheerful, skillful, companionable. Moreover, on his own testimony, our hunt had made him a confirmed Christian. Who says that hunting is barbarous pastime?

As for me, and I'm just an average sportsman, I hope that I may live to enjoy many another ducking trip to Tranquillity, and I hope that the Happy Hunting Grounds, among many other charming haunts for sportsmen, will have a place as much as possible like the Tranquillity that I know and love well.

DANKY KNOWS HIS DUCKS

Archibald Rutledge

*An encore for Mr. Rutledge, as we return to the same South Caro-
lina setting as the previous chapter. The men of the Rutledge plantation, Hampton, are interesting and vivid characters in many of
Rutledge's stories, and Danky is no exception.*

WHEN GOOD old good-for-nothing Steve took me on the delta after
the old bronzed men who there reside, he was affording me the kind
of sport that a lone hunter can often enjoy in the Santee country.
But the sport alone is not all that makes that region delightful; for,
being in a country of vast plantations, one becomes friends with the
owners of these game-haunted places, and we neighbors visit one
another, especially during the hunting season. A typical visit of this
sort was the memorable one I paid to the beloved Reeves family, at
Annandale—people so hospitable that, however generous a man may
be, after a visit with them, he instinctively resolves to do more for
the friends who come to his hearthstone.

Twilight was falling on my plantation when Dick Reeves, a dear
friend of mine from Annandale, a place across the Santee from
mine, drove up and hailed me. Now, when a fellow sportsman who
has a superb hunting preserve visits me, I try not to look too darned
expectant—though he knows and I know that I'm just naturally crazy
for an invitation to go places and bring my old duck gun along. We
passed through the innocuous weather-stage of our greeting. Then
he said, "Been killing any ducks?"

"No," I answered, as mournful as an unkissed bride.

"Well," he said, "you'd better come over tonight and stay with
us. We are going to try it early in the morning, and I want Danky
to paddle you."

Now, the name "Danky" has a fascination for me, for this old
Negro knows his ducks. When you find a Negro who really knows
game, you'll hardly find a better guide. His natural nearness to Na-

ture enables him to enter into the lives and hearts of game; he has a dim infallible prescience, an intuitive understanding that insures rare sport to the man who accompanies him. So, though I needed no special encouragement to accept the invitation, the thought of Danky lent to the whole business an extra allurement. Will I shoot ducks with Danky paddling me? Will a debutante accept a millionaire?

At twilight I reached Annandale, a beautiful plantation home in its quiet setting among the oaks and pines. About the house are japonicas and gardenias, but, my host told me, "The deer eat nearly all the leaves and flowers." On three sides the pine forests and the old fields of the planatation stretch interminably away; to the east is a long swamp, behind which lie the old ricefields, with Minim Creek and dozens of canals and smaller creeks winding through them. South of the duck country is the North Santee River; to eastward are miles of marsh, cane-brake and myrtle jungles, full of deer; to the north lies Winyah Bay.

The duck fields of Annandale are, therefore, a part of a peninsula between a bay and a great river. And ducks love Annandale almost as much as I do. To stay overnight at Annandale and to shoot ducks there in the early morning is just about my idea of dreams come true.

Into that remote and lovely hinterland the wild doings of the world never really penetrate. I recall mentioning the Depression to an old Negro. He looked puzzled, but seemed to feel obligated to say something. "It wouldn't be so bad," he ventured, "if it hadn't come at so bad a time." The closer one lives to Nature, the less he is affected by the chances and changes of life.

Now, this duck shooting at Annandale can be blind-shooting in ponds, but most hunters prefer jumping their ducks. This is a sport that has about it practically all the qualities that genuine hunting should have: constant alertness is demanded; as your canoe is softly paddled up the meandering creeks and canals you are constantly changing scene; as the ducks jump either from the water or from the marsh which borders it, you have to be handy with your old fusee. I always enjoy, too, the quiet woodsy philosophy of the Negro who is paddling me. He takes an intense personal interest in each duck, and remarks about every one as he would about a human individual.

Jumping ducks in the morning calls for an early start, and by that I mean that the hunter should be in his boat by the first streak of dawn. These ducks at Annandale have regular habits. They spend the night in these old fields and creeks, and during the day repair to the great sand-bars in the ocean, whence they return at twilight. If the weather is very rough, they may linger in the sheltered ditches and estuaries; but their standard schedule is to leave shortly after daybreak.

After we had breakfasted by firelight, my host, his brother Graham, and their sister Diana, and I got in the plantation carryall and drove through the sleeping swamp to the old rice barn, where our boats were tied up in an old canal. I remember how the Southern stars blazed, how soft and fragrant was the December air, how mysterious was the wistful landscape of that land of dreams.

Deer, retiring for their daytime siesta, crashed away through the marsh upon our approach. In the fields we could hear hosts of wild ducks still clamoring as if they were having a community bridge party. We did no talking, for in those dewy hours just before the dawn the human voice carries far and fatally.

Each one was assigned a boat and a paddler. Dick Reeves said, "Arch, I want Danky to take you into Sand Creek. It will only be a question of whether you have enough shells." He added, chuckling, "Danky knows his ducks."

The Negro who had charge of me has a great reputation in that part of the country. He heads most of the Negro lodges and burial societies, and he is the only Negro I have known who has been permitted both to be a treasurer and to keep the key of the lock-box. Two men are nearly always used to divide that delicate responsibility.

Huge in size, rather majestic in appearance, Danky might easily be an African chief. However, he is intensely, even ludicrously human, despite his imposing mien. He goes after things in a big elemental way. Dick told me that, after Danky had been toothless for years, he had been presented with his first set of plates, whereupon he celebrated by eating a whole ham!

As soon as I was in the boat and we had begun to move down the dark tide, I knew that my boatman's reputation as a ducker was already justified, for in this particular sport nearly everything depends on the skill of the boatman. The canoe must be kept absolutely steady; the paddle must not rap the sides, not make the water curl and gurgle too loudly; and the paddler's command must be such that, if ducks jump at too acute an angle to the side or behind, he can quickly yet steadily swing the boat so that the hunter is in position for a shot.

Leaving the mouth of the canal, we crossed the still misty reaches of Minim Creek. I could hear ducks all about me, and in the skies over me.

"There are plenty here," I ventured, my voice sounding like a foghorn in that immense silence.

"You must not talk, sir," whispered Danky gravely. "Ducks don't like our conversation. I will take you to them."

We entered the mouth of Sand Creek just as the first pearly pink of dawn came into the sky. This creek winds for miles and miles through the lonely reedlands, and is entered here and there by smaller waterways and by old ricefield ditches. In these retired backwaters the ducks love to drowse and idle. Here they have practically no enemies save man and bald eagle; and wherever both these enemies are found, the eagle rarely bothers unwounded ducks, lazily preferring to live on the dead and the cripples.

As we were gliding along up the glimmering creek a gun blared behind us, and suddenly the whole sky was dark with ducks. Now, I have heard a lot about the diminishing duck supply, and I have heard sportsmen asking, "Where are the ducks?" Well, a good many are at places like Annandale.

Taking advantage of the chaos of sound, Danky said, "Get ready. You will shoot at the next bend."

Before we reached the bend, out of a ditch-mouth there suddenly stormed forty or fifty small ducks. I knew from their shrill, sweet cries that they were wood ducks. I might add that during that morning's trip I must have seen several hundred of these lovely birds, which a few years ago were threatened with extinction.

As we neared the bend that Danky had warned me about, I saw a telltale rippling of the otherwise placid surface of the creek. Danky made the canoe hug the marsh shore, propelling it with eerie silence. As we made the turn, six mallards rose, brilliant in that early light. They got up in a very confused way; or perhaps I was really the one confused. I did not know which one to shoot, and while I was try-ing to make up my mind they were well on their way. I dropped one in the creek, and there he lay, a regal old drake. I felt better; for it's a bad thing, at any time and any place, to come home empty-handed. These moral victories never put any dinner on the table.

Sand Creek is not overhung by reeds and marsh alone, but by a good many trees and bushes. The ducks, therefore, in jumping, are likely to do one of two things: they will either make a fast getaway along the level of the water, almost skimming its surface; or else they will make a prodigious leap, from eight to ten feet in the air, almost straight up, before they straighten out to go places. This latter ma-neuver I have long studied very carefully, and have found that it is accomplished by a wild driving of the wings against the water. To the hunter the thing is disconcerting, and he will usually undershoot his duck. The thing to do is to let him finish that first jump, and then give it to him.

Indeed, there is a principle here, the observance of which will help many hunters to become better shots. Nearly all wild game, if flushed or started close, will uncork a frenzied maneuver; at sight of it, the hunter himself is liable to get momentarily frenzied, and shoot violently in the general direction of the cavorting game.

Well I remember standing one day beside an old pineland hunter, watching him shoot a buck. I had killed mine, and we were together when we walked up this other one. We were within twenty yards when the old stag stormed out of a patch of myrtles. He appeared to have been commissioned to carry a cablegram to the Prince of Wales or to some one else very important and far, far away. My friend had his gun on the deer before the deer had cleared the thicket. But he did not shoot. I said nothing, because I had faith in what the man was doing. At last came the gun, and down went the stag.

"You see, Arch," he drawled, "when a buck is pitching like that, you must always let him get two or three jumps out of his system. And by the time he's steady, you'll be more steady too."

Danky now gave me the same advice when he said, "Cap'n, don't shoot until they begin to get over their scare."

It was now broad daylight. I could hear my companions shooting from many parts of that immense wild marsh country; the sky was filled with thronging ducks—mallards, black ducks, widgeons, teal and an occasional canvasback. I had only one duck; and from the general nature of the bombardment, I judged that somebody must have the limit. In hunting of this sort, and indeed in most hunting, there is a friendly rivalry that makes the sport much keener than if a man were merely a lone hunter.

A little farther up the creek a duck and a drake, both blacks, swam out of the marsh. On these I made a double as they jumped.

"Now," commented Danky as he collected the pair of ducks, "they will never go to camp meetin' no mo'."

The day, which had promised to be fair, showed some rifty clouds, and a keen wind had begun to blow in from the sea.

Noticing how the ducks were circling and dropping down here and there, Danky said, "They ain't so anxious to go outside today. A duck is just like a man: he don't mind the rain so much, but he likes to keep out of the cold and wind."

As we entered the straight stretch of the creek, two mallards suddenly swerved out of the sky about two hundred yards dead ahead, took the line of the creek, and came head on for me, flying not more than four feet above the water. Of all the shots I know on wildfowl, not even excepting the one that compels you to shoot to the right and behind you, the straight-for-you seems to me most difficult. In such a case the very appearance of the bird is strange; and the hunter is put in a sort of self-defensive attitude, as if he were compelled to shoot in order to keep the swiftly oncoming projectile from knocking his block off. And you know what happens if you let such game pass you, and then whirl and try to shoot—the whirling business being especially ticklish if you happen to be in a tippy canoe.

These ducks were not merely bearing down on me; they were boring toward me. As steadily as I could, I set my sight between the closely flying pair and let drive, feeling quite a man even to have shot my gun under such circumstances.

As these fugitives were coming at a terrific pace, the momentum of the drake I killed brought him almost up against the boat; and when the duck flared, I almost felt the wind from her wings. As I gathered in my bird I listened for Danky's approval. It was not forthcoming. Deciding to prime him, I said, "We were lucky to get one. Danky."

"He is shot so hard and close, Cap'n, that I don't think you can use him," he answered, showing me the fine breast of the mallard, frayed and ragged.

Perhaps it is better to risk a miss or no shot at all than to shoot a game bird too close.

As we went on up Sand Creek I had shots at singles flying over, at singles and pairs as they jumped at the bends or at the mouths of little canals; and all the time I was shooting, I could hear my companions blazing away. I kept sending ducks to them, and they returned the compliment. Finally we came to a little lake, or slough, overhung with wild bushes. It was not larger in area than the average room. But the water in it was warm and shallow; there were exposed mud-banks on its margins; it was remote and sheltered. I believe those conditions spell "duck" pretty well.

"If we stay here a little while," Danky said, "every duck in the whole Santee country will visit here. They don't stay, but they come to see who's here. This is a camp-meetin' place."

We didn't leave the boat; we just sat there in the screen of the reeds while ducks, as Danky promised, came to investigate. If there were no law and a man were a brute, he could sit where I sat and kill a hundred big ducks in a little while.

"They ack," Danky said, "like they has los' their queen, and is looking' for her. And they always does ack that way at this place."

The sport was so abundant that I shot very carefully, and tried to select drakes only. Within a half hour I had ten in the boat. It was like blind-shooting, except for the fact that we had no decoys and we couldn't see the ducks until they were right on us. The shooting was difficult enough to make it sport.

"We have killed all I want," I told Danky. "Are we ready to head for home?"

"You is 'lowed fifteen, Cap'n," he answered, "and I'd like you to get more than the other gunners."

Good old Danky! His professional pride as my personal escort was touched. But I thought I could assuage his anguish better with a dollar than with more ducks. I laid down my gun, and we began the paddle home. On the way I might have had perhaps thirty chances, and the wood ducks I saw would make glad the heart of any lover of wildlife.

The four of us reached the old rice barn at about the same time, and our respective bags were laid out on the sunny bank for inspection. As I have said, I had ten; Dick had twelve big ducks, including one canvasback; Graham, a rare shot, had fourteen. I saw Diana's dusky guide grinning as he laid out fifteen fine mallards. "Danky, you boys is gettin' too old to paddle fo' ducks," he taunted.

But Danky was not abashed.

"Ain't dat," he said, in a large and philosophic way; "but when a man git in a game with a 'oman, he ain't got no chanst nohow."

Shouts of laughter from all of us showed our approval of Danky's penetrant view of man's place in the universe.

NOTHING TO DO FOR
THREE WEEKS

Gordon MacQuarrie

*"I left long before daylight, alone but not lonely." The opening
sentence of this, perhaps MacQuarrie's greatest story, tells us a great
deal. The President of the Old Duck Hunters' Association is gone;
he will not be making this trip. This extremely moving and eloquent
piece of writing, in my opinion, ranks in the top tier of all the literature on the outdoors. It is rich and uplifting, a reminder that by
allowing ourselves to be alone with small, familiar pleasures, we
can heal all wounds, banish fear and doubt . . . . and go on. It
originally appeared in* Field & Stream *and, of course, was a part of
Zack Taylor's superb collection of MacQuarrie stories,* The Stories
of the Old Duck Hunters & Other Drivel *(Stackpole). MacQuarrie's
own life was destined to end not long after this piece appeared. Born
with the new century, he was taken by a heart attack in 1956.*

I LEFT LONG before daylight, alone but not lonely. Sunday-morning
stillness filled the big city. It was so quiet that I heard the whistle
of duck wings as I unlocked the car door. They would be ducks
leaving Lake Michigan. A fine sound, that, early of a morning. Wild
ducks flying above the tall apartments and the sprawling factories
in the dark, and below them people still asleep, who knew not that
these wild kindred were up and about early for their breakfast.

The wingbeats I chose to accept as a good omen. And why not?
Three weeks of doing what I wished to do lay before me. It was the
best time, the beginning of the last week in October. In the partridge
woods I would pluck at the sleeve of reluctant Indian summer, and
from a duck blind four hundred miles to the north I would watch
winter make its first dash south on a northwest wind.

I drove through sleeping Milwaukee. I thought how fine it would
be if, throughout the year, the season would hang on dead center,

] 591 [

as it often does in Wisconsin in late October and early November. Then one may expect a little of everything—a bit of summer, a time of falling leaves, and finally that initial climatic threat of winter to quicken the heart of a duck hunter, namely me.

To be sure, these are mere hunter's dreams of perpetual paradise. But we all do it. And, anyway, isn't it fine to go on that early start, the car carefully packed, the day all to yourself to do with as you choose.

On the highway I had eyes only for my own brethren of the varnished stock, the dead-grass skiff, the far-going boots. Cars with hunting-capped men and cars with dimly outlined retrievers in back seats flashed by me. I had agreed with myself not to go fast. The day was too fine to mar with haste. Every minute of it was to be tasted and enjoyed, and remembered for another, duller day. Twenty miles out of the big city a hunter with two beagles set off across a field toward a wood. For the next ten miles I was with him in the cover beyond the farmhouse and up the hill.

Most of that still, sunny Sunday I went past farms and through cities, and over the hills and down into the valleys, and when I hit the fire-lane road out of Loretta-Draper I was getting along on my way. This is superb country for deer and partridge, but I did not see many of the latter; this was a year of the few, not the many. Where one of the branches of the surging Chippewa crosses the road I stopped and flushed mallards out of tall grass. On Clam Lake, at the end of the fire lane, there was an appropriate knot of bluebills.

The sun was selling nothing but pure gold when I rolled up and down the hills of the Namakagon Lake country. Thence up on blacktop from Cable to the turnoff at Drummond, and from there straight west through those tremendous stands of jack pine. Then I broke the rule of the day. I hurried a little. I wanted to use the daylight. I turned in at the mailboxes and went along the back road to the nameless turn-in—so crooked and therefore charming.

Old Sun was still shining on the top logs of the cabin. The yard was afloat with scrub oak leaves, for a wind to blow them off into the lake must be a good one. Usually it just skims the ridgepole and goes its way. Inside the cabin was the familiar smell of native Wisconsin white cedar logs. I lit the fireplace and then unloaded the car. It was near dark when all the gear was in, and I pondered the virtues of broiled ham steak and baking powder biscuits to go with it.

I was home, all right. I have another home, said to be much nicer. But this is the talk of persons who like cities and, in some cases, actually fear the woods.

There is no feeling like that first wave of affection which sweeps in when a man comes to a house and knows it is home. The logs, the beams, the popple kindling snapping under the maple logs in the fireplace. It was after dark when I had eaten the ham and the hot biscuits, these last dunked in maple syrup from a grove just three miles across the lake as the crow flies and ten miles by road.

When a man is alone, he gets things done. So many men alone in the brush get along with themselves because it takes most of their time to do for themselves. No dallying over division of labor, no hesitancy at tackling a job.

There is much to be said in behalf of the solitary way of fishing and hunting. It lets people get acquainted with themselves. Do not feel sorry for the man on his own. If he is one who plunges into all sorts of work, if he does not dawdle, if he does not dwell upon his aloneness, he will get many things done and have a fine time doing them.

After the dishes I put in some licks at puttering. Fifty very-well-cared-for decoys for diving ducks and mallards came out of their brown sacks and stood anchor-cord inspection. They had been made decent with touchup paint months before. A couple of 12-gauge guns got a pat or two with an oily rag. The contents of two shell boxes were sorted and segregated. Isn't it a caution how shells get mixed up? I use nothing but 12-gauge shells. Riding herd on more than one gauge would, I fear, baffle me completely.

I love to tinker with gear. It's almost as much fun as using it. Shipshape is the phrase. And it has got to be done continuously, otherwise order will be replaced by disorder, and possibly mild-to-acute chaos.

There is a school which holds that the hunting man with the rickety gun and the out-at-elbows jacket gets the game. Those who say this are fools or mountebanks. One missing top button on a hunting jacket can make a man miserable on a cold, windy day. The only use for a rickety shotgun is to blow somebody to hell and gone.

I dragged a skiff down the hill to the beach, screwed the motor to it, loaded in the decoys, and did not forget to toss in an old shell box for a blind seat and an axe for making a blind. I also inspected the night and found it good. It was not duck weather, but out there in the dark an occasional bluebill skirted.

I went back up the hill and brought in fireplace wood. I was glad it was not cold enough to start the space heater. Some of those maple chunks from my woodpile came from the same sugar bush across the lake that supplied the hot biscuit syrup. It's nice to feel at home in such a country.

How would you like to hole up in a country where you could choose, as you fell asleep, between duck hunting and partridge hunting, between small-mouths on a good river like the St. Croix or trout on another good one like the Brule, or between muskie fishing on the Chippewa flowage or cisco dipping in the dark for the fun of it? Or, if the mood came over you, just a spell of tramping around on deer trails with a hand axe and a gunnysack, knocking highly flammable pine knots out of trees that have lain on the ground for seventy years? I've had good times in this country doing nothing more adventurous than filling a pail with blueberries or a couple of pails with wild cranberries.

If you have read thus far and have gathered that this fellow Mac-Quarrie is a pretty cozy fellow for himself in the bush, you are positively correct. Before I left on this trip the boss, himself a product of this same part of Wisconsin and jealous as hell of my three-week hunting debauch, allowed, "Nothing to do for three weeks, eh?" Him I know good. He'd have given quite a bit to be going along.

Nothing to do for three weeks! He knows better. He's been there, and busier than a one-armed paperhanger.

Around bedtime I found a seam rip in a favorite pair of thick doeskin gloves. Sewing it up, I felt like Robinson Crusoe, but Rob never had it that good. In the Old Duck Hunters we have a philosophy: When you go to the bush, you go there to smooth it, and not to rough it.

And so to bed under the watchful presence of the little alarm clock that has run faithfully for twenty years, but only when it is laid on its face. One red blanket was enough. There was an owl hooting, maybe two wrangling. You can never be sure where an owl is, or how far away, or how many. The fireplace wheezed and made settling noises. Almost asleep, I made up my mind to omit the ducks until some weather got made up. Tomorrow I'd hit the tote roads for partridge. Those partridge took some doing. In the low years they never disappear completely, but they require some tall walking, and singles are the common thing.

No hunting jacket on that clear, warm day. Not even a sleeveless game carrier. Just shells in the pockets, a fat ham sandwich, and Bailey Sweet apples stuck into odd corners. My game carrier was a cord with which to tie birds to my belt. The best way to do it is to forget the cord is there until it is needed; otherwise the Almighty may see you with that cord in your greediness and decide you are tempting Providence and show you nary a feather all the day long.

By early afternoon I had walked up seven birds and killed two, pretty good for me. Walking back to the cabin, I sort of uncoiled. You can sure get wound up walking up partridge. I uncoiled some more out on the lake that afternoon building three blinds, in just the right places for expected winds.

This first day was also the time of the great pine-knot strike. I came upon them not far from a thoroughfare emptying the lake, beside rotted logs of lumbering days. Those logs had been left there by rearing crews after the lake level had been dropped to fill the river. It often happens. Then the rivermen don't bother to roll stranded logs into the water when it's hard work.

You cannot shoot a pine knot, or eat it, but it is a lovely thing and makes a fire that will burn the bottom out of a stove if you are not careful. Burning pine knots smell as fine as the South's pungent lightwood. Once I gave an artist a sack of pine knots and he refused to burn them and rubbed and polished them into wondrous bird-like forms, and many called them art. Me, I just pick them up and burn them.

Until you have your woodshed awash with pine knots, you have not ever been really rich. By that evening I had made seven two-mile round trips with the boat and I estimated I had almost two tons of pine knots. In even the very best pine-knot country, such as this was, that is a tremendous haul for one day; in fact, I felt vulgarly rich. To top it off, I dug up two husky boom chains, discovered only because a link or two appeared above ground. They are mementos of the logging days. One of those chains was partly buried in the roots of a white birch some fifty years old.

No one had to sing lullabies to me that second night. The next day I drove eighteen miles to the quaggy edge of the Totogatic flowage and killed four woodcock. Nobody up there hunts them much. Some people living right on the flowage asked me what they were.

An evening rite each day was to listen to weather reports on the radio. I was impatient for the duck blind, but this was Indian summer and I used it up, every bit of it. I used every day for what it was best suited. Can anyone do better?

The third day I drove thirty-five miles to the lower Douglas County Brule and tried for one big rainbow, with, of course, salmon eggs and a Colorado spinner. I never got a strike, but I love that river. That night, on Island Lake, eight miles from my place, Louis Eschrich and I dip-netted some eating ciscoes near the shore, where they had moved in at dark to spawn among roots of drowned jack pines.

There is immense satisfaction in being busy. Around the cabin there were incessant chores that please the hands and rest the brain. Idiot work, my wife calls it. I cannot get enough of it. Perhaps I should have been a day laborer. I split maple and Norway pine chunks for the fireplace and kitchen range. This is work fit for any king. You see the piles grow, and indeed the man who splits his own wood warms himself twice.

On Thursday along came Tony Burmek, Hayward guide. He had a grand idea. The big crappies were biting in deep water on the Chippewa flowage. There'd be nothing to it. No, we wouldn't bother fishing muskies, just get twenty-five of those crappies apiece. Nary a crappie touched our minnows, and after several hours of it I gave up, but not Tony. He put me on an island where I tossed out half a dozen black-duck decoys and shot three mallards.

When I scooted back northward that night, the roadside trees were tossing. First good wind of the week. Instead of going down with the sun, Old Wind had risen, and it was from the right quarter, northwest. The radio confirmed it, said there'd be snow flurries. Going to bed that windy night, I detected another dividend of doing nothing—some slack in the waistline of my pants. You ever get that fit feeling as your belly shrinks and your hands get callused?

By rising time of Friday morning the weatherman was a merchant of proven mendacity. The upper pines were lashing and roaring. This was the day! In that northwest blast the best blind was a mile run with the outboard. Only after I had left the protecting high hill did I realize the full strength of the wind. Following waves came over the transom.

Before full light I had forty bluebill and canvasback decoys tossing off a stubby point and eleven black-duck blocks anchored in the lee of the point. I had lost the twelfth black-duck booster somewhere, and a good thing. We of the Old Duck Hunters have a superstition that any decoy spread should add up to an odd number.

Plenty of ducks moved. I had the entire lake to myself, but that is not unusual in the Far North. Hours passed and nothing moved in. I remained long after I knew they were not going to decoy. All they had in mind was sheltered water.

Next time you get into a big blow like that, watch them head for the lee shore. This morning many of them were flying north, facing the wind. I think they can spot lee shores easier that way, and certainly they can land in such waters easily. In the early afternoon, when I picked up, the north shore of my lake—seldom used by ducks because it lacks food—held hundreds of divers.

Sure, I could have redeployed those blocks and got some shooting. But it wasn't that urgent. The morning had told me that they were in, and there was a day called tomorrow to be savored. No use to live it up all at once.

Because I had become a pine-knot millionaire, I did not start the big space heater that night. It's really living when you can afford to heat a 20-by-33-foot living room, a kitchen, and a bedroom with a fireplace full of pine knots.

The wind died in the night and by morning it was mitten-cold. What wind persisted was still northwest. I shoved off the loaded boat. Maybe by now those newcomers had rested. Maybe they'd move to feed. Same blind, same old familiar tactics, but this time it took twice as long to make the spread because the decoy cords were frozen.

A band of bluebills came slashing towards me. How fine and brave they are, flying in their tight little formations! They skirted the edge of the decoys, swung off, came back again and circled in back of me, then skidded in, landing gear down. It was so simple to take two. A single drake mallard investigated the big black cork duck decoys and found out what they were. A little color in the bag looks nice.

I was watching a dozen divers, redheads maybe, when a slower flight movement caught my eye. Coming dead in where eleven geese, blues, I knew at once. I don't know whatever became of those redheads. Geese are an extra dividend on this lake. Blues fly over it by the thousand, but it is not goose-hunting country. I like to think those eleven big black cork decoys caught their fancy this time. At twenty-five yards the No. 6's were more than enough. Two of the geese made a fine weight in the hand, and geese are always big guys when one has had his eyes geared for ducks.

The cold water stung my hands as I picked up. Why does a numb, cold finger seem to hurt so much if you bang it accidentally? The mittens felt good. I got back to my beach in time for the prudent duck hunter's greatest solace, a second breakfast. But first I stood on the lakeshore for a bit and watched the ducks, mostly divers, bluebills predominating, some redheads and enough regal canvasback to make tomorrow promise new interest. The storm had really brought them down from Canada. I was lucky. Two more weeks with nothing to do.

Nothing to do, you say? Where'd I get those rough and callused hands? The windburned face? The slack in my pants? Two more weeks of it . . . . Surely, I was among the most favored of all mankind. Where could there possibly be a world as fine as this?

I walked up the hill, a pine-knot millionaire, for the second breakfast.

Tom HENNESSEY —

HAIL AND FAREWELL

Nash Buckingham

This is the final chapter, friend, and as always when it's time to pick up the decoys and point the boat homewards, I find myself filled with a mixture of satisfaction and melancholy. This selection from Mark Right! *fits my mood perfectly. In fact, I consider it to be the ultimate "sunset" piece. Every time I read it, a lump forms in my throat until I am released by the story's simple message: Life is for living fully, and made even richer by sharing. When the events in this story took place, Nash and his close buddy, Hal Bowen Howard, were both fifty-three years of age. Goodbye, my friend, and good luck to you.*

Your obedient servant,
LAMAR UNDERWOOD
Amwell, New Jersey
April, 1982

TELL ME, IF you can, of anything that's finer than an evening in camp with a rare old friend and a dog after one's own heart. We talked, Hal and I, of fishing and gunning trips we'd made together for all of thirty years. Moose and salmon in New Brunswick, the high Rockies, the old E Bar X range we rode, year in and season out, together. We talked of duck shooting—the camp at Okay, of Horace and Molly at Beaver Dam, and of bird dogs that meant more than a little in our outdoor lives—Flash, and Jimmie, and Ticket. With such talk, with such a friend, comes the spirit that blends naturally with well-steamed beef and beans and corn bread, and imparts a tendency to idle amid smoke wreaths and put off doing the dishes. Of course Chub was with us.

Chub had come to me on Easter Sunday morning, flop-eared little dickens, with a winning way to the potlicker, and the spryness of a cricket, a gift from my friend. D.C., who breeds springers. He has slept every night of his life at the foot of my bed. He comes respect-fully, if at times boisterously, to family meals. He asks his own way in and out of doors by what amounts to well-sustained canine con-versation. On his own in the neighborhood, protecting a private stock of buried bones, Chub wins and loses a normal percentage of fights, all of which are strictly his own affairs because we want no apron-string dog. And how he did grow.

A lake fronts our home, and there Chub had his first lessons in retrieving—before breakfast and in late afternoon, with the swallows and blackbirds kicking up spray and the mallard decoys raising Ned lest their broods be raided. Quick enough at yard breaking, Chub nevertheless was plenty stubborn and hard-headed. Our equipment was a sixty-foot cord, a rolled Kapok boat cushion, and a keen switch, for which Chub developed a keener respect. First dash out of the box, Chub went over his head, but swam desperately and soon developed a strong stroke. The line drew him ashore when he seized his mock duck. After a series of workouts he developed a first-rate idea of what it was all about.

September first rolled around, dove-shooting season, and we were wondering what Chub would do afield, when the guns began to pop. We scattered about the wheat and millet patches that after-noon. Yonder was Hal, with little black Grover packing his camp stool, water jug, and, proudly, the famous Becker 20-bore Magnum double. Percy, gunbearer and bottles, was under the sycamore tree, and Bob at his favorite hangout by the persimmon clump. Irma and Chub and I, with little black Billy, took station up the tall hedge-row a piece, 'twixt late corn and clipped alfalfa. Chub, wildeyed with excitement, was fully aware that something vitally affecting his career was about to be pulled off. He had pawed and licked our guns like a kid with an all-day sucker.

Just then a dove darted overhead, and by great good luck I snap-pitched it into the mown field. At gun's crack, Chub, eyeing the bird, dove through the bushes and cast about vigorously in the open. Gun shy? Not that pup! Irma and I watched—fascinated. A tense half-point—there—he had it—with a quick pounce! Chub, his first bird in mouth! Falling on her knee, Irma clapped her hands and called. Head and stubby tail proudly erect, that sturdy ball of liver and white trotted straight to his beloved mistress and gravely muzzled the softly feathered quarry into her lap.

Of course, by now you've guessed what she did—put both arms around Chub's bull neck and kissed him squarely between the eyes. Dear old Hal, watching the exploit, waved his hat and shouted, "'Attaboy, Chub!" Such moments mean a lot to folks like Irma and me, hunting and breaking dogs together, going on—oh, no matter how many years. But Chub jerked away and huffily rolled reproachful eyes—much as to say, "Cut out that Little Lord Fauntleroy stuff, will ya—I'm a big dog now—come—come—no wimmenfolks business, Missus—us got a job to mind, yonder come some doves—ain't your gun loaded, Boss?"

What an afternoon that was, for sure! What a fagged puppy fell fast asleep during the drive cityward, with his lady almost tearfully unwinding a stray cocklebur or two from his hide. Thereafter, we shot doves twice a week. Hot afternoons Chub had learned to report to Irma for a drink of water from her hat crown. But we had yet to lose a drowned or crippled bird that ever hit the ground. When business got slack in our neighborhood, I frequently joined Hal and had Chub fetch for him. You can easily understand the comradeship that sprang up among us.

Came October afternoons when shooting slowed a bit. We spent a lot of time in the open, because now we could work the bird dogs into condition, along with Chub. One afternoon, Chub jumped his first rabbit and went off duty for half an hour. An occasional shrill yelp from the bottoms kept me in touch with him, however. He slunk back dejectedly and lay panting beside me in the shady leaf bed of a thick maple. Then I told him it was all right with me, just so he brought home the bacon, because, frankly, fried rabbit is another particular one of my many weaknesses.

All the while, however, my thoughts were a long way ahead—to the approaching duck shooting and what a grand time Hal and I would have with Chub.

And here we were, at long last. It is quite a "fur, hard piece," out to that shack of ours in the tall cottonwoods skirting two thousand acres of sand bar. A car doesn't dare it except in dry weather for, if a downpour catches one, chains may or may not drag one back to civilization. Shack describes our hide-away accurately: one room, with a kitchen lean-to, built on stilts fifteen feet above high-water stage of "Ol' Miss"—a mile away. West of the camp—a gut that separates Tennessee from Arkansas, by virtue of a Federal decree relocating an original riverbank line of the late fifties. To our east—willow flats, sand-bar sloughs, and, beyond, goose country and river wildfowling; fields rank with bar grass and cockleburs; habitat of swamp rabbits, occasional bobwhite bevies, and heavily spoored by coon, mink, and possum; forests jackstrawed with freshet litter and viny morass; directly overhead the great Mississippi River wildfowl migrational route.

Taking Nature's cold dare gladly, Hal and Chub and I made camp just before dusk. While Hal and I unloaded the plunder, Chub inspected every foot of the place and enjoyed it all hugely. We were soon shipshape and in behind the suppering.

Before turning in we went for a stroll, sat on a log down the float road a piece, listened to night sounds. A big packet fighting the bend current; blue geese and honkers traveling a Stygian ceiling; staccato motorboating away downriver. Chub sniffed a lot of strange sign. Then he climbed onto the log and sat beside me, a bit awed by the big stillness and cold dark. We expected ice in the morning if the breeze laid. Hal thought he would try for black ducks and geese at the sand bar's edge, with both duck and honker stools out front. I would look in first at a hidden slough down in the back gut territory. Panning nothing there, I'd walk and jump-shoot the ponds. That, I figured, would be Chub's best chance.

A knock at the door and Chub yowls, "Who's there?" "Jus' me —ol' Clab!" Big black Clab from over the levee, come to help Hal with pit digging and packing the live goose decoys.

"Yaas, suh, Boss-men, how you-all dis frawsty mawnin'?" Hal's voice rumbles from the eiderdown. "Th'ow some wood in that heater, Clab—and—th' coal-oil bottle is over yonder on the shelf."

Lamp wicks go on duty; warmth creeps into the chilly shack. Four-thirty! Two hours and more before firing time, but we've breakfast to eat and a goodly hike ahead. Clab has percolator and skillet well in hand. Long experience has taught Hal and me to eat slowly and make up time on the far end. Clab has done himself proud.

"Oughta be er cook, Boss-men," he explains, "whut d'ol' lady ain't learnt me, I got learnt in de levee camp."

I leash Chub, tuck the big gun under my other arm, and hit the trail for Old River bank. Boot-crunchings warn that there'll be skim ice on the ponds. So much the better. I slow down as the path narrows into a pit's mouth of darkness. No use to turn an ankle in the gumbo knifed with mule tracks. Chub minds his P's and Q's. I reach the "dreen" leading from the cataway pond I'm hunting, a quarter to the left. Difficult going through here, poles very close, and steering Chub no cinch. We creep finally into a clearing just beginning to gray.

Drawing a chunk to a big willow's base, I sit talking quietly to Chub. I picture Hal and Clab at the sand bar's parapet by now, with Clab shoveling furiously and Hal staking out the callers and stool. In the distance, a cotton gin begins to pant. The aviation beacon, far below, ceases to pry the night. The east springs with old rose; high across the pond two specks dart with the wavy speed of hellbats. Teal! A raucous blue heron sails low overhead, and Chub, spotting it, goes frantic. From Hal's distant sector comes a muted double bark—I can tell his 20-bore as far as I can hear it.

Ahead, down through the stems, the water is ashake. Only one thing does that—ducks! Step by step, with Chub clucked in at heel, I edge to within spotting distance. Fully a hundred dipping, chuckling, feeding mallards, completely off guard and disporting themselves gleefully! I'll put them up, quietly, maybe get a chance if they sweep back, and then sit and wait for some returns. They'll be drifting in to feed these shallows.

"Go get 'em, Chub!" No second bidding needed. Down through the cover drives my companion, and, with a roar, out pile the mallards. A group of five deserts the main body and swings south. I gamble a tall overhead try and a bird slants from the bunch. Across the gut, in Arkansas, I see it drive full tilt into the burned top of a high tree snag and hurtle from sight.

Chub and I wade the marsh, strike a beeline to the far bank, and emerge into young cane near the big landmark. "Bird," I tell him, "go find it—bird." Into the brush dives Chub—some tall woofing, and out pelts Mister Greenhead with just enough power left to escape the raging springer and gain altitude. Thirty yards away, I drop it into the water's edge. Chub's first duck. He sniffs the big drake cautiously, takes a slant at me, picks it up gingerly, and then, confidence mounting, fashions a high-headed retrieve. Everything is now all set. Chub has the idea!

Overhead a wisping of wings. They couldn't stay away very long, could they! Two mallard drakes, coming from the river, slide across, wheel, and head for the pond's far end. My call, muted at first, rises to a hail. Right-o! The lead bird topples clean across the slough; the second crashes ice into splintering crystals. Now, Chub, for your rightful baptism. Will he tackle that deep mire and keen ice? Bless his heart, I'll say so—through it in springy surges, splattering mud, half swimming, fighting his way to that feathery drift of green and brilliant blue. A snatch, and he heads shoreward.

Meeting him at water's edge, I take the drake, point, and toss a stick toward the far shore. But Chub has seen that other victim. Quick as a flash he recrosses and is back with number two. Forenoon wears away. Nine times more the big gun erupts, and Chub does his act. Mud from tail to eyebrows by now, but what of it! For us the day has ended in a blaze of glory. I pack our limit into the capacious rucksack and hit the trial. At the first water hole along the float road, Chub, rather against his will, gets a much-needed scrubbing. At the shack I skillet a snack for the two of us; Chub dozes on the veranda, while I tidy.

Then, a few shells in my pocket for chance shots at crows or geese, Chub and I hit away to circle the peninsula, survey its lower reaches, and come by to help Hal and Clab with their load. For a river flight, Hal has been shooting with fair regularity. From a vantage hide in the wood's edge we spot Hal's pit and rig, just in time to see three geese sail past and draw a salvo from the 20-gauge. One topples dead, another, hard hit, slants to the water's edge, bounces from the sand, and regains the eddy. Hal climbs from the pit and attempts what seems futile pursuit.

But he's unaware that Chub and I have cut across the sand ahead of him. Chub's taken in the whole business, and it's right down his alley. Into the shoal he pelts, swimming now toward the faintly struggling black and gray heap. If that goose has life enough left, he may hurt or scare the puppy. But luck holds. Furiously Chub tackles the heavy order, swerves, and with the honker's neck in his teeth makes a brave flight across the current. Two minutes, and Hal grabs an armful of the goose and pup. Clab has made the pickup, and we safari homeward with a fine limit of mixed black and gray mallards and four fine geese. (The other pair were Hal's first that morning.)

At the camp all is snugged, and our car breasts the levee. Clab is dropped at his cabin and minded to be on hand at the ramp, three afternoons later. In an hour Hal and I are unloading Chub at my house. We share a toddy and linger by the smoldery log fire. Chub is lost in dreams on the rug, but comes alive at time for Hal to ramble.

At the car something seems to hold the three of us. Memory, perhaps, of all our years together, and today's added score. Hal pats Chub's head affectionately and pulls his tousled ears. "Buddy," he tells him, "you're a grand fellow. We wouldn't take a fortune for you, would we, Buck?" The lake's bosom is a dying molt of flickering amber. "Good night," he calls. "We'll try 'em a couple more barrels—good night, Chub."

Still held by that vague shadow, Chub and I stand looking into the purpling dusk, after Hal, wheeling away into the gloaming; stanch, golden heart into a golden west, fading around life's bend. For Clab will wait in vain at the levee's ramp, three days from now.

Chub and I go slowly into the house, for Hal has gone—away and away and away, to that far shore already so close upon him then—where, God willing, all hunters will some day meet again.